Student Usability in Educational Software and Games:

Improving Experiences

Carina Gonzalez
University of La Laguna, Spain

A volume in the Advances in Game–Based
Learning (AGBL) Book Series

Managing Director:	Lindsay Johnston
Editorial Director:	Joel Gamon
Book Production Manager:	Jennifer Romanchak
Publishing Systems Analyst:	Adrienne Freeland
Development Editor:	Hannah Abelbeck
Assistant Acquisitions Editor:	Kayla Wolfe
Typesetter:	Henry Ulrich
Cover Design:	Nick Newcomer

Published in the United States of America by
Information Science Reference (an imprint of IGI Global)
701 E. Chocolate Avenue
Hershey PA 17033
Tel: 717-533-8845
Fax: 717-533-8661
E-mail: cust@igi-global.com
Web site: http://www.igi-global.com

Library of Congress Cataloging-in-Publication Data

Student usability in educational software and games : improving experiences / Carina Gonzalez, editor.
     p. cm.
  Includes bibliographical references and index.
  Summary: "This book explores new models of interaction and human-computer interaction paradigms as applied to learning environments"--Provided by publisher.
   ISBN 978-1-4666-1987-6 (hardcover) -- ISBN 978-1-4666-1988-3 (ebook) -- ISBN 978-1-4666-1989-0 (print & perpetual access) 1. Education--Computer network resources. 2. Teaching--Computer network resources. 3. Education--Software. 4. Educational games. I. Gonzalez, Carina.
  LB1044.87.S849 2013
  371.33--dc23
                                    2012028990

This book is published in the IGI Global book series Advances in Game-Based Learning (AGBL) (ISSN: 2327-1825; eISSN: 2327-1833)

British Cataloguing in Publication Data
A Cataloguing in Publication record for this book is available from the British Library.

All work contributed to this book is new, previously-unpublished material. The views expressed in this book are those of the authors, but not necessarily of the publisher.

Advances in Game–Based Learning (AGBL) Book Series

Robert D. Tennyson
University of Minnesota, USA

ISSN: 2327-1825
EISSN: 2327-1833

MISSION

The **Advances in Game-Based Learning (AGBL) Book Series** aims to cover all aspects of serious games applied to any area of education. The definition and concept of education has begun to morph significantly in the past decades and game-based learning has become a popular way to encourage more active learning in a creative and alternative manner for students in K-12 classrooms, higher education, and adult education. AGBL presents titles that address many applications, theories, and principles surrounding this growing area of educational theory and practice.

COVERAGE

- Curriculum Development Using Educational Games
- Digital Game-Based Learning
- Edutainment
- Electronic Educational Games
- Game Design & Development of Educational Games
- MMOs in Education
- Pedagogical Theory of Game-Based Learning
- Psychological Study of Students Involved in Game-Based Learning
- Role of Instructors
- Virtual Worlds & Game-Based Learning

IGI Global is currently accepting manuscripts for publication within this series. To submit a proposal for a volume in this series, please contact our Acquisition Editors at Acquisitions@igi-global.com or visit: http://www.igi-global.com/publish/.

Titles in this Series

For a list of additional titles in this series, please visit: www.igi-global.com

Student Usability in Educational Software and Games Improving Experiences
Carina Gonzalez (University of La Laguna, Spain)
Information Science Reference • copyright 2013 • 439pp • H/C (ISBN: 9781466619876) • US $175.00 (our price)

Interactivity in E-Learning Case Studies and Frameworks
Haomin Wang (Dakota State University, USA)
Information Science Reference • copyright 2012 • 408pp • H/C (ISBN: 9781613504413) • US $175.00 (our price)

Handbook of Research on Improving Learning and Motivation through Educational Games Multidisciplinary Approaches
Patrick Felicia (Waterford Institute of Technology, Ireland)
Information Science Reference • copyright 2011 • 1462pp • H/C (ISBN: 9781609604950) • US $475.00 (our price)

Simulation and Gaming for Mathematical Education Epistemology and Teaching Strategies
Angela Piu (University of L'Aquila, Italy) and Cesare Fregola (Roma Tre University, Italy)
Information Science Reference • copyright 2011 • 256pp • H/C (ISBN: 9781605669304) • US $180.00 (our price)

Gaming for Classroom-Based Learning Digital Role Playing as a Motivator of Study
Young Kyun Baek (Korea National University of Education, Korea)
Information Science Reference • copyright 2010 • 358pp • H/C (ISBN: 9781615207138) • US $180.00 (our price)

Ethics and Game Design Teaching Values through Play
Karen Schrier (Columbia University, USA) and David Gibson (University of Vermont, USA)
Information Science Reference • copyright 2010 • 396pp • H/C (ISBN: 9781615208456) • US $180.00 (our price)

www.igi-global.com

701 E. Chocolate Ave., Hershey, PA 17033
Order online at www.igi-global.com or call 717-533-8845 x100
To place a standing order for titles released in this series, contact: cust@igi-global.com
Mon-Fri 8:00 am - 5:00 pm (est) or fax 24 hours a day 717-533-8661

Editorial Advisory Board

Table of Contents

Section 1
Usability, Accessibility and Playability in Virtual Learning Environments and Serious Games

Section 2
Human and Social Factors in Game-Based Learning

Section 3
Experiences and Uses of Educational Videogames in Different Contexts

Detailed Table of Contents

Section 1
Usability, Accessibility and Playability in Virtual Learning Environments and Serious Games

This chapter presents an overview of accessibility and usability for educational computer-based games and the first survey of the accessibility and usability of digital games. The overview includes a discussion of accessibility and usability, both in general and in the specific context of educational games, as well as a brief presentation of issues relating to game design, including of mobile games. Since there are no previous studies of the accessibility and usability of educational computer-based games, studies of the accessibility and usability of the related areas of virtual learning environments, digital games for entertainment and PDF documents, are also presented. The overview of accessibility and usability and the results of the survey are used to draw up a structured list of 62 guidelines and recommendations, organised into three categories at the first level and ten at the second level. These guidelines and recommendations are illustrated by an example of their application to a fictitious new educational game.

This chapter explores key issues in relation to the human computer interactions that are supported through Virtual Learning Environments (VLEs). It focuses particularly on the usability of online learning environments and highlights the impact usability can have on the learning experiences of users. The authors adopt a definition of usability that relates to the usability of virtual learning environments, specifically, and provides guidance on how to assess the usability of VLEs by offering the Multidimensional Usability Model (MUM). The MUM model is designed to identify the factors that can form technological barriers to effective Human Computer Interaction (HCI). This chapter also offers an evaluation of the theoretical frameworks, criteria, and methodologies currently available; these draw on research findings from a case study focused on the usability of an existing VLE and give practical examples of the MUM approach to usability.

    Geraldine Ryan, University College Cork, Ireland
    Noirin McCarthy, University College Cork, Ireland
    Richard Byrne, University College Cork, Ireland
    Ranran Xiong, University College Cork, Ireland

Recent technological advances mean mobile phones can now be thought of as computers that fit in pockets. With the Apple iPhone and the Google Android Phone leading the way, mobile phones today offer many technological possibilities including SMS messaging, browsing the World Wide Web, watching and making videos, downloading and playing educational games, partaking in discussion forums, blogging, etc. Educators are currently looking at the mobile phone and other mobile technologies (such as netbooks, PDAs, Nintendo DS, SONY PSP, media players, iPod Touch, voting systems, and specialist cameras) as a way of immersing the student in the learning process. These new mediums allow students to record, organise, access, share, and reflect on work-based learning experiences. The aim of this chapter is to examine how universities can use mobile-learning tools, with a view to engaging students in the learning process while also developing their meaning-making system.

    José Luis González Sánchez, Universidad de Granada, Spain
    Rosa Maria Gil Iranzo, Universitat de Lleida. Spain
    Francisco L. Gutierrez Vela, Universidad de Granada, Spain

Video games are the most economically profitable entertainment industry. The nature of their design means that user experience is enriched by emotional, cultural, and other subjective factors that make design and / or evaluation difficult using traditional methods commonly used in interactive systems. It is therefore necessary to know how to apply Playability in order to design, analyze, optimize, and adapt it to a player's preferences. In this chapter, the authors present a way to perform UX based on Playability techniques by adding hedonic factors that enrich the development of video games. The aim is to easily and cost-effectively analyze the different degrees of Playability within a game and determine how player experience is affected by different game elements. These results can be applied in the educational field where the experience of the pupils with educational video games is a crucial factor for the success of the learning process.

    Amer Ibrahim, University of Granada, Spain
    Francisco Luis Gutiérrez Vela, University of Granada, Spain
    Natalia Padilla Zea, University of Granada, Spain
    José Luis González Sánchez, University of Granada, Spain

Learning through play is currently an effective and attractive educational strategy. Recently, many educational video games have failed because methods of analysis have not been used to discuss playability level in a structured way. Ensuring a good player experience characterized by playability requires cooperation and collaboration between game designers and educators. To this end, the authors have proposed a new set of patterns to support educational video game design and analysis. These patterns aim to facilitate the development of educational video games, summarize the essential information and requirements needed to understand a particular problem and the proposed solution, and present the interrelationships between educational video game components and playability attributes.

Section 2
Human and Social Factors in Game-Based Learning

Chapter 6

Geertje Bekebrede, Delft University of Technology, The Netherlands
Casper Harteveld, Delft University of Technology, The Netherlands
Harald Warmelink, Delft University of Technology, The Netherlands
Sebastiaan Meijer, Delft University of Technology, The Netherlands

Educational games are often less attractive than entertainment games in visuals, gameplay, and other aspects, but do we need entertainment-level beauties in our education or are beasts sufficient? To identify the importance of attraction for educational games, the authors offer the results of a comparative analysis of five educational games used and evaluated from 2005-2010 (N=754). They operationalized attraction through statements in which players were asked to rate the games' visual, gameplay, and user interface attractiveness. While some scholars argue that for game-based education to become successful, educational games need to be visually more attractive, the results of the analysis show the opposite. For educational games, attraction is of relatively low importance. The authors further found that gameplay is the most important aspect of attraction and visuals the least. These results contribute to the debate amongst designers and educators on what priorities to set when considering game-based education.

Chapter 7

Robyn Hromek, The University of Sydney, Australia

Games are inherently engaging and, when crafted to do so, provide an experiential, mediated learning space that is effective and fun. This chapter explores game-based learning and the role of the facilitator in optimizing learning. As referees, they make sure games proceed in a fair and orderly manner. As teachers, they look for teachable moments to 'scaffold' learning. As mentors, they debrief what happened to enhance learning and ensure psychological safety. The author reviews the literature and her practice as an educational psychologist to examine therapeutic board games and socio-emotional learning. The Life-Space Interview and Emotional First Aid are put forward as effective debriefing tools. An argument is made for the importance of face-to-face games and attention is drawn to concerns about excessive screen time.

Chapter 8

Ines Di Loreto, University of Milan, Italy

Based on the importance of social aspects for the learning process and for Digital Natives, this chapter describes a framework to create sociality inside learning environments and in particular in serious games. The described framework is based on four elements: identity, space, time, and actions. These elements (and the behaviors that emerge from them) can be used as markers in order to evaluate whether or not the system is able to facilitate social interactions. The chapter describes in particular (1) the framework for the creation of sociability in interactive systems, (2) two methods for its application in the design phase and in the development phase, (3) two experiments carried out in order to validate the above mentioned framework using a serious game called School Society, and (4) some observations on the framework and the relationship between social and learning aspects.

This chapter deals with the development of new learning environments, particularly the different aspects linked to users' collaboration in these environments. The authors believe that game-based learning can significantly enhance learning. The emergence of online multiplayer games led them to apply the metaphor of exploring a virtual 3D world, where each student embarks on a quest in order to collect knowledge related to a learning activity. In the environment, each part of the world represents a place, sometimes a collaborative place, where students are supposed to acquire a particular concept. This new way of learning changes habits, offers new opportunities to use collaborative tools, allowing the students to co-construct knowledge efficiently. In this chapter, the authors describe an example of game-based environment that they have developed. They then give examples of uses of collaborative tools in this environment and give details on how to enhance them. The authors focus on two aspects: the monitoring of the collaborative activity, where the teacher applies his/her own strategies in order to monitor the collaborative activity; and the adaptation of the game according to the learners' profiles.

Section 3
Experiences and Uses of Educational Videogames in Different Contexts

Several groupware tools have been implemented within Computer Supported Collaborative Learning (CSCL) research groups in order to test ideas and concepts currently being studied. It is very important to perform pilot-evaluations with these systems. The CSCW Lab is an environment for evaluating groupware within research groups. Four dimensions in assessing groupware were identified: context, collaboration, usability, and cultural impacts. In this chapter, the authors present a proposal to detail the collaboration level, specifically for CSCL domain applications. Understanding and analyzing the collaborative learning process requires a fine-grained sequential analysis of the group interaction in the context of learning goals. Several researchers in the area of cooperative work take as success criterion the quality of the group outcome. Nevertheless, recent findings are giving more importance to the quality of the "cooperation process" itself. The proposed model includes a set of guidelines to evaluate the usage of CSCL tools within a collaboration process defined along with the learning objectives. The authors have defined an experiment with a software tool instrumented to gather information that allowed them to verify the presence of a set of cooperation indicators, which in turn helped to determine the quality of the work process.

Chapter 11

J. Ángel Velázquez-Iturbide, Universidad Rey Juan Carlos, Spain

Antonio Pérez-Carrasco, Universidad Rey Juan Carlos, Spain

Ouafae Debdi, Universidad Rey Juan Carlos, Spain

This chapter advocates for an approach to constructing educational tools that consists in designing small systems aimed at achieving clear educational goals and evaluating them in actual teaching situations. The authors addressed this approach with a number of small systems. In this chapter, they describe their experience in the development, use, and evaluation of two educational systems: SRec and GreedEx. The former is a highly interactive program animation system of recursion, and the latter is an interactive assistant aimed at learning the role of selection functions in greedy algorithms by means of experimentation. The evaluations allowed the authors to identify faults and weaknesses of the systems, and these results were used to enhance the systems. Moreover, their approach has yielded very high values with respect to effectiveness and student satisfaction.

Chapter 12

Norena Martin-Dorta, Universidad de La Laguna (ULL), Spain

Isabel Sanchez-Berriel, Universidad de La Laguna (ULL), Spain

Jose Luis Saorin, Universidad de La Laguna (ULL), Spain

Manuel Contero, Universidad Politécnica de Valencia (UPV), Spain

Spatial abilities are critical skills in scientific and technical fields. In recent studies, the role of computer games, particularly those with 3-D simulations, have been examined for their impact on the development of spatial skills. The work presented in this chapter describes the design and user evaluation of a 3D construction mobile game called iCube. A trial version was brought out and evaluated by twenty-two students. Users pointed out that the game is useful for improvement of spatial ability and is fun. However, some difficulties arose with use of the tactile screen, as fingerprints caused problems while interacting with the game's 3D environment. The results revealed that it is necessary to have this item in mind during the game's design, where screen action is continuous.

Chapter 13

Priscila Starosky, State University of Rio de Janeiro, Brazil

Maria das Graças Dias Pereira, Papal University of Rio de Janeiro, Brazil

This chapter shows and discusses the development and implementation of a pegagogic proposition of story co-construction via Role-Playing Games (RPG), in the context of literacy with a bilingual approach for deaf individuals. The researcher, besides the experience of practicing RPG and developing a game adapted to the particularities of deaf adolescents, also analyses narrative co-construction during the multiparticipation dynamics of the game. The research was done in the Ambulatório de Surdez do Curso de Fonoaudiologia da Universidade Federal do Rio de Janeiro (Ambulatory for Deafness of the Phonoaudiology Course of the Federal University of Rio de Janeiro). In the RPG implementation phase, the participants were four deaf adolescents and a deaf teacher (as players), an RPG and education researcher (as master), the researcher (as assistant), and a LIBRAS interpreter. The results show that the game provided for interaction among the participants with relevant multiliteracy practices.

Chapter 14

Carina Soledad González-González, Universidad de La Laguna, Spain

Francisco Blanco Izquierdo, Universidad de La Laguna, Spain

Pedro Toledo Delgado, Universidad de La Laguna, Spain

Research and experience have proved that videogames can be applied effectively in a wide variety of learning contexts. With the objective to extend the use of educational videogames with hospitalized children, the authors are working on the design of social educational videogames. Their proposal follows the foundations of Digital Game-Based Learning (DGBL), the Computer Supported Collaborative Learning (CSCL), and playability. In order to test the effects of the designed prototype with real users in educational contexts, the authors carried out a pilot study about their educational 3D videogame prototype. The objective of this pilot experiment was measuring the playability and extending this evaluation to the social interactions and emotional aspects. The authors present in this chapter the principles of design of their videogame and some preliminary results about the developed study.

Chapter 15

Vicente Galiano, Miguel Hernandez University, Spain

Victoria Herranz, Miguel Hernandez University, Spain

In this chapter, the authors describe the project of a virtual world that they developed in their university and with their students. In this work, they joined concepts like social networks and virtual reality, creating a virtual model of the University Miguel Hernandez (UMH), where students are able to walk around the campus, inside the buildings, chat with other students, and moreover, use videoconferencing rooms where students talk and see other students in the same virtual world. The authors describe this project, called UMHvirtual (available in http://virtual.umh.es), which has been supervised by the authors, implemented by a group of students, and focused on all the university students.

Chapter 16

Eurídice Cabañes, ARSGAMES, Spain

Luca Carrubba, ARSGAMES, Spain

Videogames, as a new and playful interactive language, have great potential in the education field. On the one hand, we can find educational videogames to cover almost the whole spectrum of topics offered by colleges and academies (although they are used mainly at home and not in the academic environment). On the other hand, playing videogames is in itself a recreational way to generate technical competencies and teach the use of a whole new "digital language." Depending on different countries and cultures, there is a tendency to implement this technology in educational centres in varying degrees. In order to exemplify this implementation, the authors look at "Scratch," a creative videogame program for children with a big community behind it. In the conclusion, they focus on the introduction of videogame language in the educational context, not as educational videogames but as a tool to learn digital literacy and contemporary society.

Chapter 17

María Rubio Méndez, ARSGAMES, Spain
Eurídice Cabañes Martínez, ARSGAMES, Spain

There is a distinct tendency to integrate technology into the classroom, but in practice the introduction of the ICT in education is not producing the expected effects. We are confronted with the second digital divide, which consists in the dissociation of the students from the technologies introduced in the educational sphere that do not match their actual technological environment. GAMESTAR(T) has been developed in this context as an ARSGAMES project, which, taking into account the potentialities of video games for education and socialization, proposes a series of weekly meetings that include assembly meetings for decision-making about the club's rules, activities, and materials, thematic courses related to specific domains of knowledge, and the club's sessions, in which children play, assisted by monitors, in an atmosphere of critical and collective reflection. In the following, the authors examine how the club developed, which methodology was used, what problems were encountered, and the solutions applied.

Foreword

There is no doubt. Games are a powerful resource for learning. Prensky, Gee, Connolly, Piaget, and the other usual suspects on games cannot be wrong. Neither can all of the European projects funded under the large umbrella of Game-Based Learning, as well as the billion users across the world who enjoy, interact, have fun, achieve milestones and competences, improve their performance, collaborate, discuss, take initiative, and a long list of actions and benefits usually associated to gaming. eGames are attractive, addictive, and fashionable and elicit emotional reactions in players, such as wonder, the feeling of power, or even aggression. These features lead to engagement, and engagement and educational goals can mutually support each other in the same environment to achieve specific targets. In addition, they can also support rather accurate episodes of history, real systems, complex popular events, or board games, just to mention a few. With eGames, the users can also learn content, research in human relationships, improve personal and social skills, and work on strategies. Indeed, games have the power of engaging people. They are fun and provide interaction, interactivity, problem solving, story and other elements that give the user involvement, structure, motivation, and creativity, among other benefits.

Furthermore, games allow players to experience, to explore, to improve skills, to learn content, and to practice strategy. According to the literature, a digital game is a game played in an electronic platform fulfilling the following features: a) it is a voluntary action, started and completed by the user as he wants; b) it is also imaginary, parallel to the real world, replicating a universe or an activity without any consequence in real life; c) it is limited, in time and space; d) it follows a set of rules, a specific and private framework; and e) it provides an uncertain solution since every run, every play, is different and depends on unpredictable user behaviour. Beyond these generic features, educational games exhibit additional characteristics: a) an educational game starts with a premise to be solved; b) being unproductive, it does not generate any property or wealth; c) the main drive is the gaming activity itself; d) there is at least one right solution; and e) the user/player learns a skill or attains a competence, introducing new knowledge, fixing previous acquired knowledge, training skills, sharing experiences, discovering new concepts, developing outcomes.

In this context, gaming and learning become a perfect couple. In order to achieve educational goals, the game designer/teacher can use a number of interactive learning techniques, fully in connection with games. Through eGames, the player can use several interactive learning techniques, i.e. learning by doing, learning from mistakes, goal-oriented learning, role-playing, collaborative learning, and constructivist learning. An implementation of these techniques within a game could be used to support personalization, interaction, playability, and accessibility.

On the other hand, the use of educational games within lesson plans is a widely extended practice within the community of teachers. They interlace specific content and skills with a user-friendly environment where the student is able to play, try, get wrong and right, and learn. In this sense, digital generic games and simulations have a wider and more assorted approach to learning and interaction than specific eGames, since they produce didactical worth, if they are used in the right context by practitioners. Therefore, game-based learning can be deployed not only by educational software but any generic software applied with educational purposes and context. The possibility of re-purposing this kind of existing generic game and simulation in a didactical scenario and providing new pedagogical uses to them becomes a challenge and a need if we talk about virtual learning environments and practical daily experiences by teachers.

Indeed, there is a growing interest in the field of educational technologies, learning designers, and teachers in using eGames and educational simulations as a part of their regular programmes and lessons. However, the use of these resources is usually isolated from the rest of the learning experience. In face-to-face educational settings, this gap can be closed thanks to the teacher, who elicits reflection and supports the students to make connections between the game and the other resources. However, if we want to introduce games in online education, we need to take alternative approaches to fill this gap, like standards, patterns, and rich media. The main concern is to make the game another part of the process, fully integrated in the user experience, and to not let it remain as an unconnected resource. In this sense, achieving standardization, patterns, and rich media allows for the re-use and re-integration of educational resources like eGames in virtual learning environments.

This book compiles a selected number of well-written articles, which address usability in games as one of the main topics, as supported by "Section 1: Usability, Accessibility, and Playability in Virtual Learning Environments and Serious Games." In educational games there is much concern about usability. Since interaction with users, and between them, seems to be crucial for achieving a healthy and satisfactory user experience, usability is a top issue when a work-team designs a game. From the napkin mock-up to the final release, usability plays a central role. Every single aspect of the game must serve an utmost purpose. Every required skill to make a great idea comes true, must be elaborated, refined, double-checked, and integrated into the global project. From programming to graphic design, from a smart script to a captivating soundtrack, games must engage the final user and make him dive into the magic. In this context, usability becomes the key work to make all flow smoothly. Without usability, no word, comment, drawing, or background is useful. Usability becomes the connection link between all of them, since the nature of a game is to be played by a user. Without usability, the user does not get the message, does not play the script, and does not engage.

In addition to usability, other factors make interaction one of the strongest issues in any game. These are trust, social gaming, adaptation, and attraction. All of them are broadly described in "Section 2: Human and Social Factors in Game-Based Learning." Indeed, to adapt the user experience of a game to every user, it is as needed as designing individualised learning itineraries, so that everyone gets a unique relation with the game; in doing so, every student achieves personal goals based on a number of factors, i.e. records, behaviour, background, and others. In this sense, trust becomes the master line to elicit an active response from the user, e.g. a learner, especially in social gaming. Based on social exchange theory, there are four main incentive mechanisms to make users socialize and interact in communities of practice, social collaboration, and virtual learning environments: personal access, personal reputation, social altruism, and tangible rewards. All of them lean on trust as the main seed to support personal interaction.

Finally, the book provides a sound selection of "Experiences and Uses of Educational Videogames in Different Contexts," Section 3. These interesting and well-constructed experiences come from 3D educational mobile gaming, learning grammar, and role-playing or virtual worlds, to name a few. All these are practical examples of successful implementations, which combine a strong theoretical background on education and game-base learning with a fine design and development to cope with specific problems.

This book, edited by Dr. Carina Soledad González González from University of La Laguna and well provisioned by the selected authors, provides a fresh reflection on today's current development on educational software and games, based on specific experiences. I hope that the user experience with the book leads to, at least, a user experience on an implemented game in the right context. It does not matter if we play as teachers of students: in games, as well as in learning, we all are users and learners in a different step of our personalised learning process.

Daniel Burgos
International University of La Rioja, Spain

Daniel Burgos, *Prof. Dr. Daniel Burgos is Vice-Chancellor of Research and Technology, and Director of Engineering at the International University of La Rioja (www.unir.net). Previously, he worked as Director of Education Sector and Head of User Experience Lab in the Research and Innovation Department of Atos, Spain, since 2007. His interests are mainly focused on adaptive and informal elearning, learning and social networks, egames, and elearning specifications. He is or has been involved in a number of R&D projects like, Stellar, Gala, IntelLEO, Go-MyLife, Grapple, Telma, GameTEL, Pauta, Unfold, ProLearn, TenCompetence, EU4ALL, NiHao, Kaleidoscope, Suma, Sister, ComeIn, etc. He holds degrees in Communication (PhD), Computer Science (Dr. Ing), Education, and Business Administration.*

Preface

Usability is a key factor in the ability of students to efficiently and effectively acquire knowledge and skills from interactive systems. Human-Computer Interaction (HCI) provides a set of concepts and methodologies that has advanced our understanding and design of interactive systems, especially ones based on computers, devices, and displays. The design of e-learning systems should take into account the characteristics, needs, and abilities of users who interact with virtual learning environments.

As in any virtual environment, the design of e-learning systems should also be focused on the user, usable, and taking into account the characteristics and abilities of users when interacting with the virtual learning environment and educational content. e-Learning should also consider usability, i.e. efficiency, effectiveness, and student satisfaction. Jacob Nielsen defines usability as a quality attribute that sets the usability of user interfaces and is defined by five quality components: *learnability, or ability to be learned; efficiency; memorability, or ability to be remembered; to avoid user errors; and user satisfaction.*

Directly related to the concept of efficiency referred to usability, the learnability concept appears, and refers, to the speed with which someone learns to use a specific application. Learnability refers to the degree a user interface can be learned effectively and quickly, but can also refer to the efficiency with which a specific e-learning content can be learned. While usability learnability refers to the functionality, learnability also refers to the cognitive process of learning. Thus, the less effort is devoted to understand and learn the functionality of the e-learning system, the more effort you can devote to the educational content where students learn and acquire skills. In designing e-learning systems, it is important to achieve both usability and educational goals. Students should be able to easily interact with the educational content and learning environment and focus on acquiring knowledge and skills provided in training. Therefore, the main objective is to identify design solutions e-learning to reduce user frustration and increase the usability, learning, and satisfaction.

In designing usable e-learning systems, it is interesting to consider three dimensions: *the student, the content,* and *the environment.* The user or student includes user identification and discovery of their needs and characteristics. The dimension of the educational content includes identifying design guidelines, techniques, and requirements to be followed, and different aspects related to the separation of content and visualization content. This dimension of the learning environment takes into account the identification of the requirements and characteristics of the learning environment, task analysis, and interaction design. These three dimensions help provide a vision complete e-learning showing the importance of usability in e-learning.

In virtual learning environments, it is of great importance to obtain information about user behaviour and understand how students use the learning environment, and how to navigate the educational materials. Understanding user behaviour provides very useful information for usability engineers, and designers of the system determine whether the interface of e-learning system is designed well and know that tasks generate a higher rate of failure or frustration. The data collected from the student activity is a source of valuable information and relevant to the advances in the design and development of e-learning solutions and innovative tools and services to facilitate achieving the instructional and educational objectives.

Educators are increasingly using sophisticated computer games to snag and hold the interest of the "digital natives" in their classrooms. The aim of educational games is to facilitate the player's experience, meet desired objectives, and allow users to engage in education while they are enjoying themselves. Educational games seem to put learners in the role of decision maker and give them immediate feedback on their actions and decisions, inviting exploration and experimentation.

Nowadays, techniques and mechanics of videogame design have been applied to enhance non-games applications and services. This emerged concept is called "gamification." Educational gamification suggests that the use of a game-like rule systems can help students: a) to explore through active experimentation and discovery, b) to help through the mastery process and keep them engaged with potentially difficult tasks, c) to support their motivation and engagement, d) to persist through negative emotional experiences and even transform them into positive, and e) to take on meaningful roles that are fruitful for learning.

Well-designed educational computer games share characteristics with effective e-learning environments, and can also be evaluated and designed using HCI principles. Like the design of e-learning systems and other virtual environments, the design of games must take users into account. For example, elements in playability—including challenge, strategy, pace, balance, control, and progress tracking—occupy a central role in videogame design, attracting users and engaging them in play. While a heuristic may help in design, user testing is essential for measuring success.

In addition, both e-learning systems and games are being transformed as applications and developed for new environments (like virtual immersive learning environments, video-conferencing) and devices (including mobiles and tablets). These technologies may change patterns of interaction and make ubiquitous learning possible.

The purpose of this book is to cover the new models of interaction and HCI paradigms applied to learning environments, focusing on the usability design and evaluation of learning systems and educational game environments. Therefore, this book provides a picture of the state of art in the field of HCI applied to educational environments and serious games, and could help experts of the area of HCI, learning systems, and educational videogames to improve their understanding of student experiences with new learning-gaming environments and allow researchers and developers to share techniques for the design and evaluation of educational games and interactive systems.

This book is divided into three sections. The first section "Usability, Accessibility, and Playability in Virtual Learning Environments and Serious Games," offers five chapters showing the main principles and techniques about usability, accessibility, and playability in e-learning and educational videogames. The second section, "Human and Social Factors in Game-Based Learning," consists of four chapters about the study of human factors in serious games, considering the power of attraction, trust, or studying the different aspects linked to users' collaboration in these environments. The third and final section, "Experiences and Uses of Educational Videogames in Different Contexts," presents eight case studies providing readers with a rich overview of problems and experiences in the area, such as the design and usability evaluation of educational tools, 3D mobile games, laboratory experiments in CSCL activities, or applications in different contexts and individuals, such as deaf or hospitalized persons. In this way, the book is structured to first introduce the concepts and methods and then show their applications through different case studies. In summary, the chapters in this book represent some of the main areas and applications related to student usability in educational software and serious games, illustrating the key benefits and issues emerging through these research projects that share high-quality knowledge with the HCI community.

Carina Soledad González González
University of La Laguna, Spain

Acknowledgment

My sincere appreciation to all the authors, reviewers, and special invited authors for their efforts, as well as the IGI editorial staff for their involvement to realize this book.

Carina Soledad González González
University of la Laguna, Spain

Section 1
Usability, Accessibility and Playability in Virtual Learning Environments and Serious Games

Chapter 1
An Overview of Accessibility and Usability of Educational Games

Marion A. Hersh
University of Glasgow, Scotland

Barbara Leporini
ISTI – CNR, Italy

ABSTRACT

This chapter presents an overview of accessibility and usability for educational computer-based games and the first survey of the accessibility and usability of digital educational games. The overview includes a discussion of accessibility and usability, both in general and in the specific context of educational games, as well as a brief presentation of issues relating to game design, including of mobile games. Since there are no previous studies of the accessibility and usability of educational computer-based games, studies of the accessibility and usability of the related areas of virtual learning environments, digital games for entertainment and PDF documents, are also presented. The overview of accessibility and usability and the results of the survey are used to draw up a structured list of 62 guidelines and recommendations, organised into three categories at the first level and ten at the second level. These guidelines and recommendations are illustrated by an example of their application to a fictitious new educational game.

1. INTRODUCTION

1.1. Aims and Objectives: Learning through Games

A combination of increasing interest in learning through games and advances in Information and Communications Technologies (ICT) have led to the development of a number of computer-based educational games and gaming environments. This trend is likely to continue. There is also increasing recognition of the needs of disabled students and the importance of integrating them into mainstream education, as well as the importance of doing this appropriately and the associated requirement for adequate resources to support this. This makes it imperative to consider the requirements of disabled students (and staff) to

DOI: 10.4018/978-1-4666-1987-6.ch001

ensure their full inclusion while the development and dissemination of educational computer-based games and gaming environments are still at a relatively early stage.

This raises the issues of whether and, if so, how best such approaches can be used to support disabled learners. Thus, it is important to understand the underlying pedagogical assumptions on which the particular course topic or module and the use of educational digital games are based. This will also require consideration of the affect of these pedagogical assumptions on disabled students and whether it will be necessary to modify some or all of them to enable full inclusion of all disabled and non-disabled students. In addition, guidelines will be required to support the development of high quality accessible and usable educational computer-based games. Discussion of the associated resource implications is beyond the scope of this chapter.

Therefore, the overall aim of the chapter is increasing understanding of the conditions to be met for good practice in designing educational gaming environments which are effective, fun to use and fully accessible by disabled (and non-disabled) students. Specific objectives include an introduction to accessibility and usability issues for computer-based games and gaming environments, with a particular focus on the accessibility and usability requirements of disabled people. Other objectives include a presentation and evaluation of the state of the art with regards to the development of educational computer-based games and their usability and accessibility, and the development of guidelines and recommendations to be followed.

The chapter is laid out as follows. The remainder of this section gives a brief overview of the social and medical models of disability and design for all. Section 3 considers accessibility and usability, including definitions, the connections and differences between the two and accessibility guidelines and recommendations. It is motivated by a brief discussion of computer use with the support of assistive technology. Section 3 provides an

overview of educational computer-based games, including principles and categorisations, mobile digital games, collaborative and cooperative features, student assessment, the accessibility and usability, and digital games for disabled students. The section on accessibility and usability includes pedagogical usability, playability, and accessibility and usability of educational computer based games and educational games on mobile devices. Section 4 presents a number of studies of the accessibility and usability of virtual learning environments, PDF documents, and games for entertainment. Section 5 presents the first study of the accessibility and usability of educational digital games. Section 6 presents a structured list of recommendations and guidelines, and section 7 discussion and conclusions.

1.2. The Social and Medical Models of Disability

The context in which educational gaming (and other) technologies for disabled (and non-disabled) people are developed is influenced by definitions of and attitudes to disability. There are two main approaches, the medical and social models.

The medical model is based on the international classification of "impairment," "disability," and "handicap" (sometimes referred to as the ICIDH model) developed by the World Health Organisation (WHO, 1980). It views disability as residing in the individual and focuses on the person's impairment(s) as the cause of disadvantage, leading to the approaches of occupational therapy and rehabilitation. It should be noted that many organisations of disabled people dislike the term "handicap," and it should not be used.

The social model of disability emphasizes the physical and social barriers experienced by disabled people (Swain, et al., 2003) rather than their impairments and considers the problem to be in society rather than the disabled person. It comprises the two concepts of impairment and disability, with "disability" defined as the loss or reduction of opportunities to take part in the normal life of the community on an equal level with others due to physical, environmental, or social barriers. The social model is compatible with the empowerment of disabled people and user-centred and participative design approaches (Damodaran, 1996; Rowley, 1998). It was first developed by the Union of the Physically Impaired Against Segregation (UPIAS, 1976) and then modified by the Disabled Peoples International (DPI) (Barnes, 1994). In the social model, it is the steps that are the problem not the wheelchair or the lack of large print books rather than the person's eyesight.

The importance of the social model was recognised in an update of the WHO classification system. In the new version, commonly termed ICIHD2, the terms "impairment, disability and handicap" were replaced by "disability, activity and participation" (WHO, 2001). While disablement is considered to be the result of the interaction between an individual's health and contextual factors, the individual's condition rather than external factors are still the main driver of the classification. This differs from the social model in which impairment is considered simply to be part of human diversity, but disability is recognised as being created by social and community environments that have been designed without taking the needs of disabled people into account.

1.3. Design for All

Design for all or universal design involves design for usability by the wider population, including disabled people. Design for all approaches are particularly important in an educational environment to avoid disabled (or minority group) students being stigmatised or singled out by having to use significantly different learning systems from their peers or being excluded by inappropriate design leading to barriers. They should include inclusive pedagogies which avoid cultural bias and unnecessary or restrictive requirements which are

difficult for some disabled students. However, personalisation or customisation may still be required to meet the needs of the full diversity of learners and support for personalisation should be included in the design. Design for all should also be understood to include compatibility with a wide range of different assistive devices.

The following principles (Connell, et al., 1997; CEN, 2003) are relevant to the design of educational computer-based games and virtual gaming environments.

1. The same or equivalent means of use for all users.
2. A design that accommodates a wide range of user preferences and characteristics.
3. A design that is easy to understand, regardless of the user's experience, knowledge, language skills, or current level of concentration.
4. Effective communication of relevant information, regardless of ambient conditions, the senses used to access information or other factors.
5. Minimising any negative consequences or hazards of user errors, accidental or unintended actions, including through warnings and fail-safe features.
6. Efficient and comfortable use with a minimum of effort and fatigue.

2. ACCESSIBILITY AND USABILITY

2.1. User Interfaces and Assistive Technologies: Enablers and Barriers

The discussion of usability and accessibility will be introduced by a brief overview of the way in which different groups of disabled people use the various stationary and mobile devices on which digital games can be played and potential barriers and enablers to the use of these devices. The use of computer and other devices involves input devices to input, manipulate, and give commands to the computer or other game playing device and output devices to receive output from it. Non-disabled people generally use a keyboard and mouse combination, remote control, on-screen pointer, keypad or mini keyboard for input and screen and loudspeakers (either built in or stand-alone) for output.

Many disabled people access computers and other game playing devices through some form of assistive technology. Their enjoyment and learning from the game or even whether they are able to play it at all will depend on whether the game and game playing hardware and software have been designed to be compatible with and offer their full facilities when used with assistive devices. Assistive input devices and systems include the following:

1. Adapted keyboards, including for one hand use
2. Onscreen keyboards
3. Devices that require a single muscle movement e.g. binary (on/off) switch, eyegaze control device, sip and puff device
4. Joystick
5. Braille keyboard
6. Speech recognition software.

Assistive output devices and systems include the following:

1. Screen readers with voice synthesizers and/or Braille displays
2. Screen magnification devices
3. Subtitles.

Other users' accessibility requirements may involve a particular colour contrast or the avoidance of output, which includes animation, colour, and/or scrolling text. Accessible desktop and Web applications need to be well designed, and the user interface must be compatible with a number of different assistive devices. This requires the application of design guidelines for accessible and usable user interfaces.

2.2. Usability and Accessibility: Definitions, Connections, and Differences

More attention has generally been paid to accessibility than usability in both software systems and products, with the focus on Internet accessibility. However, generally valid formal definitions and official international standards have been developed for usability, but not for accessibility. Accessibility relates to the environmental characteristics of the system input and output which enable particular (groups of) users to access and use all facilities of the system, whereas usability is the ability of the system to carry out the intended function(s) or achieve specified goals effectively, efficiently, and with satisfaction when used by particular (groups of) users in their particular context (Federici, et al., 2005). There are both definitions of accessibility, which refer specifically to disabled people (W3C, 2005) and those, which refer to the general population (Jarmin, 2012).

There are a number of definitions of usability, which characterise it in terms of some combination of the prevention of errors, user confidence and control, ease of use, ease of learning, goal achievement and satisfaction (McLaughlin & Skinner, 2000; Nielsen, 1993; Quesenbery, et al., 2001; Nokelainen, 2004). The International Organization for Standardization standard ISO 92 4-11 considers usability to be 'the extent to which a product can be used by specified users to achieve specified goals in a specified context of use with effectiveness, efficiency, and satisfaction.' Nielsen's (1993, 1994) usability heuristics are probably the best-known method for testing and evaluating usability. These include: presenting information in a natural and logical order and avoiding technical terms, keeping users informed with appropriate feedback, eliminating error-prone conditions, the ability to exit easily from an unwanted state, consistency and provision of information rather than expecting the user to recall it.

Both usability and accessibility should be considered as part of good design practice and included from the earliest stages of software specification and design. Although they are frequently considered separately, there is some overlap between the concepts. However, accessibility is frequently considered a concern of disabled people and usability of non-disabled people. This ignores both the usability problems experienced by disabled people and the accessibility barriers experienced by non-disabled people, for instance due to being smaller than a generally artificially chosen design norm. It is also increasingly being recognised that many elderly people experience both accessibility and usability barriers, whether or not they are disabled.

In some cases, the barrier could be the result of either accessibility or usability problems. For instance, a disabled person who accesses the Web via a screen reader or with the images turned off experiences problems with a website that automatically transfers their previously entered name in an incorrect format to another part of the site. When they correct the name, the site queries this and the system loops with no apparent exit. This could be a usability issue due to the lack of an option to indicate that the changed version of the name is the correct one. Alternatively, the barrier could be an accessibility one if this option is provided by a clickable button icon without an alt text description, making it invisible to the user.

There have been a few small-scale studies of the relationship between website accessibility and usability. One such study involving blind and sighted people found that the problems encountered could be divided into three groups (Petrie & Kheir, 2007):

1. Problems experienced by blind people only, classified as purely accessibility issues by the authors.
2. Problems experienced by sighted people only, classified as purely usability issues.
3. Problems experienced by both blind and sighted people, classified as universal usability issues.

Universal usability is defined by Schneiderman (2000, 2003) to cover both accessibility and usability with 'more than 90% of households as successful users of information and communication technologies at least once a week.' However, households may not use ICT due to lack of time or interest rather than accessibility or usability barriers. The study finding (Petrie & Kheir, 2007) of both common and separate problems indicates the overlap between usability and accessibility. However, it does not imply that all the problems experienced solely by blind people are purely accessibility problems with no usability component or that all the common problems have no accessibility component (for blind people).

Understanding of the relationship between accessibility and usability has been furthered by the second author and colleagues (Leporini & Paternò, 2003), who have developed 16 usability criteria for blind and visually impaired users of accessible websites based on the following usability principles:

1. **Effectiveness:** Criteria which are important for users to carry out desired tasks and without which they would experience barriers, such as clear link texts (not 'click here').
2. **Efficiency:** Rules that allow users to obtain the desired information quickly, such as meaningful descriptive names for frames. The system is usable, but takes longer or is difficult to use, leading to some users giving up.

3. **Satisfaction:** Criteria which make it more enjoyable to navigate and use websites. They include the identification of actions by short sounds and the use of high contract coloured text and background to facilitate navigation by visually impaired people. However, personalisation with the option of turning on or off sounds and coloured text is required to avoid stress and accessibility barriers to some other users, particularly those with autistic spectrum conditions.

Leporini and Paternò (2008) have applied and tested these criteria with a 'control' website prototype. The study revealed that application of the criteria can lead to a very significant time saving of 34% for carrying out tasks using a screenreader and keyboard. A study by Theofanos and Redish (2003) of the gap between accessibility and usability for screenreader users led to an unstructured list of 32 guidelines aimed at improving usability for blind users. Buzzi and Leporini (2010) have discussed accessibility and usability when accessing distance-learning systems via a screenreader and Leporini and Paternò (2003, 2008) have proposed general principles from which guidelines for specific cases can be obtained.

In summary, 'accessibility' involves overcoming potential technical barriers that could prevent successful use of the system, whereas usability is ease of use with minimum effort by particular users in a particular context. Several investigations have shown that the two are complimentary and equally important in improving the user interface, interaction, and satisfaction. For instance, a study of 100 websites with 51 disabled users (Petrie, et al., 2004) reported that 45% of the difficulties encountered were on pages which complied with accessibility requirements.

2.3. Accessibility and Usability Recommendations and Guidelines

There are a number of Web accessibility guidelines and recommendations, of which the most important are due to the World Wide Web Consortium (W3C) Web Accessibility Initiative (WAI). It has produced accessibility standards and guidelines for Web content, browsers, authoring tools and other features. The W3C Web Content Accessibility Guidelines (WCAG) address the format of information in a website, including text, images, forms, and sounds. The initial WCAG 1.0 has been updated with the WCAG 2.0 (http://www.w3.org/TR/2008/REC-WCAG20-20081211). Important documents include "How to Meet WCAG 2.0," a customisable quick reference document on applying the guidelines, and Authoring Tool Accessibility Guidelines (http://www.w3.org/TR/ATAG20/).

The WCAG 2.0 guidelines are written as testable statements that are not technology specific. However, they are only a first step and testing with disabled end users is required to ensure that websites that meet the guidelines are in practice readily accessible by disabled people. Another approach involves the development of additional guidelines for particular groups of disabled people. Accessibility guidelines can be general, whereas usability is about particular users being able to reach a desired goal in a particular context. Therefore, usability guidelines should consider the target users and the particular context and goal, and may not be appropriate for other users or contexts. For instance, Leporini et al. (2008) have developed specific guidelines for Web-based search engine interfaces for screenreader users, which are based on the following main goals when accessing a Web search engine: (1) easily identifying the search form elements and (2) reading the results obtained quickly.

3. EDUCATIONAL COMPUTER-BASED GAMES AND GAMING ENVIRONMENTS

3.1. Introduction

The concept 'game' seems to be reasonably well understood, though there is not a universally accepted definition. Common elements in existing definitions include enjoyment, gratuitousness, and rules (Kickmeir-Rust, 2003). One area of contention is whether games are defined by a lack of purpose (Anon, 2011a) or the purpose of amusing or rewarding player(s) (Zyda, 2005).

Digital games have developed considerably from the early computer-based training systems based on questions with predefined answers and which offered little interaction. They now include learning environments based on virtual reality, which encourage collaboration and allow participants to learn both from their own experiences and from their peers (Felicia, et al., 2009). However, a realistic rather than public relations approach to evaluating the advantages and disadvantages of educational computer-based games is required. They are most effective when the educational content is well integrated into appropriate curricula and pedagogies (Blamire, 2010), rather than the games being used as the sole approach to teaching. This includes allowing students to create their own games or to critique games, thereby exploring the game structure as well as the subject (Oblinger, 2006). In addition, the games used should be carefully chosen for the particular students and topic. Educational games can be used to support a range of subjects, including mathematics, languages, digital skills, strategic thinking, and group decision making (Blamire, 2010). They can be used to teach facts, principles and complex problem solving techniques, improve skills and provide practical examples of concepts and rules (Felicia, et al., 2009). Simulation type games, in particular, can also provide a challenging environment in which

it is safe to make mistakes and learn from them, experience realistic simulated settings without any real life consequences (Felicia, et al., 2009) or carry out experiments that would be dangerous to perform (Ebner & Holzinger, 2007). However, the differences between carrying out an experiment 'live' and as part of a computer game should be recognised and games should therefore be used to complement rather than replace practical work.

3.1.1. Categorisation

There have been a number of different attempts to categorise both digital games in general and the different types of digital games used in learning. However, a universally accepted categorisation has not yet been developed and many of the existing attempts comprise unstructured lists, frequently with some degree of overlap between the categories. However, several categorisations link the different types of games to the type of learning they support, or provide examples of key games and texts (Blamire, 2010). The game categories include alternate reality games, simulations/microworlds, serious games, role-playing games, creative games, and authoring games. There are also a few structured approaches to classification. The lecture games taxonomy (Wang, et al., 2009) has a structured hierarchical classification based on the three levels of: (1) Player interaction: single-player, multi-player with interaction; (2) Fantasy and skills interaction: intrinsic (integrated), extrinsic (not integrated); and (3) Main game concept with ten categories linked to second level categories.

Kickmeier-Rust's (2009) hypercube taxonomy has the three inner dimensions of purpose (ranging from fun to learning or training); reality (ranging from imitation of real or fictitious contexts to abstract visualisations); and social involvement (ranging from single player games to massively multiplayer games) and the additional dimension of activity (ranging from active to passive game types). Other approaches have derived functional categories and conditions, which can be used to categorise games, including by using design patterns and game ontologies. For instance, an unstructured list of 14 different factors which can be used to describe about 50,000 functionally different categories of games has been obtained (Elverdam & Aarseth, 2007; Dahlskog, et al., 2009). These factors include the following: perspective (overall or tied to a game token), player position (absolute or relative to objects), individual or team, and type of goal(s).

3.1.2. Evaluation

Educational games can provide ongoing feedback on performance and reduce the pressure of formative assessment and allow risk-taking, mistakes, and failure rather than requiring students to obtain the correct answer the first time. The fact that exploration and trying out new strategies are not penalised can increase the potential for learning through assessment and the integration of assessment and learning (e.g. as a quiz) rather than separated from it. They can also assess performance in (simulated) real life activities e.g. planning a city rather than purely writing an essay about it. Challenge, curiosity, and enjoyment are important elements of games based learning and should also be an important feature of games based assessment, rather than assessment leading to the stress or even fear frequently associated with traditional tests and exams. In addition, assessment should not interfere with learning or restrict curiosity to the minimal requirements to pass assessments.

There has been limited work on the use of game based assessment. One of the systems that has been developed is Smart Cat Profiling from Screen Learning (2011) for assessing the skills of primary school children and as a screening tool for additional support needs or previously unnoticed impairments. The profiler is designed to be experienced as an enjoyable game and to avoid the stress normally associated with assessment. This has meant that children are not informed

that they are being assessed (Walker, 2008). This raises the issue of the ethics of assessing even small children without their knowledge. This issue becomes more pertinent in the case of older students and leads to the question of the conditions under which game based assessment is feasible or whether the stress of knowing that an assessment is being carried out negates the playful elements associated with games.

3.1.3. Collaboration and Cooperation

Collaboration and cooperation are frequently important features of both educational computer-based games and learning environments, due to their importance in the learning process. Co-operation is generally more relevant to small groups of students, who share key objectives, whereas collaboration may involve, for instance, students from different schools, who work together on a particular project (Grudin, 1994). However, it is only relatively recently that developments in ICT have enabled the provision of support for collaboration in computer games. Therefore, most recently developed, but few older, successful commercial games have a multi-player component. Interaction between players can add a social element, which provides a context and allows players to receive feedback and valuable information from each other. Social interaction outside the game can also be of value.

Collaboration and to a lesser extent co-operation can involve students playing at the same or different times and places (Johansen, 1988), for instance at the same time and place in a classroom and different times and places when playing at home. Therefore, awareness of other players can be particularly important. This includes (Endsley, 1995; Gutwin & Greenberg, 2004) knowledge about other users and of the state of the game environment, which needs to be up-to-date, as it changes over time. This knowledge is generally obtained by playing the game. Another important feature of interaction is discussion of the game on forums and social networks. Therefore, tools such as Wikis need to be designed to simplify social and game interaction and knowledge sharing for disabled as well as non-disabled users. This requires, for instance, identical information to be available through the visual, auditory, and tactile channels and the design to be optimised for access and navigation using a wide range of different input devices. Buzzi and Leporini (2009) provide recommendations for enhancing Wiki usability for blind users arising from empirical research on navigating Wikis with a screenreader.

3.1.4. Mobile Digital Games

Digital games can now be played on mobile devices. However, there are differences of opinion as to whether mobile games include games on handheld video games systems, such as Nintendo DS and Playstation portable, or are restricted to games played on mobile and smart phones, PDAs, handheld computers, and portable media players (Anon, 2011b). There are both networked versions, which use, for instance text, multi-media messages, and/or GPS location identification, and non-networked versions.

Mobile games are able to take advantage of the connectivity, location sensitivity and context awareness of mobile devices (Thomas, et al., 2007). Context awareness can include consideration of a player's progress while playing, cooperation between players and the player's relationship with objects in the game. In principle, mobile games can enhance learning by combining gaming with reflection, mediation and collaboration (Thomas, et al., 2007). However, care has to be taken to ensure that all information is presented in an accessible format and to avoid information overload or overstimulation. This may be a particular problem for some groups of disabled learners. The introduction and wide dissemination of camera phones with improved graphics and storage capabilities has increased the potential for games on mobile phones. The integration of three

dimensional application programming interfaces into mobile platforms has led to the development of games specifically for these platforms. These games tend to be small in scope and to rely on good game play rather than flashy graphics due to their lower processing power (Anon, 2011b).

3.2. Designing Games and Gaming Environments

Although not all digital games are intended to be educational, their design generally includes features that can help develop cognitive abilities. They also have many problem solving features, such as an unknown outcome, multiple paths to a goal and collaboration in the case of multiple player games (Ebner & Holzinger, 2007). It has been suggested that it is the features of challenge, fantasy and curiosity (with an optimal level of information complexity [Piaget, 1951]) that make computer applications enjoyable (Malone, 1980). There are also different understandings of 'fantasy' in the context of games. Some authors consider it unsuitable, for instance in civil engineering education (Ebner & Holzinger, 2007), whereas others (Wang, et al., 2009) include realistic fantasies such as running a store. Other features of games which are considered to encourage learning include the facts that they are immersive, have clear goals, require frequent decisions, can be adopted to each player and involve a social network.

The Imagine project on the mainstreaming of educational games noted the importance of taking differences in background, culture, language and values into account in game design to avoid misunderstandings based on, for instance, different perceptions of values, norms, artefacts, colours, and symbols (Blamire, 2010). However, there is less awareness of the importance of accessibility and usability and the need for game design, which takes account of the needs of disabled students. The designers of digital games or gaming environments should consider factors that promote learning. These include (Wang, et al., 2009) controllable levels of difficulty, the availability of hints or other instructional support when players cannot solve problems, sound instructional principles and an inspiring game concept.

There have been three main approaches to the design of educational games, all of which have some disadvantages (Moreno-Ger, et al., 2008):

1. Developing a game from existing educational content, sometimes called edutainment. Unfortunately, the resulting games may not be very interesting and entertaining, thereby losing the benefits of game-based learning.
2. Adding educational content to existing games. This will lead to high quality games, which may also be realistic and historically accurate. However, concepts may be oversimplified and little attention paid to pedagogical and educational considerations.
3. Designing new educational games to obtain an appropriate balance between fun and learning. Effective educational games require an appropriate balance between fun and education (Prensky, 2001). However, such games can be both expensive and difficult. Their design can be facilitated by the use of educational game engines with built-in features to increase their pedagogical value.

3.3. Accessibility and Usability

3.3.1. Usability

The requirement for educational media to support learning, as well as easy and effective use, has given rise to the concept of pedagogical usability (Shield & Kukulska-Hulme, 2006; Kukulska-Hulme, 2007). The following 10 categories of pedagogical usability criteria have been suggested (Nokelainen, 2004):

1. Learner, rather than teacher or designer control of the technology, with learning material presented in meaningful units.
2. Learner ownership of the goals of action and the results, including learning material that attracts learners' attention.
3. Cooperative learning, including discussing and negotiating different approaches to learning.
4. Clear goals, which are set by the learners themselves.
5. Applicability to real situations, with examples taken from authentic situations and the resulting knowledge and skills relevant to other contexts.
6. Added value for learning and relevant media elements.
7. Motivation, which affects all learning.
8. Encouragement to make meaningful use of existing knowledge.
9. Flexibility with adaptation to different learners and tasks decomposed into small, flexible learning units.
10. Accurate feedback, giving real dialogue between the user and the computer.

3.3.2. Playability

The concept of playability arose from the recognition that the usability factors of effectiveness, efficiency and satisfaction are not in themselves sufficient for digital games. However, there is some debate as to whether it is purely an extension of usability or also involves the quality of the game elements (Gónzalez Sánchez, et al., 2009). Playability has been defined as the properties that characterise the ability of a game to provide enjoyment and entertainment by being credible and satisfying for players playing individually or with others. A number of authors, including Bickford (1997), Clanton (1998), Desurvire et al. (2004), Fabricatore (2002), Federoff (2002), González Sánchez et al. (2009), IGDA (2004),

Korhonen and Koivisto (2006), Malone (1982), Norman (1990), Sanchez-Crespo Dalmau (1999), Shelley (2001), and Shneiderman (1997) have derived lists of playability heuristics or design recommendations for digital (frequently video) games in general, rather than specifically for educational digital games through analysis of existing lists and/or consultation with players. While there is some overlap between different authors' heuristics, there are also considerable differences and a comprehensive, generally accepted list has not yet been developed. In addition, the heuristics need to be validated (Desurvire, et al., 2004). Some of the heuristics and design recommendations are very detailed and clearly only relevant to games and not other ICT systems. Since the lists are generally fairly lengthy, authors have frequently divided or categorised their elements into several different groups or categories. The categories used include the game interface, game play, game story, game mechanics, and usability (Desurvire, et al., 2004; Federoff, 2002). The different authors do not always agree on which category a particular heuristic should be assigned to.

3.3.3. Accessibility and Usability of Educational Computer-Based Games and Gaming Environments

Interacting with computer games often requires high-level motor, sensory, attention and other mental skills. This may also require the use of inflexible and complicated input devices and techniques (Grammenos, et al., 2009). Thus, the accessibility and usability requirements of computer-based games frequently go beyond those of website accessibility and usability. In addition, educational games have pedagogical usability issues and associated requirements, as discussed in the previous section. Despite the increasing popularity of digital games as a major source of entertainment and the potential role of educational games, very little attention has been given to their accessibility and usability. The earliest literature dates back to only about 2004, for instance Bierre et al. (2004), Bierre (2005).

Accessibility and usability of educational computer-based games and virtual gaming environments are frequently multi-dimensional and should cover at least the following features for all disabled learners and teachers, who may be using various different assistive input and output devices (Hersh, 2008):

1. All relevant student functions.
2. All relevant administrator and teacher functions, including editing and accessible content authoring, with prompts for features such as alternative text descriptions of figures.
3. Navigation and links.
4. Collaborative and cooperative functions and tools.
5. The content and formatting of documents posted on the system.
6. System modification in the case of open source software.

There are generally benefits from a holistic approach to accessibility, particularly in the context of elearning (Kelly, et al., 2005, 2007). This should include consideration of the context in which the elearning resource or website is being used and cover the following factors:

1. The intended purpose, including the typical tasks to be performed and the intended user experience.
2. The intended audience, including their subject specific, information technology, and assistive technology knowledge.
3. The intended usage environment, including the types of browsers and assistive technology the intended audience are likely to be using.
4. The role in the overall delivery of services and information, including whether there are non-Web options.

5. The intended lifecycle of the resource, including its expected lifespan and whether it is to be developed and/or upgraded.

Design for full accessibility is particularly important in education to ensure that all students are able to concentrate on the learning process without having to try to overcome unnecessary obstacles. The situation with regards to usability is more complex. On the one hand, learning systems should be well designed so that they are not difficult or impossible to use or unnecessarily difficult to learn to use. On the other hand, there is a perspective that deep learning requires the user to be challenged to some extent and to overcome some difficulties to carry out tasks (Mayes & Fowler, 1999). This implies that an appropriate level of difficulty in using the software may be required to facilitate learning, challenge users, and make them think about the material. However, too great a level of difficulty should be avoided, as it will act as a barrier to learning. The user's prior learning and level of knowledge should be considered (Mayes & Fowler, 1999). This then shifts the focus from the design of interfaces to the design of effective tasks and support for the creation of a framework to support understanding.

However, approaches to improving accessibility have generally been based on either the use of assistive devices, such as binary switches and joysticks, (which may be used as mouse emulators) and screenreaders, or design for a particular group of disabled people, such as audio games for blind people and single switch games for physically disabled people (Grammenos, et al., 2009). While assistive devices will be required by some disabled users, using them with games for which they have not been designed is frequently unsatisfactory and can lead to longer interaction times, reduced functionality and increased errors, for instance when a mouse emulator is used to select small areas. In addition, unless textual versions of graphics are provided manually, they will not be available, as it is not (yet) possible to automatically provide such descriptions (Grammenos, et al., 2009). While the development of games for particular groups of disabled people can lead to high quality games, doing so can be expensive and contribute to social exclusion through the separation of disabled and non-disabled players (Grammenos, et al., 2009).

Every user of an elearning system needs to have access to the same educational content. This may require different media to be used to deliver content to different users to take account of their access requirements and preferences. These different versions, for instance text, sign language and other representations of non-text content, need to be educationally equivalent to the original version. However, a detailed discussion of what this means in practice is beyond the scope of this chapter.

Determining whether computer-based games are fully usable and accessible will require an evaluation process and appropriate tools and procedure to support it, as well as the involvement of both disabled and non-disabled end-users. One such evaluation tool (Silius, et al., 2003) has accessibility, informational quality, usability, and pedagogical usability sections, each with four to 12 criteria and allows criteria, which are not relevant to the particular Web-based learning environment to be filtered out. The resulting report provides a profile of the learning environment, a summary of good features and detailed guidelines on how to improve accessibility, the quality of the information, usability, and pedagogical usability.

3.3.4. Accessibility and Usability of Games on Mobile Devices

Accessibility and usability are particularly important for educational computer-based games and learning environments (as well as other learning systems) on mobile devices. The very factors, namely small size, low weight and multi-functionality, that make mobile devices attractive by making them easily portable and enabling them to be used at any time and place are potentially a source of accessibility and usability barriers, particularly to disabled and elderly people. Mobility and small size result in reduced memory and processing speed, and the need for batteries to be regularly recharged (Kukulska-Hulme, 2007), as well as small, relatively difficult to see or feel screens, keyboards and pointers. Mobile devices are used in non-ideal physical environments where there are likely to be frequent interruptions (Kukulska-Hulme, 2007), further contributing to accessibility and usability barriers. The importance of screen size has been considered in a disciplinary context (Kukulska-Hulme, 2007), but not as a wider accessibility issue with implications for the participation of disabled people in mobile learning.

Recognition of the importance of user-centred design and awareness of the context of use (Evans & Taylor, 2005; Malliou & Miliarakis, 2005) may be particularly relevant in avoiding accessibility and usability problems for disabled people and promoting successful and enjoyable mobile learning. A study of a number of mobile learning projects (Kukulska-Hulme 2007) identified four main categories of usability issues: physical attributes (e.g. size, weight, memory, battery life), content and software applications, network speed and reliability, and the physical environment. The perception of usability issues frequently depended on the context. In addition, mobile devices were often used in unpredictable real-world circumstances to which people responded constructively, but not in ways that could easily be fed back to inform the technology design (Kukulska-Hulme, 2008).

3.4. Digital Games for Disabled Students

Participation in the same activities as other students prevents stigma and encourages the inclusion of disabled students. However, there has been limited consideration of the need for design for all approaches to digital educational games. Many existing games are not particularly accessible to disabled people. For instance, they include audiovisual information without textual equivalents, such as closed subtitles, for deaf and hard of hearing people, and text or audio equivalents, such as audio descriptions, for blind people. Alternatively, they may require very fast responses and be difficult to operate with a single switch. This then raises the issue of whether all games can be made fully accessible to all users without reducing enjoyment, for instance by including the provision of high quality text and audio equivalent versions, or slowing down the game. There are clear advantages in using only educational games, which can be made fully accessible. However, there could also be benefits in providing a number of different games to support each topic or module, with the different games taking account of learners' different cognitive styles and interests. Where visual or sound effects are an important feature of the game and its attractiveness, the text and audio versions should be of equally high quality and attractiveness. Where a fast pace is an important game feature, it may be necessary to provide other means of generating excitement when the game is slowed down.

Where accessibility has been considered, it has frequently been on the basis of making digital games accessible to a particular group of disabled people e.g. blind or deaf people rather than disabled people in general. For instance, audiogames.com has a list of games, which use only sound and generally only have auditory and no visual output (http://audiogames.net/listgames. php). For each game, the type of license and genre is indicated and a link to the game home page is given. A list of 'screen-reader friendly' online games with links to the game home page can be found at (http://www.whitestick.co.uk/ongames. html). A few of the games, such as Alter Aeon, provide a support page or other features for blind and visually impaired players. However, neither of these lists indicates the educational potential of the games.

Early games had very limited audio capacities and comprised mainly text and graphics. However, the importance of audio has increased and it is now very important in modern games. It may be used to provide important information about the game, vital clues in puzzles, to convey emotion or otherwise enhance the game (Tol, 2006). Closed subtitles can be used to present text versions of speech, as well as descriptions of sounds and music. The term 'closed' indicates that viewers have to activate them and that, unlike open subtitles, they are not automatically visible to everyone. Closed subtitles are also useful in public places to avoid sound interference, to save battery power on mobile devices and where it is too noisy to hear the audio easily. Further enhancements and additional information may be required to give hearing impaired players a fully immersive game experience.

Other options, many of which are already used in some games, include the use of colour coding of the text or speaker portraits to indicate the speaker, action captions, sound balloons, sound visualisations, video clips, and visual sound indicators. Action captions are visual, generally onomatopoeic (words that imitate the sound described) representations of the sound in brightly coloured text superimposed on the scene at approximately the location of the sound. Analogously to speech balloons, sound balloons have a description of the sound in a visual container close to the sound source. Sound visualisations are single images or animations, which can be used to show hearing impaired learners how a sound behaves, for instance the speed of flow of the leak in a pipe. Animated sound balloons could be controlled by actual sounds in real time using visualisation algorithms. Video clips could be used to illustrate sounds, such as a helicopter firing a rocket. A radar map could be used to indicate the locations of important sound sources (Tol, 2006).

The inclusion of sign language would be valuable for Deaf signers, for whom the national spoken language is generally a foreign or second language and who may experience difficulties in reading and understanding text, particularly at speed. However, the technology is still under development and only a minority of deaf people sign. All the sound replacement options should be provided in closed format to avoid disturbing other players, particularly those with autistic spectrum conditions, who may be sensitive to sensory overstimulation and/or disturbed by particular colours, lighting effects, sounds, or animations.

Game accessibility for physically disabled people has two main components (Anon, 2006): accessible game control which allows users to use a wide range of different interface devices; and adapting the game or adding additional functionality, for instance the option to slow down the game in difficult passages, called 'bullet time.' Physically disabled people can use many mainstream video games, but may require specialised hardware, including mouth controllers, head and eye trackers, or control boxes that can be adapted for one-handed use. Single switch games are becoming increasing popular and information can be found at oneswitch.org.uk. They are suitable for physically disabled people who access computers using, for instance, binary switches, joysticks or sip and puff devices.

People with autistic spectrum conditions may require games to avoid overstimulation, for instance in terms of visual and sound effects. For some of them certain types of colours, lights, sounds, animation, and scrolling text may present strong accessibility barriers, though others may be fascinated by some sensory stimuli. In addition, many autistic people like the fact that (educational) games are structured, have rules and frequently require repetitive movements. There is some evidence that educational games offer students with Asperger's syndrome opportunities for exploration, learning about and participating in meaningful social interaction and collaboration in a structured environment with reduced speed social interaction, including through being part of a learning community (Loeppky, 2006).

Games for people with cognitive impairments, specific or general learning difficulties may require additional instructions and/or instructions that do not have to be read. Additionally, there may benefit from the option to subdivide activities into very small tasks, with additional prompts to reduce the need for memorisation and to support progress through these tasks.

The games UA Chess, Access Invaders, and Terrestrial Invaders have been designed to be accessible to several different groups of disabled people (Grammenos, et al., 2009). This is a considerable advance on accessibility for a particular group of disabled users, even if not the 'universal accessibility' claimed or a holistic design for all approach. User profiles are used to record and set the accessibility features required. In addition, the dialogue box for setting up the profile has a number of accessibility features to avoid accessibility barriers at the start.

The chess game UA chess runs on any browser with a Flash player plug-in. It supports users who are sighted, blind, low vision or have manual or mild memory or cognitive impairments. However, the use of flash may make it partially or totally inaccessible to some autistic players. The mouse, keyboard, any binary switch that can emulate keystrokes and speech recognition can be used to access all game functions, though the speech recognition may perform poorly. It has self-voicing capabilities and a built-in screenreader that gives auditory access to the whole interface. User preferences can be used to size the game and it can be zoomed in and out. Speech application language tags are used to support speech recognition and synthesis. Further support is provided in the form of visual, but not audio cues of the last move, the current moves, available moves, and whether the king is in check.

Access Invaders is a modified more accessible version of Space Invaders for blind and low vision users, people with manual impairments and people with cognitive impairments. It has very simple rules, logic and content and limited control options. The interface and the player's spaceship can be controlled by one or more of the following:

keyboard, mouse, joystick, game pad and binary switches. The game's pace and the aliens' shooting speed can be reduced. The aliens' positions can be located by sound due to sonification of all game elements and a reduction in the number of aliens and their spread. Blinking and flashing graphics, which can cause problems for people with autistic spectrum conditions as well as those with epilepsy, are avoided and there are options for higher contrast, larger and less complex graphics and fonts.

Terrestrial Invaders is a development of Access Invaders. Both games support multiple concurrent players and multiple enemy groups. There are options for adjusting various game features, including game speed, enemies' speed, the size of player bombs and all game graphics, the game's difficulty and the number of enemy bullets active at one time. Menus can be read aloud and automatically scanned and two types of audio description (summary and detailed) are available. Two dimensional sound can be used to locate objects on a two dimensional plane and text and/or graphics for visualising all game sounds. There are two high contrast modes (light on dark and dark on light) and the option of replacing all graphic elements by simple shapes with high contrast solid colours, which people with low vision can generally see more easily than complex graphics. Controls can be redefined, but this requires editing the XML level description files, so many users would require assistance to do this.

4. STUDIES

4.1. Accessibility of Virtual Learning Environments

To our knowledge to date, other than the survey by the authors presented in section 5, no surveys have been carried out of the accessibility or usability for disabled students of educational computer-based games or virtual gaming environments. Therefore, this section will discuss briefly surveys of the accessibility of Virtual Learning Environments (VLEs), as the closest 'relative' for which such surveys are available. VLEs have been defined by the UK Joint Information Systems Committee as places where 'online interactions of various kinds take place between learners and tutors.' They generally include teaching materials, communication, student, assessment and student management and tracking tools, as well as shared student work group areas (Dunn, 2003).

4.1.1. Surveys of Colleges and Universities in the UK

There have been two surveys of the use of VLEs in colleges and universities in the UK. The first survey (Dunn, 2003) was distributed through relevant email lists. It received replies from 23 universities, 19 colleges, and 4 independent consultants, and also carried out seven face-to-face or telephone interviews. The more recent survey (Hersh, 2008) of all the universities and an equivalent number of FE colleges in the UK received replies from 18 universities and 8 colleges. There are both significant differences and some commonality in the survey questions used. Both this fact and the small numbers of respondents make it difficult to compare the surveys or determine whether and, if so, how practice has developed over time. In addition, both surveys noted that the small scale and, in the case of the first survey, the methodology of using email lists, increased the likelihood of respondent bias in favour of institutions with more interest in accessibility and at the better practice end of the spectrum with regards to policies and implementation. Therefore, although the situation may have improved since the surveys, other colleges and universities are likely to have much greater VLE accessibility problems.

At the time of the first survey, the main VLEs in use in both universities and colleges were Blackboard (32%) and WebCT (24%). By the second survey, the situation had significantly changed. Most institutions used either Moodle or Blackboard, with the colleges having a strong preference for Moodle (75%) and the universities for Blackboard (67%). One of the respondents noted that 60% of further education colleges use Moodle, indicating that the preference found in this survey holds more generally across further education.

The common main reasons (Hersh, 2008) for both colleges' and universities' choices were ease of use, functionality (including integration with existing systems in the case of colleges), and the availability of support. Colleges were also interested in costs and the fact that Moodle was Open Source. Universities were also interested in pedagogical issues, including not constraining users to a particular pedagogical approach, and support for sophisticated course design. One college mentioned ease of use with screenreaders and two universities mentioned accessibility as being important factors. About two thirds of the institutions had considered accessibility when making decisions about which VLE to adopt, but it had been a major consideration for only a small number of them. In the first survey (Dunn, 2003) 15% of respondents considered accessibility to be a prerequisite for VLE choice; 48% considered it a factor, but not the main one, and 15% considered it unimportant.

78% of respondents in the earlier survey (Dunn, 2003) considered the VLE used by their institution to be only partially or not accessible, with problems cited including the use of frames, inaccessibility of synchronous chat functions and poor usability. Respondents considered the most urgent issue leading to VLE inaccessibility to be lack of awareness of disability and accessibility issues and how they affected elearning in general and VLEs in particular. Other reasons cited for accessibility problems included inaccessibility of the VLE product or lack of support from the developers for accessibility, lack of technical skills by content authors, inaccessible content, insufficient end-user testing, lack of management support and insufficient course development time. This illustrates the importance of choosing an appropriate VLE system, though moves to open source VLEs that can be modified have reduced the importance of this. However, a survey of the reasons for choosing a particular VLE in 100 educational institutions ranked ease of use for staff second and ease of use for students joint last (Stiles, 2002). This is probably changing, but for the wrong reasons, due to the increased perception of students as 'customers' to be satisfied. In the UK and probably many other countries there is also considerably more awareness of the needs of disabled students than of disabled staff, with most institutions providing a disability service for students, but few having one for staff.

The later survey (Hersh, 2008) found that 37.5% of the colleges and two thirds of the universities thought that the VLE they used provided particular accessibility features, half the colleges and 28% of the universities were unsure and one university believed that it did not. The accessibility features university respondents were aware of included compliance with the legal requirements of the different accessibility standards, the ability to customise the system with regards to layout, colour and text size, compatibility with screen-readers and the availability of high contrast colour schemes and keyboard accessibility features. One university respondent drew attention to the problems caused by teachers putting up inaccessible materials even if the VLE itself was accessible.

The first survey (Dunn, 2003) highlighted the need for policies, publicity, and training on accessibility issues. The second survey (Hersh, 2008) found that 83% of the universities provided recommendations and guidelines on document accessibility and 72% of them also provided training, whereas 75% of the colleges provided recommendations, guidelines and training. Half of the colleges and 61% of the universities provided recommendations and guidelines and 37.5% of the colleges and 55.6% of the universities provided training on making documents on the VLE

accessible. However, one university respondent noted that their university's guidelines were not very prominent or widely known. Some institutions integrated accessibility issues into general e-learning training and others had separate courses on accessibility. Further research is required to obtain data on take-up of these courses, the content of recommendations and guidelines and staff familiarity with them. Problems due to lack of time and resources are likely to have intensified as a result of UK government policies which have led to funding cuts and resulted in reductions in staff numbers.

4.1.2. Surveys of Disabled Students and Staff

A small-scale survey (Hersh, 2008) of the experiences of disabled students and staff of using Virtual Learning Environments (VLEs) had mixed results, including uncertainty as to whether the VLE used had features to make it easier to use by disabled people and the extent to which it was accessible. Specific problems encountered included the following:

- Little support for blind users.
- Problems with the user management system.
- Difficulties in expanding the system with new features or developing new modules.
- Difficulties in creating virtual simulations and three-dimensional virtual environments.
- Lack of knowledge of the system.

Another UK survey examined the experiences of six disabled students with different impairments of using two VLEs, one developed by the university (COSE) and a commercially available system which has since been withdrawn (Lotus Learning Space, LLS) (Stiles, 2002). A number of problems were encountered with the VLEs, the content and the university website. Accessibility requires each of these components to be accessible and problems with any one of them will cause difficulties to some disabled students. Accessibility problems in the design and organisation of Web pages can prevent disabled users navigating a virtual learning environment. Accessibility problems of varying degrees of severity were encountered with both VLEs. They included issues of compatibility with assistive software, unclear help messages, and problems with navigating the site, as well as the need for text versions of icons, clear links, British Sign Language, and the ability to personalise colour and font size. Issues of this type can make all content on a VLE inaccessible, regardless of its accessibility in itself. This makes it important that VLE developers include accessibility features and that institutions take accessibility into account when choosing a VLE. Navigation caused the most problems. Issues that require addressing include the ease with which users can change the focus (the currently 'live' part of the screen) and ensure that the focus is already set appropriately. In addition, the navigation order needs to be logical and keyboard equivalents for all menu options and keyboard shortcuts provided.

An Australian study carried out an accessibility audit of WebCT (a proprietary VLE that has now become Blackboard Learning System) (Alexander, 2002). The evaluation was from the perspective of students rather than course designers. It was based on the W3C WAI WCAG1 conformance evaluation supplemented by testing by two blind students, who used screenreaders, and one physically disabled student, who generally used the keyboard and found manipulating the mouse difficult. Numerous checkpoint failures were found at each of the three priority levels. The students also experienced a number of serious problems. The chat tool was inaccessible to JAWS users, who were unable to read text from other participants or navigate to the text input box. The main navigation frame could not be bypassed, meaning that links were read out every time a new page or course tool was accessed and the physically

disabled student had to tab through all the links or struggle to position the mouse. Screenreader users could not distinguish between institutional and personal bookmarks and text alternatives for some important items were meaningless. Course navigation options in the main window were read twice. There were no alternative text descriptions for the correct/incorrect images in the evaluation tool and it was not clear to the physically disabled user how to indicate a correct answer. The drawing and whiteboard tools were inaccessible to the blind students and very difficult to use for the physically disabled student, as they required a (difficult) mouse manipulation.

Alexander (2002) has made the following recommendations, which have been reformulated to be relevant to all VLEs rather than specifically to WebCT: (1) Active liaison with disabled students. (2) Identifying the assistive technologies which work best within the constraints of the VLE while meeting disabled students' needs. However, we recommend the choice of VLEs, which are compatible with at least the most commonly, used assistive technologies in consultation with disabled students and staff. (3) The inclusion of accessibility considerations in VLE training programmes for academic staff to ensure they know how to make course materials accessible. (4) Representations to VLE vendors and developers to improve accessibility, including by institutions lobbying as a group.

4.2. Accessibility of PDF Documents

Portable Document Format (PDF), developed by Adobe systems, is increasingly being used by both individuals and organisations for electronic documents on the Web and to distribute them over corporate networks, by email and digital media, as well as for e-books, manuals, technical documents and CD conference proceedings (on CD or on-line). Its main advantages are simplicity and preserving the appearance of the original document for printing and viewing. In addition, it offers some additional security of the document contents, though most PDF documents can now be edited.

Unfortunately, many PDF documents are created without considering accessibility, making them partially or totally inaccessible. The authors have provided simple instructions and a template for producing accessible PDF documents for conferences (Hersh & Leporini, 2009). They (Hersh & Leporini, 2008) have also reported a study of authors preparing a paper for an international conference on assistive technology for blind and deaf people using an earlier version of this template. The authors included both disabled and non-disabled people, but very few screenreader users. The investigation showed that even authors working with assistive technology for blind and deaf people found it difficult to produce a fully accessible PDF document. A particular problem seemed to be the alternative text descriptions of graphics, with some authors not providing any and others just repeating the figure caption rather than actually describing the figure. The results of this study led to revisions of the template and the production of examples of alternative text descriptions (Hersh, 2009).

Specific recommendations resulting from the study include the following (Hersh & Leporini, 2008):

1. Requesting a WORD file as well as the PDF file to enable any necessary changes to be made to make the final version accessible.
2. Provision of a style file for LaTeX, which could automatically generate the correct PDF layout and then be supplemented using the Adobe accessibility features, in addition to a WORD template.
3. Providing examples of good and bad practice in text descriptions of graphics, equations and other non-textual objects.
4. Encouraging authors to use a recent version of Acrobat Professional for the conversion

to PDF format, while recognising that cost considerations may prevent this.
5. Providing graphical illustrations of the different steps in producing an accessible PDF document.
6. Providing sample accessible PDF documents to illustrate their features.
7. Using simple language and a simple word order in the instructions and template.
8. Separating the instructions and the template, to avoid deletion of the instructions when text is inserted into the template.

4.3. Computer Games for Entertainment

4.3.1. Survey of Developers

An online survey of game developers was carried out with the support of the International Game Developers Association (Bierre, et al., 2004). 20 responses were obtained, covering a range of different types of games. Most of them were for single players and only two were multiplayer. Most of the games had accessibility features aimed at a specific group of disabled people, most commonly blind and low vision, with smaller numbers for deaf or hard of hearing people, people with mobility impairments and colour-blind people. Only a few of the games addressed disabled people with different types of impairments. The survey has been used to produce a database of games with a brief description, the accessibility features, and the disabled users they are suitable for, but an evaluation of the self-reported accessibility features has not been carried out.

4.3.2. Usability Evaluation

Usability evaluations have been carried out of three games designed for universal accessibility, with a modified version of the IBM Usability Satisfaction Questionnaires used to obtain user feedback (Lewis, 1995; Grammenos, et al., 2009).

One non-disabled, two blind and three physically disabled people, with the last group using one, two, and three switches respectively, evaluated UA Chess. The evaluation involved two rounds per player in an informal competition, with player pairs chosen randomly. Good scores were obtained on all metrics and the disabled users were enthusiastic about having the opportunity to play a computer game. Access Invaders was evaluated by three blind, three physically disabled, and three non-disabled people. While the overall reactions were positive, the blind players were concerned about the speech and sound quality and the lack of an auditory help facility. In addition, players either found the game too easy or too hard. User profiling and adapting all difficulty related parameters prior to the evaluation could have alleviated this problem. There was also a tendency for users to be less critical than they might have been otherwise due to reacting positively to the concept of accessible games.

5. STUDY OF EDUCATIONAL GAMES

5.1. Methodology

This study is based on a questionnaire sent to disabled students, parents of disabled students, teachers, lecturers, and educational experts (some of whom may themselves be disabled). It is envisaged as a pilot or exploratory study, as there is very little work in this area. English, Italian, and Polish versions of the questionnaire were produced, with the English version the original. It was translated by native speakers, some modifications were made by the first author and then the modified version was further updated by native speakers to produce the final version. The differences in the educational systems in Italy, Poland, and UK were taken into account in the different language versions. However, to avoid confusion, one terminology will be used throughout the chapter. Thus, the UK term 'secondary school' will be used, while recognising

that it is divided into lower and upper secondary schools in Italy and Poland, as well as a number of other countries. The UK terminology of Further Education (FE) colleges is also used, though there are not exact Italian and Polish equivalents, for an educational institution which provide a wide range of post-16 education, including academic, vocational, university access, undergraduate degree and lifeskills courses.

Two slightly different versions of the questionnaire were produced, for disabled students, recent students, and parents of disabled students; and teachers, lecturers and educational experts respectively. The questionnaire examined the use of computer-based games, how they supported teaching and learning, their use with or by disabled students and difficulties encountered, as well as details of existing digital games suitable for disabled students and suggestions for new games. Teachers and experts can be contacted through their work context, but making contact with disabled people or their parents is more difficult. Some of the difficulties and strategies used in making contact with disabled people are discussed in Hersh (2010, 2011). Two main strategies were used:

- Circulation to appropriate contacts, including teachers, experts and disabled students,
- Circulation on appropriate mailing lists, including of disabled students and disability studies researchers.

However, these strategies may lead to some respondent bias in favour of respondents who are interested in accessibility and usability and/or who have experience of using educational computer-based games. This is difficult to avoid and the results are therefore illustrative rather than fully representative. Questionnaire accessibility was improved by providing short instructions on completing the questionnaire at the start and giving the number of options in brackets after each single-answer multiple-choice question to inform screenreader users of the number of options to listen for. While experience with other questionnaires indicates that many Deaf signers (for whom the national written language is a second or foreign language) require signed versions or signed explanations, resource limitations prevented this. The questionnaire was deliberately kept relatively short and an attempt made to keep the language simple to improve accessibility.

5.2. Results from Teachers and Experts

45 responses were received, with 18 (40%) from disabled students and parents of disabled students and 27 (60%) from teachers and experts. Four fifths of the respondents to the teachers' and experts' questionnaire were teachers and 70% were female. A third were from Italy, just over a quarter (25.9%) from the UK and 18.5% from Poland, with other respondents from Austria, France, Slovakia and the USA. There were respondents from universities, Further Education (FE) colleges, and secondary, primary, and pre-schools. The subjects taught included engineering, mathematics, computer science, languages, communication, data security, history and geography and switchboard operation. There was also a good distribution of levels of experience, though very new teachers were less well represented. Only 11% stated they were disabled, specifically visually impaired or blind, with one of the three also having mental health issues and two of them using screenreaders.

Just under half (48.1%) used digital games, with equal numbers not using them and one person not replying. Two teachers used games involving microworlds; three games in virtual learning environments and eight other types of digital games. The games used included WheelSim Focus (for learning to use an electronic wheelchair) to teach university computer science students about usability, software development and human-computer interaction. It was considered suitable for all disabled and non-disabled students. One of the experts working with children with autism used computer programs, which support learning about emotions and the other used computer images, letters, animals and animal noises to help the children learn to recognise different animals. They drew on the children's interest in computers and the fact that the computer exercises were more interesting than paper ones to help motivate them to accomplish tasks.

An FE teacher has used Second Life when teaching degree level communications and handheld 'mind-training' games with entry-level students. While not discussing its appropriateness for disabled students, Second Life was used to give 'students practical experience of communicating in a different way and helps them to think about issues of identity.' This implies it could be used to support learning about the different ways non-disabled and disabled people communicate. The mind-training games were used as a reward and to keep students occupied, though they are designed to improve concentration. Several respondents used games to support learning arithmetic, mathematics, and English.

Nintendo Wii (Wii Sports and Wii Fit) and Nintendo DS (Brain training games and Spellbound) were used to support mathematics in FE, for instance by analysing and graphing data from the games and to support learning English by writing commentaries and articles about matches. Coolmath and www.mymaths.co.uk provided practice and feedback in FE and literacy; and numeracy games, for instance from the BBC skillwise websites, were used due to their accessible format and appropriate language. A secondary school teacher used games for simulating laboratory experiments when it was not possible to develop real ones. The main reasons for not using games or planning to use them in the future were lack of knowledge of suitable games, followed by being unsure whether they were useful. Two respondents mentioned accessibility issues. A university lecturer indicated that the regular curricula in France did not consider the specific requirements of visually impaired students and a psychologist working with disabled children that she was only aware of one program suitable for children with autism.

80% of teachers and experts who used digital games had used them with disabled students. Three of them had worked with disabled students who had experienced difficulties in accessing or using these games. Attempts at problem resolution in all three cases involved providing additional information, for instance by verbally describing what was on the screen. One respondent found this unsatisfactory, as it reduced student independence. The need for additional explanations was also commented on by other respondents, for instance for dyslexic students. However, once they started using the games, they were better for these students than having to write. Problems in the past due to general visual and physical accessibility issues rather than game specific issues were also mentioned, as was the need for games specifically for blind students with auditory output and input via the keyboard and less use of the mouse.

Only 18.5% of the teachers were aware of games suitable for disabled students. The games mentioned included WheelSim and Nintendo DS brain training games and Spellbound, with the additional information that the Nintendo games can be used by students with a hearing impairment, physical disability, or learning difficulty. Games from Komlogo and Young Digital Planet were considered suitable for stimulating speech development for disabled children with autism or Down's syndrome. Games from the American Printing House for the Blind were mentioned without further details. Virtual Laboratory can be used together with text books to learn about laboratory tools and materials in physics and chemistry. It was considered suitable for students with developmental and behavioural impairments or reduced use of their hands.

A visually impaired Polish pre-school teacher made the important point that educational games need to be accessible to disabled parents, therapists and teachers as well as students. While she did not mention this explicitly, accessibility for these groups may involve additional editing and game development functions, which may not always be required for accessibility to students. A number of programs were not compatible with her screenreader and the firms were not responsive to her suggestions for improvements. A secondary school teacher noted the need for Braille displays and screenreaders for accessibility to visually impaired students. Other comments related to educational games for use in university teaching, taking account of the excitement of on-line games and other activities and students' familiarity and comfort with social media and social networking, which are becoming important educational tools.

5.3. Results for Disabled Students and Parents of Disabled Students

Responses were received from eight parents and ten disabled university students, 60% postgraduate, 30% undergraduate, and 10% both. They were gender balanced. 40% were visually impaired and used screen magnification; 10% had a hearing impairment; 20% were physically disabled, with half of these students using an adapted keyboard and a switch, joystick or sip and puff device; 10% had both visual and physical impairments and used screen magnification; 10% had diabetes; and 10% both specific learning difficulties and a visual impairment. Half the students were studying computing science and/or mathematics. Other subjects studied included foreign languages, humanities, natural sciences, military science, and psychology.

Only 20% (two) of the students used computer-based games and neither of them had encountered accessibility or usability problems. One of them was a female PhD student with both physical and visual impairments who used a screen magnifier. She used both digital games involving microworlds and in learning environments, as she was studying them and the ways they can be used to support changes in behaviour. She used Micro-WorldsEx to help develop 'creativity, problem solving and critical thinking skills.' While she had not experienced any problems with it, she thought that visually impaired students might have difficulties with the program and require assistance to resolve them.

The other user of digital games was a female mathematics undergraduate with diabetes. She used sports games, which were 'not connected with (her) studies,' and considered they 'help (her) concentrate.' A physically disabled male computer science undergraduate also commented on the role of games in providing pleasure and rather worryingly on the need to 'endure and overcome' the 'monotony' of studying. Another student would use computer-based games if suitable ones were available. The main reasons for no future interest in using educational games were lack of time followed by lack of knowledge of suitable games. The current game users, but none of the other students, were aware of computer-based games that were suitable for disabled students. These games included The Shogun; Logistyka, Marketing and MicroWorldsEx. The first three are strategic games, which require 'cunning and logical thinking' and were considered suitable for people with mobility impairments, as they require little movement other than that of the mouse. However, it should be noted that some physically disabled people are not able to use the mouse and, unless the game is suitably designed, it may be difficult to control the game adequately using, for instance a binary switch or an eye tracker. Suggestions for new games included language learning games with graphics and games to enrich mathematics, as well as games that could be customised while playing to better meet the user's needs.

The overwhelming majority of the parents (86%) were from Italy with one from Scotland.

Just over half (57%) of their disabled children were at secondary school, with one primary school student, one student of secondary school age who was being home educated and two unspecified. All the Italian students were visually impaired or blind, with one of them using a screenreader, another screen magnification and an adapted keyboard and a third an adapted keyboard. The Scottish student was being home educated and had an autistic spectrum condition. 63% of the students used non-computer based games and three quarters have used digital games. Half the parents considered these games to be useful, a third that they were not particularly useful, and one was unsure.

The autistic student used a wide variety of games, including Simcity, Civilisation, Crosswords and World of Warcraft and Scrabble for learning across the curriculum including history, geography, sociology, decision making, communicating and basic living skills. Two of the visually impaired students used the Italian language games Picture Wizard (Mago pittore) and the Sims; and Telling the Time (Per ora) respectively. The mother of the autistic student was particularly enthusiastic about the role of digital games in learning and helping autistic children understand human interaction and test communication strategies. She noted that her son had 'developed relationships that help him make sense of the world' and that simulation games enabled him 'to experiment in a safe environment and see the impact of his actions, as well as the importance of games being 'engaging and fun' in supporting learning. Half the parents were aware of games, which were suitable for disabled students, including Claudia and 5 Fingers (5 dita). Claudia can be used by blind and visually impaired primary school students for learning geography, particularly maps and country locations. 5 Fingers can be used by visually impaired students to help them recognise letters.

6. DESIGNING ACCESSIBLE AND USABLE EDUCATIONAL GAMING ENVIRONMENTS

6.1. Guidelines and Recommendations

In this section, a number of guidelines and recommendations will be presented for designing and using educational games to make them fully accessible, usable, and playable for all students, both disabled and non-disabled. They are drawn from the results of the survey of accessibility and usability of educational computer based games reported in the previous section, as well as the guidelines, recommendations and heuristics obtained from a study of the literature. To make them more manageable the guidelines are organised into a structured list with three categories at the first level and ten different categories at the second level: (A) Underlying design (pedagogical and other principles), (B) Accessibility (support, navigation, customization, and accessibility of audio and visual elements), and (C) Playability and usability. Each of the guidelines has a letter and number to facilitate reference to it in the example in section 6.3:

A. Underlying design, pedagogical and other principles
1. **The Development of Educational Games:**
    D1. The use of inclusive design and design for all approaches, which consider user diversity in preferences and characteristics.
    D2. The provision of an enjoyable and high quality learning experience for all students.
    D3. The involvement of disabled students and teachers as experts on their own requirements.
    D4. Consideration of both general principles of accessibility and

usability, and issues specific to the particular game, the learning context it is intended to be used in and the target students.
    D5. User diversity, accessibility, and usability requirements should be seen as an opportunity to use creative approaches rather than a problem.
2. **Pedagogical Principles:**
    P1. The use of inclusive pedagogies and the avoidance of any requirements, materials or technologies which are not fully accessible to all students, unless there are exceptionally good pedagogical reasons for using them.
    P2. Ensuring that all (disabled) students have access to equivalent learning materials and experiences, preferably by using the same digital games as non-disabled students.
    P3. Flexibility with options for adaptation to the learning styles and other needs of individual students.
    P4. Learner control of the technology and goals, with learning material presented in meaningful units.
    P5. Support for cooperative learning, including discussing and negotiating different approaches to learning.
    P6. Encouragement to make meaningful use of existing knowledge and skills and familiar situations and experiences.
    P7. Meaningful and accurate feedback, giving real dialogue between the user and the computer.
    P8. Good integration of the educational and fun aspects of educational games.

B. Accessibility: support, navigation, customisation and accessibility of audio and visual elements

1. **Support:**

   S1. Clearly written and well organised documentation in a variety of different accessible formats, including plain text of varying sizes and colours, HTML, simplified language, audio and sign language.

   S2. Accessibility features announced in the game packaging and game information, with standards for categorising them.

   S3. Flexible on-line help system, with different options for accessing it. The type and extent of help provided can be set by the user profile.

   S4. The option for memory supports and regular prompts, with a choice of audio, visual or text cues.

   S5. Clearly stated rules, with simpler and more complex versions to support different types of users.

   S6. Activities broken down into tasks with user choice of task size.

   S7. Warning and fail-safe features to minimise any negative consequences of errors and unintended or accidental actions.

2. **Navigation:**

   N1. Access to all functions and system components through a range of different input devices, including the mouse, keyboard, joystick, game pad, binary switches, sip and puff device and head or eye tracker devices.

   N2. Full support for text-only navigation, including link shortcuts, hidden links and descriptive link texts.

   N3. Adaptive navigation facilities, which allow users to go directly to the content, bypassing non-essential elements.

   N4. Simple menus, which are easy to navigate and a quick start method.

   N5. Controls that can be remapped to allow users to tailor them to their needs and more than one control having the same action to reduce fatigue.

3. **Accessibility of Audio and Visual Elements:**

   A1. Choice of verbatim or summary closed subtitles (captions) for all dialogue and important sound effects.

   A2. Audio tags and support for sound location of all significant elements, including actors, doors, items, and actions.

   A3. Choice of summary or detailed audio description for graphics and rich media.

   A4. Built-in screenreader with auditory access to the whole interface.

   A5. Options for reduced graphics versions of text, particularly for use with screenreaders.

   A6. Use of wrap lines for text.

   A7. Choice of visual representations of sounds, e.g. sound balloons, sound visualisation, video clips.

   A8. Choice of high contrast modes, including black on white and white on black and scalable fonts and graphics.

   A9. Separate volume controls for music and sound effects.

4. **Customisation:**

   C1. A user profile to support customisation. Users have control over the information in the profile and can choose whether or not it is automatically updated in response to user actions and game performance.

C2. Options to turn a wide range of features on or off, including sound, graphics, blinking or flashing graphics, colour, prompts, memory cues, scrolling text, warnings, fail-safes and feedback. This provides all learners, particularly disabled ones, with the support and accessibility features they require, while avoiding accessibility barriers to disabled learners with sensory sensibilities, and enhances the experiences of all learners.

C3. Choice of different formats for game information (e.g. context, score, status of player and other characters, feedback, and goals), e.g. audio, graphical, text, tactile, sign language, or a combination.

C4. Choice of a wide range of difficulty levels, to allow advanced users to be challenged and no user to find the game too difficult. This should include the size of the tasks into which activities are decomposed.

C5. Choice of a wide range of speed options for all functions, allowing users to slow down games to take account of slow reaction times.

C. Playability and usability

1. **Game Interface:**

I1. A non-intrusive interface, which is consistent in control, visual (colour, type style, and size), audio (type and speed of voice) and dialogue design.

I2. Well organised and limited number of menu layers, which are experienced as part of the game, with advanced options at lower menu levels.

I3. Convenient, flexible, customisable and intuitive controls, which are easy to learn and can be expanded for advanced options.

I4. Readily available, unambiguous, concise and easily understandable game information (e.g. context, score, status of player and other characters, feedback and goals). Textual and spoken information in simple and precise language. All information provided in both visual and audio formats.

I5. Network effects, such as disconnections and delays, are minimised.

I6. The use of clear, simple language to communicate all information.

2. **Game Story:**

G1. A strong, meaningful, and consistent storyline, which supports the game play. Customisation allows the story to be made interesting and relevant to players.

G2. The storyline encourages player emotional involvement.

G3. The characters are interesting, can be customised to be similar or relevant to the player and develop as the action progresses. The player has control over the characters.

G4. The story unfolds through playing the game and continues to develop throughout the game, not just at the start and end.

G5. The player is in control of and able to influence the game world. The game responds in a consistent, challenging, and exciting way to player actions, and changes persist.

3. **Game Play:**

PL1. Clear goals or support for players to develop their own goals, with the main goal presented at the start of the game and further short-term goals introduced throughout the game.

PL2. Consistent, coherent, and socio-culturally relevant game elements, setting, and story. Game characters with similar characteristics have equal chances of victory. Coherence makes the game world seem real (even if in a fantasy sense) and encourages players to immerse themselves in the game world.

PL3. The game is satisfying and enjoyable to play both the first and subsequent times, with the focus on fun for the player rather than the designer. There are no repetitive or boring tasks and an appropriate level of interactivity.

PL4. Sensory appeal, including through the use of audio/visual and tactile effects, all of which are customisable and can be turned on and off.

PL5. Clearly differentiated and easy to identify game units and characters with easily understandable game roles and consistent and coherent behaviour. Any unpredictable behaviours or changes in behaviour to enhance challenge should have an understandable reason, even if this is not immediately obvious.

PL6. Clearly rendered scenarios, which are independent of the player's position, and the use of appropriate lighting, visual, audio, and tactile effects to draw attention to relevant objects.

PL7. Smooth game flow, without delays, and with few, if any, interruption. Any interruption in the game flow, such as the use of cut-scenes, exploration, learning about objects and access to fundamental items, should be relatively fast. Long non-interactive animated sequences should be avoided so as not to disrupt the game.

4. **Learnability and Challenge:**

L1. Easy to learn without a manual, but hard to master.

L2. The game and the skills required are taught before they are needed.

L3. Quick and easy involvement through interesting tutorials, sufficient information to start playing when the game is turned on, and progressive or adjustable difficulty levels.

L4. Assistance modes: training options, which allow players to play at their own pace with less pressure: on-screen hints and automatic targeting options if relevant to the game.

L5. An appropriate degree of challenge, which increases at an appropriate rate as players progress, including through the use of additional goals and varying activities and pace, so that challenges are experienced as positive and motivating.

L6. An unexpected outcome, unless counter-indicated by the player's profile, multiple ways to win and meaningful rewards, which increase player capabilities and immerse them more fully in the game.

6.2. General Principles Underlying the Guidelines and Recommendations

The guidelines and recommendations presented in the previous section are both numerous and fairly detailed. The following shorter list of more general principles may be easier for games developers to follow.

1. All information should be available in a variety of formats, including text, audio, graphical, and tactile.
2. The game should be designed to be used with a wide range of different input and output devices.
3. Features to promote accessibility should include closed captions, audio tags, high contrast colour schemes, and text descriptions.
4. A wide range of customisation options, supported by user profiles and including the options to turn various accessibility features on and off, should be available.
5. Educational games should be flexible, provide a wide range of options and avoid restrictive pedagogical assumptions, so they can be played by all learners, whether or not they are disabled or have learning difficulties.
6. The game should have a good story line, which supports the game play and into which the educational elements are integrated, with progression through the game requiring successful completion of relevant learning activities. The story and characters should be customisable, including, to increase their resemblance or otherwise increase their relevance to the players.
7. Information on all aspects of the game, including the state of the player and any other players or characters, should be readily available in simple language and a range of different formats.
8. A wide range of non-intrusive support mechanisms should be available, including interesting on-line tutorials, assistance modes, hints, and feedback in a wide range of alternative formats. The game should be designed to be interesting and exciting for both expert and novice players.
9. The game should be fully accessible, fun to play and support learning, with learning elements fully integrated into the game and equal importance given to accessibility, enjoyment and learning.

6.3. Example

The guidelines will be illustrated through application to designing a fictitious new educational game called MathsWorld. A fictitious rather than a real game was chosen for the example to avoid any ambiguity as to whether a particular guideline holds and allow application of almost all of the guidelines to be illustrated. The use of the guidelines to evaluate existing games would preferably require the involvement of a number of players and the use of surveys to obtain comments on their experiences and the extent to which they consider that particular guidelines are met. The numbers of the guidelines illustrated by a particular point are given in brackets after it. It should be noted that some of the guidelines give wider scope for interpretation than others. For instance, A1 Choice of verbatim or summary closed subtitles provides less scope for interpretation than P3 Flexibility with options for adaptation to the learning styles and other needs of individual students. In the latter case, feedback from disabled and non-disabled students will be required to determine whether any flexibility and adaptation options provided do meet their needs.

A design for all approach is taken which enables learners/players with a wide range of different characteristics and mathematical abilities, including learners with mathematics learning difficulties, to play the same game in ways that meet their learning and other needs (D1, P1, P3). Before the start of game development, an advisory group was set up, including learners with mathematics learning difficulties and other impairments, and teachers (D3, P1, P2). This group was actively involved in all stages of the development of the game. This enabled the focus to be on fun for the players rather than the designers and gives a high likelihood that the game will be fun to play both the first and subsequent times (Pl3). Additional learners, including disabled learners, and teachers were involved in testing and commenting on the game at important stages (D3, P1, P2). The modular program structure and the built-in programming redundancy will ensure that disconnections and delays are minimised (I5). Game flow was designed to be smooth with minimal, if any, interruptions (Pl7).

Players move through a well-designed and consistent real or fantasy universe by solving mathematical problems (Pl2, P8). These problems are an integral part of this universe and solving them has a direct impact on the universe and players' progress through it (D2, P8). Incorrect solutions result in the appearance of obstacles or the loss of resources and correct solutions in the provision of additional resources or other aids to progress (P7). The types of obstacles to be avoided and resources and aids removed are related directly to the type of problem(s) most recently responded to (P7, P8). Players have a wide range of different customisation options, relating to the game world, type of problems, the game interface, sensory features, and player and other characteristics (C2, D2, D4, Pl4). Customisation options for problems include choices of the difficulty level of the problems, the speed of the game, the type and frequency of hints, the type of feedback and when problems are made easier or more difficult in response to correct or incorrect answers (C4, C5, P3, L5). Customisation also enables players to choose easily identifiable characters which have similar characteristics or are otherwise relevant to them (for instance their favourite fictional or real life characters) and which have distinct, clearly defined roles (Pl2, Pl5, G3, G5). It also allows players to choose the number of characters and whether or not there is overlap between their roles (L5, C4, G5).

To simplify the procedure players can choose and modify a system defined profile. Alternatively, they can develop their own profiles (C1). Players can also choose whether or not the profile is updated in response to their actions and game performance. They also have access to their own profiles at all times (C1). Customisation options for the game interface include choice of the different formats for game information, including audio, graphical, Braille, sign language and a combination (C3). Since the technology for sign language-text and text-sign language conversion are not yet mature, the game includes a number of pre-recorded sign language messages for output, but sign language input is not supported. All game information, including on the context, player status and performance and that of other characters, is easily accessible in a range of formats as indicated above (I4).

Players can choose and, if they wish, modify one of a range of real, fantasy or fictional scenarios and characters within these scenarios or define their own characters with help from the system (G3, Pl2). They are encouraged to develop versions of the existing scenarios that are relevant to their experiences and socio-cultural context and which draw on their experiences and knowledge of situations (Pl2). Whether real, fictional or fantasy, the scenarios are designed to be consistent and coherent and to have a strong story line into which the mathematical problems are integrated (G1, G2). The mathematical problems, particularly those at the start of the game, draw on the players' existing knowledge and skills to both strengthen them and encourage the development of new knowledge and skills (P6). This is further supported by making the scenarios and problems relevant to the socio-cultural context and reported interests of the players (Pl2).

Students can play the game on their own or in groups. When playing in groups, they can do this on a competitive or co-operative basis, as well as moving between the two. There is a Maths World Forum where players can discuss both educational and social aspects of the game (P5). The main goal of moving through the game by solving mathematical problems is clearly stated in the game information and at the start of the game (Pl1). The end-point of the game and the rewards are determined by the player profile (L6). Rewards include the option to go to the next level of the game, which has more complex problems, access to additional game resources and/or a tutorial on an interesting new topic, as well as rewards, which relate specifically to the particular game scenario (L6). There is only a small set of rules. However, these rules are stated clearly on game information and at the start of the game (S5). A small number of additional rules become relevant as players move to higher levels of the game and these are also clearly stated (S5).

The game is designed to be played on a variety of different devices, including computers and mobile phones and for all functions to be accessed in a variety of different ways, including via a mouse, keyboard, joystick, game pad, and a wide variety of binary access devices, including binary switches and head and eye control devices (N1). All navigation and other functions and links can be accessed via text (N2). Players who require or prefer a non-graphical version can choose to either have a version with all graphics designed out and text-only links or a version with a choice of summary or detailed alternative text descriptions of graphics (A3, C2). Menus are optimised so that a minimum number of layers is required to access all the main functions (N4, I3, I4). More complicated or advanced options and functions are at lower levels of the menu to make it easy for players to find the more frequently used ones (I2). However, there are also options for reconfiguring the menu, as well as the other control functions (N5, I3). The choice of text-only navigation automatically configures the navigation system to go

directly to content and bypass any non-essential elements, which are also minimal (N2, N3).

Users can tailor controls to their needs, including by adjusting the operation and response speeds (C5). There are a number of different ways of doing this: directly, through the profile or by choosing an existing control configuration and modifying it if necessary. The game has closed captions for all dialogue, alternative text descriptions for all graphics and rich media and the option for the use of audio tags and support for the sound location of players and important game elements (A1, A2, A3). The default version has no blinking or flashing graphics or scrolling text, though there are options to turn these on (C2). There are options to turn on and off graphics, sound, colour, prompts, warnings, fail-safes, and memory cues, as well as to adjust the screen lighting (C2, S4, S7). Further options include the choice of high contrast visual modes and the type of high contrast e.g. white on black or black on pale yellow and the choice of visual representation of sounds and the type of representation and the option of reduced graphics versions (A5, A7). An appropriate balance between the levels of speech and sound effects can be obtained using the separate controls for speech and sounds (A9). Players can choose to enhance their experience through the use of visual, audio or tactile effects and customise the type of effects (Pl4).

Meaningful and prompt feedback is provided to players (P7). They can choose the style of feedback e.g. straightforward, consoling, critical, boosting confidence, the circumstances in which it is provided e.g. in response to every player action or when a problem has been completed and the range of possible responses and further interactions with the game in response to this feedback (P7). They can also determine the circumstances in which prompts and memory cues are provided, whether they are audio, graphical or text and the style of prompt (S4). They can also turn the incorporated closed subtitles on and off and choose whether they are verbatim or summary (A1) and have a choice of summary or detailed audio descriptions of graphics (A3). There is a built-in screenreader, which can be used to give access to all functions and features of the game (A4). Summary information about the game accessibility features will be provided as part of all game information and publicity (S2).

The game is designed so that on turning it on users are taken into the game world, given brief instructions as to how to find and answer problems and move through the game world (L2). At this point, they are given the option of continuing into the game or using the on-line tutorial (L3). This is based in the game world and uses the same type of customisation of scenarios and game characters as the game will. The initial problems are easy to give players practice in moving through the game world (L3). If a player requires more time to respond than indicated by the profile, additional information will be provided and the player will be given the option of additional time, a hint or returning to the tutorial (L3, L4). There is an on-line help system, as well as the option to ask questions on the player forum (S3, P5). There are also further tutorials and other approaches to learning both new game playing and new mathematical skills, with the option to turn this facility off (L4). Activities can also be broken down into smaller tasks, with the option of increasing the size of these tasks increasing as players gain confidence (S6). Players are presented with tutorials, other approaches to learning or information about the skills required before they need to use them in the game (L2). Full game documentation is available, though not necessary to play the game (S1). It is written in simple language and available in a variety of formats, including plain text, text plus graphics, audio and sign language (S1). The story unfolds and develops in complexity and richness as the player answers problems, whether correctly or incorrectly, and moves through the game world (G4).

7. DISCUSSION AND CONCLUSION

Computer-based games and gaming environments, especially with collaborative and cooperative interaction modalities, are an increasingly popular source of entertainment and potentially very valuable tools for learning as well as for making users aware of (new) opportunities and possibilities. On-line games and downloadable stand-alone applications are increasingly being used in education. There are also mobile games, which are being used both by individuals and collaboratively, for instance in museums. It is important that these games and associated applications are fully accessible and usable by disabled people and that disabled users are able to gain the same educational benefits and enjoyment from them as non-disabled people.

However, there are no previous studies of the accessibility and usability of educational games and even studies of the accessibility and usability of games for entertainment are sparse. The concepts of accessibility and usability express important general principles and goals. However, effective practical application of these concepts requires considerations of the particular user context. In addition, though guidelines drawn up for non-educational games are useful as a starting point for the accessibility and usability of educational games, they are not sufficient on their own and need to be augmented by principles relating to the pedagogical aspects of educational games. There is also a need for surveys and other approaches to investigate the actual experiences and problems of disabled end-users to ensure that they are fully taken account of and that the resulting recommendations and guidelines do meet their needs.

This chapter has presented an overview of accessibility and usability issues for educational computer-based games. The overview was introduced by a brief presentation of the social and medical models of disability and design for all, followed by a discussion of accessibility and usability in general. This included a very brief introduction to the use of assistive technology to access computers and the Internet, as well as the differences between and the complementary nature of accessibility and usability.

This was followed by an introduction to computer-based games and gaming environments. Mobile games, collaborative and cooperative features, and evaluation were covered, as well as accessibility and usability features in the context of e-learning, including pedagogical usability and accessibility and usability of educational computer-based games.

Brief overviews of a number of surveys in related areas carried out to date were included, as there have been no previous surveys of the accessibility and usability of educational computer based games. The overview included surveys of Virtual Learning Environments (VLEs) as the closest 'relative' of educational computer-based games and gaming environments. The surveys of VLEs were small scale, but they have shown up a number of problems including lack of knowledge of disability and accessibility issues, lack of resources and the use of inaccessible VLEs. The surveys of non-educational games indicate a strong interest in games which are accessible and that where games have considered accessibility, they have focussed on features for blind and visually impaired people rather than taking a design for all approach to the needs of all disabled and non-disabled people.

The chapter also reported a study carried out by the authors of the accessibility and usability of educational computer-based games. To the authors' knowledge, this is the first such survey. It involved disabled students, parents of disabled students, teachers, and experts in seven different countries, with most respondents from Italy, Poland, and the UK. This survey showed both the potential of educational computer based games and the lack of knowledge and sometimes also negative attitudes amongst potential users. Particular enthusiasm for computer-based games was shown by the mother of a home-educated

autistic student and it would be useful to further investigate both the use of computer based games to support the education of autistic students and their potential for making education more accessible to all disabled people.

The results of the study and a survey of the literature were used to draw up guidelines and recommendations for the accessibility, playability, pedagogical, and general usability of educational computer-based games. These guidelines were organised into a structured list of 62 items, organised, as indicated below into the three categories at the first level and ten categories at the second level:

1. **A:** Underlying design, pedagogical and other principles: the development of educational games, pedagogical principles
2. **B:** Accessibility: support, navigation, accessibility of audio and visual elements, customisation.
3. **C:** Playability and usability: game interface, game story, game play, learnability, and challenge.

A shorter list of nine general principles was also presented to provide additional support for game developers. These nine general principles summarise the 62 criteria and provide general principles for the development of accessible and usable computer games and gaming environments.

The approach to accessibility and usability in this chapter differs from other approaches, for instance that taken by the International Game Developers Association (IGDA, 2004) in being based on design for all principles which consider the needs of all learners, disabled and non-disabled, rather than focusing on the requirements of each impairment-based group of disabled people separately. It also considers accessibility, playability, pedagogical and general usability together rather than focussing solely on accessibility. The guidelines and recommendations presented in this chapter are specific to educational games, whereas the IGDA (2004) does not consider educational aspects of games. However, the guidelines and recommendations presented here could be generalised to other types of games by the removal of the section on pedagogical principles (and a small number of the other criteria).

An example has been presented to illustrate the use of the detailed set of lists of heuristics of accessibility, playability, pedagogical and general usability. It is based on the design of a fictitious new educational game and illustrates how accessibility, usability, and playability principles can be incorporated into a game. A fictitious rather than a real game has been chosen as the basis of this example to enable inclusion of almost all the guidelines and to avoid ambiguity as to whether or not particular guidelines are satisfied. Application of the guidelines to the evaluation of real games should involve surveys of the experiences of disabled and non-disabled players.

Work on the accessibility and usability of computer-based games is still at a very early stage. Further work is required, including on pedagogical issues, collaborative aspects of games and the accessibility and usability of educational games on mobile devices. In addition, there is a need for the development and validation of a list of heuristics or recommendations and guidelines that is universally accepted and which has the status of a standard. These recommendations and guidelines should cover all aspects of the accessibility and usability of digital games, including underlying principles, accessibility, pedagogical usability, playability and general usability.

The list presented here could possibly form the basis of such a list. However, validation of the guidelines to produce the final definitive list will require the involvement of disabled and non-disabled users. This involvement should include a number of large-scale surveys of the accessibility and usability of educational computer based games, the experiences of disabled and non-disabled players and the problems encountered. It should also include a number of focus groups, for instance suggesting lists of guidelines and recom-

mendations and critiquing the existing lists and adding and deleting items, based on the experience of their members. The disabled and non-disabled people involved should be very varied on factors such as gender, age, education, and employment, type of impairment and interests. This work will need to take place over a period of several years with the results of each survey used to update and improve the current set of recommendations and guidelines. An organisation such as IGDA might be able to coordinate this work.

ACKNOWLEDGMENT

We would like to thank all the people who completed questionnaires, as well as those who helped as distribute them.

REFERENCES

W3C. (2005). *Introduction to web accessibility*. Retrieved from http://www.w3.org/WAI/intro/accessibility.php

Alexander, D. (2002). An accessibility audit of WebCT. In *Proceedings of the Eighth Australian World Wide Web Conference, (AUSWEB)*. Queensland, Australia: AUSWEB. Retrieved from http://ausweb.scu.edu.au/aw02/papers/refereed/alexander/paper.html

Anon. (2006). *Gaming with a physical disability*. Retrieved from http://www.game-accessibility.com/index.php?pagefile=motoric

Anon. (2011a). *Serious game*. Retrieved from http://en.wikipedia.org/wiki/Serious_game

Anon. (2011b). *Mobile game*. Retrieved from http://en.wikipedia.org/wiki/Mobile_game

Barnes, C. (1994). *Disabled people in Britain and discrimination: A case for anti-discrimination legislation*. London, UK: Hurst & Co.

Bickford, P. (1997). *Interface design, the art of developing easy-to-use software*. Chestnut Hill, MA: Academic Press.

Bierre, K. (2005). *Improving game accessibility*. Retrieved from http://www.gamasutra.com/view/feature/2342/improving_game_accessibility.php?print=1

Bierre, K., Hinn, T., & McIntosh, M. (2004). *Accessibility in games: Motivations and approaches*. Retrieved from http://www.igda.org/sites/default/iles/IGDA_WhitePaper.pdf

Blamire, R. (2010). *Digital games for learning, conclusions and recommendations from the IMAGINE project*. Retrieved from http:www.imaginegames.eu

Buzzi, M., & Leporini, B. (2009). Editing Wikipedia content by screen reader: Easier interaction with the accessible rich internet applications suite. *Disability and Rehabilitation. Assistive Technology*, *4*(4), 264–275. doi:10.1080/17483100902903457

Buzzi, M., & Leporini, B. (2010). Distance learning: New opportunities for the blind. In Buzzi, M. (Ed.), *eLearning*. Vienna, Austria: IN-TECH. doi:10.5772/7778

CEN. (2003). *CEN workshop agreement CWA 14661: Guidelines to standardisers of ICT products and services in the CEN ICT domain*. Retrieved from ftp://cenftp1.cenorm.be/PUBLIC/CWAs/e-Europe/DFA/cwa14661-00-2003-Feb.pdf

Clanton, C. (1998). An interpreted demonstration of computer games design. In *Proceedings of the Conference on CHI Summary: Human Factors in Computing Systems*. CHI.

Connell, B. R., et al. (1997). *The principles of universal design version 2.0*. Retrieved from http://www.design.ncsu.edu/cud/about_ud/ud-principlestext.htm

Dahlskog, S., Kamstrup, A., & Aarseth, E. (2009). Mapping the game landscape: Locating genres using functional classification. In *Proceedings of DiGRA*. DiGRA.

Damodaran, L. (1996). User involvement in the systems design process-a practical guide for users. *Behaviour & Information Technology*, *15*(6), 363–377. doi:10.1080/014492996120049

Desurvire, H., Caplan, M., & Toth, J. A. (2004). *Using heuristics to evaluate the playability of games*. Paper presented at CHI 2004, Vienna, Austria.

Dunn, S. (2003). *Return to SENDA? Implementing accessibility for disabled students in virtual learning environments in UK further and higher education*. London, UK: City University London. Retrieved from http://www.saradunn-associates.net/uploads/tx_policyreports/CityEU_VLEreport.pdf

Ebner, M., & Holzinger, A. (2007). Successful implementation of user-centred game based learning in higher education: An example from civil engineering. *Computers & Education*, *49*, 873–890. doi:10.1016/j.compedu.2005.11.026

Elverdam, C., & Aarseth, E. (2007). Game classification as game design: Construction through critical analysis. In *Proceedings of DiGRA 2005*. DiGRA.

Endsley, M. (1995). Toward a theory of situation awareness in dynamic systems. *Human Factors*, *37*(1), 32–64. doi:10.1518/001872095779049543

Evans, D., & Taylor, J. (2005). The role of user scenarios as the central piece of the development jigsaw puzzle. In Attewell, J., & Savill-Smith, C. (Eds.), *Mobile Learning Anytime Everywhere: Papers from Mlearn 2004*. Mlearn.

Fabricatore, C., Nussbaum, M., & Rosas, R. (2002). Playability in action videogames: A qualitative design model. *Human-Computer Interaction, 17*, 311–368. doi:10.1207/S15327051HCI1704_1

Federici, S. (2005). Checking an integrated model of web accessibility and usability evaluation for disabled people. *Disability and Rehabilitation, 27*(13), 781–790. doi:10.1080/09638280400014766

Federoff, M. (2002). *Heuristic and usability guidelines for the creation and evaluation of fun video games*. (Master Thesis). Bloomington, IN: Indiana University.

Felicia, P. (2009). *Digital games in schools: A handbook for teachers*. London, UK: European Schoolnet EUN Partnership AISBL.

González Sánchez, J. L., Padilla Zea, N., & Gutiérrez, F. L. (2009). Playability: How to identify the player experience in a video game. *Lecture Notes in Computer Science, 5726*, 356–359. doi:10.1007/978-3-642-03655-2_39

Grammenos, D., Savidis, A., & Stephanidis, C. (2009). Designing universally accessible games. *ACM Computers in Entertainment, 7*(1), 8:1-8:28.

Grudin, J. (1994). CSCW: History and focus. *IEEE Computer, 27*(5), 19–26. doi:10.1109/2.291294

Gutwin, C., & Greenberg, S. (2004). The importance of awareness for team cognition in distributed collaboration. In Salas, E., & Fiore, S. M. (Eds.), *Team Cognition: Understanding the Factors that Drive Process and Performance* (pp. 177–201). Washington, DC: APA Press. doi:10.1037/10690-009

Hersh, M. A. (2008). Accessibility and usability of virtual learning environments. In *Proceedings of the 8th IEEE International Conference on Advanced Learning Technologies*. Santander, Spain: IEEE Press.

Hersh, M. A. (2009). *Examples of alternative text descriptions*. Retrieved August 5 2011 from http://www.elec.gla.ac.uk/Events_page/CVHI/cvhi/pages/instructions-for-authors.php

Hersh, M. A. (2010). *Methodological issues in multi-country multi-language participative research with blind and visually impaired people*. Paper presented at SWIIS 2010. Pristina, Kosovo.

Hersh, M. A. (2011). *Participative research with diverse end-user groups: Multi-language, multi-country blind and visually impaired people*. Paper presented at the 17th IFAC Congress. Milan, Italy.

Hersh, M. A., & Leporini, B. (2008). Making conference CDs accessible: A practical example. In *Proceedings of the 11th International Conference on Computers Helping People with Special Needs (ICCHP 2008)*. Linz, Austria: ICCHP.

Hersh, M. A., & Leporini, B. (2009). *Paper template*. Retrieved from http://www.elec.gla.ac.uk/Events_page/CVHI/cvhi/pages/instructions-for-authors.php

IGDA. (2004). *Accessibility in games: Motivations and approaches*. Retrieved from http://www.igda.org/accessibility/IGDA_Accessibility_WhitePaper.pdf

Jarmin. (2012). *Accessibility guide*. Retrieved from from http://jarmin.com/accessibility

Johansen, R. (1988). *Groupware: Computer support for business teams*. New York, NY: The Free Press.

Kelly, B., Sloan, D., Brown, S., Seale, J., Petrie, H., Lauke, P., & Ball, S. (2007). *Accessibility 2.0: People, policies and processes*. Paper presented at the International Cross-Disciplinary Conference on Web Accessibility (W4A). Banff, Canada.

Kelly, B., Sloan, D., Phipps, L., Petrie, H., & Hamilton, F. (2005). *Forcing standardization or accommodating diversity? A framework for applying the WCAG in the real world.* Paper presented at the International Cross-Disciplinary Workshop on Web Accessibility (W4A). Chiba, Japan.

Kickmeier-Rust, M. D. (2009). Talking digital educational games. In M. D. Kickmeier-Rust (Ed.), *Proceedings of the 1st International Open Workshop on Intelligent Personalization and Adaptation in Digital Educational Games*, (pp. 55-66). Graz, Austria: IEEE.

Korhonen, H., & Koivisto, E. M. I. (2006). *Playability heuristics for mobile games.* Paper presented at MobileHCI 2006. Helsinki, Finland.

Kukulska-Hulme, A. (2007). Mobile usability in educational contexts: What have we learnt! *International Review of Research in Open and Distance Learning, 8*(2).

Kukulska-Hulme, A. (2008). Human factors and innovation with mobile devices. In Hansson, T. (Ed.), *Handbook of Research on Digital Information Technologies: Innovations, Methods and Ethical Issues* (pp. 392–403). Hershey, PA: IGI Global. doi:10.4018/978-1-59904-970-0.ch025

Leporini, B., Andronico, P., Buzzi, M., & Castillo, C. (2008). Evaluating a modified Google user interface via screen reader. *Universal Access in the Information Society, 7*(3), 155–175. doi:10.1007/s10209-007-0111-y

Leporini, B., & Paternò, F. (2003). Criteria for usability of accessible web sites. In Carbonell, N., & Stephanidis, C. (Eds.), *User Interfaces for All.* Berlin, Germany: Springer Verlag. doi:10.1007/3-540-36572-9_3

Leporini, B., & Paternò, F. (2008). Applying web usability criteria for vision-impaired users: Does it really improve task performance? *International Journal of Human-Computer Interaction, 24*(1), 17–47. doi:10.1080/10447310701771472

Lewis, R. J. (1995). IBM computer usability satisfaction questionnaires: Psychometric evaluation and instructions for use. *International Journal of Human-Computer Interaction, 7*(1), 57–78. doi:10.1080/10447319509526110

Loeppky, S. (2006). *Gaming and students with Asperger's syndrome: A literature review.* Retrieved from http://www.usask.ca/education/coursework/802papers/loeppky/locppky.pdf

Malliou, E., & Miliarakis, A. (2005). The MOTFAL project: Mobile technologies for ad hoc learning. In Attewell, J., & Savill-Smith, C. (Eds.), *Mobile Learning Anytime Everywhere: Papers from Mlearn 2004.* Mlearn. doi:10.1109/ICALT.2004.1357716

Malone, T. W. (1980). What makes things fun to learn? Heuristics for designing instructional computer games. In *Proceedings of the 3rd ACM SIGSMALL Symposium and 1st SIGPC Symposium on Small Systems*, (pp. 162-169). ACM Press.

Malone, T. W. (1982). Heuristics for designing enjoyable user interfaces: Lessons from computer games. In Thomas, J. C., & Schneider, M. L. (Eds.), *Human Factors in Computing Systems.* Norwood, NJ: Ablex Publishing Corporation.

Mayes, J. T., & Fowler, C. J. H. (1999). Learning technology and usability: A framework for understanding courseware. *Interacting with Computers, 11*, 485–497. doi:10.1016/S0953-5438(98)00065-4

McLaughlin, J., & Skinner, D. (2000). Developing usability and utility: A comparative study of the users of new IT. *Technology Analysis and Strategic Management, 12*(3), 413–423. doi:10.1080/09537320050130633

Moreno-Ger, P., Burgos, D., Martínez-Ortiz, I., Sierra, J. L., & Fernández-Manjón, B. (2008). Educational game design for online education. *Computers in Human Behavior, 24*, 2530–2540. doi:10.1016/j.chb.2008.03.012

Nielsen, J. (1993). *Usability engineering*. New York, NY: Academic Press Ltd.

Nielsen, J. (1994). Enhancing the explanatory power of usability heuristics. In *Proceedings of CHI 1994*, (pp. 152-158). Boston, MA: CHI.

Nokelainen, P. (2004). Conceptual definition of the technical and pedagogical usability criteria for digital learning material. In *Proceedings of World Conference on Educational Multimedia, Hypermedia and Telecommunications*, (Vol. 1), (pp. 4249-4254). ACM.

Norman, D. (1990). *The design of everyday things*. New York, NY: Doubleday.

Oblinger, D. G. (2006). Digital games have the potential to bring play back to the learning experience. *EDUCAUSE Quarterly, 29*(3).

Petrie, H., Hamilton, F., & King, N. (2004). Tension, what tension? Website accessibility and visual design. In *Proceedings of the International Cross-Disciplinary Workshop on Web Accessibility (W4A)*. New York, NY: ACM Press.

Petrie, H., & Kheir, O. (2007). The relationship between accessibility and usability of websites. In *Proceedings of CHI 2007*. San Jose, CA: CHI.

Piaget, J. (1951). *Play, dreams and imitation in childhood*. New York, NY: Norton.

Prensky, M. (2001). *Digital game based learning*. New York, NY: McGraw-Hill.

Quesenbery, C., Jarrett, J., Ramsey, J., & Redish, G. (2001). *What does usability mean?* Paper presented at the Annual Conference for Social for Technical Communication. Chicago, IL.

Rowley, J. (1998). Towards a methodology for the design of multimedia public access interfaces. *Journal of Information Science, 24*(3), 155–166. doi:10.1177/016555159802400302

Sanchez-Crespo Dalmau, D. (1999). *Learn faster to pay better: How to shorten the learning cycle*. Retrieved from http://www.gamasutra.com/view/feature/3392/learn_faster_to_play_better_how_.php?page=5

Schneiderman, B. (2000). Universal accessibility. *Communications of the ACM, 43*(5), 85–91.

Schneiderman, B. (2003). Promoting universal usability with multi-layer interface design. In *Proceedings of 2003 Conference on Universal Usability*. New York, NY: ACM Press.

Screen Learning. (2011). *Smart cat profiling*. Retrieved from http://www.screenlearning.com/products/smart-cat.php

Shelley, B. (2001). *Guidelines for developing successful games*. Retrieved from http://www.gamasutra.com/features/20010815/shelley_01.htm

Shield, L., & Kukulska-Hulme, A. (2006). Are language learning websites special? Towards a research agenda for discipline-specific usability. *Journal of Educational Multimedia and Hypermedia, 15*(3), 349–369.

Shneiderman, B. (1997). Human factors of interactive software. In Shneiderman, B., Plaisant, C., Cohen, M., & Jacobs, S. (Eds.), *Designing the User Interface: Strategies for Effective Human-Computer Interaction*. Upper Saddle River, NJ: Pearson-Addison.

Silius, K., Tervakari, A.-M., & Pohjolainen, S. (2003). *A multidisciplinary tool for the evaluation of usability, pedagogical usability, accessibility and information quality of web-based courses*. Paper presented at the Eleventh International PEG Conference. Nashville, TN.

Stiles, M. J. (2002). *Disability access to virtual learning environments*. Retrieved from http://www.computing.dundee.ac.uk/projects/dmag/resources/casestudies/stilesfull.asp

Swain, J., French, S., & Cameron, C. (2003). *Controversial issues in a disabling society*. Buckingham, UK: Open University Press.

Theofanos, M. F., & Redish, J. (2003, November/December). Bridging the gap: Between accessibility and usability. *ACM Interactions Magazine*, 36-51.

Thomas, S., Schott, G., & Kambouri, M. (2007). Designing for learning or designing for fun? Setting usability guidelines for mobile educational games. In Vahey, P., Tatar, D., & Roschelle, J. (Eds.), *Learning with Mobile Devices: A Book of Papers* (pp. 173–181). Mlearning.

UPIAS. (1976). *Fundamental principles of disability*. London, UK: UPIAS (Union of the Physically Impaired Against Segregation).

van Tol, R. A. (2006). *The sound alternative*. Retrieved from http://www.accessibility.nl/games/index.php?pagefile=soundalternative

Walker, I. (2008). *The future use of educational assessment games in the foundation stage: An SSAT evaluation project*. Retrieved from http://wiki.ict-register.net/images/4/44/ScreenLearning.pdf

Wang, A. I., Øfsdahl, T., & Mørch-Storstein, O. K. (2009). *Collaborative learning through games – Characteristics, model and taxonomy*. Retrieved from http://citeseerx.ist.psu.edu/viewdoc/download?doi=10.1.1.159.4657&rep=rep1&type=pdf

WHO. (1980). *International classification of impairments, disabilities and handicaps*. Geneva, Switzerland: World Health Organisation.

WHO. (2001). *International classification of functioning, disability and health (ICF)*. Geneva, Switzerland: World Health Organisation.

Zyda, M. (2005, September). From visual simulation to virtual reality to games. *IEEE Computer*.

ADDITIONAL READING

Alliance for Technology Access, & Hawking, S. (2004). *Computer resources for people with disabilities: A guide to assistive technologies, tools and resources for people of all ages*. Alliance for Technology Access.

Asakawa, C., & Leporini, B. (2009). Screenreaders. In Stephanidis, C. (Ed.), *Universal Access Handbook*. London, UK: Taylor & Francis.

Burgstahler, S. (2002). *Universal design of distance learning, information technology and disabilities*. Retrieved from http://www.rit.edu/~easi/itd/itdv08n1/burgstahler.htm

Calabrò, A., Contini, E., & Leporini, B. (2009). Book4All: A tool to make an e-book more accessible to students with vision/visual-impairments. *Lecture Notes in Computer Science, 5889*, 236–248. doi:10.1007/978-3-642-10308-7_16

Chang, M., & Kuo, R. (2009). Learning by playing: Game-based education system design and development. *Lecture Notes in Computer Science, 5670*.

Clark, S., & Baggaley, J. (2004). Assistive software for disabled learners. *International Review of Research in Open and Distance Learning, 5*(3).

Dix, A., Finlay, J., Abowd, G. D., & Beale, R. (2004). *Human computer interaction* (3rd ed.). Upper Saddle River, NJ: Prentice-Hall.

Donker, H., Klante, P., & Gorny, P. (2002). The design of auditory user interfaces for blind users. In *Proceedings of the Second Nordic Conference on Human-Computer Interaction*. New York, NY: ACM Press.

Eagle, M. (2009). Level up: A frame work for the design and evaluation of educational games. In *Proceedings of the 4th International Conference on Foundations of Digital Games (FDG 2009)*. ACM Press.

Edmonds, C. (2004). Providing access to students with disabilities in online distance education: Legal and technical concerns for higher education. *American Journal of Distance Education, 18*(1). doi:10.1207/s15389286ajde1801_5

Ellis, B. (2007). *Barriers in games, why can't they play?* Retrieved August 3 2011 from http://www.retroremakes.com/access/

Folmer, E. (2007). *Designing usable and accessible games with interaction design patterns.* Retrieved from http://www.gamasutra.com/view/feature/1408/designing_usable_and_accessible_.php?print=1

Grammenos, D., Savidis, A., & Stephanidis, C. (2009). Designing universally accessible games. *Computers in Entertainment, 7*(1).

Hersh, M. A. (2008). Assistive technology, education and the elderly, interview. In Mordini, E., & Mannari, S. (Eds.), *Including Seniors in the Information society 28 World Leading Expert Talks on Privacy, Ethics, Technology and Aging.* CIC Edizioni Internazionali.

Hersh, M. A., & Johnson, M. A. (2003). *Assistive technology for the hearing impaired, deaf and deafblind.* Berlin, Germany: Springer Verlag. doi:10.1007/b97528

Hersh, M. A., & Johnson, M. A. (2006). *Accessibility of PDF documents.* Leeds, UK: AXMEDIS.

Hersh, M. A., & Johnson, M. A. (2007). A user-centred approach for developing and evaluating advanced learning technologies based on the comprehensive assistive technology model. In *Proceedings of the 7th IEEE International Conference on Advanced Learning Technologies, ICALT 2007.* Niigata, Japan: IEEE Press.

Hersh, M. A., & Johnson, M. A. (2008). *Assistive technology for visually impaired and blind people.* Berlin, Germany: Springer Verlag. doi:10.1007/978-1-84628-867-8

Hersh, M. A., & Moss, G. (2007). New media and the digital divide: Accessibility and usability for disabled people and women. In *Proceedings of the 4th International Conference on Cybernetics and Information Technologies, Systems and Applications, CITSA 2007.* CITSA.

Hinske, S., Langheinrich, M., & Lampe, M. (2008). Towards guidelines for designing augmented toy environments. In *Proceedings of the 7th ACM Conference on Designing Interactive Systems (DIS 2008).* ACM Press.

Kam, K., et al. (2009). Improving literacy in rural India: Cellphone games in an after-school program. In *Proceedings of the IEEE/ACM Conference on Advanced Learning Technologies,* (pp. 485-487). Washington, DC: IEEE Press.

Kim, Y. Y.-Y., & Kim, K.-H. (2010). An interactivity-based framework for classifying digital games. *International Journal Contents, 6*(4), 35–38. doi:10.5392/IJoC.2010.6.4.035

King, T. W. (1998). *Assistive technology, essential human factors.* Reading, MA: Allyn and Bacon.

Miller, C. (2009). *Games: Purpose and potential in education.* Berlin, Germany: Springer.

Molnar, A., & Frías-Martínez, V. (2011). EducaMovil: Mobile educational games made easy. In *Proceedings of the World Conference Ed-Media.* Ed-Media.

Mori, G., Buzzi, M. C., Buzzi, M., Leporini, B., & Penichet, R. V. M. (2011). Making "Google docs" user interface more accessible for blind people. *Lecture Notes in Computer Science, 6616.*

Rowe, J. P., Shores, L. R., Mott, B. W., & Lester, J. C. (2010). Individual differences in gameplay and learning: a narrative-centered learning perspective. In *Proceedings of the Fifth International Conference on the Foundations of Digital Games (FDG 2010)*. ACM Press.

Rutter, R., Lauke, P., Waddell, C., Thatcher, J., Lawton Henry, S., & Lawson, B. … Urban, M. (2006). *Web accessibility: Web standards and regulatory compliance*. Berlin, Germany: Springer.

Sánchez, J., Saenz, M., & Garrido, J. M. (2010). Usability of a Multimodal video game to improve navigation skills for blind children. *Transactions on Accessible Computing, 3*(2).

Stephanidis, C. (2009). *The universal access handbook*. Boca Raton, FL: CRC Press.

Torrente, J., del Blanco, A., Moreno-Ger, P., Martínez-Ortiz, I., & Fernández-Manjón, B. (2009). Implementing accessibility in educational videogames with <e-Adventure>. In *Proceedings of the First ACM International Workshop on Multimedia Technologies for Distance Learning (MTDL 2009)*. ACM Press.

Trewin, S., Laff, M., Hanson, V., & Cavender, A. (2009). Exploring visual and motor accessibility in navigating a virtual world. *Transactions on Accessible Computing, 2*(2).

Yesilada, Y., Harper, S., Goble, G., & Stevens, R. (2004). Screen readers cannot see (ontology based semantic annotation for visually impaired web travellers). In *Proceedings of the 4th International Conference on Web Engineering*, (pp. 445-458). Heidelberg, Germany: Springer Verlag Publishers.

Chapter 2
Usability of Online Virtual Learning Environments:
Key Issues for Instructors and Learners

Ian John Cole
University of York, UK

ABSTRACT

This chapter explores key issues in relation to the human computer interactions that are supported through Virtual Learning Environments (VLEs). It focuses particularly on the usability of online learning environments and highlights the impact usability can have on the learning experiences of users. The authors adopt a definition of usability that relates to the usability of virtual learning environments, specifically, and provides guidance on how to assess the usability of VLEs by offering the Multidimensional Usability Model (MUM). The MUM model is designed to identify the factors that can form technological barriers to effective Human Computer Interaction (HCI). This chapter also offers an evaluation of the theoretical frameworks, criteria, and methodologies currently available; these draw on research findings from a case study focused on the usability of an existing VLE and give practical examples of the MUM approach to usability.

BACKGROUND

What is a VLE?

Before we can consider the usability of Virtual Learning Environments (VLEs), it might be helpful to provide a definition for VLE. The term VLE is often interchangeable with the term Managed Learning Environment (MLE), and for the purposes of this chapter, there is an intension to clarify the distinction between the two by adopting the British Educational Communications and Technology Agency definition of an MLE as incorporating:

DOI: 10.4018/978-1-4666-1987-6.ch002

"The whole range of information systems and processes ... (including its VLE) that contribute directly or indirectly to learning and learning management' so 'in effect, an MLE might consist of a whole range of different software and systems that interrelate, share data and contribute to learning management' whilst 'VLE refers to a specific piece of software that enables learners and staff to interact, and includes content delivery and trackin" (BECTA, 2000).

If we will concentrate specifically on VLEs as the focus is on the student learning experience rather than the administrative systems that support learning. We have adopted the United Kingdom's Joint Information Systems Committee (JISC), definition for VLEs as referring to the components in which learners and tutors participate in online interactions:

"The requirements of a VLE are to control access to curriculum and learning resources, the tracking of student activity and achievement, the support for on-line learning, the recording of assessment and the use of communication tools between participants to build a sense of group identity and community of practice" (JISC, 2002).

Britain and Liber's (1999) work has helped to outline the definition further by listing the principle tools of a *prototypical* VLE as including the following:

*   Notice-board
*   Course outline
*   E-mail
*   Asynchronous and synchronous communication tools
*   Class lists and student homepages
*   Assignments and assessment tools
*   Calendar
*   Collaboration tools
*   File sharing and upload area
*   Access to multimedia resources

Defining Usability

My research work into the 'usability' of VLE's, has concentrated on an educators' perspective instead of a technologists approach. It has been found that usability can have a significant impact on learning, retention rates, and learner motivation, and it can play a key role in enhancing the positive learning experiences of students using VLE's. One of the main purposes of this chapter is to provide the reader with practical guidance on how they might apply a simple model to test the usability of a VLE and identify adjustments that might be made in order to make interfaces easier to use and learn and meet the specific needs of their students.

Perhaps before we explore the concept of usability further we should attempt to offer a definition of usability. There are as many definitions of usability as there are academics writing on the concept and it can be confusing. Perhaps a starting point is an original definition offered by Jenny Preece in 1994:

Usability is "a measure of the ease with which a system can be learned or used, its safety, effectiveness and efficiency and the attitude of its users towards it" (Preece, 1994).

We can consider this definition a helpful starting point, as the approach puts the learner at the centre of the design and evaluation process. However, in 2000, Preece (2000) developed her definition further to take into account the advent of VLE's and computer mediated conferencing tools, she defined usability in the context of online learning communities suggesting that:

"Software with good usability supports rapid learning, high skills retention, low error rates and high productivity. It is consistent, controllable and predictable, making it pleasant and effective to use" (Preece, 2000).

This definition makes the connection between usability and the learning experience. At this stage, it might also be helpful to acknowledge that many educators confuse usability with accessibility, to clarify matters further I offer the following simple distinction:

"Usability focuses on making software, websites and online applications and services easy to use" *(Frontend, 2001, p. 13).*

"Accessibility may be defined as making them equally easy for everyone to use including people who may use assistive technologies" (Frontend, 2001, p. 13).

and assistive technology can be defined as:

"Equipment and software that are used to maintain or improve the functional capabilities for a person with a disability" (Doyle & Robson, 2002).

ISSUES, CONTROVERSIES, PROBLEMS

Why Usability?

It could be argued that usability testing should be left to the experts. Undoubtedly, many software companies invest significant time and resources in testing new systems during the development stages of software creation. There have been attempts to map existing usability models to the development of VLE's (Kissane & Finn, 2003) but most educators do not feel that they have the skills and understanding to evaluate usability and therefore do not consider the issue of usability when planning to use learning technologies to support learning. However, it is clear that bad usability can have disastrous consequences on the quality of the learning experience and the retention and motivation of learners.

Educators often find themselves, unexpectedly, as the first port of call for students experiencing difficulties and frustrations as a result of poor usability of a VLE, yet they feel helpless in taking actions to improve the usability of their institutions chosen interface.

The Context

The following transcripts are from an independent usability test that was video recorded and demonstrates a simple example of 'bad' usability, the impact this can have on leaner frustration levels and the quality of the learning experience. The participants (non-expert testers) are real 'tutors' working through learning activities in a VLE that had reportedly undergone extensive 'upgrades' by the supplier in response to feedback from users and the organisation procuring the VLE.

During the usability test, two (non-expert) testers were asked to participate in a cognitive walkthrough experiment (Wharton, et al., 1992), a method that requires the tester to think out loud and verbalise how easy it is to achieve the required action/goal correctly. These transcript extracts capture the testers' verbal comments and describe their actions. On completing a series of learning activities, the testers were directed to return to a main menu to answer a series of assessment questions, as you will see the testers had difficulty locating the assessment questions within the VLE:

The testers' comments are in italics.

Non-Expert Tester 1

- Assessment *"Questions—Where are they?"*
- (She re-listened to the Learning Objective Assessment Page and said) *"But it doesn't tell you other than return to the main menu and select the questions for this module."*

- Tester was looking for a button on the bottom of screen to take her back to main menu—there wasn't one.
- What she thought was an exit button, brought up a contents list for the course.
- She then spotted Help but Help did not tell her how to get back to the Home Page, it just provided information on the course with no search facility available.

Non-Expert Tester 2

- Tester 2 said: "No navigation aid from page 25 to questions in Main Menu."
- Tester had real difficulty finding questions area—he found the Home Page (but not the Main Menu) ultimately by guesswork and trial and error. He then said: "Tried Help but Page Cannot be Displayed came up."
- Eventually he asked the usability expert where to find the questions area (i.e. via 'courses').
- When he clicked 'courses' a spurious list came up. He then said *"a Kitchen Porter would definitely think they had made a mistake."* (The usability team think there might have been a sequence bug in the VLE—this problem had occurred in another usability test).
- He went back to the Home Page then Courses again and the correct list came up, and he said, "hmm, but not into Main Menu."
- On arriving at the assessment questions, he said, "9 out of 10 learners would have given up by now. They would already be anxious about the test—there is a need here to give lots of learner reassurance."

As the above extracts demonstrate the non-expert testers were experiencing real difficulties with general navigation within the VLE, this led to confusion and frustration and impacted on their ability to complete the required assessment activities. The transcript also illustrates that even when systems are sold with assurances that they have been rigorously tested during software development, we cannot assume that the right amount or the correct type of usability testing has been built into the development phase.

To reinforce this Stuart Smith (2002) while experimenting with the interface of VLEs and dyslexic users concluded that:

"If user testing were more widely deployed in both the academic & commercial world then the VLE would be a more satisfactory product from the users viewpoint and this process would help developers have better understanding of user requirements" (Smith, 2002).

The ideal VLE from a usability point of view would be so intuitive to use and learn that users would not need instruction on how to use the environment, and would be able to navigate themselves through the environment with total control, as the software would tailor itself to the needs of the individual user. Clearly, such technology is not currently available and all VLE's have strengths and weaknesses. However, given the restrictions of current technology we recommend that educators should take up the challenge of becoming involved in usability testing while developing their curriculum for online technologies. It is within the educators' power to require VLE providers to make improvements and confront real problems that become real barriers to learning enhancement for many students.

Frameworks for Evaluating Usability

There has been a lot of work on evaluating usability over the decades and it helps to break usability down into component parts and identify the important elements. Don Norman (1999) classified

Human Computer Interaction (HCI) constraints into 3 categories:

- **Physical:** The movement of things
- **Logical:** Making actions and their effects obvious
- **Cultural:** Learned conventions, i.e. emoticons

Usability forms part of his user-centred design philosophy (Norman & Draper, 1986) and the needs, wants and limitations of a user are given extensive attention at every stage of the design process. Vilpola and Ihamäki (2004) focused on usability as *effectiveness*, *efficiency*, and *satisfaction* in which users achieve specified goals in particular environments.

In 1996, Martin Rantzer introduced the DELTA method as a framework for usability evaluation; he proposed that his method should be used from the first stage of a software development project and continues throughout a project until the user interacts with the system or interface. Rantzer argued that if usability is applied too late after the system requirements have been defined, there is a high risk of trying to improve a finished product, he used the effective analogy of "applying lipstick to the corpse" (Rantzer, 1998).

Gould and Lewis (1985) also focused on the need for early intervention and identified 3 main principles of user-centred design as:

1. An early focus on users and tasks.
2. Empirical measurement of product usage (i.e., ease of use).
3. Iterative design whereby a product is designed, modified, and tested repeatedly.

Clearly, the best approach to usability testing involves end users at the beginning of software development, and yet most of us are likely to be working with off the shelf products, and we are unlikely to be able to apply Gould and Lewis's first principle (unless using open-source software). However, Principles 2 and 3 can be tested at any stage of using a VLE. We would argue that it is never too late to usability test a VLE and even when VLE's have been procured and installed; individual educators should influence their organisations by adopting strategies to test the usability of their system with real tutors and students in real learning situations. This can be done without huge resources and lead to longer term benefits realisation.

There is growing literature indicating that the usability of most VLEs is less than satisfactory. Examples of often-cited 'bad' usability include:

- Lack of navigational control (Armitage, et al., 2003)
- Too many unnecessary features and tools (Beasley, et al., 2003)
- Counter-intuitive on-screen information, poor presentation of key information and lack of accessibility (Frontend, 2001)

VLEs that are hard to use lead to student dissatisfaction (Jones, et al., 2003; Kent, 2003) and cause real barriers to learning. Vilpola and Lhamaki (2004) stated that many of these problems occur because:

"Learning environments are not planned and tested (with) their target user group in mind" (Vilpola & Lhamaki, 2004)

This was also highlighted by Maia Dimitrova et al. (2002) in a study that explored 'expert-based methods' when evaluating e-learning applications. The findings concluded that while most usability experts were able to identify the majority of usability issues, they were less able to predict the problems that many learners encountered.

SOLUTIONS AND RECOMMENDATIONS

Usability Models

The most commonly used usability models from Dix (1993), Nelsen (1994), and Preece (1994) are theoretical models that characterise *Effectiveness, Efficiency, and Satisfaction* as the most important characteristics of usability. Dix and Nelsen's models also include *learnability*. It was important for us to consider these criteria as we developed our practical Multidimensional Usability Model (MUM).

Most of the literature on usability recommends that to conduct usability studies, *well-appointed, well-equipped, expensive laboratories with professional testing staff* are essential (Rubins, 1994). Most agree that usability testers should be close to the 'end user' and all comment on a process of finding out what the users needs are by engaging usability 'experts' to conduct reviews (Shneiderman, 1998, p. 125). However, Dumas and Redish (1999, p. 65) comment that organisations are constantly *'looking for cheaper ways to evaluate usability.'* Our experience suggests dedicated usability testing laboratories are no always required for this type of work, a comfortable office or meeting room can suffice to conduct multidimensional usability testing.

We recommend a model that is designed to be cost effective with a process that can be supported by one independent usability expert and real users (educators and learners) to test VLE software. It may be difficult to find a usability expert locally to facilitate your evaluation but according to Neilson (2000, p. 320), North America, most European countries, and the leading countries in Asia all have plenty of consultants available and experts can be contacted through Internet newsgroups and social networking sites.

THE MULTIDIMENSIONAL USABILITY MODEL

The Multidimensional Usability Model (MUM) has been devised over the last seven years, initially with work on CD-Rom and networked software projects, then developed and modified over the last three years for Web-based technologies particularly VLEs. The design of the model is such that it can easily be modified for any Human Computer Interaction (HCI) software/interface development project as it provides a flexible framework for the usability evaluation of computer software systems.

The 4 main dimensions of the multidimensional usability model are shown in Figure 1 as you will see each dimension overlaps and join in the centre. This reflects the model's complex and integrated structure of the central point where the usability expert and the 3 usability evaluation dimensions represent the point at which the final evaluation is achieved.

The expert user, the mixed mode questionnaire, the non-expert tester dimensions are intrinsic to the model. The cognitive walkthrough dimension can be omitted if required although we strongly recommend the inclusion of this dimension in order to achieve the best evaluation results. A cognitive walkthrough is the sequence of actions that a usability expert may requires a tester to perform in order to accomplish defined tasks within a carefully structured experiment, using a usability questionnaire and whenever possible video or audio recording the interaction. It is a widely accepted HCI evaluation method used to assess the usability of a system in situations where the user is not an expert (Wharton, et al., 1992). Although it is possible to use the MUM model without conducting a cognitive walkthrough experiment, it is recommended that at least one non-expert tester performs a cognitive walkthrough in each MUM study.

Figure 1. The multidimensional usability model

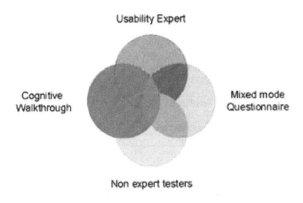

Conventional usability models call for testing to be performed by expert usability testers using a range of methods such as, the heuristic evaluation, guideline review, consistency inspection, cognitive walkthrough (Nielson & Mack, 1994) and formal usability inspection (Shneiderman, 1998, p. 126). We would argue that a conventional usability model although based on sound HCI principles is mainly concerned with the functionality of the interface/software and is not learner centred, these usability models do not take into account of the real pedagogical wants and needs of the user. We cannot improve systems that reflect and enhance real learning experiences unless we involve a real mix of users (i.e., non-experts) including educators and learners in the usability testing process.

There are three approaches to applying the MUM model:

- *Method One* is the simplest method and involves the design of a mixed-mode questionnaire (see Figure 2). The questionnaire is given out to non-expert testers for a fixed period (2 to 4 weeks) and the non-expert testers are left to complete the questionnaire in their own time, this method does not require observations or cognitive walkthrough experiments to be conducted.
- *Method Two* requires the non-expert testers to complete a cognitive walkthrough experiment following the questionnaire

with the experiment being videoed and observed by the usability expert.
- *Method Three* is a combination of methods one and two with at least one tester performing a cognitive walkthrough experiment. In each method, the questionnaire is the same.

The Usability Expert (5 Stages)

The usability expert's role is to project, manage, and facilitate the usability test and this can be viewed as having 5 stages:

1. **Mapping the VLE:** The usability expert will first conduct an evaluation of all areas in the VLE and s/he assigns a name/title to each of the VLE areas (see Figure 3), then taking the questionnaire template (Cole, 2005), the expert maps the areas and questions to the VLE (further explanation given below under mixed mode questionnaire section).

2. **Materials Production:** If a cognitive walkthrough experiment is not to be performed the expert will need to test the final questionnaire and arrange to have it distributed to non-expert testers (for Method 1 or 3).

3. **Managing the Test Users:** The expert agrees the return times for questionnaires (Method 1 or 3) and organises the arrangements for each non-expert cognitive walkthrough test (method 2 or 3).

4. **Cognitive Walkthrough:** If a cognitive walkthrough is to be performed, the expert will need to arrange an appropriate venue for the tests, one that has enough room to accommodate the non-expert tester, the expert, a computer, a video camera and any additional equipment. The expert will then observe and question the non-expert testers as they interact with the VLE interface.

5. **Data Collection and Analysis:** When all tests have been completed the expert will

Figure 2. Semantic differential scale descriptors

Annoying to Pleasant	Confusing to Clear	Difficult to Easy	Discouraging to Encouraging
Dull to Stimulating	Frustrating to Satisfying	Hard to Easy	Hard to complete to Easy to Complete
Hard to read to Easy to read	Hard to understand to Easy to understand	Inadequate to Adequate	Inappropriate to Appropriate
Inconsistent to Consistent	Never to Always	Rigid to Flexible	Terrible to Wonderful
Too Slow to Fast Enough	Unhelpful to Helpful	Unpleasant to Pleasant	Unreliable to Reliable

need to analyse the data and publish the findings.

Mixed Mode Questionnaire

The questionnaires design should include 2 elements, a user profile and an in-depth 10-point Semantic Differential (SD) measure. The Semantic Differential scale (Osgood, et al., 1957) uses a range of bipolar attitudes about a particular screen, interface, action or task. These bipolar descriptors were developed from the Questionnaire for User Interaction Satisfaction (Chin, et al., 1988; Shneiderman, 1998).

Usually a Semantic Differential scale is 7 points, we have extended this to give a wider response range. The rationale for using a 10 point (0 to 9) Semantic Differential scale instead of the standard 7 points is that this type of scale can show discrimination and the use of an even scale instead of the standard 7 point or the Questionnaire for User Interaction Satisfaction point scale (Chin, et al., 1988) does not allow participants to take a centre point as in 3 out of 5 or 5 out of 9 (Abran, et al., 2003). The 10-point MUM scale forces

participants to make finer judgments either side of the centre point (4.5) (see Figure 2).

The VLE needs to be split into areas that can be mapped directly to the questionnaire such as the list in Figure 3.

Once the VLE mapping exercise has been achieved, the questions can then be written. It will be necessary to duplicate some questions in different areas of the VLE (e.g., questions about the *organisation of information* or the *use of colour* in areas such as a 'Course Area' or a 'File Sharing Area'). This mapping is needed to ensure that the non-expert tester is prompted to cover all aspects of the test according to a usability criteria (Figure 4). The usability criterion was developed to map all the questions for each page/screen/area (Figure 4) to the VLE area (Figure 3) some duplication of mapping sections to be expected.

Each of the questions should have a comments space beneath each SD scale grid (see Figure 5) and a larger additional comments panel at the end of each section so as to elicit qualitative data.

The final task is to ensure that the questionnaire includes appropriate usability tasks, these are mapped to the cognitive walkthrough experiment and are grounded in Polson and Lewis (1990)

Figure 3. VLE areas mapping

Login & Home Page	Course Area	Assessment	Asynchronous Area
Synchronous Area	File Sharing Area	Personal Area	Help Resources
General Reactions	Accessibility Tools	System Capabilities	Overall Reactions

CE+ theory using a four step information processing model.

1. The usability expert sets a goal for the non-expert tester to accomplish within the VLE (for example, opening a document in the VLE).
2. The non-expert tester searches the interface for currently available actions (menu items, buttons, command-line inputs, etc.).
3. The non-expert tester selects the action that seems likely to make progress toward the goal.
4. The non-expert tester performs the selected action and evaluates the VLE's feedback for evidence that progress is being made toward the set goal.

The tasks should be embedded in the questionnaire at relevant and strategic points in the process, in most cases they are obvious, i.e. posting a message in a discussion board or interacting in a VLE chat room. At the end of the questionnaire, construction process the average questionnaire should contain approximately 100 questions. A complete example MUM questionnaire can be downloaded via the Internet (see Additional Reading section).

Cognitive Walkthrough Experiment

The Cognitive Walkthrough method is used to evaluate the usability of the user interface (Polson & Lewis, 1990), it requires the user to think out loud and verbalise how easy it is to achieve the required action/goal correctly. One of the main advantages of using this method is that it makes the users' goals and expectations explicit (Vilpola & Ihamäki, 2004, p. 68).

In the MUM process, the experiment can be videoed (or audio recorded) and observed by the usability expert, who acts as a prompt to make sure the non-expert tester keeps vocalising their feelings throughout the test, the expert prompts and asks questions whenever necessary.

The video recording is used mainly to capture the audio that the user and tester vocalise throughout the test but if a Liquid Crystal Display (LCD) screen is used with the computer instead of a Cathode-Ray Tube (CRT) screen, then the video camera can zoom in and focus on the screen showing exactly what the user is doing/clicking on screen. If a cathode-ray tube screen is used it will have an unwatchable rolling effect on the screen and will require the expert to code each screen the tester interacts with.

The MUM Cognitive Walkthrough process requires the non-expert tester to follow the instructions in the questionnaire, answer any questions the expert may have and complete the questions at the end of each section before moving on to the next section. On average, each cognitive walkthrough test should take between two hours and 4 hours but there is a need for regular comfort breaks especially if the tester is getting frustrated with the VLE interface, we recommend short breaks are scheduled into each hour.

The Non-Expert (Usability) Testers

There are two types of MUM testers.

Figure 4. Criteria for usability testing

Use of Images and Icons	Readability and Text Size
Use of Colour	Navigation and Instructions
Interactivity	Learning to use the VLE
System Capabilities	Organisation of information
Learning Styles	Accessibility
General Reactions	Overall Reactions

Figure 5. Example questions and SD scale

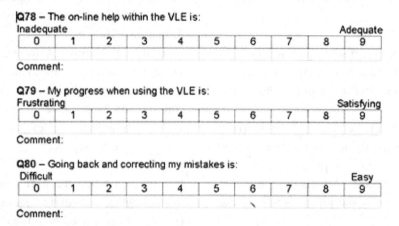

Both types of tester need to be reasonably computer literate although there is no need for them to be considered computer experts.

- **The Educator Tester:** It is important that the educator tester has limited or no VLE experience as they may bring previous technology interactions to the experiment. They should not be given any training in using the VLE prior to the test period as a well-designed VLE should be intuitive enough for the tester to easily navigate without prior instruction. The educator brings pedagogical knowledge to the test that a usability expert may not have.
- **The Learner Tester:** As the learner tester is probably using the VLE as part of a live course, it is important that they are given training on how to use the VLE. This is to ensure that they are not disadvantaged by technology in their progression through their course. The learner tester should always undertake the testing or completion of the questionnaire at the end of their period of learning.

- The educators with limited or no experience of using a VLE
- The learners who will learn using the VLE.

Data Analysis

MUM Questionnaire

After the usability study is finished, the data from each questionnaire should be analysed and a results matrix produced (see Figure 6). This matrix will identify particular problem areas of the VLE.

Any question scoring less than 4.5 mean on the Question Results Matrix (QRM) is a concern; looking at Figure 6, we see the students who had been using the VLE for several weeks scored this question 4.3 (frustrating) and the control group of educators scored the question 5.4 (satisfying) in most cases the combined results (4.7) give a more accurate picture.

Once all the questions have been analysed the questions can be mapped to the MUM usability Classification (see Figure 7). As seen from the example in Figure 6, once mapped to the usability classification this question results in a 3 category minor problem that might need further exploration, any question with a category 1 or 2 classification is a very serious usability problem and would need resolving.

RESEARCH FINDINGS

The Multidimensional Usability Model Case Study

The Multidimensional Usability Model was used in the following case study where an evaluation into the usability of the Blackboard virtual learning environment was undertaken.

The VLE was being used for the delivery of a blended course by a Higher Education Institution (HEI) in the United Kingdom. The 10-week "blended" (Rogers, 2001) course started with 16 students, delivery was by 3 face-to-face workshops and 7 online (individual and group) activities. The course focused on the underpinning pedagogies that are needed to support effective virtual learning communities.

While the course was running the usability evaluation of the VLE was undertaken to explore the usability and functionality of the software and to examine whether the users experienced any "barriers to learning" (DFEE, 1998) by using the technology. The study was conducted by a lead researcher from a different HEI, and he recruited a 6-person (non-expert) usability evaluation team, one of the testers agreed to undertake a "cognitive walkthrough experiment" and have their interactions with the VLE videoed. The group of 16 students on the course was also included in the study and they were asked to complete the MUM questionnaire at the end of their period of study.

All testers in the 6-person evaluation team were working in the education sector and chosen by the researcher because of their experience in teaching/facilitating computer-based training. Only one of the testers had ever used a VLE (WebCT) before in a pilot project a few years before. None of the group were given VLE training and all were given the MUM questionnaire and asked to explore the VLE and complete the questionnaire within a set timescale (see Figure 8), they were asked to contact the researcher if any additional help was required.

Cognitive Walkthrough Experiment

The cognitive walkthrough experiment was conducted at the participants' home where the tester came into contact with the VLE for the first time. She was using a computer that was running Microsoft Windows operating system with a Pentium 3 processor and a 512kb Broadband Internet connection, therefore it was considered unlikely that the home computer would compromise the exercise. The experiment took 3 hours to complete and was videoed with the participant vocalising her initial

Figure 6. Question results matrix[1]

Q85 – Using the VLE is:
Frustrating   Satisfying

	0	1	2	3	4	5	6	7	8	9	NR's	Means
Students	1		1	1	5		2	2			2	4.3
Control					1	2	1	1				5.4
Experiment								1				
Totals	1		1	1	6	2	3	4			2	4.7

Comment:
S: Had quite a few problems with access speed, which really frustrated me, as I didn't have a lot of time to spend waiting for something to happen.

Figure 7. MUM usability classification

	Problem Rating	Question Score
1	A Catastrophic Problem	0 to 1
2	A Serious Problem	2 to 3
3	A Minor Problem (which might or might not need attention)	4 to 5
4	A Minor Positive Finding	6 to 7
5	A Major Positive Finding	8 to 9

fccling and first impressions of the VLE interface. A MUM questionnaire (containing the same questions as the other test groups) was completed at the end of each VLE area inline with the section on the *Mixed Mode Questionnaire*.

Study Results

Upon completion of the questionnaires, the statistical data was analysed and collated with the following important outcomes and issues raised:

- Logging on to the VLE was generally considered easy with an overall mean score of 8.1. There were no major problems encountered getting into the system.

- Quite a few participants had problems with the speed of access of the VLE at certain times (total mean score 5.0). The reason for this is believed to be the number of total university students accessing the Blackboard server and overloading the university system. This was considered an issue of network infrastructure and not VLE usability.

- Initial reactions to the opening VLE pages were mixed (total mean score 5.1) with particular confusion for the walkthrough

experiment participant in what was viewed and how to proceed from the opening page.

- Generally, it was thought that the size of text and colour was readable and acceptable although a number of testers thought that the VLE should make it easy for individuals to change font size and background colours of pages & documents placed inside the VLE. The version of Blackboard tested at the time did not allow these changes. It was also commented that when tutors choose colours (of text) it should only be colours that a dyslexic or visually impaired learner would find suitable.

- The use of images was considered OK if uninspiring as most images were icons and only decorative.

- The organisation of information within the VLE was considered confusing in several areas of the environment, compounded by a lack of instruction and a poorly constructed help facility.

- Most of the functions in the Tools area were considered poorly identified, without proper instructions or help. It was difficult to understand the purpose of the tools and it was an area that nobody used.

- The synchronous chat tool (virtual classroom or V.C) was considered a poor re-

Figure 8. Questionnaire completion timescales

Usability Testers (x5)	4 week time scale
Cognitive Walkthrough Tester (x1)	4 hour videoed experiment
Students on the blended course (x16)	2 week time scale (end of course)

source that has potential if it were to be improved. It was confusing to use and lacked facilities compared to freely available synchronous communication tools. Issues such as the main panel not informing participants who was available in the virtual classroom or who was typing made using it frustrating. It was also commented that it would have been useful to be able to view work in other parts of Blackboard while working in the V.C., but this was not possible as the V.C. closes as soon as a user clicks on another part of the VLE.

Case Study Conclusions

The conclusions from these results raised some interesting issues concerning speed of access to the system, navigability, lack of instruction, issues of accessibility and the design and functionality of the communication tools.

As the participants reactions to the VLE were mixed and some participants experienced confusion in what they were viewing on the opening screens of the VLE, it was felt that there should be clear progress instructions and signposting as to where the user is at all times while in the VLE.

It was clear from this case study that certain VLE tools, options and facilities needed improvement, the case study highlights the need for VLE's to signpost learners and course developers through the environment. Blackboard Inc in a continuous cycle of upgrading there software and some or all of these issues may be addressed in future versions.

FUTURE RESEARCH DIRECTIONS

As technology has become smaller and smaller with laptops, Personal Digital Assistants (PDAs), and mobile telephones being used to access the Internet, the need for good usability increases. Buchanan et al. (2001) commented that many mobile Internet systems are difficult to use and lack flexibility and robustness and technology such as WAP phones give a poor user experience this situation has now improved. Jakob Nielson (the

Figure 9. Multidimensional usability model checklist

The Multidimensional Usability Model Checklist	Tick
Assign a usability expert to project manage the study.	
The MUM method of delivery is chosen	
Method 1	
Method 2	
Method 3	
The usability expert maps the VLE to the questionnaire template	
The usability expert tests the final questionnaire	
The usability expert identifies/selects the non expert testers	
Educator testers	
Learner testers	
The usability expert organises the Cognitive Walkthrough experiment	
Room	
Computer	
Video Equipment	
The usability expert distributes the questionnaires	
Agrees return date	
Collects Questionnaires	
The usability expert supervises the Cognitive Walkthrough experiment	
The usability expert analyses the data	
Results Matrix	
Usability Classifications	
The usability expert produces final study report	

usability consultant) has even stated that WAP was the Wrong Approach to Portability (1999).

Gabrielli et al. (2005) explored cognitive walk-through processes while evaluating an e-learning course that used PDAs for content delivery, some of their findings highlighted usability issues such as the difficulty of scrolling with a PDA stylus, PDA browser problems, poor navigation and outdoor lighting conditions making it hard to see the screen.

Diminishing screen sizes on portable devices is only one area of usability that requires more research. A wide range of innovations and refinements in technological advances in particularly the convergence of technologies in mobile phones and computer games have led to the 'Xbox generation' expecting better usability of portable devices.

Coupled to the usability of mobile devices is the expanding use of wireless technology. One of the questions being asked in British universities a few years ago was "if we have a wireless campus network, do we need so many desktop computer laboratories?"

Two of the main benefits of wireless & mobile trends are the availability of background material during lectures, and mobile devices that can be used to provide access to software can be used outside the classroom, i.e. for off campus learning, mobile access to information can promote a richer learning experience when visiting museums, theatres, and art galleries (Cover, 2003). However, there is a need to have Web pages written specially for mobile devices or at lease have scalable Web pages that can run on different devices. This has also leaded to having a mobile version of some VLE software's.

CONCLUSION

Within this chapter, I have aimed to provide the reader with an overview of usability particularly in relation to VLEs. I hope that the Multidimensional Usability Model will provide an alternative flex-ible approach to enable readers and organisations to engage in simple cost effective usability testing and lead to the development of more learner centred and pedagogically focused VLE's. It is important to remember that none of the VLEs tested so far are perfectly easy to use and learn. Don Norman (1988, p. 29) highlighted this issue when he commented that "it usually takes five or six attempts to get a product right," and we would add, even when VLE providers think they have the product right there is still more work to do adapting systems and interfaces to meet the needs of users in their varied and different learning contexts.

Finally, we offer readers who are embarking on the path of VLE usability testing, some resources (in the Additional Reading section) including a quick checklist of each step associated with the Multidimensional Usability Model (Figure 9) and a MUM mixed mode questionnaire template available for downloading from the Internet (Cole, 2005).

REFERENCES

Abran, A., Surya, W., Khelifi, A., Rilling, J., Seffah, A., & Robert, F. (2003). Consolidating the ISO usability models. In *Proceedings of the 11th Annual International Software Quality Management Conference*. Software Quality Management.

Armitage, U., Wilson, S., & Sharp, H. (2003). The effects of navigation aids on ownership for learning with electronic texts. In R. Williams (Ed.), *Proceedings of the 2nd European Conference on e-Learning*, (pp. 47-58). Reading, MA: Academic Conferences International.

Beasley, N., & Smyth, K. (2003). Students selective use of a virtual learning environment: Reflections and recommendations. In R. Williams (Ed.), *Proceedings of the 2nd European Conference on e-Learning*, (pp. 71-79). Reading, MA: Academic Conferences International.

BECTA. (2000). *Managed learning environments (MLEs) in further education: Progress report*. Retrieved 10/08/11 from http://www.jisc.ac.uk/news/stories/2000/07/circular700.aspx

Blackmon, M. H., Polson, P. G., Kitajima, M., & Lewis, C. (2002). Cognitive walkthrough for the web. In *Proceedings of the 2002 ACM Conference on Human Factors in Computing Systems (CHI 2002)*, (pp. 463-470). ACM Press. Britain, S., & Liber, O. (1999). *A framework for pedagogical evaluation of virtual learning environments*. Retrieved 10/08/11 from http://www.leeds.ac.uk/educol/documents/00001237.htm

Buchanan, G., Farrant, S., Jones, M., Thimbleby, H., Marsden, G., & Pazzani, M. (2001). Improving mobile internet usability. In *Proceedings of the 10th International Conference on World Wide Web*, (pp. 673-680). New York, NY: ACM Press.

Chin, J. P., Diehl, V. A., & Norman, K. L. (1988). Development of an instrument measuring user satisfaction of the human-computer interface. In *Proceedings of CHI*. (pp 213-218). CHI.

Cole, I. (2005). *Multidimensional usability model (MUM) questionnaire template*. Retrieved 08/08/11 from http://www-users.york.ac.uk/~ijc4/work.htm

Cover, S. (2003). Wireless networks and mobile devices. *Transformations: Liberal Arts in the Digital Age*. Retrieved 10/22/10 from http://www.colleges.org/transformations/issue1/cover/01.html

Department for Education and Employment. (1998) *The learning age: A renaissance for a new Britain*. Retrieved 20/08/11, from http://www.lifelonglearning.co.uk/greenpaper/

Dimitrova, M., Sharp, H., & Wilson, S. (2002). Educational multimedia cognitive walkthrough: Supporting experts to predict valid user problems. In *Proceedings of Human Computer Interaction 2002 (Vol. 2*, pp. 26–29). London, UK: ACM.

Dix, A., Finley, J., Abowd, G., & Beale, R. (1993). *Human-computer interaction*. Upper Saddle River, NJ: Prentice-Hall.

Doyle, C., & Robson, K. (2002). *Accessible curricula - Good practice for all*. Retrieved 06/08/11 from http://www.uwic.ac.uk/ltsu/accessible.pdf

Dumas, J. S., & Redish, J. C. (1994). *A practical guide to usability testing*. Exeter, UK: Intellect Books.

Frontend.com. (2001). *Why people can't use elearning*. Retrieved 04/08/11 from http://www.infocentre.frontend.com/uploaded_files/eLearning_white_paper.pdf

Gabrielli, S., Mirabella, V., Kimani, S., & Catarci, T. (2005). Supporting cognitive walkthrough with video data: A mobile learning evaluation study. In *Proceedings of the 7th International Conference on Human Computer Interaction with Mobile Devices & Services, MobileHCI 2005*, (pp. 77-82). MobileHCI.

Gould, J. D., & Lewis, C. (1985). Designing for usability: Key principles and what designers think. *Communications of the AMC*, *2*(3), 300–311. doi:10.1145/3166.3170

Higher Education Academy. (2010). *What is a VLE?* Retrieved 11/08/11 from http://www.ukcle.ac.uk/resources/trns/vles/one.html

Joint Information Systems Committee. (2000). *Managed learning environments (MLEs) in further education: Progress report*. Retrieved 11/08/11 from http://www.jisc.ac.uk/news/stories/2000/07/circular700.aspx

Joint Information Systems Committee. (2002). *Briefing paper no 1- MLEs and VLEs explained*. Retrieved 04/08/11 from http://www.jisc.ac.uk/uploaded_documents/bp1.pdf

Jones, P., Packham, G., Miller, C., Davies, I., & Jones, A. (2003). e-Retention: An initial evaluation of student withdrawals within a virtual learning environment. In R. Williams (Ed.), *Proceedings of the 2nd European Confrence on eLearning*, (pp. 239-248). Reading, MA: Academic Conferences International.

Kent, T. (2003). Supporting staff using WebCT at the University of Birmingham in the UK. *Electronic Journal of e-Learning, 1*(1), 1-10.

Kissane, A., & Finn, E. (2003). Development of a usability model for VLE deployment. In *Proceedings of ILTA, EdTech 2003*. Retrieved 11/05/10 from http://www.ilta.net/EdTech2003/papers/FinnKissane.doc

Moody, L., & Schmidt, G. (2004). Going wireless: The emergence of wireless networks in education. *Journal of Computing Sciences in Colleges, 19*(4), 151–158.

Nielsen, J. (1994). *Usability engineering*. Boston, MA: Academic Press.

Nielsen, J. (1999). Graceful degradation of scalable internet service, WAP: Wrong approach to portability. Retrieved 20/08/11 from http://www.useit.com/alertbox/991031.html

Nielsen, J., & Mack, R. (Eds.). (1994). *Usability inspection methods*. New York, NY: John Wiley & Sons, Inc.

Norman, D. (1988). *The design of everyday things*. New York, NY: Basic Books.

Norman, D. (1999). Affordance, conventions, and design. *Interaction, 6*(3), 38–43. doi:10.1145/301153.301168

Norman, D. A., & Draper, S. W. (1986). *User centered system design*. Hillsdale, NJ: Lawrence Erlbaum Associates.

Osgood, C. E., Suci, G., & Tannenbaum, P. (1957). *The measurement of meaning*. Urbana, IL: University of Illinois Press.

Polson, P. G., & Lewis, C. H. (1990). Theory-based design for easily learned interfaces. *Human-Computer Interaction, 5*, 191–220. doi:10.1207/s15327051hci0502&3_3

Preece, J. (1994). *Human-computer interaction*. Reading, MA: Addison-Wesley.

Preece, J. (2000). *Online communities: Designing usability, supporting sociability*. New York, NY: John Wiley & Sons.

Preece, J., Rogers, Y., & Sharp, H. (2002). *Interaction design: Beyond human-computer interaction*. New York, NY: John Wiley & Sons.

Questionnaire for User Interaction Satisfaction. (2011). *Website*. Retrieved 26/08/11 from http://lap.umd.edu/quis/

Rantzer, M. (1996). *The delta method—A way to introduce usability field methods casebook for software design*. New York, NY: John Wiley & Sons Inc.

Rantzer, M. (1998). Mind the gap: Surviving the dangers of user interface design in user interface design. In Wood, L. E. (Ed.), *Bridging the Gap from User Requirements to Design*. New York, NY: CRC Press.

Rogers, P. L. (2001). Traditions to transformations: The forced evolution of higher education. *Educational Technology Review, 9*(1).

Rubins, J. (1994). *Handbook of usability testing*. New York, NY: John Wiley & Sons Inc.

Shneiderman, B. (1998). *Designing the user interface: Strategies for effective human-computer interaction* (3rd ed.). Reading, MA: Addison-Wesley. doi:10.1145/25065.950626

Smith, S. (2002) *Access all areas: Disability, technology & learning.* Retrieved 11/08/11 from http://www.alt.ac.uk/sites/default/files/assets_editor_uploads/documents/accessallareaslow.pdf

Vilpola, I., & Ihamäki, H. (2004). *How to remove the major obstacle of learning: Poor usability.* Retrieved 11/07/11 from http://www.elearningeuropa.info/lv/node/2425

Wharton, C., Bradford, J., Jeffries, J., & Franzke, M. (1992). Applying cognitive walkthroughs to more complex user interfaces: Experiences, issues and recommendations. In *Proceedings of CHI 1992 Conference on Human Factors in Computing Systems*, (pp. 381-388). Monterey, CA: CHI.

ADDITIONAL READING

Cole, I. (2005). *Multidimensional usability model (MUM) questionnaire template.* Retrieved from http://www-users.york.ac.uk/~ijc4/

Dix, A., Finley, J., Abowd, G., & Beale, R. (1993). *Human-computer interaction.* Upper Saddle River, NJ: Prentice-Hall.

Dumas, J. S., & Redish, J. C. (1994). *A practical guide to usability testing.* Exeter, UK: Intellect Books.

Eisenberg, B., & Quarto-von Tivadar, J. (2008). *Always be testing: The Complete guide to google website optimizer.* New York, NY: Ibex.

Interaction, H. C. (2012). *Mailing lists & discussion groups.* Retrieved from http://degraaff.org/hci/communication.html

Jakob Nielsen's Usability. (2012). *Website.* Retrieved from http://www.useit.com/

Joint Information Systems Committee. (2012). *Website - Information and communications technology to support education and research.* Retrieved from http://www.jisc.ac.uk/

Nielsen, J. (1994). *Usability engineering.* Boston, MA: Academic Press.

Nielsen, J., & Mack, R. (Eds.). (1994). *Usability inspection methods.* New York, NY: John Wiley & Sons, Inc.

Nielsen Norman Group. (2012). *User-centered design and usability experts.* Retrieved from http://www.nngroup.com/

Norman, D. (1988). *The design of everyday things.* New York, NY: Basic Books.

Norman, D. A., & Draper, S. W. (1986). *User centered system design.* Hillsdale, NJ: Lawrence Erlbaum Associates.

Preece, J. (1994). *Human-computer interaction.* Reading, MA: Addison-Wesley.

Preece, J. (2000). *Online communities: Designing usability, supporting sociability.* New York, NY: John Wiley & Sons.

Preece, J., Rogers, Y., & Sharp, H. (2002). *Interaction design: Beyond human-computer interaction.* New York, NY: John Wiley & Sons.

Resalm's End Gamer's Inteface. (2012). *Psychological aspects of digital game playing.* Retrieved from http://www.lap.umd.edu/

Rhodes, J. (2009). *Selling usability: User experience infiltration tactics.* New York, NY: CreateSpace.

Rubins, J. (1994). *Handbook of usability testing.* New York, NY: John Wiley & Sons Inc.

Shneiderman, B. (1998). *Designing the user interface: Strategies for effective human-computer interaction* (3rd ed.). Reading, MA: Addison-Wesley. doi:10.1145/25065.950626

Techdis. (2012). *UK accessibility and inclusion organization.* Retrieved from http://www.techdis.ac.uk/

UK Higher Education Academy. (2012). *Website.* Retrieved from http://www.heacademy.ac.uk/

Usability First. (2012). *Website.* Retrieved from http://www.usabilityfirst.com/

Yahoo. (2012a). *Usability groups.* Retrieved from http://groups.yahoo.com/group/international-usability/

Yahoo. (2012b). *Usability groups.* Retrieved from http://groups.yahoo.com/group/london_usability/

Yahoo. (2012c). *Usability groups.* Retrieved from http://groups.yahoo.com/group/internet-usability/

ENDNOTES

[1]   In Figure 6 students are a group of learners using the VLE, control are educator testers, and experiment is a cognitive walkthrough tester.

Chapter 3
Educating University Students:
Can Mobile Technologies Help?

Geraldine Ryan
University College Cork, Ireland

Noirin McCarthy
University College Cork, Ireland

Richard Byrne
University College Cork, Ireland

Ranran Xiong
University College Cork, Ireland

ABSTRACT

Recent technological advances mean mobile phones can now be thought of as computers that fit in pockets. With the Apple iPhone and the Google Android Phone leading the way, mobile phones today offer many technological possibilities including SMS messaging, browsing the World Wide Web, watching and making videos, downloading and playing educational games, partaking in discussion forums, blogging, etc. Educators are currently looking at the mobile phone and other mobile technologies (such as netbooks, PDAs, Nintendo DS, SONY PSP, media players, iPod Touch, voting systems, and specialist cameras) as a way of immersing the student in the learning process. These new mediums allow students to record, organise, access, share, and reflect on work-based learning experiences. The aim of this chapter is to examine how universities can use mobile-learning tools, with a view to engaging students in the learning process while also developing their meaning-making system.

INTRODUCTION

In times of crisis, we change. Today, the world of education is changing. Globalisation, technological shifts, financial booms and crisis, demographic pressures and most importantly changing user expectations are all forcing education to adapt. This is particularly the case for third level education. While traditionally third level students were in their early twenties, attended University full-time and spent many hours each day in the University library, this is no longer the case. The

DOI: 10.4018/978-1-4666-1987-6.ch003

modern student inhabits a social, cultural, and technological environment (Cobcroft, et al., 2006) and is just as likely to be a shopkeeper in search of a formal training, a financial manager who wants to learn more about risk management or a solider on military duty, anywhere in the world, who wants to complete a degree in Business Strategy. Life-long education and education-on-the-move have become an integral part of the knowledge economy we find ourselves in.

Today a new way of educating and learning is appearing - mobile learning, known as m-learning. M-learning is not just learning using a portable device instead of a book, in fact, the mobile device is no more than a learning enabler. O'Malley et al. (2003, p. 6) argue that m-learning is "any sort of learning that happens when the learner is not at a fixed, predetermined location or, learning that happens when the learner takes advantage of learning opportunities offered by mobile technologies." The advantage of m-learning is that it provides the learner with a high degree of mobility, flexibility and independence. Learners of all ages, nationalities, and social groups can use unexpected idle times spontaneously for learning, obviating the need for computer access and the availability of printed learning materials.

The 21st Century educator can and should see technology as a way to engage the learner more in the education process. Being a competent educator goes beyond simply telling your students what they need to know. Each student in a class is a unique individual, who learns and processes information in a different way. It is noteworthy that educators address these different learning styles and adapt their teaching styles so as to maximise the return on each new learning opportunity. Keegan (2011) argues that there are four types of learners: visual learners (students who learn through seeing or reading), auditory learners (students who learn through hearing), reading/writing learners (students who learn by reading information and then writing it), and tactile/kinaesthetic learners (students who learn through doing). To a large

extent teaching and learning in many universities, particularly in the area of business and the social sciences, focuses around the first three of these learner types. The modern student, however, is more likely to be a tactile learner—this student learns from role-plays, practicing experiments, short lectures, and learning environments where they can view, handle, and experiment with ideas and instruments. With this in mind, this chapter examines how mobile technology can be used to enable higher order thinking and to enhance the student learning experience.

To date the majority of research in this field has examined the application of mobile learning to disengaged youths (Attewell, 2005) and primary school students (Sharples, et al., 2002; Silander, et al., 2004; Zurita & Nussbaum, 2004), with only a few studies examining tertiary students (see review in Duncan-Howell & Lee, 2007). In third level education, we now have the opportunity to design learning differently, to create extended learning communities, to link people in real and virtual worlds, to provide expertise on demand, and to support a lifetime of learning. This chapter focuses around four key issues. Firstly, we review what is meant by m-learning; secondly, we examine the key criteria required to foster and develop higher order thinking; thirdly, we examine whether m-learning can be seen as an incentive mechanism which can motivate students to immerse themselves in their education; and fourthly, we examine how modern technology can be used to enable and enhance critical learning. We begin in the next section by defining what is m-learning.

Background

Many definitions of mobile learning exist in the literature. For example, Stead (2005, p. 3) defines mobile learning as "making use of whichever devices and technologies surround our learners, in an attempt to empower and enrich their learning, wherever and whoever they are." Wexler et al. (2008, p. 256) define it as "any activity that allows individuals to be more productive when consuming, interacting with, or creating information, mediated through a compact digital portable device," while MoLeNET (2010) define it as "the exploitation of ubiquitous handheld technologies, together with wireless and mobile phone networks, to facilitate, support, enhance and extend the reach of teaching and learning." Finally, Brown and Metcalf (2008, p.3) simply define mobile learning as "knowledge in the hand." The core message provided by these definitions is that mobile learning is learning facilitated by small, high-powered, wireless devices.

Vavoula (2005), as cited in Sharples et al. (2005), in a survey of everyday adult learners, found that 72% of learning takes place at home or in the workplace. Other popular reported study environments included cafes and outdoors. Interestingly, only 1% of those surveyed said that they studied on public transport. Based on this evidence, Sharples et al. (2005) make the crucial point that it is the learner that is mobile and not necessarily the technology. They suggested that their findings indicated that either (1) mobile learning is not necessarily associated with physical movement or (2) that there was huge scope to develop new technology that would make it possible to study while travelling on busses, planes, and trains. Since this study, we have seen huge advances in mobile technologies with the introduction of such technologies as the Nintendo DS in 2004 and the Apple iPhone in 2007.

Stead (2005) argues that we should see mobile learning as a collection of new tools that can be added to an educator's toolbox. These tools should not be seen as replacements for traditional learning but instead should be seen as mechanisms that can encourage and facilitate greater engagement and understanding. For example, a lecturer can use text messaging as a skills check or for collecting feedback. Java puzzles can be used to engage tactile learners and podcasts of lectures and tutorials can be used to engage auditory learners. Mobile technology can be used to deliver

and assess learning, foster collaboration and to provide access to performance support (Brown & Metcalf, 2008). DeGani et al. (2010) note that all of the following are considered to be mobile learning devices: smartphones, netbooks, PDAs, Nintendo DS, SONY PSP, media players, iPod Touch, voting systems, and specialist cameras. Each of these tools, used correctly, provides a wonderful opportunity for academics to enliven conventional lectures and programmes.

Why is mobile learning so important? Attewell (2005, p. 13) argues that it allows "truly anywhere, anytime, personalised learning." In addition, students are often more comfortable engaging in personal or private subject areas using a mobile device than doing so using traditional methods. Cobcroft et al. (2006) suggest that students learn the most when given the opportunity to learn skills and theories in familiar contexts and environments. Gay et al. (2001) propose that by learning this way students are able to construct their interpretations of a subject and then they communicate these understandings to others. In this way, mobile learning benefits society as a whole.

Today's students have enormous access to digital technology and many of them have an innate ability to engage and adapt with this technology. Prensky (2001, p.1) describes modern day students as "digital natives" while Duncan-Howell and Lee (2007, p. 223) call them "Generation C." Generation C typically produce and share digital content such as blogs, digital images, digital audio or video files, and SMS messages. Oblinger (2004) contends that today's learners are digitally literate, always on, and mobile.

As educators, we are faced with the task to educate, engage, and challenge these students. Mobile learning can help us to interact with these 'Generation C' students. For example, the aim of educational games is to allow users to engage in education while they are enjoying themselves. Active learning requires a lot of effort for tactile learners, while playing, in many cases, is done effortlessly (de Freitas, 2006). Multiplayer online games are one of the most powerful forms of modern gaming allowing players/students to get involved and learn from a range of situations in different settings. These games have the ability to engage students to a much greater degree than any other type of in-class experiment or role-play. The games are fast and responsive to a player's moves, the advanced graphics allow players to get involved in a range of scenarios, the games can be customised and modified for different players in different ages-groups, with different skill-sets, or to highlight different knowledge concepts (Prensky, 2001). Most importantly the games can be challenging, while the ability to play in a multi-player scenarios means that players can experience a sense of excitement and real achievement if they perform well in the game/on the task. This can incite interest and can help immerse the student/player in the learning experience (see Mitchell & Savill-Smith, 2004).

So to summarise, m-learning can encourage independent learning, facilitate collaborative learning; identify problem areas where students need extra support, engage reluctant students; maintain a students interest for a longer period of time and promote self-esteem and self-confidence (Attewell, 2005; Cobcroft, et al., 2006). It can reach places traditional learning cannot (Attewell, 2005; Sharples, et al., 2005; Stead, 2005). It is user-centred (Roschelle, 2003; Sharples, et al., 2005; Taylor & Evans, 2005). It is "always-on learning, accessible to the masses, but tailored to the individual" (Thomas, 2005, p. 5).

M-learning is not a stand alone medium (Roschelle, 2003) and should only be seen as one tool in the educators' toolbox. Roschelle (2003, p. 261) tells us that mobile technologies do "not control learning." This point is reinforced by Stead (2005) who finds that students benefit the most when learning combines the mobile device with group activities, paper-based material and everything else educators normally use. It is an ideal medium for facilitating collaboration and communication (Duncan-Howell & Lee, 2007), and it can enhance

the growing shift from instructor centred teaching to constructivist learner centred education (Holzinger, et al., 2005). In the next section we examine how adults learn and, in particular, how we can enable higher order thinking and learning in universities.

LEARNING AND HIGHER ORDER THINKING

As our markets and economies develop and learn to cope with the challenges presented to them, it is more important than ever that universities equip their students with higher order thinking and problem solving skills (e.g. information research, comparing and contrasting, synthesising, analyzing, and evaluating) and enable them to apply this knowledge in a variety of ways (Cradler, et al., 2002). In this section, we examine (1) the stages of adult mental development; (2) how 'teaching for understanding' can encourage and develop higher-order thinking, and (3) how such development can be fostered in a University environment.

Robert Kegan (1982, 1994, 2009) has written extensively on the theory of adult mental development and higher order thinking. Before exploring how higher order thinking and problem solving skills can be fostered, it is important to provide an overview of Kegan's work in order to give an insight into the stages of adult mental development. An understanding of the stages of adult mental development begins with an understanding of Kegan's theory of meaning making development. This is essentially "a conceptualisation of how human beings make meaning of themselves, of others and of their experiences throughout the life span" (Ignelzi, 2000, p. 6). It captures how an individual understands themselves, their experiences, and their relationships with others. A key part of adult mental development is the idea of the transformation of the meaning-making system. Transformation or transformative learning is different to learning new information or skills.

Transformative learning occurs when there is a shift in the way a person makes meaning. According to Patten (2007, p. 1), "transformation occurs when someone is newly able to step back and reflect on something and make decisions about it." The mean-making system becomes more complex as we move through the stages of mental development. Kegan contends that there are five orders/stages of mental development; the impulsive mind, the instrumental mind, the socialised mind, the self-authoring mind, and the self-transforming mind. Very small children are normally of the first order. At this stage, they are unable to understand that things in the world have the same qualities over time; for example, when they look out of a tall building and see how small people are on the ground, they believe that people are small. In the second order, older children/young adults learn that objects stay the same (the people outside the tall building do not magically grow as we come down the elevator), their beliefs and feelings remain constant over time (e.g. they like cake), and they realise that others have opinions and beliefs that also remain the same over time (e.g. their mothers rule that bedtime is 7pm). At this stage, there is no empathy and children/adults are self-centred—a lot of time is spent trying to figure out how to get what they want. At the third stage, people no longer see others as a means to an end. Most university students and the majority of adults operate at this stage. Here, people are guided by the people and institutions, which are most important to them, and they are devoted to something that's greater than their own needs. People at this stage rely on others and what others view as correct and often find it very difficult to make independent decisions. At stage four, adults now have their own internal set of rules and regulations and they use these to make decisions. These people are "self-guided, self-motivated, and self-evaluative" (Berger, 2011, p. 6). Very few adults reach the fifth order; at this stage, an individual can see the limits of having their own internal meaning-making system. To move up

through these steps a person must transform their meaning-making system. Kegan (1994, p. 17) notes that transformative learning is characterised by a change in an individual "not just the way he behaves, not just the way he feels, but the way he knows—not just what he knows but the way he knows." Therefore, there is a shift in emphasis away from solely what the individual knows to recognising the importance of understanding how meaning is actually made at the individual level.

According to Kegan (1982, 1994) individuals actively construct their own sense of reality through their mean-making system. Ignelzi (2000, p. 7) argues that "an event does not have a particular solitary meaning attached that simply gets transferred to the individual." It is dependent upon the event and an individual's reaction to that event. According to Kegan, "The activity of being a person is the activity of meaning-making. There is no feeling, no experience, no thought, no perception, independent of a meaning-making context in which it becomes a feeling, an experience, a thought, a perception, because we are the meaning-making context" (Kegan, 1994, p. 11).

Kegan suggests that an individual's meaning-making changes and evolves during a person's lifetime. This transformative process is characterised by the transition from subject to object. To use Kegan's language, this involves a shift from what is viewed as subject to what is viewed as object (Kegan, 1994). An individual's unquestioned beliefs and assumptions about the environment around them are held as subject. On the other hand, something that is object to us can be described as "those elements of our knowing or organising that we can reflect on, handle, look at, be responsible for, relate to each other, take control of, internalise, assimilate, or otherwise operate upon" (Kegan, 1994, p. 32). This shift from subject to object is key in understanding Kegan's orders of adult mental development. Patten (2007, p. 2) argues that "this shift means that what was once an unselfconscious lens through which the person viewed the world now becomes something that can be seen and reflected upon." Where an element of an individual's meaning-making system was once subject and controlling them, it can shift to being held as object where the individual has a sense of control over the actual meaning-making system.

Kegan (1994) suggests that most University students are order three (the socialised mind) with some moving to order four (the self-authoring mind). To develop students during this period of their education means to recognise that students are at a particular stage in terms of their development and to provide them with an education that supports and accelerates their development. In an effort to begin to understand how a students' development or 'meaning-making' can be expanded, we need to consider what the mindset of a typical university student is like. In general, the typical student profile is one that is embedded in the relationships they hold, in role and rules, relationships have them rather than they have relationships. They are however able to see their needs clearly and manage them. They can see another's point of view but what matters most to them is not doing anything to damage that relationship. The person's sense of meaning making resides partly in the socialised group they are surrounded by and partly within themselves. Therefore, there is no clear coherent mean making that occurs separately to other people or sources in the surrounding environment, or the socialised group. According to Kegan et al. (1982), cited in Ignelzi (2000, p. 8), an order three person is "masterful at coordinating others' points of view and can create a shared reality with others but is limited in the ability to reflect on that shared reality and how it is influencing or determining the person's own view." What is important to understand about this stage is that individuals are 'held' by the set of beliefs and the structure provided by their socialised group.

Order four, or 'self-authorship,' is characterised by an ability of a person to know their own mind, separately but possibly in relation to the society or culture they operate in and the set of assump-

tions or beliefs that were previously held without question. There is a greater ability to explore thoughts, feelings, and other points of view and internalise them. However, individuals' no longer feel determined by others expectations, external factors, or the context they are operating in. The move from order three to order four for a student may begin by them questioning their original set of beliefs and principles and challenging existing assumptions. They will begin to look for different perspectives on situations.

Gardner and Boix Mansilla's (1994) 'Teaching for Understanding' is one approach to teaching delivery which could facilitate the transformative process and shift move to higher-order thinking. According to Perkins and Blythe (1994, pp. 5-6), "understanding is a matter of being able to do a variety of thought demanding things with a topic—like explaining, finding evidence and examples, generalising, applying, analogizing, and representing the topic in a new way." A *teaching for understanding* framework has four parts: (1) generative topics; these should be of central importance to a discipline, be interesting, and provide opportunities for students to make connections with their own experiences, (2) understanding goals; these essentially break the generative topic into a number of specific areas, (3) performances of understanding, these are clearly linked to the generative topics and understanding goals, and (4) on-going assessment; this generally involves where students are given specific criteria, feedback and the opportunity to reflect. A distinction should be made between all performances and performances of understanding (Blythe, et al., 1998). For example, some performances such as answering multiple-choice questions are too routine to be described as performances of understanding. The key point in that performances of understanding is characterised by using what an individual knows in new ways. According to Perkins (1998, p. 52), this type of learning occurs "through reflective engagement in approachable but challenging understanding performances." Blythe et al. (1998, p. 62) states that "in performances of understanding, students reshape, expand on, extrapolate from, and apply what they already know. Such performances challenge students' misconceptions, stereotypes, and tendencies towards rigid thinking." Through these performances, students can demonstrate their expanded meaning making. This is a key route through which transformative learning can occur, aiding the move towards high-order thinking.

King and Baxter Magolda (1996, p. 166) suggest that "the achievement of self-authorship and personal authority should be heralded as a central purpose of higher education." Kegan (1994) points out that many college students feel that they are 'in over their heads' in terms of their educational environment and consequently may feel anxious. He suggests that this can occur because there is a mismatch between the meaning-making system of most university students, usually order three, and the expectations of universities that all students will have order four meaning-making systems.

Ignelzi (2000) makes a number of suggestions to aid the transformative development of students from order three towards order four. He particularly emphasises the great importance of support and guidance offered to students. Simply assigning students tasks that require self-authorship without the necessary structure and support will not help students in achieving transformative learning. Instructing a student to become self-authored is not enough. He argues that students should be provided with multi-stage incremental assignments, where each stage is connected and allows the student to develop and grow. After each stage, the student should be provided with ample feedback and support to allow them to learn how to generate their own ideas and theories about the issue under examination. It is on this point that the link to a teaching for understanding framework can again be seen. Specifically performances of understanding can be designed to facilitate the move towards self-authorship. Blythe et al. (1998, p. 56) tell us that "performances of understanding require

students to go beyond the information given to create something new by reshaping, expanding, extrapolating from, applying, and building on what they already know." Kegan (1994) uses the metaphor of a bridge to emphasise the importance of assigning tasks to students that are meaningful to them but which also facilitate the development of higher-order thinking and their meaning-making system. He says we cannot simply stand on our favoured side of the bridge and worry or fume about the many who have not yet passed over. A bridge must be well anchored on both sides, with as much respect for where it begins as for where it ends (Kegan, 1994, p. 62).

In a recent study, Caret (2011) found that higher-order thinking skills improve when students are given access to computers. He argued that computer access lead to increased writing skills, a better understanding of mathematics, a greater ability to solve problems and think critically about an issue and an ability to teach others. Similarly, Coley et al. (1997) present evidence that when students are given a semi-structured assignment, which requires them to use the Internet to research a topic and share information with their classmates they become independent, critical thinkers. Modern technologies can be used to teach students how to collect data and turn it into information and knowledge (Molnar, 1997). In the next section, we examine how these technologies can be used to incentivise students to engage actively in the learning process and as a result, expand their meaning making system.

M-LEARNING: AN INCENTIVE TO ENCOURAGE LEARNING?

Education is mostly based on decision-making and perhaps one of the key ingredients for any decision is information. Holding the correct information at the right time is powerful (Rasumsen, 2007). To arrive at a decision for the best course of action, you must determine how others are going to act (or react). This requires knowledge of others' aims and the options available to them. In the university set-up, the lecturer and the student may have identical aims (e.g. the lecturer wants the student to learn as much as possible about a topic and the student also wants to learn as much as possible about that topic; here the student may be order three or possibly four on Kegans' scale of mental development), or their aims may be at odds (e.g. the lecturer wants the student to learn as much as possible, but the student wants to study as little as possible; here, the student is likely to have an order two meaning making system). If the lecturer and the student have different aims, then the lecturer may need to incentivise the student to study.

What are incentives? The Online Oxford English Dictionary (2011) defines incentives as "a thing that motivates or encourages someone to do something." Ryan and Shinnick (2008) refer to incentives as mechanisms offered to help in the decision-making process. For example, large supermarkets use loyalty cards to encourage customers to return to their store, teachers use exams to encourage students to study, parents often use treats to persuade their children to behave. The purpose of an incentive is to provide the decision maker (i.e. a manager, employee, student, child, etc.) with a reason to follow a particular course of action. Economics is to a large extent a study of incentives: incentives to work hard, to produce high quality goods, to study, to invest, to save, etc. (Laffont & Martimort, 2002). The main reason for incentives is that, used correctly, they can help to solve information problems. In education, the most common form of information is incomplete. In other words, the lecturer and the student often do not know each others' aims. This is common in the marketplace where, for example, an employer may want to maximise the value of a company but an employee may want to maximise their quality of life. In economics, this is known as the principal-agent problem. This is where the principal (i.e. the employer, the lecturer) and the

agent (i.e. the employee, the student) have different knowledge/information and different aims (Pratt & Zeckhauser, 1985). McMillan (1992) suggests that the best solution to the principal-agent problem is to use incentives to align the aims of both parties (see also Laffont & Martimort, 2002; Mirrlees, 1997; Rauh & Seccia, 2005).

Incentives and information are intrinsically linked. With full information, there is no need for incentives. The problems caused by information asymmetries have attracted a lot of attention in the economics literature (see for example Akerlof, 1970). Applied to labour markets (see for example Gibbons & Katz, 1991) this adverse selection problem argues that when an employer does not have sufficient information to judge the quality of the candidate applying for a job, then s/he may not be able to offer a tailored compensation package. Where a competitive firm is unable to distinguish high quality workers from low quality workers, they will treat them as all one group and will offer them all the same wage, thereby reducing the incentive for the high quality worker to perform well at his job (Akerlof, 1982).

There are many solutions to the problems caused by information asymmetries. For example, Spence (1971) demonstrated how better informed people in a market could credibly transmit or signal their information to less informed people. Job candidates, for example, can use their education and experience as a means of signalling their ability to prospective employers. Similarly, Rothschild and Stiglitz (1976) show that asymmetry problems can be solved through screening. This is where employers offer different employment contracts to their employees and these contracts are set up in such a way that high quality employees are incentivised to select one type of contract, whereas low quality employees are incentivised to select another type of contract (e.g. a high quality employee may select a contract which is largely commission based, whereas a low quality employee would opt for a flat wage). In a similar way, incentives can be used to encourage educators to change how and what they teach, to encourage the student to participate in active learning, and to facilitate the swift move to higher order thinking and learning.

Incentives can be classified broadly into two types—carrot incentives and stick incentives (see McMillan, 1992). Carrot incentives are often associated with rewards; rewarding those who work hard, meet deadlines and exceed expectations. Carrot incentives may take the form of money (being paid fees for offering a service), satisfaction (the pure enjoyment of performing a task), promotion, or holidays. While it is widely argued that different incentives yield vastly different results, carrot incentives are perhaps not the most common form of incentive (Dickinson, 2001). Stick incentives, on the other hand, include such things as the threat of being fired, lower wages, or unpaid leave-of-absence. Stick incentives are usually punishment incentives. Dickinson (2001) found that stick incentives yield 6% higher returns than carrot incentives, perhaps because a threat is viewed as more believable than a reward.

How can teachers get the best out of their students? Dearden et al. (2005) and Davis (1993) argue that we need to use incentives to motivate students to stay in and participate in the education process. The English Encarta Dictionary (2011) describes motivation as "a feeling of enthusiasm, interest, or commitment that makes somebody want to do something, or something that causes such a feeling." Ames (1992) agrues that motivation is the reason individuals behave in a particular manner in a certain situation. Motivation exists as part of one's goal structures, one's beliefs about what is important, and it determines whether or not one will engage in any given pursuit.

To identify the role motivation plays in the academic world one must note that motivation is often broken down into two categories, intrinsic and extrinsic motivation. According to Middleton and Spanias (1999) intrinsic motivation refers to students who are motivated to engage in academic tasks because they enjoy them. They feel that learn-ing is important with respect to their self-image and they seek out learning activities for the sheer joy of learning. A student who is intrinsically motivated is a student who genuinely enjoys learning for their own curiosity and interest to achieve their own agenda. When you are intrinsically motivated, you enjoy an activity, course or skill development solely for the satisfaction of learning and having fun, and you are determined to strive inwardly in order to be competent (Wang, et al., 2009). Extrinsically motivated students are students who are motivated by reward. When you are motivated to behave, achieve, learn or complete a task based on a highly rewarded outcome, rather than for the fun, development, or learning provided within an experience, you are being extrinsically motivated (Wang, et al., 2009). Ames (1992) described extrinsic students as students who perform goals to obtain favourable judgements from teachers, parents, and peers in order to avoid negative judgements such as poor grades. These students have an order two (instrumental mind) or three (socialised mind) meaning-making system.

Today many schools and universities use a large range of extrinsic rewards to try and enhance student learning and behaviour (Madera, 2009). These rewards include things like verbal rewards, trophies, medals, extra points for speaking in class, extra points for attending seminar sessions, fieldtrips to reward appropriate behaviour etc. While Dearden et al. (2005) find that some kind of motivation is better than none; it is essential that the correct types of incentives are used. In a study carried out by Brewster and Fager (2000), there is persuasive evidence to suggest that students who are intrinsically motivated fare better than those who are extrinsically motivated. Evidence by Dev (1997) tells us that intrinsically motivated students earn higher grades on average than extrinsically motivated students. Intrinsically motivated students are more likely to feel confident about their ability to learn new material and are more likely to persist with and complete assigned tasks than extrinsically motivated students.

Extrinsic rewards are particularly effective if the students are reluctant learners or if they have low interest in a subject (Brewer, et al., 1995). The concern about these rewards arises when we examine their impact on students who are already intrinsically motivated and interested in the subject. Madera (2009) and Dev (1997), amongst others, find that using extrinsic rewards to engage students in learning can lower achievement and negatively affect student motivation. Madera (2009) notes that extrinsic rewards may create a performance rather than a process orientation, they may diminish the value of a task and thus discourage interest, they lose their power when withdrawn, and they may serve as de-motivators when individuals are already interested in a topic (here she suggests that we often lose interest in something if it becomes part of our job).

The differences between intrinsic and extrinsic motivators primarily lie within the reason for doing something. In order for us to change or improve behaviour, we have to understand the reason for the behaviour. So how do we make our students become intrinsically motivated? Pokay and Blumenfeld (1990) suggest that students exhibit intrinsic characteristics if they are interested in the subject or course material or if they have achieved high grades. Similarly, Biggs (1999) points out that student's perform better if they are given learning materials consistent with their interests. Therefore, the obvious course of action is to find some mechanisms, which engage students in the subject and consequently increase their interest in learning. One means of engaging today's student is through the use of m-learning. Wang et al. (2009) note that students need to get 'hooked' in the first class session, and they need continuous encouragement to stay involved. Cole et al. (2004) emphasise the importance of motivation. They argue that students who are motivated to use the mobile applications tend to achieve higher levels of performance as indicated on the mid-term exam, final exam, and ultimate course grade. It is most important that a reward system

(i.e. extrinsic motivation) is used at the beginning to engage the students with the new technology, but lecturers should aim for students' self-motivation afterwards (i.e. intrinsic motivation).

So can we view m-learning itself as a 'carrot' incentive to encourage learning? Many studies show that, on average, a student can concentrate for up to 20 minutes (Toma, 2007). A thirty-minute training session is considered the most efficient and effective, where this session includes a five minutes warm up—organizing—and a five minute warm down—reviewing—period. To motivate and maintain learning it is important that instructors engage with alert minds, in fact, forced learning with tired minds can be counterproductive and create a sense of disappointment in the user (Garris, et al., 2002). Sustained motivation is also very important. Key motivation factors include creating a sense of challenge, creating opportunities to explore and discover new information and learner control. Therefore, it is best to allow users to discover information, to think through problems and to have fun while learning. This in turn can foster higher-order thinking and can facilitate the movement from an order two meaning-making system to an order three meaning making system. These objectives can easily be obtained using digital technology. In a way, digital media provides a platform, which can be used to engage the student and may incentivise students to become intrinsically motivated.

Can m-learning incentivise higher-order learning in University settings? Kukulska-Hulme et al. (2009) purport that the aim of most University m-learning projects is to facilitate active engagement and participation by students. Kukulska-Hulme and Traxler (2007) maintain that mobile technologies can support diverse teaching and learning styles, and lend themselves particularly well to personalised, situated, authentic and informal learning, while Traxler (2007) argues that mobile devices change the nature of knowledge and discourse, and consequently the nature of learning and learning delivery. The CEO Forum

(2001) emphasises "technology can have the greatest impact when integrated into the curriculum to achieve clear, measureable educational objectives," while Mann et al. (1999) have shown that students' exam results increase when basic technology skills are integrated into the objectives of a curriculum.

Limited attention has been given in the literature to the impact of m-technology on learning (Perkins & Saltsman, 2010). McKinney et al. (2009) compared the performance of students who attended a lecture with the performance of students who missed this lecture but listened to it later on a Podcast stored on iTUNES University. iTUNES University is a website with downloadable educational podcasts, that is sponsored by Apple Computers, Inc. Students can listen to podcasts stored on this website wherever and wherever they choose. The study of 66 students revealed that those who listened to the podcasts scored significantly higher than those who attended the lecture. In addition those who listened to the podcasts and actively engaged by taking notes scored significantly higher than those who only listened to the podcasts but took no notes. Moreover, Cradler and Cradler (1999) found that students who are encouraged to actively engage in learning through technology increase their research skills and their ability to apply learning to real-world situations. They also improve their organisational skills and express a greater interest in the content of the module.

Cole et al. (2004) argue that m-technology can enhance learning by connecting the material to student's intrinsic motives (e.g. their career goals and aspirations). A study by Vogel et al. (2007) noted that mobile devices can incentivise learning, and most importantly can incentivise intrinsic as well as extrinsic motivation towards learning. In a study of 1600 business students in the City University of Hong Kong, they noted that those students who were motivated to use the mobile applications tended to achieve higher levels of performance as indicated on both the mid-term and final exam. While students were given some extrinsic motivation to engage in this new learning process (they received e-tokens based on the degree of application success and top ranking students were recognised on the e-token website) most students engaged in the progress for alternative intrinsic motives (the authors noted that most students did not upload their results to receive e-token credit).

The results to date are positive and indicate that m-technology can incentivise both extrinsic and intrinsic learning. By combining m-technologies with traditional lectures, university lecturers now have a greater ability to facilitate higher-order thinking and learning. Students in large lecture theatres no longer need to be passive observers; lecturers can use clickers, mobile phones, on-line simulations, etc. to engage the student in the learning process. Moreover, learning is not only confined to the lecture theatre and lecture time, students can now listen to podcasts, complete on-line quizzes and polls, use on-line simulations, participate in on-line tutorials, collect and analyse live data, etc. All of these projects encourage self-guided exploration and have a capacity to foster and develop intrinsic motivation (Vogel, et al., 2007). In the next section, we examine the worldwide availability and accessibility of these modern technologies and we examine how mobile technologies can be used to help students immerse themselves in their education.

IMMERSING USERS USING TECHNOLOGY

Mobile technology has the means to encourage higher-order thinking and to develop problem-solving skills. In addition, Cradler (1994) argues that the development of content and problem-solving strategies can help prepare students for the workforce. To be able to use the technology students must be able to access it and therefore we begin this section by examining the availability

Table 1. Technology access (per 100 inhabitants)

	Households with Fixed Broadband Access[a]	Mobile Phone Fixed Contract[b]	Mobile Phone Pre-paid Card[b]		Households with Fixed Broadband Access	Mobile Phone Fixed Contract	Mobile Phone Pre-paid Card[b]
Australia	62.0	102	49	Korea	95.9	90	2
Austria	57.8	119	44	Luxembourg	71.1	142	65
Belgium	63.4	96	53	Mexico	13.7	65	60
Canada	66.9	62	14	Netherlands	77.0	113	59
Chile	14.8	84	63	New Zealand	63.0	102	69
Czech Rep.	48.9	127	66	Norway	77.8	110	30
Denmark	76.0	116	18	Poland	51.1	109	70
Finland	73.7	115	10	Portugal	46.2	127	97
France	57.5	87	28	Slovak Rep.	41.7	113	57
Germany	64.6	118	65	Slovenia	56.1	96	37
Greece	33.1	145	103	Spain	51.3	108	59
Hungary	50.9	110	68	Sweden	79.5	112	51
Iceland	86.7	105	44	Switzerland	71.0	109	7
Ireland	53.7	117	87	Turkey	16.5	85	69
Italy	39.0	151	134	UK	69.5	121	78
Japan	60.0	84	2	US	63.5	87	15

Data Source: [a]OECD Broadband Statistics [www.oecd.org/sti/ict/broadband]
[b]OECD Communications Outlook 2009 [www.oecd.org/sti/telecom/outlook]

of mobile phone and broadband connections. Following this, we examine how mobile technology can be used to engage students within and outside the classroom.

Access to Mobile Technology

To engage with m-learning, we must have access to the technology. Table 1 shows the huge disparities in access to technology around the world. For example, while 95.9% of inhabitants in Korea have access to broadband only 13.7% of inhabitants in Mexico have this access. Luckily, this level of disparity does not seem to exist for mobile phones with inhabitants in most countries owning more than one mobile phone. For example, in Greece, for every 100 inhabitants there are 145 fixed contract mobile phones and 103 pre-paid mobile phones. At the start of 2011, it was estimated

that there were 5.3 billion active mobile phone subscriptions across the globe (ITU, 2010). Given this data there is no doubt that we are becoming a much more mobile society and there is great scope for the education sector to take advantage of the availability of this technology.

Mobile phones are on their way to becoming the primary way we connect to the Internet. While data collection on mobile Internet connections is at an early stage, we can see from Table 2 how Korea has the greatest number of subscriptions. With the younger generations driving this trend (EIAA, 2010) mobile learning is enjoying a similar growth (DeGani, et al., 2010).

Our interest and involvement in mobile technology, particularly for social purposes, is exploding. For example, today Facebook has over 500 million active users worldwide and over 100 million of these currently access Facebook through

Table 2. Dedicated mobile data subscriptions (subscriptions per 100 inhabitants)

	Dedicated Mobile Data Subscriptions		Dedicated Mobile Data Subscriptions
Australia	21.2	Netherlands	5.3
Belgium	2.2	Norway	10.1
Canada	2.4	Poland	6.5
Denmark	19.1	Portugal	12.1
Germany	8.3	Slovak Republic	5.4
Hungary	4.2	Spain	12.1
Iceland	8.9	Sweden	23.3
Ireland	11.4	Switzerland	3.8
Italy	8.6	United Kingdom	6.9
Korea	78.6	United States	12.2
Luxembourg	1.4		

Data source: OECD Broadband statistics [www.oecd.org/sti/ict/broadband]

Data Notes: Please note this data is in the early stages of collection and is therefore not complete. Detailed notes for this data are available at www.oecd.org/sti/ict/broadband

their mobile phone (ContestSweepstakes, 2011). Similarly, on 3rd May 2011 it was estimated that over 175 million people currently have a Twitter account and this increases by approximately 300,000 every day. According to the Huffpost Tech (2011) in the past year, the average number of tweets per day has nearly tripled from 50 million to 140 million, and there has been a 182% increase in the number of users tweeting from their mobile devices.

The use of mobile technology is gradually increasing and diversifying across every sector of education, and across both the developed and developing world. For example, Daichendt (2011) reports that Universities in the United States use mobile technology for a number of general issues such as: mobile safety alerts, class scheduling, deadline reminders, helping new students adjust to campus life, campus maps, athletic schedules, etc. In addition, university lecturers are using it to podcast their lectures, to send and receive assignments, to facilitate class debates and to communicate with their students.

McMahon and Pospisil (2005) argue that access to this range of technology has developed the students' ability to multitask. Young people today are constantly staying in contact via text messaging, emails, and websites like Facebook. Often they use these medium while simultaneously playing computer games, listening to music, and watching television (Cobcroft, et al., 2006). This skill creates an avenue for third level education to push the boundaries of learning by allowing students to concentrate more actively on their personal learning experience. In the next section, we look at some of the ways mobile phones can be used to engage the student learner.

CAN THE MOBILE PHONE ENHANCE LEARNING?

There are many types of learning including "listening, observing, imitating, questioning, reflecting, trying, estimating, predicting, speculating, and practicing" (Prensky, 2005, pp. 1). The mobile phone can allow for all of these learning types while also enhancing and supporting many traditional learning modes (Brown & Metcalf, 2008). Wang, Shen, Novak, and Pan (2009) argue that active learning techniques can greatly benefit students. Bailey (2004) contends that active engagement in the learning process helps students to acquire knowledge, to develop their critical thinking skills, to solve problems and to think independently. In this section, we focus on how a mobile phone (or Smartphone) can be used to enhance the students learning experience.

According to the Horizon Report (2011), mobile phones will outnumber computers within the next year. They argue that the huge advantage of mobile phones for education is that they combine many technologies such as an electronic book reader, annotation tools, applications for creation and composition, and social networking tools, while digital capture and editing bring rich tools for video, audio, and imaging. Mobile technology can be particularly useful when a lecturer is trying to engage, coach and motivate a large class. Ruhl and Suritsky (1995) assert that classroom interaction in the form of question and answer sessions or role-plays can greatly enhance a students learning and improve their attention during a lecture. It can also help the lecturer to ascertain quickly if the learning outcomes for the module are been achieved and if students are motivated by and interested in the material.

Currently there are two key executable mobile learning modes: (1) Short Message Service (SMS) based learning and (2) connecting-browsing learning (including quasi-mobile learning on the campus wireless network basis). SMS-based mobile learning provides for voice services and text messaging. Many of the text messaging services can be automated so the student can submit answers to multiple-choice questions using their phone and then immediately get a reply indicating whether the answer is correct (Attewell, 2005). This allows the student to be more engaged in the process and also speeds up the learning process (compared to providing the questions on a paper handout and then collecting and grading the questions by hand). SMS-based mobile learning does not allow for the transmission of multimedia

teaching resources and displays. With the recent and continuing improvements in communications chips and digital signal processors, we are starting to see more and more mobile phones allowing for browsing-based mobile learning. Therefore, the learner is increasingly able to access the Internet through their mobile device, visit the teaching server and then browse, search and implement real-time interaction, which is similar to ordinary Internet users.

Many studies have found that using SMS messaging for multiple choice questions, quizzes, and in-class polls and can improve a students learning experience. For example, Thornton and Houser (2005) conducted an experiment using 44 female English as a Foreign Language students. These students were send three short text messages, at predefined times, containing practice exercises. The majority of students reported reading all three text messages at once. Similarly in another experiment conducted in 2005 which compared the efficacy of text message exercises to paper exercises Thorton and Houser found that those who received their exercises via text messages scored higher on the final exam than those who received paper copies of their exercises. A similar study by Katz and Yablon (2010) found that students who studied English using a mobile phone claimed that it allowed for flexible learning, was user-friend and learner centred, allowed for learner autonomy, control and motivation. They also found that students preferred SMS messaging over emails as a learning tool. There are some drawbacks to the use of SMS messages for education, for example, Draganova (2009) points out that the cost of sending messages can prevent some students from engaging with this medium. In addition, lecturers can find it difficult to aggregate these messages and give feedback in real-time.

An alternative use of the mobile phone is to use it to connect to the Internet. Many University campuses now provide some rooms with WiFi networks thus providing free broadband for staff and students. This means that programme and module specific applications can be built and used, many of which can provide appropriate automatic individual feedback to the students' mobile phones while also providing the lecturer for the module with an idea of the students' misunderstandings (Lee, et al., 2008). Applications can be used to submit assignments, answer quizzes, look up campus maps, watch podcasts of lectures, tutorial and discussion forums, and check class schedules and grades. In addition polling software can be used, such as uHavePassed (see http://luziaresearch.com/), allowing all students to participate in-class quizzes.

Social media platforms such as Facebook and Twitter can be used to encourage communication and discussion between (1) lecturers and students and (2) between peers. Similarly, blogs can be used for lecturers and students to express their opinion on either course material or on other general interest stories. Groups based on a common interest can easily be created on Facebook. Manlow et al. (2010) find that students are often very proactive when using Facebook, many set-up forums and then invite their classmates and friends to join these forums. Facebook can then be used to post messages on the forum 'wall,' send instant messages to all group members, or send an individual message to any one member of the group. Like Facebook, Blogging has become increasingly popular since 1999. Blogging using a mobile phone has become known as moblogging. Tomita (2009, p. 1) defines this as any "activity that occurs away from your normal blog-writing place whose purpose is to create content for your blog." Software such as TypePad and Kablog are commonly used to upload material, which can include text, photos, or short videos. These types of social media allow students to engage in topical discussions, develop and sharpen their critical reasoning skills and build social networks.

Video conference software such as Skype, SightSpeed, and Yahoo Messenger offer an exciting opportunity for mobile learners. Lecturers can deliver lecturers, tutorials, feedback sessions etc.

using this software while students can partake in the live session from anywhere in the world using their mobile device. Similar software such as WebEx allows lecturers to record these sessions and post them online so student can watch them at any time of the day or night. Using these technologies students can ask questions, they can deliver part of the on-line class themselves, they can complete tasks and feedback their replies and/or they can be asked to answer multiple-choice questions at any stage of the lecture with immediate feedback about the reply. In many cases, students can either type their question or ask their question aloud to the person delivering the session thereby allowing even the shyest person to engage.

Using technology students located on the four corners of the earth can get the sense of being in the one place at the one time, even when attending a class in person isn't possible, practical, or desirable. This mobile technology can connect teachers and learners worldwide in a way that if implemented correctly can enhance the learning experience. Clearly, technology as a stand-alone tool cannot create higher order thinkers, however, it can facilitate the learning process and provide mechanisms, which allow for new ways of thinking, communicating, innovating, and creating knowledge. Such mechanisms can change a persons' meaning-making system and allow them to move up Kegans' orders of adult mental development.

Not all aspects of using a mobile phone for education are positive. Laxton and Coulby (2009) examined the success of using such devices with 137 students across a range of medical programmes. They found that student bored of the devices after a period of time particularly when they encountered technological problems. In addition, they noted that the adaptation of material for the devices was much more cumbersome than expected and this often resulted in the frustration of lecturers trying to adapt material. Whittlestone (2009) stresses that successful mobile applications in education must have (1) a reference point from which users can compare the attributes of the mobile application in terms of their needs and wants for carrying out a specific task or learning a concept with the method they used previously, (2) must provide a return on their investment (for example, will engaging in a forum connect the student to the key researchers in that area?), (3) must be set up in such a way that access to information is simple but the completion of a task is challenging enough to keep the learner engaged but not so challenging to dissuade them from partaking, and (4) must be embedded into the core of the 'learning ecosystem.'

USING MOBILE-TECHNOLOGIES IN THE CLASS ROOM

To be effective users of mobile-technology, we must first understand how a student learns. There are many theories of learning including student-based learning, teacher-based learning, process-based learning, classroom-based learning, phenomenographic model-based learning, and institutional system-based learning (see Biggs, 2011). In brief, *student based learning* argues that the qualities inherent in the student (such as their ability, prior knowledge, motivation, teach-ability, quantitative or qualitative outlook on learning, and learning style) have an important effect on their ability to learn and these factors outweigh education factors. *Teacher-based learning* theory argues that the teacher and his/her teaching skills is the key determinant of how a student learns and performs. *Process-based theories* are based upon the idea that information-processing skills and strategies drive the ability to learn. In other words, the ability of the student to learn depends on their ability to learn and apply techniques (e.g. learning how to solve/derive a model). There is some support for this approach in the literature and authors such as Biggs (1988) noted that skills training can work if it is given appropriate contextual and motivational backup. Biggs (2011) argues that

for this approach to work and indeed to improve learning we need to integrate the teaching based, student-based, and process-based approaches. In other words, for this approach to work there needs to be student and teacher buy-in and commitment. The *classroom-based theory* (Biggs, 1993) argues that student ability, teaching method and learning approaches and outcome as interactively related and this relationship develops throughout a class/module. This is a recursive model where the teacher sets a task and then closely monitors and tweaks this task as they monitor student behaviour and learning. The *phenomenographic model* (Marton, 1988) argues that learning should be studied from the point of view of the learner (not the teacher or researcher). The aim of this model is to move beyond surface learning. Here "learners may comprehend, more or less, the teacher's perspective, but they genuinely learn only what they construct from their own perspective" (Biggs, 2011). In this model, we begin with the students perceptions of the task so the students' construction of meaning is important. Learning is context dependent—an honours student will see things differently than a pass student. This approach does not offer solutions to the 'how can I teach better' question as it sees each student and situation as different, however, it suggests that students learn cumulatively and in clear stages. The final model is the *institutional model*. Reid (1987) argues that there are three components to the institution model; the rhetoric, the technology, the social system. Under this approach, our attention is drawn to how systems, such as the use of an external examiner, may constrain teaching and learning. Assessment tasks and related feedback are often set with both the external examiner comment and the students needs taken into consideration. Harris and Bell (1986) and Masters and Hill (1991) as cited in Biggs (2011) argue that personalised assessment tasks (e.g. diaries, self-assessment, peer assessment, etc.) are often discouraged even though they incentivise higher order learning processes. This is often due to quality control and accountability.

Given that Universities world-wide are moving towards a greater degree of accountability it is important that any new technologies introduced motivate learners, engage them in their personal learning process with a view to facilitate higher-order thinking, and assess students in an open and fair manner. Within education the motivation to learn is promoted when (1) a learner's curiosity is aroused due to a gap in their knowledge, (2) the knowledge to be learned is perceived to be meaningful, (3) they believe they can succeed in mastering the task, (4) they anticipate and experience satisfaction by engaging in the task, and (5) when after being motivated to strive for a goal the learner is self-motivated to achieve it (i.e. intrinsically motivated) (see Keller, 2008). Effectively motivated students should perform better in examinations.

Mayer et al. (2009) argue that one of the simplest ways to motivate a group of students whilst simultaneously fostering learning is through the use of questioning. Many authors have found that students who answer an adjunct question while reading a piece of text perform much better in final examinations (see for example Anderson & Biddle, 1975; Dornisch & Sperling, 2006). Indeed this research notes that students perform better on tests of incidental learning (i.e. tests covering content that is different to the content in the adjunct questions) when the questions are placed after the lesson rather than before it. In addition, students perform better on conceptual questions rather than factual questions. Wiser and Graesser (2007) argue that teaching students how to answer questions during learning is an effective way to promote active learning. In addition, Roediger and Karpicke (2006) find evidence that students perform better in examinations if they take a practice test, without feedback, than if they just study the material covered in class, while Roy and Chi (2005) find that students perform better, when they are required to explain their answer aloud.

How can we implement such active learning in large lecture halls? Limited research has been conducted on the effectiveness of clickers (aka personal response systems) at university level. While much of the research in this area has focused how helpful the students found the remote controls (see for example Beekes, 2006; Draper & Brown, 2004); a paper by Mayer et al. (2009) investigates their educational value. To facilitate learning using this method Mayer et al. (2009, p. 52) report that lecturers need to "organize the material for the lecture into a coherent representation in the students working memory" and then "integrate this representation with existing knowledge from long-term memory." Questioning can be used to meet these objectives. To be able to answer the questions students need to select the relevant material, mentally organise this material and then integrate it with their prior knowledge. In a study of 385 University students (139 who did not use clickers and were not asked questions in class, 111 who were asked questions throughout the class, 111 who were asked questions and used clickers) Mayer et al. (2009) noted that clicker-supported questioning method improved academic achievement.

With a similar questioning method in mind, Wang et al. (2008) designed a mobile phone application called Lecture Quiz. Its purpose is to promote student participation and encourage variation in how lectures are taught in higher education. The game is essentially a multi-player game, allowing an unlimited number of users to play simultaneously via their mobile phone. One of the benefits highlighted of the Quiz game approach is that it can be used in any course, regardless of subject. The level of challenge can be adjusted by the types of questions asked and the number of response alternatives provided. Two types of game modes are tested. The first was Score Distribution. Here students' responses were displayed on a 3D bar chart, with the bars representing the distribution of the various alternatives. In the Last Man Standing mode, the players have to answer correctly to get through to the next round. Communication between the student game client and server was conducted over either the available WiFi network or telecom network. The game was tested in a Software Architecture lecture at the Norwegian University of Science and Technology and received positive student feedback regarding the concept, engagement, and playability.

The TVREMOTE Framework was designed by Bär et al. (2005). The framework is designed to allow students to provide feedback to lecturers via their mobile phone. Questions can be submitted electronically and multiple-choice questions can be given. The advantage of this system from a lecturer's point of view is that they can get a clear view of the number of correct and incorrect answers. Another framework using SMS based technology is called *PLS TXT UR Thoughts* piloted by Markett et al. (2006) to promote the use of student initiated interactivity loops. However a purpose built display to manage and display the students SMS messages is required. Both an in-class interface and after class interface are required to capture the initial message and then to allow other students or the lecturer to respond to the initial message.

Today as m-technology assess rises and the cost of using this technology falls more and more universities are actively engaging in the m-learning process. It is important to note that for these technologies to work lecturers and administrative support must work in harmony so as to create an unambiguous and seamless learning environment. In addition, students need to be correctly incentivised and motivated to engage with the technology and to discover and develop their personal meaning-making system.

FUTURE RESEARCH DIRECTIONS

Information and communication technologies are the enablers of change in our universities, firms, and market places. They facilitate knowledge creation in innovative societies (OECD, 1996). While they do not create change, they act as the tools, which can release people's creative potential and knowledge. According to Seppälä and Alamäki (2003), mobile technology is only beginning to take its first steps in academic teaching and learning. The opportunities it creates have been recognised and the idea of a wireless campus is spreading to universities.

As soon as the term 'm-learning' appeared, many researchers began to investigate how new technologies could be used to enhance education field. Some of these studies took a teaching and cognition perspective, examining the feasibility of applying mobile devices in the actual teaching and learning, while others analysed the learning characteristics of learners and examined that situations where mobile devices would be most effective. Experimental results (see for example Lai, et al., 2007) show that with the support of new technology, the learning effect has been increased significantly, which provides a good prerequisite for further study and application of mobile learning. Today mobile learning is at a critical stage in its growth, evolution, and adoption.

M-learning development is highly correlated with the successful development of user-friendly, affordable, and efficient mobile learning technologies. For m-learning, there are several indispensable conditions: we need lighter mobile devices such as smartphones or handheld devices, iPads, E-books; we need to be able access the Internet at any time, so WiFi or 3G wireless Internet access is necessary; and the capacity of mobile device storage needs to be large enough to store applications, programme material and specialised software. As each of these conditions improves, we are faced with a new set of challenges. For example while Brown and Metcalf (2008) argue that the main challenges and concerns regarding mobile deployment still include screen size, battery life, costs, and security, with each new device and increased competition these items continue to improve. This in itself is a challenge—particularly for early adopters of the technology. Attewell (2005) points out that a major dilemma faced by his project team was whether to develop materials, which could be used in the current market or to future proof their materials by trying to predict the type of devices that might be available in three to four years time. Therefore, it is no surprise that some researchers are still sceptical about the use of mobile devices.

In terms of future research, it is critical to study the opportunities which new technology might bring to improve the quality of teaching and learning (Seppälä & Alamäki, 2003). It is particularly important to explore how students themselves use communication technology and how they experience it (Downes, 1999). It is important that before we adopt new technologies that we ask ourselves what is the rationale for using m-learning? Will the use of these technologies and learning styles enhance and enrich our learning experiences or are they a passing gimmick? How will they impact on the quality of communication and interaction both between peers and between staff and students? What impact will these technologies have on examinations—can we teach using these technologies but then examine without them? How will the re-design of material to suit these technologies impact on the depth and breadth of knowledge taught on University programmes? Facer et al. (2005) and Cobcroft et al. (2006) point out that the lack of teacher confidence, training, and technical difficulties with devices may impact negatively on their uptake and use. As a result do lecturers/universities need be incentivised to embrace this technology—for example, is there funding for training programmes?

CONCLUSION

Mobile technology enables 'user-led' learning and education. Students can create their own content, collaborate with their peers, and actively participate in the learning process. These new technologies can help lecturers to engage the student, assess their learning on a continual basis, teach

them concepts and allow them practice what they are learning (Stead, 2005). Since the purpose of learning is to develop human capacity, it is important in this knowledge economy that we find tools which will allow greater and more efficient access to learning. Mobile technologies offer this opportunity on two fronts: firstly, Cradler et al. (2002) argue that it enables the development of critical thinking skills by using the technology to present, publish, and share results of projects; and secondly, Sharples et al. (2005) argue that the new learning environment integrates learning that takes place at the university, at home, on a bus/train, in the park or anywhere thus enabling a truly flexible learning environment.

In order to use mobile technology effectively, an understanding of the stages of adult metal development and how to develop higher-order thinking in a University environment is important. Kegan (1994) suggests that most University students are order three (the socialised mind) with some moving to order four (the self-authoring mind). King et al. (1996) make the point that the achievement of self-authorship should be one of the primary goals of higher education. The 'teaching for understanding' approach has been identified as one way of facilitating a move towards higher-order thinking, with performances designed to offer students the opportunity to demonstrate their expanded meaning making systems. Kegan (1994) suggests that these tasks should be meaningful but also facilitate the development of higher-order thinking. Support and guidance offered to students is essential to aid their transformative development.

In third level institutions, mobile technologies allow us to access a new wider audience, including those who are working full-time and cannot commit to a fixed class schedule. It allows learners to engage in learning at times when formerly they would have been doing something else—waiting for the bus, sitting on a train, or even lazing in bed on a Sunday morning. It also allows us to interact, motivate, and engage students, especially in a large class where the student traditionally was a passive audience member. Mobile phones can be used for an array of tasks including podcasting lectures, quizzes, surveys/polls, collaborative and problem based learning, coaching, mentoring, providing support, and feedback, sending updates about lecture times, venue, required readings, etc., creating immersive experiences using simulations and games.

In the future mobile technologies are likely to change the way we examine material. DeGani et al. (2010) argue that it will allow us move away from tracking what the student knows and instead examine what the student is capable of in terms of their skills and competencies. Using these new technologies students will be able to build up a record of their achievements (e.g. recording of group presentations and work placement exercises, submission of multiple-choice questions, photographs of fieldwork) so they will be able to demonstrate what they can do. This will allow students to think for themselves, relate their ideas among their peers, use evidence they collate critically and draw conclusions from it, and most importantly, it will allow them monitor their own understanding and learning strategies.

It goes without saying that these new technologies are creating some challenges for third level educators (Corbeil & Valdes-Corbeil, 2007). For example, they make it easier for the student to cheat - how can you stop a student 'googling' the answer before they complete the online quiz? They can give a competitive advantage to a student who is technically minded while at the same time can create huge challenges for non-technically minded staff attempting to convert their materials into a standard media-friendly platform (which could be outdated quickly with rapid technology upgrades). However bearing these items in mind, as the size and quality of mobile phones and global broadband connections improve mobile technology will become an intrinsic part of our learning environment. With these developments, it is important that we move to examining issues such as cost, compatibility, equity of access, security, privacy,

and ethical concerns. Other aspects which need to be addressed include an investigation into the impact of this type of learning technology on the different learner types e.g. does it hinder the female, non-technical, visual/auditory learners) and what situations is it most suited too?

REFERENCES

Akerlof, G. A. (1970). The market for lemons: Quality uncertainty and the market mechanism. *The Quarterly Journal of Economics*, *84*(3), 488–500. doi:10.2307/1879431

Akerlof, G. A. (1982). The short-run demand for money: A new look at an old problem. *The American Economic Review*, *72*(2), 35–39.

Ames, C. (1992). Classrooms: Goals, structures, and student motivation. *Journal of Education & Psychology*, *84*, 261–271. doi:10.1037/0022-0663.84.3.261

Anderson, R. G., & Biddle, W. B. (1975). On asking people questions about what they are reading. *Psychology of Learning and Motivation*, *9*, 90–132. doi:10.1016/S0079-7421(08)60269-8

Attewell, J. (2005). *Mobile technologies and learning: A technology update and m-learning project summary*. London, UK: Learning and Skills Development Agency. Retrieved May 6, 2011 from http://www.m-learning.org/docs/The%20m-learning%20project%20-%20technology%20update%20and%20project%20summary.pdf

Bailey, D. (2004). *Active learning*. In R. Hoffman (Ed.), *Encyclopaedia of Educational Technology*. Retrieved May 6, 2011, from http://edweb.sdsu.edu/eet/

Bär, H., Tews, E., & Rößling, G. (2005). Improving feedback and classroom, interaction using mobile phones. In *Proceedings of the IADIS International Conference on Mobile Learning*, (pp. 55-62). IADIS.

Beekes, W. (2006). The "millionaire" method for encouraging participation. *Active Learning in Higher Education, 7*, 25–36. doi:10.1177/1469787406061143

Berger, J. G. (2011). *Key concepts for understanding the work of Robert Kegan*. Report by Kenning Associated. Retrieved on June 20, 2011 from http://wiki.canterbury.ac.nz/download/attachments/6358104/Berger+Kegan+key+concepts+kb.doc

Biggs, J. (1999). What the student does: Teaching for enhanced learning. *Higher Education Research & Development, 18*(1), 57–75. doi:10.1080/0729436990180105

Biggs, J. (2011). *Student learning research and theory - Where do we currently stand?* Retrieved November 6, 2011 from http://www.londonmct.ac.uk/deliberations/ocsld-publications/isltp-biggs.cfm

Biggs, J. B. (1988). The role of the metacognition in enhancing learning. *Australian Journal of Education, 32*, 127–138.

Biggs, J. B. (1993). From theory to practice: A cognitive systems approach. *Higher Education Research & Development, 12*, 73–86. doi:10.1080/0729436930120107

Blythe, T. (1998). *The teaching for understanding guide*. San Francisco, CA: Jossey-Bass Publishers.

Brewer, E. W., Hollingsworth, C., & Campbell, A. C. (1995). Incentive motivation psychology: An exploration of corrective learning behavior. *Journal of Southeastern Association of Educational Opportunity Program Personnel, 14*(1), 33–51.

Brewster, C., & Fager, J. (2000). *Increasing student engagement and motivation: From time-on-task to homework*. Northwest Regional Educational Laboratory. Retrieved May 6, 2011 from www.nwrel.org/request/oct00/textonly.html

Brown, D., & Metcalf, J. (2008). Mobile learning update. *Learning Consortium Perspectives*. Retrieved on May 6, 2011 from http://masieweb.com/p7/MobileLearningUpdate.pdf

Caret. (2011). *Student learning*. Report by Centre for Applied Research in Information Technology. Retrieved on June 20, 2011 from http://caret.iste.org/index.cfm?fuseaction=evidence&answerID=7#references

CEO. (2001). *The CEO forum school technology and readiness report: Key building blocks for student achievement in the 21st century*. Retrieved May 6, 2011 from http://www.cckln.edu.hk/libweb/Search%20Subject/All%20teachers/21st%20century%20learning/sch%20technology%20report.pdf

Cuberoft, C., Towers, S., Smith, J., & Burns, A. (2006). *Literature review into mobile learning in the university context*. Retrieved September 25, 2008, from http://eprints.qut.edu.au/archive/00004805/01/4805.pdf

Cole, M. S., Feild, H. S., & Harris, S. G. (2004). Student learning motivation and psychological hardiness: Interactive effects on students' reactions to a management class. *Academy of Management Learning & Education, 3*, 64–85. doi:10.5465/AMLE.2004.12436819

Coley, R., Cradler, J., & Engel, P. (1997). *Computers and classrooms: The status of technology in U.S. schools*. Princeton, NJ: Educational Testing Service.

ContestSweepstakes. (2011). *Article history and statistical data about Facebook and Twitter*. Retrieved May 6, 2011 from http://contestsweepstakes.co.tv/article-211-history-and-statistical-data-about-facebook-and-twitter

Corbeil, J. R., & Valdes-Corbeil, M. E. (2007). Are you ready for mobile learning? *EDUCAUSE Quarterly, 30*(2), 51–60.

Cradler, J. (1994). School-based technology use planning. *Educational IRM Quarterly, 3*(3-4), 12–16.

Cradler, J., McNabb, M., Freeman, M., & Burchett, R. (2002). How does technology influence student learning? *Learning and Leading, 29*(8), 46-49. Retrieved May 6, 2011, from http://caret.iste.org/caretadmin/resources_documents/29%5F8%2Epdf

Cradler, R., & Cradler, J. (1999). *Just in time: Technology innovation challenge grant year 2 evaluation. Report for Blackfoot School District No. 55*. San Mateo, CA: Educational Support Systems.

Daichendt, L. (2011). *Mobile technology use in education*. Retrieved on May 6, 2011 from http://marketingwithnewtechnology.wordpress.com/2011/01/26/mobile-technology-use-in-education/

Davis, B. G. (1993). *Tools for teaching*. San Francisco, CA: Jossey-Bass Publishers.

Dearden, L., Emmerson, C., Frayne, C., & Meghir, C. (2005). *Education subsidies and school dropout rates*. Working Paper vol. 05/11. Washington, DC: Institute for Fiscal Studies.

deFreitas, S. (2006). *Learning in immersive worlds: A review of game-based learning*. London, UK: Joint Information Systems Committee. Retrieved on May 6, 2011 from http://www.jisc.ac.uk/media/documents/programmes/elearninginnovation/gamingreport_v3.pdf

DeGani, A., Martin, G., Stead, G., & Wade, F. (2010). *E-learning standards for an m-learning world – Informing the development of e-learning standards for the mobile web*. Tribal Education. Retrieved on May 6, 2011 from http://www.m-learning.org/images/stories/Final_mSCORM_paper.pdf

Dev, P. C. (1997). Intrinsic motivation and academic achievement: What does their relationship imply for the classroom teacher? *Remedial and Special Education, 18*(1), 12–19. doi:10.1177/074193259701800104

Dickinson, D. L. (2001). The carrot vs. the stick in work team motivation. *Experimental Economics, 4*, 107–124. doi:10.1007/BF01669275

Dornisch, M., & Sperling, R. A. (2006). Facilitating learning from technology enhanced text: Effects of prompted elaborative interrogation. *The Journal of Educational Research, 99*, 156–165. doi:10.3200/JOER.99.3.156-166

Downes, T. (1999). Playing with computing technologies in the home. *Education and Information Technologies, 4*(1), 65–79. doi:10.1023/A:1009607432286

Draganova, C. (2009). *Use of mobile phone technologies in the classroom context, in mobile learning cultures across education, work and leisure*. Paper presented at the 3rd WLE Mobile Learning Symposium. London, UK. Retrieved on June 15, 2011 from http://symposium.londonmobilelearning.net/?page=Programme

Draper, S. W., & Brown, M. I. (2004). Increasing interactivity in lectures using an electronic voting system. *Journal of Computer Assisted Learning, 20*, 81–94. doi:10.1111/j.1365-2729.2004.00074.x

Duncan-Howell, J., & Lee, K. T. (2007). *M-learning innovations and initiatives: Finding a place for mobile technologies within tertiary educational settings*. Paper presented at the ASCILITE Annual Conference. Singapore. Retrieved on May 6, 2011 from http://www.ascilite.org.au/conferences/singapore07/procs/duncan-howell.pdf

EIAA. (2010). *New decade heralds the age of digital mobility*. Retrieved on May 6, 2011 from www.eiaa.net/news/eiaa-articlesdetails.asp?lang=1&id=216

English Encarta Dictionary. (2011). *Motivation.* Retrieved on May 6, 2011 from http://encarta. msn.com/encnet/features/dictionary/dictionary-home.aspx

Facer, K., Faux, F., & McFarlane, A. (2005). *Challenges and opportunities: Making mobile learning a reality in schools.* Retrieved on May 6, 2011 from http://www.mlearn.org.za/papers-full.html

Gardner, H., & Boix Mansilla, V. (1994). Teaching for understanding within and across the disciplines. *Educational Leadership, 51*(5), 14–18.

Garris, R., Ahlers, R., & Driskell, J. E. (2002). Games, motivation, and learning: A research and practice model. *Simulation & Gaming, 33*(4), 441–467. doi:10.1177/1046878102238607

Gay, G., Stefanone, M., Grace-Martin, M., & Hembrooke, H. (2001). The effects of wireless computing in collaborative learning environments. *International Journal of Human-Computer Interaction, 13*(2), 257–276. doi:10.1207/S153275901-JHC1302_10

Gibbons, R., & Katz, L. (1991). Layoffs and lemons. *Journal of Labor Economics, 9*(4), 351–380. doi:10.1086/298273

Harris, D., & Bell, C. (1986). *Evaluating and assessing for learning.* London, UK: Kogan Page.

Holzinger, A., Nischelwitzer, A., & Meisenberger, M. (2005). Mobile phones as a challenge for m-Learning: Examples for mobile interactive learning objects. In *Proceedings of the 3rd International Conference on Pervasive Computing and Communications Workshops.* Kauai Island, HI: IEEE.

Ignelzi, M. (2000). Meaning-making in the learning and teaching process. *New Directions for Teaching and Learning, 82,* 5–14. doi:10.1002/tl.8201

ITU. (2010). *Key global telecom indicators for the world telecommunication service sector.* International Communications Union. Retrieved on May 6, 2011 from http://www.itu.int/ITU-D/ict/statistics/at_glance/KeyTelecom.html

Katz, Y. J., & Yablon, Y. B. (2010). Affect and digital learning at the university level. *Campus-Wide Information Systems, 28*(2), 114–123. doi:10.1108/10650741111117815

Keegan, C. (2011). *Student learning styles.* Retrieved on May 6, 2011 from http://www.ast.org/pdf/TeachandLearn_Stu.pdf

Kegan, R. (1982). *The evolving self: problem and process in human development.* Cambridge, MA: Harvard University Press.

Kegan, R. (1994). *In over our heads: The mental demands of modern life.* Cambridge, MA: Harvard University Press.

Kegan, R., & Lahey, L. (2009). *Immunity to change: How to overcome it and unlock the potential in yourself and your organisation.* Boston, MA: Harvard Business School Press.

Kegan, R., Noam, G., & Rodgers, L. (1982). The psychologic of emotion: A neo-piagetian view. In Chichetti, D., & Pogge-Hesse, P. (Eds.), *Emotional Development.* San Francisco, CA: Jossey-Bass Publishers. doi:10.1002/cd.23219821606

Keller, J. M. (2008). First principles of motivation to learn and e[3] learning. *Distance Education, 29*(2), 175–185. doi:10.1080/01587910802154970

King, P. M., & Baxter Magolda, M. B. (1996). A development perspective on learning. *Journal of College Student Development, 37,* 163–173.

Kukulska-Hulme, A., Sharples, M., Milrad, M., Arnedillo-Sánchez, I., & Vavoula, G. (2009). Innovation in mobile learning: A European perspective. *International Journal of Mobile and Blended Learning, 1*(1), 13–35. doi:10.4018/jmbl.2009010102

Kukulska-Hulme, A., Traxler, J., & Pettit, J. (2007). Designed and user-generated activity in the mobile age. *Journal of Learning Design, 2*(1), 52–65.

Laffont, J. J., & Martimort, D. (2002). *The theory of incentives*. Princeton, NJ: Princeton University Press.

Lai, C.-H., Yang, J.-C., Chen, F.-C., Ho, C.-W., & Chan, T.-W. (2007). Affordances of mobile technologies for experiential learning: The interplay of technology and pedagogical practices. *Journal of Computer Assisted Learning, 23*, 326–337. doi:10.1111/j.1365-2729.2007.00237.x

Laxton, J., & Coulby, C. (2009). *Mobile learning and assessment: The student perspective in mobile learning cultures across education, work and leisure*. Paper presented at the 3rd WLE Mobile Learning Symposium. London, UK. Retrieved on June 15, 2011 from http://symposium.londonmobilelearning.net/?page=Programme

Lee, S. W., Palmer-Brown, D., & Draganova, C. (2008). Diagnostic feedback by snap-drift question response grouping. In *Proceedings of 9th WSEAS International Conference on Neural Networks*, (pp. 208-214). WSEAS.

Madera, C. E. (2009). I will never teach the old way again classroom management and external incentives. *Theory into Practice, 48*(2), 147–155. doi:10.1080/00405840902776483

Manlow, V., Friedman, H., & Friedman, L. (2010). Inventing the future: Using social media to transform a university from a teaching organization to a learning organization. *Journal of Interactive Learning Research, 21*(1), 47–64.

Mann, D., Shakeshaft, C., Becker, J., & Kottkamp, R. (1999). *West Virginia basic skills/computer education program: An analysis of student achievement*. Santa Monica, CA: Milken Family Foundation.

Markett, C., Arnedillo Sánche, I., Weber, S., & Tangney, B. (2006). Using short message service (SMS) to encourage interactivity in the classroom. *Computers & Education, 46*(3), 280–293. doi:10.1016/j.compedu.2005.11.014

Marton, F. (1988). Describing and improving learning. In Schmeck, R. R. (Ed.), *Learning Strategies and Learning Styles*. New York, NY: Plenum.

Masters, G. N., & Hill, P. W. (1988). Reforming the assessment of student achievement in the senior secondary school. *Australian Journal of Education, 32*, 247–286.

Mayer, R. E., Stull, A., DeLeeuw, K., Almeroth, K., Bimber, B., & Chun, D. (2009). Clickers in college classrooms: Fostering learning with questioning methods in large lecture classes. *Contemporary Educational Psychology, 34*, 51–57. doi:10.1016/j.cedpsych.2008.04.002

McKinney, D., Dyck, J. L., & Luber, E. S. (2009). iTunes university and the classroom: Can podcasts replace professors? *Computers & Education, 52*, 617–623. doi:10.1016/j.compedu.2008.11.004

McMahon, M., & Pospisil, R. (2005). Laptops for a digital lifestyle: Millennial students and wireless mobile technologies. In *Proceedings of ASCILITE 2005*. Retrieved May, 6, 2011, from http://www.ascilite.org.au/conferences/brisbane05/proceedings.shtml

McMillan, J. (1992). *Games, strategies and managers: how managers can use game theory to make better business decisions*. Oxford, UK: Oxford University Press.

Middleton, J. A., & Spanias, P. A. (1992). Motivation for achievement in mathematics: Findings, generalizations, and criticisms of the research. *Journal for Research in Mathematics Education, 30*(1), 65–88. doi:10.2307/749630

Mirrlees, J. A. (1997). Information and incentives: The economics of carrots and sticks. *The Economic Journal, 107*(444), 1311–1329. doi:10.1111/j.1468-0297.1997.tb00050.x

Mitchell, A., & Savill-Smith, C. (2004). *The use of computer and video games for learning: A review of the literature.* London, UK: Learning and Skills Development Agency. Retrieved on May 6, 2011 from http://www.m-learning.org/archive/docs/The%20use%20of%20computer%20and%20video%20games%20for%20learning.pdf

MoLeNET. (2010). *Case studies of innovative e-learning.* Lifelong learning programme. Retrieved on May 6, 2011 from http://www.northamptoncollege.ac.uk/facilities/MoLeNET.aspx

Molnar, A. S. (1997). Computers in education: A brief history. *T.H.E. Journal, 24*(11), 63–69.

O'Malley, C., Vavoula, G., & Glew, J. Taylor, J., Sharples, M., & Lefrere, P. (2003). *Guidelines for learning/teaching/tutoring in a mobile environment.* Mobilearn project deliverable. Retrieved on May 6, 2011 from http://www.mobilearn.org/download/results/guidelines.pdf

Oblinger, D. G. (2004). The next generation of educational engagement. *Journal of Interactive Media in Education, 8.* Retrieved on May 6, 2011, from http://www-jime.open.ac.uk/2004/8/oblinger-2004-8-disc-paper.html

OECD. (1996). *The knowledge-based economy.* Paris, France: Organisation for Economic Cooperation and Development.

Oxford English Dictionary. (2011). *Incentives.* Retrieved on May 6, 2011 from http://oxforddictionaries.com/view/entry/m_en_gb0404550#m_en_gb0404550

Patten, T. (2007). *How consciousness develops adequate complexity to deal with a complex world: The subject-object theory of Robert Kegan.* Retrieved on May 20, 2011 from http://terrypatten.typepad.com/iran/files/KeganEnglish.pdf

Perkins, D. (1998). What is understanding? In Wiske, M. S. (Ed.), *Teaching for Understanding: Linking Research with Practice.* San Francisco, CA: Jossey-Bass Publishers.

Perkins, D., & Blythe, T. (1994). Putting understanding upfront. *Educational Leadership, 51*(5), 4–7.

Perkins, S., & Saltsman, G. (2010). Mobile learning at Abilene Christian University: Successes, challenges, and results from year one. *Journal of the Research Center for Educational Technology, 6*(1), 47–54.

Pokay, P., & Blumenfeld, P. C. (1990). Predicting achievement early and late in the semester: The role of motivation and use of learning strategies. *Journal of Education & Psychology, 82,* 40–43. doi:10.1037/0022-0663.82.1.41

Pratt, J., & Zeckhauser, R. (1985). *Principals and agents: The structure of business.* Boston, MA: Harvard Business School Press.

Prensky, M. (2001). Digital natives, digital immigrants. *Horizon, 9*(5), 1–6. doi:10.1108/10748120110424816

Prensky, M. (2005). What can you learn from a cell phone? Almost anything! *Innovate, 1*(5). Retrieved on June 20, 2011 from www.marcprensky.com/.../prensky-what_can_you_learn_from_a_cell_phone-final.pdf

Rasumsen, E. (2007). *Games and information: An introduction to game theory.* Oxford, UK: Blackwell Publishing.

Rauh, M. T., & Seccia, G. (2005). *Incentives, monitoring, and motivation.* Working Paper, No. 0506008, EconWPA: Game Theory and Information. Retrieved May 6, 2011 from http://129.3.20.41/eps/game/papers/0506/0506008.pdf

Reid, W. A. (1987). Institutions and practices: Professional education reports and the language of reform. *Educational Researcher, 16*(8), 10–15.

Report, H. (2011). *One year or less: Mobiles.* Retrieved on June 20, 2011 from http://wp.nmc.org/horizon2011/sections/mobiles/

Roediger, H. L., & Karpicke, J. (2006). The power of testing memory: Basic research and implications for educational practice. *Perspectives on Psychological Science, 1*, 181–210. doi:10.1111/j.1745-6916.2006.00012.x

Roschelle, J. (2003). Unlocking the learning value of wireless mobile devices. *Journal of Computer Assisted Learning, 19*(3), 260–272. doi:10.1046/j.0266-4909.2003.00028.x

Rothschild, M., & Stiglitz, J. E. (1976). Equilibrium in competitive insurance markets: An essay on the economics of imperfect information. *The Quarterly Journal of Economics, 90*, 629–650. doi:10.2307/1885326

Roy, M., & Chi, M. T. H. (2005). The self-explanation effect in multimedia learning. In Mayer, R. E. (Ed.), *The Cambridge Handbook of Multimedia Learning* (pp. 271–286). Cambridge, UK: Cambridge University Press. doi:10.1017/CBO9780511816819.018

Ruhl, K., & Suritsky, S. (1995). The pause procedure and/or outline: Effect on immediate free recall and lecture notes taken by college students with learning disabilities. *Learning Disability Quarterly, 18*, 2–11. doi:10.2307/1511361

Ryan, G., & Shinnick, E. (2008). The power of incentives in decision making. In Adam, F., & Humphreys, P. (Eds.), *Encyclopaedia of Decision Making and Decision Support Technologies.* Hershey, PA: IGI Global. doi:10.4018/978-1-59904-843-7.ch081

Seppälä, P., & Alamäki, H. (2003). Mobile learning in teacher training. *Journal of Computer Assisted Learning, 19*, 330–335. doi:10.1046/j.0266-4909.2003.00034.x

Sharples, M., Corlett, D., & Westmancott, O. (2002). The design and implementation of a mobile learning resource. *Personal and Ubiquitous Computing, 6*(3), 220–234. doi:10.1007/s007790200021

Sharples, M., Taylor, J., & Vavoula, G. (2005). *Towards a theory of mobile learning.* Paper presented at the mLearn Conference. Cape Town, South Africa. Retrieved on May 6, 2011 from http://www.mlearn.org.za/CD/papers/Sharples-%20Theory%20of%20Mobile.pdf

Silander, P., Sutinen, E., & Tarhio, J. (2004). *Mobile collaborative concept mapping – Combining classroom activity with simultaneous field exploration.* Paper presented at the 2nd IEEE International Workshop on Wireless and Mobile Technologies in Education. Retrieved on May 6, 2011 from http://ieeexplore.ieee.org/stamp/stamp.jsp?arnumber=01281347

Spence, M. (1971). Job market signalling. *The Quarterly Journal of Economics*, *87*, 355–374. doi:10.2307/1882010

Stead, G. (2005). *Moving mobile into the mainstream*. Paper presented at the 4th World Conference on mLearning. Retrieved on May 6, 2011 from http://www.mlearn.org.za/CD/papers/Stead.pdf

Taylor, J., & Evans, D. (2005). Pulling together: keeping track of pedagogy, design and evaluation through the development of scenarios - A case study. *Learning, Media and Technology*, *30*(2), 131–145. doi:10.1080/17439880500093588

Tech, H. (2011). *Twitter user statistics show stunning growth*. Retrieved on May 6, 2011 from http://www.huffingtonpost.com/2011/03/14/twitter-user-statistics_n_835581.html

Thomas, S. (2005). Pervasive, persuasive eLearning: Modelling the pervasive learning space. In *Proceedings of the 3rd International Conference on Pervasive Computing and Communications Workshops (PERCOMW 2005)*, (pp. 332–336). Kauai Island, HI: PERCOMW.

Thornton, P., & Houser, C. (2005). Using mobile phones in English education in Japan. *Journal of Computer Assisted Learning*, *21*(3), 217–228. doi:10.1111/j.1365-2729.2005.00129.x

Toma, A. L. (2007). *A case study - Training aviation English to on-the-job Brazilian pilots*. Paper presented to the second ICAO Aviation language Symposium. Montreal, Canada. Retrieved on May 6, 2011 from http://www.icao.int/icao/en/anb/meetings/ials2/Docs/1.Lage.pdf

Tomita, D. K. (2009). Text messaging and implications for its use in education. In *Proceedings of TCC 2009*. Retrieved on June 20, 2011 from http://etec.hawaii.edu/proceedings/2009/Tomita.pdf

Traxler, J. (2007). Defining, discussing, and evaluating mobile learning: The moving finger writes and having writ. *International Review of Research in Open and Distance Learning*, *8*(2), 1–12.

Vogel, D., Kennedy, D. M., Kuan, K., Kwok, R., & Lai, J. (2007). *Do mobile device applications affect learning?* Retrieved from http://ln.academia.edu/DavidMKennedy/Papers/1045642/Do_mobile_device_applications_affect_learning

Wang, A. I., Ofsdahl, T., & Mørch-Storstein, O. K. (2008). *An evaluation of a mobile game concept for lectures*. Paper presented at the 21st Conference on Software Engineering Education and Training. Retrieved from November 8, 2011 from http://www.computer.org/portal/web/csdl/doi/10.1109/CSEET.2008.15

Wang, M., Shen, R., Novak, D., & Pan, X. (2009). The impact of mobile learning on students' learning behaviours and performance: Report from a large blended classroom. *British Journal of Educational Technology*, *40*(4), 673–695. doi:10.1111/j.1467-8535.2008.00846.x

Wexler, S., Schlenker, B., Bruce, B., Clothier, P., Adams Miller, D., & Nguyen, F. (2008). *Authoring and developing tools*. eLearning Guild Research. Retrieved May 6, 2011 from http://www.cedmaeurope.org/newsletter%20articles/eLearning%20Guild/elg_360_tools_final.pdf

Whittlestone, K. (2009). *Principles behind the mobile killer application in education in mobile learning cultures across education, work and leisure*. Paper presented at the 3rd WLE Mobile Learning Symposium. London, UK. Retrieved on June 15, 2011 from http://symposium.londonmobilelearning.net/?page=Programme

Wiser, R. A., & Graesser, A. C. (2007). Question-asking in advanced learning environments. In Fiore, S. M., & Salas, E. (Eds.), *Toward a Science of Distributed Learning* (pp. 209–234). Washington, DC: American Psychological Association. doi:10.1037/11582-010

Zurita, G., & Nussbaum, M. (2004). A constructivist mobile learning environment supported by a wireless handheld network. *Journal of Computer Assisted Learning*, *20*(4), 235–243. doi:10.1111/j.1365-2729.2004.00089.x

KEY TERMS AND DEFINITIONS

Adult Mental Development: How humans grow and change over their lifetime.

Extrinsic Motivation: Extrinsic motivation refers to motivation that comes from outside an individual and includes rewards such as money or grades.

Incentive: Financial compensation, public recognition or other benefits used to reward higher levels of performance and/or new ideas or contributions.

Incentive Theory: Incentive theory is an element of human resources or management theory. It states that firm owners should structure employee compensation in such a way that the employees' goals are aligned with owners' goals. It is more accurately called the principal-agent problem.

Intrinsic Motivation: Intrinsic motivation refers to motivation that comes from inside an individual.

Meaning-Making: How individuals actively generate an understanding about themselves, their experiences and the world around them.

Transformative Learning: A shift in the process of *how* a person makes meaning at an individual level.

Orders of Consciousness: These represent different forms of meaning making and mental organisation that affect how individuals feel, understand themselves, related to others and their environment.

Teaching for Understanding: A framework that is used to lead students towards doing a variety of new, thought-provoking things with a topic, with a shift in emphasis from pure knowledge of information to actual understanding, and demonstrating this.

Chapter 4
Enriching the Experience in Video Games Based on Playability Development Techniques

José Luis González Sánchez
Universidad de Granada, Spain

Rosa María Gil Iranzo
Universitat de Lleida, Spain

Francisco L. Gutierrez Vela
Universidad de Granada, Spain

ABSTRACT

Video games are the most economically profitable entertainment industry. The nature of their design means that user experience is enriched by emotional, cultural, and other subjective factors that make design and / or evaluation difficult using traditional methods commonly used in interactive systems. It is therefore necessary to know how to apply Playability in order to design, analyze, optimize, and adapt it to a player's preferences. In this chapter, the authors present a way to perform UX based on Playability techniques by adding hedonic factors that enrich the development of video games. The aim is to easily and cost-effectively analyze the different degrees of Playability within a game and determine how player experience is affected by different game elements. These results can be applied in the educational field where the experience of the pupils with educational video games is a crucial factor for the success of the learning process.

INTRODUCTION

Video games are highly interactive systems whose main goal is to entertain users (players) that interact with them in order to have fun. Nowadays, video games are the most economically profitable entertainment industry. The use of new technology and teaching methods that help improve the learning process has resulted in the inclusion of videogames as active elements in the classroom. Videogames are ideal learning tools since they provide training skills, promote independence,

DOI: 10.4018/978-1-4666-1987-6.ch004

increase and improve students' concentration and attention and increase social connections. However, their use in education generally involves significant problems. Firstly, most existing educational videogames are basically multimedia didactic units, which have lost the essence and attributes of videogames. Secondly, the devices on which these didactic games run are simple PCs, which generally do not spark children's interest like other devices. The result is that educational games offer players a less positive experience than other kinds of videogames. However, we cannot forget the experiences of the pupils who play the games are crucial factors that affect the success of the video game ad didactic tool. In the educational field is very difficult to evaluate the positive motivation or the degree of satisfaction for players. To analyze and design better experiences based on playability techniques in this type of games is a must.

User Experience (UX) is understood as a set of sensations, feelings, or emotional responses that occur when users interact with the system. UX focuses more on the subjective aspect of the interaction process, and goes beyond the traditional study of skills and cognitive processes of users and their rational behaviour when interacting with computers (ISO 9241, 2010). Due to the nature and design of videogames, user experience should be enriched by recreational, emotional, cultural, and other subjective factors that make analysis and evaluation difficult using traditional methods commonly used in interactive systems.

Player eXperience (PX or User Experience in Video Games) depends not only on the product itself, but also on the user and the situation in which he or she uses the product. Players cannot be designed. Players are different. Some are able to easily use a game to perform a challenge while others simply cannot. The stimulation that a video game provides depends on the individual user's experience with similar products. Users compare games and have different expectations. Furthermore, they have different goals, and so they use a game in different ways. Furthermore, PX evolves

over time. The first time users try a game they may find it confusing and have a rather negative experience. When they later become accustomed to the game, discover the wealth of features and potential it has to offer, and learn how to handle it, they may become emotionally attached to it, and thus the PX would become more positive.

User Experience (UX) should be taken into account throughout product development (hardware or software), so as to achieve the optimum experience for the player. The current importance of video games in society justifies the need for models that characterize the overall experience, and mechanisms for designing and analyzing the Experience throughout the video game development process become a must. The purpose of this chapter is to present a Playability Model for the design and evaluation of user experience in videogames, with the following objectives:

- To analyze how the game experience presents characteristics that are not explicit in the quality standards models and why the usability or quality in use is not sufficient in video games context without the inclusion of cross-cultural features or emotional factors.
- To analyze the hedonic properties that characterize the experience with video games.
- To be able to measure the degree of 'quality of the game experience' within an electronic entertainment system: Playability.
- To present a Playability Model for entertainment systems, including different attributes, facets and metrics to characterize the player experience with videogames.
- To show how to use the Playability Model and Playability Techniques in a User Centred Video Game Development Process.
- To apply this model for evaluating and improving playability in the video game development process, in order to improve the user experience.

The objectives of designers when developing a video game are likely to be diverse and subjective, but one objective they have in common is to make the player feel good when playing the game. Analyzing the quality of a video game purely in terms of its Usability is not sufficient; it is important to consider not only functional values but also a set of specific non-functional values, given the hedonic properties of videogames. Additional factors for consideration might include, for example, emotional response, social and cultural background, etc. In other words, the PX (Player Experience, or UX in Video Games) is generally much more complex than the UX in desktop software. In this chapter, we describe a Playability model, which offers a set of properties to describe the Player Experience and different facets for analysing PX and its relationship to the most common elements of a video game architecture. We also introduce the most important objectives for applying playability ideas within a Player Centered Video Game Development Process and discuss the Requirement Specification step and the Analysis and Evaluation phases.

This chapter reflects the importance of a Playability Framework and techniques for improving the design, thus helping to obtain the playability requirements and evaluate the final experience in video games. Understanding and evaluating the user experience in video games is important for developing more efficient and successful products in terms of entertainment. In this chapter, we demonstrate the importance of rich evaluation to obtain as much information as possible about the user experience in video games.

In first section, we discuss about the User Experience in Video Game, especially how emotions and cross-cultural factors can affect to the overall experience in games. Then, we present a Playability Model to characterize the User Experience in Video Games. Later, we apply the Playability Model in a Video Game Development Process with the objective of enriching the experience. Finally, we discuss about our proposals

in conclusion and future works related with this chapter will be presented.

Why is it necessary to obtain a positive experience in educational video games? Yes, Always! To reach a good experience is the main objective as video game developers. But, for example, in the educational field, good experiences increment the efficacy of the learning process. With good experience, educational videogames unite the characteristics of games for entertainment and educational tools, having the following properties (McFarlane, 2002):

- **Academic Success:** Pupils that use video games show an improvement in reading comprehension abilities.
- **Cognitive Abilities:** Pupils develop their cognitive abilities using game environments based on discovery and creativity.
- **Motivation:** Games are a means of encouraging children; they make the learning process easier and considerably increase attendance levels.
- **Attention and Concentration:** Children's attitude towards games means that their attention and concentration increase in order to solve concrete problems.

Results discussed in this chapter can be directly used in the efficient development of video games for educational or sanitary rehabilitation, using the Player Centered Video Games Development Process. In these kinds of games, a positive experience implies greater efficiency of the video game as a didactic tool. A correct experience level means that the main activity of the user is playing the game, the consequence of which is that the child learns the educative contents in an implicit way. This is denominated "Learning by Playing, Playing To Learn," whereby the videogame acts as a "mediator" in the learning process. Knowledge is obtained through the game contents, and cognitive abilities are developed as a result of playing the videogame (Malone & Lepper, 1987; González Sánchez, 2008).

USER EXPERIENCE IN VIDEO GAMES

Player eXperience (PX or User eXperience in Video Games) depends not only on the product itself, but also on the user and the situation in which he or she uses the product. A formal definition for UX has been issued by ISO 9241-210 (2010, clause 2.15): *"a person's perceptions and responses that result from the use and/or anticipated use of a product, system, or service."* Furthermore, User Experience (UX) manifests as quality of design, interaction and in the value of using a product. One of the challenges related to UX is how to select appropriate measures to address the particularities of a design and evaluation context. UX is focused more on the subjective part of the user when he or she interacts with an application. The user's emotional response is the result of three different factors: the emotions evoked by the product during the interaction process, the user's mood, and the user's feelings associated with other circumstances prior to use of the system. Hence, UX goes beyond the traditional study of skills and cognitive processes of users and their rational behaviour when interacting with computers (Law, 2009). The main goals of several studies realized by the HCI Community are centered on concepts such as utility, usability, communicability, emotion during use, cross-cultural factors, the desirability of the product, the value of the product, accessibility, ease of use, the flexibility and adaptation to the user's profile, safety, and confidence in the interaction process (Hassenzahl, 2003). Videogames are interactive systems designed to exploit the user experience when used by players, because their main objective is to exploit the emotions/feelings of the user and ensure fun and entertainment for the player (Barr, 2007).

It is important to ascertain and analyze what a user feels or how to correctly design and evaluate the experience (player experience) with these systems. User Experience in video games is enriched by the playful nature of game systems, together with the characteristics that give identity to the game, such as game rules, goals, challenges, rewards, GUI, dialog systems, etc., which are unique to each game and make the experience with every game different for each player, who will also have different experiences from one another. The design and evaluation are also enriched by hedonic properties such as emotional response and cross-cultural factors that provoke different experiences in players. In the field of video games, the main goal is much more indefinite and subjective than in other interactive systems such us Desktop Systems: to feel good and have fun, in other words: 'entertainment.' This objective is generally linked to the socio-cultural profile of the player and is exploited by the elements of the video game. If we can evaluate and identify the player emotion, we can detect if the game entertains to players or if the player are satisfied during the playtime. We can detect if objective properties of the experience, such us usability are affected by different emotional state, reducing the subjectively of the results. Cultural factors offer the possibility to contextualize the experience to specific player's profiles.

The 'Player eXperience' (PX) with a video game can be quite extensive, subjective and more specific when compared with a traditional interactive system, requiring the identification of a property to analyze and measure these types of experiences. The property that characterizes the Player Experience or User Experience in entertainment systems is commonly called Playability and it can be used in the design process or at the evaluation stage to ascertain the experience that players feel when playing a video game.

It is important to mention some important characteristics of the hedonic properties of the Player Experience. In this section, we introduce two of the most influential hedonic properties affecting user experience in video games: Emotions and Cross-Cultural Properties.

User Experience and Emotions

Nicole Lazzaro (2008) defined player experience in the following way: "A game's value proposition is how it makes its players think and feel. Players don't buy games, they buy experiences." Lazarro's theory of fun focuses on experiential emotion rather than the game mechanics themselves.

Emotion is the complex psychophysiological experience of an individual's state of mind, interacting with biochemical (internal) and environmental (external) influences. The user's emotional response to the interactive process is a factor that can cause that player to love or hate a video game. There are numerous studies about "emotions" in the literature, with a consensus on the definitions of this term and properties to characterize it. An emotional response or feeling is a psychological reaction related to the needs, objectives, and concerns of an individual and is composed of behavioural, physiological, cognitive, and affective dimensions, in response to stimuli that occur when a user is interacting with a product and the emotion is specific to each individual (Brave & Nass, 2002; Mehrabian, 1994).

Norman (2004) has mentioned many features of emotion that motivate players. Emotions such as beauty, fun, and pleasure work together to produce enjoyment and a state of positive affect. Norman introduced the idea that a design should address three different levels of cognitive and emotional processing: visceral, behavioural, and reflective:

- Visceral Emotions are related to how a player wants to feel and other sensory aspects.
- Behavioural Emotions characterise what a player wants to do. They are associated with behaviour of the player with the game and the interaction process.
- Reflective Emotions are related to the culture and background of the users

To measure the emotional response we can use oral self-tests, where respondents use a numerical scale to record their emotions (Mehrabian, 1994; Desmet, 2001). The main criticism of these kinds of techniques is that they only register the emotional states that the user is aware of, yet they are popular because they are easy to perform. Since emotions are automatic and dynamic, it is important to capture the moment when they occur. We can make use of emotions heuristics to analyse facial expressions (De Lera & Garreta, 2007) or use Emoticon cards (Emocards) to identify visually how the user feels with the system and then compare the results with other methods previously mentioned (Desmet, 2001).

User Experience and Cross-Cultural Factors

Sociocultural background can lead to differences in UX. For example, why is a game successful in Japan and not in Europe? Hofstede considers culture as a term referring to mental programming (Hofstede, 1991). Every person has patterns of thinking, feeling, and action that act as "mental software." Videogames can be re-designed based on cultural patterns in light of these cultural meta-models, according to the cultural background of the target market. It is not an easy task to design a video game, especially for a multinational company, which includes profiles of users from different cultures. Moreover, the designer must collaborate with the application development team, and may thus be in contact with people from very different backgrounds. In this kind of scenario, all members of the team should be knowledgeable about how cultural factors influence the field of design.

There are numerous parameters and variables when designing an interface, including cultural features. These influence a user's understanding of the interface, in some cases leading to a complete misunderstanding of it, as will be seen in some examples. Cultural features are extracted from sociological models (Trompenaars & Hampden-Tuerner, 2010; Hofstede, 1991) and include those which characterize a number of different user experiences:

- **Individualism Versus Collectivism:** This focuses on the degree of personal independence. For example, China is a typical example of collectivism whereas Germany is an example of individualism.
- **Power Distance:** This is the degree to which people accept great differences between the most and least powerful members of society.
- **Uncertainty Avoidance:** This is the degree to which a nation establishes universal rules
- **High Context Versus Low Context:** This refers to communication norms where the perception of what is aggressive or insulting can change depending on the explicitness of the actions in a game.
- **Achievement and Quality Of Life:** A good quality of life allows the achievement of personal goals and freedom from social and cultural constraints.
- **Universalism Versus Uniqueness:** A system should be as adaptable and universal as possible, and not be limited to one group of people, society, or culture.
- **Affective Versus Neutral:** This is the degree to which a person can openly talk about their emotions in a culture.
- **Achievement Versus Ascription:** This expresses the degree to which a culture takes into account a person's achievements reflected in social status.

When collecting information about the cross-cultural factors which affect player experience (especially with regards to emotion, socialization, immersion, and social and cultural attributes) it is advisable to use heuristics/questionnaires which evaluate the social-cultural influence using a three dimensional approach (Chen, 2005):

- **In-Game Environment:** Includes factors embedded in the game that are developed during game design.
- **External Environment:** Includes external factors such as social, political, legal, and ideological issues, etc.
- **User Profiles:** Includes the cultural background of players, conventions, game-playing contexts, attitudes and habits towards games, and the role of games in everyday life.

Playability and the Player Experience in Video Games

In this chapter, we argue that an analysis of the quality of a game in terms of usability or quality of use is not sufficient to characterize the overall user experience due to the hedonic factors that identify it. To ensure the experience is positive, a set of attributes and properties must be established to identify the player experience during video game use and indicate whether a game is 'playable' or not, i.e. player experience is characterized by the Playability of the video game.

Playability is a term used in the design and analysis of video games that describes the quality of a video game in terms of its rules, mechanics, goals, and design. It refers to all the experiences that a player may feel when interacting with a game system. Playability is a key factor in the success of the video game due to its ability to ensure that the game engages, motivates, and entertains the player during playing time. Currently, game designers and game developers work to produce game content that ensures optimal playability and game experience. Playability is affected by the quality of the storyline, responsiveness, pace, usability, the possibilities to customize it, control, intensity of interaction, intricacy, and strategy, as well as the degree of realism and the quality of graphics and sound. Playability is a live topic in the scientific community; it has been studied from different points of view and with different objectives.

Every game must try to achieve good playability, because it reflects the pleasurable experience, sensations, and feelings felt by a user when playing the videogame. According to the philosophy of videogames, a player must have the best experience possible. Educational game designers/developers must design and develop a high quality videogame that is fun and entertaining for the player. Only in this way can the player experience be improved and with it the success of the game as an educational tool.

Playability: Background

In this section, we briefly describe the most representative works for each specific line of research. The most important references on playability are compiled in Bernhaupt (2010), Nacke (2009), Isbister & Schaffer (2008).

It is worth mentioning the work of Rollings (2003), which contains three key elements for identifying the playability of a videogame. These are:

- **Core Mechanics:** Game rules, objectives and goals to achieve.
- **Storytelling and Narrative:** Story line and narrative technique used in the video game.
- **Interactivity:** Set of elements that the player can see, hear and interact with in the virtual world.

In *The Art of Game Design* (Crawford, 1984) the author indicates that playability happens when the gameplay is right and is properly executed, thus observing the importance of interaction with the elements of the video game. For Swink (2007), playability is based on the combination and proper structuring of the game elements during the playtime. Furthermore, Akihiro Saito (2008) indicates that the player experience is identified by "Gamenics": the quality of play, the quality of the platform on which a game runs and the

mechanics of the game (GAme + MEchanics + electroNICS).

Norman (2004) and Lazzaro (2008) propose that one of the secrets of playability is the management of emotions and the motivation of the player. Regarding the interactive and use components, we should highlight the need for the correct level of "flow" and immersion during the playtime (Csikszentmihalyi, 1990). Regarding "Flow" Theories, Playability according to Järvinen (2002) is "a collection of criteria with which to evaluate a product's gameplay of interaction." Järvinen identified four types of playability for the purposes of evaluation. They are:

- **Functional Playability:** This refers to the functional aspects that affect gameplay. It relates to the game controls and is close in meaning to traditional usability. Analyzing functional playability means, for example, evaluating how well the input-device is configured to producing the desired gameplay.
- **Structural Playability:** This concerns the game mechanics. The game rules and the patterns that emerge from them give structure to a game. The rules define the game, and actions in the game are only relevant when they are understood in the context of these rules. The actions form patterns that look the same in several sessions of the game.
- **Audio-Visual Playability:** This can drastically change gameplay. The visual spectrum ranges from photorealism to cartoon style and can drastically influence which kind of customers the game appeals to. By analyzing audiovisual playability, it is possible to ascertain if the sound and graphic is the best for the desired gameplay, or if there are confusing elements in the game world.
- **Social Playability:** This relates to the desired context of use (for example, com-

puter or television, single player or multiplayer, etc.) and player communication. Communication can take place both in game (in multiplayer games) and off game. Off-game communication includes, for example, forums, mailing lists, and the official game website where players can share and discuss their experiences of the game. It is important to offer both in game and off game communication.

Other works on Playability and player experience define playability as "the usability in the context of video games," in which usability is understood as a traditional property of the UX. One of the most referenced works in this area is Federoff's (2002) proposal. Federoff focused on developing a set of heuristics to measure "playability" based on Nielsen's twelve main points (Nielsen, 1993) in a video game context. Following the line of heuristics and evaluation criteria of playability and usability in video games are the works by Desurvire and Wiberg (2009), Korhonen (2007), and Pinelle (2008). Moreover, it is possible to find style guides that promote playability and accessibility in video games (IGDA, 2004).

Some interesting works focus more on how to evaluate the player experience, model the emotional state of a user by applying biometric techniques (Mandryk, 2006; van den Hoogen, 2008) or analyse the user experience through specific game and gameplay metrics (Canossa & Drachen, 2009).

We should also mention examples of guidelines and patterns proposals for game developers to increase the usability (playability) in video games (Björk, 2003; Nokia, 2010) or to readapt the experience according to the cross-cultural and location factors of the user (Chen, 2005).

Playability Model and Facets that Characterize Experiences in Video Games

As previously mentioned, the User Experience is characterized by two main points of view: process of use and product quality development. These are enhanced and enriched by the user's emotional reactions, and the perception of non-instrumental qualities. Playability is based on Usability in video games, but in the context of video games, it goes much further.

Furthermore, Playability is not limited to the degree of 'fun' or 'entertainment' experienced when playing a game. Although these are primary objectives, they are very subjective concepts. It entails extending and formally completing the characteristics of User Experience with players' dimensions using a broad set of attributes and properties in order to measure the Player Experience.

There is a clear need for a common or unambiguous definition of playability, attributes to help characterize the player experience, properties to measure the development process of the video game, and mechanisms to associate the impact/influence of each video game element in the player experience. We consider this a significant lack, since the different definitions of playability require different criteria to measure it: there are no universals.

González Sánchez (2009a, 2009b) presents a playability model to characterize PX in video games, introducing the notion of facets of playability, which integrates methodological approaches into the game development process. To achieve the best player experience, they propose a set of attributes to characterize the playability. Playability is defined as 'a set of properties that describe the Player Experience using a specific game system whose main objective is to provide enjoyment and entertainment, by being credible and satisfying, when the player plays alone or in company.' Playability describes the Player Experience using the following attributes and properties, Figure 1.

- **Satisfaction:** This is defined as the gratification or pleasure derived from playing a complete video game or from some aspect of it. Satisfaction can be measured using the following properties:
  - **Fun:** The main objective of a video game is to entertain; hence, a video game that is no fun to play could never satisfy players.
  - **Disappointment:** It is important to ensure that players do not feel such disappointment when playing a video game that they abandon it altogether.
  - **Attractiveness:** This refers to attributes of the video game that increase the pleasure and satisfaction of the player.
- **Learnability:** This is defined as the player's capacity to understand and master the game's system and mechanics (objectives, rules, how to interact with the video game,

etc.). To characterise Learning the following properties can be used:
  - **Game Knowledge:** A player's prior knowledge of a video game will influence the degree to which they are affected by the learning curve proposed by the game.
  - **Skill:** This is demonstrated by how the player plays. Once a player has understood and assimilated the game's objectives and rules (cognitive skill), how they address the game's challenges to achieve the different objectives and rewards is a matter of skill (interactive skill).
  - **Difficulty:** This may be higher or lower depending on how steep the learning curve is, relative to the player's skills and how long he or she has been playing. A high Difficulty level

Figure 1. Playability model to characterize the player experience in video games

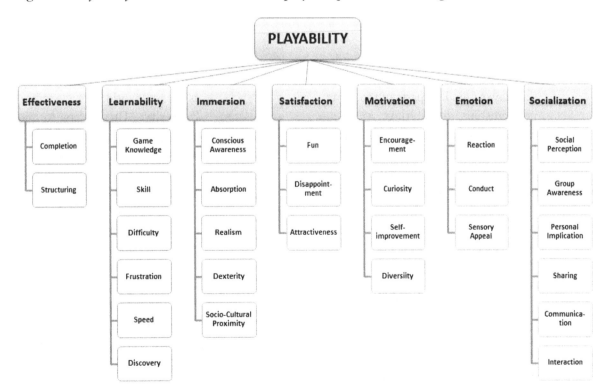

can encourage a player to make a greater effort to learn how to play.

- **Frustration:** This property is often part of the learning process, produced by the player's feelings of unease when unable to achieve a particular challenge or objective, or when failing to understand certain concepts.
- **Speed:** The speed with which new concepts and contents are introduced into the game directly affects the learning process.
- **Discovery:** The different game resources support better assimilation of the game's various contents so that the player needs progressively less time to improve his or her abilities to achieve the game's objectives.

- **Effectiveness:** This is defined as the time and resources necessary to offer players a fun and entertaining experience whilst they achieve the game's various objectives and reach the final goal. It can be identified using the following properties:
  - **Completion:** A video game is more effective if the percentage of Completion is high. In other words, it can be considered effective in that the player found no parts of the game uninteresting. Structuring: a video game is comprised of well structured elements (i.e., where, when and how they appear in the Gameplay) when it achieves a good balance between the various objectives to be achieved and the different challenges to overcome, such that the player remains engaged and enjoys himself throughout the entire game time.
  - **Immersion:** This is defined as the capacity of the video game contents to be believable, so that the player becomes directly involved in the virtual game world. The following prop-

erties are proposed to characterise Immersion:

- **Conscious Awareness:** The degree to which the player is consciously aware of the consequences of his actions in the virtual world. Understanding what happens as a result of performing a particular action helps the player imagine what to do next and to develop the necessary abilities to overcome challenges.
- **Absorption:** A player who is completely absorbed is involved in the Gameplay to such a degree that all his or her abilities and attention are focused on overcoming the game's challenges.
- **Realism:** The more realistic a video game (regarding the use of controls, presentation of contents, or atmosphere), the greater the player Immersion. Realism helps to focus the player on the game's challenges, rules and objectives by making the virtual world as believable as the real world.
- **Dexterity:** This refers to the player's ability to interact with the game's controls (interactive dexterity) and perform different movements and actions in the virtual world in which they are immersed (virtual dexterity).
- **Socio-Cultural Proximity:** Video games have more, or less, immersive efficacy depending on the degree of socio-cultural proximity to the player, being appropriate to their age or gender, for instance. The metaphors and atmosphere used in

the game, even when realistic, can still reduce Immersion of the player if they do not reflect certain socio-cultural characteristics that the player can identify with.

- **Motivation:** This defines the set of game characteristics that prompt a player to realise specific actions and continue undertaking them until they are completed. It has the following properties:
  - **Encouragement:** The degree of encouragement is affected by the level of confidence a player feels when facing new game challenges and the possibility of reaching new game objectives.
  - **Curiosity:** This can be generated by the inclusion of optional features, objectives, and challenges. These offer the player the freedom to interact with a greater number of elements and maintain a player's sense of intrigue as to what will come next.
  - **Self-Improvement:** This occurs when the player or their character develops their ability and skills, be it to overcome specific challenges, or simply because the player enjoys employing a particular skill. Diversity: A greater number of different elements makes the game more attractive to players and reduces the likelihood of monotony.
- **Emotion:** This refers to the player's involuntary impulse in response to the stimulus of the video game that induces feelings or a chain reaction of automatic behaviours. Emotion can be measured with the following properties:
  - **Reaction:** The player reacts to a video game because the system is a source of different stimuli. The play-

er's initial reaction may then trigger different emotions.
  - **Conduct:** Video games are behavioural mechanisms in that they are able to influence the conduct of the player during Game Time by leading them through different emotions.
  - **Sensory Appeal:** The aesthetic elements should stimulate a player's interest and desire, and increase the emotions and attraction that he or she feels towards the game., and different sensory channels should be used, e.g. the audiovisual channel, to induce emotions in the player while he or she is playing the game..
- **Socialization:** This defines the set of game attributes, elements and resources that promote the social dimension of the game experience in a group scenario. This kind of collective experience enables players to appreciate the game in a different way, through relationships that are established with other players (or with other characters from the game). Socialization is also at work in the connections that players make with the characters of the video game. Examples of this might include: choosing a character to relate to or share something with; interacting with characters to obtain information, ask for help, or negotiate for some items; and how the influence of a player on game characters may or may not facilitate the achievement of certain objectives. Socialization can be analysed using these properties:
  - **Social Perception:** This is the degree of social activity undertaken and understood by players, who experience a more extensive game in a multiplayer context than they do playing on their own.

- ◦ **Group Awareness:** This refers to players' conscious awareness of being part of a 'team,' and sharing common objectives, challenges and game elements. Players must understand that they are a part of a group and that the success of the group depends on achieving shared objectives.
- ◦ **Personal Implication:** The player needs to be aware that individual achievement leads to group victory. Hence, game resources need to be developed to help raise the player's awareness of their role in the group's success, and their identification with it.
- ◦ **Sharing:** When a player plays within a group, the objectives and different resources, and how these are managed, are shared by the group.
- ◦ **Communication:** Multiplayer video games should offer communication mechanisms that enable optimal interchange of information among players.
- ◦ **Interaction:** How the rules of the game are perceived by the group or how members will interact to achieve the objectives, i.e. the way in which characters or players relate to each other allows objectives and challenges to be overcome in different ways according to the interests fostered by interaction among group members. We highlight the following types of interaction: Competitive (when a player plays to achieve personal success, when one player wins the rest of the group generally loses); Collaborative (individual success is replaced by group success. Here the notion of ´team´ applies; the entire group shares and achieves a com-

mon goal) and Cooperative (players can have their individual goals whilst forming a group to benefit themselves, thanks to the help of other members, a team approach is not essential to achieve the player's objective, rather it arises only circumstantially).

This model offers the possibility of ensuring the quality of game play elements based on international standards, by establishing a connection between playability and quality in use, considering the properties and attributes of playability as an extension of the Quality in Use standard for videogames (ISO 25010, 2011; González Sánchez, 2009c). This can be characterised with the following properties:

- **Effectiveness:** The degree to which specific users (players) can accurately and fully achieve the proposed goals in the context of use, the video game.
- **Efficiency:** The degree to which specific users (players) invest sufficient resources to achieve the proposed goals in relation to the effectiveness achieved in a context of use, the video game. This factor is determined by the ease of learning and immersion.
- **Context Coverage:** The degree to which the video game can be used in different contexts or by different player or game profiles.
- **Freedom from Risk:** The acceptable level of risk to the player health, the context environment or data in a context of use, the video game.
- **Satisfaction:** The degree to which users (players) are satisfied in a context of use, the video game. This factor considers various attributes such as fun, attractiveness, motivation, emotion, or sociability.

Following the definition of Quality in Use, Playability can be defined as *"the degree in which specific players achieve specific game goals with effectiveness, efficiency, flexibility, security and, especially, satisfaction in a playable context of use"* (González Sánchez, 2009c).

Playability analysis is a very complex process due to the different perspectives that we can use to analyse the various parts of a video game architecture. In Gonzalez Sanchez (2009a, 2009b), a classification of these perspectives is based on six Facets of Playability. Each facet allows us to identify the different attributes and properties of Playability that are affected by the different elements of video game architecture. These Facets are:

- **Intrinsic Playability:** This is the Playability inherent in the nature of the video game itself and how it is presented to the player. It is closely related to Gameplay design and Game Mechanic.
- **Mechanical Playability:** This is the facet related to the quality of the video game as a software system. It is associated with the Game Engine.
- **Interactive Playability:** This facet is associated with player interaction and video game user interface development. This aspect of Playability is strongly connected to the Game Interface.
- **Artistic Playability:** This facet relates to the quality of the artistic and aesthetic rendering in the game elements and how these elements are executed in the video game.
- **Intrapersonal Playability or Personal Playability:** This refers to the individual outlook, perceptions and feelings that the video game produces in each player when they play, and as such has a high subjective value.
- **Interpersonal Playability or Social Playability:** This refers to the feelings and perceptions of users, and the group aware-ness that arises when a game is played in company, be it in a competitive, cooperative, or collaborative way.

The overall Playability of a video game, then, is the sum total of values across all attributes in the different Facets of Playability. It is crucial to optimise Playability across the different facets in order to guarantee the best Player Experience.

ENRICHING THE VIDEO GAME DEVELOPMENT PROCESS

Nowadays, the methodologies used in video game development are similar to those used in software development, but with the addition of certain elements or phases reminiscent of film production: screenplay, scenery recreation, virtual world and character design, etc. Can Playability and the best UX be guaranteed in the development phase of every video game?

We argue that Playability should be considered in every phase of video game development in order to guarantee quality of the User Experience. Typically, Playability is only checked in the test phase of the product, using evaluation techniques to test specific aspects of the video game, but it is necessary to introduce hedonic factors, such us emotions and cross-cultural factors, into these phases. We assert that the design of video games, as interactive systems, should be focused on users by involving them directly in the development process, from initial specification through to final test stage in order to improve their experiences (pragmatic and hedonic experiences). We propose the use of a Player-Centred Video Game Development approach, using the principles of Playability and UX throughout the different phases of development in order to achieve a high quality player Experience, in the same way as other interactive systems, such us desktop systems, mobile systems or Web applications (González Sánchez, 2009b).

Figure 2. User centred videogame development process to optimize the experience

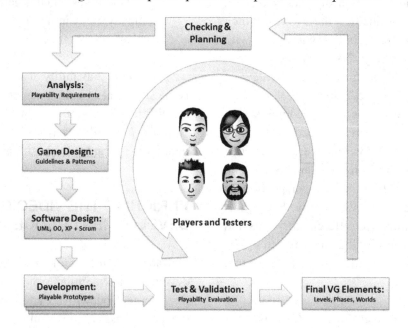

Using this core idea, we introduce playability and UX into the principal videogame development phases, following the User Centred Development Process. In this section, we focus on how to achieve better experiences throughout the principal stages of this process: Requirements, Design, and Test. At each stage, we provide different examples of how to apply PX and Playability techniques in order to adapt the game to players and thus improve the final experience, Figure 2.

Analysis and Video Game Requirements

It is necessary to start with a game specification that includes the Requirements of Playability deduced from the Facets of Playability, analysing which attribute is affected by which specific video game element or which playability attributes are affected by a specific requirement. It is very important to analyse the requirements of each game stakeholder, to obtain the overall information and the best specification of the experience.

In an educational field, for example, it is important to use different groups of players in order to determine their game preferences, and to consult teachers for information about how the educational contents should be taught in the game.

Table 1 shows an example of the requirements specification of playability using facets of playability to analyse each attribute in the videogame "Leoncio and the Lost Vowels Island" (Figure 3) (González Sánchez, 2008). These playability requirements were derived using the facets of playability to classify the teacher's ideas about the game structure, our game design concepts (how to structure the game rules, objectives, and dynamics in the videogame device, etc.) and the children's concepts of the "perfect" game to play with a video console.

It is also possible to introduce priority rules or levels (for example, High, Medium, Low, or numerical scales), to classify the requirements. By means of different videogame prototypes, we can indicate that the requirements are crucial to developing a positive experience from the first iteration of the User Centred Development Process.

Furthermore, it is highly advisable to specify different games characteristics according to the

Table 1. Playability requirements in "Leoncio and the lost vowels island"

Facets	Attribute	Requirement to be achieved	Associated VG Element	Priority Level
Playability Inter-active	*Satisfaction*	Using the stylus and game pad	Challenges and Input Sub-System	H
	Learnability	Tutorials in the initial level	Rules and Mechanics	M
	Effectiveness	Using the stylus as a pencil	Input system	M
	Immersion	Using two screens: Cause and Consequence	Output Sub-System	H
	Motivation	Hearts, coins and visual and audible rewards	Rewards	H
	Emotion	Facial expressions and line colors	User Interface	L
	Socialization	Using the microphone and sending messages	Output Sub-System	L
Mechanical Play-ability	*Satisfaction*	No delay or sync appreciation	Rendering Engine	H
	Learnability	Adjusting the number of concepts according to difficulty	A.I. Engine	M
	Effectiveness	Surround areas for tactile detection of each pictogram	Game Engine	H
	Immersion	Stylus recognition and voice controls.	I/O Control System	H
	Motivation	Minimum load times among phases	Game Engine	M
	Emotion	Fade effects to change the phase in "mysterious way"	Game Engine	H
	Socialization	Using WI-FI for multiplayer.	I/O Control System	M

user emotional response (emotional game impact) and different adaptations based on the socio-cultural background of different users, in order to correctly specify the hedonic aspect of the player experience.

At the end of the specification phase, all requirements should be evaluated with a team of test players to ensure that the elements used in the video game produce the best experience during playtime. This 'requirements check' can

Figure 3. One level of "Leoncio and the lost vowels island"

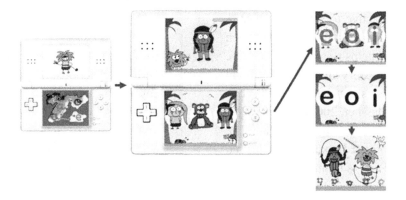

be enhanced by an "interview," which helps collect information about players' preferences and incorporate these preferences into the GDD (Game Design Document). This process allows the basic requirements for achieving a positive experience to be met thanks to the complete specification of the playable requirements in the GDD.

Video Game Design

In the creative video game design phase, we propose the adaptation of Game Patterns (Björk, 2003), introducing Playability attributes and properties to improve the efficiency and the effectiveness, in Playability terms, of these patterns. Game Style Guides (Nokia 2010; González Sanchez, 2010) are necessary in order to design appropriate and playable elements according to the context of the game or player profiles.

During the Videogame Design process, the videogame theories and playability concepts mentioned in previous sections should be used in order to obtain the most successful videogame possible. To obtain the best experience possible, it is essential that a player's motivation, attention, concentration, and emotion improve while playing the game.

Furthermore, all playability and experience techniques should be applied following a User Centred Design. This means basing development on prototype iteration in order to improve the experience through the best playable video game elements.

The first step is to create a complete storyline, which should be attractive to a future player. A good story offers a "good connection" between game and player and helps to achieve a positive player experience. The story thus provides crucial motivation mechanisms that interest the user in playing the game (Glassner, 2004). In this way it is guaranteed that if the user enjoys the game, he or she should be motivated, excited and thrilled by it and thus experience is improved (Provenzo, 1991).

The next step is the Gameplay Design. This includes all player experiences during the interaction with the game, such as goals, rules, learning curve, etc. The term is used to describe the overall experience of playing the game excluding the aspects of graphics, sound, and the storyline.

In Gameplay Design, for example, there are some critical factors, which improve the experience that are easily recognized in video games:

- **Feedback:** The game must offer feedback for each action. This feedback focuses on the ability of the game to capture a player's attention and make playing it easier. To develop this feedback, different game interaction methods are used as support tools as well as the user's profile.
- **Motivation:** It is important that players do not get frustrated by their mistakes. Errors should be corrected without causing disappointment or discouragement.
- **Hero:** In some games, it is advisable to use a main character or hero who acts as a guide. Users should see themselves reflected in this hero. The hero is the mediator in the game process and the one who carries out the actions; the hero should be very expressive, with gestures and facial expressions promoting positive action assimilation and emotional feedback.
- **Phases and Levels:** Each game must have goals. The game process should increment, based on multi-levels or missions where the difficulty level increases gradually. At each level, it should be clearer how to play the game.
- **Rewards:** To give rewards for correctly performed actions: animations, songs, videos, points, objects, money, and even gifts in the real world. Rewards offer an extra motivation-satisfaction factor; they allow us to create mechanisms that encourage the player to improve and advance in the game.

- **Real Interaction:** The mechanism for performing an action in the game should have the same structure as the mechanism that would be used to solve it in the real world. This improves the immersion factor and helps focus the player on the game process.

Using this design guide it is possible to create a videogame taking into consideration the objectives that define a positive experience: Entertainment, motivation, and enthusiasm from overcoming challenges.

The videogame has patterns of interaction that demonstrate applicable solutions for how determined aspects or actions of a game should be used. Game design patterns are powerful tools that can be used to build a real gaming future, by providing utility, flexibility and scalability of the game design (Ibrahim, 2011). They provide a common ground for designers, testers, programmers, developers, and players alike to understand, interpret, evaluate, and share their ideas. It is advisable to introduce Playability attributes and UX properties in order to improve the pragmatic and hedonic factors of the gameplay experience. Patterns are generic solutions with the objective of improving the experience. Game developers can use patterns as inspiration by simply choosing a set randomly and inventing a game from them. A more structured approach may be to study an individual game design pattern and trying to implement it in a novel way. In Table 2, we show an example of a Video Game Pattern.

We also advise using storyboards or graphics specification techniques to specify the emotions and feelings and testing them with different players, for example using Emotional Scripts (Callele, 2006) or Emocards (Desmet, 2011), see Figure 4.

Furthermore, the cross-cultural factor is significant as it has a major influence on the final experience in videogames. It is important to take into account aspects and elements such as colour, layout, or writing style, which should be modified following recommendations for the design of cross-cultural interfaces (Collazos & Gil, 2011). For example of this we can study the differences between the Sony PlayStation websites for Japan, USA and Europe or how games change characters or icons depending on the cultural context or market of the players. The following list includes some important cross-cultural or location suggestions with examples for enriching the user experience in games:

- **Message and Information:** The Arab culture can be considered as an example. The alphabet is the first great difference. If the message is originally in another language, it must be translated. However, there are variants of languages (for example, American/British English, Spanish/Latin American Spanish) which make translation difficult. Thus, the message must be contextualized. Global companies such as McDonalds have successfully addressed this problem, using "Cajita Feliz" in Guatemala and 'Happy Meal' in countries where, although English is not spoken as a first language (for example, Spain), it is completely understood. Everything is translated in the Guatemalan website, including the logotype ("I'm lovin' it"—"me encanta").

- **Layout and Colour:** Arab users read and write from right to left, a fact that conditions the layout. A western user accessing a website portal such as Jazeera.net will observe that logotype is on the right, sentences are aligned to the right, image numbers are in reverse order, news is laid out in a reverse format to that of a western site, among many other details. Globally, the design is symmetrical to a "western" site because of the direction of reading and writing.

Table 2. Example of a video game pattern to improve experience (Björk, 2008)

Pattern Name:	Paper – Rock – Scissors

• **Description:** This pattern is based on the children's game of the same name. Players try to outwit each other by guessing what the others will do, and by tricking other players into incorrectly guessing their own action. The original game is very simple; after counting to three both players make one of three gestures, depicting rock, paper or scissors. Rock beats scissors, scissors beat paper and paper beats rock. The essence of the pattern is that there is no winning strategy: players must somehow determine which choice is the best in each given moment. This game pattern is well-known within the game design community (sometimes called "triangularity," see Crawford) and is a mnemonic name for the logical concept of non-transitivity (esentially, even if A beats B and B beats C, A doesn't beat C).
• **Examples:** Quake (relation between weapons and monsters), Drakborgen, SimWar, protogame to show non-transitivity (Dynamics for Designers, Will Wright, GDC 2003)
• **Consequences:** The Paper-Rock-Scissors pattern can either be implemented so that choices have immediate consequences (as in the original game) or long-term effects. In both cases it promotes Tension, either until the moment when the choices are revealed or until the success of the chosen strategies is evident. A paper-rock-scissor pattern introduces Randomness unless players can either gain knowledge about the other players current activities or keep a record of other players' behaviour, otherwise a player has no way of foreseeing which tactics will be advantageous. If the game supports knowledge collection, the correct use of the strategies allows for Game Mastery.
• **Using the Pattern:** Games with immediate consequences from choices related to Paper-Rock-Scissor usually allow users to keep records of other players' behaviour. Quick Games using the pattern, such as the original game, are usually played repeatedly, meaning some form of Meta Game can be used to allow players to gain knowledge of their opponents' strategies. A common way of implementing the pattern for long-term effects is through Investments to gain Asymmetrical Abilities, either through Proxies or Character Development. See Dynamics for Designers (Will Wright) for an example based on proxies. For this kind of pattern use, players can be given knowledge about other players through Public Information or in the case of games with Fog of War through sending Proxies. Allowing players to keep a record of other players' behaviour is redundant if play commences face-to-face, otherwise some form of Personalization is required.
• **References:**
• Kreimeier, B. The Case For Game Design Patterns: www.gamasutra.com/features/20020313/kreimeier_01.htm
• Wright, W. Dynamics for Designers. Presentation at GDC 2003. http://www.gdconf.com/archives/2003/Wright_Will.ppt
• Orthogonal Unit Differentiation, Harvey Smith. Presentation at GDC 2003. http://www.gdconf.com/archives/2003/Smith_Harvey.ppt
• Chris Crawford. The Art of Computer Game Design

• **Semantic and Design:** For example, Legend of Darkness is a Korean game. The developers redesigned the story and gameplay for a US audience. To this aim, they incorporated a greater emphasis on role-playing, politics, and religion and added elements of "Gaelic and Lovecraftian horror." The result (Dark Ages) remains successful in the US.

• **Use the Correct Images:** Images are used to show features of collectivism/individualism. Many portals use either images of individual users or groups for the same company depending on the country. Asian cultures are the prototype of collectivism; they use groups of people in their interfaces.

• **Genre:** Sexist stereotypes are widely used; however, the perception of what is sexist changes depending on the country. Nonetheless, perceptions of sexual stereotypes change between countries. Identical content can be found offensive in different countries, for example the representation

Figure 4. Using interactive and emotional script and story board (left) and emocard (right)

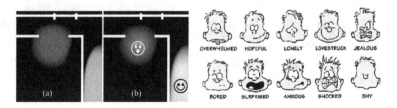

of housewives. Concepts of what constitutes sexism change between Europe and the USA. Portals selling soap, appliances, perfumes etc. use these concepts daily.

- **How to see, how to Read:** The direction of reading / writing even affects the information structure. Asian countries use a wide variety of horizontally disposed menus.
- **Focus on the Market:** The game EverQuest ranks high in the western digital market, yet was not even listed on the top 10 list in China, where the top two digital games are "Lineage" and "Mu." However, in the oriental version of Everquest II, the characters were redesigned according to Chinese player's preferences (see Figure 5) and it was consequently much more successful in the Chinese market.

To achieve a good experience we must integrate cross-cultural and localisation features into the videogame design, as has been seen previously.

Video Game Test and Experience Evaluation Based on Playability

We recommend evaluating and testing the Playability and Player Experience during the entire development process in order to ensure the quality of Playability/Experience in every playable video game element or game content in the final product.

When evaluating Playability and PX it is important to use a unified tool to develop a pre-test, test, and post-test in order to analyze the player experience using pragmatic and hedonic properties of the UX. PHET (Playability and Hedonic Evaluation Tool) offers the possibility to organize and collect the necessary information for the evaluation process and create different reports (González Sánchez, 2010, 2011a). PHET allows the creation of different types of questionnaires and heuristics and relates them with Playability metrics, attributes, and factors in order to obtain information about which attributes and properties have greater influence on the overall player experience, and what video game elements have more emotional impact or cultural relevance for players. PHET also offers the possibility to use different points of view to realize and classify the heuristics and questionnaires and perform an analysis of PX using the Facets of Playability. These facets allow us to relate the results of the PM with the different elements of a video game ontology Each facet permits identification of the different attributes and properties of Playability that are affected by the different elements of the video game architecture. Furthermore, PHET offers the possibility to include information about different profiles, such as *Player Profile* (information about players: each player has his/her own social or video game backgrounds which can lead to different game experiences); *Video Game Profile* (each game is based on a series of specific core/mechanical properties that provokes different experiences); or *Platform Profile* (platform on which the game is played). Using this information

Figure 5. Example of localization and redesign of game characters, focusing on US and Chinese markets (Chen, 2005)

a PX analysis can be developed which designs the best set of questionnaires, metrics, or heuristics for PX evaluation. Finally, it is also possible to obtain graphical reports, which represent the player experience, using a Surfaces of Playability option based on the facets or attributes of the Playability Model that we have been introduced in this chapter.

When testing or evaluating experience, a Playability Model is used to achieve the following objectives:

- Analyse the player experience in a quantitative/qualitative way using the playability model.
- Test the effects of certain elements of a video game on overall player experience.
- Identify problems that may cause a negative player experience.
- Complete the functional assessment and objectives of QA systems with non-functional evaluations that are closer to the experience for each player profile.
- Offer reports that provide complete information of every aspect of the player experience.

In typical Playability and PX evaluation, there are four steps to test pragmatic and hedonic attributes (González Sánchez, 2011b):

- **Pre-Test:** Questionnaires and a short test to obtain information about player profiles. These should be completed with emotional information and multicultural background influences.
- **Test:** To collect information in real time about player experience while users play a video game. Observation techniques should be used to measure facial and corporal expressions or biometric constants and the gameplay actions should be analysed with playability metrics.
- **Post-Test:** Players are given different questionnaires or heuristics and interviews

to be completed, particularly, with subjective information related to hedonic properties (hedonic properties are a crucial factor in motivation, emotion, and satisfaction attributes). The questionnaires should be guided by the Facets of Playability.

- **Reports:** To obtain a number of reports about the PX including information about which playability attributes have more influence, or which type of elements are more valued by players. Special emotional and cultural information can be obtained using emocards.

It is highly advisable to work with different player profiles (game stakeholders) so that the results are representative of the context of real-life video game use. To obtain the maximum information about UX we suggest using different player profiles: 'expert' (or "gamer," a person who is a good player, knows the game platform perfectly and is comfortable with difficult game challenges) and 'casual' (a person who plays infrequently and looks for quick entertainment). For the evaluation process, information about all game players is required—not only experienced ones—in order to analyse the experience for all possible player profiles and identify which elements of the video game affect the results.

To evaluate the player experience for a given video game, five to ten sessions of play lasting thirty minutes are recommended, using normal levels of difficulty throughout the game.

The objective of the *Pre-Test* is to collect information about the profile of participants using multimedia questionnaires (images, pictures, music, videos, etc.). The test provides important results about emotional state or socio-cultural background that may influence player experience, for example: preferences for different game genres, initial emotional state, the adequacy of the game hero and the context of the video game (what feeling or emotions do the characters transmit? where is the game set [place]? Is the look appropriate?). The player's answers to these questions can provide information about the social and cultural properties or emotional influences (hedonic dimension) that produce better immersion in the video game.

During the *Test*, users play the videogame. Their facial and body expression should be recorded and their heart rate monitored. The aim is to detect visceral and emotional reactions occurring during the interaction process, their relationship with the user's biometric data and how these emotions can affect the strategies used to overcome game challenges following the guidelines proposed in (De Lera & Garreta, 2007; Hupont, 2010). With these techniques, we can obtain information about the experience in real time, Figure 6. We can observe, for example, when players are uncertain, looking around to capture all screen elements, how stress increases with the arrival of challenges at the level climax, provoking surprise and agitation in the player (for example, lifting of the eyebrows), or how the stress caused by the challenges increases the player's

concentration (for example, players press the pad quicker and more violently than at the beginning of the game). Furthermore, two types of strategies may sometimes be detected: a defense strategy or a direct and violent confrontation. The degree of immersion can be indicated by an increase in heartbeats per minute or how stress becomes satisfaction, which may be expressed as a slight smile or slight gasp. It is interesting to note that the strategy depends on cultural factors such as gender and other factors, which may be related to the survival instinct of the user when faced with real challenges.

It is essential to complete the biometrics reactions with a thorough analysis of the actions of the player during the playtime. To perform the gameplay analysis we can use Playability Mode Properties Measurements (González Sánchez, 2009a, 2010), see Table 3 or Playability Quality in Use Metrics, Table 4 (González Sánchez, 2009c). Other metrics to analyse the experience and the game actions can be found in Mandryk

Figure 6. Real time information on UX using biometric data

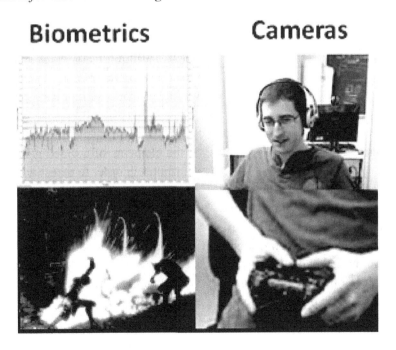

Table 3. Example of measurement of playability in a video game using playability properties

Attribute	Property	Example of how to measure
Satisfaction	*Fun*	High percentage of game completed.
	Frustration	Amount of time invested in different challenges is high.
Learning	*Game Knowledge*	Number of special movements used is high.
	Skill	Time needed to overcome a challenge is low.
	Difficulty	Number of attempts made to overcome a challenge is high.
	Frustration	Time spent and attempts made to overcome challenge are both high.
	Speed	Number of new concepts to use is high.
	Discovery	Number of tutorials available is high.
Effectiveness	*Completion*	Percentage of game world left unexplored is low.
	Structuring	Intervals between goals and challenges are optimised.
Immersion	*Conscious Awareness*	Analysis of possible actions to be done by players.
	Absorption	High percentage of accomplished goals.
	Realism	Navigation and control analysis.
	Skill	High precision in actions or in overcoming challenges.
	Socio-Cultural Proximity	Ethnographic and cultural analysis.
Motivation	*Frustration*	Low percentage of game played.
	Curiosity	Percentage of virtual world discovered is high.
	Self-Improvement	Number of items obtained is progressively higher.
	Diversity	High number of different items and actions used.
Emotion	*Reaction*	Emotional tests via reactions during the game.
	Conduct	Behavioural test on the player, post-game.
	Sensory Channels	Sensory perception analysis: sight, hearing or touch.
Socialization	*Social Perception*	High number of shared resources for players
	Group Awareness	Analysis of group information, statistics and resources.
	Personal Implication	Analysis of individual contribution to the group.
	Sharing	Analysis of which resources are shared, and how.
	Communication	Number of messages and notes among team members.
	Interaction	Analysis of social rules and objectives of the game.

(2006), van den Hoogen (2008), and Canossa and Drachen (2009).

In the *Post-Test*, informal interviews and questionnaires are used to obtain information about the player experience. The evaluation process is performed using a list of questions, with the aim of investigating the degree of each attribute of playability in order to obtain a measurement of the player experience. The process is guided by Facets of Playability; so it is possible to relate the elements of a video game to playability attributes in order to detect which parts of a video game have a positive or negative influence on the overall playability using PHET. The questions and heuristics are designed to extract information about the pragmatic and hedonic PX dimensions. The evaluation mode is also important so that the evaluator can choose the appropriate test for the 'test-users.'

Table 4. Example of metrics associated with playability quality model

	Metric name	Purpose	Formula	
Effectiveness	*Goal effectiveness*	What proportion of the goals are achieved correctly?	$M1 = |1-\Sigma Ai|$ Ai proportional value of each missing	M1 ϵ [0, 1], the closer to 1 the better
	Goal completion	What proportion of the goals are completed?	X = A/B A = n. of goals completed B = total number of attempted goals	M1 ϵ [0, 1], the closer to 1 the better
	Attempt frequency	What is the frequency of attempts?	X = A/T A = n. of attempts made by the player T = time or number of goals	Expert player closer to 0. At the beginning > 0
Efficiency	*Goal time*	How long does it take to complete a goal?	X = Ta	Novice players will have more time
	Goal efficiency	How efficient are the users?	X = M1/T	X ϵ [0, 1], closer to middle value
	Relative user efficiency	How efficient is a player compared to an expert?	X = A/B A = ordinary player's goal efficiency B = expert player's goal efficiency	M1 c [0, 1], the closer to 1 the better
Context coverage	*Accessibility*	What proportion of the goals can be achieved by using alternative ways of interaction?	X = A/B A = goals with alternative interactions B = total number of goals	M1 ϵ [0, 1], the closer to 1 the better
	Personalization	What proportion of the personalization options are used by the players?	X = A/B A = personalized elements B = elements in the game	M1 ϵ [0, 1], if closer to 1 original interaction way, perhaps should be changed
Freedom form risk	*User health and safety*	What is the incidence of health problems among users of the product?	X = 1 – A / B A = number of players reporting errors B = total number of players	M1 ϵ [0, 1], the closer to 1 the better
	Software damage	What is the incidence of software corruption?	X = 1 – A / B A = n. occurrences of soft. corruption B = total number of usage situations	M1 ϵ [0, 1], the closer to 1 the better

continued on following page

Table 4. Continued

	Metric name	Purpose	Formula	
Satisfaction	*Satisfaction scale*	How satisfied is the player?	$X = A/B$ A = questionnaire producing psychometric scales B = population average	X>0 the larger the better
	Satisfaction questionnaire	How satisfied is the user with specific software features?	$X = \Sigma Ai /n$ A i= response to a question B = number of responses	Compare with previous values, or with population average
	Discretionary usage	What proportion of potential users choose to use the system?	$X = A/B$ A = number of times that specific software functions are used B = number of times players are intended to be used	M1 ∈ [0, 1], the closer to 1 the better
	Socialization	What proportion of potential users choose to use the system?	$X = A/B$ A = number of times that game is used in a collaborative environment B = number of times that game is used	M1 ∈ [0, 1], the closer to 1 collaborative game, closer to 0 personal game

Some of the questions are based on validated heuristics/questionnaires works (González Sánchez, 2011a; Desurvire & Wiberg, 2009; Korhonen, 2007; Pinelle, 2008), which are readapted/extended to follow the facets, and associate them with the Playability Model and the ontology of the video game elements. In Table 5 we present some characteristic heuristics guided by Facets that are used by PHET to evaluate the user experience.

According to Nielsen a maximum of five expert evaluators are recommended. Indeed, a greater number of evaluators does not guarantee an improved result (Nielsen, 1993). For this type of evaluation, we require information of all game players, not only experienced ones, in order to analyze the experience for all possible player profiles and identify which elements of the video game affect the results (i.e. 'expert,' a person who is a good player or 'casual,' a person who plays infrequently and looks for quick entertainment). We recommend a maximum number of players

to obtain maximum information from the video game experience (more than 20 is desirable).

To generate the reports we require a tool to describe and analyse the Player Experience, and PHET (references) can provide enough information to do this. Examples of the summary of scores describing player experience can be seen in Figure 7. A special PHET report called 'Surfaces of Playability' is used to represent the experience using Playability's Attributes and Facets. We can also obtain information about Quality in Use Factors and Properties.

Another advantage of PHET is the identification of the most value game elements. With this tool, we can observe how the most valued video game element was the game platform. This result can be obtained thanks to the integrity rules of the ontology and their relation to the Playability Model, Facets, and design of questionnaires.

The evaluation results of experience, playability or quality in use automatically obtained

Table 5. Examples of some heuristics guided by facets of playability that are used by PHET

Facets of Playability	Evaluation Heuristics
Intrinsic Playability	The game mechanics are appropriate for the nature of the video game. The game can be replayed by offering new challenges. The game has a help manual. The game has different difficulty levels and/or a difficulty system that adapts the challenges to the player's skills. The game provides a means to facilitate the memorization of the items displayed and assimilate their subsequent use.
Mechanical Playability	The game engine satisfies the player and exploits the full platform resources. The game provides a balanced IA system to readapt the challenges to the player actions. The game offers dynamic context-sensitive help for overcoming specific challenges. The game offers correction mechanisms for player control and actions. The graphics and textures are rendered without appreciable errors for the players.
Artistic Playability	The game story and narrative are age appropriate/pleasing to the player. The game story captures the player's attention and the important elements are remarked during the play time. The game music is consistent with the challenges and immerses the player in the game dynamic. The visual elements (graphics, sprites, animations, etc.) are age appropriate / attractive to the player. The game does not reveal future story events that may affect the player's interest.
Interactive Playability	The game control system, menus and dialogs are attractive and enjoyable for the player. User achieves learning and memorization of game controls and IU in a pleasing and entertaining way. The controls and menus follow the standards of the game genre. The game interface is not intrusive for players. The game controls and menus can be customized and mapped according to the player's preferences.
Interpersonal Playability	The time spent on game and amusement obtained is high. The percentage of unblocked game is high. The amusement caused by the challenge is high. The actions and precision of movements for overcoming the challenges are high. The number of attempts at every challenge is generally low.
Intrapersonal Playability	New game objectives, rules and challenges are easily identified when several players play the game. The 'full' game story is complete for all players or can be completed by every player sharing the story events. The social interaction among other players or characters in the new dynamic of play is attractive to the player. There are game elements to identify the identity of each player within the virtual world. The social game controls with other players or characters differ little from the individual game system.

by PHET must be completed using additional information obtained through questionnaires/interviews and emocards and other suggestions from players. This permitted us to evaluate the degree of playability of a particular video game in depth and analyze the overall experience. With questionnaires and heuristics, we have obtained information of pragmatic value about the experience, but with emocard and real time biometrics factor, we can obtain information about the hedonic information of the player experience.

Using the Emocards, we are able to analyze factors that are difficult to assess objectively us-ing a number on a scale of values. However, at the same time, players are able to easily identify the emotional impact they have felt. Examples of these questions and answers can be seen in Figure 8. For example, with the results of emocards we can reaffirm the positive feedback from users with regards to the setting and context as well as sound effects and music in general (high level of satisfaction, mainly characterized by a state of pleasure, which varies between excitation and neutral state) (González Sánchez, 2011b).

The analyses of the hedonic factor help us to identify if the game satisfies players. We con-

Figure 7. UX representation using surfaces of playability for evaluation of Disaster: Day of Crisis: attributes of playability (left) and facets of playability (right) (González Sánchez, 2010)

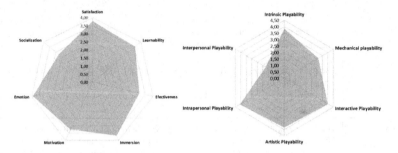

sider that enriching the PX analysis with multicultural and emotional factors (hedonic properties) helps us to establish information about player preferences and likes.

The Playability techniques demonstrated in this work can assist in the improvement of a video game as a product by enhancing the final experience, where the cultural or emotional impact can influence how a game should be designed or modified according to different player profiles or the market in a cost-effective manner.

Conclusion and Future Work

This work reflects the importance of analysing the experience that players have with video games in a pragmatic and hedonic way, and demonstrates how to analyse both the value of this experience and which elements of a game are the most/least

playable. Understanding and evaluating the user experience in video games is important for developing more efficient and successful products in terms of entertainment where cultural influence and emotional impact are crucial properties. Video Games are special interactive systems developed to entertain the user, thus we need to enrich the development process in order to determine the entire Player Experience.

We have presented the concept of Playability as a crucial characteristic of Player Experience in video games, outlining the attributes and properties that characterise it in order to measure and guarantee an optimum Player Experience. To facilitate the analysis of Playability, we have proposed six Facets of Playability in order to study every property in each attribute and identify the elements necessary to achieve a positive overall Playability in different video games. We

Figure 8. Examples of the emotional impact in a Castlevania: Lords of Shadow: castle recreation (left) and sound effects (right) (González Sánchez, 2011b)

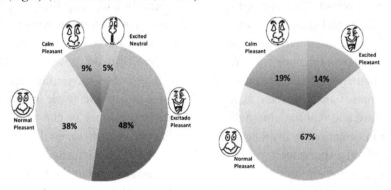

also complete the information about PX with measurement techniques (metrics, questionnaires, tests, software patterns, style guides, and heuristic techniques) thus ensuring optimum *Playability* of the videogame end product.

To acquire more information about the player experience, we propose the enhancement of the development process with hedonic factors (for example, techniques of emotional design and cross-cultural analysis) to increase the efficiency of experience development. An example of this includes the use of Emocards, tracking the player response in real time, and measuring biometric constants. The measurement and analysis process is considered to be easy and cost effective to perform, thus making it appropriate for agile development based on playable video game prototypes. Through practical examples, we have demonstrated the importance of this kind of evaluation for the development of a product that can provide better overall experiences or specific experiences (for example, fear or sudden intense excitement), depending on the target market.

The enrichment of the development process with Playability techniques will help game developers improve the final player experience in different stages of the development and in the overall final product.

As further work, we aim to evaluate the "forms" of the surface of playability in order to find common patterns in the user experience which can help us promote a certain experience in predefined player profiles. We are working on including hedonic factors to represent different feelings and emotions more efficiently using emocards and multidimensional emotions representation in order to complete the PHET report information. To realize this, we are also currently adapting different emotional and cross-cultural evaluation techniques and dimensions to characterize the interaction experience in more detail and extract rich patterns.

We are also currently updating and completing the different development phases of the Player Centered Video Game Development Process, particularly the requirement analysis and evaluation of experience. We are working on including the use of agile methodology to help us iterate on different game prototypes, we are incorporating hedonic factors to guarantee the experience in order to evaluate and improve playable prototypes and readapt the user experience to the possible changes in requirements and preferences which can occur when players test the game.

In the field of Educational Video Games (EVG) there is a lack of methodologies that provide the necessary constructs and support for the different design tasks. We are working to incorporate new attributes in the Playability Model to describe Educative Playability as well as new Facets to analyse the Player Experience in these kinds of game (Ibrahim, 2011). In educational games, a positive experience leads to greater efficiency as a didactic tool, in accordance with the philosophy of "Learning by playing, playing to learn." We are also working to introduce special patterns for improving player experience in the EVG field, in addition to determining how playability guidelines should be designed in order to be useful to educational videogame developers while also being useful for evaluating the achievement of playability. In addition, we are incorporating playablity techniques to improve experience in multiplayer video game with collaborative activities. To this aim, we are developing an architecture and development methodology following the ideas described in (Padilla Zea, 2009, 2011).

Finally, we are currently applying Quality in Use Techniques and Hedonic Factors of UX to improve the playability and the experience in educational and sanitary rehabilitation video games where a positive experience is a crucial factor for the success of the f video games as support tools.

ACKNOWLEDGMENT

This research is financed by the Spanish International Commission for Science and Technology (CICYT), the DESACO Project (TIN2008-06596-C02), and OMediaDis (TIN2008-06228).

REFERENCES

Barr, P., Noble, J., & Biddle, R. (2007). Video game values: Human–computer interaction and games. *Interacting with Computers, 19*(2), 180–195. doi:10.1016/j.intcom.2006.08.008

Bernhaupt, R. (Ed.). (2010). *Evaluating user experience in games: Concepts and methods*. London, UK: Springer.

Björk, S., Lundgren, S., & Holopainen, J. (2003). Game design patterns. In *Proceedings of Level Up 1st International Digital Games Research Conference*. Utrecht, The Netherlands: Dordrecht.

Brave, S., & Nass, C. (2002). Emotion in human-computer interaction. In Jacko, J., & Sears, A. (Eds.), *The Human-Computer Interaction Handbook: Fundamentals, Evolving Technologies and Emerging Applications*. Englewood Cliffs, NJ: Lawrence Erlbaum Associates.

Callele, D., Neufeld, E., & Schneider, K. (2006). Emotional requirements in video games. In *Proceedings of the 14th International Requirements Engineering Conference*, (pp. 292-295). Washington, DC: IEEE.

Canossa, A., & Drachen, A. (2009). Play-personas: Behaviours and belief systems in user-centred game design. In T. Gross (Ed.), *Proceedings of the 12th IFIP TC13 Conference on Human-Computer Interaction (INTERACT)*, (pp. 510-523). Berlin, Germany: Springer.

Chen, M., Cuddihy, E., Thayer, A., & Zhou. (2005). *Creating cross-cultural appeal in digital games: Issues in localization and user testing*. Paper presented at the 52nd Annual Conference for the Society for Technical Communication (STC). Retrieved July 07, 2011, from http://www.mark-dangerchen.net/pubs/Game_Slides_final3.ppt

Collazos, C. A., & Gil, R. M. (2011). Using cross-cultural features in web design patterns. In *Proceedings of Eighth International Conference on Information Technology: New Generations*, (pp. 514-519). Las Vegas, NV: IEEE Press.

Crawford, C. (1984). *The art of computer game design*. Berkeley, CA: McGraw-Hill/Osborne Media.

Csikszentmihalyi, M. (1990). *Flow: The psychology of optimal experience*. New York, NY: Harper and Row.

De Lera, E., & Garreta-Domingo, M. (2007). Ten emotion heuristics: Guidelines for assessing the user's affective dimension easily and cost-effectively. In *Proceedings of the 21st British HCI Group Annual Conference on People and Computers*, (pp. 163-166). Swinton, UK: British Computer Society.

Desmet, P. M. A., Overbeeke, C. J., & Tax, S. J. E. T. (2001). Designing products with added emotional value: Development and application of an approach for research through design. *The Design Journal, 4*(1), 32–47. doi:10.2752/146069201789378496

Desurvire, H., & Wiberg, C. (2009). Game usability heuristics (PLAY) for evaluating and designing better games: The next iteration. In Ozok & Zaphiris (Eds.), *Proceedings of the 3rd International Conference on Online Communities and Social Computing*, (pp. 557-566). Berlin, Germany: Springer-Verlag.

Federoff, M. (2002). *Heuristics and usability guidelines for the creation and evaluation of fun in video games*. (Master of Science Thesis). Indiana University. Retrieved Februry 08, 2009, from http://citeseerx.ist.psu.edu/viewdoc/download?doi=10.1.1.89.8294&rep=rep1&type=pdf

Glassner, A. (2004). *Interactive storytelling: Techniques for 21st century fiction*. Boca Raton, FL: CRC Press.

González Sánchez, J. L. (2010). *Jugabilidad: Caracterización de la experiencia del jugador en videojuegos*. (PhD Thesis). University of Granada. Granada, Spain. Retrieved March July 15, 2010, from http://hdl.handle.net/10481/5671

González Sánchez, J. L. (2011) *Jugabilidad y videojuegos: Análisis y diseño de la experiencia del jugador en sistemas interactivos de ocio electrónico*. Barcelona, Spain: Lambert Academic Publishing GmbH & Co (Ed.)

González Sánchez, J. L., Gil Iranzo, R. M., & Gutiérrez Vela, F. L. (2011). *Enriching* evaluation in video games. In P. Campos et al. (Eds.), *13th IFIP TC13 Conference on Human-Computer Interaction*, (pp. 519–522). Springer.

González Sánchez, J. L., Montero, F., Padilla Zea, N., & Gutiérrez, F. L. (2009). Playability as extension of quality in use in video games. In *Proceedings of the 2nd International Workshop on the Interplay between Usability Evaluation and Software Development (I-USED)*, (Vol. 490), (pp. 37 – 43). Berlin, Germany: Springer.

González Sánchez, J. L., Padilla Zea, N., & Gutiérrez, F. L. (2009). Playability: How to identify the player experience in a video game. In T. Gross (Ed.), *Proceedings of the 12th IFIP TC13 Conference on Human-Computer Interaction 2009*, (pp. 356-359). Berlin, Germany: Springer.

González Sánchez, J. L., Padilla Zea, N., & Gutiérrez, F. L. (2009). From usability to playability: Introduction to player-centred video game development process. In M. Kurosu (Ed.), *Proceedings of the Human-Computer Interaction International - Human Centered Design 2009*, (pp. 65–74). Berlin, Germany: Springer.

González Sánchez, J. L., Padilla Zea, N., Gutiérrez, F. L., Cabrera, M., & Paderewski, P. (2008). Playability: The secret of the educational videogame design. In T. Conolly & M. Stansfield (Eds.), *2nd European Conference on Games Bases Learning (ECGBL 2008)*, (pp. 147-156). Paisley, UK: ECGBL.

Hassenzahl, M. (2003). The thing and I: Understanding the relationship between user and product. In Blythe, M., Overbeeke, C., Monk, A. F., & Wright, P. C. (Eds.), *Funology: From Usability to Enjoyment* (pp. 31–42). Dordrecht, The Netherlands: Kluwer Academic Publishers. doi:10.1007/1-4020-2967-5_4

Hofstede, G. (1991). *Cultures and organizations: Software of the mind*. London, UK: McGraw-Hill.

Hupont, I., Cerezo, E., & Baldassarri, S. (2010). *Sensing facial emotions in a continuous 2D affective space*. In *Proceedings of the International Conference on Systems, Man, and Cybernetics*, (pp. 2045-2051). IEEE Press.

Ibrahim, A., Gutiérrez, F. L., González Sánchez, J. L., & Padilla Zea, N. (2011). Playability design pattern in educational video games. In T. Conolly & M. Stansfield (Eds.), *5th European Conference on Games Bases Learning (ECGBL 2011)*. ECGBL.

IGDA. (2004). *Accesibility in games: Motivations and approaches*. Retrieved March 15, 2010, from http://www.igda.org/accessibility/

Isbister, K., & Schaffer, N. (Eds.). (2008). *Game usability: Advancing the player experience*. New York, NY: Morgan Kaufmann.

ISO/IEC 25010. (2011). *Software product quality requirements and evaluation (SQuaRE): Software product quality and system quality in use models.* ISO.

ISO/IEC 9241-210. (2010). *Ergonomics of human–system interaction: Human centred design for interactive systems.* Clausule 2.15.

Järvien, A., Heliö, S., & Mäyrä, F. (2002). *Communication and community in digital entertainment services.* Retrieved May 10, 2011, from http://www.arts.rpi.edu/public_html/ruiz/public_html/EGDFall09/readings/Creating%20communityUniv.of%20Tampere.pdf

Korhonen, H., Paavilainen, J., & Saarenpää, H. (2009). Expert review method in game evaluations - Comparison of two playability heuristic sets. In *Proceedings of the 13th International MindTrek Conference: Everyday Life in the Ubiquitous,* (pp. 74-81). New York, NY: ACM Press.

Law, E., Roto, V., Hassenzahl, M., Vermeeren, A., & Kort, J. (2009). Understanding, scoping and defining user experience: A survey approach. In *Proceedings of the 27th International Conference on Human Factors in Computing Systems (CHI 2009),* (pp. 719-728). New York, NY: ACM.

Lazzaro, M. (2008). The four fun key. In Isbister, K., & Schaffer, N. (Eds.), *Game Usability: Advancing the Player Experience* (pp. 315–345). New York, NY: Morgan Kaufmann.

Malone, T. W., & Lepper, M. R. (1987). Intrinsic motivation and instructional effectiveness in computer-based education. In Snow, R. E., & Farr, M. J. (Eds.), *Aptitude, Learning and Instruction: Conative and affective process analyses* (pp. 243–286). Hillsdale, NJ: Lawrence Erlbaum Associates.

Mandryck, R. L., Inkpen, K. M., & Calvert, T. W. (2006). Using psychophysiological techniques to measure user experience with entertainment technologies. *Behaviour & Information Technology, 25*(2), 141–158. doi:10.1080/01449290500331156

McFarlane, A., Sparrowhawk, A., & Heald, Y. (2002). *Report on the educational use of games: An exploration by TEEM of the contribution which games can make to the education process.* Retrieved April 13, 2011, from http://www.teem.org.uk/publications/teem_gamesined_full.pdf

Mehrabian, A. (1994). *Manual for the revised trait arousability (converse of the stimulus screening).* Monterey, CA: Alta Mesa Road.

Nacke, L., Drachen, A., Korhonen, H., Kuikkaniemi, K., Niesenhaus, J., & van den Hoogen, W. … de Kort, Y. (2009). DiGRA panel: Playability and player experience research. In *DiGRA Breaking New Ground: Innovation in Games, Play, Practice and Theory.* London, UK: Brunel University.

Nielsen, J. (1993). *Usability engineering.* San Francisco, CA: Morgan Kaufmann Publishers.

Nokia. (2010). *Game design and user experience.* Retrieved March 15, 2010, from http://library.forum.nokia.com/index.jsp?topic=/Design_and_User_Experience_Library/GUID-21B5CE2C-7141-41CF-A669-2006502C151E.html

Norman, D. A. (2004). *Emotional design: Why we love (or hate) everyday things.* New York, NY: Basic Books.

Padilla Zea, N. (2011). *Metodología para el diseño de videojuegos educativos sobre una arquitectura para el análisis del aprendizaje colaborativo.* (PhD Thesis). University of Granada. Granada, Spain.

Padilla Zea, N., González Sánchez, J. L., Gutiérrez, F. L., Cabrera, M., & Paderewski, P. (2009). Design of educational multiplayer videogames: A vision from collaborative learning. *Journal Advances in Engineering Software, 40*(12), 1251–1260. doi:10.1016/j.advengsoft.2009.01.023

Pinelle, D., Wong, N., & Stach, T. (2008). Heuristic evaluation for games: Usability principles for video game design. In *Proceedings of the The 26th Annual CHI Conference on Human Factors in Computing Systems,* (pp 1453-1462). New York, NY: ACM Press.

Provenzo, E. (1991). *Video kids.* Boston, MA: Harvard University Press.

Saito, A. (2008). Gamenics and its potential. In Isbister, K., & Schaffer, N. (Eds.), *Game Usability: Advancing the Player Experience* (pp. 357 381). New York, NY: Morgan Kaufmann.

Swink, S. (2007). *Game feel: The secret ingredient.* Retrieved May 13, 2011, from http://www.gamasutra.com/view/feature/2322/game_feel_the_secret_ingredient.php

Trompenaars, F., & Hampden-Tuerner, C. (2010). *Riding the waves of innovation: Harness the power of global culture to drive creativity and growth.* New York, NY: McGraw-Hill.

Van den Hoogen, W. M., Ijsselsteijn, W. A., & de Kort, Y. A. W. (2008). Exploring behavioral expressions of player experience in digital games. In A. Nijholt & R. Poppe (Eds.), *Proceedings of the Workshop on Facial and Bodily Expression for Control and Adaptation of Games,* (pp. 11-19). Enschede, NL: IEEE.

Chapter 5
Playability Design Patterns:
An Approach to Facilitate the Design of Educational Video Games

Amer Ibrahim
University of Granada, Spain

Francisco Luis Gutiérrez Vela
University of Granada, Spain

Natalia Padilla Zea
University of Granada, Spain

José Luis González Sánchez
University of Granada, Spain

ABSTRACT

Learning through play is currently an effective and attractive educational strategy. Recently, many educational video games have failed because methods of analysis have not been used to discuss playability level in a structured way. Ensuring a good player experience characterized by playability requires cooperation and collaboration between game designers and educators. To this end, the authors have proposed a new set of patterns to support educational video game design and analysis. These patterns aim to facilitate the development of educational video games, summarize the essential information and requirements needed to understand a particular problem and the proposed solution, and present the interrelationships between educational video game components and playability attributes.

INTRODUCTION

The field of Educational Video Games (EVGs) is unique, with different objectives, designs, and forms of presentation, which distinguish it from other kinds of video games and which vary according to the requirements of the user. EVGs

are a combination of two components that are different in nature: learning and playful. This multidisciplinary nature of EVGs makes them difficult to design and implement. EVGs are a wonderful way to promote enjoyable learning, and there are currently many on the market. However, are all EVGs successful and do they always keep the player interested and motivated? Here, we emphasize that the success of an EVG depends

DOI: 10.4018/978-1-4666-1987-6.ch005

on the fun a player has while learning. From our point of view, this requires an implicit learning process and an innovative approach, which effectively integrates and balances fun challenges with the educational objectives. Accordingly, it involves providing attractive aspects that traditional methods of teaching cannot offer, so that while students play an EVG they are learning without even realizing it.

Unfortunately, one important issue that no existing educational video game methodology addresses is: how to create good, effective designs from the point of view of playability and player experience, which are very important for EVGs. This is the challenge that successful, experienced games designers face. To overcome the problem we propose the use of design patterns as an effective model to support the design and analysis of EVGs so that the video game experience and the efficiency of the learning process may be improved. Design patterns originated as a way to democratize design knowledge, by exposing the timeless principles at the heart of expert knowledge and making them accessible to all. Design patterns help to develop better games, and are good tools for recording and reutilizing design experience, providing the explanation and evaluation of important and recurrent designs. Using design patterns in EVG provides us with the ability to describe the interaction between the EVG components and the use of these components by the player to affect EVG Playability.

In this chapter, we present the way in which design patterns support Player Experience based on playability characteristics of EVGs, and how they help video game designers to combine and focus their game ideas. We have developed a collection of design patterns that describe solutions to reoccurring educational playability problems in EVGs. Our patterns have been collected from the analysis of existing educational video games. Our proposal gathers together whatever is suitable and useful for EVG design patterns from a set of works that relate to different video game

genres, interactive systems, hypermedia systems and multimedia systems. Furthermore, we have introduced a taxonomy for grouping the proposed patterns into a flexible, interactive structure related to EVG elements, which makes it easy to select an appropriate pattern for a specific EVG problem.

Design Patterns: Related Works

Design patterns have been suggested as a shared language of design experience. The idea of design patterns originated with the work of the architect Christopher Alexander (Alexander, et al., 1977). It was done with the explicit aim of externalizing knowledge to allow the accumulation and generalization of solutions and to allow all members of a community or design group to participate in the discussion relating to the design. As such, design patterns can be seen as a methodological tool to support the creation of an explicit design language. In general, a design pattern is defined as a high-level specification for solving a problem during the design phase.

Alexander describes patterns as being not merely informal guidelines, but a formalized arena of discourse. Once a pattern is identified and formalized, it can be easily referenced by domain experts and objectively compared to other formalized patterns in its ability to satisfy design goals. Alexander described design patterns as a formal design tool for use in the field of architecture in the book *A Pattern Language* (Alexander, et al., 1977). In it, he wrote the sentence that would prove to be the foundation for the entire use of design patterns in software development in the decades to come:

Each pattern describes a problem which occurs over and over again in our environment, and then describes the core of the solution to that problem, in such a way that you can use this solution a million times over, without ever doing it the same way twice.

However, Alexander's proposal has since been adopted by both design and software engineering professionals. Design patterns in video games have been a topic of discussion for some time now. Using patterns in EVGs allows the integration of educational content and video game design ideas, and in this way, they help us to balance the game challenges and the learning objectives in EVGs. The idea of applying the design patterns approach to produce game designs was first described by a practitioner within the game industry (Kreimeier, 2002) and an extensive collection has been developed for gameplay design patterns (Björk & Holopainen, 2004). Rogers (2010) provides a complete guide to video game design from ideas to characters, mechanics, and level design. Church (1999) proposed tools to help designers understand game design and to maximize the player's feeling of involvement and self.

Björk and Holopainen defined design pattern in their book *Patterns in Game Design* as the following: "Game design patterns are semiformal interdependent descriptions of commonly reoccurring parts of the design of a game that concern gameplay." They also presented a large collection of game design patterns that were compiled by analyzing existing games, explaining the template used for the game design patterns that followed, and suggesting means for identifying patterns and applying them to the design of a game (Björk & Holopainen, 2004).

Smith has also proposed some formal design tools, outlining the premise behind his "Systemic Level Design" (Smith, 2002) and "Orthogonal Unit Differentiation (O.U.D.)" (Smith, 2003). Common to these two proposals is the concept of design patterns, although he does not specifically call them that.

Church (1999) introduced Formal Abstract Design Tools (FADTs) as a way to achieve a shared design vocabulary. Falstein attempted to find a list of 400 rules that apply to game design by including rules that make a good game (Falstein,

2002). Church and Falstein have proposed the same objectives; to define a way to describe and share game design knowledge. In his book, *Art of Game Design: A Book of Lenses*, Schell presented a hundred ways to look at game design from a multiplicity of angles (Schell, 2008). Several other books have also been written about game design (Rollings & Adams, 2003; Koster, 2004).

Kiili (2010) considered that the objective of patterns was to fulfill the need for a common tool to facilitate the interaction between designers and to develop high quality educational games. He defined pattern design in educational games in this way: "Educational game design patterns are semiformal interdependent descriptions of commonly reoccurring parts of the design of an educational game that concern and optimize gameplay from an educational perspective focusing on the integration of engagement and learning objectives." He categorized educational game design patterns as follows:

- **Integration Patterns:** Describe solutions that harmoniously integrate game elements and learning objectives.
- **Cognition Patterns:** Describe solutions that trigger reflective and metacognitive processes in players.
- **Presentation Patterns:** Describe solutions that decrease the extraneous cognitive load.
- **Engagement Patterns:** Describe solutions that motivate players to perform better in a game, facilitate reciprocal learning, and increase playing time.
- **Social Patterns:** Describe solutions that facilitate learning or teaching through social activities and socially constructed game elements.
- **Teaching Patterns:** Describe solutions that facilitate teachers' work by providing observation, assessment and participation possibilities.

All the works discussed in this section form a solid base and present attractive ways to build a video game. Kiili presented a new taxonomy for EVG design from an educational perspective, and aimed to integrate the fun and educational aspects of EVGs. However, because the current trend in video game design is player-centered, we believe there is a need to create a set of patterns grouped using a new classification related to all aspects of the Game-Player interaction. This set of patterns should take into account the need to promote and maintain the playability of an EVG, to build and improve the player experience of the game process and facilitate the game development process. We have therefore focused on existing patterns found in the works presented above and similar works, as well as those found in educational multimedia systems and hypermedia systems that have been previously used to develop an interactive educational environment (Lyardet, et al., 1998; Kreimeier, 2002).

Design Pattern Importance

Learning through play is currently an effective and attractive educational strategy. During our research, we found many EVGs that appeared on the market before their efficacy had been ensured. As a result numerous games have failed, due to the lack of game design methods to convert designers' objectives into reality (Egenfeldt-Nielsen, 2011), as well as the fact that analyzing methods are rarely used discuss the level of playability in EVGs in a structured way. Another problem arises from the fact that an EVG is a combination of fun and learning. Thus, a good EVG development process requires cooperation and synergy between game designers and educators in order to ensure a good player experience (Padilla Zea, 2011).

To this end, we have proposed a set of player centered design patterns that support EVG design and analysis, i.e. game design and analysis that places the player experience first and foremost. Björk and Holopainen (2004) have mentioned several points that demonstrate the need for design patterns that do not depend on a designer's experience:

- **Problem-Solving for Game Interaction Design:** Patterns contain descriptions of identifiable elements of interaction within a game together with approaches to ensure the presence of those elements.
- **Inspiration:** A collection of patterns is in essence a list of concepts that other game designers have found useful for designing games.
- **Creative Design Tool:** Patterns are analyzed in the specific context for designers and potential subpatterns are identified. The subpatterns are identified through analysis and are chosen based on their feasibility. This activity continues recursively until an initial design has been completed.
- **Communicating with Peers:** Patterns offer definitions of elements found in many games. Describing one's design in terms of patterns offers one possibility to describe the design in a standardized format to make the understanding and comparison of different designs easier.
- **Communicating with Other Professions:** Using patterns for the design of the actual game play can make the transfer between different parts of a project group easier as the general working technique is familiar and gaining a basic understanding of patterns from another discipline is usually easy.

Based on the above, we present our opinion regarding design patterns in video game design. Design patterns provide many benefits during the design and analysis of video games:

- Design patterns allow new perspectives for both design and analysis, and provide a network of relations between different game design concepts.

- Design patterns are formal tools used for solving known problems, i.e. they function as a design toolbox. Patterns allow different levels of abstraction in order to address a specific game design problem, and offer the best way to solve issues related to software development using a proven solution.
- Design patterns facilitate the development of highly cohesive modules, which may be used many times in different contexts and applications.
- Using patterns describes many design decisions that cannot be recorded through the use of primitive methods.
- Patterns have the ability to increase the opportunities for communication and reduce misunderstandings between educators, designers, and players, leading to more efficient communication between them.
- Each pattern allows some aspect of the system structure to change independently of other aspects.

PLAYABILITY AND DESIGN PATTERNS

A Tool to Improve the Player Experience

Having identified that games exhibit some unique playability problems, e.g. the lack of a player role in the game design or the inability to provide the player with the proposed content, we considered that there was a clear need to develop a collection of design patterns that specifically addresses playability and player experience in video games.

The need for EVGs arises from the failure of e-learning systems and technology enhanced learning process to engage students and keep them motivated to study (Parker, 2003; Prensky, 2001). In this work, we emphasize the properties

of player experience that are necessary to obtain a successful video game, where this experience is related to all aspects of interaction between the video game and the player. Accordingly, the solution should ensure optimal player experience and be able to blend the educational objectives with playful challenges, present the game objectives, and provide interesting choices, immediate support and assistance, and an attractive learning environment.

We consider that the design of EVGs is ideal for developing design patterns because it is able to:

- Support an innovative approach that effectively integrates and balances fun challenges with educational objectives.
- Support the playability attributes and build an optimal experience by including a game design that motivates players.
- Provide a common vocabulary between game developers and designers in this rapidly expanding field.
- Guide the test and evaluation of the game experience and the efficiency of the learning process.

Playability

From the previous section, we can highlight the player's role in the structure of an EVG. The role of the video game is also important as a means to entertain and teach players, as well as to improve the user experience during playing time. The current trend in video game design is player-centered, which takes the player experience into account for a game to be successful. We present the player experience as an extension of the User Experience, where user experience is understood as a set of sensations, feelings or an emotional response experienced by users when they interact with a system (Law, et al., 2009). The term player experience—based on definitions of user experience (Nielsen-Norman, 2007)—refers to "all aspects related to the player that are affected by and interact with the playing environment." These aspects represent pragmatic and hedonic features of the interaction process such as: sensation, feelings, emotional response, assessment, user satisfaction, and the experience obtained during playing time (González Sánchez, et al., 2011). A video game with good playability provides a player with positive experiences of the aforementioned aspects.

Playability in EVGs is not limited to playful objectives but must take into account educational objectives, such as learning while having fun, improving the abilities of students to solve complex problems, reinforcing players' skills, and improving player experience. We thus propose the definition of playability in EVGs to be "the set of properties that describe the player experience in the gaming environment, the main goal of which is to provide enjoyment and learning in a playable and learnable context for the duration of play." This definition retains "fun" as a subjective concept and includes educational goals. Thus, playability in EVGs is an extension of playability in videogames. In this way, we have proposed a set of characterizations to identify and qualify new attributes and properties, which are suitable for defining playability in EVGs based on those that have been presented for video games (Ibrahim, et al., 2011; González Sánchez, 2010):

- **Satisfaction:** The gratification or pleasure derived from playing a complete video game or from some aspect of it.
- **Learnability:** The player's capacity to understand and master the game system and mechanics (objectives, rules, how to interact with the video game, etc).
- **Effectiveness:** The resources needed to offer players a new experience (fun and learning) while they achieve the game's various objectives and reach the final goal.
- **Immersion:** The capacity of the EVG contents to be believable, such that the player becomes directly involved in the virtual

game world. By using this property, we measure the ability of EVGs to implicitly present the educational aspects.
- **Motivation:** The set of game characteristics that prompt a player to realize specific actions and continue undertaking them until they are completed. The motivation to play produces indirect motivation to learn.
- **Emotion:** This refers to the player's involuntary impulse in response to the stimulus of the EVG that induces feelings or a chain reaction of automatic behaviors.
- **Socialization:** The set of game attributes, elements, and resources that promote the social dimension of the game experience in a group scenario. Socialization is the ability to support students learning from one another.
- **Supportive:** The ability of an EVG to keep the player motivated, to teach players/students effectively and encourage them to continue learning and achieve the learning objectives.
- **Educative:** The educational characteristics of the game and the ability of the player to be aware of, understand, master and achieve the learning goals.

Design Pattern and Playability

The integration of playing and learning is the main objective of an EVG. In this article, we highlight the properties of player experience, which result in a successful game. Player experience is related to all aspects of interaction between the video game content and the player. As previously mentioned, the goal is to ensure an optimal player experience while blending educational objectives with fun challenges. To achieve this, we suggest a set of design patterns based on the playability attributes as a tool to reduce the complexity of EVG design, as well as to help the player improve his/her experience during playing time. A feature of game design patterns is that adding new patterns does not restrict or specialize the nature of the game, but rather expands it. This is because a pattern describes a particular aspect of playability and its effects on player experience.

We thus present a new taxonomy of design patterns, which were compiled by analyzing the existing exiting game design patterns and the current problems that face EVG designers. Each pattern in our proposed set describes a part of the possible interaction between a player and the game. These patterns are related and when used together they are able to improve player experience and effectively resolve EVG problems. Design patterns provide video game designers with the opportunity to play a powerful role in constructing and improving game playability. Design can be reactionary, responding only to current conditions, or it can be visionary, by presenting solutions to problems yet undefined.

The new set of patterns has been created so that the following points are considered: appeals to both cognition and emotion; improves upon the player's previous experience; fosters creativity and collaboration between designers in order to produce the best player experience possible; presents a game structure that is able to bridge the gap between the required experience and the player experience; facilitates the evaluation of the experience and the effectiveness of the game. Using design patterns should increase designers' experience, helping them to ascertain what is meaningful to the end user and how to present it in the best possible way.

DESIGN PATTERN PROPOSAL FOR EDUCATIONAL VIDEO GAMES

In the previous sections, we have mentioned the need to develop EVGs as a system of both learning and entertainment, and have emphasized the role of player experience to ensure that these two objectives are achieved and a successful video game obtained. To achieve learning and enter-

tainment in a gaming environment, an integrated set of patterns must be suggested to support the player experiences based on the playability attributes in EVGs.

In this chapter, we aim to propose design patterns, documented in a standard format, as solutions to common design problems. We use patterns as a tool for problem solving, to support creative and effective design, to build a repository of knowledge and encourage reuse of best practices, and as a way to share designers' experience. By using the patterns described in this chapter, it should be possible to develop a structure that helps build both entertaining and productive educational video games.

Elements of a Design Pattern

Christopher Alexander stated that, at the very least, a design pattern should contain the following components (Alexander, et al., 1985): a name, a problem statement, a proposed solution, the consequences of using the pattern, and the relation with other patterns. Several other pattern templates include other elements, or subdivide these elements. Based on the above, we here present our pattern template. To facilitate the development and use of EVG patterns, our template consists of the following main elements (see Table 1).

Design Pattern Taxonomy

We believe that the best way to classify the patterns is related to "Educational Playability." In this way, we associate the proposed patterns with the situations and the game elements, which are closed to the player's experience during the game. We believe that this aspect is most important to develop effective and motivating learning games. In this context, we have classified the proposed patterns within a flexible interactive structure based on playability attributes and related to all aspects of EVGs, as follows:

Table 1. Design pattern components

Name	The design pattern name should be short, specific, and idiomatic. The main purpose of naming is to provide intuitive names that may provide mnemonic support after the pattern description has been read.
Problem	The design pattern problem is a question that reflects the discussed problem in the pattern. It must be straightforward and simple so that the reader has a clear understanding of the pattern's content.
Description	This is a reflection of the content and the goal of the pattern. It is an explanation of the pattern problem. It does not provide a solution, but helps infer the result of applying the pattern. It contains information on how the pattern affects the structural framework of the game. The description is complemented with other pattern elements (Name and Problem) to provide the reader with a clear explanation of the pattern's objective.
Solution	This is an abstract structure that briefly describes the suggested solutions for resolving or avoiding a particular pattern problem. It provides a number of ways to solve the current problem as well as a number of design choices specific to it. In other words, it presents the way in which the pattern may be useful for solving design related issues.
Elements of the Game Affected	Presents the EVG elements (Amory, 2006; Amory & Seagram, 2003) that are affected by the pattern and have related to the discussed problem and the proposed solution.
Playability Elements Affected	Describes the effects of applying the proposed solution on the player experience and which playability attribute will be in the range of the pattern influence. In other words, it determines the playability attributes that are related to the discussed problem.
Relations with other patterns	Defines the relationships between the different patterns, which can be divided in this way: Inter-Pattern relation is the solution to a problem, which results from applying another pattern; Relate-Pattern relation is a set of patterns that serve the same objectives, and Co-Pattern relation helps another pattern to resolve a problem.
Consequences	Presents the effects that applying the proposed solution has on player experience.
Example	This part of the pattern is optional. The example is a supplementary part of the general pattern image and its aim is to give the developer a better understanding of the pattern.

- **Interactive Integration:** Describes those patterns that focus on EVGs as a combination of fun and educational elements. It presents the structure of EVG objects, where educational and fun aspects are given more emphasis than in other types of games.
- **Active Support:** Describes those patterns that help and support players to understand what they are doing and learning during the game's progress. This discourages the player from stopping the game, and encourages him or her to think about the decisions, actions, or strategies that must be taken in the next step.
- **Knowledge Realism:** Describes those patterns that ensure the quality of the EVG content, by presenting accurate knowledge related to the real world. This gives the user confidence as it enables him or her to check the accuracy of obtained information.
- **Beneficial Play:** Describes those patterns that provide players with incentives (reward, fun, pleasure) to encourage them to advance in the game, and consequently, in their knowledge and skill acquisition.
- **Knowledge Growth:** Describes those patterns that focus on the use of EVGs to give players new knowledge and skills, and to improve and develop previous knowledge.
- **Social Awareness:** Describes those patterns that present and use the social features of EVGs to facilitate learning or teaching through social activities and their role in strengthening the player experience.

Table 2 presents the proposed taxonomy of design patterns, the common problems, the suggested solutions in each group, and EVG elements that are related to the discussed problem.

PROPOSED DESIGN PATTERNS

The specification presented in Table 2 shows how to classify the proposed patterns and how the EVG can be designed as a result. We subsequently present a description of the proposed patterns based on the suggested template in more detail.

We are currently in the process of defining and analyzing patterns in order to build a comprehensive collection of interrelated patterns based on aspects related to player experience and educational playability. Our proposed set of patterns has been constructed by examining different elements and features of EVGs, board games and card games, and we, therefore, believe that it has the potential to be helpful in the design of EVGs.

Interactive Integration

Balanced EVG

- **Problem:** How do we create a game in which all fun and educational aspects are included?
- **Description:** EVGs have playful and educational contents, and producing an EVG in which both these aspects are included is very difficult, as both contents form the EVG and determine the success or failure of the game. Thus, failure to balance these contents impacts negatively on player experience.
- **Solution:** Creating a successful EVG requires that the balance of EVG contents (fun and educational) is ensured. This can be achieved in a number of ways: presenting the EVG contents in the same stage in a way that they do not conflict with each other, and without one dominating the other during the entire game, or at any game stage; emphasizing the need for game contents to be well-structured and carefully-chosen throughout the videogame design to produce an integrated EVG; Presenting educational content indirectly and adding playful content with the goal of maintaining the game story; Keeping these contents compliant in terms of goal visualizing and achieving.
- **Elements of the Video Game Affected:** Applying this pattern affects the challenge type and frequency, the presented tasks, and the game objectives in all game steps.
- **Playability Elements Affected:** This pattern should provide a degree of fun to encourage and motivate players to continue playing. In this way, it ensures the EVG's effectiveness as an educational system. It is related to the attributes Satisfaction, Motivation, Effectiveness and Educative.
- **Relations with Other Patterns:** This pattern is directly related to the Interface Structure pattern. The Co-Pattern relation between these two patterns produces the best integration between video game components, and also ensures that an interactive playing environment is presented to players.
- **Consequence:** This pattern ensures that players are entertained and provided with interesting content. It also ensures that the playful and educational contents are balanced in order to produce a successful EVG. The use of the pattern facilitates cognitive immersion and game mastery.

Interface Structure

- **Problem:** How do we produce an appropriate and attractive player interface?
- **Description:** One of the problems facing EVG designers is how to present the huge

Table 2. Design pattern taxonomy

Taxonomy	Pattern Problems	Patterns	EVG Elements
Interactive integration	Create an EVG in which all fun and educational aspects are included, Present the educational content indirectly, Produce a appropriate player interface, Generate a good player experience.	Balanced EVG, Interface Structure, Adaptive Content	Tasks, Disposition, Objective, Challenges.
Active support	Feedback, Keep the player informed about his or her status, Present the necessary information to support the game progress. Incentives to reward players	Related Support, Reward	Feedback, Score, Active Reward.
Knowledge realism	Give players new, correct knowledge, Effect of game reality on player experience.	Knowledge Correctness, Game Reality	Reward, Realism, Challenges, Rules.
Beneficial play	Use game activities to teach, Keep player motivated during playing time and progress in the game.	Incremental Learn, Motivated Play	Reward, Challenges.
Knowledge Growth	Support players to become aware of and to obtain new knowledge. Improve player experience and awareness.	Skills Improvement, Embedded Learning	Challenges, Feedback.
Social awareness	Use social aspect to improve player experience.	Shared Experience	Group challenges, Dependence among members.

number of different EVG components (playful and educative elements), and keep these components related and consistent so that players are engaged throughout the game.

- **Solution:** An appropriate player interface can be designed in different ways: ensuring the suitability and compatibility of content objects, presenting attractive elements, considering the aesthetic and cognitive aspects that attract a player, introducing EVG objects and challenges in an attractive way, so that the presentation of EVG contents motivates players and keeps them immersed. Furthermore, integrating all these aspects in the player interface can facilitate and accelerate the learning process.
- **Elements of the Video Game Affected:** This pattern is directly related to the disposition of EVG objects (e.g. Playful, Education), and how we can present the different objectives and challenges during the learning and gaming process.

- **Playability Elements Affected:** Good presentation of game components is very important in order to keep the player motivated and immersed. Thus, a successful player interface can affect the following playability attributes: Immersion, Learnability, Effectiveness, Motivation, and Supportability.
- **Relations with Other Patterns:** This pattern has a Co-Pattern relation with Balanced EVG and, as mentioned above, these two patterns play an important role in the success of an EVG. This pattern and the Balanced EVG pattern present the game elements in a complementary way.
- **Consequence:** The result of the Game interface design pattern is an interface that is comfortable to use, that aids and assists successful task completion, and that reflects the interrelationship of the game objectives and the game environment.

Adaptive Content

- **Problem:** How can the EVG actively provide players with the proposed content?
- **Description:** EVGs may offer different levels of difficulty in order to engage different types of players. Presenting several levels of difficulty (e.g. easy, normal and difficult) is not enough to engage the player in the game. The game chooses a difficulty level at start-up, and it is usually not possible for a player to change difficulty levels without starting over.
- **Solution:** In addition to providing different game levels, EVGs should adapt the difficulty level to the player throughout the game. This adaptation may be introduced in several ways, based on player performance during both the learning and playing process. Player performance and the skills developed can determine the content that should be presented to the player. Adjusting the level helps to reduce player errors, as well as ensuring the quality of the content provided. It also provides a means for players to customize their characters using a comprehensive list of abilities and allow those abilities to be improved as play progresses. This pattern ensures that a player's curiosity is maintained while playing a game.
- **Elements of the Video Game Affected:** Many video game elements affect this pattern, such as game challenges, game roles, game objectives and game history. All of these elements encourage players to actively participate in the game.
- **Playability Elements Affected:** The difficulty of the game and the suitability of the level to player experience are very important in ensuring player satisfaction, motivation and immersion and their effects on the educative attributes of playability.

- **Relations with Other Patterns:** This pattern is related to the other patterns of the interactive integrations category through the Pattern-Related relation.
- **Consequence:** It is essential to apply this pattern to ensure the complete absorption of a player in the game events, and to avoid negative emotions that may arise when a player faces game challenges.

Active Support

Reward

- **Problem:** How can we provide players with incentives that encourage them to explore the game world?
- **Description:** Due the great complexity of EVG content, players must be stimulated in different ways in order to become immersed in the game and motivated to play.
- **Solution:** Players should be rewarded for being active in the virtual world in such a way that all players are encouraged to discover and achieve the game's objectives, and continue playing throughout the different levels. Rewards should ensure that the game is fun. Rewards that are not fun do not help a player. Providing rewards for good and appropriate behaviors eventually transforms initially fun activities into work. Rewards should be introduced when player achieves a goal during the game or at the end of a level. Rewards should also provide meta-information during the playing time, and refresh vital resources that are needed for the game to progress.
- **Elements of the Video Game Affected:** This pattern is related to Game Objectives and Game Challenge, which affect player satisfaction during a game level.
- **Playability Elements Affected:** The effects of this pattern include educational

and playful playability attributes, such as Satisfaction, Motivation and Educative.

- **Relations with Other Patterns:** This pattern has a Co-Pattern relation with Related Support.
- **Consequence:** The main objective of this pattern is to encourage the player to participate in the different tasks and events of an EVG, and to change player behaviors and reactions based on the gaming process. With this incentive, we create interesting, imaginative, narrative descriptions of scenes and character actions.

Related Support

- **Problem:** How do we help the player's progress in the virtual game world?
- **Description:** It is sometimes the case that a player requires certain information in order to understand his or her situation during the game, and take a decision or determine what must be done next. It is therefore necessary to provide support for every situation a player may encounter.
- **Solution:** Player support can be provided in many ways, such as giving feedback about the effect of each game object, or making feedback non-ambiguous and comprehensive. In a multi-player game, feedback about an action must be provided to all players in the shared workspace, not just the user who performed the action. Messages may also be used to explain the player's action and situation, and the score list displayed so that a player knows his or her score and position during the playing time. Moreover, players should have access to complete game information, and additional help should be accessible while playing. For example, an information screen can be present at the end of each level to notify the player about status, position, score and provide a brief description

of the next level. This pattern aims to prevent players from encountering difficulties and leave the game. It thus reduces the need for human assistance, in contrast to traditional E-learning systems.

- **Elements of the Video Game Affected:** This pattern depends on the game elements that help players to overcome all game steps, such as game feedback and game score. It is also related to game rules and game control, which are very important for mastering the game process.
- **Playability Elements Affected:** This pattern is very important in the learning process due to its relation with player satisfaction and the emotions generated in a player during the game. In this way, it affects player immersion and the educative playability attributes.
- **Relations with Other Patterns:** This pattern has a Relate-Pattern relation with Knowledge Correctness and Incremental Learning. Together, these patterns aim to improve the player experience during the playing time.
- **Consequence:** This pattern can prevent players from encountering difficulties, and thus reduces the need for human assistance.

Knowledge Realism

Knowledge Correctness

- **Problem:** How can the player be given new, correct knowledge during playing time?
- **Description:** Players may create new knowledge using their imagination while they are playing. This knowledge may be wrong, yet it is often kept in a player's memory after the game has ended, and in this case the game content constitutes a negative influence on the learning process. It is therefore essential that the presenta-

tion of game content progresses correctly throughout the game.

- **Solution:** To ensure that new, correct knowledge is presented to players throughout the game, a way to check the accuracy of the knowledge gained while playing should be provided. To do so quizzes and tests can be used, as well as activating the use of the gained knowledge during the different game levels to overcome the challenges faced. It is also important to maintain knowledge accuracy by changing the incorrect knowledge and skills that a player may have unintentionally acquired. This should be achieved by providing information about the objectives of each level at important points during the game, allowing comparison between the player's actual situation and the ideal situation.

- **Elements of the Video Game Affected:** To ensure the game's success, this pattern must take into account how players can control and master the game. It is thus related to the following game elements: Reward, Objectives, Game Structure, Game Challenges, and Rules.

- **Playability Elements Affected:** This pattern supports logical and strategic thinking, which requires the player to be aware of the presented content while playing. This pattern is therefore related to playful and educational playability attributes, such as Supportability, Educative, Effectiveness, and Learnability.

- **Relations with Other Patterns:** This pattern has common objectives with other patterns of the proposed set, such as Game Reality and Related Support. The Relate-Pattern relation connects these patterns.

- **Consequence:** The main advantage of this pattern is to support logical and strategic thinking, where a player is able to compare knowledge gained with knowledge that must be gained.

Game Reality

- **Problem:** How can the useful aspects of game realism be used and managed to improve player experience?

- **Description:** In many cases players use their real-life situations to build strategies in the virtual game world, and compare the presented EVG contents with real life. Thus, the reality of an EVG should be exploited due to the great effect that it can have on the player experience.

- **Solution:** EVGs are set in the real world, but an overlay is applied which gives players more information than is available to them in the real world. All or part of the game world is defined by this, and it can be ensured by establishing some basic principles of the real world. This effectively activates players' primer experience (real world experience), and gives them the ability to set up the game environment by themselves, helping them to understand how the hybrid relation between real world and game world is defined. This pattern makes real-world situations and simulations available within a game, tells a real story and presents a realistic sequence of events throughout the game.

- **Elements of the Video Game Affected:** This pattern is related to all EVG elements that give a game aspect of reality, such as Game Realism, Game Challenges, Game Objective, Game Rules, Game History, and Game Reward.

- **Playability Elements Affected:** This pattern motivates the player's understanding and awareness of the presented content, establishing some basic principles of the real world to activate his primer experience. It can affect Satisfaction, Effectiveness, Learnability, and Educative.

- **Relations with Other Patterns:** This pattern is very important to the patterns Knowledge Correctness and Player Experience Development.

- **Consequence:** This pattern motivates players to be conscious of the presented content, and to be able to use his or her real experience in the virtual game world.

Beneficial Play

Incremental Learning

- **Problem:** How can a player's desire to achieve the educational content of an EVG be increased?

- **Description:** We know that not all types of knowledge can be learned incrementally (educational content has serious aspects that can be reduce its interactivity). Games have characteristics that contribute to accelerating the learning process when gradually increase the player's skills level during playing time.

- **Solution:** In order to motivate and encourage players to achieve the proposed educational content, EVG designers must use curiosity, challenges and rewards to increase the players' skill levels. Designers must also determine the point at which players find the game challenging and interesting, in order to increase the degree of interaction between players and the game and thus encourage the achievement of game content. In other words, improving the player experience level involves increasing the educational content of the game. It is therefore clear that the role of motivational properties in EVGs is to engage players and keep them immersed so they continue playing. Players thus have a sense of achievement and feel good accordingly.

- **Elements of the Video Game Affected:** Different elements of EVGs are involved in the success of this pattern, such as Game

Reward, Game Challenges, Game structure and Game History.

- **Playability Elements Affected:** This pattern relies on player motivation and emotion in order to draw players into the virtual game world. It is also based on the emotional response of a player when he or she faces and overcomes the proposed challenges. It thus affects such playability attributes as: Effectiveness, Motivation, Emotion and Satisfaction.

- **Relations with Other Patterns:** This pattern is related to Knowledge Correctness, Player Experience Development, Game Reality and Interface Structure, through the Relate-Pattern Relation.

- **Consequence:** The sense of achievement that results from applying this pattern is very helpful for encouraging players to continue playing and become immersed in the game events.

Motivated Play

- **Problem:** How can the player be kept motivated to play and achieve the EVG contents?

- **Description:** Maintaining the same level of player absorption throughout the different game levels is related to the game structure. In EVGs, keeping a player immersed and interested during playing time is very difficult due to the cognitive over-load which results from the learning process.

- **Solution:** In order to keep a player motivated, we suggest providing fun and enjoyment to concentrate his or her attention on game goals. This can be achieved in many ways with different effects on different players. This may appear as concentrating on the playful side more than on the educational content, but it is the best way to introduce the educational content implicitly. EVGs can be engaging, and even addictive, and learning can be indirectly motivated by good presentation of game mystery, curiosity, and rewards. These give players satisfaction and pleasure and reduce the frustration that may be felt from the educational side of EVGs. Presenting different features, objectives, and challenges also gives players a wide range of interaction with the elements of play. It can also be beneficial to give a player a lot of freedom to create his or her profile and customize the virtual environment.

- **Elements of the Video Game Affected:** Many aspects and elements of EVGs are involved in motivating a player to continue playing and achieving the proposed objectives, including Game Challenges, Game Objectives, Game Reward, Game Challenges, Game Structure, Sound, and Visual effects.
- **Playability Elements Affected:** This pattern requires several playability attributes to be successful, such as Playability Motivation, Immersion, Satisfaction and Supportability, where all these attributes are related to the game aspects that support player immersion and motivation during playing time.
- **Relations with Other Patterns:** Related Support is connected to this pattern through the Relate-Pattern relation. Related Support and Motivated Play aim to keep the player playing for the maximum possible time to achieve the proposed objective.
- **Consequence:** Introducing this pattern creates the opportunity for players to become involved in the mechanism of game tasks, by using methods of encouragement and incentives during the game.

Knowledge Growth

Embedded Learning

- **Problem:** How can the educational content of an EVG be presented throughout the game?
- **Description:** Not all types of interaction are fun. In an educational video game, interaction is related to global game features, such as design, goal structure, and challenges. When a player finds a game enjoyable and stimulating, he or she has a desire to learn more and explore the educational content.
- **Solution:** Due to the serious nature of the educational content, players do not have control over this area, and player interaction with this aspect of the game is reduced. As such, it should be hidden during the learning process, allowing the player to interact with and understand the content and encouraging and motivating him or her to explore the game world and to achieve the content's objectives. More playful than educational elements should also be introduced based on player performance. This is known as "Hide educational complexity," and it can be used as an indicator of the player's interaction with the presented contents and the amount of educational elements in the game.
- **Elements of the Video Game Affected:** This pattern is related to game elements that have an effective role in player performance during playing time, such as Game Structure, Game Objectives, and Educational Challenges.
- **Playability Attributes Affected:** Managing the relation between the EVG elements "playful" and "educative" is very important in this pattern, as is the diversity of the presented game elements during game progress. Thus, this attribute involves

the use of these playability attributes: Supportability, Educative, Effectiveness, and Immersion.

- **Relations with Other Patterns:** This pattern is related to Balanced and Interface Structure through the Pattern- Related Relation. These three patterns aim to effectively present the game content during the playing and learning process.
- **Consequence:** Using this pattern increases the player's ability to achieve the educational content, and maintains his or her interest in playing.

Skills Improvement

- **Problem:** How do we support the player to become aware of new game knowledge and obtain it?
- **Description:** EVGs constitute an appropriate support to the strengthening or teaching of new knowledge and skills, as they captivate and engage players for hours. In this way, they develop and improve player knowledge and awareness during playing time.
- **Solution:** Improving the previous skills and knowledge of a player involves evaluating these skills and basing the game content presented to a player on this evaluation, as well as adjusting the level of difficulty and complexity to suit the player's skills. Thus, a player's previous knowledge is linked to the knowledge presented in the game so that the player is stimulated into using his or her current experience. Improving players' skills also requires the use of game characteristics that accelerate the learning process, and gradually encourage the player to pass the game levels and achieve the desired goals of the EVG.
- **Elements of the Video Game Affected:** Improving player skills and knowledge is linked to the different game elements that

can activate the player experience, such as Game Challenges, Feedback, Game Roles and Game Objectives.

- **Playability Elements Affected:** This pattern is affected by all playability attributes that activate and motivate the player knowledge, and thus it relates to Supportability, Motivation, and Satisfaction.
- **Relations with Other Patterns:** This pattern has a Relate-Pattern Relation with Related Support, Game Reality, and Knowledge Correctness.
- **Consequence:** This pattern focuses on reinforcing player skills and improving his or her prior experience. It also facilitates reflective thinking and creativity, as well as giving players the opportunity to concentrate entirely on subjects that increase their skills.

Social Awareness

Shared Experience

- **Problem:** How can the social characteristics of EVGs affect the Player Experience?
- **Description:** In EVGs, different players' experiences of playing a game can be communicated to each other, however just being in the same game does not count as shared experience. It is therefore very important to encourage the interchange of skills and knowledge between players.
- **Solution:** Social skills are vital for game playability and prove that shared experience adds value to the achievement of the game objectives. Social skills can be developed by presenting the concepts of interaction, competition, collaboration, and cooperation to achieve the same goals, which lead to strategic knowledge by improving the interactivity among players. Furthermore, shared experience can be attained by giving a shared reward to

the group that achieves the game goals, this reward may be any type of temporary advantage.

- **Elements of the Video Game Affected:** Many elements of a game have social aspects that are involved in the design of this pattern, such as Group challenges, Dependence among members, Game Rewards.
- **Playability Elements Affected:** This pattern explains the role of shared experience in achieving different game goals, and how this leads to strategic knowledge by improving collaboration and interactivity among players. It is related to Playability Socialization, Supportability.
- **Relations with Other Patterns:** It has a Relate-Pattern Relation with Reward and Knowledge Correctness.
- **Consequence:** In an EVG design, this pattern uses strategic thinking and new skills of players to improve collaboration and cooperation among them.

CONCLUSION

The design and creation of an EVG is far from simple. Nowadays, several methodologies provide the necessary constructs and support for the different design tasks. During our research, we have perceived the need for a unified vocabulary and common concepts regarding EVGs and game design. Game design patterns are powerful tools that can be used to build a real gaming future, by providing utility, flexibility, and scalability of the video game design.

Design patterns appear to be ideally suited to the role of enabling design-level conversation across the disciplines involved in EVGs. Yet, in order to fulfill this role, it is necessary to develop a set of design patterns using the educational playability principles. However, we believe there are

many more patterns waiting to be formalized and many more to discover in the domain of EVG. The format and scope of our patterns may contribute to the development of a larger number of patterns than those currently available. Furthermore, the proposed pattern template aims to facilitate the development and use of EVG patterns, and to present a comprehensive explanation and description of the proposed patterns.

This set of patterns plays a powerful role in constructing and improving the player experience by analyzing the existing game design problems and effectively resolving them. Our proposed patterns offer an attractive structure for creating EVGs that are effective to play and learn, that bridge the gap between player experience and game experience, and that consider the playability attributes and properties to develop the player experience.

We have classified the collection of patterns into six groups related to the playful and educational contents. These patterns reflect the characteristics of complex design; they respond to the need for adaptation, emergence, and the expression of educational values in complex video game design. They also address important concerns in EVGs and can be used together to build complex but effective video games, resulting in EVGs with fewer playability problems, and potentially leading to improved player experience.

ACKNOWLEDGMENT

This work is financed by the Ministry of Education and Science, Spain, as part of DESACO Project (TIN2008-06596-C02-2) and the F.P.U Program.

REFERENCES

Alexander, C., Davis, H., Martinez, J., & Corner, D. (1985). *The production of houses*. Oxford, UK: Oxford University Press.

Alexander, C., Ishikawa, S., & Silverstein, M. (1977). *A pattern language: Towns, buildings, construction.* Oxford, UK: Oxford University Press.

Amory, A. (2006). Game object model version II: A theoretical framework for educational game development. *Educational Technology Research and Development, 55*(1), 51–77. doi:10.1007/s11423-006-9001-x

Amory, A., & Seagram, R. (2003). Educational game models: Conceptualization and evaluation. *South African Journal of Higher Education, 17*(2), 206–217.

Björk, S., & Holopainen, J. (2004). *Patterns in game design.* New York, NY: Charles River Media.

Church, D. (1999). Formal abstract design tools. *Game Developer, 3*(8), 28. Retrieved November 8, 2011, from http://www1.cs.columbia.edu/~cs4995/files/Doug_Church_FADT.pdf

Falstein, N. (2002). Better by design: The 400 project. *Game Developer Magazine, 9*(3), 26.

González Sánchez, J. L. (2010). *Playability the characterization of player experience in video game.* (Doctoral Dissertation). Granada University. Granada, Spain. Retrieved November 8, 2011, from http://digibug.ugr.es/handle/10481/5671

González Sánchez, J. L., Gil Iranzo, R., & Gutiérrez Vela, F. L. (2011). Enriching evaluation in video games. *Lecture Notes in Computer Science, 6949,* 519–522. doi:10.1007/978-3-642-23768-3_72

Ibrahim, A., Gutiérrez, F. L., González Sánchez, J. L., & Padilla Zea, N. (2011). Playability design pattern in educational video game. In *Proceedings of the European Conference on Games Based Learning (ECGBL 2011).* Athens, Greece: ECGBL.

Ibrahim, A., Gutiérrez, F. L., González Sánchez, J. L., & Padilla Zea, N. (2012). Educational playability analyzing player experiences in educational video game. In *Proceedings of The Fifth International Conference on Advances in Computer-Human Interactions ACHI 2012.* Valencia, Spain: ACHI.

Kiili, K. (2010). Call for learning-game design patterns. In Edvardsen, F., & Kulle, H. (Eds.), *Educational Games: Design, Learning, and Applications* (pp. 299–311). New York, NY: Nova Publishers.

Koster, R. (2004). *Theory of fun for game design.* New York, NY: Paraglyph Press.

Kreimeier, B. (2002). *The case for game design patterns.* Retrieved November 8, 2011, from http://www.gamasutra.com/features/20020313/kreimeier_01.htm

Lyardet, D., Rossi, G., & Schwabe, D. (1998). Using design patterns in educational multimedia applications. In *Proceedings of ED-MEDIA 1998.* Freiburg, Germany: ED-MEDIA.

Padilla Zea, N. (2011). *Methodology for the design of educational video games on architecture for the analysis of collaborative learning.* (Doctoral Dissertation). Granada University. Granada, Spain.

Padilla Zea, N., González Sánchez, J. L., Gutiérrez, F. L., Cabrera, M. J., & Paderewski, P. (2009). Design of educational multiplayer videogames: A vision from collaborative learning. *Advances in Engineering Software, 40*(12), 1251–1260. doi:10.1016/j.advengsoft.2009.01.023

Parker, A. (2003). Identifying predictors of academic persistence in distance education. *Journal of the United States Distance Learning Association, 17*(1), 55–62.

Prensky, M. (2001). *Digital game-based learning.* New York, NY: McGraw-Hill.

Rollings, A., & Adams, E. (2003). *Andrew Rollings and Ernest Adams on game design.* Indianapolis, IN: New Riders.

Schell, J. (2008). *The art of game design: A book of lenses.* Burlington, MA: Morgan Kaufmann Publishers.

Smith, H. (2002). Systemic level design for emergent gameplay. In *Proceedings of the Game Developers Conference 2002.* Retrieved November 8, 2011, from http://www.gamasutra.com/features/slides/smith/index.htm

Smith, H. (2003). Orthogonal unit differentiation. In *Proceedings of the Game Developers Conference 2003.* Retrieved November 8, 2011, from http://www.planetdeusex.com/witchboy/gdc03_OUD.ppt

Section 2
Human and Social Factors in Game-Based Learning

Chapter 6
Beauty or the Beast:
Importance of the Attraction of Educational Games

Geertje Bekebrede
Delft University of Technology, The Netherlands

Harald Warmelink
Delft University of Technology, The Netherlands

Casper Harteveld
Delft University of Technology, The Netherlands

Sebastiaan Meijer
Delft University of Technology, The Netherlands

ABSTRACT

Educational games are often less attractive than entertainment games in visuals, gameplay, and other aspects, but do we need entertainment-level beauties in our education or are beasts sufficient? To identify the importance of attraction for educational games, the authors offer the results of a comparative analysis of five educational games used and evaluated from 2005-2010 (N=754). They operationalized attraction through statements in which players were asked to rate the games' visual, gameplay, and user interface attractiveness. While some scholars argue that for game-based education to become successful, educational games need to be visually more attractive, the results of the analysis show the opposite. For educational games, attraction is of relatively low importance. The authors further found that gameplay is the most important aspect of attraction and visuals the least. These results contribute to the debate amongst designers and educators on what priorities to set when considering game-based education.

INTRODUCTION

The "beauty" of a game is difficult to judge. It is subjective, for sure, but it can even be questioned whether it is possible to capture the beauty of a game in words. This problem goes beyond games. It is applicable to any form of art, from movies to music. Just as it is hard to explain why the *Mona Lisa* is such a beautiful painting, it is similarly hard to tell why *Angry Birds* is a beautiful game. Theories of design and arts help to analyze aspects of the beauty after the fact of creation (and sometimes centuries beyond), but never fully capture the emotional aspects of getting involved with the aesthetic values of an artifact.

While this difficulty exists, in the entertainment game industry an extensive reviewing practice

DOI: 10.4018/978-1-4666-1987-6.ch006

has come into being, in which games are judged by several quality criteria. Criteria concern for example graphics, gameplay, and audio. The eventual judgment is often if not always represented numerically, in the form of a percentage or a number ranging from one to five or one to ten. Such representations not only express the feeling a reviewer has about a game, it also facilitates comparisons between games. Although one should certainly be careful in making any firm statements, ratings suggest that games with high ratings are good games, often stated in the textual evaluation as very beautiful ones. If many reviewers agree on this, the achieved inter-subjectivity essentially suggests this is generally true. For entertainment games, a plethora of portals exist that review games in these manners. Well-known portals are *GameSpot*, *IGN*, and *The Edge Magazine*.

For educational games, such a reviewing practice does not exist. Yet, these types of games have often been blamed for being "ugly." Most early educational games, preferably called "educational software" or "edutainment" by game designers, were considered poor games by the standards of the entertainment industry (Egenfeldt-Nielsen, 2007). In the past decennium we have witnessed a revival of the use of games for serious purposes (Harteveld, 2011), and one of the key ideas of this new movement concerns a closer approximation to the standards of the entertainment industry (see also Sawyer, 2002). Having the right educational content embedded in a game is not believed to be sufficient anymore. The games themselves should also be engaging and immersive, or simply fun.

Aspiring to achieve the quality of entertainment games is admirable, but educational game designers have limited resources, a narrow target group, and an unprofitable business model (if at all) at their disposal. With this in mind, some think that the solution should be sought in repurposing existing entertainment games for education (Van Eck, 2009). While in certain situations this could very well be a solution, in many if not most others a customized game is needed. Considering this problematic situation, the question should be raised to what extent the beauty of an educational game

really matters. The use, purpose, and setting of an educational game is quite different from that of an entertainment game. For educational games, a "beast" of a game might be just as effective as a "beauty." In case beauty matters, it would be useful for educational game designers as well as for the educators selecting games to know what they need to focus on. Prioritization is needed, and thus it would be valuable to know whether certain aspects require more attention than others.

This is an urgent matter. While the attention for game-based education is still rising, and many applications are finding their way into schools and universities, it might turn out not to be sustainable. Creating a game is hard work and requires much investment. While new technologies address this issue by making it easier for users to create games, and profitable business models may arise in the educational market, game-based education will remain an intensive educational method in usage but especially in design. Nobody wants to create a "beast" of a game, but if creating a "beauty" is not feasible and not necessary, why pursue it?

In this chapter our purpose is to determine whether an educational game's attractiveness is of importance, i.e. whether it contributes to the effectiveness of using games in education. Our research question concerned therefore: What are the effects of the attraction of educational games on the educational effectiveness? Since 2005, we have been using and evaluating a variety of digital games in higher education. By comparing game results, we are able to answer our research question and conclude whether game-based education requires beauties or if beasts are sufficient. Before we get to this, we will first explain what we mean by "beauty," what games have been used and evaluated, and how we compared the games.

ATTRACTION DEFINED

To investigate the importance of creating a "beautiful" game in higher education, it should first of all be clear what aspects make a game potentially beautiful. As stressed before, it is quite difficult and very subjective to judge the beauty of a game (or any other artifact). In entertainment game reviews, beauty is also never specified, if even a specification is given at all. Most reviewers speak of "awesome visuals," "slick visuals," or "a great style." This makes it a difficult concept to research.

To avoid the problems of trying to define beauty, we will continue to speak of *attraction* (or attractiveness). While the beauty of something is difficult to disentangle, it is possible to identify aspects that players find attractive in games. By identifying these aspects, it becomes clear what needs to be considered for determining the importance of attraction of educational games. As no reviewing practice exists at the moment for educational games, we decided to find inspiration for defining attraction by looking at the reviewing practices of entertainment games. This choice seemed justified, as entertainment games are seen as a reference point in terms of attraction for educational games.

Generally, three types of practices can be distinguished. The first is to only provide a rating. This practice is used by *The Edge Magazine*. It describes the game and then rates the game from 1 to 10. A second, used by *GameSpot* amongst others, is to provide a rating *and* give a summary with positive and negatives (or loves and hates) about the game. These two practices hardly help us in our efforts to define attraction. The third practice does. This involves rating a number of aspects of the game, next to an overall rating. *IGN* is an example of a game review portal that uses this practice.

No complete agreement exists, however, on what aspects need to be included. Of the seven game review portals we considered (i.e. besides *IGN* this concerned *Game Informer*, *Impulse Gamer*, *GamerReview*, *Videogametalk*, *Game Boyz*, and *Gaming Target*), none of them uses the exact same aspects. Despite this, much overlap still exists. Four aspects are mentioned in at least six of the seven portals: the visuals (or graphics), gameplay, sound (or audio), and replay value.

Other aspects that are mentioned more than once concern playability and presentation.

For our purposes, we decided to focus on three particular aspects, visuals, gameplay, and user interface. The latter is a combination of playability and presentation, as used in the above-mentioned game review portals. In this section, we explain what these aspects are. We also explain why we did not include any of the other aspects, such as sound and replay value.

Visuals

So what attracts players to games? The visuals of a game are mostly highlighted in the entertainment industry but also by players themselves. Both seem to have a never-ending desire for bigger, better, and more graphics. When a new game comes out, it is the first aspect that players will talk about. To give an example, just recently a trailer of the newest game in the *Tombraider* franchise was released. On *GameSpot*, this is what a player said who liked it:

This looks awesome, I'm so glad that Lara looks more realistic and not like a brown haired Barbie doll anymore, it was time for a change – by Eric_Drav3n on June 13, 2011

And this is what a player said who did not like a part of the game:

The fire that defies physics kinda bothers me – allan_delacruz on June 13, 2011

The latter comment also highlights the obsession with realism that players and the industry have, and which is one of the driving forces behind the development of computer technology. Many players and designers want their games to be as realistic as possible. Water needs to look and behave as in the physical world. The same goes for fire, trees, and other features. The Holy Grail would then be the "holodeck" (see also Murray,

1997). This is a technology from the *Star Trek* series, in which complete worlds are simulated in a room. These simulated worlds are not distinguishable from the worlds outside of it. They are very realistic. Currently, the latest realism advances are made on facial gestures (see *L.A. Noire*) and crowd simulation (see *Assassin's Creed*).

However, visuals are not only about looking realistic and showing off the latest technological possibilities. Visuals also include style and art and excelling in this could lead to a visually appealing game by itself. With style, we refer to the type of visuals the game has—what "look" it has. Some look more cartoony, others for instance very abstract. With art, we refer to the quality of the visuals. Whether realistic or not, the artwork of a game, how the game world is visualized, with what colors, detail, and so forth, has an impact on the attractiveness as well.

Many casual or indie games, games that are developed with a small budget, rely especially on style and art to attract players. Also in big entertainment games, it matters. The first comment about the new *Tombraider* game indicates that the player not only finds the game more realistic, he also likes the new style of it.

Gameplay

While the industry, players, and certain scholars are very much concerned with visuals, others like to de-emphasize its importance to games (Dormans, 2012; Juul, 2005; Poole, 2000). They like to point out that games are more about rules and interaction. In addition, if visuals are so important, what explains the success of card and board games and certain digital games, such as *Tetris* and more recently *Angry Birds*? These games do not show off the latest visual capabilities; they are "just" fun to play.

Quite elucidating is also that players tend to ignore the visuals the longer they play a game. A great example concerns players who play 3D shooters, such as *Counter-Strike* (Retaux &

Rouchier, 2002). They tend to lower the visuals, by adjusting the settings, to be able to have a faster frame rate. They are more focused on how they interact with the rules than with the game's fictional world (see also Juul, 2005).

This means visuals are not the only aspect that attracts players to games. It may sometimes lure players in, but it is not what keeps them playing. We tend to call this other attractive aspect *gameplay*. Like beauty, gameplay is difficult to define (Harteveld, 2011). It concerns how the game is played. More specifically, it is a combination of the challenges offered by the game, the player's options to deal with these, the player's choices, and the rules that determine what happens next. Salen and Zimmerman called this a "system of experience that always includes some kind of sensory input, player output, and internal player cognition" (2004, p. 316). Some players referred to the importance of this attraction aspect next to visuals in their comments about the upcoming *Tombraider* game:

It's about time they revamped Tomb Raider ... It looks awesome. Hope the gameplay is at par with the visuals – by Lethal Intake on June 18, 2011

Therefore, when can we then talk of *good* gameplay? For this, we could turn to the well-known theory of flow (Csikszentmihalyi, 1991). If a player is continuously involved in the system of experience it offers, the player will find him-/herself loosing track of time and looking back at play as "fun." According to Csikszentmihalyi, this is the result of being in a state of flow: a quite positive mental state caused by the system of experience not being too hard, nor too easy. It was just right. The player was challenged enough without feeling incompetent.

Something else of importance is what Sid Meier, designer of *Civilization* and many other games classic games, said about good gameplay (Rollings & Morris, 2004, p. 38). According to him, games need to provide for "a series of interesting choices." With this, he meant that players should be able to make a difference in the game environment and not know upfront what choice they should make. In other words, a game needs to be interactive and encompass uncertainty (Harteveld, 2011). Overall, for good gameplay to occur, a game should put players into a state of flow and provide interesting choices.

User Interface

Yet an engaging system of experience is arguably not the only determinant of good gameplay. How a player is able to deal with a game's challenges and its outcomes is not only dependent on how these challenges and possible outcomes have been defined and coded into a game. The way the player interacts with the system of experience is arguably just as important. Put most simply, the way a player can actually interact with the game world and its system of experience is also very important for a player to be attracted to it.

While in the game review portals this is referred to as "presentation" or "playability," in game design this is often referred to as user interface design. While for analog games, this is about what and how paraphernalia are used (Meijer, 2009); for digital games, this facet of designing a game pertains to how the player actually uses the hard- and software. For example, it is about whether the game's hardware controls work intuitively or whether the game's visual user interface is intuitive enough, such as the positioning of interaction buttons. This has arguably an important impact on a game's attractiveness next to visuals and gameplay as well.

We consider user interface a separate aspect of attractiveness. However, as suggested above, one could also consider it an integral part of designing a game's system of experience. Without a hard-/software user interface that players would deem intuitive, the players would find it much harder to actually learn and interact with the game's system of experience. Imaging playing *Tetris* where the

arrow buttons are reversed. The arrow button pointing upwards now actually leads a brick to fall down to the floor. This is hardly intuitive and, more importantly, makes it much harder for a player to actually engage with the system of experience, i.e. the act of observing a brick, figuring out where to put it, and then positioning it accordingly. This integration possibility is probably why some of the game review portals have not included this aspect as much as any of the others.

Other Aspects?

We realize that other aspects of attractiveness could be defined and taken into account. One obvious other aspect of attractiveness, and frequently mentioned by the game review portals, is sound. Sound plays an important role in games as it can further immerse the player into the game world and its system of experience (see also Schuurink, Houtkamp, & Toet, 2008). Indeed, we do not want to suggest that any other possible aspect of attractiveness (sound or otherwise) is insignificant. In this chapter, we choose to focus solely on the aforementioned three key aspects of attractiveness for two reasons. Firstly, it is a simple matter of demarcation. The choice keeps our analysis and hence this chapter palpable. By focusing "only" on the aforementioned three elements of attractiveness we are able to rigorously test whether they generally have an effect on a game's deemed effectiveness.

Secondly, it is a matter of appropriateness. As explained in the next section, the educational games we apply in our analysis have no or only very limited sound design. In the games where sound was incorporated, the sounds were actually brief sound effects integrated into the game's user interface. Put simply, the sounds encompassed audible button effects appropriate for the button's action (e.g. sound effects for acknowledgement, cancellation, construction, demolition, etc.). As such, the sounds were "merely" meant to increase the intuitiveness of the game's user interface. In addition, some entertainment game value, such as replay value, simply not appropriate to many educational games. The games we used were only applied once and so replay value does not play a role. Thus, given the nature of the games we have selected for our analysis, it is most appropriate to focus solely on visual, gameplay and user interface attractiveness.

Having explained our choice for defining a game's attractiveness, we can move on to explaining how we then actually test its effects on the students' opinions about the game's effectiveness. In the following section, we explain the five educational games we analyzed by describing their main topic and learning goals, as well as how they could be scored on visual, gameplay and user interface attractiveness from a designer's perspective.

EDUCATIONAL GAMES IN HIGHER EDUCATION

From 2005 onwards most game sessions in which Delft University of Technology (DUT) was involved, have been evaluated with a standard questionnaire (see Bekebrede, 2010). In total, eight different types of digital games have been evaluated this way and the database includes already more than 1,500 participants. Two games, one about water management (*Water Game*, Tygron Serious Gaming, 2011), another about railway station management (*SprintCity*, Vereniging Deltametropool, 2011), were omitted for the purposes of this chapter. They were not used in higher education but only in professional settings. Some of the included games were deployed in professional settings as well. The data from these sessions have also been omitted from the analysis.

A third game named *Cyberdam* (Stichting RechtenOnline, 2011) was solely used in higher education. *Cyberdam* is actually a "frame game" (Leigh & Kinder, 1999; Thiagi Inc., 1999) that has been adapted and repurposed numerous times at several educational institutes in the Netherlands

and beyond (Warmelink & Mayer, 2009). Unfortunately, the standard questionnaire was adapted for this specific game in ways that it became unsuitable for comparison with the other games on attraction. Because of its clear visual non-attractiveness (or ugliness), this game remains interesting and we will discuss it in the discussion section at the end of this chapter.

In this secion we describe the five games that we included into our analysis: *Ventum Online* (CPS – TU-Delft Centre for Serious Gaming, 2011c), *Sim-MV2* and its twin brother *SimPort-MV2* (CPS – TU-Delft Centre for Serious Gaming, 2011b), *Construct-IT* (CPS – TU-Delft Centre for Serious Gaming, 2011a), and *Sharkworld* (RANJ Serious Games, 2011). Except for *Sharkworld*, which was developed by Ranj Serious Games, all other games were developed by DUT in collaboration with Tygron Serious Gaming. Researchers at DUT were responsible for content and game design. Visual design and programming were done by Tygron Serious Gaming. For Ventum Online another company called IJsfontein was involved. They took care of the visuals. All games are played on a PC with a keyboard and mouse.

In addition, and again except for *Sharkworld*, the setup and procedure of the games are much alike. Typically, the games are played with 20 to 40 students in one large room. Students play in groups and have one or more laptops at their disposal, on which they can play the game. As all students play the game in the same room, the games do not only take place behind the laptop screens. Within and between groups face-to-face communication takes place and other physical paraphernalia, such as drawing boards, are also available. The games are facilitated by two to three teachers, who take up a role in the game as well and can intervene when needed. Each game is divided into several (iterative) rounds or stages, and in between and at the end an extensive debriefing is led by the teachers. In the debriefing, the teachers ask the students to reflect on their experiences. The entire process of gameplay and debriefing lasts one whole day (7-8 hours).

In describing the games more specifically, we start with an introduction of what the goal is *within* and *of* the game, i.e. what players need to do in the game and what they should learn from the game. After that, we describe gameplay, visuals, and user interface. The order in which we present these games is based on their visual extensiveness. As game designers, we consider *Ventum Online* to be the visually least extensive game, and *Sharkworld* the most extensive.

Ventum Online

In the game *Ventum Online,* players form a consortium of four companies with the goal of designing and building an offshore wind farm. A wind farm is an area encompassing numerous power-generating windmills. The learning purpose of the game is to let players practice managing a large engineering project where several stakeholders with different interests are involved. Oftentimes three different consortia are formed in a single game session. Up to three students play one stakeholder within each consortium. During the debriefing, differences and similarities are discussed between the consortia.

The gameplay can be described in two ways. First, the game offers five different screens that represent five different stages of the game. In the first "Instruction" screen, players can find technical and organizational information about the project; in the second "Forming a consortium" screen, players can work on what the consortium feels are the intentions of the project and the (financial, legal, communication) rules under which the stakeholders need to collaborate; in the third "Tender" screen, players can make choices concerning the technical design of the wind farm, budget, and time; in the fourth "Designing the wind farm" screen, players finalize their technical design choices; and finally, in the fifth "Test report" screen, players can view results from the tests of their preliminary technical designs. The game ends when all five stages have been processed.

The second most important element of gameplay concerns how players relate to and interact with each other. A consortium consists of four stakeholders: a holding company and three technical companies that can each provide the resources and expertise required for building the wind farm (i.e., the foundations, tower, and rotor blades). Thus, each stakeholder has its own information to share and input to provide. Aside from communicating face-to-face, players can also use an in-game messaging system, allowing them to share specific game data as well. During the game, the consortium is further fed with market news and feedback from the government (played by the course teacher and/or game facilitator) concerning the consortium's proposed tender. To make sure players interact and come to decisions, they play under time pressure.

The game's visuals are relatively simple. It is basically a website designed with Adobe Flash. As screenshot 1 shows, in terms of visuals the game encompasses above-all tables and input fields, some simple images with in most cases an esthetic purpose only, and some graphs with a more substantive purpose. While simple, the visuals are colorfully designed (though mostly in different shades of green, unsurprisingly) and the overall style is very consistent, as shown in Figure 1.

The user interface consists of four main parts, as Figure 1 also shows. Of course, the game's user interface depends strongly on both gameplay and visuals. At the top, users find six buttons. The first five pertain to the aforementioned five stages of the game. The sixth button is the game's end screen. It shows the results of the consortium (e.g., the technical and financial performance of the project) at the end of the game. On the left, players see stage-specific information. On the top right, players have stage-specific interaction possibilities. Finally, on the bottom right players can read market news and use the internal messaging system.

Figure 1. Screenshot of ventum online

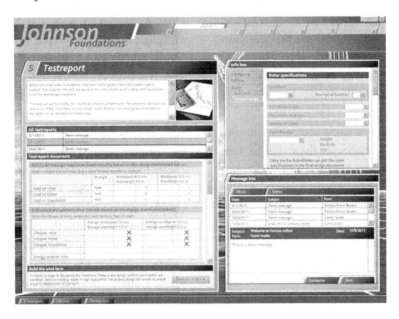

Sim-MV2

In the game *Sim-MV2,* players are employees of the Port of Rotterdam (PoR) responsible for designing, building, and exploiting a new port area called Second Maasvlakte. A group of up to six students play one instantiation of the game. Within each group, each player takes up one of the following roles: General Director, Commercial Director, Director of Infrastructure and Management. Similarly to *Ventum Online*, the game allows players to practice managing a large engineering project where multiple stakeholders are involved. It also allows players to explore possible design strategies for the new port area and the consequences of those strategies. As such, the game is also meant to let players explicitly experience the complexity and uncertainty that comes with doing such a large engineering project.

Gameplay can again be described in two ways. Like *Ventum Online*, gameplay is based on a number of different activities. In the case of *Sim-MV2* it is governed by three activities. In the first "Strategy" activity, players decide on the project's strategy. For instance, players may want

to immediately start contacting and/or contracting clients for the port area when the building starts, or they may want to wait to see which clients get in touch with them. In the "Building" activity, the players start building the port area, which entails land reclamation, basic infrastructure development (roads and rails), and plot allocation. The latter consists firstly of generally designating certain types of clients (e.g. logistical, natural resource refinement) and secondly of actually designating the specific clients that the company manages to contract. In the "Negotiation" activity, players can get in touch with potential clients, negotiate terms, and finalize contracts. Unlike *Ventum Online*, players starts with defining the strategy after that the simulation time starts and they can start building and negotiating.

As this description of gameplay activities already suggest, the amount of possibilities and decisions for the port area project is quite high. This is where the second element of gameplay comes in. Like in *Ventum Online*, this element pertains how players relate to and interact with each other. The aforementioned game roles each have quite a lot of work to do. Thus, players need to divide roles among themselves and work in parallel on them. The fact that each role has its own laptop on which the game is run supports this division of labor. Moreover, players work under time pressure. They need to have an up-and-running port area within 30 years, while the game operates at up to 10 minutes per year.

Again, the game's visuals are quite simple, though slightly more elaborate than *Ventum Online*. Visuals consist mostly of tables and input fields, even though they have been again colorfully designed. The game also includes graphs that have a substantive purpose (e.g. customer satisfaction and financial performance over the years). The biggest visual difference with *Ventum Online* is that *Sim-MV2* has a top-down, two-dimensionally and dynamic visual display of the new port area. The visual display has a substantive purpose as it is based on the decisions players have made and the players have to use it when allocating plots.

Conceptually, the user interface is also similar to *Ventum Online* (see Figure 2). Like the latter, *Sim-MV2* has a top bar with several buttons that relate to the game's stages. On the left players are offered information and interaction possibilities dependent on the stage they are in. In the Building and Negotiation activities, players see the visual display of the port area. On the right, players are presented with the choices they can make within the chosen stage, e.g. choices in building packages or clients to contact. Finally, a bottom bar shows some further information, i.e. market news, financial state of the company, and overall customer satisfaction.

SimPort-MV2

In 2006, work started on an upgrade of *Sim-MV2* to *SimPort-MV2*. The new version had the same in-game and learning goals. In this upgrade, the actual PoR organization was involved, leading to a slight change in content and gameplay. However, the basic structure of gameplay–the three activities and division of labor–did not change.

Visually the game's changes were most extensive. The game's visuals still consists of the aforementioned elements, i.e. the tables, input fields, and graphs, as well as a two-dimensional and dynamic visual display of the port area. Yet another element was added. A three-dimensionally rendered and dynamic visual display of the port area also became available. Upon opening the two-dimensional visual display, players could zoom in upon which the three-dimensional display would show (see Figure 2). This way players could more clearly see the consequences of their design choices within the port area. Additionally, the menus received a facelift. The design looks sharper, cleaner, more crisp, and above all, more professional. This version was not only developed for use in education, it also had to be used to train professionals of the PoR. These visual changes made *SimPort-MV2* look and feel more as a simulation, while *Sim-MV2* looks and feels more as a game.

In terms of user interface, the game also differs from its predecessor and especially in the drawing of the clients in the map. The drawing was one of the unclear elements of Sim-MV2 and one of the reasons to redesign the game. In SimPort-MV2 players click on the area to define the clients space. Yet, unlike the two-dimensional display, the three-dimensional display did not offer any further interaction possibilities. It served only an informational purpose, rendering the actual change in user interface minimal.

Construct-IT

In *Construct-IT* groups of up to three students take up the role of one of the stakeholders who are together responsible for re-designing and re-constructing an existing port area, this time the port of Scheveningen near The Hague. Stakeholders concern the municipality of The Hague and companies with residential, commercial, cultural, and recreational interests. Its learning purpose is similar to the other games in the sense that

Figure 2. Screenshot of SimPort-MV2

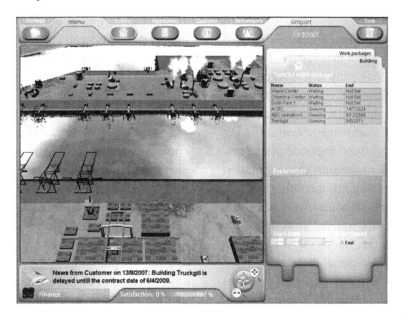

the players have to experience the complexity of working together with different stakeholders. However, compared with the first it is much less focused on technical complexity and more on the negotiation between different actors. With both it differs in the type of stakeholders involved. The stakeholders in *Construct-IT* diverge in interests much more; they are even conflicting, while in the other games, the participants are part of a similar company or consortium. This makes the social complexity somewhat larger. The game was based on the game engine and code framework of *SimPort-MV2* to allow for rapid development. Since *SimPort-MV2*'s engine and code structure formed the basis of *Construct-IT*, the game's visuals and user interface were quite identical to *SimPort-MV2*. It makes use of the same screen layout and the same three-dimensionally rendered and dynamic visual display of the port area. The visuals look only a bit more updated, making this a slight improvement over its source of inspiration.

In terms of gameplay, differences become more apparent. Basically, players now only have to come to an agreement about how they are going to re-design the port area. To achieve this, the game is divided into three stages. In the first stage players decide on a project setup and col-

laboration strategy, just like in *Sim(Port)-MV2*. However, in the subsequent iterative stages of design and negotiation, players need to take the wishes of the other stakeholders into account in order to get the general and their own goals realized. These wishes are defined in the location, type, and amount of new housing, the location, size, and purpose of the industry and shopping areas, and the preservation of historical valuable locations and artifacts, within the new port area. Trade-offs have to be made, as only a limited budget is available. The municipality takes the lead in the negotiation between the stakeholders to get agreement on the re-design and planning of the port area. This can be done by having a general meeting, chaired by the municipality. Also agreements between two or three stakeholders can be possible, which will affect the general process arranged by the municipality. The game ends when all stakeholders have agreed about the complete re-design and planning of the port.

Due to budget and time limitations, the game was released without any thorough testing. As a result, the game still has some minor bugs and these may have a detrimental effect on the game's experience.

Sharkworld

In the game *Sharkworld* (see Figure 3), players take on the role of project manager working for a Dutch installation company that is responsible for converting a former Olympic location in China into a shark aquarium. The game allows players to practice project management skills, i.e. decision-making while working under time pressure and dealing with uncertainty (having limited experience, experiencing an unfamiliar culture, obtaining ambiguous information). Unlike the other games, this game was not customized for education at DUT. In fact, its original purpose was to make students in vocational technical schools enthusiastic about being a project manager. Due to its success, the game found a widespread use. Aside from universities such as DUT, even some consultancy firms started to use the game in their training programs (Harteveld, Bekebrede, Lo, Plomber, & Jordaan, 2011).

Furthermore, unlike the previous games, the game is single-player and completely computerized. Thus, the game can be played at the students' own discretion, both in terms of time and place. Players take five days to play the game. During those five days, play consists of interacting with the game software on a computer with Internet connection as well as several other forms of interaction. Players can be called or sent text messages on their mobile phone, or they can be e-mailed.

Gameplay effectively consists of making decisions about certain questions and challenges that the game raises by selecting one of a number of choices. To aid the player in making these decisions, information about the actual project, the involved stakeholders, or Chinese culture is available. The decisions made have an influence on how the project unfolds and on the performance criteria. Success is measured on hard project management criteria, like planning, budget, and quality, but on softer criteria as well. Performance also depends on the satisfaction of the project team, the client, and the player's boss.

Of all games, this game is visually the richest. Its main screen looks like a Flash-based interactive website, much like the other games, and it also uses graphs, tables, and other managerial information schemes. Yet the game makes extensive use of video footage with real-world actors (see Figure 3). Although some of the footage is fixed, others depend on the decisions players make. For example, if players decide to fire an employee,

Figure 3. Screenshot of Sharkworld

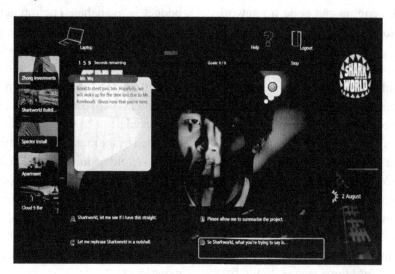

they will get to see different footage than if they decided otherwise.

As to the user interface, the main game screen displays the questions or challenges in the center of the screen and the possible choices for decisions below them. Players can change location by selecting one of the available locations on the left side of the screen. A top bar offers several general game functions (see Figure 3) and access to the player's laptop, which has information about the project. Aside from general functions such as a help and logout icon, the rest of the screen offers important information, such as the available time to answer a question and the goals reached within the game.

RETROSPECTIVE DATA ANALYSIS

To understand the importance of attraction, we wanted to look back at the data of the five selected games we just described. Each of these games has been evaluated with a standard pre- and post-questionnaire. The standard pre-questionnaire includes variables on the background of the participants (e.g. age, gender, game experience), attitudes towards games and the subject at hand, and expectations of the game. The standard post-questionnaire asks for students' judgments about game use and quality, as well as what they have learned. The questionnaires were taken before the start of the game session and at the end. We used PASW Statistics 18 (formerly known as SPSS) to analyze the results.

Before we get to the results, in this section we describe how we used the data for the purposes outlined in this chapter. We found five statements in the standard post-questionnaire of relevance and we will elaborate on the use of these below. Each statement is assessed with a 5-point Likert scale (from totally disagree to totally agree). After that, we will provide some more context of the use of these games, as these could lead to possible biases.

Attraction and Effectiveness Variables

Earlier we defined attraction into three aspects: visuals, gameplay, and user interface. Each aspect contributes to what players find attractive in a game and is considered a predictor variable in our analysis to determine the importance of attraction of educational games. With visuals this is about the style and art of a game, how the game looks. This could be very realistic, but it does not need to be. For good gameplay, players need to get into a flow and should be offered interesting challenges. Finally, with the user interface we refer foremost to having a clear and intuitive interaction with the game's hard- and software. We found three statements, one for each aspect, that reflect these aspects. They are mentioned in Table 1.

It is important to emphasize that the statements have been chosen in retrospect. This means that they have not been designed for the research purpose as outlined in this chapter. If they would have been, the statements would have been phrased differently and more variables would have been considered. At present, each concept is only represented by a single variable, which is statistically not very strong. Furthermore, by no means do the statements fully represent the theoretical aspects of attraction. For example, user interface encompasses much more than navigation and visuals much more than only style attributes. Despite these limitations, with this dataset we are still able to give a clear indication about what the importance is of attraction. As the topic is highly relevant to game-based education, such an indication is very valuable.

To determine the effects of the attraction variables on the effectiveness of the games, we took two other statements that we used as outcome variables for the success of an educational game. Both statement and their variables are also mentioned in Table 1. The first variable is "learning." Educational games are supposed to be learned from and they serve their purpose especially well

Table 1. Overview of the considered variables and their statements

Variable	Statement
Visuals (predictor)	Style attributes used on the computer screens are attractive and suitably designed.
User interface (predictor)	Navigation through the user screens (interfaces) was logical and easy to use.
Gameplay (predictor)	The simulation game was built up in an interesting and motivating way.
Learning (outcome)	Working on this simulation game improved my learning process.
Fun (outcome)	I had fun working on this simulation game.

when it helped the students in understanding the course material. For this reason, a statement on the post-questionnaire was included about to what extent playing the game helped them in their learning process.

Another variable we used to determine a game's success concerns "fun." Although fun is a bit of a contested term, without doubt it plays an important role in playing games (Harteveld, 2011). This is definitely true for entertainment games but also for educational games. It is often thought of as an important contributor to learning (Koster, 2005) and a moderate correlation has been found between learning and fun for games (Bekebrede, 2010). As game attraction is often related to fun, this variable proofs an additional check to the results on the learning variable and will provide for further evidence on what designers and educators need to prioritize on.

As regards to our research purpose, we formulated two hypotheses. The first hypothesis concerns:

H_1 = An educational game's attractiveness has no influence on learning.

We base this on the suggestion that students know very well that the game has an educational purpose and should be judged as such. They know how to separate the "triple A" entertainment games that they play at home and the ones they play at school. Players are more intelligent than what most scholars assume (see also Sicart, 2009). Even when asked if they find the game attractive, they will probably consider the educational context they play it in rather than an entertainment context.

Of course, when players are asked to judge educational games outside their context, then it becomes different. In such cases, attraction will probably have a determining role. This is also the reason why scholars may think that the large pile of educational games are too unattractive. They base this on the judgment of players who have not played this as part of a curriculum.

Our second hypothesis relates to the hierarchy in attraction. For similar reasons, we think that students value visuals as less important than user interface and gameplay. Visuals are probably contributing to the experience, but if they want to go for visuals, they would rather play an entertainment game, not some educational game at school.

H_2 = Visual attractiveness is of less importance than user interface and gameplay attractiveness when playing educational games.

Possible Biases

In understanding and interpreting the results of our study, we think it is important to highlight some possible biases that may influence the outcomes presented in this chapter. To begin with, most participants were students at DUT (91%). Others were exchange students or students from the nearby Erasmus University Rotterdam, where once a session of *Ventum Online* was played. Due to a large male population at the university, the data reflects a bias in gender. Of all 754 participants, 81% is male. Other biases might stem from the year the game was played in, the participants' age, and the course it was used in. An overview of this variety is provided in Table 2, along with the participant numbers.

The year in which a game was played might be a bias, because every year game technology improves significantly. The games in our study did not. This means that students in later years may have had higher expectations and standards regarding what they consider attractive and found the games not up to par with what they play at home. In earlier years, this may have been less of an issue.

The year could matter for another reason as well. Many scholars believe that newer generations who have grown up with digital games have developed certain learning and social interaction styles that affect how they generally wish to work, learn and be educated (see e.g. Beck & Wade, 2004, 2006; Prensky, 2001, 2006; Tapscott, 1998, 2008; Veen & Vrakking, 2006). Different terms are used to denote this new generation, e.g. the Net Generation, Digital Natives, Homo Zappiens, or simply the Game Generation. It might well be that we were dealing with a Game Generation inherently more positive about the use of games in education. However, in previous research we found that such a possible "generation" does not exist, at least not within this dataset (Bekebrede, Warmelink, & Mayer, 2011).

In a similar vein, age could make a difference as well. Younger students may be more attracted by visuals; older students by content. By using an ANOVA analysis, we found a significant difference between the participants' ages of *Sharkworld* and *Sim-MV2* and the other games, $F(4, 540)=8.60$, $p<.001$. This difference is explainable, because *Sim-MV2* and *Sharkworld* were respectively largely and solely used in a bachelors course. All other games were used in masters courses.

This difference in age appears to matter, because the participants of *Sim-MV2* and *Sharkworld* indicated that they on average play more digital games than all others at home, just for fun. The amount of time playing entertainment games is thus higher for bachelors students than masters students. The difference is, however, only really significant in comparison to the participants of *Ventum Online*.

As for the courses, they differ within and between some of the games. In addition, most of the games were applied in courses for students in Policy Analysis (PA), the others for students in Civil Engineering (CE) or Inter-Faculty students (IF). Despite these differences, the use of the game has been largely the same: to provide an experience and understanding of real-world complexity. In all instances, the games were used

Table 2. Overview of the basic characteristics of the games

Game	Year	Age (M, SD)	Course	Participants (*n*)
Sim-MV2 (S-MV2)	2005; 2006	22.5 (2.5)	Materials and Ecological Engineering (CE); Functional Design (PA)	141
SimPort-MV2 (SP-MV2)	2006-2009	23.5 (3.2)	Functional Design (PA); Ports and Waterways (CE); Politics of Policy Analysis (PA)	165
Ventum Online (VO)	2006-2009	23.8 (2.4)	Materials and Ecological Engineering (CE); Strategic Management of Large Engineering Projects (PA)	360
Construct-IT (C-IT)	2009; 2010	23.9 (2.5)	Process management (IF)	65
Sharkworld (SW)	2010	21.2 (16)	Tools, Skills and Techniques for Consultants (IF)	23

to put the theoretical content of the courses into some perspective. Nevertheless, we are very much aware that the course and type of students may have been an influential factor.

To see whether it matters we looked at whether the results differed amongst participants for *Sim-MV2*, *SimPort-MV2*, and *Ventum Online*. It turns out that differences exist. For *Sim-MV2* and *SimPort-MV2* differences can be attributed to the bachelor group of students. Generally, they were more positive and found it easier to play. For *Ventum Online* there are differences between the Policy Analysis (PA) and Civil Engineering (CE) students. The latter found the game easier and more motivating and indicated to have learned less.

All of this shows that some diversity exists amongst the samples used in the database and that this diversity affects the outcomes of a game experience. Of course, in this chapter it is not our goal to offer a complete analysis of all predictors for determining the effectiveness of an educational game. Thus, for sake of simplicity, we do not take this diversity further into account.

IMPORTANCE OF ATTRACTION

So, regarding our five educational games, did attraction play a meaningful role? We will provide an answer to this and its related questions below. First, we analyze the differences between the selected games. This way we can see to what extent the results match our own preconceived notions of the games' attractiveness. Subsequently, we look into the relationships between the results to be able to accept or reject the hypotheses put forward in the previous section.

Differences Between Games

Due to the ordinal nature of the scales, we applied non-parametric statistics to compare the five games on each of the variables (see Table 1). A Kruskal-Wallis (K-W) test was first conducted to see if differences generally existed. After that, Mann-Whitney tests were performed for posthoc analysis (with a customary Bonferroni correction to control for Type I errors). The results are shown in Table 3. Also visible in this table are the descriptives of each variable per game. For pragmatic reasons we have used means and Standard Deviations (SD). The differences are in some cases quite subtle. The differences would have been even less clear if we would have applied other types of descriptives, such as the median and the interquartile range.

Based on this comparison we ranked the selected games as shown in Table 4. In the table we have also ranked the games on overall attraction. This variable includes the total scores on visual, gameplay, and user interface attractiveness. When developing the rankings, we used the mean statistics offered in Table 3. The game with the highest mean gets the highest ranking, and vice versa. For attraction overall, the scores on the three attraction aspects were summed. The game with the lowest score was ranked first; the game with the highest score was ranked last.

Although generally speaking all games have been judged favorably, differences exist as well. The Kruskal-Wallis test shows significant results on every one of them. While the overall variance differs widely, if we look into the paired differences by performing the Mann-Whitney tests, we find that only a few are really significant. If we look at visual attractiveness, the differences are almost non-existent. Almost, since the best-judged game, *Ventum Online*, outshines the least judged game *Sim-MV2*. Thus, interestingly, although this game was visually extensively upgraded, apparently players did not value this so highly. Visually they seemed content with the old version.

The findings also show that visuals did not account for gameplay. Except for its successor, *Sim-MV2* performed better in terms of gameplay than all other games. Its successor also performed well, but unlike its predecessor it did not perform better than *Construct-IT*, a derivative from this

Table 3. The descriptives per game and the statistical results on their differences

Variable	S-MV2 Mean (SD)	SP-MV2 Mean (SD)	VO Mean (SD)	C-IT Mean (SD)	SW Mean (SD)	K-W test	Posthoc tests
Visuals	3.61(.67)	3.68(.70)	3.88(.81)	3.84(.92)	3.55(.86)	001	VO > S-MV2
User interface	3.60(.72)	3.53(.94)	3.74(.83)	3.28(.11)	3.68(1.2)	.011	VO > C-IT
Gameplay	4.32(.54)	4.09(.68)	3.52(.81)	3.92(.78)	3.55(.86)	< .001	S-MV2 > VO/C-IT/SW SP-MV2 > VO/SW
Learning	3.89(.71)	3.63(.70)	3.61(.85)	3.56(.83)	3.41(.96)	.008	S-MV2 > VO
Fun	4.16(.59)	4.13(.74)	3.68(.81)	3.98(.67)	3.45(.86)	< .001	S-MV2/SP-MV2 > VO/SW

game. Furthermore, *Sim-MV2* had the highest scores on learning and fun, indicating that visual attractiveness might not matter that much.

With regards to learning, we only found a significant difference between *Sim-MV2* and *Ventum Online*. This is an interesting result, because the latter game performs best on two of the attraction variables, i.e. visual and user interface attractiveness. On average, *Ventum Online* was not judged the worst, yet it was the only one that scored significantly poorer than *Sim-MV2*. *Sim-MV2* probably did not outperform the other relatively lower performing games *Construct-IT* and *Sharkworld* due to the relatively small sample sizes of these latter games.

With regards to fun, it seems that gameplay is a driving force. *Sim-MV2* as well as *SimPort-MV2* outperform *Ventum Online* as well as *Sharkworld*. The reason why *Sharkworld* may have been deemed less fun (and scored lower on learning) is probably due to its easiness. Players want to be challenged (see Koster, 2005). This is what

makes games fun. For *Ventum Online* the reverse was true, for at least some players. In this game, players are confronted with the complexity of large-scale engineering projects, in particular the technical complexity of wind farm design. This proved to be very or even overly challenging for particularly policy analysis students.

Construct-IT is an interesting case. In terms of learning and fun it pars with its alternates (*Sim-MV2, SimPort-MV2, Ventum Online*), yet it did not score so well on user interface and gameplay attractiveness. Yet this also does not surprise us too much. The game had some flaws and should have been further tested before it was really used in education.

From this ranking, we can draw two conclusions:

Our preconceived notions of what is considered attractive is completely different from what players judge as attractive. The game we thought to be very attractive, *Sharkworld*, (from all three perspectives) actually ranks lowest. The game we

Table 4. Rankings of the five games on scores for all five variables and on overall attraction

Rank	Visuals	User interface	Gameplay	Learning	Fun	Attraction overall
1.	VO	VO	S-MV2	S-MV2	S-MV2	VO
2.	C-IT	SW	SP-MV2	SP-MV2	SP-MV2	S-MV2
3.	SP-MV2	S-MV2	C-IT	VO	C-IT	SP-MV2
4.	S-MV2	SP-MV2	SW	C-IT	VO	C-IT
5.	SW	C-IT	VO	SW	SW	SW

thought would rank lowest, *Ventum Online*, was a clear winner.

Attraction seems not a strong determinant for fun and learning. The best performing game on visual and user interface attractiveness scored average on these variables.

To solidify these findings we look into the relationships between the variables.

Relationships Between Variables

To accept or reject our hypotheses about the importance of attraction and the order of importance of the attraction aspects, we created two models using multinomial logistic regression analyses. To construct each model we used a backward stepwise method and treated the three attractiveness variables as main predictors for the two outcome variables. Given our interest in exploring the potential effects of any of these variables, and in developing a model rather than testing an existing one, this method of logistic regression is arguably best (Field, 2009). For both models, we thus treated the visual, gameplay, and user interface attractiveness statements as covariates with main effects. For the first model, the general learning statement concerned the outcome variable, while for the second this was general fun statement. The results of both models are presented in Table 5.

In both models, the visual attractiveness variable was removed. This is a clear indication that for fun as well as learning visual attractiveness do not play a large (direct) role. It is of course still possible that visual attractiveness affects some other variable, which in turn influences perceived learning and/or fun. It could also be that visual attractiveness has an interactive effect on learning and/or fun together with one or more other variables. We have not investigated these possibilities as they go beyond the goal of this book chapter.

The models' test scores (see Table 5) show that both models somewhat fit the actual data. The model chi-squares are quite high, but the Cox and Snell and Nagelkerke scores are not,

indicating that statistically there are indeed further predictors for both outcome variables. Thus, the two remaining covariates user interface and gameplay attractiveness are the most significant of all three, yet they only slightly predict deemed learning and fun.

So what makes an educational game truly fun to play? Moreover, how do we ensure a truly educational experience? Based on just these variables presented here, the results presented in Table 5 show that for fun to occur, students need to deem the game motivating and interesting and its user interface fine. Visual attractiveness plays no role. For learning to occur user interface is clearly a less significant predictor. An interesting and motivating game best ensures a highly valued educational experience.

Looking back at our two hypotheses posed earlier, we thus must reject the first hypothesis. Attraction matters when considering gameplay an aspect of attraction. Gameplay has a moderate effect on how educational games are experienced (fun and educational). However, attraction matters much less than many scholars may have expected. The relative unimportance of especially visual and even user interface attractiveness is something designers and players of educational games should keep in mind.

Thus we can accept the second hypothesis. We can accept the idea that visual attractiveness is of less importance than user interface and gameplay attractiveness when playing educational games. A slight subtle amendment should be made though, as user interface plays a bigger part in deeming an educational game fun than deeming it generally instructive.

DISCUSSION

To analyze the importance of attraction of educational games we have disentangled attraction into three aspects: visuals, user-interface, and gameplay. The first refers to the visuals, style, or

Table 5. Overview of both models. In both models the reference category is 'strongly disagree.'

Choice	Covariates	Learning model χ^2 (8)=113, p<.001, N=630 R^2=.17 (Cox & Snell), .18 (Nagelkerke)			Fun model χ^2 (8)=203, p<.001, N=668 R^2=.26 (Cox & Snell), .29 (Nagelkerke)		
		β	*p*	Exp(β)	B	*p*	Exp(β)
Disagree	Intercept	-2.74	.15		-1.10	.52	
	User interface	.383	.43	1.47	.556	.24	1.74
	Gameplay	1.43	.011	4.19	.400	.44	1.49
Neutral	Intercept	-2.33	.21		-3.83	.026	
	User interface	.239	.62	1.27	1.01	.029	2.73
	Gameplay	1.79	.001	5.96	1.31	.009	3.69
Agree	Intercept	-4.22	.023		-5.93	.001	
	User interface	.394	.41	1.48	1.14	.013	3.14
	Gameplay	2.36	< .001	10.6	2.04	< .001	7.72
Strongly agree	Intercept	-11.9	< .001		-13.85	< .001	
	User interface	.940	.061	2.56	1.49	.002	4.44
	Gameplay	3.32	< .001	27.6	3.39	< .001	29.6

look of the game; the second to how pleasantly the interaction with the computer takes place; and the third is about playing the game itself. This definition was suitable for our purposes, but the concept can be developed and elaborated further. As we noted before, more attraction aspects could be thought of.

For examining the role of these three aspects, we examined our database, consisting of many digital games that have been used and evaluated in higher education. We found a number of variables that expressed statements in line with each of the aspects. As mentioned earlier, this means that no specific research was set up to look into the importance of attraction. Such a specific study may reveal much stronger results, especially since we are now basing the results on only a couple of statements. However, our database consists of a large number of participants, which gives a strong case for the results presented here. A specific study will probably not have the luxury of so many participants, at least not on a short term.

One of the clearest and most revealing results provided in this chapter concerns the relative low importance of visual attractiveness. Even upgrading a game from 2D to 3D purely for the sake of attractiveness has largely no impact. Something else that struck us is that what we consider to be attractive, was not attractive for the students. The students especially praised the looks of one game, *Ventum Online*, which was basically a flash-based website and nothing more. One could argue that overall all of the selected games are quite similar in terms of visuals, thus rendering statistical analyses rather weak. Still, if this were true, one would still expect visual attractiveness to contribute to a fun and instructive experience. This was not the case.

An aspect of attraction that seems to contribute is gameplay. Expressed as the extent to which students found it motivating and interesting to play the game, this aspect contributed moderately to fun as well as learning. This is not a complete surprise. What otherwise explains for the successes of games such as *Tetris* and *Angry Birds*? Although the latter has great visuals as well, it is especially the simple yet very engaging gameplay that attracts players to these games. Also striking is that the game with the highest scores on gameplay, has the highest scores on learning as well as fun. Designers and users of educational games should be paying more attention to this type of attraction than to any other.

Designers and educators should not neglect the last attraction aspect, i.e. user interface. While like visuals it is hardly related to learning, it does contribute slightly to learning and certainly to the fun that players experience. It seems that for learning to occur, players are able to overlook the flaws of a game's user interface, such as *Construct-IT*, but they do take it into account as to the extent they found the experience pleasurable. As fun and learning are moderately related to each other as well, user interface has some indirect effect on learning.

A number of factors could have influenced the results presented here. We already mentioned age and the type of course the students were following as well as the year in which the game was used. The period 2005-2010 might not seem that long, but in the world of games, it is. Consistent with some of our beliefs regarding the influence of the usage year, the game that performed best on learning and fun, *Sim-MV2*, was the one used in the earlier years, 2005 and 2006. Aside from maybe not having too much expectations about playing a game at the university, the students were one of the first to play a digital educational game in the first place and this novelty may have positively influenced their perceptions.

But many more factors could be thought of, such as the teachers involved, the debriefing session at the end of the game, and the group dynamics in each session (Kriz & Hense, 2006). When using games in education, it is hard or even problematic to pinpoint one or two factors that explain a game's success in terms of deemed fun and learning effect. In this regard our study is somewhat limited by not taking all possible factors into account. On the other hand, for our purposes

it was not necessary to do this. We simply wanted to see the importance of attraction in this complex picture of what makes an educational game work.

While other factors could have played a role, we think our findings are trustworthy. We substantiate this by looking at another game that was used in our education: *Cyberdam*. This game was inspired by the Scottish game environment *Ardcalloch* (Mayer, Bekebrede, & Warmelink, 2009) with the aim of using it in Dutch higher education. Similar to *Ardcalloch*, *Cyberdam* is a fictional city used for educating students on the law and policy-making involved in particularly urban reconstruction projects. It has a simple website, consisting of text and a map (see Figure 4). In terms of attraction, this game is *the beast* amongst all other games in our dataset.

Unfortunately, when evaluating this particular game the statements on visual and user interface attractiveness were not used. However, the others were, and from this, we can still get some sense of what a beast like this does in education. In total, we gathered 455 responses. Compared with the other games the students found *Cyberdam* on average less interesting and motivating (M=3.17, SD=.99). They indicated that they learned less from it (M=3.55, SD=.94) and had less fun playing it (M=3.46, SD=.95). While these results are still largely positive, every other game performs significantly better on gameplay and fun, except for *Sharkworld*. This is just as what one would expect.

However, on learning none of the games differ significantly, except for *Sim-MV2*. This is quite shocking. A simple educational game with no attractive features at all performs statistically similar to much more attractive games. Only the best performing game—the beauty—turns out to outperform it. This indicates that much effort should be put into attraction will it significantly make a difference in learning. It also indicates what we have been arguing so far: for educational games, attraction is not that important.

Figure 4. Screenshot of Cyberdam

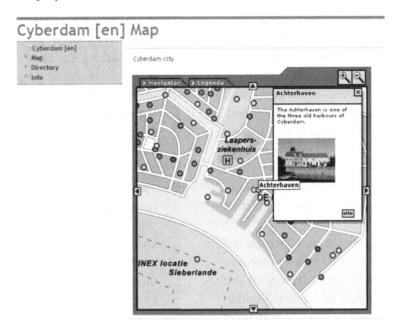

We emphasize that our research concerned the context of *higher* education. It may well be that for other types of education, especially where students are less motivated to learn, attraction will make more of a difference. In general, students in higher education are arguably more intrinsically motivated and are interested in the topics they study. They do not need any extras to make the game more fun and engaging. From our experience, we know that students may find such extras even annoying (Harteveld, et al., 2011).

A final reservation that needs to be made concerns on how the games have been evaluated. The use of Likert-scales have their obvious limitations, with participants tending to agree on statements and also tending to avoid on any of the extremes (i.e. totally disagree or totally agree). However, more important is that they reflect players' judgments and these may have been made with different contexts in mind. In judging for example the visuals, some students may have used other educational software they use as a benchmark and not any of the entertainment games they know, while others may have done the latter. In addition,

students' perception of learning may not reveal what they actually have learned. In addition, it could very well be that they learned the wrong things. In our analysis, we have assumed that each and every one of the games discussed is valid.

CONCLUSION

The purpose behind this chapter was to scientifically scrutinize the extent to which it is important to make digital games in education attractive. Many scholars have been arguing that the digital games used in education are not up to par with the entertainment games. According to them, they should be to make sure students will want to play these games and learn from them. In the entertainment industry, a strong focus is placed on attraction, especially on visuals. As players also learn from entertainment games, the argument goes that educational games should be attractive as well. Our research shows that this is everything but true.

In our research, we looked back at how a selected number of games were experienced by students. The games differ widely in content, form, and attraction. Some of them were in 3D, while others consisted of a simple website. Despite these differences, every one of them can be considered successful for the educational purpose it was used. In fact, with regards to learning, except for one the games do not differ from each other. Even concerning how much fun the students experienced with the games, the results hardly differed. These results prove that for educational games attraction seems unimportant.

Upon further investigation, in which we decomposed attraction into three different aspects, i.e. visuals, gameplay, and user interface, we found that visuals do not contribute anything to learning as well as fun. User interface played a part, but it was a very limited one when it concerned learning. For fun it was certainly relevant, although much less than gameplay. The latter was moderately influential for how much students deemed to have learned and had fun. Consistent with this finding, the game with the highest scores on gameplay also scored highest on learning and fun.

Do these results mean that we should not consider attraction when designing educational games? To this question, we answer with a clear no. Attraction still matters, especially given how we have included gameplay into our definition of attraction. Yet it is just relatively less important than one may think upfront. From our findings, we can give educational game designers and educators the following words of advice:

N1. In using or designing an educational game focus especially on the content and use of the game and not on whether "it looks awesome."

If games are correctly embedded within a course, the students will learn from it–even from a very "ugly" game.

N2. In considering attractive features focus most of all on the gameplay–how the game is played. Having an interesting and motivating experience contributes much more to the educational game experience than other aspects of attraction, such as the visuals and user-interface.

N3. Upon considering visuals, be simple and consistent. The game with the most visual praise had simple visuals yet a consistent style. For some educational games 3D is unavoidable, but when it can be avoided, a nicely designed website could sometimes be much more effective.

Our research has its limitations. It is based on a retrospective data analysis and uses only a few statements to draw conclusions from. Despite all of this, the results clearly indicate that like in our everyday relationships and the *Beauty and the Beast* fairytale, with educational games beauty also comes from within.

REFERENCES

Beck, J. C., & Wade, M. (2004). *Got game: How the gamer generation is reshaping business forever*. Boston, MA: Harvard Business School Press.

Beck, J. C., & Wade, M. (2006). *The kids are alright: How the gamer generation is changing the workplace*. Boston, MA: Harvard Business School Press.

Bekebrede, G. (2010). *Experiencing complexity: A game-based approach for understanding infrastructure systems*. Delft, The Netherlands: Next GenerationInfrastructures Foundation.

Bekebrede, G., Warmelink, H. J. G., & Mayer, I. S. (2011). Reviewing the need for gaming in education to accommodate the net generation. *Computers & Education, 57*(2), 1521–1529. doi:10.1016/j.compedu.2011.02.010

CPS – TU-Delft Centre for Serious Gaming. (2011a). *Construct-IT*. Retrieved July 18, 2011 from http://cps.tbm.tudelft.nl/site/content/construct-it

CPS – TU-Delft Centre for Serious Gaming. (2011b). *Simport – Maasvlakte 2*. Retrieved July 18, 2011 from http://cps.tbm.tudelft.nl/site/content/simport-maasvlakte-2

CPS – TU-Delft Centre for Serious Gaming. (2011c). *Ventum online*. Retrieved July 18, 2011 from http://cps.tbm.tudelft.nl/site/content/ventum-online

Csikszentmihalyi, M. (1991). *Flow: The psychology of optimal experience*. New York, NY: HarperCollins.

Dormans, J. (2011). Beyond iconic simulation. *Simulation & Gaming, 42*(5), 610–631.

Egenfeldt-Nielsen, S. (2007). *Beyond edutainment: The educational potential of computer games*. London, UK: Continuum Press.

Eric_Drav3n, allan_delacruz, & Lethal Intake. (2011, June 13 & 18). *Comments on the stage demo of the newest Tombraider game*. [Online forum comment]. Retrieved July 18, 2011 from http://www.gamespot.com/ps3/action/tombraider-2012/video/6318948/tomb-raider-e3-2011-stage-demo

Field, A. (2009). *Discovering statistics using SPSS* (3rd ed.). London, UK: SAGE.

Harteveld, C. (2011). *Triadic game design: Balancing reality, meaning and play*. London, UK: Springer.

Harteveld, C., Bekebrede, G., Lo, J. C., Plomber, A.-J., & Jordaan, B. (2011). *Make it fun or real: Design dilemmas and their consequences on the learning experience*. Paper presented at ISAGA 2011: Bonds and Bridges. Warsaw, Poland.

Juul, J. (2005). *Half-real: Video games between real rules and fictional worlds*. Cambridge, MA: MIT Press.

Koster, R. (2005). *A theory of fun for game design*. Scottsdale, AZ: Paraglyph Press.

Kriz, W. C., & Hense, J. U. (2006). Theory-oriented for the design of and research in gaming and simulation. *Simulation & Gaming, 37*(2), 268–283. doi:10.1177/1046878106287950

Leigh, E., & Kinder, J. (1999). *Learning through fun and games*. Sydney, Australia: McGraw-Hill.

Mayer, I. S., Bekebrede, G., & Warmelink, H. J. G. (2009). Learning in a virtual world: An introduction . In Warmelink, H. J. G., & Mayer, I. S. (Eds.), *Learning in a Virtual World: Reflections on the Cyberdam Research and Development Project* (pp. 1–22). Nijmegen, The Netherlands: Wolf Legal Publishers.

Meijer, S. (2009). *The organization of transactions: Studying supply networks using gaming simulation*. Wageningen, The Netherlands: Wageningen Academic Publishers.

Murray, J. H. (1997). *Hamlet on the holodeck: The future of narrative in cyberspace*. Cambridge, MA: MIT Press.

Poole, S. (2000). *Trigger happy: The inner life of videogames*. London, UK: Fourth Estate.

Prensky, M. (2001). *Digital game-based learning*. New York, NY: McGraw-Hill.

Prensky, M. (2006). *Don't bother me mom – I'm learning!* St. Paul, MN: Paragon House.

Retaux, X., & Rouchier, J. (2002). Realism vs surprise and coherence: Different aspects of playability in computer games. In *Proceedings of Playing with the Future: Development and Directions in Computer Gaming*. Manchester, UK: Centre for Research on Innovation and Competition.

Rollings, A., & Morris, D. (2004). *Game architecture and design: A new edition*. Indianapolis, IN: New Riders Publishing.

Salen, K., & Zimmerman, E. (2004). *Rules of play: Game design fundamentals*. Cambridge, MA: MIT Press.

Sawyer, B. (2002). *Serious games: Improving public policy through game-based learning and simulation*. Washington, DC: Woodrow Wilson International Center for Scholars.

Schuurink, E., Houtkamp, J., & Toet, A. (2008). Engagement and EMG in serious gaming: Experimenting with sound and dynamics in the levee patroller training game. *Lecture Notes in Computer Science, 5294*, 139–149. doi:10.1007/978-3-540-88322-7_14

Serious Games, R. A. N. J. (2011). *Sharkworld – A project management game*. Retrieved July 18, 2011 from http://www.sharkworldgame.com/index.php

Sicart, M. (2009). *The ethics of computer games*. Cambridge, MA: MIT Press.

Stichting RechtenOnline. (2011). *Welkom bij de cyberdam user group*. Retrieved July 18, 2011 from http://www.cyberdam.nl/

Tapscott, D. (1998). *Growing up digital: The rise of the net generation*. New York, NY: McGraw-Hill.

Tapscott, D. (2008). *Grown up digital: How the net generation is changing your world*. New York, NY: McGraw-Hill.

Thiagi Inc. (1999). *Framegame game booklets*. Retrieved July 18, 2011 from http://www.thiagi.com/framegames.html

Van Eck, R. (2009). A guide to integrating cots games in your classroom. In Ferdig, R. E. (Ed.), *Handbook of Research on Effective Electronic Gaming in Education* (pp. 179–199). Hershey, PA: IGI Global. doi:10.4018/978-1-59904-808-6.ch011

Veen, W., & Vrakking, B. (2006). *Homo zappiens: Growing up in a digital age*. London, UK: Network Continuum Education.

Vereniging Deltametropool. (2011). *Project SprintStad*. Retrieved July 18, 2011 from http://www.deltametropool.nl/nl/sprintstad

Warmelink, H., & Mayer, I. (Eds.). (2009). *Learning in a virtual world: Reflections on the cyberdam research and development project*. Nijmegen, The Netherlands: Wolf Legal Publishers.

Chapter 7
Facilitation of Trust in Gaming Situations

Robyn Hromek
The University of Sydney, Australia

ABSTRACT

Games are inherently engaging and, when crafted to do so, provide an experiential, mediated learning space that is effective and fun. This chapter explores game-based learning and the role of the facilitator in optimizing learning. As referees, they make sure games proceed in a fair and orderly manner. As teachers, they look for teachable moments to 'scaffold' learning. As mentors, they debrief what happened to enhance learning and ensure psychological safety. The author reviews the literature and her practice as an educational psychologist to examine therapeutic board games and socio-emotional learning. The Life-Space Interview and Emotional First Aid are put forward as effective debriefing tools. An argument is made for the importance of face-to-face games and attention is drawn to concerns about excessive screen time.

INTRODUCTION

Children of the new millennium grow up in a world of accelerating technology, full of smartphones, laptops, IPods, and a seemingly endless stream of information on the Internet. It is not unusual for tech-savvy kids to multi-task their homework, social media and music. The comment is often made that screen-based media have created a cohort of learners not easily engaged by traditional methods and teachers are looking for new ways to engage students. Young people are looking for meaningful ways of relating to what they are learning, no longer content with traditional 'book learning.' Experience-based learning strategies are finding a place in modern classrooms as teachers use multimedia presenta-

DOI: 10.4018/978-1-4666-1987-6.ch007

tions, role-plays, games, drama, group work, and interactive technologies. Schools are not alone in embracing these approaches. Simulations and games are making an impact on how business, ecology, society, and dental technology, for example, are taught (Castella, et al., 2003; Tsuchiya, 2005; Vahed, 2008). Games have been integral to human culture throughout history as evidenced by ancient philosophies and archeological finds. Essentially, games are a social experience and can be used to teach just about anything and when facilitators guide the learning, a sense of connectedness and trust develops. Games provide a semi-naturalistic space where players can rehearse new skills in a safe environment and facilitators are well placed to monitor the psychological safety of players. Unpredictable learning contexts arise and skilled facilitators use these opportunities to mediate the learning experience. Social competence and emotional resilience are critical in a changing world that relies increasingly on collaborative approaches to learning and the workplace. Children who lack these skills need a safe and engaging forum in which to learn. Establishing rapport can be tricky if young clients are oppositional and do not want the extra attention being provided however playing a game together quickly disarms resistance, especially if they are playing with a small group of peers. Before they know it, they are having fun, talking about the issues, and learning new skills. Therapeutic board games are specifically designed to teach social and emotional skills like anger management, friendships, resilience, helpful thinking, and social problem solving.

The purpose of this chapter is to consider board games as a tool for teaching socio-emotional skills to children and young people and to outline the ways in which facilitation can enhance this process. It looks at the advantages of experience-based learning and how a skilled facilitator can influence outcomes for players within the 'zone of proximal learning.' It also examines the skills, attitudes, and values of effective facilitators with a focus on debriefing emotional crises. While

the focus is on face-to-face board games, other experience-based learning strategies should also benefit from effective facilitation. In this emerging age of the 'e-world,' accessed largely through screens, it is becoming increasingly important for facilitators to alert players to the potential dangers of excessive screen-time. The chapter closes by impressing on players and facilitators the importance of monitoring their physical, psychological, and social wellbeing and not neglect face-to-face social contact.

BACKGROUND

2.1 Experience-Based Learning: A New Paradigm

Until the late 1960s the dominant paradigm for teaching and learning involved information transfer from experts to learners using instructional technologies like books, lectures, and articles, with success most often measured by written examination. While these methods are common in educational settings today, pedagogy has moved on to broader understandings of the teaching and learning process. Cognitive theorists like Vygotsky (1978), Gardner (1999), and Goleman (1996) discuss the social and emotional environment and its impact on learning. Intelligence is now seen as a multi-facetted concept with emotional intelligence emerging as a pivotal factor. This diverse view calls for more complex approaches such as those provided by 'experience-based learning.' Rubens (1999) sees experience-based learning as having potential to address the limitations of traditional paradigms. According to Rubens, the fundamentals of experience-based learning are found in the writings and practices of Aristotle, Socrates, Dewey (1938), Mead (1934), Lewin (1951), and Kolb (1984). Experience-based learning is interactive and relational and uses instruction technologies like simulations, games, role-plays, case studies, scenarios, multi-media presentations, encounter groups, to name a few (Cameron, 2008). It is also a pervasive and subtle process, resembling life in many ways. Herein lies the potential for experience-based learning to impact on the socio-emotional learning of children. Table 1 sets out the limitations of traditional paradigms and the potential of experience-based learning.

Socio-Emotional Learning: Fun and Games

Play is the language of children and crucial to their development. The reciprocity between play and learning prepares them for the physical, social, cognitive, and linguistic worlds of their future (Smilansky & Shefatya, 1990; Cheok, et al., 2008). In the natural setting of a child's game language develops, hypotheses are tested, problems are solved and thoughts are constructed. 'Scripts' of language are created to reflect shared cognitive themes and cultural understandings (Fromberg, 1992). Whenever two or more players are involved, they are learning how to get along, practicing skills like turn taking, explaining, negotiating, accommodating and sharing. Piaget (1962) suggests that one of the functions of childhood games is to practice working with rules and self-discipline, which ultimately underpin social order. Longitudinal research by Pellegrini and

Kato (2002) concluded that being able to play games well in the schoolyard predicts adjustment to school in general and social competence in boys in particular. Play and games are similar in that they resemble life and explore life-issues; they are interactive, relational, and experiential; they provide a space for experimentation; there is an element of chance; they are usually fun and are intrinsically rewarding. What distinguishes a game from unstructured play is the set of explicit rules, goals, and consequences that impact on the player's roles. There is a beginning and an end, players assume roles, rules govern the play, and rights, responsibilities and consequences are set out. To be engaging, games need a balance between chance, competition, skill, and strategy, with hope and fun built in. Robertson (2010), a game engineer from the UK, provides a word of caution about the 'pointification' of games. An over-focus on points, badges, awards, and levels in a game can interfere with the learning objectives.

The fun and humor of a game stimulates creativity as the brain moves from a cognitive, rule bound state to a more fluid, relaxed state where the whole body is engaged in problem solving (Prouty, 2000). When positive emotions flow, they become enduring personal resources—physical, intellectual, social, and psychological—that can be drawn on later to help people survive and

Table 1. Attributes of traditional and experience-based learning

TRADITIONAL PARADIGM	EXPERIENCE-BASED LEARNING
Teaching and learning = stimulus and response	Learning mediated by socio-emotional and physical environments
Passive, memory-based learning	Active, collaborative, critical thinking, analysis, problem solving, evaluation
Learner watches and listens to 'expert' teacher	Learner interacts and collaborates with adults and peers
Learning viewed predominately in the cognitive domain	Learning linked to cognitive, affective and behavior domains
Learners learn what teachers teach Standardization leads to mediocrity	Diverse learners and environments lead to creativity
Knowledge often assessed by written examination	Knowledge assessed through application – projects, presentations
Predictable, static, unchallenging = boring	Fun, challenging, relevant, multi-media = engaging
Books, articles, lectures, examinations	Simulations, games, role-plays, case studies, encounter groups, multi-media

thrive (Fredrickson & Joiner, 2002). Positive relationships create a sense of belonging and a secure base from which to deal with life's challenges. Emotional resilience refers to the internal and external adjustments made when adapting to adversity and change. A protective social network for example, guards against victimization, or the ill effects of a learning difficulty. Blum (2000) followed a cohort of children over their lifetimes and identified a range of personal, family and peer/adult factors that were common in resilient young people. The research emphasizes the importance of creating opportunities for skill development and for involvement in humanitarian activities, adventure, and fun. Games-based learning with effective mediation is a fun way to help develop skills (Table 2).

Therapeutic Board Games and Socio-Emotional Learning

Games, psychodrama, role-plays, and simulations have been used to develop insight, empathy, prosocial skills, and improve behavior (Bellinson, 2006; Dromi & Krampf, 1986; Sheridan, et al., 1995; Hromek, 2004; Tingstrom, et al., 2006). Malouff and Schutte (1998) field-tested therapeutic games by evaluating the types of experiences produced in the games and the extent to which players enjoyed them. The results supported the effectiveness of therapeutic games with children, adolescents, and adults. In a meta-analysis of moral education interventions, Schlaefli (1985) concluded that programs that involved moral dilemma discussion, psychological development, and ran for a course of 3 to 12 weeks with a

Table 2. Resilience factors in children and opportunities provided by games

RESILIENCE	GAMES-BASED LEARNING
self-efficacy	skills gained through modeling, guided practice, role-play increases confidence
social skills	turn-taking, listening, sharing, negotiating, resolving conflict, apologizing, encouraging
emotional literacy	identifying emotions in self and others, perspective and empathy
sense of humor	fun and humor are fundamental to games
positive attitudes	solution-focused, positive interactions are encouraged
average to above intelligence	reasoning, attention, perseverance, problem solving, explaining involved in playing games
even temperament	emotional regulation required
work success	development of a pro-social skill-set is fundamental to working together - social skills, emotional regulation, perseverance
talents	confidence and skills gained through persistence in a safe environment
school: positive early experience, connectedness, academic success	collaborative, positive, fun-based activities lead to a sense of connectedness
family: warm relationships, connectedness, qualities valued by family	a skill-set is developed for maintaining positive relationships at home and school
social opportunities: leadership, talent, positive relationships, adventure, fun, humanitarian pursuits, success, coaching responsibility	games provide the opportunity for positive relationships, confidence, helping skills, values clarification, moral development and fun

skilled facilitator produced significant results. Recent studies have shown that players' short-term behaviors are predicted by the pro-social or the violent content of the games they played. In addition, players with high pro-social game exposure had higher pro-social traits and behaviors over time (Gentile, et al., 2009; Greitemeyer & Osswald, 2010). Added to this is the importance of studying faces, eye contact, voice tone, and touch in establishing empathy with others (Greenfield, 2010). Playing face-to-face game provides these experiences.

Therapeutic board games are psycho-educational tools that teach a range of social interaction and emotional regulation skills. Issues addressed include friendships, teasing, anger, sportsmanship, anxiety, depression, and happiness (Hromek, 2005). The teaching points are embedded on the board-face and in cards that are turned over during a game. Social dilemmas and challenges are discussed in the game-space, which also allows behavior rehearsal, emotional regulation, collaboration, and self-reflection. Each game becomes an 'experiment' in which players make comparisons and try new strategies while watching the 'experiments' of others. Learning operates at several levels within the game:

- The *psycho-educational* level where skills are directly taught. Players practice socio-emotional skills embedded in the game, for example, saying something funny in response to a tease or solving a dilemma in a pro-social manner;
- The *interactional* level between players—talking, listening, role-playing, problem solving, regulating emotion, tolerating frustration, showing respect;
- The *mediated* level where facilitators model behaviors and scripts, provide hints and guided discussion and debrief players to enhance learning.

FACILITATION AND DEBRIEFING

Social Cognitive Learning and the Zone of Proximal Development

Studies in the fields of primate cognition and artificial intelligence draw on the theories of Lev Vygotsky about the mind. Vygotsky (1986) argued that cognitive development takes place within a dynamic interplay of socio-historic environments and biophysical factors. He saw the mind as being constructed from the outside through interactions with the 'life-space.' Language develops initially for social contact and control and later as *egocentric speech, which* directs thinking. Language is the primary tool for mediating between the elementary mental functions (perception, attention, memory) and the higher skills (consciousness, meaning, intentionality), that is, between "*stimulus and response.*" Language scripts create "mind schema" that mediate between thoughts, feelings, and behaviors and regulate human social behavior in both helpful and unhelpful ways (Corsaro, 1985; Snow, 1989). This process of internalization occurs within the *zone of proximal development* that surrounds the learner and the challenge. Similarly, the social cognitive learning theories of Bandura (2001) suggest that children's learning depends on their social milieu as much as their internal, inherited characteristics. By observing and imitating the interactions of those around them, children integrate behavior into a framework of internal meaning. Bandura concluded that programs based on modeling, coaching, behavior rehearsal, and social reinforcement yield significant results in the development of pro-social and positive emotional skills. Teaching, modeling and coaching increase emotional literacy and compensate for temperamental dispositions and social disadvantages (Kagan, 1998; Karoly, et al., 1998).

Within the *zone of proximal development*, facilitators mediate learning by scaffolding words and resources around the learner. Scripts, hints, encouragements, explanations, models, role-plays, and problem solving strategies influence thought concepts and behaviors and assist the integration of ideas into a framework of internal meaning. So, rather than simply telling a child how to solve a problem, it is possible to encourage higher mental functions and emotional regulation within the *zone of proximal development*. For example, asking a group of young players "Who wants to go first?" creates a social dilemma. Each child is likely to want the first turn and will go through an internal dialogue about the importance of being fair while struggling with self-interest, all within an emotional milieu of excitement and other feelings. They will be making decisions about whether to cooperate with the majority solution or to "make a fuss" and protest their rights, prolonging the conflict and delaying the game. This opportunity would have been missed if the facilitator simply chose who would go first. It is at this point that facilitators can guide discussion about fairness, waiting for your turn or whether going first really does matter.

Role of the Facilitator

Klabbers (2006) sees games as a *magic circle* in which players create a real situation with feelings, and the possibility of learning as much about themselves as the topic being explored in the game. Facilitation is crucial to psychologically safe learning environments and is arguably the most important part of all experience-based learning interventions (Crookall, 1995). Game-spaces need to be emotionally safe, where aims and objectives are clear, rules are applied fairly, and collaboration, cooperation, and perseverance are encouraged. To this end, facilitation should be engaging, with "flair and panache" and the safety of players foremost (Jones, 1999). According to Jones, effective facilitators set the scene and "sit back" in a curious, philosophical manner, waiting for the "teachable moments" that arise in the *zone of proximal development*. Mistakes are welcomed as opportunities for growth through

problem solving approach to debriefing that is designed to help make connections between the experiences in the game and real-life situations. Jones (2004) makes the point that emotions are often feared in games. Facilitators may not want to "lose control" by allowing a situation in which emotions may come to the surface. This means some of the most powerful learning, for both individuals and groups, is lost. Understanding the players and their individual characteristics, developmental stages and varying capacities to participate, reflect, and draw conclusions is therefore important. Also, facilitators should be aware of the situations that may cause stress in a game, for example when players are asked to give personal opinions, disclose feelings, provide anecdotes, or "put on the spot" (Hill & Lance, 2002). Being alert and responding immediately to possible issues of harm while avoiding shame or embarrassment can provide a break or "out" for participants. When teaching socio-emotional skills, the following set of values, skills, and attitudes apply (Table 3).

The Life Space Interview (LSI) and Emotional First Aid (EFA) as Debriefing Tools

Debriefing is a powerful learning tool to use in the face of emotional crises. Rather than sidelining the emotions that are, whether we admit it or not, always present in games-based learning situations, it addresses them with thought to the values held by the young person being debriefed. The LSI is a verbal technique for working with children in emotional crisis. It was initially developed by Fritz Redl (1966) and has been refined since by others (Watson, 1992; Wood & Long, 1991). They are immediate, meaningful, solution focused interviews that encourage empathy and provide emotional space for restitution. The events surrounding a crisis are debriefed in order to expand understanding of the young person's behavior and the responses of others. Emotional flooding can

Table 3. Facilitator attitude, skills, and values

Attitude	Respectful, curious, neutral, philosophical stances reduce stress and create safe spaces for players to try new skills
Immediacy	Teachable moments arise within a game and between players and can be used to enhance learning
Language	Inclusive and non-judgmental language encourages responsibility and the development of empathy
Scripts	Scripts help manage anger, frustration or conflict: *1. it's hard to wait but I can do it* *2. don't worry, calm down, it's not worth it* *3. not everyone can finish first*
Making connections	Comments on learning, commonalities and shared feelings help to make connections
Modeling	Courtesy, rule-keeping, turn-taking, apologizing, resolving conflict, smiling, having fun
Participation	Full participation shows what is expected and increases the sense of belonging and equality
Reading and language skills	Poor readers may need help when cards are used. New concepts may need explanation
Cheating	A curious, philosophical attitude defuses the situation. Allow the group to decide on the response to cheating
Winning and losing	Winning is not the main object in games-based learning. The emphasis is on having fun and learning. However players are interested in who finishes first or who has the most tokens. Acknowledge feelings, use scripts *I didn't finish first but it was fun anyway* *Winning is fun but it doesn't matter*
Managing difficult behavior	Negotiate rules at the beginning like taking turns, speaking respectfully and listening. Stop unruly games, ask what needs to happen in order to play, invite players back later. Reduce the group size
Minimize harm	Discuss importance of trust, gain agreement with the rules. Deal with put-downs immediately. Avoid 'loss of face' and shame. Facilitate restitution of relationship
Debrief	Debrief difficult issues immediately. Discuss positive experiences and skills learnt. Use a Life Space Interview with individual players as required
Incentives	Young players enjoy incentives like stickers. This adds to the fun and ameliorates the pain of not finishing first. Older children find games intrinsically motivating

interfere with this process and EFA is required to support the young person while they regulate their emotions. Sometimes this can take a while and the LSI may have to be held at a later time. EFA acknowledges the physiological nature of the emotional response and the need for time and space in order for the young person to calm down and think straight (Hromek, 2007). Once calm, the process of decoding the feelings behind actions and identifying the central issues and values can begin. Problem solving creates alternative behaviors for a young person to consider and choose. Repairing and maintaining relationships is an important part of the debriefing. The pivotal part of the LSI is the discussion about the values the young person

is upholding. This face-saving step acknowledges that their concerns are important and that they can be addressed in pro-social ways.

LSIs can be used as brief interventions during a game or as private, in-depth interviews afterwards. The steps of the LSI are as follows:

- **Emotional First Aid:** If there is a flood of emotion, use reflective listening to empathize. Encourage self-soothing strategies like a drink of water, taking a walk, breathing to reduce the physiological response. Flooding can last for 20 to 30 minutes and time and space may be needed during this phase.

- **Focus on the Incident:** Talk, listen, and reflect to understand the facts. This assures the young person of your unbiased attention.
- **Identify the Values Being Upheld, for Example, Fairness and Respect:** Decide on therapeutic goals, like anger management, social skills, assertive communication.
- **Use Problem Solving Strategies:** Brainstorm alternatives, evaluate consequences, explore restitution, make a plan.
- **Plan for Success:** Rehearse the plan, anticipate other people's reactions, accept consequences.
- **Finish in a Calm, Responsible, Matter of Fact Manner:** And resume previous activity.

Safety Issues in Digital, Screen-Based Gaming

The 'digital natives' in our schools and homes will grow up with all the benefits that digital screen-based technologies have delivered over the past twenty years and into the future. Interactive whiteboards, computers, social media, the Internet, online learning represent new ways of connecting with all types of learners in the classroom, preparing them for futures their parents cannot imagine. While most young people are able to play with and use these new technologies responsibly, maintaining active lives, friendships and success at school, there is a small percent who experience significant social, emotional, physical, and behavioral problems associated with excessive screen-based game time (Vorderer & Bryant, 2006). Withdrawn, uncommitted individuals who experience failure at school or work, loss of relationships, deterioration in health and wellbeing and compulsively play for long periods are at risk of problematic Internet, screen-based use. For some players it is a simple lack discipline and time management skills, however for 5 to 10 percent of gamers they will be experiencing a serious disability, often oblivious to the problem. Facilitators and parents need to be aware of these potentially serious issues emerging in the wake of a rapid increase in the amount of time children and young people are spending in front of screens.

- **Social:** An association has been found between increased screen time and poor attachment to parents and peers (Richards, et al., 2010);
- **Behavioral:** According to research by Holtz and Appel (2011), online gaming, Internet use, and playing first-person shooter games are predictive of externalizing behavior problems like aggression, delinquency. Online role-playing games are predictive of internalizing problem behaviors like withdrawal, depression, and anxiety. Importantly, when parents and children talked about Internet activities, fewer problem behaviors were reported;
- **Psychological:** Problems have been identified in the development of the self in some adolescents who spend excessive amounts of time playing online role-playing games (Alison, et al., 2006). Internet addiction is associated with symptoms of ADHD and depressive disorders (Ko, 2008; Yen, 2007);
- **Brain Function:** Heavy use of the Internet is linked to the shrinking of brain tissue (Yuan, et al., 2011). Carr (2008) writes about loss of concentration, superficial thinking, and shallow interactions brought about by problematic Internet use. Greenfield (2008), a neuroscientist, claims that the Internet and other screen-based activities are literally changing the brain in unprecedented ways. The Internet is replacing memory for some users and has become a primary form of external memory, where information is stored collectively outside ourselves (Sparrow, 2011);

- **Sleep:** Internet addiction is strongly associated with excessive daytime sleepiness in adolescents (Choi, et al., 2009);
- **Attention:** Viewing television and playing video games are associated with increased subsequent attention problems in childhood (Swing, et al., 2010);
- **Vision:** A strong association was found between prolonged hours on the computer or TV, fast food eating, poor lifestyle habits, and low vision (Bener, et al., 2010). Physical activity has a beneficial influence on retinal microvascular structure, whereas screen time has adverse effects (Gopinath, 2011);
- **Addiction:** Holden (2001) suggests that out-of-control gambling, eating, sexuality, and Internet use may share the same neurobiological mechanism with substance dependence and can be termed "behavioral addiction." Digital devices feed the primitive brain whenever points are gained, levels reached, or message signals are received. This releases dopamine, a pleasure creating neurotransmitter, which acts as a reward. Excessive Internet video game players have higher reward dependency and an increased prevalence of dopamine (Han, et al., 2007; Thaleman, et al., 2007). The 'endless' nature of Massive Multiplayer Online Role Playing Games keeps players at the screen for longer than they may have planned, even when they believe they shouldn't (Porter, et al., 2010);
- **Obesity:** Daley (2009) concludes that while 'exergaming' may increase heart rate, it is no substitute for sports and other activities. Other researchers find a correlation between screen-time and obesity (Krebs & Jacobson, 2003).

Teaching about the potential risks and actions that may mitigate against them is an important role for the facilitator. Facilitators, parents, and young people should be alerted to the dangers and encouraged to manage gaming exposure, for example:

- Ask about the games young people are playing, how long do they play, do they have good posture, take breaks, and look into the distance. Keep a diary of play-time if needed;
- Keep computers in common areas while children are young so parents or teachers can monitor content and play-time;
- Negotiate and enforce play-time limits;
- Monitor social interactions, school performance, health, and wellbeing;
- Seek help if the young person is showing signs of social withdrawal, reduced performance at school, or other physical symptoms.

CONCLUSION

Intuitively, we know that playing games with children is an excellent way to engage them. Games are fun, and as a subset of experience-based learning, they provide highly motivating and meaningful opportunities for social interaction, connectedness and co-operation between players. With careful design, just about any teaching content can be presented as a game, including the psychological skill-set required for positive relationships and emotional wellbeing. Pro-social skills and emotional regulation are pivotal to success in modern learning and work environments and early intervention is essential to assist children and young people with deficits in these areas. Theory and research validate games-based learning experiences as effective ways for young people to learn the social and emotional skills that will help them succeed. The power of using games to teach socio-emotional learning lies in the interactional nature of playing a game together. What is also clear from the literature and from experience is the pivotal role of facilitators. By modeling, coaching, teaching, refereeing, debriefing, and so forth, facilitators enter the *zone of proximal development,* enhancing the experience of players by developing positive relationships and strengthening emotional resilience. A vital role exists for the facilitator to enhance the learning that is taking place within a game, both at the skill-based level and at the interactional level and to provide opportunities to extend and embed this in the formal and informal curriculum and the myriad of interactions that occur in every day school life. This article has presented theoretical and practical evidence to support using this highly motivating approach to teaching socio-emotional learning and the pivotal role of the facilitator in enhancing the learning in the games and the safety of the players.

REFERENCES

Allison, S., von Wahlde, L., Shockley, T., & Gabbard, G. O. (2006). The development of the self in the era of the internet and role-playing fantasy games. *The American Journal of Psychiatry, 163*(3), 381–385. doi:10.1176/appi.ajp.163.3.381

Bandura, A. (2001). Social cognitive theory: An agentic perspective. *Annual Review of Psychology, 52,* 1–26. doi:10.1146/annurev.psych.52.1.1

Bellinson, J. (2002). *Children's use of board games in psychotherapy.* Northvale, NJ: Jason Aronson Inc.

Bener, A., Al-Mahdi, H. S., Vachhani, P. J., Al-Nufal, M., & Ali, A. I. (2010). Do excessive internet use, television viewing and poor lifestyle habits affect low vision in school children? *Journal of Child Health Care, 14*(4), 375–385. doi:10.1177/1367493510380081

Blum, R. (2000). *Healthy youth development: Resiliency paradigm for adolescent health development.* Paper presented at the 3rd Pacific Rim Conference of the International Association for Adolescent Health. Christchurch, New Zealand.

Cameron, B. H. (2008). Experience-based learning. In Tomei, L. A. (Ed.), *Encyclopedia of Information Technology Curriculum Integration* (pp. 308–315). Hershey, PA: IGI Global. doi:10.4018/978-1-59904-881-9.ch052

Carr, N. (2008). Is Google making us stupid? *Atlantic (Boston, Mass.), 302*(1), 56–63.

Carr, N. (2010). *The shallows: What the internet is doing to our brains.* New York, NY: Norton and Company Inc.

Castella, J. C., Trung, T. N., & Boissau, S. (2005). Participatory simulation of land-use changes in the mountains of Vietnam: The combined use of an agent-based model, a role-playing game and a geographic information system. *Ecology and Society, 10*(1), 27. Retrieved from http://www.ecologyandsociety.org/vol10/iss1/art27/

Cheok, A., Ishii, I., Osada, J., Fernando, O., & Merritt, T. (2008). Interactive play and learning for children. *Advances in Human-Computer Interaction.* Retrieved from http://www.hindawi.com/journals/ahci/2008/954013/

Choi, K., Son, H., Park, M., Han, J., Kim, K., Lee, B., & Gwak, H. (2009). Internet overuse and excessive daytime sleepiness in adolescents. *Psychiatry and Clinical Neurosciences, 63*(4), 455–462. doi:10.1111/j.1440-1819.2009.01925.x

Corsaro, W. A. (1985). *Friendship and culture in the early years.* Norwood, NJ: Ablex.

Crookall, D. (1995). *Debriefing: The key to learning from simulation/games.* Thousand Oaks, CA: Sage.

Daley, A. (2009). Can exergaming contribute to improving physical activity levels and health outcomes in children? *Pediatrics*, *124*(2), 763–771. doi:10.1542/peds.2008-2357

Dewey, J. (1938). *Experience and education*. New York, NY: Collier.

Dromi, G. P., & Krampf, Z. (1986). Programming revisited: The miftan experience. *Social Work with Groups*, *9*, 91–105. doi:10.1300/J009v09n01_08

Fredrickson, B. L., & Joiner, T. (2002). Positive emotions trigger upward spirals toward emotional well-being. *Psychological Science*, *13*, 172–175. doi:10.1111/1467-9280.00431

Fromberg, D. P. (1992). A review of research on play. In Seefeldt, C. (Ed.), *The Early Childhood Curriculum: A Review of Current Research* (2nd ed., pp. 42–84). New York, NY: Teachers College Press.

Gardner, H. (1999). *Intelligence reformed: Multiple intelligences for the 21ˢᵗ century*. New York, NY: Basic Books.

Gentile, D. A., Anderson, C. A., Yukawa, S., Ihori, N., Saleem, M., & Ming, L. M. (2009). The effects of prosocial video games on prosocial behaviors: International evidence from correlational, longitudinal, and experimental studies. *Personality and Social Psychology Bulletin*, *35*(6), 752–763. doi:10.1177/0146167209333045

Goleman, D. (1996). *Emotional intelligence: Why it can matter more than IQ*. London, UK: Bloomsbury.

Gopinath, B., Baur, L. A., Wang, J. J., Hardy, L. L., Teber, E., & Kifley, A. (2011). Influence of physical activity and screen time on the retinal microvasculature in young children. *Arteriosclerosis, Thrombosis, and Vascular Biology*, *31*, 1233–1239. doi:10.1161/ATVBAHA.110.219451

Greenfield, S. (2008). *Creating creative brains*. Paper presented at CCI's Creating Value: Between Commerce and Commons conference. Brisbane, Australia. Retrieved July 11, 2011, from http://cci.edu.au/presentations/creating-value-conference-presentations

Greitemeyer, T., & Osswald, S. (2010). Effects of prosocial video games on prosocial behavior. *Journal of Personality and Social Psychology*, *98*(2), 211–221. doi:10.1037/a0016997

Han, D. H., Lee, Y. S., Yang, K. C., Kim, E. Y., Lyoo, I. K., & Renshaw, P. F. (2007). Dopamine genes and reward dependence in adolescents with excessive internet video game play. *Journal of Addiction Medicine*, *1*(3), 133–138. doi:10.1097/ADM.0b013e31811f465f

Hill, J. L., & Lance, C. G. (2002). Debriefing stress. *Simulation & Gaming*, *33*, 490–503. doi:10.1177/1046878102238613

Holden, C. (2001). Behavioral addictions: Do they exist? *Science*, *294*, 980-982. Retrieved July 18, 2011 from http://www.sciencemag.org

Holtz, P., & Appel, M. (2011). Internet use and video gaming predict problem behavior in early adolescence. *Journal of Adolescence*, *34*(1), 49–58. doi:10.1016/j.adolescence.2010.02.004

Hromek, R. P. (2004). *Planting the peace virus: Early intervention to prevent violence in schools*. Bristol, UK: Lucky Duck.

Hromek, R. P. (2005). *Game time: Games to promote social and emotional resilience for children aged 4-14*. London, UK: Paul Chapman.

Hromek, R. P. (2007). *Emotional coaching: A practical programme to support young people*. London, UK: Paul Chapman.

Jones, K. (1999). With appropriate panache. *Simulation & Gaming*, *30*, 327–331. doi:10.1177/104687819903000307

Jones, K. (2004). Fear of emotions. *Simulation & Gaming, 35*, 454–460. doi:10.1177/1046878104269893

Kagan, J. (1998). *Galen's prophecy.* Boulder, CO: Westview Press.

Karoly, L. A., Greenwood, P. W., Everingham, S. S., Hoube, J., Kilburn, S. R., Rydell, C. P., & Chiesa, J. (1998). *Investing in our children: What we know and don't know about the costs and benefits of early interventions.* Santa Monica, CA: RAND.

Klabbers, J. H. B. (2006). *The magic circle: Principles of gaming and simulation.* Rotterdam, The Netherlands: Sense.

Ko, C., Yen, J., Chen, C., Chen, C., & Yen, C. (2008). Psychiatric comorbidity of internet addiction in college students: An interview study. *CNS Spectrums, 13*(2), 147–153.

Ko, C., Yen, J., Chen, S., Yang, M., Lin, H., & Yen, C. (2009). Proposed diagnostic criteria and the screening and diagnosing tool of Internet addiction in college students. *Comprehensive Psychiatry, 50*(4), 378–384. doi:10.1016/j.comppsych.2007.05.019

Kolb, D. A. (1984). *Experiential learning: Experience as the source of learning and development.* Englewood Cliffs, NJ: Prentice-Hall.

Krebs, N. F., & Jacobson, M. S. (2003). Prevention of pediatric overweight and obesity. *Pediatrics, 112*(2), 424–430. doi:10.1542/peds.112.2.424

Lewin, K. (1951). *Field theory in social science: Selected theoretical papers.* New York, NY: Harper & Row.

Malouff, J., & Schutte, N. (1998). *Games to enhance social and emotional skills: Sixty-six games that teach adolescents and adults skills crucial to success in life.* Springfield, IL: Hares C. Thomas.

Mead, G. H. (1934). *Mind, self and society.* Chicago, IL: University of Chicago Press.

Milbourne, L. (2005). Children, families and inter-agency work: Experiences of partnership work in primary education settings. *British Educational Research Journal, 31*(6), 675–695. doi:10.1080/01411920500314653

Pellegrine, A. D., & Kato, K. (2002). Short-term longitudinal study of children's playground games across the first year of school: Implications for social competence and adjustment to school. *American Educational Research Journal, 39*(4), 991–1015. doi:10.3102/00028312039004991

Piaget, J. (1962). *Play, dreams and imitation in childhood.* New York, NY: W. W. Norton.

Porter, G., Starcevic, V., Berle, D., & Fenech, P. (2010). Recognizing problem video game use. *The Australian and New Zealand Journal of Psychiatry, 44*(2), 120–128. doi:10.3109/00048670903279812

Prouty, D. (2000). Creativity. *Zip Lines: The Voice for Adventure Education, 40*, 9–11.

Redl, F. (1966). *When we deal with children.* New York, NY: The Free Press.

Richards, R., McGee, R., Williams, S. M., Welch, D., & Hancox, R. J. (2010). Adolescent screen time and attachment to parents and peers. *Archives of Pediatrics & Adolescent Medicine, 164*(3), 258–262. doi:10.1001/archpediatrics.2009.280

Robertson, M. (2010). *Can't play, won't play.* Retrieved July 18, 2011, from http://www.hide-andseek.net/2010/10/06/cant-play-wont-play/

Ruben, B. D. (1999). Simulation, games, and experience-based learning: The quest for a new paradigm for teaching and learning. *Simulation & Gaming, 30*, 498–505. doi:10.1177/104687819903000409

Schaefli, A., Rest, J. R., & Thomas, J. (1985). Does moral education improve moral judgement? A meta-analysis of intervention studies using the defining issues test. *Review of Educational Research, 55,* 319–352.

Sheridan, M. K., Foley, G. M., & Radlinski, S. H. (1995). *Using supportive play model: Individualised intervention in early childhood practice.* New York, NY: Teachers College Press.

Smilansky, S., & Shefatya, L. (1990). *Facilitating play: A medium for promoting cognitive, socio-emotional and academic development in young children.* Gaithersburg, MD: Psychosocial and Educational Publications.

Snow, C. E. (1989). Understanding social interaction and language acquisition: Sentences are not enough. In Bornstein, M. H., & Bruner, J. S. (Eds.), *Interaction in Human Development* (pp. 83–103). Hillsdale, NJ: Lawrence Erlbaum.

Sparrow, B., Liu, J., & Wegner, D. M. (2011). *Google effects on memory: Cognitive consequences of having information at our fingertips.* Retrieved July 14, 2011 from http://www.sciencexpress.org

Swing, E. L., Gentile, D. A., Anderson, C. A., & Walsh, D. A. (2010). Television and video game exposure and the development of attention problems. *Pediatrics, 126*(2), 214–221. doi:10.1542/peds.2009-1508

Thalemann, R., Wölfling, K., & Grüsser, S. M. (2007). Specific cue reactivity on computer game-related cues in excessive gamers. *Behavioral Neuroscience, 121*(3), 614–618. doi:10.1037/0735-7044.121.3.614

Tingstrom, D. H., Sterling-Turner, H. E., & Wilczynski, S. M. (2006). The good behavior game: 1969-2002. *Behavior Modification, 30,* 225–253. doi:10.1177/0145445503261165

Tsuchiya, S. (2005). Utility deregulation and business ethics: More openness through gaming simulation. *Simulation & Gaming, 36*(1), 114–133. doi:10.1177/1046878104272667

Vahed, A. (2008). The tooth morphology board game: An innovative strategy in tutoring dental technology learners in combating rote learning. In M. Stanfield & T. Connolly (Eds.), *2nd European Conference on Games Based Learning,* (pp. 467-480). Reading, UK: Academic Publishing Limited.

Vorderer, P., & Bryant, J. (Eds.). (2006). *Playing video games: Motives, responses, and consequences.* Mahwah, NJ: Lawrence Erlbaum Associates, Inc.

Vygotsky, L. S. (1976). Play and its role in the mental development of the child. In Bruner, J. S., Jolly, A., & Sylvia, K. (Eds.), *Play – Its Role in Development and Evolution* (pp. 537–554). New York, NY: Basic Books. doi:10.2753/RPO1061-040505036

Vygotsky, L. S. (1986). *Thought and language.* Cambridge, MA: MIT Press.

Watson, I. (1992). Techniques for helping and controlling children who hate: The craft of Fritz Redl. *Australian Journal of Guidance & Counselling, 2,* 63–70.

Wood, M., & Long, N. (1991). *Life space intervention.* Austin, TX: PRO-ED.

Yen, J., Ko, C., Yen, C., Hsiu-Yueh Wu, H., & Yang, M. (2007). The comorbid psychiatric symptoms of internet addiction: Attention deficit and hyperactivity disorder (ADHD), depression, social phobia, and hostility. *The Journal of Adolescent Health, 41*(1), 93–98. doi:10.1016/j.jadohealth.2007.02.002

Yuan, K., Qin, W., Wang, G., Zeng, F., Zhao, L., & Yang, X. (2011). Microstructure abnormalities in adolescents with internet addiction disorder. *PLoS ONE, 6*(6). doi:10.1371/journal.pone.0020708

Chapter 8
Social Interactive Systems Design for Serious Games

Ines Di Loreto
University of Milan, Italy

ABSTRACT

Based on the importance of social aspects for the learning process and for Digital Natives, this chapter describes a framework to create sociality inside learning environments and in particular in serious games. The described framework is based on four elements: identity, space, time, and actions. These elements (and the behaviors that emerge from them) can be used as markers in order to evaluate whether or not the system is able to facilitate social interactions. The chapter describes in particular (1) the framework for the creation of sociability in interactive systems, (2) two methods for its application in the design phase and in the development phase, (3) two experiments carried out in order to validate the above mentioned framework using a serious game called School Society, and (4) some observations on the framework and the relationship between social and learning aspects.

INTRODUCTION

A learning environment can be defined as a context of structured activities, *intentionally* set up, where the learning process takes place. Based on this concept of learning *process* the learning environment could be also defined as a *space for action* designed to stimulate and support the building of knowledge, skills, motivation, and

attitudes. In this *space for action*, exchanges and interactions occur between students, teachers and the objects of knowledge basing on common goals and interests. The role and the importance of sociality (peer to peer or structured exchanges) for learning purposes in learning environments has been investigated by several authors (from Piaget, Vygotskij, Wersch, to Lewin, Dewey, Rogers, Goleman). For these authors internal

DOI: 10.4018/978-1-4666-1987-6.ch008

factors of the individual (knowledge, emotions, representations, ratings), as well as external stimuli (cognitive conflicts, situated learning, cooperative actions) are reasons for the action. In our previous definition, the learning process structures a *space for action* in which social aspects also have to be take into account. In the *social space for action,* students have the opportunity to have meaningful experiences in the cognitive, affective/emotional, interpersonal/social plan. For these reasons, it is important to create environments able to integrate social aspects in the learning process even when the learning environment is a "virtual" one.

Moreover, current learning environments have to meet the demands of the current generation of young people, the so-called Digital Natives. The term Digital Natives is used here to refer to the current generation of youngster, i.e. people born during or after the general introduction of digital technology who, interacting with digital technology from an early age, have a greater understanding of its concepts. This generation has different needs from previous ones because they have never been exposed to previous ways of interaction. As we will see in the following section for this generation, the role of sociality in virtual environments is taken for granted. Acceptance of a new tool, whether it be for entertainment purposes or for learning purposes, is strictly linked to its level of sociality (see Section "Digital Natives and Their Needs"). An application that fails to present familiar "social" features at the very least would be considered as backward and may be rejected. Therefore, the importance of social aspects for learning purposes interconnects with the importance of social aspects for the current generation.

This chapter presents a framework for building Social Interactive Systems (SIS) addressing the needs of Digital Natives. This means that the focus of this chapter will be more on the integration of social aspects in learning environments than on the effectiveness of the learning aspects.

The framework tested in the experiments described in this chapter is based on four elements:

identity, space, time, and actions. These elements were the result of a detailed analysis of social software used by Digital Natives (see Section "The Framework: Defining 'Indicators' for Social Presence"). In order to test the framework we used a serious game (i.e. a game with a primary purpose other than pure entertainment) called School Society for two experiments. In short, School Society is a virtual world inhabited by avatars representing the students. The aim of the game is to become the best student (i.e. the best ranked student) in this virtual world (see Section "The Framework and Serious Games as Learning Environment"). School Society was conceived on the basis of the framework and developed specifically for the experiments.

For the first experiment described in this chapter, we focused on applying the framework to create an early evaluation for a designed application (i.e. an evaluation before starting the development, see Section "Defining an Application 'Expected Profile'") and evaluated the ease of use of such a method. The second experiment was carried out after the development of School Society in order to demonstrate that the absence of one of the elements of the framework could considerably influence the use and the acceptance of the application. The main idea behind the two experiments was to compare the early evaluation of potential sociability with the actual application in order to understand if they are really linked (see Section "General Discussion").

The rest of this chapter is structured as follows. The next section will deal with current generation and their use of 'new' technologies highlighting the importance of games in Digital Natives' lives. The chapter will then describe the framework for the creation of Social Interactive Systems (hereafter SIS) whose intended target is the current generation of young people, the so-called Digital Natives. The following sections will describe different methods using the framework in the design and post-design phase of an application in order to evaluate its sociability. The serious game created to evaluate our framework (School Society) and the experiments carried out to validate it are the subject of the subsequent sections, and the final section will draw some conclusions regarding the role of sociability in serious games and its relationship with the learning aspect from a design point of view.

Motivation: From Interactive Systems to Social Interactive Systems – Digital Natives

As much as been written on the importance of social learning (apart from the works cited in the introduction we can cite Sefton-Green [2004], Scanlon et al. [2007], Eisenstadt [2007]), in this section we prefer to focus on the importance of social aspects for current era and Digital Natives.

In fact, studying the current era we realize that particular people are using new technologies in a particular social way. In order to describe the current generation we can adopt a technological (and cultural) perspective.

"Today's 24-year-old was born in 1985—10 years after the first consumer computers went on sale and the same year that the breakthrough 'third generation' video game, Nintendo's 'Super Mario Brothers,' first went to market. When this 24-year-old was a child, the basic format of instant messaging was developed, and when he entered kindergarten in 1990, Tim Berners-Lee 'wrote a computer program' called the World Wide Web. At the dawn of high school (in 1999), Sean Fanning created the Napster file-sharing service. When he graduated from high school four years later, his gifts might have included an iPod (patented in 2002) and a camera phone (first shipped in early 2003). Our 24-year-old college student saw the rise of blogs (already two-years-old in 2000), RSS feeds (coded in 2000), Wikipedia (2001), social network sites (Friendster was launched in 2002), tagging (Del.icio.us was created in 2003), free online phone calling (Skype software was made available in 2003), podcasts (term coined in

2004), and the video explosion that has occurred as broadband Internet connections become the norm in households (YouTube went live in 2005)" (Rainie, 2006).

If this timeline puts 24-year-olds in technological perspective, it does this all the more for teens. For the current generation—the so called Digital Natives for Prensky (2001), Generation Z for Mitchell (2008), or Net Generation for Tapscott (2008)—technologies that are still considered transformative by their parents and grandparents are a basic part of their everyday lives. Internet and cell phones are to Digital Natives what the Radio and TV were to other generations—the latest products. Moreover "they have never known any other way of life" (Palfrey, 2008). Not only are they used to 'new ways' of interaction, they have never experienced the 'old ways' so most of the old interaction paradigms make no sense for them.

We can thus state our first reason for rethinking the way we create and evaluate SIS:

- *"The current generation is used to pervasive social interactions and has never experienced previous ways of interactions"*
- **Digital Natives and Games:** The last assertion means that if a designer wants to design for Digital Natives he has to understand what 'interaction' means to them. As games are one of the most used software by Digital Natives this section will focus on analyzing their use in order to understand the way Digital Natives interact with them. In order to analyze this topic we can refer to two studies: the first one (Horrigan, 2007) states that for college students gaming is virtually commonplace. Thanks to a plethora of technologies (video game consoles, computers, handheld devices, Internet) a range of entertainment options is at their disposal, a range that is much wider than the one available to their predecessors.

Furthermore, today's college students are using technologies to entertain themselves wherever they may be. Computer, video and online games are woven into the fabric of everyday life for college students, and are a social/socializing activity. The same could be said for teenagers (Pew Internet American Life Project, 2007). Video gaming is pervasive in the lives of American teens—young and older teens, girls and boys. Opportunities for gaming are everywhere, and gaming is a social activity and a major component of their overall social experience.

From these two studies, we can draw two elements, which characterize the current generation.

- *"An overwhelming majority of Digital Natives play video games,"* and
- *"An integral part of Digital Natives' video game experience is social."*
- **Digital Natives and Their Needs:** Summarizing, the context Digital Natives are living in is characterized by social *and* playful ways of interaction. Current digital cultures—such as blogging and gaming—take social features for granted and they are expected to be available in any application. Because of the above described scenario an application that fails to present familiar social features at the very least, would be considered as backward, and may be rejected. In the same way, Digital Natives are naturally used to interacting with different devices. The learning curve of new technologies is very low (e.g. the one for touch screen technologies), and Digital Natives expect to interact easily with them.

Regarding the social aspect, applications with a high learning curve ratio may therefore also be rejected. Finally, games (and the fun factor associated with games) are one of their favorite activities, and while this does not imply the rejection of 'serious' applications, 'fun' applications (i.e. applications with interaction that is entertaining—the so-called gamification) have more of a chance of being accepted. As we can see, these three elements add a high level of complexity to the creation of SISs whose target is Digital Natives. There is therefore a need for design methodologies that are able to thoroughly address the above-described elements as a whole.

The Framework: Defining 'Indicators' for Social Presence

The framework conceived to address digital natives' social needs is based on four elements: identity, space, time, and actions. These elements are drawn from an empirical analysis of current social software and supported by major findings from psychology and sociology (Di Loreto, 2010). We can summarize the work that led to the creation of the framework this way: current social software were analyzed and Digital Natives involvement in the use of the same (i.e. Digital Natives' % respect to general users' population) was taken into account. All available features were listed, given a different weight based on Digital Natives' % of use, then grouped. This grouping allowed for the emergence of the 4 above mentioned elements. The software most used by Digital Natives had in common the fact that it allowed for identity representation, place customization, persistence and memory and a high level of interactivity at different levels. However, each kind of software had a different balancing in reference to the 4 elements. This means that the element balancing in social software based on micro actions such as Facebook is not the same as the one for the Second Life virtual world. We could then derive from this that the elements we found represented core features of any Social Interactive Systems (SIS) targeted towards young generations and that each kind of social software had its own 'preferred' configuration. The 4 elements also represent interesting evaluation criteria for the potential sociability of the application to be designed at an early stage. In fact, software evaluation is usually performed a posteriori. On the contrary, we claim that an a priori evaluation of social systems may be useful. In fact, while users are able to evaluate the quality of their experience, for the most part they are not able to understand which feature/characteristic causes poor performance. This does not mean that a user centered design approach (see e.g. Vrendenburg, et al., 2001) is not useful when designing software with social aspects. On the contrary an in depth analysis of users' needs is at the heart of any application development. However, between user centered design and user satisfaction measurement we want to add an intermediate layer. An additional level of an early evaluation approach can, for example, help designers to anticipate several problems that could arise *before* starting the implementation stage enabling them to return to the design phase to add missing elements, keeping development cost down (see Section "General Discussion").

The semantics of each element, which makes up the framework is described in more detail below.

- **Identity:** Our point of view about identity is the same as social psychology's later approaches, which consider individual and social identity not as stable characteristics, but rather as a dynamic phenomenon (Harré, 1991). In these approaches, the choice about what possible self to show is driven by *strategic moves* (e.g., what features are more relevant and effective for self-presentation) *that participants can make within a particular situation*. For example, in describing everyday interactions (Goffman, 1959) distinguished between two ways of expressing information: information that is given and information that is given off. Information that is given is the conscious content of communication, the voluntary symbolic actions that are mutually understood. While information that is given is considered to be within the actor's control, information that is given off is per-

ceived by the audience to be unintentionally communicated. To give an example, the explicit specification of a social network of acquaintance can be seen as information that is given off. If it is true that social networks are built via a series of invitations, usually members also have some control over the visibility of their network for others. This means that, for impression management, a user will show only networks he/she wants to show. In this case, there is 'given' information (the user chooses what to show about his/her identity), but also 'given off' information (derived e.g., from the kind of groups a user decided to show). From a design point of view, we can say that, allowing both kinds of identity representation becomes the starting point for an evolving social identity. For additional studies on the identity topic see for example Turkle (1997), Widdicombe (1998), Wenger (1999).

- **Space:** If studied carefully the language we use to describe our experience of the virtual environment is a reflection of an underlying conceptual metaphor: 'Cyberspace as Place' (Lakoff, et al., 1988). This means that we are transferring certain spatial characteristics from our real world experience over to the virtual environment. The metaphor 'Cyberspace as Place' leads to a series of other metaphorical inferences. Cyberspace is like the physical world: it can be 'zoned,' trespassed upon, interfered with, and divided up into a series of small landholdings that are just like real world property holdings. Although we linked the terms space and place in the last paragraphs, for SISs to function well it is important to distinguish between them. In actual fact the literature dealing with space and place is extremely large and diverse. A converging definition of the difference between space and place does not exist, however we can list some interesting definitions adapted from Carmona (2003). Spaces are the basic divisions of our surroundings; place is our history and adaptation of them (landscape historian JB Jackson), space is the scene of being; place is a site where human modes of being are well provided for (Heidegger). By imbuing them with meaning, individuals, groups or societies change 'spaces' into 'places' (urban designer Edward Relph). Finally, place is complex, inextricably multi-dimensional, lived, experienced, meaningful (with multi-meanings of course). This means that while space is a well-defined topographical entity, place is the result of human inhabitation, (social) interaction, and the like. We claim that in order to design a social system, it is essential to allow by design the creation of public (at different levels) spaces for aggregation but also the creation of private places (Wenger, et al., 2002). Besides, the lever of personalization can be used in order to allow the shift from spaces to places. Only by taking possession of the space, and manipulating it to turn it into something we like, can we transform it into a place. For additional studies on the space topic see for example Bentley et al. (1995), Blythe et al. (2008), Dourish et al. (2004), Dourish (2006).

- **Time:** As we have seen, in order to create a social identity in an online environment several elements are required. One of these is the persistence of personal identity in the system. In a non-persistent world, it is not possible to have a history of actions and thus allow, for example, the creation of a reputation like in real life. In addition, Danet et al. (1997) argued that the 'flow experiences,' a state of total absorption and a lack of awareness of time passing, is associated with synchronicity. The idea of synchronicity is linked to the idea of tem-

porality, a linear procession of past, present, future. This particular nuance (synchronicity as process) is very interesting if we consider the fact that interaction with media and media perception has changed. In fact, advances in technology and the speed of network connections are blurring distinctions between synchronous and asynchronous communications (Joinson, 2003). Synchronous and asynchronous communications are thus processes that happen during time. The idea of synchronicity as a process is totally consistent with the idea of persistence and is another element supporting social awareness. For additional studies on the time topic, see for example Preece (2001), Rheingold (1993), Gunawardena (1997).

- **Action:** In this part, we discuss physical and psychological mechanisms that regulate human actions in order to understand why the action element has to be considered as a pillar for SIS design. The first theory we want to describe is the so-called *thinking through doing*. This theory describes how thought (mind) and action (body) are deeply integrated and how they co-produce learning and reasoning (Klemmer, 2006). Piaget (1952) postulated that cognitive structuring requires both physical and mental activity. In a very basic sense, humans learn about the world and its properties by interacting within it. As a second support, we can cite *embodied cognition*. Theories and research of embodied cognition regard bodily activity as being essential to understanding human cognition (Pecher, et al., 2005). While these theories address cognition through action in physical environments, they also have important implications for designing interactive systems. In fact, body engagement with virtual environments constitutes an important aspect of cognitive work. Because an action is always an action-over-something, the kind of interaction spaces and objects we create in a social system will influence what cognitive work the user will do over the system. For additional studies on the action topic, see for example Dourish (2006), Vallacher et al. (1985, 1987).

The Overall Framework

Table 1 summarizes the critical factors that have to be taken into account when building an SIS and give several examples of features that could be used by a designer to stress a particular element. In addition, we can consider each of the above-described elements as a line (an axis) that starts from the lack of presence of the element to the fulfillment of its presence for a social system (see Figure 1). For example, for the concept of identity: when totally missing it represents anonymity while when fulfilled represents social presence (with intermediate points such as personal identity construction). For the concept of space: when missing it represents a topographical space while when fulfilled represents social places (with intermediate points such as third places and personal places). For the concept of time: its total absence is system 'amnesia' while its fulfillment is memory (with intermediate points linked more or less to the concept of persistence). Finally, for the concept of action: its total absence is the obstruction of action (i.e. my user can only look at my application) while its fulfillment is social actions (with intermediate points such as public personal actions and the like). Figure 1 also highlights that the total framework is not simply a list of elements (i.e. its application doesn't mean putting the four elements in your system one after the other) but is created through the delicate balance between them. It is up to the designer to choose which element of the framework to stress or not during the creation of a dynamic experience, such as a serious game with social integrated features.

THE "PROFILE" OF AN APPLICATION

The use of the above-described axis in conjunction with Table 1 can help to analyze existing applications. In the rest of this section we will show how using Second Life and Facebook, two very popular social applications (Table 2).

The analysis of the two above-mentioned applications was made following these steps:

1. A complete list of the features implemented in the system was filled.
2. Each feature was positioned in the 'right' cell of Table 1 (i.e., identity features into the identity field, and so on). Table 2 shows a short example of this table filling.
3. Features belonging to the same elements were compared and regrouped. For example 'changing the face appearance' can be considered as a subpart of 'changing the avatar appearance,' and the like. This is a very important step, in order to not count two times the same element.
4. The final features were totaled (i.e., how many features impact the identity construction, and so on).
5. The resulting scores were used for creating a radar graph basing on the axis in Figure 1.

The result of the analysis is shown in Figure 2. In this way a 'Profile' of each application based on the framework was obtained. What is interesting for the purpose of this chapter is to compare the two profiles. Facebook can be defined as an 'Everyday application' where actions (and identities) are the main elements. As the name implies, an 'Everyday application' is one that is used every day (or most days) by its users. This means that each and every day they do something with it. Communicating with coworkers, sharing what they ate for breakfast, sharing the pictures of last holidays, and the like (i.e, they make micro-actions). An interesting aspect in Facebook's profile is the time axis. In Facebook, by default only a limited number

Table 1. Critical factors for building an SIS

Identity		
Factors	**Features for Identity construction**	**Social Implications**
Public Textual Claims	- Screen names - Personal profile (age, sex,etc.) - Resumé - Status . . .	Explicit self expression and Behavioral residue (e.g., 'the status makes us think that the user is always upset', etc.)
	- Networks membership declaration - Post and Comments - Online Status . . .	Explicit self expression and Collateral information (e.g, 'I know user's interests through his groups and comments', presence awareness, etc.)
Public Visual Claims	- Avatar - Pictures - Interposed avatar - Environment graphical personalization . . .	Explicit self expression and Collateral information (e.g., 'know me through my friends',reputation, etc.)
Space		
Factors	**Features for Space/Place shift**	**Social Implications**
Public Places	- Public (part of) Homepages (i.e., the public result of a personalized homepage) - Personal Home in games - Personal Content maps/ . . .	Explicit personalization and Behavioral residue (e.g., 'the homepage lets me know what your interests are', social sense of presence, etc.)
Private Places	- Personal (part of) Homepages i.e., the private result of a personalized homepage) . . . (same features as Public Places, with the setting private)	No impact on the social part. However personal impact on the shift Space/Place
Third Places	- Chat - Cantina's in games - Forum - (World/concept) Maps . . .	Social sense of presence. Understanding of community's interests, etc.
Time		
Factors	**Features for Time construction**	**Social Implications**
Persistence	- Logs - Chat logs - Posts - Interface/system changes . . .	Explicit self expression and Behavioral residue (e.g., the homepage personalization, my posts, etc.)
Memory	- Information retrieval tools - People retrieval tools . . .	Shared memory and knowledge for the Community/Social Network
Action		
Factors	**Features for Actions**	**Social Implications**
Signs of life	- Online presence - Latest posts - Leader boards - Reputation systems . . .	Emergence of a 'live' network of users, etc.
Passive/active behavior shift	- In(visibility) of private/public activities - Lurking	Social and individual participation emerge and is not 'pushed'.
Different level of relationships	- Chatting - Gift-giving activities - Online presence - Friends and followers . . .	Balancing between emergence and clear statement of a network, etc.

of feeds are shown on the homepage. The older posts are in fact hidden every time a new post is added. In this case, the general idea is to focus on the 'here and now' created on the later posts and pushing conversation around them rather than on the persistence. As you can see, Facebook is not a 'persistent' application even though it has some kind of 'memory.' On the contrary, Second Life is a virtual world where you are engaging in a set of complex activities (for example, building a whole area in a collective way). However the system does not allow for an internal management of the history of the actions (e.g., it is not possible to retrieve old chats). For this reason most of the people engaged in Second Life activities use external 'memory' applications (such as blogs) in order to build the memory of their actions. In the end, both the applications have a 'low' value in the time element of the profile. However, while in Facebook's case the lack of memory is not a problem (as said it is an everyday application in which you make 'small' actions: taking quizzes,

Figure 1. A graphical representation of the four elements through axis

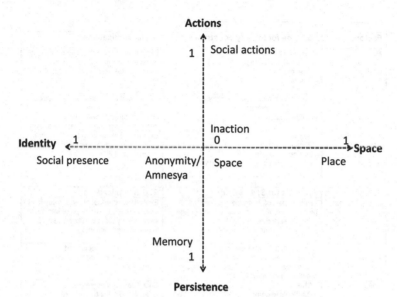

post comments, and the like), in Second Life this lack of memory is a real problem (proved by the use of external blogs). For this reason, we can say that while the profile of the Facebook application for the time part is a good one, the Second Life one is not.

Defining an Application "Expected Profile"

The fact that the balance between the four factors is context dependent (i.e., that from the time point of view the Facebook profile is a good one while the Second Life one is not) leads to the consequence that creating a Social Interactive System does not mean 'making the four elements equal' (i.e., having a radar graph balanced over the four axis) for all the social applications. This means that different kinds of application will have different kinds of 'profiles' (based on the four elements). To summarize, there is not one social interactive design solution for all. For this reason it is very important before filling in the elements table to have a conceptual phase, which defines your 'Expected Application Profile' (i.e., you have to know what you want to create and what

Table 2. An example of table filling

Time		
Factors	**Facebook**	**Second Life**
Persistence	- Posts - Interface/system changes	- Logs (only for advanced users) - Chat logs (only for advanced users)
Memory	- People retrieval tools	- People retrieval tools
Action		
Factors	**Facebook**	**Second Life**
Signs of life	- Online presence - Latest posts	- Online presence
Passive/active behavior shift	- In(visibility) of private/public activities - Lurking	
Different level of relationships	- Chatting - Gift-giving activities - Online presence - Friends and groups	- Chatting - Gift-giving activities - Online presence - Friends and groups

Figure 2. The application profile for Facebook and Second Life

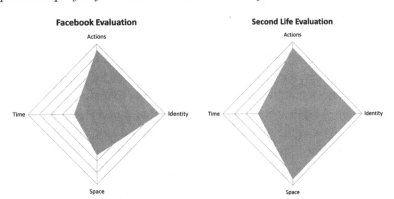

the consequences are of different balancing). In fact, for your system sociality could be something as simple as experiencing the game while being aware of others co-existing in the same world. For example, it is a matter of fact that many players of Massive Multiplayer Online (MMO) games (like World of Warcraft—WoW) will never really interact with other players. At the same time, the experience for them is increased due to the social nature of the environment (i.e., the fact that there are other players that they may come across and interact with, even if it is in a very simple way). In this case the 'Expected Profile' for the application is a social environment that is low on (social) active choices but high on passive experiences (e.g., being aware of others' presence) (Metcalf, 2007). On the contrary, if you want to create a game that is half way between a persistent world and a casual game (as in most of the games developed for browsers), the 'Expected Profile' will focus on actions and space more than on identity. In other words: you can minimize some aspect of the framework but you cannot 'ignore it.'

Defining SIS through "Family Resemblance"

However, saying that before filling in the table the designer has to create an 'Expected Profile' for the application gives rise to the necessity to find a way to distinguish between a *good* 'Expected

Profile' from a *bad* one based on the particular context and on the particular purpose of the application. In order to overcome this difficulty a field study on already existing applications was conducted. During the analysis of the social ap plications used for the framework creation, a set of common uses of the four elements emerged. These configurations are common to the *good* (from the sociability point of view) profiles, and are absent in the *bad* ones. To be specific, the analysis highlighted a minimal 'configuration' for each kind of SIS (social networks for general purposes, virtual worlds, and so on).

The idea of basic elements shared between applications can lead to the concept of 'patterns.' However the idea of pattern does not underline the fact that some elements are shared between the different kinds of applications (e.g., that the use of a high level of identity features is common to virtual worlds but also to social networks). For this reason is preferable to adapt Wittgenstein's idea of 'Family Resemblance' to Social Interactive Systems Design.

Family resemblance (German Familienähnlichkeit) is a philosophical idea proposed by Ludwig Wittgenstein with the most well known exposition being given in the book Philosophical Investigations (Wittgenstein, 1991). The idea itself takes its name from Wittgenstein's metaphorical description of a type of relationship he argued was exhibited by language. Wittgenstein's point was that things, which may be thought to be connected by one essential common feature, may in fact be connected by a series of overlapping similarities, where no one feature is common to all. If we gather five members of the same family, they probably look alike, although there is no distinctive feature that they all share in common. A brother and a sister might have the same dark eyes, while that sister and her father share a slightly turned-up nose. They have a group of shared features, some of which are more distinctly present in some members of the family, while some features are not present at all. Games, which Wittgenstein used to explain the notion, have become the paradigmatic example of a group that is related by family resemblances. Wittgenstein asks himself the question: how do we define a 'game'? Solitaire is a game, so is basketball, chess, bingo, poker, pick-up-sticks... If these are all games, they must have something in common, something that makes them games. If we analyze a set of games what emerges is the picture of overlapping sets of features which come together to form an interlinked array. By the time we get to Game 4, none of the properties in Game 1 are even there—they share no properties, yet they are both games.

Wittgenstein's main idea is to decide whether something is a game not by asking if it has this or that property, but by seeing if it might fit into such an array.

To 'translate' Wittgenstein's idea in our SIS world: the elements of our Table 2 are the single letters of our array. The 'Expected Profile' for the application is the set of elements of the array (for example Game 1). Now, what is interesting in this approach is that Game 1 and Game 2 share a set of common elements. This implies the necessity

to decide in what moment Game 1 differs from Game 2 or, out of metaphor, in what moment a Virtual World like Second Life is different from a MMORPG like World of Warcraft. The current most diffused SIS are analyzed in Table 3 and Table 4 in order to underline their family resemblance. Weights were calculated in the same way as for the Second Life and Facebook profile. To make the analysis table more readable a legend for the used abbreviations follows (see Table 3). Before continuing the analysis, it is important to clarify that this is a simplified table. In an accurate analysis elements with M and 1 need to be detailed.

Once deconstructed into their sub-elements it is clear that M can be considered as a sub-set of 1 because M elements possess at least one element of the 1 set. For reasons of clarity, this in depth analysis was not detailed in the table. However, also an analysis of the simplified Table 4 can underline some 'family resemblances.' For example for social networking websites (such as LinkedIn, Facebook, and MySpace), the minimal configuration is IDM1-SM1-TM-AMM. Second Life shows a configuration (ID1-S1-TM-A1) nearer to WoW (IDMM-SM1-TM-A1) and Facebook (ID1-SMM-TM-A1) than to the other Virtual Worlds (for example Habbo - IDM1-SM1-TM-AM1).

Following this kind of 'family resemblance,' Second Life seems to be something of a cross between games and social networks. And so on. This way, the kind of SIS is not defined by looking at a definition but by seeing where it fits into this 'family' of activities called 'Social Interactive Systems.' This means that Social Interactive Systems show 'Family resemblance' but do not share all the same properties. In a simplified

Table 3. The legend for family resemblances

Game 1	*Game 2*	*Game 3*	*Game 4*
ABCD	BCDFG	CFGHIJK	HIKLM

Table 4. Family resemblances for some of the most used online SIS

Abbreviation	Description
ID0	indicates the absence of any social identity representation element
IDM1	indicates the presence of at least one social identity representation element
IDMM	indicates the presence of several social identity representation elements
ID1	indicates the presence of all the social identity representation elements
S0	indicates the absence of any space/place shift
SM1	indicates the presence of at least one space/place shift element
SMM	indicates the presence of several space/place shift elements
S1	indicates the presence of all the space/place shift elements
T0	indicates the absence of any persistence
TM	indicates the at least the persistence of the environment
T1	indicates the presence of all the time elements
A0	indicates the absence of any action
AM1	indicates the presence of at least a social action
AMM	indicates the presence of several social actions elements
A1	indicates the presence of all the social actions elements

way, if I am going to create a social network for friendship purposes I will create something *with at least* the IDM1-SM1-TM-AMM profile. Note that the 'minimal' configuration may not be the better configuration (i.e., the fact that all the current Social Networks share this configuration does not mean that this is the best one). The framework is not the knowledge of the minimal configuration: it is the knowledge of the consequences of the absence of each element. Only the designer's expertise can decide where to put the limit for the minimal configuration. To summarize: there is no 'Expected Profile' useful for all the kinds of e.g., social networking applications. However for each axis the impact of each configuration (each subset of 'family resemblance') over the social experience can be detailed.

AN EARLY EVALUATION FOR AN APPLICATION

As we have seen, the above-described framework can be used in the phase of design of a social application but also for evaluation purposes. This section will go into more detail regarding this aspect, as the framework can be helpful in evaluating the 'potential sociability' of an application. If the use of all the four elements is fundamental in the building of *good* (successful from the social

point of view) applications, a way to measure their absence/presence at early stages can help to avoid developing *unsuccessful* systems (i.e., systems that are destined to have a negative impact on sociability). This section thus proposes an 'Early Evaluation Method' (from here on EEVa method) based on the framework. Normally, software development starts with a design document. Using the design document, engineers decide on a set of software requirements. To accomplish this, they employ use cases and other tools of analysis. After that, they design the software (and finally someone develops it). The main problem of this approach is that the starting design document provides information about the application from the perspective of the designer (who could be a computer scientist but also a pedagogue, and the like). Let us use a game design as an example. The game designer seeks to create a game with a map editor, a character editor, several levels, and a complex world. This means that the game design document provides information about the game as an artistic entity. However, the requirements that are drawn from this document constitute the first important step in transforming the vision of the game into technical specifications. For this reason, after the design phase each developer faces the problem of how to translate the design in natural language into software requirements. In order to overcome this difficulty, an interesting approach is the use of the *stripes* concept. In Flynt's definition, a stripe is 'a set of functionalities embodied in a single component of the system' (Flynt, 2004). More specifically, a stripe embodies a subset of the functionalities described in the requirements document (for example the GUI—Graphical User Interface—can be a stripe). Generally, the first stripe consists of only the most general system features, such as the framework of the application. With each successive stripe, the features addressed become more refined. The level of detail and complexity grows with each stripe, but because the detail and complexity are layered, at no point does complexity become overwhelming. While it is true that the stripes approach calls for designing all stripes before beginning software construction, it also involves an approach that is iterative and incremental. In fact, after the creation of the stripes, priorities are given to their development. In addition, priorities can also be given to the setting of features they embody. This kind of management creates an incremental approach at both levels: the single stripe and the whole system. The interesting part of this approach (i.e., the part that suggested a possible link with the framework described in this chapter) is its incredible use of the concept of 'chains of actions.' The problem with the same approach is that it does not give any (more or less) formal way to translate the natural language design into stripes. For this reason, the need arises to develop a method for *translating* the design into stripes. In order to make this translation, an iterative phase of pre-design was inserted between the concept development and the classical computer scientist design phase. The idea behind this insertion is to use the pre-design phase to translate the design into requirements in the following way. The designer takes the natural language specifications; he/she analyzes them through a schema based on the framework and finds the actions that characterize the design. Each of these actions can be defined as a 'sub-stripe' (i.e., a part of the total stripe). For example, the path to follow in order to complete a quest in a game can be seen as a stripe (find a better sword, find the monster, kill the monster, acquire experience), while the fact that it is possible, for example, to kill monsters in order to fulfill your quest, is a sub-stripe. Once the designer has defined all the sub-stripes for the design he/she joins them into a set of chained actions that will result in the stripes (for example the quest we mentioned above). The analysis of each stripe will allow the designer to de-construct them into features (note again that features can be common to different stripes) and components. In our previous example, the system that manages experience every time you kill a monster can be seen as a feature. Obviously, this feature can be shared by other stripes. In order to follow the path described, a detailed list of actions for helping the 'translator' in his deconstruction was created (see also Table 5).

As a first step, the 'translator' does a very simple thing: he/she takes the design and highlights actions (i.e., verbs) in natural language. For each action, he/she then defines the elements that impact on the framework using the field of the table. The 'Who,' 'Interaction space,' and 'When' elements, for example, help to define the persistence (or not) of the action and if the action concerns identity or space (who is acting: the user, the system and the like, and 'over what' he is acting: the avatar, the system the Graphical User Interface and the like). The application of this method is linear (in fact, the 'translator' analyzes the document paragraph after paragraph). The result of the application is a set of very detailed sub-stripes. Once detailed, sub-stripes can be used in order to make the 'Early Evaluation' of the designed application (Figure 3). In fact, filling in the schema for each sub-stripe implies 'explicit' actors/agents (of the action) and objects. However, in order to complete the 'Early Evaluation' only the sub-stripes that fall under the label of the four elements of our framework are analyzed. For example, the fact that the system has a splash screen can be counted as an action but not as an action that impacts on the system. Then, we can provide

Table 5. The schema for the sub-stripes creation

SIS Name	Description/Focus	Elements
Facebook	Social Networking(friendship)	ID1-SMM-TM-A1
ANobii	Collection (books)	IDM1 -S1-T1-AM
Flickr	Collection(photos)	IDM1 -SMM-T1-A1
MySpace	Social -Networking(show-business)	ID1-S1-TM-AM
LinkedIn	Social Networking(business)	ID1-SM1-TM-AMM
Bebo	Social Networking(friendship)	IDM1-S1-T1-AMM
Friendster	Social Networking(friendship)	IDM1-SM1-TM-AMM
Gaia Online	Virtual World(general/game)	ID1-SM1-TM-AM1
World of Warcraft	MMORPG	IDMM-SM1-TM-A1
Habbo	Virtual World(general)	IDM1-SM1-TM-AM1
Second Life	Virtual World(general)	ID1-S1-TM-A1
Netvibes	Aggregator	IDM1-S1-TM-AM1
Ning	Social Network Generator	IDM1-SM1-TM-AM1
Stumble Upon	Collection(site preference)	IDM1-SMM-TM-A1
Twitter	Micro-blogging	ID1 - SMM -TM- A1
Windows Live spaces	Blogging	ID1-SM1-TMM-AM
del.icio.us	Collection(links)	IDM1-SM1-T1-AMM
Wikipedia	Collection (enciclopedia)	IDMM-S1-T1-AM

weights, ranging from 0 to 1 to each sub-stripe. The translator will give 1 to the ID field if and only if the element impacts on the system, otherwise he/she will give 0. The same will be done for the other elements. Once the weights are given, the final action is simply to sum up all the weight present in the different columns of Figure 4. The four obtained weights can then be graphically represented through the four axes. At this point of the explanation, the need arises to clarify two things. Firstly, In Flynt's textbook there are other described frameworks (i.e., function, object-oriented, patterned). The decision to use the Stripes method is linked, as said before, to the fact that this kind of development is compliant with the concept of activity (action) present in the framework. Secondly, Flynt does not offer a method for translating the design into requirements. The adoption of an iterative pre-design phase, the creation of the translation method, and the early evaluation method that will be described in following sections are additions made by the authors. To summarize, the above-described process for the 'EEVa Method' can be described as (see Figure 3):

- **Step 1:** The translator analyses the natural language design in a linear way and under-lines all the actions (verbs). If something is not clear, the translator can pose questions using the issue field.

- **Step 2:** for each highlighted action, the translator fills in the schema in Figure 2. In particular, for each action he/she answers: Who makes the action? Is it a persistent action? What does the action impact on?

- **Step 3:** The translator gives weight to each sub-stripe, based on his answers.

- **Step 4:** The obtained weights are summed up and graphically represented.

- **Step 5:** The designer analyses the graphic and compares it to the 'Expected Profile.' Note that if there is no 'Expected Profile' this step of the process requires the presence of an expert of the framework and its family resemblance.

If the analysis it is not compliant with the desired result, the design has to be reworked and then the process re-applied for the added/modified parts starting from Step 1. On the contrary, if the analysis is considered suitable, the designer can continue his work.

- **Step 6:** Once all the sub-stripes have been obtained the designer regroups them into

Figure 3. The overall steps for the EEVa method

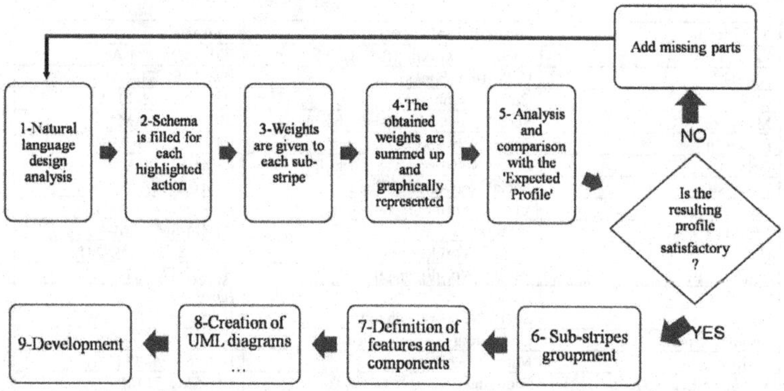

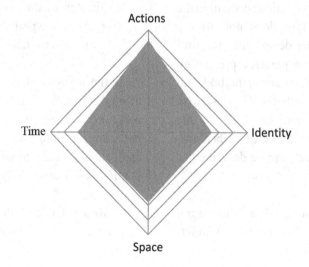

stripes, using the Who and What fields as guidelines.

- **Step 7:** For each stripe the designer defines the linked features, and then the derivatives of the components.
- **Step 8:** Using the defined objects the designer creates UML diagrams (dependencies, use-cases, etc.).
- **Step 9:** Development starts.

Note that the part strictly linked to the framework is only the first cycle (from Step 1 to Step 5). The other steps are a consequence of the stripes approach.

It is also worth noting that Early Evaluation is not an obligatory step when using the framework but it could be very useful in order to avoid developing an application and then having to return to modify it after development.

THE FRAMEWORK AND SERIOUS GAMES AS LEARNING ENVIRONMENT

While the previous sections described in detail the possible methods used to evaluate sociability in a learning environment, the next sections

Figure 4. The expected profile for the school society virtual world

will describe the experiments used to validate the above-described methods. In particular, the experiments rely on the conception and development of a serious game called "School Society."

While the term serious game is established nowadays, there is no current single definition of the concept. However, following Zyda (2005), we can say that when comparing serious games with computer games, serious games have more than just a story, art, and software. It is the addition of (any kind of) pedagogy activities, which makes games serious. A serious game was chosen to put the framework to the test since games are already a known language for Digital Natives, and using one would therefore reduce the learning curve of the application. In addition, games are goal oriented and this aspect can help the user in his understanding of what to do with the system. These two points could be allowing Digital Natives to concentrate on the practical and social use of the system rather than on how it functions. The appropriation curve was considered an important point for the experiment due to two previous experiences with other different kinds of social systems. In the first case (De Cindio, et al., 2008)—being the analyzed system a tool for community creation—the time spent by users to establish social connections was high. People had to get to know each other before starting to share common interests. In this case, the absence of a common goal did not encourage communication exchanges. In the second case (Ripamonti, et al., 2009) while the experiment was held in the virtual world of Second Life (which allows for very easy content creation and has many projects which become a means for shared communication) the absence of a single purpose lengthened the time of the experiment. In other words, the fact that a 'Resident' (i.e. an inhabitant of Second Life) can choose what to do with his in-world life had consequences similar to the first experiment: users spent of a lot of time on world exploration. Note that we are not saying that those kinds of systems are not suited for experiments; we are only saying

that from our experience games are more suited for quick experiments than other kind of environments. In the case of our experiment, we collected an interesting amount of data to analyze—more than 20,000 actions on the system in one week. These few data seems to suggest that is preferable to use serious games for experimentations than use other types of learning environments. As said before, the serious game was created ad hoc based on the framework and then used for two experiments: one focused on applying the framework to create an early evaluation of potential sociability, the other to validate/invalidate the early evaluation analyzing the actual sociability.

Before describing the two experiments, the next part will briefly describe the School Society environment.

The Framework in Action: The Gameplay for the School Society World

When the user enters the world for the first time, an animated intro scene describes how the world was created. Sometime in the future humankind has managed to practically destroy the world via magnetic weapons. The world was knocked off its axis and continents have sunk into the ocean. Only small islets remain (loosely inspired on Alexander Key's novel: The Incredible Tide). Several decades later, the survivors have managed to remodel their lives. They have built homes on the islets, as well as shops and a school. The top, elite students of this school are recognized worldwide as the best people in the world: the Legendary Eagles.

From a graphical point of view, the structure of the world reflects the cataclysm. Each Resident (students or teachers who inhabit the world) lives on his little island detached from the rest of the world and he has his own canoe that allows him to travel. In the world, the Resident is represented through an avatar (3rd person perspective). Apart from studying, there is no final aim in School

Society. Each Resident can find his own way to inhabit this word.

Based on family resemblances, the best combination for a virtual world—as School Society is—is a balanced one. This means that School Society must neglect none of the four aspects (Figure 4). Note that for another kind of game (for example a casual one) configuration should change. Hereafter a subset of game design elements (both from the framework application and from the gameplay point of view) linked to the framework are described in more detail.

- **Space in Action:** The public buildings enclosed in the world are a Pub, a Market, and a School. The basic idea was to use the Pub as a potential 'third place' (Oldenburg, 1989) for the world. In fact, the Pub is a place where a student can 'informally' meet people he does not know. On the contrary, the Market is only a space to buy items for competitions. Finally, the school is the more 'formal' space. In addition, School Society's world has its own newspaper called the 'Gazette,' which is the 'voice' of the world. Any interesting event that has occurred in the world can be found in it. This journal is a kind of herald that publicizes 'public' activities (in-world events such as tournaments) but also 'private' activities (what your friends have done). The result is a dynamic public and private space that changes over time and is the 'memory' of the interactions within the world. Each public building is managed by an NPC (Non Playing Character) with different personalities (from the chatty to the unsociable). These NPC do not exhibit autonomous behavior and they do not influence game evolution (which is, contrarily, influenced by players' interactions/aggregations). Their role is more linked to players' gratification (see Identity in Action) and personal evolution.

- **Identity in Action:** Each student can personalize the avatar he created when he entered the world whenever he wants. Moreover, a student can use the gold he has earned through quizzes to buy objects in the market, which he can then use to add personal items to his avatar. Finally, there are elements that link together space and identity. First of all, as an element of identification, the student's home is indicated as 'My home.' In addition, when he/she reaches a public place, an NPC welcomes him. NPC behavior is then influenced by players' achievements but only locally (i.e. it is not dependent on a group of players' achievements).

- **Activity in Action:** Several actions taken by participants have an impact on the world ranking in both a direct and indirect way. In the School Society world, there are two ranks: the top 10 best students and the top 10 best fighters. Fighters are people who are the best in the 'recreational' part of the game. This ranking is influenced by the equipment (bought or exchanged) each player owns. The other ranking, however, is influenced by the 'serious' part i.e. the quizzes taken by students. Quizzes are the means to gain currency to buy new equipment, while fights are a means to rise in rank in order to unlock new and more difficult quizzes. In addition, in the school building students can take part in a set of social actions: participate in tournaments and challenge the professor. In the first activity, the student is alone against other students. If he can beat all the other participants, his success is published in the world journal, the 'Gazette.' In this case, the social aspect is driven through competition. The other activity is literally a social one. If a professor is available, students can organize themselves in groups and challenge the teacher. Therefore, while the students take quizzes created by the teacher, the teacher will answer a quiz created by the students. For each answer the team gives, the time available to the teacher to solve the quiz increases or decreases (based on right or wrong answers). If the team is able to leave the teacher no time to solve the quiz, the team will be the winner of the contest and rewarded with the Medal of Honor, 'Where Eagles Dare.' In this case the bravery is also publicized in the 'Gazette' (and so will be publicly visible).

- **Time in Action:** First of all the game's world is a persistent one. This means that each time the player disconnects from his account, the game will save his status: his modifications, his avatar's appearance, his experience, and so on. Persistence in virtual worlds is linked to the importance of a community memory. An example of the impact that the lack of community memory can have on a virtual world life is well illustrated by the fact that in Second Life, where it is not possible to easily retrieve old information, community building/ memory is supported by external sites.

Figure 4 shows the final profile for School Society and summarizes the elements described in previous paragraphs. For this reason, we decided not only to make the world a persistent one but also to make all old 'copies' of the Gazette and Pub chats available for consultation. In this way, all public events, all competition winners and the like are stored (and if necessary retrieved) creating a memory for the community.

A First, Basic Experiment

The gameplay described in the previous section is a shortened version of the one used for School Society development. This means that developers received requirements in natural language. Due to space restrictions, we cannot go into detail

about how the choice of each element added to the gameplay was made. However, it is important to know that the early evaluation process was applied incrementally to create the final profile (for more details on the topic see Di Loreto 2010b, 2010c). A summary of this first experiment is described below.

- **Subjects, Procedure, and Materials:** First of all, the textual description of a School Society was prepared by a team of researchers made up mainly of pedagogues (2 people) and game designers (2 people). The actual game design document was about 20 pages (4000 words and 15 figures). A computer science engineer with 3 years' experience was specifically hired to produce the serious game specifications starting from the game design document. The methodology was introduced to him during a half-day training session conducted by the author. The engineer was allowed to ask questions about the game design document raising issues only by using a standard issue tracking system. The identities of the engineer and game design authors were not revealed to each other to prevent indirect interactions and all interactions occurred expressly through the issue tracking system. The production of the final serious game specification was performed in two phases:
  - **Phase 1:** The engineer produced all stripes and automatically drew the application profile. The result of this phase was then transmitted to game design authors who provided feedback in order to correct what was missing and guide the next phase. At this stage, they were allowed to make changes to the original game design document.
  - **Phase 2:** The engineer takes into account phase 1 feedback and makes re-

visions to produce a new set of stripes and a new application profile. Again, these results were presented to game design authors. At this point, the game designers declared themselves satisfied with the design.

The study was limited to two phases but one notices that this is an iterative process that can be iterated more than twice. Phase 1 lasted three weeks and was three times longer that phase 2. This is due mainly to the learning curve of the methodology and also to the fact that most of stripes were produced during phase 1 and only a few were modified and added from phase 1 and 2.

- **Results and Basic Discussion:** The final evaluation was conducted using interviews with the engineer and game design authors. During the interview, the engineer addressed several points regarding his experience with the presented methodology. The engineer already had some experience in developing large software systems and was therefore aware of the cost of implementation and revision of software systems. Consequently, he pointed out that the early evaluation performed between phase 1 and phase 2 helped to revise some fundamental decisions without having to conduct costly implementations. In addition, the engineer also pointed out that having extracted all stripes and grouping them into clusters makes it very easy to build a detailed storyboard of the serious game and facilitates the implementation phase.

In fact, during the implementation all stripes are translated into features that are implemented by developers. This deconstruction can also help to adopt an iterative approach by deciding what features to implement for each release. The application profile was considered by game designers as an interesting medium to communicate with

the engineer. In fact, they were given feedback that represents, to some extent, the interpretation of the engineer. For instance after phase 1, game designers noticed that several points concerning social interactions were missed by the engineer. In fact, phase 1 game design clearly mentioned the need for chat between players. Since this description was not that significant, the engineer did not create a specific stripe. When analyzing the early evaluation of phase 1, game designers discovered this omission and decided to add a description of a pub to the game design to allow players to socialize. This generated specific stripes in phase 2.

Experiment 1: Create an Early Evaluation for an Application

A single experiment obviously does not guarantee the usability of the method. For this reason, another experiment was carried out. The experiment is described in depth in Di Loreto (2010b). Hereafter, a summary of the experiment with its major findings.

- **Subjects:** The participants of the experiments were 26 computer scientists from France and Italy. The gender distribution of participants was 22 (85%) males and 4 (15%) females, with an average age of 27 years. 15 of them were master students in computer science, while the rest of the participants were professionals working in the sector.
- **Procedure and Materials:** Two 3h ad hoc sessions conducted by the same person (one for the French native speakers, another for the Italian ones) were held to introduce participants to the method. At the end of the session, each of the participants received a file summarizing the framework, the method, and the 'Expected Profile' concept.

Participants were then asked to apply the method to the School Society natural language design, and to follow a defined procedure. At this moment, they were also given an 'Expected Profile' for this application. At the end of the experiment, participants were asked to fill in a survey and another discussion session was held. No time constraints were given and the participants were not asked to develop the application. On the contrary, participants were asked to deliver the final excel sheets with the elaborated sub-stripes and stripes, as well as the UML diagrams.

- Results and Basic Discussion: Ease of use (based on the survey completed by participants) rated 2.5 (scale 0-4). On average students rated it lower than professionals. However, lower marks were given by two professionals. The reason for this mark (in participants' words) is that they are used to a non linear-analysis of the design. This means that after reading specifics, they immediately produce UML or E-R diagrams without intermediate steps. For them the way they were asked to think was too detached/far from the way they were used to thinking.

- Regarding perceived usefulness of the method, 75% (20) of participants rated it as Very Useful, 25% Quite Useful. In addition, the two people who rated it as very difficult to use, rated it Quite Useful. One of the reasons for noting this was the perceived importance of analyzing the design as carefully as possible before programming in order to avoid errors during the software development. One of the more 'enthusiastic' stated: 'It allows you to clarify the requirements of your application in your head before committing to designing the architecture. If necessary you could then fix, add or remove features depending on your objectives.'

- 97% of participants considered the time used for applying the EEVa Method the right amount of time for an early evaluation. The same number of participants asserted that the method forced them to look at the design more carefully than in normal cases.

- An interesting point to note (although not strictly linked with the framework) is that while students regrouped the sub-stripes practically in the same way, professionals were very creative. While this is not relevant for the EEVa method evaluation, this is an indicator that the remaining part of the stripe method can also be applied in a flexible way. However, as has been underlined by participants, the method does not have any specific tool or guideline that prevents one from creating a badly formed stripe. Thus a complete understanding of the UML design process is necessary in order to fully appreciate this method.

- Strictly speaking about the evaluation of the EEVa Method, all the participants found it very easy to evaluate the application.

Experiment 2: Evaluate the Real Use of the System

The main interest in the early evaluation is to compare it with the actual implementation and use of the system. For this reason, we carried out another experiment after the development of School Society in order to demonstrate that the wrong balance of the elements could considerably influence the use and the acceptance of the application. In this case, as opposed to the previous one, we tested the importance of each axis. A detailed description of the experiment could be found in Di Loreto (2010c). For the purposes of this chapter, we will detail only the systems usage and some remarks on framework elements assessed with the experiment.

- **Subjects:** The participants in the experiments were 60 students of the University Institute of Technology (IUT) of Montpellier. The gender distribution of participants was 42 (70%) male and 18 (30%) female, with an average age of 20.
  - Students were divided into four groups:
    - **Group 1:** Full vision over the system
    - **Group 2:** Vision of the system without Identity features
    - **Group 3:** Vision of the system without Space features
    - **Group 4:** Vision of the system without Time features

All the groups were able to access social actions (pub, school, and the like). In fact, social actions were used as a point of reference in order to compare the different groups' performances (e.g., the same pub, the different number of chats opened by different groups)

- **Procedure and Materials:** At the beginning of class, subjects in all groups were introduced to the virtual world of School Society. The students were then asked to use the systems for two months. A pre-defined set of tasks was used to populate four preparatory quests in order to structure the participants' interaction with the system. These tasks covered all of the major functional areas of the system to ensure an average knowledge of the system. The rest of the interactions were 'free' for the students, they just had to inhabit the world, as they liked. The idea was that if the students did not feel the absence of a feature they would not ever look for it (i.e., if they did not feel the necessity to use a chat, they would never open a chat).

At the end of the two months, students were asked to evaluate their experience in School Society. Data on the experiment were collected through two channels. In fact, the survey method was coupled with tracking methods based on technological features (log files, number of sessions, sessions' length, and the like) and based on Preece (2001) ideas. The general idea was that by cross referencing users' feedback and number of interactions (qualitative and quantitative data) it would be possible to understand whether or not the designed social system really works from the social point of view.

- **Results and Discussion:** First of all, Figure 5 shows the trend of general system usage (the number represented in the y-axis is the number of total general actions that impacted over the system, i.e. caused some change). As we can see, there is a general increase in the trend, with a peak on November 10, when the first (and only) 'Challenge the prof' was announced. This trend was mostly due to the number of private messages exchanged. This suggests that participation should be seen as a discrete phenomenon rather than as a 'continuum,' with peak moments when the local actors are more inclined to participate. The first peak, on the contrary, is linked to the 'appropriation' of the system: each group 'played' with practically all the features in the system. In this lapse of time, the average length of a session is 20 min., while for the rest of the experiment it decreased to 8 min. per session.

On the other hand, the number of sessions per day increased. In general, throughout the whole experiment Group 1 maintains a greater number of actions than the other three groups. Group 3 (space block) overtakes Group 2 (identity block) in activities when identity issues start to matter (the challenge). In addition, it is possible that the

Figure 5. System usage during the two months of the experiment

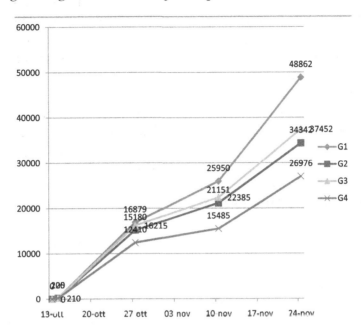

fact that the students were from the same degree course provided support through real identities to virtual identities (this will explain why until the challenge there was practically no difference between group 2 and 3). To summarize, commenting on this graph we can say that: (1) there is a general trend that underlines the fact that the totally supported group used the system more than the other three groups, (2) in some circumstances, the influence of lack of identity is more evident than in others, (3) the lack of time features had a deeper impact than the other two blocks.

- **Some Remarks on the Four Elements:** In order to understand if and why Identity and Space personalization influenced students' experience a set of open questions were submitted to each group. To one of the questions in the survey "What do you think about the fact that you can personalize your avatar?" the most common answer (68%) was that they are used to doing it (as for the rest they added adjectives such as fun, useful and the like). Groups with space

elements did not talk about habits of use but more about the fun linked to personalization (35%) and visiting friends' houses (45%). Finally, groups with time features talked about usefulness (65%) of public information. We would like to underline that these were open questions, so the fact that they shared the use of the same classes of adjectives can be seen as relevant.

In addition, in putting together the data from the survey and the system usage the experiment underlined that there seems to be a kind of hierarchy in the elements described in our framework. Oversimplifying, if we say that the Social Actions aspect has priority 0 (with no social action there is no social system), the time (persistence/memory) aspect seems to have priority 1, the identity aspect priority 2, and space priority 3 (depending on circumstances this latter priority can shift). Obviously, while the fact that the presence of all the four aspects influenced the number of interactions (compared to the lack of one of the features) is proved, the hierarchy issue is an open issue. It would be very interesting to measure if this kind of hierarchy is the norm in an environment different from a Virtual World (for example, Wikipedia).

What is certain is that the time aspect is essential for catching the peak moments and the identity element is essential to manage issues related to trust. At the same time, space and identity impacts on the perceived 'property' of the application.

GENERAL DISCUSSION AND LIMITATIONS OF THE FRAMEWORK AND ITS METHODS

The central part of the use of the framework is the understanding of the consequence of the absence of one element of the framework. In the first described experiment, participants had to compare the profile resulting from the EEVA with a given one and decide to improve the design or not. In order to do this, most of them were not willingly to 'extract' the information about the framework from the supplied files and relied on their memory (i.e., on things learned during the first 'live' session). It is our opinion that this kind of approach can be a limitation. The expertise in dealing with the framework and family resemblance for an 'evaluator' is very important. In fact, only an 'expert' can answer questions such as: What happens in the case of an application that is between a general social network and a virtual world? Which profile is the best? And so on. While detailed guidelines for specific classes of applications and fully structured examples can surely reduce the steepness of the method's learning curve, only an in depth knowledge of the framework can create a good Social Interactive Systems analyzer.

From the practical point of view, one evident limitation of this EEVA method is the fact that, while it can be applied to whatever natural language design you want (from games, to social networks, to accounting software), you need a natural language design. Now, in real life most small projects start with an idea that is re-worked

while developing (i.e., parts are added from time to time). In this case, the EEVa delays the developing starting point too long. In fact, the method schedules for cycling the EEVa each time you add consistent parts to the natural language design. If the added parts are too little the number of cycles becomes overwhelming. To summarize, this method is better applied to complex software development, which requires written requirements. Nevertheless, the need for an EEVa able to analyze the 'social potentiality' of the application still remains. Insofar as we know, there are no methods on this subject.

The last comment on this method regards the 'public.' During the first described experiment we saw the emergence of three sub-sets of population. One can be called 'the students.' They had to be guided more during the application of the method and they produced more uniform groups of stripes. The other one can be called 'conservative professionals'—for them applying the EEVa method was too far from the way they are used to developing software. Note that they were not the older professionals involved in the experiment, so this is not a matter of age. Finally, there is a population of 'flexible professionals' who added their own expertise to the experiment. Actually, this is a 'method for everyone' (especially if levels of automation for the analysis are added), but not a method useful in the same way for everyone. 'Flexible professionals' are the best candidates for the 'position' of 'profile analyzers.' During the experiment they were proactive (every single one of them read the written guidelines on the framework) when analyzing the resulting profile. Students, on the contrary, really need a set of examples to rely on, and they were not able to explain why the profile needed improvement. While this is also a way to apply the method, it is certain that the other one leads to a deeper understanding of the resulting profile consequences in terms of 'potential sociability.' In fact, while this chapter has only shown the ease of use and the learnability of the method, the real purpose of the proposed 'Early Evaluation Method' is to evaluate 'potential sociability' of an application in order to avoid time (and money) consuming developments. In order to be able to do this, the EEVa Method is useful, but the knowledge of the framework is essential.

FUTURE RESEARCH DIRECTIONS

It is then possible to say that while the framework itself could be considered as 'stable,' the evaluation methods could be improved. In addition, the idea for the framework described in this chapter started from the consideration that social elements are an important element to be addressed when designing a social software for learning purposes. We can thus say that social elements in a to-be-developed software have to be addressed at the same time as the learning aspects. At first glance, it seems that the research problem will only be linked to the integration of social aspects with learning aspects. We can than think about extending the 'Early Evaluation' method in order to include a framework able to assess learning aspects for a particular kind of learning environment. While this is surely an issue to be addressed, a usable learning system calls for a still more complex framework. In fact, not only does a learning environment for Digital Natives have to cross social and learning aspects but also to define interaction methods. As we described in Section "Digital natives and games," the way they interact with a system is "playful." How can we integrate this playfulness aspect in the evaluation of the learning environment? One of the possible solutions could be to "adapt" complex software systems by creating different profiles based on the four dimensions of the framework in order to answer to different needs. However this implies an understanding about what it means to create a playful learning environment. My personal approach is more towards gamification than towards serious games,

but as said, this is a personal approach. Another issue involving interaction is more linked to the "physical" aspect. Digital Natives are used to a plethora of interaction that are beyond the WIMP (Windows, Icons, Menu, Pointer) interaction. From a research point of view, it could be interesting to ask ourselves: Do these ways of interaction have to be taken into account from the moment of evaluation t? Does the developed application have to be "hardware independent"? Are they an additional element to be taken into account after the software evaluation moment in order to constrain or extend the profile? And so on.

REFERENCES

Bentley, R., & Dourish, P. (1995). Medium versus mechanism: Supporting collaboration through customisation. In *Proceedings of the Fourth Conference on European Conference on Computer-Supported Cooperative Work,* (pp. 133-148). ECSCW.

Blythe, M., Bardzell, J., Bardzell, S., & Blackwell, A. (2008). Critical issues in interaction design. In *Proceedings of HCI 2008, Culture, Creativity and Interaction Design.* HCI.

Carmona, M., Heath, T., & Tiesdell, S. (2003). *Public places urban spaces: The dimensions of urban design.* Burlington, MA: Architectural Press.

Danet, B., Ruedenberg-Wright, L., & Rosenbaum-Tamari, Y. (1997). Hmmm... where's that smoke coming from? Writing, play and performance on internet relay chat. *Journal of Computer-Mediated Communication, 2.*

De Cindio, F., Ripamonti, L. A., & Di Loreto, I. (2008). The interplay between the actual and the virtual citizenship in the milan community network experience. In Aurigi, A., & Cindio, F. D. (Eds.), *Augmented Urban Spaces: Articulating the Physical and Electronic City.* London, UK: Ashgate.

Di Loreto, I. (2010). *From interactive systems to social interactive systems*. (PhD Thesis). Università degli Studi di Milano. Milan, Italy.

Di Loreto, I., & Gouaich, A. (2010°). *An early evaluation method for social interactive systems*. N°ARR-10016(2010)001-010[lirmm-00486932 - version 1].

Di Loreto, I., & Gouaich, A. (2010b). An early evaluation method for social presence in serious games. In *Proceedings of the 2nd International Conference on Computer Supported Education CSEDU 2010*. CSEDU.

Di Loreto, I., & Gouaich, A. (2010c). A framework for designing social interactive systems. In *Proceedings of ICTEL 2010 Athens - 1st International Conference on Technology-Enhanced Learning*. ICTEL.

Dourish, P. (2006). Re-space-ing place: "Place" and "space" ten years on. In *Proceedings of the 2006 20th Anniversary Conference on Computer Supported Cooperative Work*, (pp. 299-308). New York, NY: ACM.

Dourish, P., Finlay, J., Sengers, P., & Wright, P. (2004). Reective HCI: Towards a critical technical practice. In *Proceedings of CHI 2004 Conference on Computer Human Interaction 2004*. CHI.

Eisenstadt, M. (2007). Does elearning have to be so awful? Time to mashup or shutup. In *Proceedings of the Seventh IEEE International Conference on Advanced Learning Technologies (ICALT 2007)*, (pp. 6-10). IEEE Press.

Flynt, J. P. (2004). *Software engineering for game developers*. New York, NY: Thomson.

Goffman, E. (1959). *The presentation of self in everyday life*. New York, NY: Doubleday.

Gunawardena, C. N., Lowe, C. A., & Anderson, T. (1997). Analysis of a global online debate and the development of an interaction analysis model for examining social construction of knowledge in computer conferencing. *Journal of Educational Computing Research, 17*, 395–429. doi:10.2190/7MQV-X9UJ-C7Q3-NRAG

Harré, R., & Langenhove, L. V. (1991). Varieties of positioning. *Journal for the Theory of Social Behaviour, 21*(4), 393–407. doi:10.1111/j.1468-5914.1991.tb00203.x

Horrigan, J. (2007). *Older Americans and the internet: A typology of information and communication technology users*. Retrieved from http://www.pewinternet.org/PPF/r/213/reportdisplay:asp

Joinson, A. N. (2003). *Understanding the psychology of internet behaviour: Virtual worlds, real lives*. New York, NY: Palgrave Macmillan.

Klemmer, S. R., & Hartmann, B. (2006). How bodies matter: Five themes for interaction design. In *Proceedings of Design of Interactive Systems (Vol. 74*, pp. 140–149). DIS.

Lakoff, G., & Turner, M. (1988). Categories and analogies. In Helman, D. H. (Ed.), *Analogical Reasoning: Perspectives of Artificial Intelligence, Cognitive Science, and Philosophy (Vol. 3)*. Chicago, IL: University of Chicago Press.

Metcalf, C. (2007). *Investigating the sharing practices of family & friends to inform communication technology innovations*. Retrieved from http://blogs.motorola.com/default.asp?item=638638

Mitchell, D. (2008). Generation z striking the balance: Healthy doctors for a healthy community. *Australian Family Physician, 37*(8), 665–667.

Oldenburg, R. (1989). *The great good place: Cafes, coffee shops, bookstores, bars, hair salons, and other hangouts at the heart of a community*. New York, NY: Paragon House.

Palfrey, J., & Gasser, U. (2008). *Born digital: Understanding the first generation of digital natives*. New York, NY: Basic Books.

Pecher, D., & Zwaan, R. A. (2005). *Grounding cognition: The role of perception and action in memory, language, and thinking*. Cambridge, UK: Cambridge University Press. doi:10.1017/CBO9780511499968

Pew Internet American Life Project. (2007). *Teens and social media*. Retrieved from http://www.pewinternet.org/pdfs/PIPTeensSocialMediaFinal.pdf

Piaget, J. (1952). *The origins of intelligence in children*. London, UK: International University Press. doi:10.1037/11494-000

Preece, J. (2001). Sociability and usability in online communities: Determining and measuring success. *Behaviour & Information Technology, 20*(5), 347–356. doi:10.1080/01449290110084683

Prensky, M. (2001). Digital natives, digital immigrants part 1. *On The Horizon – The Strategic Planning Resource for Education Professionals, 9*(5), 1-6.

Rainie, L. (2006). *Digital natives invade the workplace*. Retrieved January 13, 2009 from http://www.informationweek.com/news/internet/ebusiness/showArticle.jhtml?articleID=192700574

Rheingold, H. (1993). *The virtual community: Homesteading on the electronic frontier*. New York, NY: Perseus Books.

Ripamonti, L. A., Di Loreto, I., & Maggiorini, D. (2009). Augmenting actual life through MUVE. In Whitworth, B., & de Moor, A. (Eds.), *Handbook of Research on Socio Technical Design and Social Networking Systems*. Hershey, PA: IGI Global. doi:10.4018/978-1-60566-264-0.ch033

Scanlon, E., & O'Shea, T. (2007). New educational technology models for social and personal computing. In *Proceedings of the Seventh IEEE International Conference on Advanced Learning Technologies (ICALT 2007)*, (pp. 11-14). ICALT.

Sefton-Green, J. (2004). *Literature review in informal learning with technology outside school*. NESTA Futurelab Research Report 7. Retrieved on April 7, 2009 from http://www.nestafuturelab.org/research/reviews/07_01.htm

Tapscott, D. (2008). *Grown up digital: How the net generation is changing your world*. New York, NY: McGraw-Hill.

Turkle, S. (1997). *Life on the screen: Identity in the age of the internet*. New York, NY: Simon & Schuster.

Vallacher, R. R., & Wegner, D. M. (1985). *A theory of action identification*. Mahwah, NJ: Erlbaum.

Vallacher, R. R., & Wegner, D. M. (1987). What do people think they're doing? Action identification and human behavior. *Psychological Review, 94*, 3–15. doi:10.1037/0033-295X.94.1.3

Vredenburg, K., Isensee, S., & Righi. (2001). *User-centered design: An integrated approach*. Upper Saddle River, NJ: Prentice Hall.

Wenger, E. (1999). *Communities of practice: Learning, meaning, and identity*. Cambridge, UK: Cambridge University Press.

Wenger, E., Mcdermott, R., & Snyder, W. M. (2002). *Cultivating communities of practice.* Boston, MA: Harvard Business School Press.

Widdicombe, S. (1998). Identity as an analysts and a participants resource. In *Identities in Talk* (pp. 191–206). London, UK: Sage. doi:10.4135/9781446216958.n12

Wittgenstein, L., Anscombe, G. E. M., & Anscombe, E. (1991). *Philosophical investigations: The German text, with a revised English translation 50th anniversary commemorative edition* (3rd ed.). New York, NY: Wiley-Blackwell.

Zyda, M. (2005). From visual simulation to virtual reality to games. *Computer, 38*(9), 25–32. doi:10.1109/MC.2005.297

KEY TERMS AND DEFINITIONS

Digital Natives: From a vital statistic point of view, the so-called Digital Natives generation includes people born between 1981 and 2000. As Palfrey and Gasser claim, digital natives are connected to one another by a common culture. Major aspects of their lives—social interaction, friendships, and civic activities—are mediated by digital technologies.

Expected Profile: In this chapter, the Expected Profile of an application is the way the designer decides to balance the four elements in the Conceptual Phase, knowing the effects of this balancing.

Identity: In this chapter, the term Identity means more than the classical 'profile.' In addition, the global identity is more than the personal identity: it's also the social identity constructed through time in our system because of the interaction. So, in a SIS identity emerge: (1) from our explicit identity claims, (2) from the 'performances' (actions) we do with our personal identity, and (3) from the social identity the others build around us.

Impression Management: Impression management refers to the activity of controlling information in order to steer others opinions in the service of personal or social goals. Although people can manage impressions of almost anything (e.g., a clothing brand, a political position, etc.), people most commonly manage the impressions others form of themselves, a sub-type of impression management that is often termed self-presentation.

Persistence: In the chapter, time refers to persistence. In fact, not only communications are processes that happen during time (and for this reason require the permanence of the system you use to communicate). In addition, permanent records (such as posts) are useful if we need a 'memory' in our environment in order to create the basis of a community or a social network.

Place: The chapter, more than how to build a space, talks about how to allow the shift from spaces to places. Places normally show three characteristics elements: (1) largely exist within spaces, (2) are complex, inextricably multi-dimensional, lived, experienced, appropriated, and (3) have social meaning.

Self-Representation: Self representation is the image the subject has of him or herself based on his or her own interpretation. In this chapter we use the term in order to indicate the act of actively represent this interpretation of the self.

Space: In computer science, the term Space is used as a metaphor for appropriating the virtual environment. The use of the term Space allows, for extension, the use of expression such as: navigation, trespassing the boundaries, and the like.

Stripe: In real life, a stripe is a long, straight region of a single color. In the same way in Flynt's definition a stripe is 'a set of functionality embodied in a single component of the system.' More specifically, a stripe embodies a subset of the functionality described in a requirements document (for example the GUI—Graphical User Interface).

Virtual World: A virtual world is a synchronous, multi-user system that offers a persistent spatial environment for iconically represented participants. They are also called 'synthetic worlds.'

Chapter 9
Enhancement of Adaptation and Monitoring in Game-Based Learning Environments

Thibault Carron
Université de Savoie, France

Jean-Charles Marty
Université de Savoie, France

ABSTRACT

This chapter deals with the development of new learning environments, particularly the different aspects linked to users' collaboration in these environments. The authors believe that game-based learning can significantly enhance learning. The emergence of online multiplayer games led them to apply the metaphor of exploring a virtual 3D world, where each student embarks on a quest in order to collect knowledge related to a learning activity. In the environment, each part of the world represents a place, sometimes a collaborative place, where students are supposed to acquire a particular concept.

This new way of learning changes habits, offers new opportunities to use collaborative tools, allowing the students to co-construct knowledge efficiently. In this chapter, the authors describe an example of game-based environment that they have developed. They then give examples of uses of collaborative tools in this environment and give details on how to enhance them. The authors focus on two aspects: the monitoring of the collaborative activity, where the teacher applies his/her own strategies in order to monitor the collaborative activity; and the adaptation of the game according to the learners' profiles.

INTRODUCTION

Recent years have seen a rise in learning with Computer-Based Learning Environments. These environments provide functionalities that are recognized as being valuable, but students tend to consider them as unexciting. Observing the emergence and success of online multiplayer games with our students—the so-called "digital natives" (Rosenbloom, 2007; Purdy, 2008; Scott, 2007)—we decided to develop one as a support for our course. This led us to apply the metaphor

DOI: 10.4018/978-1-4666-1987-6.ch009

of exploring a virtual world, called Learning Adventure, where each student collects knowledge related to a learning activity. It is our view that the way to acquire knowledge during a learning session is similar to the exploration of a virtual world, pursuing knowledge quests. This approach reveals advantages, such as a recreation-type process, a large usability of the tool, or its adaptation to the student's speed.

This new way of learning changes habits, offers new opportunities to use collaborative tools, allowing the students to co-construct knowledge efficiently (Lou, 2000). However, it is often difficult for users to know how to use these tools effectively, especially because the interactions take place in a social context (Hadwin, 2010). In this chapter, we describe an example of Game-Based environment that we have developed. We then give examples of uses of collaborative tools in this environment and give details on how to enhance them. We focus on two aspects: the monitoring of the collaborative activity, where the teacher applies his/her own strategies in order to monitor the collaborative activity; and the adaptation of the game according to the learners' profiles. We explain the way for obtaining factual indicators of collaboration that are useful for the monitoring process and how to fill and update the fields of the User Model for adaptation purpose. We illustrate these two issues through two experiments carried out in the Learning Adventure environment.

A Game-Based Learning Environment: Learning Adventure

In this section, we describe a Game-Based Learning Environment that we have developed. This environment will serve as an example for illustrating the ideas described later in the chapter. We explain the links between a learning session and the objects in the Game and we give details on the enactment of a learning session with students. We then describe how the collaboration takes place in Learning Adventure (LA).

LA is a Game-Based Learning Management System representing a 3D environment where the learning session takes place (see Figure 1). A particular map (environment with lakes, mountains, and hills) is dedicated to a particular learning activity, for a particular subject. Each part of the map represents the place where a given (sub) activity can be performed. The map topology represents the overall scenario of the learning session, i.e. the sequencing between activities. There are as many regions as actual activities, and the regions are linked together through paths and Non-Player Character (NPC) guards, showing the attainability of an activity from other ones. An example of a scenario seen as a map topology is presented in Figure 2. Similar models that link pedagogical issues with game elements can be found with a more general point of view in Amory (1999) and more precisely concerning this approach in Carron (2008).

The environment is generic in the sense that it is not dedicated to a particular teaching domain. With the help from a pedagogical engineer, the teacher adapts the environment before the session by setting pre-requisites between sub activities and by providing different resources (documents, videos, quizzes) linked to the course. Experiments have been set up for learning English as well as Project Management or Object Oriented Concepts in Computer Science.

Learning Adventure is based on a role-play approach (Baptista, 2008). Players (students or teachers) possibly represented by their own avatars, can move through the environment, performing a sequence of sub activities in order to acquire knowledge. Activities can be carried out in a personal or collaborative way (see Dillenbourg, 1996, for a list of cooperation abilities): one can access knowledge through objects available in the world, via help from the teachers, or from work with other students. In order to communicate with other players a chat tool is available. It is also possible to construct group knowledge with specific tools. We detail two examples of such

Figure 1. A screenshot of an activity in learning adventure

tools later in the chapter (the "post it wall" and the "collaborative feather").

It is possible for the students to embark several knowledge quests in parallel. That is why it is important for them to be aware of the current active quests (right part of Figure 1). In order to facilitate the navigation inside the game, the objects or NPCs to be reached in the active quests are displayed on a compass (upper right corner of Figure 1).

COLLABORATIVE TOOLS FOR LEARNERS

As stated above, collaborative learning allows the acquisition of new skills from interaction with other group members. A consensus must be reached and the whole group is responsible for the failure or success of the collaborative tasks (Fischer, 1980; Mooney, 2000). In this section, we describe briefly two collaborative tools included in

Figure 2. An example of a scenario seen as a map topology

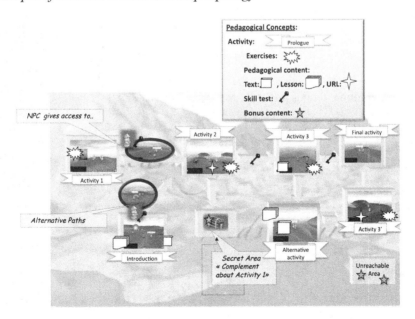

Learning Adventure. We then relate odd behaviors that we have encountered with users during our experiments and propose two general directions to consider when designing collaborative tools: the monitoring and the adaptation.

A Simple Tool: The "Post-It Wall"

In Learning Adventure, we have designed a collaborative tool called the post-it wall (see Figure 3). The idea of the tool is quite simple. It allows the same features than a board in a meeting room with post-it notes. People can stick post-it notes on a wall and move them to rearrange the ideas. Of course, when someone moves a note, all the people involved in the activity notice the change. All the participants in a "post-it wall" activity have the same view of the wall at any moment. This tool is often used when students need to organise ideas.

This tool is mainly used as a brainstorming tool, and supports the two steps of the brainstorm-

ing: the creativity step and the organization step. In the creativity step, each participant can write on a post it and put it on the board. As usually in this kind of tools, there is no criticism allowed in order to facilitate the creativity aspects. That is why there is no functionality for annotation or vote. The organization step suggests the clustering of post-it notes, which is possible by moving the notes on the wall. This is a minimal (but useful) facility.

A More Elaborated Tool: The Collaborative Feather

Designing new sessions for students with Learning Adventure reveals new needs, especially when collaboration is addressed. The "post-it wall" was a first simple example, but more complicated tools are also emerging. For instance, the co-edition of document is very often required in collective knowledge acquisition, especially in the

Figure 3. A screen shot of the "post-it wall"

reformulation phase, when the group explains the path followed to reach an objective.

Collaborative tools are difficult to use, mainly because of the group regulation. However, the CSCL community works hard on that subject. While designing the collaborative feather, we have tried to take into account the characteristics of such tools. For instance, we have separate workspaces for personal thinking and for collaborative ideas. We also maintain a common view on the collaborative space (every user of the tool has the same vision than the others).

Short Description of the Tool

This tool aims at helping a small group of people (5 to 8) to provide an outline of a document. Every member of the group takes place in front of a free board (see Figure 4). Clicking on the board gives access to the collaborative session.

One must understand that there are three different spaces used in this tool:

- Each participant has his/her personal space. A rough notebook is a good metaphor for this space. One can scribble ideas in this space before proposing an idea to the rest of the group. This space is displayed in the lower part of Figure 5.

- A collaborative workspace. The ideas proposed to the group appear in this space. Discussions around these ideas can be stimulated through actions available in the space menu. One can ask for explanation on the idea, provide a positive or a negative comment (the colour of the feather changes). Only the ideas are displayed on the board, but one can see the discussions around an idea by clicking on it. Vertical lines are displayed on this space in order to classify the ideas and construct the outline of the document in a hierarchical manner. As in the post-it wall, the users are able to move the ideas and to align them with others, to re-order them. The ideas aligned on the same line are at the same level in the outline (chapter / sub chapter / sub sub

Figure 4. General view of the "collaborative feather"

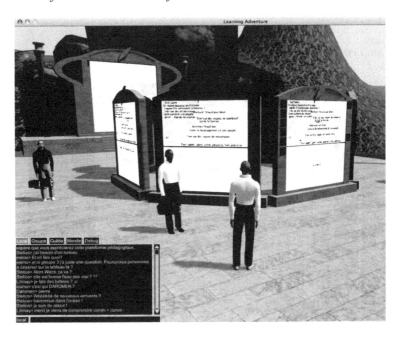

chapter). This space is displayed in the higher part of Figure 5.

• A "marble space" where the ideas, validated by the whole group, are engraved. This space is not a collaborative one. It contains the decisions of the group (from a vote on the collaborative space) and the history of all the discussions of the ideas. Hopefully, the marble space contains an outline of the document at the end.

Generally, the participants in an activity mediated by the collaborative feather want to produce a document outline. They propose ideas, comment, clarify other members' ideas, and organize them in order to produce a group result. Sometimes, the ideas have been generated through another tool. In that case, a member of the group (e.g. the teacher or the team leader) put all the ideas in the collaborative space and the aim of the group is to classify them in a hierarchical way.

How Can We Go Further with Such Tools?

We describe some experiments that we had set up with these tools more precisely later in the

chapter. We would like to stress what happened related to socially shared regulation.

With the post-it wall, odd behaviors drove the teacher to monitor the activity. For instance, some students tend to start the activity before the others arrive (some are still doing the previous activities). The first students were first manipulating the post-it notes inefficiently, moving notes that someone else just positioned elsewhere. However, they quickly understood how to self regulate the activity through the chat and obtained an acceptable diagram before the others students joined them. The teacher was faced to a real problem here, because some students were unable to participate to the collaborative activity. This can be due to a bad design of the pedagogical scenario in the game (it seems that collaborative activities in this kind of environments are optimal with 5 students). However, the teacher can monitor the activity, by organizing groups into subgroups, or by proposing a new quest to the students that have already discovered the solution. In order to do so, s/he must be aware of who was involved much in the activity. S/he thus needs awareness information, graphic widgets, e.g. a pie chart, in which each division shows the percentage of actions on the wall for one student. This "magic"

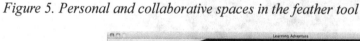

Figure 5. Personal and collaborative spaces in the feather tool

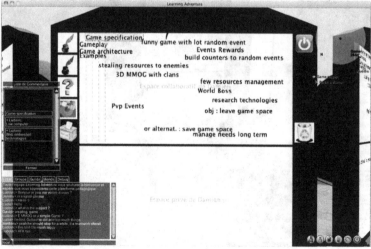

information can be obtained from the actions performed by each user in the environment. We explain the process of understanding these data traces in the next part. The monitoring of collaborative activities can thus sometimes enhance the group production. This is possible by providing the teacher with awareness information calculated from learners' traces, in real time.

With the Collaborative Feather, all the participants in the activity had the same role. There is no lead in the group since we wanted to experiment auto regulation within this tool. The role is in fact a very temporary role, assigned for doing a particular action, and this is precisely the fact of doing the action that changes the role. One can consecutively play the role of a leader when one asks for a vote, of an idea producer when one proposes an idea, of a clarifying person when one asks questions. The tool accordingly sets the appropriate rights. This approach is similar to the one taken in (Hadwin, 2010) when they declare their role when using a structured forum. Another important topic in CSCL deals with the property of the ideas produced by a group. It seems that the idea becomes the group idea only if it has been discussed within the whole group. From the three different workspaces used in the collaborative feather, it is clear that the property of an idea shifts from personal idea to group idea, since the idea is discussed, refined, classified (collaborative space) and belongs finally to the whole group once it has been validated (marble space).

In some cases, it is interesting to analyze the main roles played by the different actors during the session. Who were the leaders? Who organized the work? Who gave strength to the document, reinforcing the ideas? No doubt that these interesting information can help a lot in self organization by suggesting names of students that have skills not available in the group. This information can also point out that there are some worrying facts linked to self-regulation. We can notice that some students' involvements in the activity are very low. There are two ways of managing this fact:

Either we consider that this non involvement is not a problem and that the group will re organize activities later; or we need to avoid this by developing collaborative tools embedding regulation features that react to threshold (here a low level of participation) by asking questions to such students.

The environment will change and adapt according to the users' actions or behaviors. There is a real need for keeping a user model, containing both knowledge and behavioral information concerning a particular user. This information is used to adapt dynamically the environment to obtain an adequate level of activity for all the individuals in the group.

Now, we give more details about these two topics: Indicators and User Models.

INDICATORS

The tracing activity is an appropriate way for reflecting in depth details of the activity and for revealing very accurate hints for the teacher. Unfortunately, traces are objects very difficult to manage and understand. Carron (2006), France (2006), and Marty (2007) have already proposed some trace visualizations as a solution to specific observation problems. The purpose here is to be more general and offer observation features on any pedagogical tool.

As a matter of fact, we have chosen an approach that is as generic as possible and thus possibly independent from our application. The idea is to equip any application (here, the whole of the learning Adventure environment) with a tracing possibility. This implies the definition of an API of required basic observations. For instance, in the learning adventure environment, actions such as "entering a new zone (workshop)" or "correctly answering a quiz" may be traced and thus collected by specific elementary probes.

Basically, in our environment, we defined 17 elementary probes that may be flagged at any moment by any client of our application. As seen in Table 1, each probe contains some parameters and has a particular aim in order to complete a specific category of awareness, which is not often addressed (see Gutwin, 2002, for awareness definition).

As said before, we have developed new collaborative tools for the Learning Adventure Environment (Figure 6). These tools are also equipped with specific probes. For example, for the feather tool, we are able to know who provides new ideas, asks for explanation on the idea, provides a positive or a negative comment, structures the ideas, etc. Figure 7 and Figure 8 show indicators using these "pieces of information."

For a teacher, the expectations concerning the perception through the system are somewhat difficult to express. The level of what needs to be perceived may vary, as is also the case in traditional teaching: a teacher may want to observe basic facts (e.g., who starts a new activity) or more abstract facts (e.g., who regularly cooperates before answering a quiz properly). The API provides the users with elementary probes. They are

thus useful for observing basic facts. However, they may not be helpful enough when the level of abstraction needed is higher. For instance, being aware only of a student consulting a help file can be not very meaningful. However, if the same observation occurs just after s/he has given a wrong answer and then followed that with a success in the same activity, the teacher may be reassured as to the usefulness of the help file related to the activity. The combination of these three indicators (simple probes) allows to create a complex probe and thus to provide a higher-level explanation about the on-going activity.

As stated previously, 17 basic indicators (simple probes) have been extracted from your learning environments (see Table 1) and 3 operators have been proposed: AND, OR, THEN to combine one probe with another. All these indicators may be combined with each other to define new complex probes and their representation. Figure 6 shows an example of such a definition with the administration tool. The new indicator is available in the educational platform, with the same properties

Table 1. List of awareness indicators

Probe Name	Parameters	Awareness category
WorkshopArriving	<UserName>, <WorkshopName>	Group-structural awareness
WorkshopLeaving	<UserName>, <WorkshopName>	Group-structural awareness
WorkshopAnswering	<UserName>, <WorkshopName>	Group-structural awareness
WorkshopAnsweringWithContent	<UserName>, <WorkshopName>, <AnswerContent>	Social awareness
WorkshopTeacherValidating	<UserName>, <WorkshopName>, <TeacherName>	Group-structural awareness
WorkshopTeacherValidatingWithContent	<UserName>, <WorkshopName>, <TeacherName>, <Comment>	Social awareness
WorkshopCorrectlyAnswering	<UserName>, <WorkshopName>, <Boolean>	Group-structural awareness
StudentConnecting	<UserName>	Informal awareness
HelpConsulting	<UserName>, <HelpName>	Group-structural awareness
Chatting	<UserName>, <ChannelName>	Group-structural awareness
ChatContentListening	<UserName>, <ChannelName>, <SentMessage>	Social awareness
GroupCreating	<GroupName>, <GroupType>, <UserName1>, <UserName2>...	Group-structural awareness
GroupSplitting	<GroupName>, <GroupSplitter>, <UserName1>, <UserName2>, ...	Group-structural awareness
StudentDeconnecting	<UserName>	Informal awareness
TeacherConnecting	<TeacherName>	Informal awareness
TeacherDeconnecting	<TeacherName>	Informal awareness
TeacherHelpCalling	<UserName>, <TeacherName>	Social awareness

Figure 6. How to build up indicators from these traces

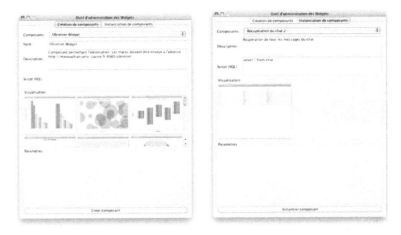

as the basic probes (Figure 7). In particular, the new ones can be reused to create a more complex probe or indicator. Thanks to this mechanism, the set of indicators naturally increases with the help of the users, guided by the needs of observation in the platform.

HOW TO FEED IN USER MODELS: STATIC AND DYNAMIC VIEWS

In LMS, the concept of learner profile or student model is used to represent the characteristics of a learner (Brusilovsky 2001; Rueda 2003; Vassileva 2003). These numerous characteristics can be classified into several categories: common characteristics, preferences, skills, and behaviors. We thus set out in this part what is inside the user model and a possible classification of the attributes

Figure 7. Individual view of user's actions in the feather tool

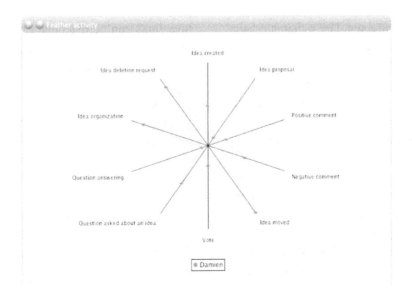

Figure 8. Collective view of users' participation to a kind of action

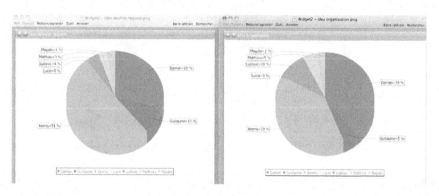

(characteristics) of the user. Then, we point out which improvements to current user model require attention in order to update it.

Categories of a User Model

A student is identified and represented by specific, generally static, information, especially in an academic domain. These common characteristics of the user model are important from an administrative point of view and are always present in a user model in order to identify a person individually.

A student is described by his/her name, student ID, past and current courses, diplomas, etc. Such information may be collected automatically from administrative services, or the system can explicitly ask the user him/herself when a new account is created in the learning game. These characteristics are often used to adapt an application, making the system user-friendly (usage of the name, of the address to find local references, etc.).

The second category of user characteristics deals with the user's preferences. In this category, we can find the User Interface Preferences (fonts, colours) or the subjects the user is keen on (if they are related to the application, of course). Some preferences may be implemented in order to provide the student with adapted graphical interfaces or adapted modality of information presentation (text, image, sound, video) (Brusilovsky, 2001). This is particularly pertinent in pedagogical sys-

tems where knowledge acquisition is enhanced by a way of teaching that is adapted to the personal means of information memorization (Choukroun, 1985) of the user (visual, auditory, data format, etc.). This approach is, however, seldom used because the teacher needs to provide the same information in many formats or modalities, which is very time consuming.

In our Game-Based Learning Management System, the third part of the user model containing information on the user skills refers to the knowledge acquired by a student. The characteristics contained in this part change more often than those described in the previous two parts. User skills are widely used to personalize the path for knowledge acquisition, and to adapt the form of presentation. (Brusilovsky, 2001) explains in detail how links can be extended or hidden according to the user's knowledge of a particular concept. In video games, especially RPG, the progression in the game is directly controlled by the skills of the avatar. For example, it is impossible to reach an island if your avatar does not swim or does not have access to a boat. The "swim skill" has to be acquired in order to explore this island.

In order to make our Learning Games adaptable, and to make the activity requisites possible, we base our user model on the same concept: a learner is defined with skills (and different levels for each skill) that allow access to new exercises or to a part of the game world. As in traditional teaching, where some exercises require specific knowledge, the scheduling of exercises depends on the skills of the student and the game world is automatically adapted to each student according to his/her user model. It is possible to see a skill level as a key enabling the following exercises (and following part of the world).

Finally, the fourth part contains characteristics deduced from the behaviour of a user (talkative, cooperative, slow). We can even imagine civic characteristics as, shown in Kahne (2009) or found in Salen (2007) via the RPG Gamestar Mechanic. This part is particularly useful in new learning systems where the collaboration and the social aspects are central. It is therefore important for a teacher to be aware of the different behaviours of his/her students: collaborative, talkative, hesitant, etc.

These characteristics are crucial for regulating a learning activity (Marty, 2007). As a matter of fact, previous works, experimentations and teachers' feedback have elicited several requirements concerning student representation in learning games. For instance, a teacher can define in his/her learning scenario (definition of the sequencing of the actions in the game) that an activity is available only if the cooperation inside a group of students reaches a certain threshold. Moreover, each exercise may bring a new skill and thus a new field in the user model. Specific behaviours may be observed or expected from a learning scenario. Therefore, we propose to see the user model as a declarative object. In function of the pedagogical scenarios already accomplished, each student will have specific content in her/his user model (see Figure 9).

Nevertheless, as in commercial websites or in collaborative platforms for knowledge management for example, the main and well-known problem of a user model is to keep it updated (Fink, 2000).

Updating the Characteristics of the User Model

In order to motivate the students, the need of a correct UM is crucial. As a matter of fact, they are fond of seeing their avatar evolving. On the other part, this information is important for the teacher to be able to provide a student with adapted content (resources, exercises, scenarios). First of all, the difficulty concerning IT platform using a user model is to get information in a user-friendly manner and to fill the first fields. Next, as said before, the problem is to keep it updated. Therefore, we imagined two concepts to achieve these goals.

The first one is used at the end of the "warm-up part" as a sort of reward proposed by a mysterious NPC who has detected some particular skills for the student: a specific test will be proposed (see Figure 10 and results in Figure 9). Indeed, this first playable part called the Newbie Park allows us to describe main functionalities, explain the use of some specific collaborative tools that are present in this game or this particular learning session. Moreover, as in many collaborative sessions, this part can be seen as a "warm-up activity" in order to get student minds into an adequate "ready to play for learning" state.

For instance, as we will see in the next part concerning experiments, the learning session concerns Project Management. Therefore, we decided to implement in the user model, the specific behaviours determined in Belbin (2004, 2010) that may appear in a project team (plant, monitor evaluator, team worker, resource investigator, co-ordinator, implementer, completer finisher, shaper). A team role came to be defined as "A tendency to behave, contribute, and interrelate with others in a particular way." Moreover, the author proposed a specific questionnaire based on 7 questions (Belbin's Team-Role Self Perception Inventory) that allow us to fill project management fields for each student. Indeed, different individuals display different Team Roles to varying degrees. Only 5-10 minutes are necessary to

Figure 9. Example of a UM in learning adventure

fill this questionnaire and the results are very interesting for the students because explanations concerning the highest values obtained are displayed at the end.

Naturally, this is particularly essential in project management (the theme of this learning game session) but also more generally in collaborative work. Moreover, we focused here on a specific theory but alternatives exist like Honey's five team roles or other personality tests (Maslow hierarchy of needs self-test, McGregor's XY Theory, etc.).

The second concept relies on the fact that, as shown before, it is possible to obtain information from traces left by the users when using the learning game. Our approach consists in taking advantage of the traces left by the players participating in the mediated learning activity to identify, to observe the actions, the behaviour and the answers of the students in order to get clues and to update some fields of the UM. Moreover, some of these pieces of information may also possibly be used to update the UM of each student. For example, the value of the field "cooperative" of a student accompanying another one of the same group to show/give her/him a specific resource available in the map will be enhanced when such behaviour is detected.

Adaptation of the Game According to the Learners' Profiles

As explained before, there is an obvious need for awareness, especially for the teacher. This lack of awareness is related both to the knowledge acquired by a particular student and to the behaviour s/he exhibited in the game. In the light of this statement, we consider that it is crucial to exploit the information collected in the user model to adapt the game. For example, when several fails are detected, adapted content is proposed (new courses, other easier exercises, help from the teacher if present in the game); when monopolistic behaviour concerning the use of a collaborative tool is detected, new specific quests are proposed, some actions are disabled, etc. We have also proposed additional collaborative content for the (detected) leader of a group.

Moreover, thanks to collaboration indicators with observation of user behaviours, we are able to identify such problems in teamwork, search and find in the UM of the learners present in the game an adapted profile.

For example, in our experiment, when particular events occur, we notify the teacher of possible lack or problem in team constitution in

Figure 10. Filling the UM thanks to a personality questionnaire

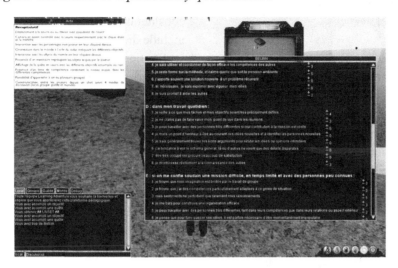

regard of particular aspects collaborative activity (e.g., a team has difficulties to propose innovative solutions, to respect delay, or some students are chatting too much). As a consequence, the teacher is able to suggest/impose a team reorganisation by proposing a new member with the right profile for optimisation purpose.

User Model: View of a Distributed Collaborative Tool

The user model thus becomes a key object in our game architecture, and students and teachers may follow-up and evaluate the learning progression through the User Model (UM).

As the user model becomes central in this approach, there are crucial needs that must be satisfied. We thus consider that all this information should be gathered in the user model seen as a unique object that should be persistent. On that point, we agree with Vassileva's idea: the user model is decentralised in new learning environments and belongs to the user (Vassileva, 2003). The user model can be a way of representing the student, bringing together the relevant characteristics for the learning aspects (skills, behaviours, preferences).

This approach leads to systems where the user model is not directly integrated in the learning tools, but is accessible through inter-process communication. Kobsa demonstrates in Kobsa (2001) the advantages of such a distributed approach.

First, the user model must be updated with respect to the effective activity, and second, the different users must be able to visualise the result easily. We thus propose a way to visualize such user models directly in the game, making a complete immersion of the students and the teacher possible. Moreover, as we will see, these artefacts, representing learning progression, knowledge, or behaviours may also be visible to other students and are additional elements that enhance collaboration. Indeed, although a user model is generally considered as a private, more or less realistic view of a user, we propose to take advantage of observation in learning games and extend our vision of a user model by adding another specific fundamental point of our learner model. It concerns the concept of interactive future views. As we will see presently, rules may be used to help the learner to reach goals proposed by the "virtual" views.

Static and Dynamic View of a User Model

From our point of view, as the user model is an object known to the users, it can also be a reactive object, and in this chapter, we propose a way to express intentions by acting on the user model. For instance, a teacher can express his/her intentions for a particular student skill to be improved. The learning scenario will thus be adapted to take this constraint into account.

As we can see, the user's characteristics are numerous and it is a challenge for the game designer to present them to the users without obliging them to change their focus of attention. In addition to the current trends in the user model field, there is a real need for considering the user model as a real object, central in the system. As seen, this object is used to adapt the learning aspects in the game and the game itself. However, as a real object, we should also perform actions on it, such as interaction or visualisation. The interaction with the user model opens new perspectives in which the user can act on his/her own representation, expressing wishes on what skills s/he would like to enhance.

From what we have described, it is clear that the user model is an important piece of information for the user. This model can serve in other learning environments to personalize them but also as data for expert research (we here approach the field of knowledge capitalization). As a matter of fact, the user can see the user model of the learning game as a kind of passport describing his/her skills and behaviour. If s/he is interested in providing this passport to someone else, this object can be used as a real collaborative tool. In a pedagogical set-up, the teacher and the student both have a view as to how the student can improve his/her personal skills and behaviour. These views are not necessarily the same. A student may want to focus on one improvement such as "be even better in computer programming" whereas the teacher finds it more important for this student to "improve his/her foreign language ability" or to

"adopt a more collaborative behaviour." All these considerations led us to extend our user model to include different views.

Starting from the current user model (real view) for a particular student (calculated as defined previously), the student would like to improve certain characteristics of his/her avatar (exactly as a user tries to make his/her avatar evolve in an RPG, which is a fundamental motivation point in such games). By defining these desired improvements, s/he defines his/her personal target, a future virtual user model view. In parallel, the teacher can have his/her own vision of the improvements needed and defines the academic target, a future virtual user model view. This object can thus take several forms and can be a negotiation object for making an action plan for the improvement of a particular student. This is richer than a simple mark report, because the behavioural aspects are present, too.

In Carron (2009) and Marty (2011), we proposed an adapted and user-friendly representation of the user model which is important to keep the learner immersed in the game; linking the standard user model formalization (text, xml) with a graphical one.

CASE STUDIES

Short Description of the Experiment

Case 1

Conditions and Methodology of the Experiment

This experiment was carried out in 2010 in our university with six groups of fifteen students with their teacher. The students were 18 years old and familiar with computer use. Each student accessed the virtual environment through his/her workstation, and had a personal (adapted) view on the world (see Figure 11). These students used the environment for approximately two hours and half. They were explicitly allowed to communicate through the chat tool provided with the system and were warned that they would be observed concerning the use of the system. The students were free to refuse this observation (the same practical work was available outside the learning environment), but everyone agreed to follow the proposed protocol. However, the first part of the session deals with a fifteen minutes introduction practice called the "Newbie Park" in order to discover and explain step by step the basic functionalities of the game (collect bag, quest book, skill book) and specific collaborative tools (post-it wall, white board, etc.).

Pedagogical Objectives

The aim of the session (role-playing game) was to assess the knowledge and know-how of the students about Object-Oriented Concepts. A story guided the knowledge quest thanks to metaphors. The challenge is encouraged through NPCs who propose a coherent contest. Indeed, in one of the activities for learning one of these concepts in this environment, the students were asked to use this post-it wall to provide the class diagram of an ecosystem whose components were present in the game. The solution had to be the result of the common thinking from a group of fifteen students. The final objective was, here to fight an evil character: "the boss" thanks to a correct diagram displayed on the post-it wall. Immersion is reinforced when the users' actions have a direct impact on the objects of the world. As said before, the teacher was present in the game via an avatar: it was possible to chat with him, to ask for help for example. In terms of monitoring example, the teacher were warned thanks to dedicated indicator of a monopolistic attitude of a learner and a supplementary specific quest was proposed to this student in order to let the others use the post-it wall. Naturally, this quest was created with this pedagogical scenario but was just not available for all students.

Technical Considerations

The whole environment is coded in JAVA developed with the help of an engineer and students on placement (internship). The network part relies

Figure 11. Conditions of the experiments

on the Red Dwarf project (http://www.reddwarf-server.org/). The whole environment is based on client-server architecture.

Correct actions are automatically rewarded with the relevant skill level up. The learner's user model is consequently updated in the game.

The second case study deals with a similar experiment concerning Project Management.

Case 2

Conditions and Methodology of the Experiment

This experiment was carried out in 2011 in our university with co-located settings. The conditions and methodology were almost the same than the one described before. The main difference lies on the fact that three groups of five students were created at the beginning of the session and maintained all along the experiment as justified in Gress (2010). Moreover, the end of the first part allowed to fill a questionnaire to initiate some values of the user model as explained before.

Pedagogical Objectives

The pedagogical scenario contains two distinct phases: First, the students are asked to design a game from blocks obtained in the game. Then they must organize the first steps to take in the Scrum methodology in order to implement this game.

In the first activity in this scenario, the students were asked to find 3 parts of game bricks classification (Djaouti, 2011) whose components were hidden in the game (see Figure 12). Then they had to design a game based on these bricks. The collaboration for this design was effective through the specific collaborative tool called collaborative feather. The solution had to be the result of the common thinking from a group of five students (see Figure 11).

Once a proposition has been elaborated, the project management part could begin. The learning content only dealt with "SCRUM elementary concepts." For each team, five parts of SCRUM lessons were dispatched in the world (resources, examples, part of lecture); one specific for each student of a same group. With that information and the concept elaborated in the previous part of the session, each group had to produce three key documents of the SCRUM method: the Product Backlog Product, the First Sprint, and the Sprint Backlog (Kniberg, 2007). In terms of adaptation thanks to user profiles, we detected the leader of each team (highest value thanks to questionnaire and specific actions done using the collaborative feather such as "ask for a vote to validate the work") and gave new collaborative goal to these students. The aim of the session was to assess the knowledge and know-how of the students about the latter and to see how teamwork could be self-regulated thanks to specific functionalities of collaborative tools.

Evaluation and Results

Concerning these two experiments, two ways of evaluation were chosen: First of all, quantitative thanks to collaborative indicators elaborated with traces left by the users when collaborating and another part, qualitative with questionnaires and explicit feedback of the teacher.

At the end of the experiment, the students were asked to fill in questionnaires to give feedback about their feelings concerning their work session. The questionnaire (ranking and open-ended questions) evaluated aspects relating to several parts of the learning game (pedagogical content, scenario-story, collaborative activities and specifically collaborative tools, and user model evolution). As usual in our experiments, the final question let the students propose improvements concerning weak and strong points of the game. For example, they found that the visualization of the questionnaire must be improved.

The initial objective concerning collaboration perception was reached. The students were unanimous in preferring to work with this envi-

Figure 12. Searching and finding game bricks

ronment rather than do conventional practical work on workstations, and more generally were very enthusiastic about this kind of experiment. Apart from their perception of the scenario, male and female students appear to react similarly to this learning game, but as usual, this may be due to the small sample size, which is not a true representation of the population, as it is now well known that specific gender aspects have to be taken into account (Hayes, 2008). It was already the case last year.

From the teacher's point of view, in the light of previous experiments (Marty, 2009; Bisognin, 2010), it was mandatory to have tools supporting him in the monitoring task with the help of an updated user model for each student: this was naturally a main goal for these experiments. As explained before, several indicators or observation widgets (see Figure 7 and Figure 8) were therefore set up in our environments in order to meet this requirement. The results were very satisfying but the set up of such tool and experiment is extremely time-consuming for the teacher. In addition, we are expecting a quick dynamic scenario editor in order to elaborate/modify new accurate quests during the session. We will only see later if all these facilities may be reused easily in other domains.

Other experiments are currently planned in the context of other projects.

FUTURE RESEARCH DIRECTIONS AND CONCLUSION

In this chapter, we have illustrated a way of regulating a collaborative session thanks to information found both in the game during the pedagogical session and in user model of the learners. We focused on two aspects: the monitoring of the collaborative activity, where the teacher applies his/her own strategies in order to monitor the collaborative activity; the adaptation of the game according to the learners' profiles. We explained the way for obtaining factual indicators of collaboration that are useful for the monitoring process and how to fill and update the fields of the User Model for adaptation purpose. Finally, we illustrated and validated from a technical point of view these two issues through two experiments carried out in the Learning Adventure environment. This environment is collaborative, multiplayer and fully observable thanks to traces left during the game. These traces allow us to elaborate collaborative indicators. Moreover, the feedback collected from these experiments; we are able to obtain new factual indicators of collaboration exploiting traces left by the users.

In the PEGASE project, supported by the French Ministry for the Economy, Industry, and Employment, we are also applying this work to another domain: Product Lifecycle Management to conduct the change in industry. Another scenario was imagined, developed, and proposed for that purpose but the use of profiling is based on same concepts.

As stated previously, this environment is still being developed and will be aimed at proposing both specific collaborative tools and facilities for helping the teacher to regulate a learning session. We have shown an example based on the values of fields presented in the user model but we may also imagine self-regulation or auto regulation by the use of specific rules as it can be use in Artificial Intelligence. Self-regulation, co-regulation, and socially-shared regulation are precisely described in Hadwin (2010).

Some drawbacks persist: we must recognize that it is very difficult for the teacher to be present in the game, help the students, and regulate the session even with these specific tools. For the moment, not very well-integrated indicators are present because they are very time-consuming to develop. We currently think that we can develop some specific generic indicators dedicated to only classical fields of the user model. An interesting perspective could be to develop and propose directly within the indicators some basic regulation actions such as "send message to user," "propose new content," "change the user from group," or "enable/disable such facility/ies for this student." We are also working on a user-friendly editor separating educational concepts and game aspects into two levels. From our point of view, flexibility is a key point for these new learning environments.

ACKNOWLEDGMENT

We would like to thank G. Dalla Costa, J. Depoil, L. Kepka, and L. Michea for their great help in developing the Learning Adventure Platform.

REFERENCES

Amory, A., Naicker, K., Vincent, J., & Adams, C. (1999). The use of computer games as an educational tool: Identification of appropriate game types and game elements. *British Journal of Educational Technology*, *30*(4), 311–321. doi:10.1111/1467-8535.00121

Baptista, R., & Vaz de Carvalho, C. (2008). Funchal 500 years: Learning through role play games. In *Proceedings of ECGBL 2008*. Barcelona, Spain: ECGBL.

Belbin, R. M. (2004). *Management teams: Why they succeed or fail* (2nd ed.). London, UK: Butterworth Heinemann.

Belbin, R. M. (2010). *Team roles at work* (2nd ed.). London, UK: Butterworth Heinemann.

Bisognin, L., Carron, T., & Marty, J.-C. (2010). Learning games factory: Construction of learning games using a component-based approach. In *Proceedings of the European Conference on Games Based Learning (ECGBL)*. Copenhague, Denmark: ECGBL.

Brusilovsky, P. (2001). Adaptive hypermedia. *User Modeling and User-Adapted Interaction*, *11*(1/2), 87–110. doi:10.1023/A:1011143116306

Carron, T., Marty, J.-C., & Heraud, J.-M. (2008). Teaching with game based learning management systems: Exploring and observing a pedagogical dungeon. *Simulation & Gaming*, *39*(3), 353–378. doi:10.1177/1046878108319580

Carron, T., Marty, J.-C., Heraud, J.-M., & France, L. (2006). Helping the teacher to reorganize tasks in a collaborative learning activity: An agent-based approach. In *Proceedings of ICALT,* (pp. 552–554). IEEE Computer Society.

Carron, T., & Martym, J.-C. (2009). User modelling in learning games. In *Proceedings of the European Conference on Games Based Learning (ECGBL)*. Graz, Austria: ECGBL.

Choukroun, J., & Lieury, A. (1985). Rôle du mode de présentation (visuel, auditif, audio-visuel) dans la mémorisation d'instructions. *L'année Psychologique, 4*, 503-516. Retrieved April 24th 2009 from http://www.persee.fr/web/revues/home/prescript/article/psy0003-50331985num85429110

Dillenbourg, P., Baker, M., Blaye, A., & O'Malley, C. (1996). The evolution of research on collaborative learning. In *Learning in Humans and Machine: Towards an Interdisciplinary Learning Science* (pp. 189–211). Dublin, Ireland: Emerald Group. doi:10.1007/978-1-4020-9827-7_1

Djaouti, D., Alvarez, J., & Jessel, J.-P. (2011). Classifying serious games: The G/P/S model. In Felicia, P. (Ed.), *Handbook of Research on Improving Learning and Motivation through Educational Games: Multidisciplinary Approaches* (pp. 118–136). Hershey, PA: IGI Global. doi:10.4018/978-1-60960-495-0.ch006

Fink, J., & Kobsa, A. (2000). A review and analysis of commercial user modeling servers for personalization on the world wide web. *User Modeling and User-Adapted Interaction, 10*(2-3), 209–249. doi:10.1023/A:1026597308943

Fischer, K. W. (1980). A theory of cognitive development: The control and construction of hierarchies of skills. *Psychological Review, 87*(6), 477–531. doi:10.1037/0033-295X.87.6.477

France, L., Heraud, J.-M., Marty, J.-C., Carron, T., & Heili, J. (2006. Monitoring virtual classroom: Visualization techniques to observe student activities in an e-learning system. In *Proceedings of the ICALT*, (pp. 716–720). IEEE Computer Society.

Gress, C. L. Z., Fior, M., Hadwin, A. F., & Winne, P. H. (2010). Measurement and assessment in computer-supported collaborative learning. *Computers in Human Behavior, 26*(5), 806–814. doi:10.1016/j.chb.2007.05.012

Gutwin, C., & Greenberg, S. (2002). A descriptive framework of workspace awareness for real-time groupware. *Computer Supported Cooperative Work, 11*, 411–446. doi:10.1023/A:1021271517844

Hadwin, A. F., Oshige, M., Gress, C. L. Z., & Winne, P. H. (2010). Innovative ways for using gStudy ot orchestrate and research social aspects of self-regulated learning. *Computers in Human Behavior, 26*(5), 794–805. doi:10.1016/j.chb.2007.06.007

Hayes, E. (2008). Girls, gaming and trajectories of IT experience. In Kafai, Y., Heeter, C., Denner, J., & Sun, J. (Eds.), *Beyond Barbie and Mortal Kombat: New Perspectives on Gender and Gaming* (pp. 217–230). Cambridge, MA: MIT Press.

Kahne, J., Middaugh, E., & Evans, C. (2009). *The civic potential of video games*. Cambridge, MA: MIT Press.

Kniberg, H. (2007). *Scrum and XP from the trenches: How we do scrum*. Enterprise Software Development Series.

Kobsa, A. (2001). Generic user modeling systems. *User Modeling and User-Adapted Interaction, 11*(1-2), 49–63. doi:10.1023/A:1011187500863

Lou, Y., Abrami, P. C., & Spence, J. C. (2000). Effects of within-class grouping on student achievement: An exploratory model. *The Journal of Educational Research, 94*, 101–112. doi:10.1080/00220670009598748

Marty, J.-C., & Carron, T. (2011). Observation of collaborative activities in a game-based learning platform. *Transactions on Learning Technologies, 4*(1), 98–110. doi:10.1109/TLT.2011.1

Marty, J.-C., Carron, T., & Heraud, J.-M. (2009). Observation as a requisite for games based learning environments. In *Games Based Learning Advancements for Multisensory Human Computer Interfaces: Technics and Effective Practices* (pp. 51–71). Hershey, PA: IGI Global. doi:10.4018/978-1-60566-360-9.ch004

Marty, J.-C., Heraud, J.-M., France, L., & Carron, T. (2007). Matching the performed activity on an educational platform with a recommended pedagogical scenario: A multi source approach. *Journal of Interactive Learning Research, 18*(2).

Mooney, C. (2000). *Theories of childhood: An introduction to Dewey, Montessori, Erikson, Piaget and Vygotsky*. Minneapolis, MN: Readleaf Press.

Purdy, J. A. (2008). *Serious games: Getting serious about digital games in learning*. Retrieved from http://www.corpu.com/newsletter%5Fwi07/sect2.asp

Rosenbloom, A. (2007). Interactive immersion in 3D computer graphics. *Communications of the ACM, 47*(8), 28–31. doi:10.1145/1012037.1012058

Rueda, U., Larranaga, M., Arruarte, A., & Elorriaga, J. A. (2003). Dynamic visualization of student models using concept maps. In *Proceedings of the 11th International Conference on Artificial Intelligence in Education*, (pp. 89-96). AIE.

Salen, K. (2007). Gaming literacies: A game design study in action. *Journal of Educational Multimedia and Hypermedia, 16*(3), 301–322.

Scott, G. (2007). *Games get down to business: Simulations growing in popularity as younger workers move up the corporate ranks*. Retrieved on the 16 June 2007 from http://www.theglobe-andmail.com/servlet/story/RTGAM.20070502.wgtgames0502/BNStory/GlobeTQ/home

Vassileva, J., McCalla, G., & Greer, J. (2003). Multi-agent multi-user modeling. *User Modeling and User-Adapted Interaction, 13*(1), 179–210. doi:10.1023/A:1024072706526

Zimmerman, B. J. (1990). Self-regulated learning and academic achievement: An overview. *Educational Psychologist, 25*, 3–17. doi:10.1207/s15326985ep2501_2

KEY TERMS AND DEFINITIONS

Collaborative Activity: Several learners (from 2 to 15) work together in order to achieve a specific goal.

Collaborative Tool: An interactive piece of software present in the game to support collaborative activity.

Trace Observation: Each action done in the game is traced in order to be observed by another actor (i.e. the teacher) and to give, during the game, clues concerning the learning activity.

Section 3
Experiences and Uses of Educational Videogames in Different Contexts

Chapter 10
Laboratory Experiments in CSCL Activities

César A. Collazos
Universidad del Cauca, Colombia

Marcos Borges
Universidade Federal do Rio de Janeiro, Brazil

Luis A. Guerrero
Universidad de Costa Rica, Costa Rica

Neide dos Santos
Universidad do Estado do Rio de Janeiro, Brazil

Jose A. Pino
Universidad de Chile, Chile

Sergio Zapata
Universidad Nacional de San Juan, Argentina

Flavia M. Santoro
Universidad do Rio de Janeiro, Brazil

Wilson Sarmiento
Universidad Militar Nueva Granada, Colombia

ABSTRACT

Several groupware tools have been implemented within Computer Supported Collaborative Learning (CSCL) research groups in order to test ideas and concepts currently being studied. It is very important to perform pilot-evaluations with these systems. The CSCW Lab is an environment for evaluating groupware within research groups. Four dimensions in assessing groupware were identified: context, collaboration, usability, and cultural impacts. In this chapter, the authors present a proposal to detail the collaboration level, specifically for CSCL domain applications. Understanding and analyzing the collaborative learning process requires a fine-grained sequential analysis of the group interaction in the context of learning goals. Several researchers in the area of cooperative work take as success criterion the quality of the group outcome. Nevertheless, recent findings are giving more importance to the quality of the "cooperation process" itself. The proposed model includes a set of guidelines to evaluate the usage of CSCL tools within a collaboration process defined along with the learning objectives. The authors have defined an experiment with a software tool instrumented to gather information that allowed them to verify the presence of a set of cooperation indicators, which in turn helped to determine the quality of the work process.

DOI: 10.4018/978-1-4666-1987-6.ch010

1. INTRODUCTION

Several groupware tools have been implemented within Computer-Supported Cooperative Work (CSCW) and Computer-Supported Collaborative Learning (CSCL) research groups in order to test ideas and concepts currently being studied. It is very important to perform pilot-evaluations with these software tools. Yet the evaluations must be done following some methodology so that the results make sense and can be used to enhance the research. The demand for groupware evaluation can be observed by the number of papers and research reports addressing this issue and by the recent workshops totally to this theme (Knutilla, Steves, & Allen, 2000; Steves & Allen, 2001; Pinelle & Gutwin, 2000).

The CSCW Lab is an environment for evaluating research products. The main goals are to guide groupware researchers in establishing a method for designing and conducting their evaluations and to be a repository of groupware evaluation knowledge. It intends to study existing methodologies applied to groupware evaluation as well as to define new methods, instruments, and/or tools. An ontology that comprises the concepts related to groupware evaluation was defined and four main dimensions were identified: context, usability, collaboration, and cultural impacts (Araujo, Santoro, & Borges, 2002).

Besides the dimensions, there are issues related to specific groupware domain applications that should be considered when designing an evaluation process. Therefore, since the CSCW Lab is a general environment, it is necessary both to analyze particular domains and specialize each of the four dimensions. They will be combined defining and applying appropriate methods.

One of the dimensions in assessing groupware is the level of collaboration that the group achieves while working with the software support. In this chapter, we present a proposal to detail the collaboration level of the CSCW Lab specifically for the CSCL domain applications. The model includes a set of guidelines to evaluate the usage of a CSCL tool within a collaboration process defined along with the learning objectives.

The rest of the chapter is divided into nine more sections: Section 2 describes the CSCW Lab, which is the context of our work; Section 3 presents the proposal for the collaboration dimension. In Section 4, we present the stages of cooperative learning process. Sections 5 and 6 present the metrics and indicators proposed. Section 7 shows the software tool developed to validate the model. In Sections 8 and 9, the experiment and the results are described. Finally, we give some conclusions and further work in Section 10.

2. THE CSCW LAB

The CSCW Lab is a laboratory for conducting groupware pilot evaluations. Besides the physical space, it includes guidelines and instruments for executing groupware evaluations. Groupware evaluation involves a great amount of effort. The planning, design, accomplishment, and replication of an evaluation are costly activities (Ramage, 1999). The design of the experiment is an activity that should be carefully performed in order to guarantee that the results and measures obtained are relevant for interpretation.

The CSCW Lab is also a repository of information about groupware evaluations. The aim of this repository is to collect information about evaluations design, their results, and interpretations. Browsing this repository, evaluators can find guidelines for planning their own evaluations. Data of past evaluations could be used to compare against their own evaluation.

The strategy chosen to build this repository or knowledge base was to define and populate an ontology (Araujo, Santoro, & Borges, 2002). The dimensions in the CSCW Lab ontology are the core elements, associated with the other common concepts that exist in evaluations in general: instruments, data, products, results interpretations, and so forth (Figure 1).

Figure 1. The CSCW lab ontology

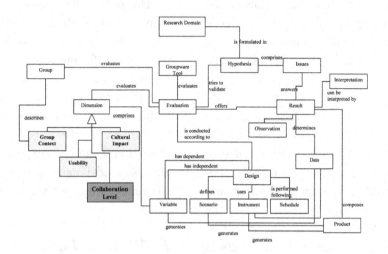

The four dimensions identified were a first step towards building a conceptual framework for our studies in the CSCW Lab. We consider that while evaluating groupware we may also address how to: describe and evaluate the context in which the application will be used; to evaluate the application's usability strengths and weaknesses; to evaluate the level of collaboration achieved while using the application; and to evaluate the technological and cultural impact achieved with its use over the course of time. Each dimension can be viewed as a step of a method for conducting groupware pilot-evaluations (Araujo, Santoro, & Borges, 2002).

These dimensions have a close relationship with each other. For instance, depending on the group characteristics (its context), the reaction to using a specific tool can be quite different. Groups that are highly committed to an activity may try to overcome any usability problems that exist in the supporting tool. If a tool has too many usability problems, collaboration may be completely compromised. If a high level of collaboration is achieved through the use of a groupware tool, the cultural impacts can be of a greater dimension.

The dimensions are quite adequate to configure the evaluation process of a groupware tool; however, we need to detail each one for the different kinds or domains of groupware applications.

Each dimension implies defining specific methods and issues to assess it. In this chapter, we focus on the third dimension: level of collaboration. Collaboration may occur at many levels and depends a lot on the nature and objectives of the group task. To evaluate collaboration it is first necessary to state what the measures or variables that determine how people collaborate. For instance, in a discussion forum, one possibility to measure collaboration is to count the number of contributions generated by the group. However, collaboration in a forum is only effective if contributions are not only inserted but also read by the other participants.

Measuring collaboration also involves subjective metrics. Usually, people are able to get the feeling on the degree of collaboration their group mates are providing. By introducing instruments such as questionnaires or by incoporating direct observation, evaluators can be aware of participants' satisfaction and have an indication about the collaboration that occurs among group members.

Evaluating the collaboration process is a complex task. We decided to start our studies about collaboration within the context of a groupware support in CSCL based on our previous experience on this subject (Araujo, Santoro, & Borges, 2002; Collazos, Guerrero, Pino, & Ochoa, 2002; Guerrero, Alarcon, Collazos, Pino, & Fuller, 2000a, 2000b; Santoro, 2001). Besides, the analysis of the CSCL area reveals the existence of a great number of cooperative environments. However, the way activities are proposed within a CSCL environment may not lead to collaboration, as several authors reported when evaluating the use of the environments in real situations (Guzdial, 1997). Therefore, it would be a great contribution to this area to define a method for evaluating the usage of educational groupware. The next step is to extend the research to other domains of groupware application.

3. THE COLLABORATION DIMENSION IN CSCL DOMAIN

Cooperative learning is a complex phenomenon. Since the advent of computer supported collaborative work, the investigation of computer supported collaborative learning has been of major interest. It has been conclusively argued that a focus on the process of collaboration is necessary in order to understand the value of working together with peers for learning (Muhlenbrock & Hoppe, 1999). Collaboration is the mutual engagement of participants in a coordinated effort to solve a problem together (Roschelle & Teasley, 1991). Understanding and analyzing the cooperative learning process and group dynamics requires a fine-grained sequential analysis of the group´s interaction in the context of learning goals (Soller & Lesgold, 2000). The Computer-based learning topic originates from different academic backgrounds mainly Computing, Psychology, and

Education. Despite being inter-linked, problems may arise due to the different paradigms to which these disciplines belong. Indeed, on the issue of which criteria should be adopted for the evaluation of CSCL, three distinct schools of thought emerge: technical, social-psychological, and cognitive.

Several researchers in the area of cooperative work take the quality of the group's outcome as success criteria. Traditional group work in solving problems tends to emphasize the product of the design and development process, but not the work process itself (Linn & Clancy, 1992). Nevertheless, recent findings are giving more importance to the quality of the cooperation process itself (Johnson & Johnson, 1978).

Success in cooperative learning means both learning the subject matter (collaborating to learn), and learning how to effectively manage the interaction (learning to collaborate) (Collazos, Guerrero, Pino, & Ochoa, 2002). The effects of the collaboration process cannot be measured along a single variable (Salomon, 1995); rather, a chain reaction occurs in which each event gives meaning to the next. Thus, selecting variables is a difficult task.

A cooperative learning process is typically composed of tasks that must be carried out by the cognitive mediator or facilitator and by the group of apprentices (Johnson & Johnson, 1978). In order to evaluate the cooperative learning process, Collazos et al. (Collazos, Guerrero, Pino, & Ochoa, 2002) divide it into three phases according to its temporal execution: pre-process, in-process, and post-process. Thus, pre-process tasks are mainly coordination and strategy definition activities and post-process tasks are mainly work evaluation activities. The group members will perform the tasks concerning the in-process phase, to a large extent. It is here where the interactions of cooperative work processes take place. Guerrero et al. (Guerrero, Alarcon, Collazos, Pino, & Fuller, 2000) have defined an Index of Collaboration based on the structure of a cooperative learning of the in-process phase. The indicators are based on the following activities proposed by Johnson and Johnson: use of strategies, intra-group cooperation, reviewing the success criteria and monitoring. The fifth indicator is based on the performance of the group.

Various approaches for analyzing group-learning interaction have been proposed. Some of them are discussed below to present an overview of how this interaction is considered from different perspectives.

Barros and Verdejo (1999) have proposed an asynchronous newsgroup-style environment enabling students to have structured, computer-mediated discussions on-line. Evaluating the interaction involves analyzing the conversation to compute values for the following four attributes: initiative, creativity, elaboration, and conformity. Katz (1999) developed two rules learning systems, String Rule Learner and Grammar Learner. These systems learn patterns of conversation acts from dialog segments that target particular pedagogical goals. Inaba and Okamoto (1997) describe a model that draws upon the ideas of finite state machines and utility functions. They used a finite state machine to control the flow of conversation and to identify proposals, while applying utility functions to measure participants' beliefs with regard to the group conversation.

Muhlenbrock and Hoppe (1999) have developed a framework system for computer-supported cooperative learning and working. The system has been used in determining conflicts in focus setting as well as initiative shifts in aggregation and revision phases during some cooperative sessions on problem solving. Constantino-Gonzalez and Suthers (2001) developed a system that evaluates a new approach to supporting collaboration that identifies learning opportunities based on studying differences among problem solutions and on tracking levels of participation.

Soller and Lesgold (2000) have developed an approach to analyze cooperative learning using Hidden Markov Models. Additional work is needed to understand how students communicate and collaborate, and to apply this knowledge to develop computational methods for determining how to best support and assist the collaboration learning process.

Santoro (2001) investigated a few methods for evaluation of cooperative learning processes. A compilation of them generated a set of criteria and measure units. The collaboration levels to be evaluated within the groups are based on four categories of study: communication, collective knowledge building, coordination, and awareness. The communication is related with the interaction in terms of the quality of messages exchanged among participants (e.g., content, coordination, or socialization messages). The collective knowledge building is observed from the contributions of the participants on discussions and on the artifacts produced. The contributions on other members' contributions such as comments and suggestions are also considered; it means the process of sharing ideas and building something together. The coordination means the ways groups articulate and design their strategies to solve the problems. The awareness is the perception of each group member about the process, the participation, and the way the group carried out the work. We suppose that these issues can indicate whether a group is more or less collaborative.

Taking into account characterization of cooperative learning presented by Johnson and Johnson, we present a refinement of an Index of Collaboration proposed by Collazos at al. (Guerrero, Alarcon, Collazos, Pino, & Fuller, 2000) as a method for CSCL evaluation in the context of CSCW Lab. The main objective is to evaluate the cooperative learning process. We have made an experiment with a tool instrumented to gather information that allowed us to verify the presence of cooperation indicators, which in turn allow us to determine the quality of the cooperative work process.

4. STAGES OF COOPERATIVE LEARNING PROCESS

A cooperative learning process is typically composed of several tasks that must be developed by the cognitive mediator or facilitator, and by the group of apprentices, defining naturally two categories of tasks. In order to evaluate the cooperative learning process, we divide it into three phases according to its temporal execution: pre-process, in-process, and post-process. Thus, pre-process tasks are mainly coordination and strategy definition activities and post-process tasks are mainly work evaluation activities. Both phases, pre-process and post-process, will be accomplished entirely by the facilitator. The tasks concerning to the in-process phase will be performed, to a large extent, by the group members. It is here where the interactions of cooperative work process takes place, so that, our interest concentrates in the evaluation of this stage. In order to specify this division, we present the structure of a cooperative learning activity proposed by Johnson and Johnson in Adams and Hamm (1996), and next we classify each activity according to the stage we have identified[1]:

- Design the content and main tasks objectives to be accomplished by cooperative groups (pre-process).
- Specify the size of the groups. It is suggested to be up to 6 people depending on the nature of the task and the time available (pre-process).
- Arrange the groups. Designate the students to compose each group or allow them to form the groups by their own (pre-process).
- Arrange the room for the cooperative learning activity. The facilitator must be "attainable" by every group and their members can seat together with out interrupt other groups (pre-process).
- Distribute the instructional material. This can be achieved of several forms (pre-process).

- Design roles, such as: speaker, facilitator, recorder, executor, and observer (pre-process).
- Specify the task directives: define the game rules (pre-process).
- Apply strategies like positive interdependence of the goal, motivation of the peers and support to learning. Create a product related to a goal system where rewards are based on individual and group results (it is defined in the pre-process, but evaluated in the in-process phase).
- Organize the intra-group cooperation, which means, define the collaboration strategies that are going to be used by the members of the group (pre-process, the definition of cooperation strategies occurs in the in-process phase).
- Test the success criteria explaining the guidelines, limits, and roles (pre-process, in-process, and post-process phases). The success criteria must be defined at the beginning of the activity, and must be reviewed during the activity to check if the common goal is being reached, and after the activity, to check if the common goal was reached.
- Determine the desired behavior (pre-process, definition of desired behavior occurs in the in-process phase).
- Monitor the students; for example, verify that the previous point is fulfilled (phase of in-process).
- Provide assistance when someone asks for it (in-process phase): it is provided to the whole group by the facilitator or peers.
- Intervene when groups have problems to collaborate (in-process phase).
- Terminate an activity (post-process phase).
- Evaluate the quality of learning accomplished by the students (post-process phase).
- Encourage students to perform an evaluation on how well does the group work altogether (at the end of the in-process phase).

- Provide and foster feedback. Discuss how the activities could be improved (at the end of in-process phase).

These activities define the structure of any cooperative learning activity that takes place in small groups, and in synchronous learning scenarios (face-to-face, same time, same place). We are interested in the evaluation of the activities that correspond to the in-process phase. Based on these, we will define some collaboration indicators.

The following section presents a software tool used as an instrument to evaluate the presence or absence of our indicators of collaboration. In Section 5, we define these indicators.

5. THE INDICATORS

In a previous work (Guerrero, Alarcon, Collazos, Pino, & Fuller, 2000), we defined an Index of Collaboration based on the structure of a cooperative learning activity explained in Section 4 (in-process phase). That Index was the average result of five identified indicators based on the some activities proposed by Johnson and Johnson in Adams and Hamm (1996).

In this chapter, we present a refinement of the Index of Collaboration, defining a set of indicators which main objective is to evaluate the cooperative learning process. Four of the indicators are based on the following activities proposed by Johnson and Johnson in Adams and Hamm (1996): use of strategies, intra-group cooperation, checking the success criteria, and monitoring. The fifth Indicator is based on the performance of the group. Next, we are going to explain in detail each one of these indicators.

5.1. Applying Strategies

To produce a single product or put in place an assessment system where rewards are based on individual scores and on the average for the group as a whole, it is necessary to apply strategies, such

as positive goal interdependence, peer encouragement, and support for learning.

According to Fussell (Fussell, Kraut, Lerch, Scherlis, McNally, & Cadiz, 1998), the discussion of the strategy to solve the problem, helps the group members to construct a shared view or mental model of their goals and tasks required to execute, this mental model can improve the coordination, because each member knows how their task fits into the global team goals. A team's learning potential is maximized when all the students actively participate in the group's discussions. Building involvement in group discussions increases the amount of information available to the group, enhancing group decision making and improving the students' quality of thought during the learning process (Jarboe, 1996).

In this context, due to its high degree of interdependence, we have proposed the following percentage composition: 20% problem solution (to consider the success or failure in solving the labyrinth), and 80% strategy applied. For this last item (strategy applied), we consider 20% use strategy, 5% quality of strategy, 25% maintain strategy and 30% communicate strategy. This will be our first cooperation indicator (CI1).

5.2. Intra-Group Cooperation

This activity corresponds to the application of cooperative strategies defined previously during the process of group work. If each group member is able to understand how her task is related with the global team goals, then every one can anticipate their actions, requiring less coordination efforts. This indicator also includes help that each player requires from her peers to reach her partial goal when acting as a coordinator.

A group achieves interdependence when the members of the group perceive that their goals are positively correlated such an individual can only attain her goal if her team members also attain their goals (Deutsch, 1962). In cooperative learning, these goals correspond to each member's need to understand her team members' ideas, questions, explanations, and problem solutions.

We have defined the indicator as: 80% application of cooperative strategies and 20% providing help. The former represents a good coordination procedure and a shared strategy, therefore should be reflected in an efficient and fluid communication were the messages among group members are precise, accurate and opportune, thus requiring fewer messages (1 – (Work strategy messages)/(Work messages)). The latter, ratio represents the involvement and concern degree of players in their role of collaborator (coordinator assistant), based on the ratio between the number of work messages and the total amount of messages spawned by the group.

5.3. Success Criteria Review

This activity corresponds to review the boundaries, guidelines, and roles of the group activity. They may include summarizing the outcome of the last task, assigning action items to members of the group, and noting dates for expected completion of assignments. The beginning and ending of any group collaboration involve transition tasks such as taking roll, requesting changes to an agenda, and locating missing meeting participants.

5.4. Monitoring

The monitoring is understood as a regulatory activity. The objective of this activity is to oversee that the group maintain the chosen strategies to solve the problem, keeping focused on the goals and the success criteria. In this sense, our fourth cooperation indicator (CI4) will be related to the number of coordination messages, where a few amount of messages means a best coordination (1 – (Coordination strategy messages)/(Coordination messages)).

5.5. Performance

Baeza-Yates and Pino (1997) made a proposal for the formal evaluation of cooperative work. They take into account three aspects: Quality (how good is the result of cooperative work), Time (total time elapsed while working), and Work (total amount of work done). The performance indicator (CI5) will be the average between the aspects Quality, Work, and Time.

6. METRICS

In order to analyze each one of the Indicators, we define some metrics that are indicators of system, user, and group performance that can be observed, singly or collectively, while executing group activities (Table 1). Metrics—such as time, length of turn, and other countable events—are directly measurable and can often be collected automatically (Drury, Hirschman, Kurtz, Fanderclai, Damianos, & Linton, 1999).

The Table 1 metrics comprises the observable data elements that were identified as useful indicators of system and group performance. In Table 1, each metric with the corresponding definition is presented.

All these metrics should be captured during an interaction mediated by groupware and the results obtained should be analyzed. Therefore, we describe a collaborative tool built in order to validate the proposed model.

7. CHASE THE CHEESE

Since our goal is to study the cooperative learning process, we developed a tool to capture data from groups engaged in such type of learning. We chose a small case in which a group of persons have to

Table 1. Metrics of performance

Metric	Meaning
Number of Errors	Total hits over an obstacle.
Solution of the problem	The group is able to solve the game.
Movements	Total movements of the mouse
Queries	Total queries to the scores
Use strategy	Outline a strategy of the problem solution in an explicit way.
Maintain strategy	Use the strategy defined during all the game
Communicate strategy	Negotiate, reaching consensus and disseminate information about strategy.
Strategy messages	Messages that propose guidelines to reach the group goal.
Work strategy messages	Messages that help the coordinator to make the most suitable decisions. Those are sentences in present tense and have the aim to inform the group about the current state of the group task.
Coordination strategy messages	Messages that correspond to activities which its main purpose is to regulate the dynamics of the process, and are characterized by prescribed future actions.
Work messages	Messages received by the coordinator.
Coordination messages	Messages sent by the coordinator.
Success criteria review messages	Messages that review the boundaries, guidelines and roles of the group activity.
Lateral messages	The kind of particular messages (i.e. social messages, comments) and conversations that are not focused on the solution of the problem.
Total messages	Total number of the messages received and sent by the group during the activity.

do some learning in order to do a joint task. The task is a game of the labyrinth type.

Four persons play the game—called Chase the cheese—, each with a computer. The computers are physically distant and the only communication allowed is computer-mediated. All activities made by participants are recorded for analysis and players are made aware of that.

Players are given very few details about the game. The participants while playing must discover the most part of the game rules. They also have to develop joint strategies to succeed. Therefore, people can only play the game once.

7.1. System's Functionality

Figure 2 shows the game interface. By the left, there are four quadrants. The goal of the game is to move the mouse (1) to its cheese (2). Each quadrant has a coordinator—one of the players—permitted to move the mouse with the arrows (4);

the other participants—collaborators—can only help the coordinator sending their messages which are seen at the right-hand side of the screen (10). Each player has two predefined roles: coordinator (only one per quadrant and randomly assigned) or collaborator (the three remaining).

The game challenges the coordinator of a quadrant in which the mouse is located because there are obstacles to the mouse movements. Most of the obstacles are invisible to the quadrant coordinator, but visible to one of the other players. In each quadrant, there are two types of obstacles through where the mouse cannot pass: general obstacles or grids (6) and colored obstacles (7). This is one of the features of the game, which must be discovered by the players. The players must then develop a shared strategy to communicate obstacle location to the coordinator of the current quadrant. No message broadcasting is allowed, so players have to choose one receiver for each message they send (9). Since each par-

Figure 2. Game interface

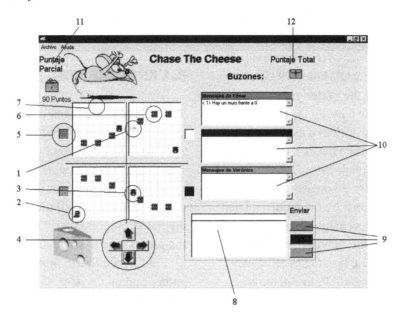

ticipant has a partial view of the labyrinth, she must interact with his or her peers to solve the problem. In order to communicate with them, each player has a dialogue box (8) from which she can send messages for each of them explicitly (once at a time) through a set of buttons associated to the color of the destiny (9). For example, in Figure 1, she can send messages to the players with colors blue, red, and green.

Each player has a color associated to her. Her quadrant shows the corresponding color (5). When starting to move the mouse, the coordinator has an individual score (11) of 100 points. Whenever the mouse hits an obstacle, this score is decreased 10 points. The coordinator has to lead the mouse to the cheese (in the case of the last quadrant) or to a traffic light (3), where the mouse passes to another quadrant and her role is switched to collaborator and the coordinator role then, is assigned to the next player (clockwise). When this event occurs, the individual score is added to the total score of the group (12). Both scores, partial and total, are hidden, if a player wants to see them, he or she must pass the mouse over their icon unfolding the score by two seconds. If any of the

individual scores reaches a value below or equal 0, the group loses the game. The goal of the game is to take the mouse to the cheese and do it with a high total score (the highest score is obviously 400 points).

7.2. Gathered Information

The application presents a structured chat-style interface (9) that serves as the basis for interpreting the group conversation. The application records every message sent by any member of the group. Along with each message, it registers the time of occurrence, sender, addressee, and current quadrant (the mouse location—X and Y position—when the message was sent). In addition, it records the partial scores and total score by quadrant. The tool also registers the start and the end time of the game, the time spent in each quadrant, and the number of times that each player looks at the partial and total scores by quadrant.

Because each player has a partial view of the game obstacles, to solve the problem they have to interact closely with their group peers. Due to this necessity, the game presents a strict positive interdependence of goals. If the group is able to solve the game, we can say that their members have built a shared understanding of the problem (see Dillenbourg definition of collaboration [Dillenbourg, Baker, Blake, & O'Malley, 1995]). They must have understood the underlying problem: the coordinator does not have all the information needed to move the mouse in her quadrant without hitting any obstacle, so she needs the opportune assistance from each collaborator.

Quality of strategies is measured by three factors: fewest errors done by the group (related to the best score), achievement of the main goal (the group can solve the labyrinth) and fewest movements of the mouse (related to efficiency).

In the game, the success or failure of the group, related to the partial and global goals, is shown in the scores obtained (partial and global scores). In addition, the messages analyzed review boundaries, guidelines, and roles of the activity. The third cooperation indicator (CI3) reflects the interest in the individual and collective performance. The more concerned the player is with the goals of the team, the most queries to the scores she will do, and the most messages of this kind will have. CI3 is defined through a range from 0 to 1 where 1 means a high number of score queries and a high success criteria review messages. If a player does not sustain the expected behavior, the group will not reach the common goal. Therefore, the monitoring indicator will be measured by the coordination messages.

In regard to the tool, Quality can be measured by three factors: fewest errors done by the group (related to the best score), achievement of the main goal (the group can solve the labyrinth) and fewest movements of the mouse (related to efficiency). The tool records the playtime since the first event (movement of the mouse or a message sent by any player); until the group reaches the goal (cheese) or looses the game (a partial score goes down to zero). In this view, the "best" group does the

work faster. The work is reflected by the amount of messages sent by the members of the group.

8. EXPERIMENTAL DESIGN

The experiment had four phases. In the first phase the group received a brief description of the software tool, in the second phase, group members were assigned to network workstations, in separate rooms (synchronous distributed interaction). From this point on, all the communication were mediated by computer. During the third phase, the group tried to solve the labyrinth.

Finally, the fourth phase corresponded to the gather and analysis of data recorded in the tool logs. We made also a final interview to the participants to foster a self-evaluation of the experience. This gave us a general overview of the problem perceived by each member of the team. By that time, we have applied the experiment to eleven groups, as we describe:

- A group of post-graduated students, from the course "Collaborative Systems" at the Pontificia Universidad Católica de Chile, with some experience on collaborative work techniques (group 0).
- A group of people randomly selected, who have not met among them and, of course, they never have worked as a group before (group 3).
- A group of friends that has worked in group many times before the experience and has a good personal relationship (group 4).
- Four groups of high school students from Cumbres de Santiago with an average age of 15 years old. Two of these were randomly selected (group 1 and 2) and the remaining ones were friends (groups 5 and 6).
- Four groups of graduate students, from the Universidad de Chile (Groups 7, 8, 9, 10).

9. ANALYSIS OF RESULTS

9.1. Applying Strategies

The objective is not only to show which group got the best or worst score, but to analyze each one of the elements that are part of this indicator and so, determine why some groups are better than others. The Table 2 shows us the results obtained.

In effective groups since the collaborative work viewpoint, goals are clarified and modified so that there is the best possible match between individual and group goals, and they are structured cooperatively so all members are committed to achieve them. The results show us that groups are ineffective, because, although all groups had a great score in the maintenance aspect, the communicating results were low. We can infer members accepted imposed goals, which are competitively structured competitively structured, so each member attempted to achieve his personal goal first.

We could not find that conflict of interest was negotiated through integrative negotiation and agreement, that is to say there was not a mediated process. It was common to observe, that the first coordinator tried to impose her viewpoint, and the work of the coordinated members, were to follow up the instructions given by the first member. Normally, it was possible to find out at the beginning of the session imperative messages, like: "Let's label the columns with letters and the rows with numbers," or "I will move first and then you are going to send me your coordinates," but it was to difficult to find out messages that could induce to negotiate a position, like: "I propose that our strategy.... do you agree?" or "What do you think?" Therefore, we can observe that the communication is not two-way and open with the possibility to express feelings as well as ideas, but is one-way, where only ideas are expressed and feeling ignored. Although the participation was distributed among all members, the person who had more power tends to impose her viewpoint among all members of the group.

The group that got the best score was the group 5 (CI1= 0.75), so, we could think that it is a good group in this aspect (applying strategies), but if we analyze in detail this indicator, we can infer this is a good work group, but not a good collaborative group.

This group was ineffective as a collaborative group, because, although they have the best score in the maintenance aspect, this result is not as good as we think, due to the fact that in a collaborative activity it is not only important to understand the

Table 2. Applying strategies results

Group	Solution	Use	Quality	Maintain	Communicate	CI1
0	1	1	0.62	0.62	0.36	0.69
1	0	0	0.5	0.68	0.41	0.31
2	1	1	0.95	0.65	0.26	0.68
3	0	1	0.52	0.59	0.36	0.48
4	1	1	0.87	0.64	0.37	0.71
5	1	1	0.74	0.74	0.43	0.75
6	1	1	0.56	0.71	0.35	0.71
7	1	0	0.5	0.60	0.32	0.47
8	0	0	0.4	0.61	0.35	0.27
9	0	0	0.4	0.65	0.35	0.28
10	1	0	0.5	0.62	0.34	0.48

problem, but to share that understanding with the teammates, and this group could not build an effective communication method among group members. This group, compared to the group 8, which got the worst score (CI1=0.27), used a better strategy (according to our quality metric), maintained it, but the problem was that although it was one of the groups that tried to promote some kind of discussion around the strategy definition, finally the decision was imposed without a integrative negotiation.

It was common to find out groups that although defined a strategy in the first quadrant, and some members of the group understood the strategy, do not obtained a high score, why? Because, in spite some members of the group understood the strategy, all member of the group did not understand this one. We could observe, for example, a group, where two of the members understood the strategy, and during the first two quadrants, the partial results were very good. The problem appeared in the third quadrant, because the coordinator—who had not understood the strategy—began to make some movements according to her viewpoint, and obviously, the group could not solve the labyrinth. The problem in this group was although some members understood the strategy; do not care if the rest of the group members had understood the strategy. Therefore, it is not only important to understand the problem, but to be aware that the rest of the people, during a collaborative activity, can understand the problem situation.

A team's learning potential is maximized when all group members participate in the group's discussions. Building involvement in-group discussion increases the amount of information available to the group, enhancing group decision making and improving the participants' quality of thought during the learning process (Jarboe, 1996). For this reason, encouraging active participation could increases the likelihood that all group members will understand the strategy, and decreases the likelihood that only a few participants will un-

derstand the strategy, leaving the others behind. Unfortunately, this aspect there was not present during the activity within the analyzed groups.

9.2. Intra-Group Cooperation

This indicator brings us information about the application of cooperative strategies defined previously during the process of group work. The Table 3 shows us the results obtained.

Respect to this indicator, we can conclude that almost all groups got a good score. These results showed us, that there was an interest to solve the problematic situation among all members of the groups. It was common to observe that when someone asked information about something, the other members of the group were able to solve her doubts, for this reason, all the questions (when were proposed) were solved by all members of the group.

Analyzing and observing the members' actions, we could find out an established dialogue pattern. When a participant requested help, at least she received one answer of the rest of the participants. It is important to note that these answers were timely. Let us show some of these dialogue patterns.

Table 3. Intra-group cooperation results

Group	I2
Group 0	0.69
Group 1	0.71
Group 2	0.62
Group 3	*0.61*
Group 4	0.74
Group 5	0.84
Group 6	0.72
Group 7	0.80
Group 8	0.75
Group 9	0.75
Group 10	0.80

Coordinator: Can I move to the right?
Player 2: I don't have obstacles.
Player 3: I don't have obstacles.
Player 4: In that position there is an obstacle.

All the answers were given in a minor interval, so the coordinator could infer what movement she could do, and all participants are helping to solve the problematic situation.

Members of the group who were not influenced by interdependence engage in promotive interaction; they verbally promoted each other's understanding through support, help and encouragement (Johnson, Johnson, & Holubec, 1990). Therefore, it was common to observe that if a member of the group did not understand the answer to a question or solution to a problem, her teammates made special accommodations, sending special messages like: "Remember, you need to send me your locations obstacles" or "You can not move" to address her misunderstanding before the group moves on. Therefore, to ensure that each member of the group receives the help she needs from her peers is key to promoting effective collaboration interaction, we can conclude all groups were good according this indicator.

9.3. Success Criteria Review

This indicator brings us information about the interest of participants to check their roles, performance, and results in order to achieve the main goal. The Table 4 shows us the results obtained.

This indicator gives an understanding of the performance analysis group did during the group activity. Group processing and performance analysis exists when groups discuss their progress, and decide what behaviors to continue or change (Johnson, Johnson, & Holubec, 1990). Therefore, it is necessary that people evaluate the results obtained before in order to continue evaluating students' individual and group activities and to provide feedback. It is also necessary that members of the group take turns questioning, clarify-

ing, and rewording their peers' comments to ensure their own understanding of the team's interpretation of the problem and the proposed solutions. "In periods of successful collaborative activity, students' conversational turns build upon each other and the content contribute to the joint problem solving activity" (Webb, 1992). Unfortunately, it did not happened within the analyzed groups.

If we observe the results obtained, we could infer there were some groups who had a perfect performance in this indicator (groups 5, 6), but if we analyzed in detail the objective of this Indicator, and observe the log's groups, we can conclude that this aspect was not enough, as we would like. The results obtained are relative scores, that is to say, according to the analyzed groups, the best groups were 5 and 6, but that not means they are good groups according this indicator, only reflects we need to do more experiences in order to determine to "ideal group," and according to that group make relative comparisons. The groups with the best score were groups that reviewed the partial and total score during the process of collaborative activity, but rarely or never, were interested to evaluate the results obtained in order to re-define the next movements, or to provide some feedback to the members of the group. It was not common,

Table 4. Success criteria review results

Group	CI3
Group 0	0.2
Group 1	0.2
Group 2	0.2
Group 3	0.5
Group 4	0.8
Group 5	*1*
Group 6	*1*
Group 7	*0.2*
Group 8	*0.2*
Group 9	*0.2*
Group 10	*0.2*

to find out messages such as: "We are losing our score is decreasing, so we need to define our next movement." Only in two groups (5, 6) appeared some messages such as: "Our score increased," "We are loosing," but unfortunately, these groups no offered opportunities to analyze the situation, clarify and define a new model of solving the problem situation.

9.4. Monitoring

This indicator gives us an understanding of the maintaining the chosen strategies to solve the problem by the group. The Table 5 presents the results we have obtained. These results indicate us, that members of the group were interested to maintain the strategy, so there was a direct relation between this indicator and the aspect of maintenance within Applying strategies indicator (the group that got the best CI4, got the best score in the maintenance part of CI1). In addition, it is important to mention that the group, which got the best scores, was those ones, which had been working together for a long time, so they have a good connection between the members of the group. In spite of good scores obtained by all groups in this indicator, it is important to note, that as CI3 (Success criteria review), the results don not indicate that we have good monitoring groups, it only shows us that for example, group 5 was better than group 3. In cooperative learning groups, members were required to acquire group skills, like how to provide effective leadership, decision-making, trust building, communication, and conflict-management (Johnson, Johnson, & Holubec, 1990).

The combination of knowing how to manage intellectual disagreements and how to negotiate/mediate conflicts among participants' wants, needs, and goals ensures that the power of cooperative efforts will be maximized. The productiv-

ity of groups increases dramatically when members are skilled in how to manage conflicts constructively. Unfortunately, the groups selected, in spite that some of them had worked together, still have the characteristics of "work groups" and are not collaborative groups. It was common to find, according to the analysis of the messages, that leadership is delegated and based upon authority, participation is unequal with high powered members dominating, characteristics typical of ineffective collaborative groups (Morrison, 2001).

The same analysis gave us an understanding of the role of the coordinator in every quadrant, and the function of the coordinator was to contribute to maintain the harmony within group, avoiding discussions or conflicts, but one of the most important aspects within a cooperative activity is the promotion of creative conflicts. Cooperation and conflict go hand-in-hand (Johnson & Johnson, 1995). The more group members care about achieving the group's goals, and the more they care about each other, the more likely they are to have conflicts with each other. How conflict is managed largely determines how successful cooperative efforts tend to be. For this reason, we can conclude that groups still are working as work groups, and still have not acquired the collaborative status.

9.5. Performance

Our last indicator gives us an understanding of the fulfillment of the group. Table 6 presents the results obtained.

This indicator shows us the results of the group's outcome. Notice that the group, which got the worst score, was the group that almost got the best score in the other indicators. That observation, could inform us that the performance of a group is not related with the learning of the same.

Table 5. Monitoring results

Group	CI4
Group 0	0.75
Group 1	0.80
Group 2	0.80
Group 3	0.74
Group 4	0.78
Group 5	0.86
Group 6	0.85
Group 7	0.80
Group 8	0.82
Group 9	0.81
Group 10	0.83

10. CONCLUSION AND FUTURE WORK

In this chapter, we presented a model for evaluating the collaborative dimension of a CSCL tool within the context of the CSCW Lab (Araujo, Santoro, & Borges, 2002). This model includes a set of five Indicators, which allows the evaluation of the Collaboration Level process of a group working on a given task in order to learn a subject.

We also presented a software tool to enable a collaborative work computer-based activity, and

to gather information concerned to it, in order to validate the indicators proposed. It is also important to headline that the personal style and individual behavior of every member of the group influence the cooperative work process. We can observe stability in the performance of the tasks accomplished by each one of the group members, as much in their coordinator role like in their collaborator role. This stability is also observed in the personal styles and communication skills.

The results suggest that the shared construction of a strategy to fulfill a group work, understood and adopted by every member of the group, is related to a successful process, to the individual construction of cognitive context, and to the experiences shared by the group members. Also, it enhances the elaboration process of strategies and facilitates its application. This fact is reflected in the performed language utterances: those are homogeneous, direct and unambiguous when referred to the common problem features.

The participant groups are ineffective collaborative groups, because according to Johnson and Johnson (1978), in cooperative learning situations, students have two responsibilities: 1) learn the assigned material, and 2) ensure that all members of the group learn the assigned material (Johnson & Johnson, 1978), and the second

Table 6. Performance results

Group	Quality	Time	Work	CI5
0	0.87	0.86	0.22	0.65
1	0.5	0.82	0.4	0.57
2	0.95	0.99	0.13	0.69
3	0.52	0.67	0.72	0.63
4	0.62	0.42	0.95	0.66
5	0.74	0.83	0.27	0.61
6	0.56	0.81	0.19	*0.52*
7	0.5	0.87	0.23	0.53
8	0.4	0.81	0.4	0.54
9	0.4	0.82	0.4	0.54
10	0.5	0.78	0.3	0.53

aspect is something that never occurred during the cooperative learning process of analyzed groups.

It is important to notice that although we are proposed a set of indicators, there is a relation between them. There is a direct relationship between the monitoring indicator and the maintenance of the strategy, and between the intra-group cooperation and communication of the strategy.

The work within the CSCW Lab is been carried out in two main directions: the first one is the development of the ontology, which will help to understand the complexity of groupware evaluations; the second one is the study of specific methodologies to support several domains. The research done until now is based on defining and refining these methodologies, besides projecting the experimental environments. The next steps are to perform several experiments and analyze the results in order to validate our proposal.

ACKNOWLEDGMENT

This work was partially supported by Universidad del Cauca, Vicerectoria de Investigaciones de la Universidad del Cauca, grants CICYT TIN2011-26928, LACCIR, and MECANISMO PARA LA INTERPRETACIÓN DE EMOCIONES EN LA EVALUACIÓN DE USABILIDAD DE ENTORNOS VIRTUALES DE APRENDIZAJE, Id 2011ER98673 of Ministerio de Educación Nacional (Colombia).

REFERENCES

Adams, D., & Hamm, M. (1996). *Cooperative learning, critical thinking and collaboration across the curriculum* (2nd ed.). London, UK: Charles C. Thomas.

Araujo, R. M., Santoro, F. M., & Borges, M. R. S. (2002). The CSCW lab for groupware evaluation. In *Proceedings of 8th International Workshop on Groupware – CRIWG 2002*. La Serena, Chile: Springer-Verlag.

Baeza-Yates, R., & Pino, J. A. (1997). A first step to formally evaluate collaborative work. In *Proceedings of the ACM International Conference on Supporting Group Work* [Phoenix, AZ: ACM Press.]. *Group, 1997*, 55–60.

Barros, B., & Verdejo, M. F. (1999). An approach to analyze collaboration when shared structured workspaces are use for carrying out group learning processes. In *Proceedings of the International Conference AI-ED 1999*, (pp. 449-456). AI-ED.

Collazos, C., Guerrero, L. A., Pino, J., & Ochoa, S. (2002). Evaluating collaborative learning processes. In *Proceedings of the 8th International Workshop on Groupware (CRIWG 2002)*, (pp. 203-221). La Serena, Chile: Springer Verlag.

Constantino-González, M., & Suthers, D. (2001). Coaching web-based collaborative learning based on problem solution differences and participation. In *Proceedings of the International Conference AI-ED 2001*, (pp. 176-187). Dordrecht, The Netherlands: IOS Press.

Deutsch, M. (1962). Cooperation and trust: Some theoretical notes. In M. Jones (Ed.), *Nebraska Symposium on Motivation* (pp. 275-320). Lincoln, NE: University of Nebraska Press.

Dillenbourg, P., Baker, M., Blake, A., & O'Malley, C. (1995). The evolution of research on collaborative learning. In Spada, H., & Reimann, P. (Eds.), *Learning in Humans and Machines*. Dublin, Ireland: Emerald Group. doi:10.1007/978-1-4020-9827-7_1

Drury, J., Hirschman, L., Kurtz, J., Fanderclai, T., Damianos, L., & Linton, F. (1999). Methodology for evaluation of collaboration systems. *ACM SIGGROUP Bulletin, 20*(2), 50–51.

Fussell, S., Kraut, R., Lerch, F., Scherlis, W., McNally, M., & Cadiz, J. (1998). Coordination, overload and team performance: Effects of team communication strategies. In *Proceedings of CSCW 1998*. Seattle, WA: CSCW.

Guerrero, L., Alarcón, R., Collazos, C., Pino, J., & Fuller, D. (2000a). Evaluating cooperation in group work. In *Proceedings of CRIWG 2000*. Madeira, Portugal: IEEE Computer Society Press.

Guerrero, L., Alarcón, R., Collazos, C., Pino, J., & Fuller, D. (2000b). Evaluating cooperation in group work. In *Proceedings of the Sixth International Workshop on Groupware, CRIWG 2000*. Madeira, Portugal: IEEE Press.

Guzdial, M. (1997). Information ecology of collaborations in educational settings: Influence of tool. In *Proceedings of CSCL 1997*. Toronto, Canada: CSCL.

Inaba, A., & Okamoto, T. (1997). The intelligent discussion coordinating system for effective collaborative learning. In *Proceedings of the IV Collaborative Learning Workshop in the International Conference AI-ED 1997*. Kobe, Japan: AI-ED.

Jarboe, S. (1996). Procedures for enhancing group decision making. In Hirokawa, B., & Poole, M. (Eds.), *Communication and Group Decision Making* (pp. 345–383). Thousand Oaks, CA: Sage Publications.

Johnson, D., & Johnson, R. (1978). Cooperative, competitive, and individualistic learning. *Journal of Research and Development in Education, 12*, 8–15.

Johnson, D., & Johnson, R. (1995). *My mediation notebook* (3rd ed.). Edina, MN: Interaction Book Company.

Johnson, D., Johnson, R., & Holubec, E. (1990). *Circles of learning: Cooperation in the classroom* (3rd ed.). Edina, MN: Interaction Book Company.

Katz, S. (1999). The cognitive skill of coaching collaboration. In *Proceedings CSCL 1999*. Mahwah, NJ: Lawrence Erlbaum Associates.

Knutilla, A. J., Steves, M. P., & Allen, R. H. (2000). Paper In *Proceedings of the Workshop on Evaluating Collaborative Enterprises 2000*. Infrastructure for Collaborative Enterprises.

Linn, M. C., & Clancy, M. J. (1992). The case for case studies of programming problems. *Communications of the ACM, 35*(3), 121–132. doi:10.1145/131295.131301

Morrison, T. (2001). *Actionable learning: A handbook for capacity building through case based learning*. Tokyo, Japan: Asian Development Bank Institute.

Muhlenbrock, M., & Hoppe, U. (1999). Computer Supported interaction analysis of group problem solving. In Hosadley & Roschelle (Eds.), *Proceedings of CSCL 1999*, (pp. 398-405). CSCL.

Pinelle, D., & Gutwin, C. (2000). A review of groupware evaluations. In *Proceedings of Ninth IEEE WETICE 2000 Workshops on Enabling Technologies: Infrastructure for Collaborative Enterprises*. Gaithersburg, MD: IEEE Press.

Ramage, M. (1999). *The learning way: Evaluating co-operative systems*. (Phd. Thesis). Lancaster University. Lancaster, UK.

Roschelle, J., & Teasley, S. (1991). The construction of shared knowledge in collaborative problem solving. In C. O'Malley (Ed.), *Proceedings of CSCL 1991*, (pp. 67-97). Berlin, Germany: Springer.

Salomon, G. (1995). *What does the design of effective CSCL require and how do we study its effects?* Retrieved from http://www-cscl95.indiana.edu/cscl95/outlook/62-Salomon.html

Santoro, F. M. (2001). *A cooperation model for project-based learning.* (Doctoral Thesis). COPPE Sistemas, UFRJ. Rio de Janeiro, Brazil.

Soller, A., & Lesgold, A. (2000). Modeling the process of collaborative learning. In *Proceedings of the International Workshop on New Technologies in Collaborative Learning.* Tokyo, Japan: ACM.

Steves, M. P., & Allen, R. H. (2001). *Evaluating collaborative enterprises – A workshop report.* Retrieved from http://www.mel.nist.gov/msidlibrary/doc/steves01b.pdf

Webb, N. (1992). Testing a theoretical model of student interaction and learning in small groups. In Hertz-Lazarowitz, R., & Miller, N. (Eds.), *Interaction in Cooperative Groups: The Theoretical Anatomy of Group Learning* (pp. 102–119). Cambridge, UK: Cambridge University Press.

ENDNOTES

[1]   Johnson and Johnson do not make this phase differentiation.

Chapter 11
Experiences in Usability Evaluation of Educational Programming Tools

J. Ángel Velázquez-Iturbide
Universidad Rey Juan Carlos, Spain

Antonio Pérez-Carrasco
Universidad Rey Juan Carlos, Spain

Ouafae Debdi
Universidad Rey Juan Carlos, Spain

ABSTRACT

This chapter advocates for an approach to constructing educational tools that consists in designing small systems aimed at achieving clear educational goals and evaluating them in actual teaching situations. The authors addressed this approach with a number of small systems. In this chapter, they describe their experience in the development, use, and evaluation of two educational systems: SRec and GreedEx. The former is a highly interactive program animation system of recursion, and the latter is an interactive assistant aimed at learning the role of selection functions in greedy algorithms by means of experimentation. The evaluations allowed the authors to identify faults and weaknesses of the systems, and these results were used to enhance the systems. Moreover, their approach has yielded very high values with respect to effectiveness and student satisfaction.

1. INTRODUCTION

Currently, universities intensively use computer systems in order to improve, simplify, and even accelerate teaching and learning tasks. These systems are technologically sophisticated, and this trend seems to continue in the future. Unfortunately, many educational systems suffer from one of these drawbacks: either they are not targeted to educational goals, or they are not tuned to actual use, in real-world teaching situations.

An approach to deal with this problem consists in designing small systems aimed at achieving

DOI: 10.4018/978-1-4666-1987-6.ch011

clear educational goals and evaluating them in actual teaching situations. Having clear educational goals as the main part of their specification results in very effective tools for the tasks they were intended. Furthermore, taking into consideration practical issues (such as installation, internationalization, etc.) removes obstacles for their adoption by other teachers. Finally, the evaluation of these systems allows tuning them for effective use, but it also allows discovering incomplete support to certain tasks or additional features that were not envisioned by their developers.

Our group has addressed this approach with a number of small systems. This chapter illustrates the issues pointed out above, such as designing educational software based on educational goals, consideration of real-use issues, and evaluation of the tools. As driving examples, we show our experience in the development, use, and evaluation of two educational systems: SRec (Velázquez-Iturbide, Pérez-Carrasco, & Urquiza-Fuentes, 2008) and GreedEx (Velázquez-Iturbide & Pérez-Carrasco, 2009). The former is a highly interactive program animation system of recursion and the latter is an interactive assistant aimed at learning the role of selection functions in greedy algorithms by means of experimentation.

The chapter is structured as follows. In the second section, we introduce some concepts, which are necessary to understand the chapter, namely programming and algorithms, software visualization, learning goals, systems for programming education, and usability. In the third and fourth sections, we describe the respective features of the SRec and GreedEx systems, and show the results of evaluating them for usability. The fifth section contains a discussion of the results, presenting them to other developers as lessons learnt. Finally, we outline our conclusions and identify lines of future research.

2. BACKGROUND

In this section, we introduce some issues, which are preliminary with respect to the rest of the chapter. Firstly, some concepts of programming and algorithms are briefly introduced, such as recursion and greedy algorithms. Secondly, the main concepts on visualization and animation are given. Thirdly, Bloom's taxonomy is outlined as a framework to state learning goals. Fourthly, we review the myriad of existing systems for programming education, with an emphasis on their explicit learning goals. Finally, the usability methods we have used will be identified and placed in the context of the usability methods currently available, mainly expert evaluations, questionnaires, and observations.

2.1. Programming and Algorithms

Programming and algorithms are core topics in Computer Science (CS) education (ACM, 2008). We only introduce here some concepts, which are relevant for the rest of the chapter, namely recursion and greedy algorithms.

Recursion is a linguistic mechanism consisting in defining something in terms of itself. Recursion is strongly discouraged for definitions in general, and dictionaries try to avoid it. However, in mathematics and computer programming, recursion is a valuable tool for definitions and for problem solving. Some recursive definitions are surprisingly clear, being the Fibonacci series a paradigmatic example.

Recursion is one of the most difficult concepts in procedural programming and therefore it has received much attention from CS educators. Many conceptual models have been created in order to facilitate student learning. Most conceptual models have a strong visual component, e.g. the copies model or recursion trees. See the review by Pérez-Carrasco and Velázquez-Iturbide (2012).

Algorithms are detailed descriptions of solutions to problems stated in terms of input data-output data. Algorithms have several properties that can be modeled mathematically, e.g. correctness and efficiency. They can also be subject to experimentation, allowing the empirical study of their properties.

Optimization problems have a third property, namely optimality. A number of design techniques exist that deal with optimization problems, being the greedy technique, dynamic programming and branch-and-bound three well-known techniques. In particular, greedy algorithms have a simpler behavior than other algorithms, thank to the outstanding role played by optimal selection functions. A selection function allows selecting the next best candidate for a given problem at each stage of the algorithm. Consequently, a greedy algorithm is a loop where an optimal selection function determines the best candidate in the current iteration. More information about greedy algorithms can be found in textbooks on algorithms (Brassard & Bratley, 1996; Cormen, Leiserson, Rivest, & Stein, 2009; Sahni, 2005).

2.2. Software Visualization

A visualization is a graphical display of some artifact or phenomenon. An animation is a sequence of displays. When the artifact to display is a piece of software (i.e. a program or an algorithm), the animation typically shows the successive states of its execution.

The main goal of animation systems is to show conceptual, visual models to students. Interaction of the student with the animation system can be used to assist in different learning goals and therefore to support different teaching methods or educational tasks.

A distinction is commonly made between program animation and algorithm animation (Stasko, Domingue, Brown, & Price, 1998). The

former term refers to an animation where the visualizations have a direct correspondence with the elements of the code. The latter term is used when the visualizations illustrate the behavior of code but without a direct correspondence to it. Program visualization systems typically run any program satisfying some restrictions, gather relevant data to display, and generate visualizations of the successive states of the program, according to some predefined graphical representation. An algorithm animation is usually hand-made to illustrate a single specific algorithm.

Animations must be as interactive as possible in order to engage the learner (Naps, et al., 2003). Some interactions can be easily provided for any animation, e.g. zooming or customizing graphical attributes. However, each kind of animation better supports different kinds of interaction. Program animations are more adequate for interactive analysis of the running program. Examples of corresponding interactions are highlighting selected parts, or hiding (or showing) some parts. Algorithm animations are more adequate for understanding. Examples of corresponding interactions are linking related information or asking prediction questions in some steps of the animation.

2.3. Learning Goals

Our hypothesis is that the use of explicit, clear pedagogical goals increases the quality and effectiveness of an interactive system. Some important consequences follow. Firstly, its visualization and interaction requirements can be more easily identified. Secondly, educational activities can be checked for alignment with the educational goals of our system. Finally, broadening the range of intended educational goals may result in broadening the range of features supported by the interactive system.

We have developed two interactive systems based on the assumption of this hypothesis. Before introducing the systems, we should adopt a framework to specify their learning goals. We have found especially valuable Bloom's taxonomy (Anderson, et al., 2001; Bloom, Furst, Hill, & Krathwohl, 1956), which allows estimating the cognitive level reached for a student in a certain matter. It distinguishes six levels, assuming that a student who reaches a level also dominates the lower ones:

- **Level 1 or Knowledge Level:** The student is able to recognize or recall information without being necessary any kind of understanding about it.
- **Level 2 or Comprehension Level:** The student is able to understand and explain the meaning of the information received.
- **Level 3 or Application Level:** The student is able to select and use data and methods to solve a given task or problem.
- **Level 4 or Analysis Level:** The student is able to distinguish, classify, and relate the information given and decomposing a problem into its parts.
- **Level 5 or Synthesis Level:** The student is able to generalize ideas and apply them to solve a new problem.
- **Level 6 or Evaluation Level:** The student is able to compare and evaluate methods or solutions to solve a problem or choose the best one.

Bloom's taxonomy is one of the most commonly used by CS education researchers. It has been used in programming for different purposes: to design their courses, to evaluate students, or as a reference to design educative systems. As any pedagogical framework, it is controversial (Fuller, et al., 2007) but it is very popular because it provides a comprehensive and clear framework.

2.4. Systems for Programming Education

There is consensus among CS educators about the fact that programming is a subject matter that is difficult to learn (Fincher & Petre, 2004). Consequently, there are many proposals to improve this situation. They may be roughly classified into three main categories: studies about students' difficulties, innovative teaching methods, and educational technology. For the purposes of this chapter, we focus on the last approach. In turn, there are many kinds of systems and tools to assist in programming teaching and learning. The most common systems are programming environments and debuggers (Deek & McHugh, 1998). Other common, less general systems are programming environments for novices (Fincher & Utting, 2010), automatic assessment systems (Ihantola, Ahoniemi, Karavirta, & Seppälä, 2010), and program and algorithm animation systems (Shaffer, et al., 2010). This trend in developing new, innovative systems will continue in the future: see COALA (Jurado, et al., 2009) or HabiPro (Vizcaíno, Contreras, Favela, & Prieto, 2000) just to name two.

In general, programming tools are designed with generic goals in mind (e.g. to assist in developing programs) or trying to respond to technological challenges (e.g. to allow developing programs collaboratively). However, their educational goals hardly are explicitly stated. In general, the reader has to deduce these goals from the tool description. For instance, animations are typically aimed at the comprehension level, debuggers at the analysis level, and programming environments at the synthesis level.

One outstanding exception is problets (Dancik & Kumar, 2003), which are applets explicitly designed to assist at the application level for well-delimited topics. Typically, a problet allows randomly generating instances of a problem involving a concept, a question to be answered, some kind of visualization or interaction to help solving the problem, and feedback to the student's answer.

2.5. Usability

Although there are many definitions of the term *usability*, the most widely used can be found at the ISO 9241 standard (ISO, 1998): "The extent to which a product can be used by specified users to achieve specified goals with effectiveness, efficiency, and satisfaction in a specified context of use." *Effectiveness* is defined as the accuracy and completeness with which users achieve specified goals; *efficiency* is defined as the resources expended in relation to the accuracy and completeness with which users achieve those goals; and *satisfaction* is defined as "freedom from discomfort, and positive attitudes towards the use of the product." These definitions are broad enough to embody the features interactive systems must exhibit for successful use. Of course, these general features can be instantiated in several, more specific ways: learnability, memorability, flexibility, robustness, safety, etc. However, for the purposes of this chapter, it is not necessary go deeper into this discussion.

There are a number of methods to evaluate the usability of a system. We focus here on two classes of evaluation: evaluations with experts, and evaluations with end users. In an educational setting, the role of experts is usually taken by teachers, and that of end users by teachers or students.

Evaluations with experts are often used in the initial stages of development of a system. In heuristic evaluations, the expert uses a set of guidelines (called heuristics) that the interactive system should fulfill, e.g. consistency or conformance to standards. In walkthrough evaluations, the expert

identifies problems while she is performing a task as a final user.

Evaluations with end users can be conducted at any stage of the system development, but at least they should be conducted at the final stage of development. Instrumentation can be made in different ways, from more objective methods (e.g. observations) to more subjective ones (e.g. questionnaires).

3. THE SREC SYSTEM

In this section, we describe our experience designing and evaluating the SRec system. More details can be found elsewhere about the system itself (Velázquez-Iturbide, et al., 2008; Velázquez-Iturbide & Pérez-Carrasco, 2010), its implementation (Fernández-Muñoz, et al., 2007) or its evaluation (Pérez-Carrasco, Velázquez-Iturbide, & Urquiza-Fuentes, 2010).

3.1. Specification and Learning Goals

The SRec system (Velázquez-Iturbide, et al., 2008) was the first step in a research effort aimed at supporting the teaching of algorithms using program visualization techniques. Its domain is the set of recursive functions, as a first step towards the visualization of some algorithm design techniques based on recursion (e.g. divide and conquer).

The learning goal of SRec can be placed at the analysis level: the student must be able to analyze the behavior of recursive algorithms. In addition, the system must be able to generate animations without effort from the user (Ihantola, et al., 2005). This is an important requirement to foster system adoption from instructors (Naps, et al., 2003). Finally, some educational requirements were also stated: support to documentation tasks (e.g. exporting visualizations) and to internationalization (currently, it supports English and Spanish).

3.2. Description of SRec

Figure 1 shows the user interface of SRec after executing the Ackerman function with parameters 2 and 4.

Three areas can be clearly distinguished, apart from the window title, the main menu and the icon bar. Just under the icon bar, the animation bar contains several controls that allow playing an animation in both directions and with different levels of detail. The left area of the user interface of SRec is the code panel, which consists of an editor at the top of the panel and a message area at the bottom. The editor contains the code of the class that has been loaded and the message area displays any message produced by the Java virtual machine. The right panel of the user interface displays the current state of execution, in one of the graphical representations supported. SRec supports an overview+detail interface (Card, Mackinlay, & Shneiderman, 1999) to display large recursion trees (see Figure 1). SRec supports the simultaneous, synchronized display of two graphical representations, i.e. multiple views (Stasko, et al., 1998), although one of them is collapsed in Figure 1 to facilitate the display of the large recursion tree.

SRec visualizes algorithms coded in the Java language. It supports three graphical representations of recursion (namely, the activation tree, the control stack and the trace). In order to generate an animation, the user must load a Java class into SRec, select the method to execute, and introduce its actual parameters. Then, SRec launches the execution of the selected algorithm. Transparently to the user, SRec gathers during the execution all the information necessary to display its associated recursive process. After finishing the execution, SRec creates the different views in its main window, and the user may animate the execution in the activated views.

The user can save a visualization to load it and use it in the future. This way, it is not necessary to create a visualization from scratch. Consequently, teachers can create a library of algorithm animations ready to load and use, thus saving lecture time. Students can also save their visualizations to submit them to the teacher as an attached file in an email message where questions are asked about the execution of the corresponding algorithm.

Figure 1. User interface of the SRec system

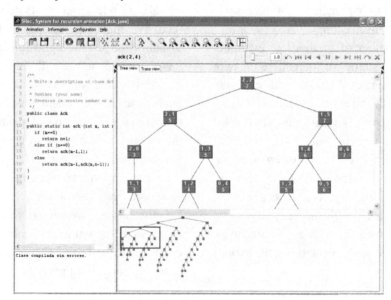

The visualizations support a high number of interactions (Velázquez-Iturbide & Pérez-Carrasco, 2010): filtering data, selection of recursive calls, rearrangement of layout, navigation in space, customization options, etc. Consequently, teachers and students have available a high number of possibilities for analysis.

Finally, SRec includes a number of educational facilities. Thus, SRec is internationalized to support multiple languages (currently, English and Spanish). SRec also allows exporting the contents of the views to standard graphical formats either as visualizations or as animations. This support is useful for both teachers and students as it makes easy documenting reports, slides, or Web pages.

3.3. Usability Evaluations

We have conducted two main classes of usability evaluations:

- **Expert evaluations:** These evaluations had three goals, although only one or two goals were simultaneously sought in a single evaluation session: testing, heuristic usability, or walkthrough usability. The first kind of evaluation checked whether the system satisfied its specification. The two other kinds of evaluations were more typical usability evaluations. All of these evaluations were conducted by the instructor of the course. We have not accounted the number of evaluations conducted, but they can be counted in many tens.
- **Evaluations with final users:** They evaluated in one or several lab sessions the satisfaction of students with SRec. They were conducted with questionnaires, which gave us feedback about user acceptance, evaluation of the main features and elements, and open suggestions. We have conducted five evaluations with students.

Each session was two hours long. Students were given the assignment statement, the SRec system, a report model, and an opinion questionnaire. They had to perform three tasks:

1. Use SRec to solve a problem on a recursive algorithm.
2. Fill and deliver a short report on their findings, using a given template.
3. Unless stated otherwise, fill and deliver an opinion questionnaire about the assistant.

A summary of the evaluations follow:

1. **May 2007:** 7 participants in a single session. The goal was to debug a wrong algorithm. All student work was done individually.
2. **December 2007:** 28 participants in a single session. The goal was to remove redundancy in a multiple-recursive algorithm. The assignment and the report were done in pairs, but the questionnaire was answered individually.
3. **November 2008:** 33 participants in a single session. Delivery was similar to the previous evaluation.
4. **November-December 2009:** Two sessions, with 28 participants in the first one and 25 in the second one. The first session was intended to facilitate familiarization of the students with the tool. The goals of the sessions were to design a lineal and a multiple recursive algorithm, respectively. Delivery had similar characteristics to the second evaluation and it was required in both sessions, but the questionnaire of the first session was simpler than the questionnaire of the second session, as it did not ask to assess the system elements.
5. **October 2010:** Three sessions, with 41, 53, and 49 participants, respectively. The goal of the two first sessions was to debug a wrong algorithm, and the goal of the third session was to design a divide-and-conquer

algorithm. The questionnaire was only required in the third session, being delivered analogously to the second evaluation.

The opinion questionnaires used in these sessions consisted of multiple-choice questions, with values in a Linkert scale ranging between 1 (very bad) to 5 (very good), and open questions. Multiple-choice questions ask the students' opinion about general issues (easiness of use, utility and satisfaction) and about specific elements of the system. Open questions ask positive or negative claims of the student.

Some evaluations were also conducted using other methods: comparison with other systems, evaluation of effectiveness to visualize textbook examples, analysis of logs, and observations. We summarize here the comparison with other systems. However, we do not give details about the other evaluation methods because their findings were limited or we have not analyzed exhaustively their results yet.

A comparison of the system with other systems reported in literature allowed identifying clearly the strengths and limitations of SRec (Velázquez-Iturbide & Pérez-Carrasco, 2010). The nine selected systems were either program visualization systems supporting the visualization of recursion or educational systems intended to learn recursion. The comparison was conducted with respect to the following features: selection of the methods to visualize, support to parameter types and values, way of constructing the visualizations, conceptual models supported, animation functions, and interaction functions. SRec is one

of the most highly ranked systems for any feature but support to parameter types and values: SRec only supports primitive data types, while other systems support any type.

3.4. Usability Results

Let us review students' satisfaction, according to the answers to questionnaires along the five evaluations.

Table 1 shows the evolution of the numerical values obtained for multiple-choice questions about general issues. Notice that two questionnaires were filled in the two sessions of the fourth evaluation. Notice also that two questions were always asked about the usefulness of SRec, so two values are shown at the second row of Table 1. These questions about usefulness varied with each session, as different tasks were assigned.

Notice that the values obtained in all the questions were high. The highest value corresponds to facility of use (4.14). Notice also that the lowest values were obtained in the first evaluation, when the system was less mature. It is also interesting to note that the values obtained in the second session of the fourth evaluation were lower than the values obtained in the first session. This variation is probably due to the higher complexity of the corresponding task.

We also assessed the quality of the different elements of SRec. The results are shown in Table 2, sorted in descending order of marks. The five best-ranked elements correspond to core elements of the SRec system.

Table 1. Evolution of values obtained for SRec in general questions

Question	Mean 1	Mean 2	Mean 3	Mean 4.1	Mean 4.2	Mean 5	Global mean
Easy to use	3.88	4.50	4.20	4.39	3.90	3.94	4.14
It has aided me in several tasks	2.63 / 4.13	4.29 / 4.36	4.19 / 4.04	4.32 / 4.25	3.83 / 3.68	4.10 / 4.00	3.99
Overall, I liked it	3.63	4.26	3.95	4.07	3.85	3.84	3.93

Table 2. Evolution of values obtained about the quality of specific elements of SRec (G means "general mark," Q means "mark of quality," and E means "mark of how easy it is to use")

Question	1G	G	G	Q	E	Q	E	Mean
Generation process of visualizations	-		4.00	4.05	4.16	4.22	4.20	4.16
Animation controls	4.00	4.50	-	4.22	3.94	3.96	3.96	4.08
Recursion tree view	4.25	4.43	4.00	4.11	4.22	3.82	4.00	4.06
Control stack view	4.00	4.04	-		-		-	4.03
Trace view	3.75	4.00				-	-	3.95
Main menu structure	3.75	4.07	-	4.11	3.95	3.78	4.00	3.94
Loading/saving a visualization	-	-	4.14	4.26	4.21	3.73	3.71	3.90
Chronological view	-		-	3.89	3.89	3.92	3.86	3.89
Exportation of a visualization	-	-	4.00	4.06	3.83	3.57	3.61	3.73
Interaction with panels (moving, scroll…)	3.63	3.89	3.80	4.00	3.94	3.57	3.55	3.72
Configuration of visualizations	3.88	3.82	3.76	4.00	3.89	3.57	3.49	3.70
Icons	-	3.86	3.57	4.05	4.05	3.59	3.49	3.70
Data structure view	-	-	-	3.74	4.00	3.63	3.63	3.70
Control of information displayed	-	-	-	3.61	3.61	3.35	3.51	3.48
Zoom configuration	-	-	3.71	3.71	3.71	3.24	3.33	3.44
Interface for large trees	-	-	3.86	3.56	3.50	2.82	3.27	3.27

We explored the mean of the marks given by all the students to all the elements of SRec. These data, shown in Table 3, are grouped in intervals. Table 3 shows percentages of people whose personal mean is inside the correspondent interval. Notice two facts: the absence of marks below two and a general tendency to lower values.

Finally, some open questions were included. The results obtained follow:

- **Positive Aspects:** Students highlight that SRec is easy to use, the recursion trees, and the expressiveness and usefulness of visualizations in general.

- **Parts that the User Would Suppress:** There is large variability among the five evaluations, due to the evolution of the system. Some answers were given by just one student. Other answers recurrently appear in the different evaluations (e.g. configuration options), but again from few students. Representative examples are: configuration of typography, the control stack view, the trace view, and some icons.

Table 3. Evolution of personal mean of SRec

Interval	Evaluation 1	Evaluation 2	Evaluation 3	Evaluation 4	Evaluation 5
[4.0 – 5.0]	85.71%	57.14%	61.90%	50.00%	18.07%
[3.0 – 4.0)	14.28%	42.86%	33.33%	45.45%	79.59%
[2.0 – 3.0)	0.00%	0.00%	4.76%	4.55%	2.04%

- **Negative Aspects, Parts Difficult to use, and Parts that the User Would Incorporate:** Students identified different issues that were improved, incorporated, or corrected into successive versions of SRec. There is large variability among evaluations, due to this evolution of the system. Some examples are: the user identification of the Java JDK directory, the creation process of GIF animations, the non-integrated code editor, and the handling of large recursion trees. Some parts still have to be further improved, such as the code editor, the handling of large trees, or the dialog to launch an animation. Finally, many students have also advocated for some visualization facilities, which are incompatible with our implementation approach (e.g. highlighting the algorithm statements as execution progresses or visualizing the contents of local variables).

We must also highlight a common situation, where some students do not know the full functionality of the system and ask for improvements or facilities that the system actually supports. This situation has been partially remedied by making each evaluation consisting of several sessions, where the first session is intended to let the student become familiar with the system.

One consequence of the iterative evaluation of SRec was its evolution to support a broader class of interactions with visualizations to analyze algorithms. Answers to open questions were especially useful. Table 4 summarizes the evolution of the functions provided by SRec. A cell with an X means that the system in the corresponding column supports the function in the corresponding row. When the cell of the following system contains the following letter in the alphabet (Y, Z), a major change has been implemented, whereas a single quote (X', X") denotes a minor change.

4. THE GREEDEX SYSTEM

In this section, we describe our experience designing and evaluating the GreedEx system. More details can be found elsewhere about the system itself (Velázquez-Iturbide & Pérez-Carrasco, 2009), the underlying experimental method (Velázquez-Iturbide & Debdi, 2011), or its evaluation (Velázquez-Iturbide, Lázaro-Carrascosa & Hernán-Losada, 2009).

4.1. Specification and Learning Goals

Some years ago, we conducted a study on the features of textbooks figures illustrating the most common algorithm design techniques (Fernández-Muñoz & Velázquez-Iturbide, 2006). A surprising result was that there is not any commonly accepted visual representation to illustrate and explain the greedy technique. As an alternative way of addressing the active learning of greedy algorithms, we challenged students to identify the key element in the design of greedy algorithms, namely optimal selection functions. In our method, students must find out optimal selection functions by means of experimentation (Velázquez-Iturbide & Debdi, 2011).

The GreedEx system was developed as an interactive tool to support our experimental method (Velázquez-Iturbide & Pérez-Carrasco, 2009). We may specify its learning goals as:

- **Comprehension Level:** The student must be able to understand the problem, a basic greedy algorithm that solves it, and candidate selection functions.
- **Analysis Level:** The student must be able to analyze the effect of using different selection functions in a basic greedy algorithm.
- **Evaluation Level:** The student must be able to evaluate and select the optimal selection functions.

Table 4. Evolution of the functions supported by different versions of SRec

	SRec v.1.0	SRec v.1.1	SRec v.1.2
Support for recursive algorithms	X	X	X
Support for recursion with several methods	X	X	X
Recursion tree view	X	Y	Z
Global+detail view	X	X	X
Control stack view	X	X	X
Trace view	X	X	X
Basic control for animation	X	X'	X'
Configuration of visualizations	X	X'	Y
Filters for methods and parameters	X	Y	Y
Zoom	X	X	X
Load and save visualizations	X	X	X
Code editor	X	X	Y
Interactive help	X	X	X
Internationalization	X	X	X
Errors information (compile time and run time)	X	X	X
Animated GIF exportation	X	Y	Z
Visualization exportation	X	X	Y
Configuration management	X	X	X
Summary of visualization data		X	X
Semantic information about tree nodes		X	X
Highlighting nodes		X	X
Chronological view			X
Data structure view			X
Panels relocation capacity			X
Usage registration capacity (log files)			X
Java Virtual Machine autosearch			X

The system supports algorithm animation. Some educational requirements were also stated: support to documentation tasks (e.g. exporting visualizations) and to internationalization (currently, it supports English and Spanish).

4.2. Description of GreedEx

Figure 2 shows the user interface of GreedEx at an intermediate state of execution of a greedy algorithm for the activities selection problem (Cormen, et al., 2009).

Three areas can be clearly distinguished, apart from the window title, main menu, and icon areas. The top area is the visualization panel, which graphically displays data. The lower left area is the theory panel, which consists of two tabs: the problem tab contains the problem statement (visible in the figure), and the algorithm tab contains its code in Java pseudocode. Finally, the lower right area is the table panel, with four tabs containing the input data table (visible in the figure), the results table, the summary table, and the abridge table.

When the user launches the application, only the theory panel hosts visible contents. Its two tabs can be read to understand the problem. Afterwards, the user may generate input data from three sources: interactively, randomly, or from a file. Some limits are imposed over data size to keep data manageable for learning and for visualization.

Input data are displayed in the visualization panel. The user may then choose any selection function from those available at the application (eight for the activity selection problem). Every time the user selects a selection function, she may execute it flexibly with four execution/animation controls: step forward, full forward, step backward, and rewind. As animation controls are clicked, the visualization is updated accordingly. After a selection function has been completely executed, the results of the algorithm are stored in the results table and in the summary table. The abridge table shows the percentage of optimal results obtained by each selection function along the user executions.

Additional facilities are provided for faster experimentation: executing all the selection func-

Figure 2. User interface of the GreedEx system

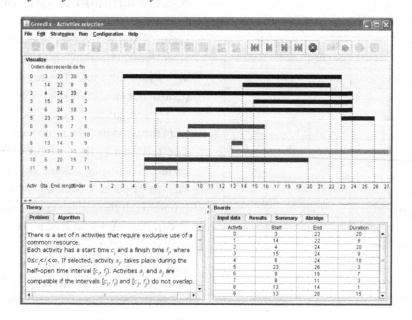

tions, executing a subset of the selection functions, and generating and executing all the selection functions over a very high number of input data.

Finally, GreedEx includes a number of educational facilities. GreedEx is internationalized to support multiple languages (currently, English and Spanish). GreedEx also allows exporting visualizations, animations, and tables to standard graphical formats. This support is useful for both teachers and students as it makes easy documenting reports, slides or Web pages.

4.3. Usability Evaluations

Evaluations of GreedEx were very similar to evaluations of SRec. We have conducted three classes of usability evaluations:

- **Expert Evaluations:** They were similar to expert evaluations of SRec.
- **Evaluation of Reports:** The reports delivered by students in lab sessions of a course on design and analysis of algorithms were graded, as a part of the course grading. Consequently, the reports delivered by

students in three sessions were used as a measure of the effectiveness of GreedEx. Notice, however, that these sessions involved concepts that students were not fluent with. Therefore, the analysis of the reports must be taken with caution as they often reveal conceptual misunderstandings, rather than tool deficiencies.

- **Evaluations with Final Users:** They evaluated the satisfaction of students with GreedEx and were similar to evaluations of SRec. We have conducted five evaluations with students, typically in a single session. (In fact, some systems which were antecessors of GreedEx were used in the first four evaluations, but these systems are almost identical to GreedEx in most regards. These systems are called AMO and SEDA).

Evaluation sessions with students were similar to the evaluation sessions of SRec: they were two hours long had a similar structure. A summary of the five evaluations follow:

1. **January 2008:** Knapsack problem. 46 participants. The assignment and the report were done in pairs, but the questionnaire was answered individually.
2. **May 2008:** Activity selection problem. 13 participants. All student work was done individually.
3. **January 2009:** Activity selection problem. 31 participants. Similar to the first evaluation.
4. **November 2009:** Activity selection problem. 27 participants. Similar to the first evaluation.
5. **November 2010:** Two sessions, with 23 participants in the first one and 36 in the second one. The first session was intended to facilitate familiarization of the students with the experimental method and GreedEx given the knapsack problem. The second session was devoted to experimentation with the activities selection problem. Both the report and the questionnaire were only required in the second session, with similar delivery characteristics to the first evaluation.

4.4. Usability Results

We present the results of usability evaluations with respect to student effectiveness and satisfaction. In general, the results have been extremely positive.

Firstly, let us review students' effectiveness. For this analysis, we may classify the students' answers we found in reports into four categories:

1. Students who performed well.
2. Students who used consistently the experimental method, but proposed suboptimal selection functions.
3. Students who did not use consistently the experimental method, but they do not exhibit further misunderstandings.
4. Students who exhibited major misunderstandings.

These categories evolved as shown in Table 5. Part of the success is due to the fact that the teacher adapted his teaching method to avoid misunderstandings, but the tool was the instrument for experimentation.

Secondly, let us review students' satisfaction, according to students' answers to the questionnaire. Table 6 shows the evolution of the numerical values obtained in multiple-choice questions about general issues. Notice that the values obtained in all the questions were very high. The highest value corresponds to its facility of use (4.45).

It also was assessed the quality of the different elements in GreedEx. The results are shown in Table 7, sorted in descending order. The eight best-ranked elements correspond to key elements in the experimental method supported. In addition, the fifth worst ranked correspond to secondary elements of the applications or to static elements.

Finally, some open questions were included. The results obtained follow:

- **Positive Aspects:** Students highlight that it is a simple, pleasant, and easy-to-use system. They also appreciate their visualizations and its usefulness to compare results.
- **Parts that the User Would Suppress:** There also is large variability among evaluations. Some answers recurrently appear in the different evaluations (e.g. configuration of colors) but from few students.

Table 5. Evolution of percentages of categories of students' answers

Category	1st session	2nd session	3rd session
1	22.22%	28.57%	47.83%
2	5.555%	23.81%	39.13%
3	16.67%	23.81%	13.04%
4	55.555%	23.81%	0%

Table 6. Evolution of values obtained for GreedEx in general questions

Question	Mean 1	Mean 2	Mean 3	Mean 4	Mean 5	Global mean
Easy to use	4.54	4.64	4.42	4.38	4.29	4.45
It has aided me in analyzing the effect of each selection function	4.20	4.50	4.36	4.19	4.43	4.34
It has aided me in identifying optimal selection functions	4.55	3.60	4.04	4.04	4.57	4.16
Overall. I liked it	4.25	4.27	4.32	4.19	4.12	4.23

- **Negative Aspects, Parts of Difficult use, and Features that the User Would Incorporate:** Most aspects identified by students were used as a base to specify future improvements. Consequently, there is large variability among evaluations, due to the evolution of the systems. For instance, some students suggested improving the visualization format.

One consequence of the iterative evaluation of GreedEx has been its evolution to better support the underlying experimental method. Answers to open questions were especially useful. Table 8 summarizes the evolution of the functions provided by GreedEx and its predecessors. A cell with an X means that the system in the corresponding column supports the function in the corresponding row. When the cell of the following system contains the following letter in the alphabet (Y, Z), a major change has been implemented, whereas a single quote (X', X") denotes a minor change. A juxtaposition of letters (XY) means that GreedEx has integrated features present in either AMO or SEDA.

Table 7. Evolution of values obtained about the quality of specific elements of GreedEx

Question	Mean 1	Mean 2	Mean 3	Mean 4	Mean 5	Global mean
Tab with results table	4.28	4.18	4.36	4.31	4.00	4.23
Execution/animation of the algorithm			4.33	4.19	4.00	4.17
Introduction/generation of input data	4.30	4.45	4.04	3.96	4.07	4.16
Structure of the main menu	4.00	4.45	4.11	4.08	4.04	4.14
Tab with summary table			4.39	3.88	4.14	4.14
Tab with input data table	4.03	4.18	4.07	4.15	4.11	4.11
Panel for data visualization	4.17	4.18	4.46	4.00	3.89	4.14
Selection of selection functions			4.07	4.00	4.00	4.02
Algorithm tab (code)	3.80	4.09	4.11	3.85	3.93	3.96
Icons	380	4.64	3.96	3.77	3.61	3.96
Problem tab (explanation)	3.60	3.91	3.82	3.58	3.89	3.76
Interactive help			3.81	3.40		3.61
Export facilities / Storage format in file	3.48	4.00	3.93	3.76	2.82	3.60

Table 8. Evolution of the functions supported by GreedEx and its antecessors

	AMO	SEDA v.1	SEDA v.2	GreedEx v.1	GreedEx v.2
Main menu	X	Y	Y'	Z	Z'
Icons	X	Y	Z	Y'	W
Configuration	X	Y	Z	X'	X'
Visualization panel	X	Y	Y'	X'Y''	X'Y''
Problem tab	X	Y	Y	X	X
Algorithm tab	X	Y	Y	X	X'
Data table	X	Y	Y	Y	Y
Results table	X	Y	Y'	X'Y'	XY'Z
Enter/generate input data	X	Y	Y'	X'Y'	X'Y'
Modify input data	X	X'	X'	X'	X'
Animation	X	Y	Y'	Y''	Y''
Save data/results	X	X'	X'	X'	X''
Internationalization		X	X	X	X
Deleting operations on tables		X	X	Y	Y
Connection tables-visualizations		X.	Y	Y	Y
Export visualizations		X	Y	Z	Z
Summary table			X	X'	X'
Previous/following selection function			X	X	X
Execute all the selection functions			X	X	X'
Execute a subset of the selection functions			X	X	X'
Abridge table				X	X'
Intensive execution				X	X'
Export tables					X

5. LESSONS LEARNED

The results with both systems have been quite successful. In this section, we discuss these results, presenting them to other developers as lessons learnt.

An important issue was the design of the systems from clear educational goals stated in terms of Bloom's taxonomy. This specification was especially important in the case of GreedEx, which was designed to support experimental tasks for specific problems. Experimentation is a complex task that requires learning skills at several levels. The specification allowed us to identify the different elements that would be necessary in the

future system to achieve such goals. Furthermore, students' suggestions were incorporated in the light of the educational goals.

A second issue is that both systems were designed under a simplicity principle, which made them appealing to students. We have shown that extending SRec with more functions resulted in a more complex system. According to our experience, we may identify at least two approaches to careful extension. The first one consists in incorporating only those features that are necessary to better fulfill the educational goals. The second approach consists in reminding that the incorporation of new functions must be accompanied with a reexamination (and possible rearrangement) of the structure of the whole system, playing the main menu and the icons an important role.

Another feature of SRec and GreedEx that made them attractive to students is visualizations, which provide an aesthetically more pleasant experience than other programming tools. Again, this feature must be carefully integrated to keep the system simple and effortless.

A third issue is that educational technology must be accompanied with adequate teaching methods. This proved to be especially important for GreedEx. Data gathered in the different evaluations were critical to intervene in different ways and to improve both the system and the teaching method. In particular, the students' reports allowed identifying misunderstandings, which were used by the teachers to improve their teaching method.

A fourth issue is the complementary role played by expert evaluations and questionnaires with final users. The former kind of evaluation was very important to guarantee system consistency. The latter kind of evaluation was important to identify lacks or incorrect design decisions in the systems. Open questions in questionnaires allowed us to obtain very useful information about the deficiencies of the system. GreedEx deficiencies were remedied by introducing new features or by modifying existing ones. A number of relevant elements were introduced to better support the intended tasks, such as some tables or execution operations. However, the whole design of the system was kept simple. As a consequence, satisfaction results from students are invariantly very high.

Finally, it must also be noticed the limitations of the evaluation methods that we selected. Firstly, the evaluation methods must often be tuned to be effective. Holding several evaluations gives the opportunity to obtain experience and enhance the evaluation procedure. For instance, the convenience of a familiarization session became evident to us after several evaluations. Secondly, questionnaires yield quantitative but subjective measures that give a partial view of the system usability. Other evaluation methods, such as observations, interviews or analysis of logs, may deliver richer information. However, they require longer time for analysis and more people to conduct the evaluations, which are not always available or are not worth the effort.

6. CONCLUSION

We have advocated for an approach to constructing educational tools that consists in designing small applications aimed at achieving clear educational goals and evaluating them in actual teaching situations. We have also described our experience in the development, use, and evaluation of two educational systems: SRec and GreedEx. Two main kinds of usability evaluations were conducted, namely expert evaluations and questionnaires with students. The results obtained show highly successful results of this approach with respect to effectiveness and student satisfaction. We have also discussed the limitations of the evaluation methods we have used.

We hope that our experience will be illuminating for other researchers willing to develop innovative educational systems. The combined use of clear educational goals, evaluation of systems in actual teaching situations and adaptation of teaching method and schedule has proved to constitute a good path to enhanced learning.

In the future, we plan to enhance our two systems in more ambitious directions. We plan to extend SRec to better support divide-and-conquer algorithms and to support the construction of dynamic programming algorithms. With respect to GreedEx, we plan to extend it for collaborative deliberation among the students in a lab group. Finally, we also plan to extend the range of evaluation methods, either as complements or alternatives to the current ones. For instance, the combined use of observations and logs can be a good way of obtaining an accurate record of students' activity in a session.

ACKNOWLEDGMENT

This work was supported by research grants TIN2008-04103 and TIN2011-29542-C02-01 of the Spanish Ministry of Science and Innovation.

REFERENCES

ACM Interim Review Task Force. (2008). *Computer Science curriculum 2008: An interim revision of CS 2001*. New York, NY: ACM & IEEE Computer Society. Retrieved February 26, 2011, from http://www.acm.org//education/curricula/ComputerScience2008.pdf

Anderson, L. W., Krathwohl, D. R., Airasian, P. W., Cruikshank, K. A., Pintrich, P. R., Raths, J., & Wittrock, M. C. (2001). *A taxonomy for learning, teaching and assessing: A revision of Bloom's taxonomy of educational objectives*. New York, NY: Longman.

Bloom, B., Furst, E., Hill, W., & Krathwohl, D. R. (1956). *Taxonomy of educational objectives: Handbook I – The cognitive domain*. Reading, MA: Addison-Wesley.

Brassard, G., & Bratley, P. (1996). *Fundamentals of algoritmics*. Hertfordshire, UK: Prentice-Hall.

Card, S. K., Mackinlay, J. D., & Shneiderman, B. (Eds.). (1999). *Readings in information visualization*. San Francisco, CA: Morgan Kaufmann.

Cormen, T. H., & Leiserson, C. E. Rivest. R. L., & Stein, C. (2009). *Introduction to algorithms* (3rd ed). Cambridge, MA: The MIT Press.

Dancik, G., & Kumar, A. (2003). A tutor for counter-controlled loop concepts and its evaluation. In *Proceedings of the 33rd ASEE/IEEE Frontiers in Education Conference – FIE 2003*, (vol. 1), (pp. T3C 7-12). Kansas City, MO: Stipes Publishing.

Deek, F. P., & McHugh, J. A. (1998). A survey and critical analysis of tools for learning programming. *Computer Science Education*, *8*(2), 130–178. doi:10.1076/csed.8.2.130.3820

Fernández-Muñoz, L., Pérez-Carrasco, A., Velázquez-Iturbide, J. Á., & Urquiza-Fuentes, J. (2007). A framework for the automatic generation of algorithm animations based on design techniques. In Duval, E., Klamma, R., & Wolpers, M. (Eds.), *Creating New Learning Experiences on a Global Scale – EC-TEL 2007* (pp. 475–480). Berlin, Germany: Springer-Verlag. doi:10.1007/978-3-540-75195-3_40

Fernández Muñoz, L., & Velázquez Iturbide, J. Á. (2006). Estudio sobre la visualización de las técnicas de diseño de algoritmos. In *Proceedings of Actas del VII Congreso Internacional de Interacción Persona-Ordenador – Interacción 2006*, (pp. 315-324). Salamanca, Spain: AIPO.

Fincher, S., & Petre, M. (Eds.). (2004). *Computer science education research*. London, UK: Rouledge Falmer.

Fincher, S., & Utting, I. (Eds.). (2010). Special issue on initial learning environments. *ACM Transactions on Computing Education, 10*(4).

Fuller, U., Johnson, C. G., Ahoniemi, T., Cukierman, D., Hernán-Losada, I., & Jackova, J. (2007). Developing a computer science-specific learning taxonomy. *SIGCSE Bulletin*, *39*(4), 152–170. doi:10.1145/1345375.1345438

Ihantola, P., Ahoniemi, T., Karavirta, V., & Seppälä, O. (2010). Review of recent systems for automatic assessment of programming assignments. In *Proceedings of the Tenth Koli Calling Conference on Computer Science Education – Koli Calling 2010*, (pp. 86-93). New York, NY: ACM Press.

Ihantola, P., Karavirta, V., Korhonen, A., & Nikander, J. (2005). Taxonomy of effortless creation of algorithm visualization. In *Proceedings of the 2005 International Workshop on Computing Education Research – ICER 2005,* (pp. 123-133). New York, NY: ACM Press.

ISO. (1998). *ISO 9241-11: Ergonomic requirements for office work with visual display terminals (CDTs): Part 11: Guidance on usability.* Geneva, Switzerland: International Standards Organization.

Jurado, F., Molina, A. I., Redondo, M. A., Ortega, M., Giemza, A., Bollen, L., & Hoppe, H. U. (2009). Learning to program with COALA: A distributed computer assisted environment. *Journal of Universal Computer Science, 15*(7), 1472–1485.

Naps, T., Roessling, G., Almstrum, V., Dann, W., Fleischer, R., & Hundhausen, C. (2003). Exploring the role of visualization and engagement in computer science education. *ACM SIGCSE Bulletin, 35*(4), 131–152. doi:10.1145/782941.782998

Pérez-Carrasco, A., & Velázquez-Iturbide, J. Á. (2012). Interactive learning of recursion. In *Educational Stages and Interactive Learning: From Kindergarten to Workplace Training.* Hershey, PA: IGI Global. doi:10.4018/978-1-4666-0137-6.ch015

Pérez-Carrasco, A., Velázquez-Iturbide, J. Á., & Urquiza-Fuentes, J. (2010). Multiple usability evaluations of a program animation tool. In M. Jemni, D. Kinshuk, Sampson, & J. M. Spector (Eds.), *The 10th IEEE International Conference on Advanced Learning Technologies, ICALT 2010,* (pp. 452-454). Los Alamitos, CA: IEEE Computer Society.

Sahni, S. (2005). *Data structures, algorithms, and applications in Java* (2nd ed.). Summit, NJ: Silicon Press.

Stasko, J. T., Domingue, J., Brown, M. H., & Price, B. A. (Eds.). (1997). *Software visualization.* Cambridge, MA: The MIT Press.

Velázquez-Iturbide, J. Á., & Debdi, O. (2011). Experimentation with optimization problems in algorithm courses. In *Proceedings of the Internacional Conference on Computer as a Tool – EUROCON 2011.* Lisbon, Portugal: University of Lisbon.

Velázquez-Iturbide, J. Á., Lázaro-Carrascosa, C. A., & Hernán-Losada, I. (2009). Asistentes interactivos para el aprendizaje de algoritmos voraces. *IEEE Revista Iberoamericana de Tecnologías del Aprendizaje, 4*(3), 213–220.

Velázquez-Iturbide, J. Á., & Pérez-Carrasco, A. (2009). Active learning of greedy algorithms by means of interactive experimentation. In *Proceedings of the 14th Annual Conference on Innovation and Technology in Computer Science Education – ITiCSE 2009,* (pp. 119-123). New York, NY: ACM Press.

Velázquez-Iturbide, J. Á., & Pérez-Carrasco, A. (2010). InfoVis interaction techniques in animation of recursive programs. *Algorithms, 3*(1), 76–91. doi:10.3390/a3010076

Velázquez-Iturbide, J. Á., Pérez-Carrasco, A., & Urquiza-Fuentes, J. (2008). SRec: An animation system of recursion for algorithm courses. In *Proceedings of the 13th Annual Conference Innovation and Technology in Computer Science Education – ITiCSE 2008,* (pp. 225-229). New York, NY: ACM Press.

Vizcaíno, A., Contreras, J., Favela, J., & Prieto, M. (2000). An adaptive collaborative environment to develop good habits in programming. In G. Gauthier, C. Frasson, & K. VanLehn (Eds.), *5th International Conference on Intelligent Tutoring Systems, ITS 2000,* (pp. 262-271). Berlin, Germany: Springer-Verlag.

ADDITIONAL READING

Ala-Mutka, F. M. (2005). A survey of automated assessment approaches for programming assignments. *Computer Science Education, 15*(2), 83–102. doi:10.1080/08993400500150747

Ben-Bassat Levy, R., & Ben-Ari, M. (2008). Perceived behavior control and its influence on the adoption of software tools. In *Proceedings of the 13rd Annual Conference on Innovation and Technology in Computer Science Education – ITiCSE 2008,* (pp. 225-229). New York, NY: ACM Press.

Benson, L., Elliott, D., Grant, M., Holschuh, D., Kim, B., & Kim, H. … Reeves, T. C. (2002). Usability and instructional design heuristics for e-learning evaluation. In *Proceedings of the Communications of World Conference on Educational Multimedia, Hypermedia and Telecommunications – ED-MEDIA 2002,* (pp. 1615-1621). Norfolk, VA: AACE.

Bower, M. (2008). A taxonomy of task types in computing. In *Proceedings of the 13rd Annual Conference on Innovation and Technology in Computer Science Education – ITiCSE 2008,* (pp. 281-285). New York, NY: ACM Press.

Costabile, M. F., De Marisco, M., Lanzilotti, R., Plantamura, V. L., & Roselli, T. (2005). On the usability evaluation of e-learning applications. In *Proceedings of 38th Hawaii International Conference on System Sciences – Track 1,* (vol. 1). IEEE.

Debdi, O., & Velázquez-Iturbide, J. Á. (2011). *Una evaluación de usabilidad de GreedEx: Serie de Informes Técnicos DLSI1-URJC, 2011-01.* Universidad Rey Juan Carlos. Retrieved November 10, 2011, from http://www.dlsi1.etsii.urjc.es/doc/DLSI1-URJC_2011-01.pdf

Denning, P. J., Comer, D. E., Gries, D., Mulder, M. C., Tucker, A. B., Turner, A. J., & Young, P. R. (1989). Computing as a discipline. *Communications of the ACM, 32*(1), 9–23. doi:10.1145/63238.63239

Douce, C., Livingston, D., & Orwell, J. (2005). Automatic test-based assessment of programming: A review. *ACM Journal of Educational Resources in Computing, 5*(3).

Gross, P., & Powers, K. (2005). Evaluating assessments of novice programming environments. In *Proceedings of the 2005 International Computing Education Research Workshop – ICER 2006,* (pp. 99-110). New York, NY: ACM Press.

Hundhausen, C., Douglas, S., & Stasko, J. T. (2002). A meta-study of algorithm visualization effectiveness. *Journal of Visual Languages and Computing, 13,* 259–290. doi:10.1006/jvlc.2002.0237

Kelleher, C., & Pausch, R. (2005). Lowering the barriers to programming: A taxonomy of programming environments and languages for novice programmers. *ACM Computing Surveys, 37*(2), 83–137. doi:10.1145/1089733.1089734

Pears, A., Seidman, S., Eney, C., Kinnunen, P., & Malmi, L. (2005). Constructing a core literature for computing education research. *ACM SIGCSE Bulletin, 37*(4), 152–161. doi:10.1145/1113847.1113893

Robins, A., Roundtree, J., & Roundtree, N. (2003). Learning and teaching programming: A review and discussion. *Computer Science Education, 13*(2), 137–172. doi:10.1076/csed.13.2.137.14200

Squire, D., & Preece, J. (1996). Usability and learning: Evaluating the potential of educational software. *Communications of the Computer & Education, 27*(1), 15–22.

Urquiza-Fuentes, J., & Velázquez-Iturbide, J. Á. (2009). A survey of successful evaluations of program visualization and algorithm animation systems. *ACM Transactions on Computing Education, 9*(2).

Velázquez-Iturbide, J. Á. (2010). *Una tercera evaluación de usabilidad de SEDA: Serie de Informes Técnicos DLSI1-URJC, 2010-01*. Universidad Rey Juan Carlos. Retrieved November 10, 2011, from http://www.dlsi1.etsii.urjc.cs/doc/DLSI1-URJC_2010-01.pdf

Velázquez-Iturbide, J. Á., Lázaro-Carrascosa, C. A., & Pérez-Carrasco, A. (2009). *Dos evaluaciones de usabilidad de SEDA: Serie de informes técnicos DLSI1-URJC, 2009-05*. Universidad Rey Juan Carlos. Retrieved November 10, 2011, from http://www.dlsi1.etsii.urjc.es/doc/DLSI1-URJC_2009-05.pdf

Velázquez-Iturbide, J. Á., & Pérez-Carrasco, A. (2009). Experimental inquiry into greedy algorithms. In *Proceedings of the 2nd Workshop on Methods and Cases in Computing Education – MCCE 2009*, (pp. 1-6). Retrieved November 10, 2011, from http://es.scribd.com/doc/14226792/MCCE-2009-Proceedings

Wing, J. M. (2006). Computational thinking. *Communications of the ACM, 49*(3), 33–35. doi:10.1145/1118178.1118215

KEY TERMS AND DEFINITIONS

Algorithm Animation: Visualization of a piece of software illustrating the main ideas or steps (i.e. its algorithmic behavior), but without a close relationship to the source code.

Computer Science Education Research: Research field that has emerged in last years at the intersection of computer science and the social sciences, such as pedagogy and psychology.

Evaluation with Experts: Evaluation of an interactive system conducted by an expert in the problem domain or task. Evaluations with experts are often used in the initial stages of development of a system.

Evaluation with End Users: Evaluation of an interactive system conducted by a person representative of the intended users of the system. Evaluations with end users can be conducted at any stage of the system development, but at least they should be conducted at the final stage of development.

Greedy Technique: Algorithm design technique suitable for optimization problems. Its main design element is a selection function, which allows selecting the next best candidate for a given problem at each stage of the algorithm.

Human-Computer Interaction: The field that addresses the study, planning and design of the interaction between people (users) and computers. It is at the intersection of computer science, behavioral sciences, and design.

Learning Taxonomy: Theory that allows classifying into several levels the students' mastery of a subject matter. Well-known examples are Bloom's and SOLO taxonomy.

Program Visualization: Visualization of a piece of software so that the representation has a close relationship to the source code.

Recursion: A linguistic mechanism consisting in defining something in terms of itself. In mathematics and computer programming, recursion is a valuable tool for definitions and for problem solving.

Usability: The extent to which a product can be used by specified users to achieve specified goals with effectiveness, efficiency, and satisfaction in a specified context of use.

Chapter 12
User's Experience with a 3D Educational Mobile Game to Support Spatial Instruction

Norena Martin-Dorta
Universidad de La Laguna (ULL), Spain

Isabel Sanchez-Berriel
Universidad de La Laguna (ULL), Spain

Jose Luis Saorin
Universidad de La Laguna (ULL), Spain

Manuel Contero
Universidad Politécnica de Valencia (UPV), Spain

ABSTRACT

Spatial abilities are critical skills in scientific and technical fields. In recent studies, the role of computer games, particularly those with 3-D simulations, have been examined for their impact on the development of spatial skills. The work presented in this chapter describes the design and user evaluation of a 3D construction mobile game called iCube. A trial version was brought out and evaluated by twenty-two students. Users pointed out that the game is useful for improvement of spatial ability and is fun. However, some difficulties arose with use of the tactile screen, as fingerprints caused problems while interacting with the game's 3D environment. The results revealed that it is necessary to have this item in mind during the game's design, where screen action is continuous.

INTRODUCTION

Over the last half century, spatial abilities have been given increasing recognition and, despite the fact that not so much attention has been paid to them as to verbal and numeric abilities, research accentuates their importance in the traditional fields of engineering, technology, and art, as well as in almost any other aspect of life. As it has repercussions in almost all scientific and technical fields, spatial abilities remain an active field of study, especially in the engineering domain.

DOI: 10.4018/978-1-4666-1987-6.ch012

Spatial skills may be associated with success in scientific areas (Smith, 1964). Non-academic activities, such as playing with construction toys as a young child and playing three dimensional computer games seem to have strong relationship with spatial visualization ability. The interest of video or computer games for improving spatial skills has been analyzed by numerous research (Deno, 1995; Sorby, 2007).

Several authors have analyzed the impact of games on education and there is wide empirical evidence supporting the positive effects of computer games as instructional tools (Amory, Naicker, Vincent, & Adams, 1999). Various experiments have tested tools in handheld devices, indicating that they strengthen and support learning in fields such as languages, science and mathematics. Mobile devices allow for learning everywhere; when walking, in the street, on the bus, in the school, or even on the subway (Salinas & Sánchez, 2006), creating the potential for a new phase in the evolution of technology-enhanced learning, marked by the continuity of learning experiences across different environments (Chan, et al., 2006). The use of touchscreen handheld devices, such as smartphones and tablets computers appears to be one of the most significant tendencies in the current market. The majority of manufacturers are in favor of incorporating touch screens to their new devices. Market tracker iSuppli Corp. expects smartphone shipments to rise 105% from 246.9 million in 2010 to 506 million units in 2014. Shipments of tablet computers like the iPad are expected to grow from 19.5 million units in 2010 to 208 million units in 2014, according to Gartner Inc. media analysts (Gartner, 2010).

Most recent research in the field of spatial abilities focuses on how these relate to new technologies (Rafi, Samsudin, & Ismail, 2006; Rafi, Samsudin, & Said, 2008; Martin-Dorta, Saorin, & Contero, 2008; Rafi & Samsudin, 2009). The possibility of using games to develop cognitive skills opens up enormous opportunities to connect education to the daily life experiences of learners and their learning styles. This, in turn, could increase their motivation for and commitment to learning (Sánchez & Olivares, 2011).

Based on the above mentioned findings and on our experience in developing multimedia spatial ability training tools (Martin-Dorta, Saorín, & Contero, 2008; Martin-Dorta, et al., 2010; Martin-Dorta, et al., 2011; Martin-Dorta, Saorín, & Contero, 2011), the present study tries to join the potential of touchscreen handheld devices, digital games and playing with construction toys to develop spatial skills. In the following sections, we present an overview of spatial ability and digital games, the architecture of the system designed, description of the applications and the study with users to know their experience with the mobile game.

SPATIAL ABILITIES

The ability to represent and process spatial information is important for many common activities. Through a survey of engineering professionals, Jensen (1986) found out that spatial abilities are the most important engineering graphic skills that an individual needs to be able to succeed in the engineering profession. Engineers use spatial reasoning and visualization in tasks like designing and documenting parts to be assembled, imagining the shape of cut hillsides for highway construction, laying out circuit designs, or finding optimal crystal configurations. In many engineering disciplines, students need to imagine objects in different orientations, translate two-dimensional drawings into three dimensions. These skills have been positively correlated with retention and achievement in engineering, mathematics, and science disciplines (Hsi, Linn, & Bell, 1997).

Spatial ability is an important human aptitude, which plays significant roles in how individuals perceive, organize, and interact with their environments (McGee, 1979). Clements and Battista (1992) define spatial reasoning as consisting of "cognitive processes by which mental representations for spatial objects, relationships, and transformations are constructed and manipulated." Linn and Peterson (1985) similarly state that spatial reasoning "refers to skill in representing, transforming, generating, and recalling symbolic, nonlinguistic information." According to Thurstone (1941), spatial ability itself can be further divided into three skills: recognizing an object from different angles, imagining movement or displacement of internal parts of a spatial configuration, and determining spatial relationships with respect to one's own body. During the middle of the 20th century, research focused on determining the factor structure of spatial ability. Investigators such as Guiforld and Lacey (1947), Zimmerman (1954), Thurstone (1950), and French (1951) all found that large batteries of spatial tests yielded evidence for separable subcomponents of spatial ability (spatial visualization, spatial relations, spatial orientation).

Researchers generally agree that spatial ability plays a crucial role in determining students' achievement in engineering courses. Gimmestad (1990) found that a student's score on a spatial ability test was the most powerful predictor for students' success in an engineering design graphics course among investigated variables. Shea, Lubinski, and Benbow (2001) reported that spatial ability is a significant predictor of academic performance in the Science, Technology, Engineering, and Mathematics (STEM) disciplines, including engineering.

Research also suggests that some factors, such as spatial activities, music experiences, and family spatial opportunity can relate to performance of spatial ability measured by spatial tests. Results from a meta-analysis conducted by Baenninger and Newcombe (1989) provided evidence that experience of spatial activities is positively related to spatial task performance. Specifically, young children develop spatial abilities as they actively manipulate objects (Clement, 1998). More use of three-dimensional objects could explain higher spatial ability scores of children (Mitchelmore, 1980).

DIGITAL GAMES TO SUPPORT SPATIAL INSTRUCTION

Numerous studies have indicated that spatial abilities can be improved through training. Many computer applications (e.g., computer-aided design and drawing) and computer games require spatial processes such as mental rotation and spatial visualization (Quaiser-Pohl, Geiser, & Lehmann, 2005). Baartmans and Sorby (1996) also believe that experience in computer games is beneficial to developing spatial skills. For example, playing the computer game "Tetris," which requires rapid rotation and placement of seven differently shaped blocks, and the game "blockout," which requires mental-rotation of geometric figures (De Lisi & Cammarano, 1996), improves spatial-test performance (Ogakaki & Frensch, 1994).

Furthermore, since the mid-nineties, several institutions and investigators have suggested novel tools for improving spatial abilities. Illuminations (National Council of Teachers of Mathematics, 2000) is a website that was created by the United States National Council of Teachers of Mathematics and the Marco Polo Foundation. The site includes the "Isometric Drawing Tool," an interactive applet that allows you to dynamically create isometric drawings on a template of dots. Crown (2001), developed a number of Web-based games using simple JavaScript code to enhance visualization skills in engineering graphics. Various games in the field of multi-view drawings, auxiliary views construction, manipulation of parts, and a reference coordinate system in a three dimensional space are developed. The experimental study shows a positive impact on student's spatial abilities. Michigan Technological University offers interactive modules for learning the engineering graphics concepts (Sorby, Wysocky, & Baartmans, 2003). Moran, Rubio, Gallego, Suarez, and Martín (2008) have created a set of applications to improve students' spatial perception using three flash-based Web applications: view table, views of a cube and the development of a tetrahedron. The Freudenthal

Institute for Science and Mathematics Education of Utrecht University (2009) host two on-line java applications: "*Building with blocks*" and "*Building houses with sides*." These applets are about building models with blocks. A Web-based multimedia application optimized for handled devices show effective to improve spatial visualisation scores. Students value positively the course accomplished and they expressed their preference for these multimedia contents over the conventional pencil and paper formats, and for the on-line learning over a face-to-face course (Martin-Dorta, Saorín, & Contero, 2011).

In recent studies, the role of computer games, have been examined for their impact on the gender differences in spatial skills. Terlecki and Newcombe(2005) found that computer experience substantially mediates the gender difference in spatial ability observed on the Mental Rotations Test (MRT). Terlecki, Newcombe, and Little (2008) conducted a study with collegeage students using 3-D Tetris as a spatial skills training aid. Undergraduates participated in repeated testing on the MRT or played the videogame Tetris. Analyses showed large improvements in mental rotation with both repeated testing and training; these gains were maintained several months later. MRT scores of men and women did not converge, but men showed faster initial growth and women showed more improvement later. Feng, Spence, and Pratt (2007) found that playing an action video game can virtually eliminate gender difference in spatial attention and simultaneously decrease the gender disparity in mental rotation ability. In summary, research consistently shows that video game exposure is related to improvements in spatial skills.

Background of this Work

In the autumn of 2007 a pilot study was carried out with volunteer freshman Civil Engineering Degree students at the University of La Laguna in Spain. We selected the Mental Rotation Test (MRT) and the Differential Aptitude Test spatial relations subsection (DAT-SR) to detect the students with lower spatial abilities and to evaluate the outcomes of the remedial course we designed. We pre-tested 47 students and we chose the lowest-scoring students to attend an intensive remedial course. 12 of them completed the course voluntarily, with ages between 18 and 20 years. The course was carried out on desktop computers in a university classroom. It was organized in two sessions of three hours, developed in two weeks with the on-line applets "*Building with blocks*" and "*Building houses with sides*" of the Freudenthal Institute for Science and Mathematics Education of Utrecht University (Wisweb, 2009). This pilot study shows a significance increase of spatial test scores. The course was effective to improve spatial skills. Students were surveyed, and they all considered necessary that the university offers such courses for students with difficulties in spatial ability. 85% of them prefer electronic course on PC or mobile devices. 75% of surveyed students felt that the overall course satisfaction was good and 25% found it excellent.

In that experience, we found out, through observation of the learners, the tasks with immediate feedback and ratings generate a high degree of motivation in students. Furthermore, we believe that these exercises could be transferred to handheld devices: mobile phones, Personal Digital Assistants (PDAs), games consoles, or MP3/MP4 players. We performed a preliminary analysis to determine the devices on which we could develop the tool, as well as the format, the programming language and the exercises that could be implemented.

Based in that first study, between 2008 and 2009, we designed a new game, implementing and testing two mobile applications to spatial training (Martin-Dorta, et al., 2010; Martin-Dorta, Saorín, & Contero, 2011). It is important to emphasize that these are the first ones specifically targeting development of spatial abilities with mobile phones. The first application, called Vizualization, is a multimedia Web-based tool optimized for handled devices. That study shows a significant improvement in average spatial visualization scores among the experimental group in comparison with the control group. Students value positively the course accomplished, and they expressed their preference for these multimedia contents over the conventional pencil and paper formats, and for the on-line learning over a face-to-face course. They also consider that having materials of this kind available in their study programme subjects and the possibility of accessing this material at any time and in any place to be a positive aspect. The second application, jCube, a Java game for Windows mobile phones, was tested with users using satisfaction questionnaires and observation records in order to evaluate it. The results show a high degree of satisfaction with the application and that users realize how useful this game can be for the proposed aims.

With the emergence of the new mobile operating systems, like Apple's iOS and Google's Android, and the proliferation of touch screen devices, we think that these new interfaces could improve the user's experience with the spatial instruction games. With this objective and based on our experience, we began with the design of the application described below (iCube).

SYSTEM DESIGN

A mobile spatial instruction system, which includes a 3D mobile game (iCube) (1), a computer application (Building 3D Desktop) (2), a server application (3), and a database (4) is presented. Figure 1 shows the detailed system architecture and below is a brief description of how it works.

The applications that make up this system were programmed in different platforms. iOS SDK was used for mobile game, using Xcode development environment; Java 2 Standard Edition (J2SE) for desktop application and Java 2 Enterprise Edition (J2EE) for server application. We used an iPod Touch device to test the trial versions of the mobile application. The data exchange between the applications of this system was carried out by means of http connections. This allows the interconnection between the components of this system using different technologies: Wi-Fi, GPRS, 3G, etc. *XML* (Extensible Markup Language) was used to transport and store data.

The Game: iCube

The game is an application for iPhone and iTouch devices where user must solve a set of exercises about building models with unit-sized cubes in a 3D environment. Figure 2 shows the game operation procedure.

Figure 1. System architecture

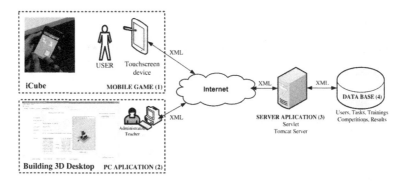

Figure 2. Steps of the game

Exercises are set on competitions which user can download once logged into the system (Step 0). There are two game modes: training and competition (Step 1). The training exercises are designed so that the user can become familiarized with the game environment (Step 2). They are available locally on the mobile device. The competitions are sets of tasks, created by the teacher or administrator, which the user has to download, by logging in to the system with a username and password. Users can only complete a competition once, and then go on to other competitions that the teacher or system administrator has activated (Steps 3 and 4). Competition results are sent to the server with data on times and scores. The application has a help function to explain how the game works (Step 2). Each exercise has an overall score of one point if exercise is correct and zero if it is wrong as well as time used for completing it (Step 4).

Two types of exercises have been developed so far, which basically consist of building 3D models with cubes in a 3D scene:

- **Type 1:** *Coping 3D Model*. This consists of copying the proposed 3D model (as seen on Figure 3).
- **Type 2:** *Three views*. This consists of building a 3D model using three orthogonal views, front, top, and right. To develop this project we used the first angle projection, the ISO standard primarily used in Europe with three standard views: front view, top view and right view (see Figure 3).

The tasks use two screens: screen 1 shows 3D scene where the user builds the model, and screen 2 shows the suggested exercise. The user is forced to do a mental retention to solve the exercise.

Computer Application: Building 3D Desktop

The PC application allows register new users, create tasks and competitions in an interactive 3D environment, and activate them so that they are available for downloading (see Figure 4).

Figure 3. Types of exercises (a) screen 1: suggested task; (b) screen 2: 3D plan where the student solves the task

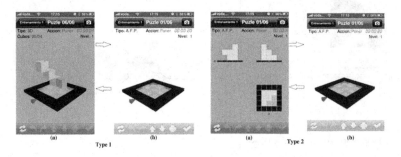

Figure 4. (a) Users' management in the PC application, (b) creating exercises in the PC application, (c) creating competitions in the PC application, and (d) users' statistics in the PC application

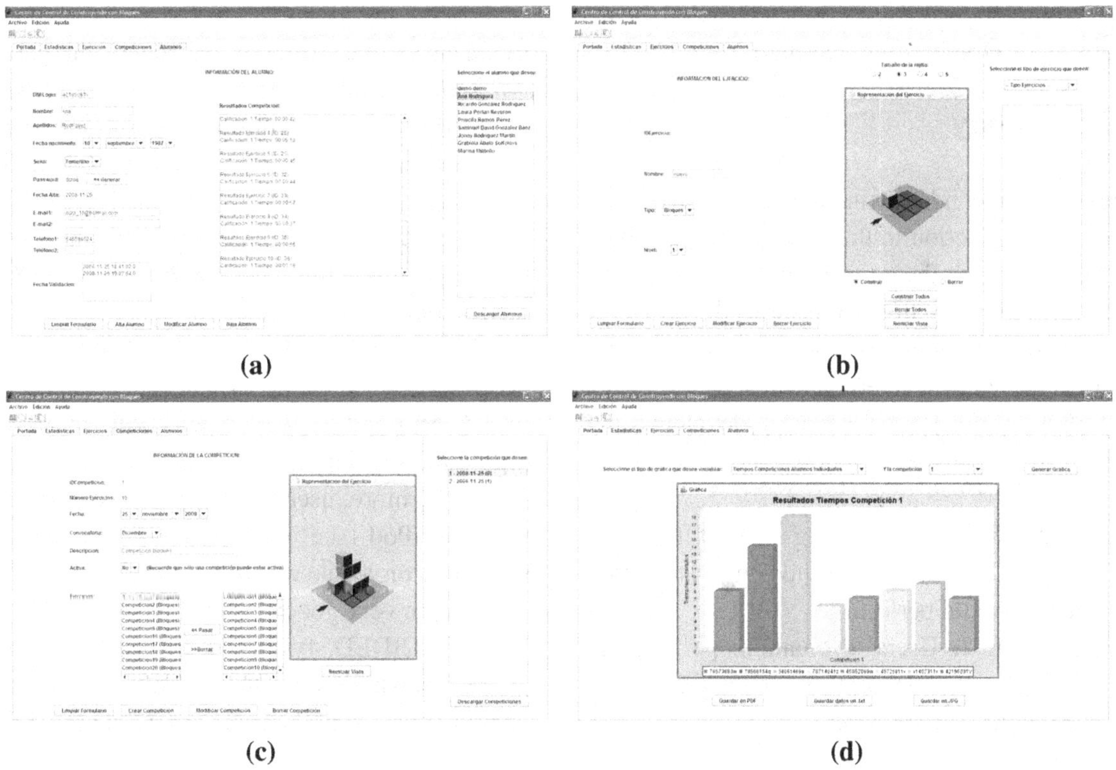

(a)

(b)

(c)

(d)

The administrator or teacher also has to group tasks together in Competitions and activate the Competition that he/she wants to make available for downloading with the mobile application. Authorized users can download task collections (Competitions) if the teacher has activated the application for them. The PC application offers users' statistics (scores and times) in graph format, and allows data to be viewed and exported in ".txt" format, so that they can be processed on a spreadsheet or with statistical software.

GAME EVALUATION

A study with users allows obtaining both objective and subjective information from the users, as well as checking application's usability. In this stage of development it is interesting knowing users' experiences with the game for targeting further investment necessary for application's improvement. Tests were performed by users, and questionnaires were used as a rating method for the mobile application. Targets approached are mainly two:

1. Improving user experience with application.
2. Spotting bugs and troubles on application for future versions' improvement.

Participants and Devices

A study was conducted on 22 undergraduate students from La Laguna University in Spain. Of the 22 participants, 16 were males, and 6 females, with ages ranging from 22 to 28, and an average age of 23.8. All of them are students from technical engineering degrees and are taking part in a seminar named 'New Tools in Teaching and Learning of Graphic Engineering I.'

Methodology

The study was conducted in a lab setting and began with an introduction to the objectives of iCube. Participants were then given a demonstration of the device in which they were shown how to use an iPod Touch for given a set of tasks (e.g. Internet navigation, wireless Internet access, etc.). Study with users in this project has been developed in several stages, as we see below.

- **STAGE 1:** Establishing project targets, getting lab ready and choosing tasks that users should perform.
- **STAGE 2:** Users' evaluation: performed by users on laboratory, collecting data through questionnaires.
- **STAGE 3:** Collect data: Summarizing bugs found and proposing solutions.
- **STAGE 4:** Application improvement: Programming and implementing suggested enhancements.
- **STAGE 5:** Game's final version.

A first trial version of the mobile game was brought out and evaluated by 22 users. A second trial version was then released based on the correction of detected bugs and suggestions made on the first version. Users were asked to complete the four training tasks available on the device and two competitions: 10 type 1 tasks and 10 type 2 tasks. At the end of the evaluation, participants were given a questionnaire to complete. The questionnaire comprised items that rated six categories of usability of iCube's various features on a scale of 1 to 5. Participants were also asked to provide qualitative comments that they felt were not raised during the evaluation.

Results and Analysis

Figure 5 shows global rating of application made by 22 users over different aspects of the game. All items are rated between 1 and 5 in a Likert scale where lowest rating is given to the worst consideration (left) while highest belongs to the best considered (right). User satisfaction was measured using an adapted version of the QUIS Questionnaire (Chin, Diehl, & Norman, 1988).

The figure shows overall rating that users have made of several iCube aspects. All items have been rated by more than 50% of users with scores of 4 (Very) and 5 (Very much) with an 81.8% regarding it as very useful and extremely useful.

Furthermore, users evaluate their experience with the iPod (see Table 1, Item n° 1 and 2), scoring it on a Likert scale, which ranges from very bad to very good (1=VERY BAD, 2=BAD, 3=UNDECIDED, 4=GOOD, 5=VERY GOOD). Overall satisfaction with the device used was rated by 91.43% of the users as GOOD or VERY GOOD (Item n° 1). Wi-Fi network was the worst rated (Item n° 2).

End-user satisfaction measure with the mobile game use a five-step Likert scale (1=STRONGLY DISAGREE, 2=DISAGREE, 3=UNDECIDED, 4=AGREE, 5=COMPLETELY AGREE). It is noticeable that around 70% of them felt able to understand and solve all exercises (Item n° 3 and 4) and even 69.7% agrees this tool stimulates their interest (Item n° 5). About mobility on application use, 86.4% agrees that it can be used anywhere (Item n° 6). Most of them regard application as a tool that can develop their spatial ability (Item n° 7) and 77.2% totally agrees on recommending it to their fellow university members (Item n° 8).

When asked about the positive and negative aspects of the application and their suggestions for its improvement, their answers have been summarized in Table 2 belonging to open questions, which users wrote in free text. About positive tool's aspects, they pointed out that game is useful for improvement of spatial ability being a fun

Figure 5. Game's overall usability scores

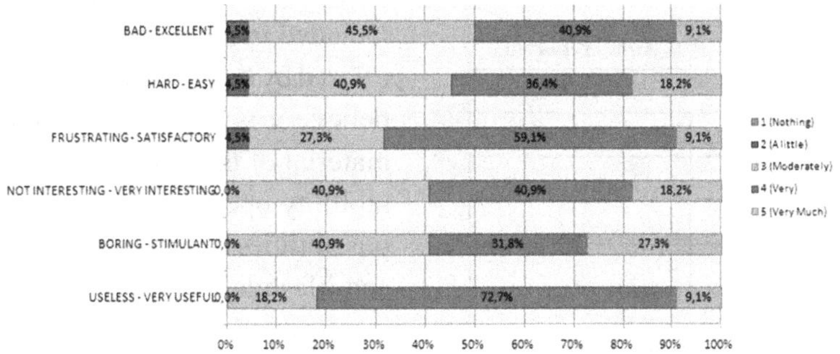

application. However, about negative aspects of it, some difficulties arose with use of tactile screen as the fingerprints caused problems while interacting with the game's 3D environment. It is necessary having in mind this item in games' design where screen action is continuous. That is why 13 users report 'trouble while adding/erasing cubes.' Suggestions as well as improvement proposals are related to detection of dust on screen caused by intensive use. This problem causes some users have a troublesome feeling when trying to add or delete cubes in the 3D environment.

CONCLUSION AND FUTURE RESEARCH DIRECTIONS

This study developed a system architecture, which includes a mobile game, iCube. We improved user experience with the game and fix bugs and troubles on application to obtain a final version. Data obtained from questionnaires allows us stating that this interactive mobile game done on handheld touch screen devices motivated the students that took part in it, generating a high degree of satisfaction. It is necessary take into

Table 1. Students' answers to attitude questionnaire regarding the game experience (N=22)

Item nº	Statement	1	2	3	4	5	Mean	Std Dev
1	How do you rate your experience with the touch screen device?	0	1	4	15	2	3.82	0.66
2	How do you rate the device's Wi-Fi connection?	0	4	8	10	0	3.27	0.77
3	I understand exercises	0	1	1	13	7	4.18	0.73
4	I felt capable of solving tasks	0	0	2	11	9	4.32	0.65
5	The game stimulates my interest	0	0	6	14	2	3.82	0.59
6	It is important to have access to the contents for using it anywhere (at home, bus, train, etc.)	0	0	3	8	11	4.36	0.73
7	I think it´s a nice tool for development of spatial ability	0	0	1	12	9	4.36	0.58
8	I would recommend this course to my colleagues	0	1	4	12	5	3.95	0.79

Table 2. Students' answers to attitude questionnaire regarding the game experience

Ítem	Times reported
ICube app positive aspects	
Useful for spatial ability improvement	14
Nice help supplied. Easy to learn	6
Fun app	7
Good interface app	4
ICube app negative aspects	
Trouble when adding/erasing cubes	13
Confusing interface for exercise access. Not enough help	5
Landscape screen format not suitable for app	2
3D surfing on environment	7
Interface: Cubes color, weariness by screen size, buttons	3
Suggestions, improvement proposals	
Help/system info improvement	6
Results' sending improvement	4
Interface improvement: Cubes, colours, audio, button, surfing on 3D environment	12
New exercises added, exercises time assignment	4

account fingerprint in touch/tactile apps, where screen actions are continuous because the user experience could be noticeably worsened.

It is important emphasizing that this game offers a new context for developing spatial abilities: in first place it offers the use of a new hardware device, the handheld touch screen devices, while it also offers mobility for the teaching-learning process and a distance learning course which can be used on the subway, bus, tram, or any place where a wireless Internet access is available (Wi-Fi, 3G, GPRS, etc.). There are many studies and developments done for spatial training, but it is the first one specifically targeting development of spatial abilities with mobile devices.

This work has been led by interest in developing material that includes development of spatial visualization related skills, promulgated by the EHEA (European Higher Education Area) and included in the new Engineering degree courses offered by the Spanish Ministry of Education. We believe it is necessary keeping development of material of this kind that provides students with mobility opening up new teaching and learning possibilities according to actual students habits and lifestyle.

We continue to work towards improving and complementing the developed application in different aspects, which will form our future lines of research in order to:

- We will be upgrading to add additional functions in the future and create new types of task.
- Verify the effectiveness of the mobile game through spatial visualization enhancement.
- Assess users' work overload with respect to the number of exercises and level of difficulty in each competition.
- Test our tool among middle and secondary school students.
- Develop an English version of the application, considering the third angle projection system.
- Test and port the mobile game in other devices (such as iPad and other tablets).

ACKNOWLEDGMENT

This work is supported by ESREVIC Project Enhancing Spatial Reasoning and Visual Cognition with advanced technological tools (Ref. TIN2010-21296-C02-02) from the Spanish Ministry of Science and Innovation under the National Plan for Scientific Research, Development and Technological Innovation 2011-2013.

REFERENCES

Amory, A., Naicker, K., Vincent, J., & Adams, C. (1999). The use of computer games as an educational tool: Identification of appropriate game types and game elements. *British Journal of Educational Technology*, *30*(4), 311–321. doi:10.1111/1467-8535.00121

Baartmans, B. G., & Sorby, S. A. (1996). *Introduction to 3-D spatial visualization*. Englewood Cliffs, NJ: Prentice Hall.

Baenninger, M., & Newcombe, N. (1989). The role of experience in spatial test performance: A meta-analysis. *Sex Roles*, *20*, 327–344. doi:10.1007/BF00287729

Chan, T. W., Roschelle, J., & Hsi, S., Kinshuk, Sharples, M., Brown, T., et al. (2006). One-to-one technology-enhanced learning: An opportunity for global research collaboration. *Research and Practice in Technology-Enhanced Learning*, *1*(1), 3–29. doi:10.1142/S1793206806000032

Chin, J., Diehl, V., & Norman, K. (1988). Development of an instrument measuring user satisfaction of the human-computer interface. In *Proceedings of the SIGCHI Conference on Human Factors in Computing Systems*, (pp. 213–218). SIGCHI.

Clements, D., & Battista, M. (1992). Geometry and spatial reasoning. In Grouws, D. A. (Ed.), *Handbook of Research on Mathematics Teaching and Learning* (pp. 420–464). New York, NY: Macmillan.

Clements, D. H. (1998). *Geometric and spatial thinking in young children*. Retrieved from http://eric.ed.gov/PDFS/ED436232.pdf

Crown, S. (2001). Improving visualization skills of engineering graphics students using simple javaScript web based games. *Journal of Engineering Education*, *9*(3), 347–354.

De Lisi, R., & Cammarano, D. M. (1996). Computer experience and gender differences in undergraduate mental rotation performance. *Computers in Human Behavior*, *12*, 351–361. doi:10.1016/0747-5632(96)00013-1

Deno, J. A. (1995). The relationship of previous experiences to spatial visualization ability. *Engineering Design Graphics Journal*, *59*(3), 5–17.

French, J. W. (1951). The description of aptitude and achievement tests in terms of rotated factors. *Psychometric Monograph, 5*.

Freudenthal Institute for Science and Mathematics Education of Utrecht University. (2009). *Wisweb*. Retrieved July 15, 2011, from http://www.fi.uu.nl/wisweb/en/welcome.html

Gartner Inc. (2010). *Gartner says worldwide media tablet sales on pace to reach 19.5 million units in 2010*. Retrieved August 15, 2011, from http://www.gartner.com/it/page.jsp?id=1452614

Gimmestad, B. J. (1990). Gender differences in spatial visualization and predictors of success in an engineering design course. In *Proceedings of the National Conference on Women in Mathematics and the Sciences*, (pp. 133-136). St. Cloud, MN: Women in Mathematics and the Sciences.

Guilford, J. P., & Lacy, J. I. (1947). *Printed classification tests. AAF Aviation Psycological Progess Research Report, No. 5*. Washington, DC: US Government Printing Office.

Hsi, S., Linn, M. C., & Bell, J. E. (1997). The role of spatial reasoning in engineering and the design of spatial instruction. *Journal of Engineering Education*, *86*(2), 151–158.

Jensen, J. J. (1986). The impact of computer graphics on instruction in engineering graphics. *Engineering Design Graphics Journal*, *50*(2), 24–33.

Linn, M. C., & Petersen, A. C. (1985). Emergence and characterization of sex differences in spatial ability: A meta-analysis. *Child Development, 56*(6), 1479–1498. doi:10.2307/1130467

Martin-Dorta, N., Sanchez-Berriel, I., Bravo, M., Hernandez, J., Saorin, J. L., & Contero, M. (2010). *A 3D educational mobile game to enhance student's spatial skills*. Paper presented at 10th IEEE International Conference on Advanced Learning Technologies. Sousse, Tunisia.

Martin-Dorta, N., Saorin, J., & Contero, M. (2008). Development of a fast remedial course to improve the spatial abilities of engineering students. *Journal of Engineering Education, 27*(4), 505–514.

Martin-Dorta, N., Saorin, J. L., & Contero, M. (2011). Web-based spatial training using handheld touch screen devices. *Journal of Educational Technology & Society, 14*(3), 163–177.

Mitchelmore, M. C. (1980). Three-dimensional geometrical drawing in three cultures. *Educational Studies in Mathematics, 11*, 205–216. doi:10.1007/BF00304356

Morán, S., Rubio, R., Gallego, R., Suárez, J., & Martín, S. (2008). Proposal of interactive applications to enhance student's spatial perception. *Computers & Education, 50*(3), 772–786. doi:10.1016/j.compedu.2006.08.009

National Council of Teachers of Mathematics. (2000). *Illuminations*. Retrieved October 8, 2009, from http://illuminations.nctm.org/ActivityDetail.aspx?ID=125

Okagaki, L., & Frensch, P. A. (1994). Effects of video game playing on measures of spatial performance: Gender effects in late adolescence. *Journal of Applied Developmental Psychology, 15*(1), 33–58. doi:10.1016/0193-3973(94)90005-1

Quaiser-Pohl, C., Geiser, C., & Lehmann, W. (2005). The relationship between computer-game preference, gender, and mental-rotation ability. *Personality and Individual Differences, 40*(3), 609–619. doi:10.1016/j.paid.2005.07.015

Rafi, A., & Samsudin, K. (2009). Practising mental rotation using interactive desktop mental rotation trainer (iDeMRT). *British Journal of Educational Technology, 40*(5), 889–900. doi:10.1111/j.1467-8535.2008.00874.x

Rafi, A., Samsudin, K., & Said, C. (2008). Training in spatial visualization: The effects of training method and gender. *Journal of Educational Technology & Society, 11*(3), 127–140.

Rafi, A., Samsudin, K. A., & Ismail, A. (2006). On improving spatial ability through computer-mediated engineering drawing instruction. *Journal of Educational Technology & Society, 9*(3), 149–159.

Sánchez, J., & Flores, H. (2006). Aprendizaje móvil de ciencias para ciegos. In Sánchez, J. (Ed.), *Nuevas Ideas en Informática Educativa* (pp. 11–21). Santiago, Chile: LOM Ediciones.

Sánchez, J., & Olivares, R. (2011). Problem solving and collaboration using mobile serious games. *Computers & Education, 57*(3), 1943–1952. doi:10.1016/j.compedu.2011.04.012

Shea, D. L., Lubinksi, D., & Benbow, C. P. (2001). Importance of assessing spatial ability in intellectually talented young adolescents: A 20-year longitudinal study. *Journal of Educational Psychology, 93*(3), 604–614. doi:10.1037/0022-0663.93.3.604

Smith, I. M. (1964). *Spatial ability- Its educational and social significance*. London, UK: The University of London Press.

Sorby, S. (2007). Developing 3D spatial skills for engineering students. *Australasian Association of Engineering Education, 13*(1), 1–11.

Sorby, S., Wysocky, A., & Baartmans, B. (2003). *Introduction to 3D spatial visualization: An active approach.* Clifton Park, NY: Thomson Delmar Learning.

Terlecki, M. S., & Newcombe, N. S. (2005). How important is the digital divide? The relation of computer and videogame usage to gender differences in mental rotation ability. *Sex Roles, 53*(5/6), 433–441. doi:10.1007/s11199-005-6765-0

Terlecki, M. S., Newcombe, N. S., & Little, M. (2008). Durable and generalized effects of spatial experience on mental rotation: Gender differences in growth patterns. *Applied Cognitive Psychology, 22*, 996–1013. doi:10.1002/acp.1420

Thurstone, L. L. (1950). *Some primary abilities in visual thinking.* Tech. Rep. No. 59. Chicago, IL: University of Chicago.

Thurstone, L. L., & Thurstone, T. G. (1941). *Factorial studies of intelligence: Psychometric monographs 2.* Chicago, IL: University of Chicago Press.

Zimmerman, W. S. (1954). Hypotheses concerning the nature of the spatial factors. *Educational and Psychological Measurement, 14*, 396–400. doi:10.1177/001316445401400220

ADDITIONAL READING

Achtman, R. L., Green, C. S., & Bavelier, D. (2008). Video games as a tool to train visual skills. *Restorative Neurology and Neuroscience, 26*(4-5), 435–446.

DeshPande, A., & Huang, S. (2009). Simulation games in engineering education: A state-of-the-art review. *Journal of Computer Applications in Engineering Education, 19*(3), 399–410.

Dondlinger, M. J. (2007). Educational video game design: A review of the literature. *Journal of Applied Educational Technology, 4*(1), 21–31.

Gee, J. P. (2008). Learning and games. In Salen, K. (Ed.), *The Ecology of Games: Connecting Youth, Games, and Learning* (pp. 21–40). Cambridge, MA. MIT Press.

Ghiselli, E. E. (1973). The validity of aptitude tests in personnel selection. *Personnel Psychology, 26*.

Mohler, J. L. (2008). A review of spatial ability research. *Engineering Design Graphics Journal, 72*(3), 19–30.

Shah, P., & Miyake, A. (Eds.). (2005). *The Cambridge handbook of visuospatial thinking.* Cambridge, UK: Cambridge University Press. doi:10.1017/CBO9780511610448

Smith, I. M. (1964). *Spatial ability- Its educational and social significance.* London, UK: The University of London Press.

Chapter 13

Role-Playing Game as a Pedagogical Proposition for Story Co-Construction:
A Brazilian Experience with Deaf Individuals in an Educational Context

Priscila Starosky
State University of Rio de Janeiro, Brazil

Maria das Graças Dias Pereira
Papal University of Rio de Janeiro, Brazil

ABSTRACT

This chapter shows and discusses the development and implementation of a pegagogic proposition of story co-construction via Role-Playing Games (RPG), in the context of literacy with a bilingual approach for deaf individuals. The researcher, besides the experience of practicing RPG and developing a game adapted to the particularities of deaf adolescents, also analyses narrative co-construction during the multiparticipation dynamics of the game. The research was done in the Ambulatório de Surdez do Curso de Fonoaudiologia da Universidade Federal do Rio de Janeiro (Ambulatory for Deafness of the Phonoaudiology Course of the Federal University of Rio de Janeiro). In the RPG implementation phase, the participants were four deaf adolescents and a deaf teacher (as players), an RPG and education researcher (as master), the researcher (as assistant), and a LIBRAS interpreter. The results show that the game provided for interaction among the participants with relevant multiliteracy practices.

DOI: 10.4018/978-1-4666-1987-6.ch013

INTRODUCTION

In the book *Castle of Crossed Destinies*, Ítalo Calvino narrates a game played in a tavern where the characters sat around a table and told their stories. However, for some unknown reason, they were unable to speak, so they used tarot cards in order to narrate their adventures. The author places the characters inside a castle, in which this game is played by means of card combinations that form a magic "square." Destinies were set, via this card game, which construed different interwoven tales.

The pedagogical proposition presented here follows Calvino's idea, and at the same time involves game together with story construction. In this study, games are understood as a *locus* for the creation of multiple meanings, assuming that meaning spans our language use practices, and it is always linked to a context, due to the other's presence, and because it is inserted in a given socio-historical process (Duranti, 1986).

Games, like story telling, are essential for gaining experience as well as achieving language and narrative structure development in children. It is through listening and sharing stories that children achieve narrative competence plus organize their world experiences (Klapproth, 2004; Bruner, 1992; Perroni, 1992). According to neo-Vygotskians, these activities are social and crucial during childhood, having an important role for children's linguistic-cognitive development, since it is through them that meaning direct actions, i.e., thought and language in social interaction are developed in an interdependent way. Interactionist approach research done with hearing and deaf children show that games with and without rules used in teaching/learning contexts stimulate both language acquisition and socialization processes (Vygotsky, 1998; Leontiev, 2001; Kishimoto, 2002; Ochs, 2002; Scollon, 2002; Saliés & Starosky, 2008).

Considering that most children who are born deaf in Brazil and in the world have hearing parents, and for this reason have late access to sign language and to their parents' oral/written language, studies involving socio-linguistic and educational processes among deaf children, youngsters and adults are a must. Accordingly, researchers who focus on deaf individuals education (Skliar, 2005, 1999; Skliar & Lunardi, 2000; Perlin, 2005; Klein, 2005; Kauchakje, 2003) are discussing the need to implement pedagogical practices that take into consideration deaf's identity and culture in literacy processes.

From this point of view, in this study, we will present and discuss both construction and implementation processes of a pedagogical proposition for stories co-construction via Role-Playing Game (RPG) as part of a literacy process for deaf teenagers. RPG may be understood as a game and at the same time as a collective story telling that generates infinite possibilities of interwoven narrative creation, forming a texture of meanings, as in Calvino's game.

The research had to be done in four different phases that dealt with specific issues and aims, taking into consideration the following points: 1) researcher learning of the game; 2) creation of a role-playing game for deaf teenagers who participate in the research; 3) RPG implementation created by deaf teenagers and other participants (researcher, RPG master, deaf teacher and Brazilian Sign Language interpreter); and 4) reflection and RPG approach as a pedagogical practice in the context of deafness.

In the following sections, we will discuss the basic concepts for the conception of the game proposition, involving some aspects of RPG as socialization practice, establishing its relation to multiliteracy concept. Afterwards, we will focus on this research context and motivation, participant profiles, and we will discuss the different phases mentioned before and their unfolding.

ROLE-PLAYING GAME: TO PLAY IS TO TELL A STORY

Born in the USA in the 1970s, due to the influence of war games and J.R.R. Tolkien—author of box-office success *Lord of the Rings*—literature and Norse mythology, a Role-Playing Game (RPG) is a game whose objective is narrative creation and character interpretation. The first RPG created in the USA was titled Dungeons and Dragons (D&D). RPG games in Brazil began only by the end of the 1980s – beginning of 1990s. One of the most important Brazilian RPGs is *Tagmar e Desafio dos Bandeirantes* (Tagmar and the Explorer's Challenge – Pereira, et al., 1992), the first set in a medieval context and the second using national theme and characters. This was very important for RPG in Brazil, because the game could reach the working class, allowing for the beginning of RPG players association, the so-called RPGians (Pavão, 2000).

Role-Playing Game has both pretending game and game with rules features, therefore, though the situation is explicitly a pretending game, there are pre-determined rules. Vygotsky, together with his disciple Leontiev (2001), argued that an imaginary situation turns into an activity in a pretending game, and that this is the moment when the child creates a laboratory in which s/he interprets a series of representations of the real world. Later, the authors describe the children's actions while playing games with rules, which demand awareness of the representations of the pretending games. This awareness is related to interaction strategies, since the participants have to evaluate their own representation as well as the other's representation in order to achieve the communicative purpose (Saliés & Starosky, 2008). However, besides being considered a *cooperative game*, RPG is also understood as a *method* in which the participants, through the characters action control and helping each other, collectively create and share a story (Rodrigues, 2004; Pereira, 2003).

RPG stories are fictional narratives that are built via an adventure proposed by a main narrator—the *master*—and are interpreted by the players who construe characters for themselves. RPG has a *setting*—world, historical period, social situation, or social group; *characters*—this is the interface between the player and the game, i.e., the way the player takes part; *rules*—they consist of a system that simulates the reality as in a pretending game; *plot*—narrative's sequence of events directed by causality, created by masters and players; and *scenario*—a combination of all components providing the elements for the construed stories (Pereira, 2003).

According to Robin Law's argument in his book *Robin's Laws of Good Game Mastering* (2002), the master is the central character who provides for players' involvement and participation, as well as for the good result of the game, i.e, that the game is fun. In his effort to involve the players, one of the actions developed by him is to describe in detail the places and situations in which the characters will act. According to Pavão (2000), the master's role is to direct the narrative and at the same time seduce the players so as they participate in the adventure, allowing for their actions to interfere in the plot he has in mind. Therefore, according to the author, the master must not be autoritarian, so he must not claim to be the sole author of the story, but be flexible, helping for the enrichment of the story construction.

There are four different kinds or formats of RPG: "Pen and Paper RPG," "Live-Action RPG," "Computational RPG," and "Massively Multiplayer RPG" (Dormans, 2006). In this research, we discuss the more traditional type, which is the "Pen and Paper RPG," also called "Tabletop RPG," where all players sit around a table and usually use written support (book) that describes the setting and the rules system, a sheet describing a character and data that will provide for the success or failure of an action. In a book, or whatever the RPG support (site, comic book, etc.), there is a partial description of the setting where the narrative will be based on. Stories created by players and by the master must be coherent with this setting (e.g., vampires and zombies for horror setting). The story begins to be told by the narrator, but the players are free to decide what the characters speak and do in the story. Therefore, RPG is a playful means to generate narratives whose main characteristcs are socialization, interactivity, narrative construction, and hypermedia (Pereira, 2007).

Socialization is understood here as an essentially motion process which is developed through practices and experiences in social groups. Hypermedia feature is closely related to the concept of multiliteracy because it is understood as a conjoined and interactive way of multimedia in which RPG becomes a verbal-audio-visual text, including written text, images, narrative, and character interpretation by players and master. This practice is aligned to the review of pedagogical literacy concept based on the multiple practices of world interaction, due to globalization, technology, and increase of social-cultural diversity. This new concept is called multiliteracy, and it is understood as text reading and creation using different semiotic codes (New London Group, 1996). Several studies also focus games as a literacy practice in different educational contexts and syllabus in native language, literature, history, geography, among others (Ritchter, 1998; Ricon, 2004; Pereira, 2003, 2008; Oliveira, 2003; Guimarães & Simão, 2008).

RPG interactive feature is construed through the effort of the master together with players acting in relation to the other game elements. Pereira (2008) argues that the interactivity concept used to understand the dynamics involved in RPG story collective construction corresponds to the third level of text overture proposed by Plaza (2003) in his discussion on reader and text. On this level, it is possible to make text changes or structural additions, i.e., change the plot. This is the overture level found in RPG, on which master and players interact and act their roles creating stories using a

setting. According to Pereira, RPG's participants could be called interactors because they have this form of joint acting.

Being tabletop RPG an oral game, centered in a dialogue between master and players/characters, it has potential to develop communicative skills, particularly regarding oral narrative construction. Observing the language acquisition process among deaf children, the appropriation of a narrative discourse is one of the linguistic skills that is affected by late exposition to sign language. Thus, the need to conceive RPG as a multiliteracy practice in pedagogy for deaf individuals is emphasized, providing for the use of multisemiosis in order to develop narrative skills.

In the following section, we will introduce the institutional contex and the participant profiles to whom the game was prepared and implemented as a pedagogical proposition, as well as the research phases.

WHY RPG FOR DEAF INDIVIDUALS?

The motivation to study games among children and teenagers who are deaf in a therapeutical/educational context is due to the fact that one of the authors of this chapter works (Starosky, 2005; Starosky, et al., 2006) as a phonoaudiologist for an institution which assists deaf individuals and their families. During this experience in the *Ambulatório de Surdez do Curso de Fonoaudiologia da Faculdade de Medicina da Universidade Federal do Rio de Janeiro* (Ambulatory for Deafness of the Phonoaudiology Course in the Medical School of the Federal University of Rio de Janeiro), it was observed the need for improvement in the therapeutic-pedagogic work done with deaf children and teenagers who go to the institution.

The work activities in the Ambulatory for Deafness are performed by a multidisciplinary team and it is part of the *Serviço de Fonoaudiologia do Hospital Universitário Clementino Fraga Filho—UFRJ* (Phonoaudiology Service of the

Clementino Fraga Filho University Hospital—Federal University of Rio de Janeiro—UFRJ). The professional team comprises two research phonoaudiologists, an interpreter psychologist (i.e., with LIBRAS high proficiency, acting as simultaneous interpreter), a deaf educator and an interpreter educator. In this context, phonoaudiological and pedagogical assistance take part of a working programme for deaf children, teenagers, and adults with bilingual approach.

Usually, children and adults assisted in the ambulatory are pre-lingual deafs (i.e., children with congenital deafness, or who became deaf before language acquisition). They simultaneously have pegagogical assistance in LIBRAS (Brazilian Sign Language), which is considered L1, and phonological assistance, that aims at Portuguese acquisition—L2, both oral and written.

When watching the activities performed with teenagers in the ambulatory, it could be noticed that the phonoaudiological assistance which aimed at developing L2 (oral and written Portuguese) was taken as a priority. However, this approach did not try to follow up the literacy level, nor the communicative competence, neither took advantage of, nor involved the language practices the teenagers have in their first language (LIBRAS). The observation of the institution context and particularly thinking about this pedagogical-therapeutic "mismatch" are the source for conceiving this research proposition.

Four pre-lingual deaf adolescents, the deaf educator, and the interpreter psychologist participate in the research process—the latter ones part of the ambulatory team. Three of the four deaf teenagers are male and are having assistance in the ambulatory for more than two (2) years. The fourth teenager was invited to participate by one of the ambulatory teenagers. All are proficient in LIBRAS and study in a school for deaf individuals—*Instituto Nacional de Educação de Surdos*, Rio de Janeiro, Brazil (National Institute for Deaf Individuals Education), and three of them use the sign language as first language, except for the

invited teenager who said that she more frequently speaks in oral Portuguese. All the teenagers participant of the study have a hearing family. They constantly use the sign language at school, while interacting with deaf friends and schoolmates, and less frequently among their family members.

During this research, the adolescents' age was 14 to 16 years old. The age group was determined based on description of game development used in this study (Vygotsky, 1998a, 1998b; Leontiev, 2001; Elkonin, 1998), since games with predetermined rules are activities for children that go to school (from 6 years old on) and remain as a playful activity until adulthood, similar to RPG case (Pereira, 2008; Pavão, 2000).

CONSTRUING RPG FOR DEAF INDIVIDUALS

The Researcher as an Artisan

The study consists of a qualitative research considering its hybrid aspect, involving collective interpretation, participation, and construction in a longitudinal and exploratory process. Thus, the methodological practices used were not defined *a priori*, but construed during the process. The qualitative researcher is seen as a *bricoleur* (artisan—its meaning in popular French), or a patchwork maker who interweave and "sew" different methodological tasks, theoretical paradigms and narrative performances that will turn the research into an interactive process of reflexive construction (Denzin & Lincoln, 2006).

A theoretic-methodological mosaic was construed in the course of the research, including a change in the researcher role that passed from observer to constructor. The transformation was dynamic and involved participation in a community of practice (RPG players), pedagogical tool design (RPG construction for deaf adolescents), and implementation of a pedagogical activity using this tool.

The Researcher Adventure as a Player

Since the objective was to establish a pedagogical activity for deaf adolescents following the RPG pattern, we observed that the theoretical knowledge of the game was not enough—it was necessary to practice RPG as a playful activity. Thus, another question arose as critical to this research process continuity: *How is RPG practice from the player's point of view*? Consequently, a new objective was established: the researcher should *experience* the game.

The practicing and understanding RPG experience was done through the researcher participation as a player in a RPG group that was part of the project *Incorporais—Brasil Barroco* (Incorporeal—Baroque Brazil) research (Godinho, 2007).

During this experience, the researcher participated as a player in four RPG game sessions that had as master and assistant two RPG and education experienced researchers and two young university students, who were regular RPG players. However, the only beginner in RPG, the researcher took part of that "community of practice" during the process. Community of practice may be understood, according to Wenger (2001), as a community in which people interact and construe relationships around a subject domain. The mutual engagement characterizes these groups and it is associated to the notion of pertainment and affiliation. The members of a community of practice are involved in a task to be performed, i.e., a collective enterprise. Therefore, to be an RPGian means to take part in a community of practice that has a particular way of interaction, and that has as the main enterprise narrative collective creation.

After this experience, the researcher developed a point of view about RPG practice inside out and from outside, considering that, besides participating in the game as a player, she also could analyse her own participation, as well as the rest of the group, focusing on interaction and RPG stories co-creation features. The practical knowledge development of the study object was critical for the later phase of the research: the development of an RPG for deaf teenagers.

RPG: "Tina and the Mystery Hunters in the Mill of Fear"

After the RPG group experience, the process of creation/preparation of an RPG game to be used as pedagogical activity with deaf adolescent began. Three other RPG and education researchers from the project *Incorporais: técnicas de narrativas interativas para temas transversais* (Incorporeal: interactive narratives techniques for crossing themes)[1] also participate in this process.

In the beginning, an interview was done with the four adolescents and the deaf educator with the purpose of maping some literacy practices which comprised what they read, watched on television and in the movies, what were their favorite sites in the Internet, etc. This interview would be used as reference to choose the game setting that was going to be created: fantasy, science fiction, historical, among others. It was observed a preference for horror and adventure genres[2] (e.g., Harry Potter, Spider Man, Batman, Skrik, Scream) and the contact with Comics literature, mainly *Turma da Mônica* (Monica's Gang) while referring to movies, TV shows, games and readings that the participants said were part of their daily habits. However, none of the teenagers, nor the deaf teacher had played RPG before. With the exception of the teacher, none of the adolescents knew the term.

In the beginning of the discussion about what would be the appropriate game support to be used (media on/in which the setting is described), we thought about creating a video in LIBRAS or with teletex subtitles. Later, after a long discussion on the feasibility of creating a video as support, we agreed that to use comics would be better, since comics also have a strong visual content, which makes possible for a diverse form of literacy, centered in the image, therefore, easier for deaf adolescents to understand (Gesueli & Almeida, 2003). Furthermore, comics are often used in the participants' literacy practices.

Thus, we tried to establish a scenario/setting for the game, which involved comics and fantasy aspects that pre-exist among the participants (Law, 2002). It was chosen, then, an adventure series in the form of comics, "*Turma da Tina e os caçadores de enigmas: Mistério Cósmico*" (Tina's Group and the Mystery Hunters: Cosmic Mystery – Maurício de Souza Produções, 2007), which has an adventure scenario, it was sort of funny at the same time, and the adolescents already knew the characters. Tina's Group series comics are a modern version of the traditional comics for teenagers, and it is developed in three monthly volumes/magazines. In the selected story, the main characters (Tina, Pipa, Zecão, Rolo, Jaiminho, and Rúbia) are young undergraduated students who are led by a Journalism student (Tina) in the search of an alleged alien whose spaceship had fallen in Brazil. The mini-series is full of movie citations (Star Wars, Blair Witch Project, Signs, among others), and of real facts, places, and people (*chupacabra* (goat sucker), Cape Canaveral, USA, etc.).

In order to add the horror genre to the adventure, we mixed the adventure *O Engenho* ("The Mill"—adventure from *Desafio dos Bandeirantes* RPG, by Pereira, Andrade, & Ricon, 1992), that had a touch of horror, in which the story "is construed under a thriller and tension mood" ("*é construída sobre um clima de suspense e tensão,*" p. 18). The *Desafio dos Bandeirantes* ("Challenge of the Brazilian Pathfinders") was issued in December 1992, the fourth RPG published in Brazil and first with national themes. It is a historical fantasy RPG placed in a mythical version of the colonial Brazil (at that time called *Terra de Santa Cruz*—Land of the Saint Cross), around the year of 1650. *O Engenho* is an adventure that is placed in an old abandoned sugar cane mill, and the plot was created to be played according to the *Desafio dos Bandeirantes* rule system and setting.

From this mix of settings and genres, the adventure *Tina e os Caçadores de Enigmas no Engenho do Medo* ("Tina and the Mystery Hunters in the Mill of Fear") was born, having a plot created by one of the researchers who during the activity was the master of the game.

Considering that the master of the game (research assistant) was a Portuguese speaker and that the players spoke LIBRAS, the communication among them had to be done via interpreter. Thinking about this and how the experience of the deaf individuals who speak sign language is mainly visual, we develop a series of visual and concrete supports, which would be used by the master during the game, so as to help and improve the interactional process. In order to achieve that, we had the participation of a graphic designer, also an RPG player, who created a board representing the master's house of the mill's plantation, one of the setting main locations of the adventure. The board was divided in parts regarding the floor plan of the houserooms, based on the drawings of the support book *O Desafio dos Bandeirantes – O Engenho* (Pereira, et al., 1992). The purpose was that the players/characters went throughout the rooms of the abandoned mill master house on the first and second floors (Figure 1 and Figure 2), according to the players choice, being able to visualize one by one while exploring the place.

In order to have the characters acting (PCs—Player Character and some NPCs—Non-Player Character) on the board, it was fabricated bidimensional miniatures that could be in a stand up position and that could be handled at the players will (Figure 3). Other objects (Figure 4) and images that represented crucial elements in the plot—the blue satin ribbon, shrine pendant collar, candle, old book, abandoned mill picture, supporting characters (NPCs), and mill objects—were

Figure 1. First floor of the abandoned mill master house

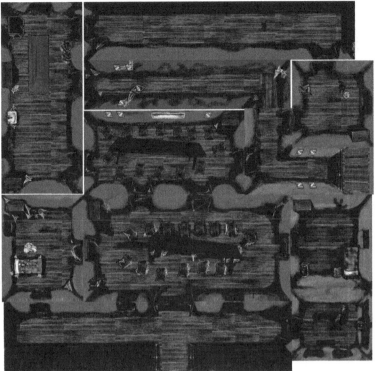

used to increase the master's narrative and mediate the narrative co-construction process. Therefore, all elements used in the setting/scenario (comics, objects, images, and the board) will be considered mediators[3], as well as the other participants.

RPG's characters usually are created by the players (PCs) based on the proposed scenario/setting and on the rule system. However, due to the participants' lack of experience in this playful practice and to the small amount of time to develop the project, we chose to have "ready" characters, who would be the already known

Figure 2. Second floor of the abandoned mill master house

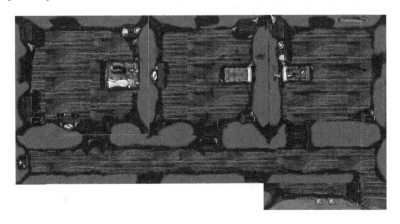

Figure 3. Fabricated bidimensional miniatures

Tina's Group characters, skipping the creation phase. The characters delivered by the master to the players had parameters[4] (points for skill, power and luck, and a list of skills) that could be improved during the game by the interactors. Considering that the main purpose of the activity was story co-creation through interaction, the rules that involved dice and character skills were adapted according to *Sistemas Incorporais* (Incorporated Systems – Godinho, 2008), and they were applied and presented by the master to the players during the game only when the character's actions could lead to partial failure or success.

Figure 4. Other objects and images that represented crucial elements in the plot

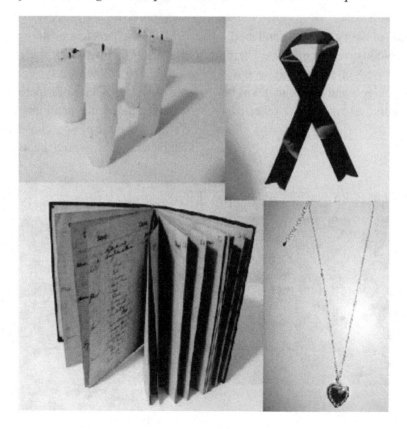

Methodologic Design for Game Implementation

The implementation of the pedagogic activity was done in three phases of the research. In the first phase, called *Pre-Game*, the deaf learners went through a narrative activity before the game, and this consisted of a re-telling of the comics the adolescents had read (Turma da Tina e os caçadores de enigmas: Mistério Cósmico), used as support for the game setting.

The second phase was called *Game* or *Campaign*, and comprised the moment when the RPG game was played. The third, considered a *Post-Game*, was the moment when the participants read the other Tina's Group mini-series in three volumes/magazines (*Tina e os caçadores de enigmas: Criaturas Lendárias* (Tina and the Mystery Hunters: Legendary Creatures), March and April 2008, Maurício de Souza Editora and Panini Comics). However, unlike the first, the third phase consisted of re-telling differently the story that was read. The proposition was that the adolescents read only the first and second mini-series magazines and re-told them creating a different ending. This way the proposition could achieve its purpose, which was to analyse the teenagers' narrative and creation skills during the process, which included RPG experience.

The pre-game phase began in September 2008 through meetings with the researcher, the interpreter, and the research assistant, as well as the distribution of comics to the adolescents and to the teacher. Two meetings were done with the interpreter psychologist so as she could understand the context in which she would act. There were done systematic meetings with the research assistant to finish the visual material. In October 2008, after the deaf teenagers and the teacher read the comics, there was an appointment with each individual separately. In this meeting, the teeangers re-told the story they have read to the researcher and they could clarify any doubts they had concerning setting and characters.

During game or campaign phases, six session games were played, in which the deaf adolescents and the teacher acted as players interpreting the characters (PCs). The game master was the assistant researcher (Projeto Incorporais). The researcher acted as an observer and assistant to the master, and the interpreter psychologist performed the simultaneous translation-interpretation from LIBRAS to oral Portuguese and vice versa, being a mediator of the communication/interaction among players and master.

In March 2009, when the activities started at Ambulatório da Surdez, started the post-game phase that began with the distribution of the two first volumes of *Tina e os caçadores de enigmas: Criaturas Lendárias*. It was presented to the adolescents a proposition to create a new ending for the story. After the reading, each teenager presented her/his story with the alternative ending created by them.

Besides the meetings with the adolescents who took part in the three phases of the RPG implementation as a pedagogic proposition, it could be seen that all the other research phases were parts equally important of this process: the researcher observation in the RPG group, the collective preparation/creation of the game in a deafness context, the meetings with the team that participated in the campaign phase, and the interview done with the research assistant and with the deaf teacher after a session of visioning[5]. This process of knowledge construction may be related to the image of a crystal that reflects the image in a series of angles (Denzin & Lincoln, 2006), i.e., the author-researcher tells her/his story from different points of view. Thus, apart from the reflections from the researcher point of view, the other participant evaluations will be presented in the final reflections.

RESULTS

Co-Creation of Stories by Means of RPG

In the pedagogic proposition presented, it was enhanced the phases through which the adolescents and mediators were getting to know the setting, the characters background and how they participated in the RPG campaign. In the first session, game, or campaign phase, the master was the main director of the activity that involved the RPG introduction: characters acting, simulation rules (dice), and the players and master roles. The knowledge through practicing the game, however, it was established during the activity, i.e., the proposition was that they would learn the RPG game through playing it. The reseacher, who acted as an assistant, gave support to the master delivering the mediator material (objects, images, board, etc.), and made comments along the game, when she thought fit.

The interaction among the Portuguese speakers (master and assistant) and LIBRAS users (adolescents and teacher) was mediated by the interpreter. It was the first time the master met deaf individuals who speak through sign language.

Before the game started, each player could choose one of the main characters scenario proposed and create a sign[6]: *Tina, Rolo, Zecão, Pipa,* and *Jaiminho* (PCs). At this point, the master warned the players that the choice should be based on the knowledge plus identification with the character's background they learned by reading the comics. Instead of creating a character, as usually done in RPGs, in this proposition the players should evoke the shared knowledge about existing characters background. On the other hand, the adolescents showed understanding that the character choice could influence the relation among them along the game.

Since it is common in deaf communities to establish signs to be used as names, the signs created for the characters were related to their bodily caracteristics (see Figure 3). Therefore, having a comic book as game scenario support was also critical to construe the knowledge that was being used during narrative co-construction. To deaf individuals who speak sign language, visual contact/ experience is the basis for linguistic-discursive processes and, in this particular case, the comic's images provided for the construction of characters evaluation and profile were this basis. In that relies the relevance of conceiving the proposition as a multimodal that combines oral/written language (Portuguese), visual-spatial language (LIBRAS), images (comics), among others.

After choosing characters, each player received her/his character sheet consisting of numerical parameters: *skill, power,* and *luck.* The master established the meaning of these parameters linking them to a hyppothetical situation as a result of rolling the dice (e.g., being able to jump over a wall), in which a character could succeed or not.

Then the game started. The master narrated an initial event through character interpretation/ action that unfolded a series of events, all of them related to another character who was missing (NPC). This initial event consisted of a critical situation related to the plot, the *problem-event.* In terms of co-narration, initial events consisting of a problem generate cognitive and social impact among the participants of the interaction (Bruner, 1996; Ochs, et al., 1986; Duranti, 1986), encouraging them to move on, prepare or change the narrative course in the search for a solution.

During the campaign, resulting from the problem-event, the story was gradually co-construed in the interaction of players, master, assistant, and interpreter through the way they handled the board, character miniatures plus mediator images and objects. RPG hypermediatic features (Pereira, 2008), therefore, are vital in the construction of meaning and understanding of objectives and purposes to be achieved by the players.

When observing the story created as a whole, it was possible to divide it in four acts that differ in theme and that were called: First Act—*The Trip*;

Second Act—*The Path*; Third Act—*The Mill*; and Fourth Act—*Don Gaspar's Curse*.

In the First Act, multiple forms of narrative and interaction arose while the adolescents and the teacher were learning *how* to play RPG. The notion of narrative continuity for actions/events that relates the plot to a particular sequence was being construed, resulting from the proposition the master delivered that the characters would take a trip to the abandoned mill in search of a missing character. While they were playing, master and players narrated the majority of the actions in the present tense, since they were simulations of imaginary situations. Most part of the narration that is co-construed in RPG is not a recollection, but a creation. This new way of narrating shows that the interactors constantly seek the new because there is no reference to the past, and the creation of scenes and characters acting is instantaneous.

The master, during the problem-event narrative, acted as a performer of the character's speech, i.e., he acted it. Game/theater framework, therefore, is construed at the moment the master changes his voice tone, posture, and facial expressions, and begins to use direct speech (he acts the character role). The players could see this particular way of acting and started doing the same: performed interpretations and used direct speech to act their characters.

During the second act of the story, the players showed more autonomy in their character acting co-construction, not needing frequent incentive questions from the master. Thus, the events sequence became more dynamic, faster, as the objects and/or characters arose and got into the narrative setting (fictional contexts). The players entered in the imaginary space/time—the path—and acted with characters appropriated for this domain. People, in general, enter in new domains while reading, telling, or listening to a story. The actor acts in other "worlds" when s/he acts her/his role on stage. However, in RPG, participants read, listen, narrate, and act in an interactional-narrative seesaw with multiple schemata, each with its own space/time domain.

The participant roles became different and particular along the story co-creation. The master became stronger as the sole narrator of time and physical features of the settings (context/direction), actions and NPCs feelings, and even of some PCs feelings. The players reacted to this and narrated their character directions and actions, as well as evaluated what was happening, and their character actions, both PCs and NPCs.

RPG feature as an "open" story, i.e., narrative co-creation through master and players' interaction in a scenario becomes evident. Many paths can be sought, depending on the choice of action of each player/character. The master's role is to be authorial without authoritarism (Pavão, 2000), using players participation to make them maintain the narrative continuity and solve the mystery.

Another important point observed during the game was how oral language and sign language speakers interacted. The sign language visual feature was so strong in the game process and narrative co-construction that, together with the master's gesture repertoire[7], LIBRAS[8] signs arose, concurrent to his speech, in order to involve and help the construction of meaning. Likewise, deaf adolescents also use oral Portuguese in specific moments. In addition to that, there was the sign language visual-spatial feature, which was imposed to the process of interpretation, acquiring a meaning re-structuring function. Therefore, all the game and narrative construction processes were mediated and influenced by the interpreter participation and by the code change during the interaction among deaf (players) and hearing (master and assistant) individuals. Thus, the proposition to use RPG as a pedagogic tool with LIBRAS and Portuguese speakers is conceived according to multiliteracy approach as well as multicultural practice, where different cultures meet and construe "*práticas e textos em gêneros dessa esfera também diferenciados*" ("different practices and texts in this sort of genres," Rojo, 2009, p. 111).

In the Third Act, the board was used as a mediator object so as the players/characters could explore the abandoned mill settings visually. This was the co-construed narration point that was most explored in terms of the physical scenario that would take the interactors to the mystery solution. The mill rooms were presented one by one, according to characters choices of directions they would go to explore the place. The visualization of the settings provided for a series of paralel stories that built a puzzle. The links the players/characters have made through context/direction that was presented, supported by images, objects and board, also provided for coherence among the narrated actions and the solving of the problem-event. This form of co-narration remit us to the concept of *visual literacy* (Hughes, 1998; Reily, 2003) and the use of multisemiosis in different literacy practices.

The master kept on using images, bidimensional miniatures, board, and objects as mediators for narrative co-construction, using the multisemiosis, not only oral speech, as a basis for meaning texture. Then, in the fourth act, the solution of the story is achieved, through characters/players actions based on previous links. In order to achieve one of the objectives (kill Don Gaspar—NPC) to solve the problem that was construed in the paralel story of the mill of fear (the curse), the interactors began to end the narrative that was co-construed during the game. The gap between the knowledge the master had of the plot and the exploratory actions on the part of the players/characters was almost filled. Almost because perspectives, visions, understandings, and solutions are not homogeneous, nor cohesive. The "door" the game provided between real and fictional worlds stays open and may be crossed at any time by the players who, from now on, are aware of its existence.

RPG as Metanarrative and Cross Culture

This last session presents the participants evaluation about their experiences in the activity performed. We focus, therefore, on how RPG, as a pedagogic proposition, besides generating entertainment and fun, may be used as a metacognitive activity. As Bruner (1996), we understand that metacognition is related to metanarrative and metalanguage:

In this kind of mental activity, the object of the thought is the thought itself. But the metacognition can also aim at language codes whose terms the thoughts are organized (...) the object of metacognition is to create alternative ways of conceiving reality construction. Metacognition, from this point of view, provides for a rational basis for interpersonal negotiation of meanings, a way to achieve mutual understanding, even if the negotiation fails regarding consensus achievement (Bruner, 1996, p. 195).

At the end of the first game session, the assistant asked the adolescents what they thought about the experience. The answers are shown in Table 1.

The adolescents made very positive evaluations in their first contact with the game. However, particularly in turn 8, it can be seen the way the activity is understood by them. Aspects involved in Adolescent 2 answer show how the game affected the players, and that it may be understood as a metanarrative activity, i.e., the adolescent reflected about the skills involved in the game co-narration: solve problems, make decisions together, and examine clues. Further, he also linked the metanarrative activity to the research purpose: *"It looks like the university is interested in how it happens."*

If we consider that, in general terms, language, and particularly stories, organize our experiences, the forms by which we see and face the world and reality, when narrating real or fictional stories,

Table 1. Answers about the experience

Interactor	Transcription[9]
Assistant	Last question. Did you like the experience?
Adolescent 1	*Yes.*
Adolescent 2	*It was cool, it was perfect.*
Adolescent 3	*It was a good experience.*
Adolescent 1	*It was very good.*
Adolescent 3	*I liked being Rolo.*
Adolescent 1	*I liked everything, I loved it.*
Adolescent 2	*What I liked most was having to solve problems, make decisions together, "let's follow the ribbon lady?" and all the clues we had to exam. It looks like the university is interested in how it happens.*

with different purposes, we engage in metacognitive activities. We thought *about* and *through* what we narrate.

Master and deaf teacher also evaluate the activity. However, there was visioning session with both of them, in which they had the opportunity to see again some moments of the game they participate through video recording. After watching themselves in the game interaction, they were asked to analyse their experience regarding the implementation of the proposition. The following Speech 1 concerns the master's evaluation on his first contact with deaf individuals, LIBRAS speakers, and how the interaction got more intense along the game sessions. He also discussed the first contact the deaf adolescents and teacher had with RPG practice, as follows:

Speech 1 (Master)

Well, it was an experience at the same time like, challenging, at the same time rewarding, you know. Why challenging? Challenging because, you see, um, (it brought) to me another world, you know, another sort of (attention), another contact. (...) There was a sincrony among me, the interpreter, and them, so we kept on tying the knots. Even more so in the later sessions. The interpreter was still

important, but I could feel a direct connection between me and them, and remember that I had no knowledge of sign language whatsoever, but we, let's put it this way, began to establish ways so as I could communicate with them. (...) Another aspect that I think is an interesting contribution was the fact to present them a game they didn't know, didn't have access. (...) And they enjoyed it. My most remarkable experience was when we finished (and they) "so, when we will do it again?" (...) Coming from them, obviously, the desire to do it again, that means we possibly got the right path, that it was fun. (...) Even for me, in a special way, at the end we sort of have a communication, to be able to communicate with them, to understand them, then I think I could see how it is to help build a bridge between two cultures.

While positioning himself as helping "build a bridge between two cultures," the master enhances the multicultural approach. Once more, we emphasize that the meeting among deaf individuals, sign language speakers, with the hearing individual, who represents the community of practice of "RPGians," provided for a local cross culture, relevant to form more flexible and democratic citizens. The assistant/master also explores the fun and the motivation that the game aroused in the participants, as in other playful practices.

The master's second speech (Speech 2) concerns the deaf adolescents and teacher in the process of story co-construction through the game. He enhances the autonomy the players had while creating the story and the "incorporation" of the characters, acting in a multimodal way and positioning themselves between the action of playing and narrating.

Speech 2 (Master)

I play RPG for about fourteen years. And I would tell them that they were excellent considering they are beginners. I have friends who play RPG that until now have a great problem, they are sort of blocked, have problems of creativity of imagination... (...) But, after the first session, the second, third, I think they incorporated very well the characters and the interaction with the story. (...) The way they started to loosen up in the story, the way they narrated, played, and so on, which are things I see among people playing RPG. They begin, like, to free these aspects and to give life to these aspects in them. Even more so in the end, in the last sessions, they were playing perfectly well, loosening up, speaking, talking, (looking for) these features, these aspects of narrating, of loosening up, that was what I saw in them.

Observing the way the master evaluates the activity—"rewarding and challenging" (Speech 1)—and to the series of aspects about the proposition implementation explored in his speech, it could be seen that his experience was complex and involved construction of new and different ways of acting as "RPG master." It also involved a new form of seeing these local cultures that constitute this new practice. However, it must be focused how the imagination and narrative skills of the deaf adolescents speakers of sign language that, according to the master's evaluation, are the very same of hearing individuals, considering his experience with the latter, even being able to surpass them.

In the following session, the deaf teacher speech about her experience as a player in the RPG implementation is presented.

Speech 3 (Deaf Teacher)

In the beginning, I chose to be quiet, because I didn't know RPG. (...) I didn't know what it was, had a lot of doubts (...) I agreed because I like comics (...) But the research brought us something new and that helped me, because to work with books and magazines I already knew. The book brings character stories, what is their work and only that. Now, the RPG story was different, totally different. (...) It reminded me of the stage, it

looks very similar to it, it seems that we all sit in a circle and begin to play, to remember what was the magazine story and to relate it to the game, following the context. (...) In the beginning I thought it was going to be hard, but along the game I could manage and it was fun, I learned many things, and it helped think on how to tell a story, always keeping it inside the context. (...) After a while, we discovered other stories, then he uses the story to make us get to know it, learn, develop. That was very good. RPG is very important.

The deaf teacher, in her speech, brought an account concerning knowledge of a new game. Between her initial action—"be quiet"—and final result—"learn many things"—the teacher got involved with news forms of narrating, understanding and evaluating the activity as "something new," "it reminded me the stage," "it was very good," "RPG is very important." The teacher's speech shows the relevance of the activity as a multimodal pedagogic practice, relevant, and new in her working context.

We finish this analysis of participants evaluation citing Bruner (1996) who discusses on how the look into narratives may generate pedagogic practices, based on knowledge construction from the point of view of daily life, not only considering scientific methods. We argue that, through the analysis of RPG implementation in the context of deafness, there are opportunities for development and learning that these practices may generate:

We dedicate great pedagogic effort to teach science methods and rational thinking (...) However, we spend most part of our lives in this world built according to narrative rules and resources. There is no doubt that education could provide for richer opportunities than it does in order to create metacognitive awareness necessary to face the world of narrative and its concurrent aspirations (Bruner, 1996, p. 196).

CONCLUSION

By means of construction and implementation of this pedagogic practice, the importance of RPG for the discoursive and linguistic-cognitive development in deaf adolescents could be seen. However, the path for the research construction process had to start with the researcher's experience as an RPG player, so it could be taken later to deaf educational context. The deaf teacher participation was also a kick-off to arise the awareness in the other educators, both in clinical and pedagogic contexts working with deaf children and teenagers, to use RPG as a multiliteracy practice.

From the methological point of view, the researcher qualitative approach as artisan improved the ability to prepare the research from the perspective of the many "layers" on which the researcher assumes different roles and tasks. In this approach, the researcher assumes an active posture concerning context and interaction with the other participants in the construction of propositions, analyses, and reflections that constitute the study.

However, the possibilities for reflection about the implementation of the proposition of using RPG in an educational context are not over with this research. Other aspects like the construction of participant's identity positioning during the game, implementation of the proposition involving digital media and other age groups are aspects that should also be studied later. Therefore, other propositions like this one should be implemented in different institutional contexts, in order to investigate forms of narrative in LIBRAS and other aspects in literacy practices among deaf children and adolescents.

REFERENCES

Bettocchi, E. (2006). *Brasil barroco: Um jogo de luz e sombras*. Retrieved from http://www.historias.interativas.nom.br/incorporais

Bruner, J. S. (1975). The ontogenesis of speech acts. *Journal of Child Language*, *2*, 1–19. doi:10.1017/S0305000900000866

Bruner, J. S. (1977). Early social interaction and language development. In Schaeffer, H. R. (Ed.), *Studies in Mother-Child Interection*. London, UK: Academic Press.

Bruner, J. S. (1990). *Acts of meaning*. Cambridge, MA: Harvard University Press.

Bruner, J. S. (1996). *Cultura da educação*. Lisboa, Portugal: Edições 70.

Calvino, I. (1991). *O castelo dos destinos cruzados*. São Paulo, Brazil: Companhia das Letras.

Denzin, N. K., & Lincoln, Y. S. (Eds.). (2006). *O planejamento da pesquisa qualitativa: teorias e abordagens*. Porto Alegre, Brazil: ARTMED.

Dormans, J. (2006). On de role of de die: A brief ludologic study of pen-and-paper roleplaying games and their rules. *The International Journal of Computer Game Research*, *6*(1). Retrieved from http://gamestudies.org/0601/articles/dormans

Duranti, A. (1986). The audience as co-author: An introduction. *Text*, *6*, 239–247. doi:10.1515/text.1.1986.6.3.239

Elkonin, D. B. (1998). *Psicologia do jogo*. São Paulo, Brazil: Martins Fontes.

Gesueli, Z. M., & Almeida, R. S. (2003). *As histórias em quadrinhos eletrônicas e o processo de letramento de alunos surdos*. Retrieved from http://www.alb.com/anais14/Sem10/C10019.doc

Godinho, E. B. (2008). *Incorporais RPG: Design poético para um jogo de representação*. Rio de Janeiro, Brazil: Pontifícia Universidade Católica do Rio de Janeiro.

Guimarães, D. S., & Simão, L. M. (2008). A negociação intersubjetiva de significados em jogo de interpretação de papéis. *Psicologia: Teoria e Pesquisa (Brasília)*, *24*(4), 433–439. doi:10.1590/S0102-37722008000400006

Hughes, P. (1998). Exploring visual literacy across the curriculum. In Evans, J. (Ed.), *What in the Picture Books*. London, UK: Paul Chapman Publishing.

Kauchakje, S. (2003). Comunidade surda: As demandas identitárias no campo dos direitos, da inclusão e da participação social. In Silva, I. R., Kauchakje, S., & Gesueli, Z. M. (Eds.), *Cidadania, Surdez E Linguagem: Desafios e Realidades* (pp. 57–76). São Paulo, Brazil: Plexus.

Kishimoto, T. M. (2002). Bruner e a brincadeira. In Kishimoto, T. M. (Ed.), *O Brincar e suas Teorias* (pp. 139–154). São Paulo, Brazil: Pioneira Thomson Learning.

Klapproth, D. M. (2004). *Narrative as social practice: Anglo-Western and Australian Aboriginal oral tradition*. Berlin, Germany: Walter de Gruyter Gmbh & Co.

Klein, M. (2005). Os discursos sobre surdez, trabalho e educação e a formação do surdo trabalhador. In Skliar, C. (Ed.), *A Surdez: Um Olhar Sobre as Diferenças* (3rd ed., pp. 75–94). Porto Alegre, Brazil: Mediação.

Law, R. (2002). *Robin's Laws of good game mastering*. New York, NY: Steve Jackson Games.

Leontiev, A. N. (2001). Os princípios psicológicos da brincadeira pré-escolar. In Vygotsky, L. S., Luria, A. R., & Leontiev, A. (Eds.), *Linguagem, Desenvolvimento e Aprendizagem* (7th ed.). São Paulo, Brazil: Ícone.

Maurício de Souza Produções. (2008a). *Tina e os caçadores de enigmas: Criaturas lendárias, número 1, março*. Rio de Janeiro, Brazil: Maurício de Souza Editora e Panini Comics.

Maurício de Souza Produções. (2008b). *Tina e os caçadores de enigmas: Criaturas lendárias, número 2, abril*. Rio de Janeiro, Brazil: Maurício de Souza Editora e Panini Comics.

Maurício de Souza Produções. (2007a). *Tina e os caçadores de enigmas: Mistério cósmico, partes 1 e 2, número 1, agosto*. Rio de Janeiro, Brazil: Maurício de Souza Editora e Panini Comics.

Maurício de Souza Produções. (2007b). *Tina e os caçadores de enigmas: Mistério cósmico, partes 3 e 4, número 2, setembro*. Rio de Janeiro, Brazil: Maurício de Souza Editora e Panini Comics.

Maurício de Souza Produções. (2007c). *Tina e os caçadores de enigmas: Mistério cósmico, partes 5 e 6, número 3, outubro*. Rio de Janeiro, Brazil: Maurício de Souza Editora e Panini Comics.

Mercer, N. (1994). Neo-Vygotskian theory and classroom education. In Stierer, B., & Maybin, J. (Eds.), *Language, Literacy and Learning in Educational Practice* (pp. 92–110). Clevedon, UK: Multilingual Matters.

New London Group. (1996). *New literacies end classroom practice*. Retrieved from http://www.newliteracies.com.au/what-are-new-literacies?/138/

Nicotti, J. A., Gonzaga, S., & Gonzaga, P. (Eds.). (2006). *Contos do amor jovem*. Porto Alegre, Brazil: Leitura XXI.

Ochs, E. (2002). Becoming a speaker of culture. In Kramsch, C. (Ed.), *Language Acquisition and Language Socialization*. New York, NY: Continuum.

Ochs, E., Smith, R., & Taylor, C. (1986). Dinner narratives as detective stories. *Cultural Dynamics*, 2, 238–257. doi:10.1177/092137408900200206

Oliveira, T. (2003). *RPG (roleplaying game): A aventura do letramento e de (re)construção de identidades sociais no contexto escolar*. Rio de Janeiro, Brazil: Universidade Federal do Rio de Janeiro.

Pavão, A. (2000). *A aventura da leitura e da escrita entre mestres de role playing games (RPG)*. Rio de Janeiro, Brazil: Entre Lugar.

Pereira, C. E. K. (2003). *Construção de personagem & aquisição de linguagem: O desafio do RPG no INES*. Rio de Janeiro, Brazil: Pontifícia Universidade Católica do Rio de Janeiro.

Pereira, C. E. K. (2007). TNI (técnicas para narrativas interativas). *Rio de Janeiro, 33*(3), 72-85.

Pereira, C. E. K. (2008). *Uma ponte pela escrita: A narratividade do RPG como estímulo à escrita e à leitura*. Rio de Janeiro, Brazil: Pontifícia Universidade Católica do Rio de Janeiro.

Pereira, C. K., Andrade, F., & Ricon, L. E. (1992). *O desafio dos bandeirantes: Aventuras na terra de Santa Cruz*. Rio de Janeiro, Brazil: GSA.

Perlim, G. (2005). Identidades surdas. In Skliar, C. (Ed.), *A Surdez: Um Olhar Sobre as Diferenças* (3rd ed., pp. 51–74). Porto Alegre, Brazil: Mediação.

Perroni, M. C. (1992). *Desenvolvimento do discurso narrativo*. São Paulo, Brazil: Martins Fontes.

Plaza, J. (2003). Arte e interatividade: Autor-obra-recepção. *Concinnitas, 4*, 7–34.

Reily, L. H. (2003). As imagens: O lúdico e o absurdo no ensino de arte para pré-escolares surdos. In Silva, I. R., Kauchakje, S., & Gesueli, Z. M. (Eds.), *Cidadania, Surdez e Linguagem: Desafios e Realidades* (pp. 161–191). São Paulo, Brazil: Plexus.

Richter, M. G. (1998). Role-play e ensino interativo de língua materna. *Linguagem & Ensino, 1*(2), 89–113.

Ricon, L. E. (2004). Oficina - Transformando conteúdos curriculares em narrativas. In Zanini, M. C. (Ed.), *Anais do Simpósio RPG & Educação*. São Paulo, Brazil: Devir.

Rodrigues, S. (2004). *Roleplaying game e a pedagogia da imaginação no Brasil*. Rio de Janeiro, Brazil: Bertrand Brasil.

Saliés, T. M. G., & Starosky, P. (2008). How a deaf boy gamed his way to second-language acquisition: Tales of intersubjectivity. *Simulation & Gaming, 39*(2), 209–239. doi:10.1177/1046878107310609

Schneuwly, B., & Dolz, J. (2004). *Gêneros orais e escritos na escola*. São Paulo, Brazil: Mercado de Letras.

Scollon, R. (2002). Cross-cultural learning and other catastrophes. In Kramsch, C. (Ed.), *Language Acquisition and Language Socialization*. New York, NY: Continuum.

Skliar, C. (1999). A localização política da educação bilíngüe para surdos. In Skliar, C. (Ed.), *Atualidades da Educação Bilíngüe para Surdos* (*Vol. 1*, pp. 7–14). Porto Alegre, Brazil: Mediação.

Skliar, C. (2005). Um olhar sobre nosso olhar acerca da surdez e das diferenças. In Skliar, C. (Ed.), *A Surdez: Um Olhar Sobre as Diferenças* (3rd ed., pp. 5–6). Porto Alegre, Brazil: Mediação.

Skliar, C. B., & Lunardi, M. L. (2000). Estudos surdos e estudos culturais em educação: Um debate entre professores ouvintes e surdos sobre o currículo escolar. In C. B. F. Lacerda & M. C. R. Góes (Eds.), *Surdez: Processos Educativos e Subjetividade*, (pp. 11-22). São Paulo, Brazil: Editora Lovise.

Starosky, P. (2005). *Jogos de brincar são jogos de linguagem – O papel da repetição no desenvolvimento de L2 de uma criança surda: Uma abordagem terapêutica interacional mediada por jogos com regras*. Rio de Janeiro, Brazil: Instituto de Letras da Universidade do Estado do Rio de Janeiro – UERJ.

Starosky, P., Saliés, T. M. G., & Goldfeld, M. (2006). Brincar é coisa séria! O desenvolvimento de L2 de uma criança surda. In M. Goldfeld, & S. Frota (Eds.), *Enfoques em Audiologia e Surdez*, (pp. 418-456). São Paulo, Brazil: Editora AM3 Artes.

Vygotsky, L. S. (1998a). *A formação social da mente* (6th ed.). São Paulo, Brazil: Martins Fontes.

Vygotsky, L. S. (1998b). *Pensamento e linguagem* (2nd ed.). São Paulo, Brazil: Martins Fontes.

Wenger, E. (2001). *Communities of practice: Learning, meaning and identity.* Cambridge, UK: Cambridge University Press.

ENDNOTES

[1] We thank Carlos Eduardo K. Pereira, Eliane B. Godinho e Rian Rezende. *Programa de Apoio à Melhoria do Ensino nas Escolas Públicas* (Improvement of Education in Public Schools Program), coordinator: Eliana Lucia Madureira Yunes Garcia, Pontifícia Universidade Católica do Rio de Janeiro (FAPERJ, no.: E-26/110.233/2007).

[2] According to Schneuwly e Dolz (2004), genres are related to a form of narration, which is related to literature culture of fiction. Nicotti *et al.* (2006) argues that the horror genre incites scare, horror, and fear in the audience, provoking thought among the audience about events beyond daily experiences or imagination.

[3] The word mediator is used in this chapter according to socio-interactional basis and the *zone of proximal development* and *scaffolding* concepts (Mercer, 1994; Vygotsky, 1998a, 1998b; Bruner, 1975, 1977).

[4] "(...) components for definition of the system (heroic function, relational function, competences, and skills), abstract concepts that show the character profile, to which quantitative value (cost and modifying numbers) and qualitative (levels) are established to help decide if the actions performed by the characters were successful or not." *("componentes definíveis do sistema [função heróica, função relacional, competências e habilidades], conceitos abstratos que traçam o perfil da personagem, aos quais se atribuem valores quantitativos [custos e modificadores numéricos] e qualitativos [níveis] que auxiliam a decidir se as ações realizadas pelas personagens foram ou não bem-sucedidas"* - Bettocchi, 2006).

[5] An Applied Linguistics proceeding which consists of producing and/or recording the report of the participants invited to watch a video recording of an interaction in a pedagogic context or any other one in order to express their opinions and perceptions about the interactional processes.

[6] In sign language, names from oral language are substituted for signs (using phonological/chirological parameters as hand configuration, articulation points, movement, orientation, face, and body expression), instead of being represented by fingerspelling (finger representation of graphemes).

[7] Spontaneous gestures, part of body, and facial expression.

[8] Words, lexical items.

[9] The deaf adolescents spoke in LIBRAS, which in this transcription is presented translated to Portuguese.

Chapter 14
Integrating the Principles of DGBL, CSCL, and Playability in the Design of Social Videogames:
A Case Study

Carina Soledad González-González
Universidad de La Laguna, Spain

Francisco Blanco Izquierdo
Universidad de La Laguna, Spain

Pedro Toledo Delgado
Universidad de La Laguna, Spain

ABSTRACT

Research and experience have proved that videogames can be applied effectively in a wide variety of learning contexts. With the objective to extend the use of educational videogames with hospitalized children, the authors are working on the design of social educational videogames. Their proposal follows the foundations of Digital Game-Based Learning (DGBL), the Computer Supported Collaborative Learning (CSCL), and playability. In order to test the effects of the designed prototype with real users in educational contexts, the authors carried out a pilot study about their educational 3D videogame prototype. The objective of this pilot experiment was measuring the playability and extending this evaluation to the social interactions and emotional aspects. The authors present in this chapter the principles of design of their videogame and some preliminary results about the developed study.

DOI: 10.4018/978-1-4666-1987-6.ch014

INTRODUCTION

Mobile and digital technologies have changed the youth and the ways they interact and communicate with others, how they learn, and in some cases, their attitudes and behaviours. Additionally, the use of technology eases closer communications among the patients and their schools, also allowing the reduction of the feeling of isolation of the minors with long term or chronic illnesses. Thus, we can affirm then that the use of mobile and digital technologies is an opportunity for the hospitalized minors to communicate, interact, improve their skills, and learn about the causes and consequences of their illness.

During long periods of hospitalization, the children are prone to develop stress and anxiety caused by physical discomfort of the illness and the treatments, fear of medical procedures, separation of their families, the change of their environment, and being confined with restricted movements. The lack of face-to-face interaction and little communication with the family can contribute to the low morale that obstructs the efficiency of the medical treatment or can cause psychological traumas. A recommended solution is to compensate this situation with toys and promote game activities that have proved to be therapeutic that involve love and fun, raise the morale, augment tolerance to pain, and improve the fulfilment of the treatments. In this sense, the use of new technologies, and in particular, videogames, can become an element of compensation, because playing is a vital part in the process of healing for a kid and may work as a 'social companion' for the minor in a moment of necessity, particularly when there is not anyone else around.

On the other hand, the research is focused on the search of forms to help people to learn to solve problems and allow them to adopt new reasoning forms (Pivec & Pivec, 2009; Dondi & Moretti, 2003) and transform to the learning process in interesting, easy, and fun. In this sense, the videogames can be really powerful learning tools.

The idea of using games as learning tools can be traced back to seminal works by Malone in the early 1980s, which remained mostly underground until the beginning of the century. However, in the last five years, we have experienced a dramatic growth in the academic field that argues for the application of game-based learning approaches in education. The argument is no longer about whether we should be using games, but about how we should be using them, how we should design them, and how we should integrate them with the existing curriculum.

According to Prensky (2005), there are two main reasons for the use of videogames as tools for the support of the study: (1) the new students have changed radically, and (2) these students need to be motivated through new forms to learn. The videogames with educative goals in addition to the "entertainment" are named "serious games" (Michael & Chen, 2006).

The lack of motivation for studies by hospitalized minors can change with the use of tools and methodologies, which pay special attention to isolation. In this sense, to mitigate the isolation, the use of methodologies and techniques originated from the collaborative learning that make possible and necessary the interaction with other students (Soller & Lesgold, 2000) is ideal. Furthermore, because of the hospitalized minor's situation heterogeneity, it is difficult for the teachers to give an educative answer adequate to the particular circumstances of each student. In addition, the circumstances that surround the hospitalized student can change fast in short periods of time. The emotional state, necessities, and skills can be seriously affected, and, as consequence, the systems that interact must adapt immediately to the new circumstances.

In the SAVEH project, we have designed a package of technological solutions not just for those kids that meet in the hospital classrooms, but also for those that stay at home, their friends, family, classmates, etc. (González, et al., 2011). Some of the tools specifically developed include:

a) an educative platform for the coordination of the education process of each one of the students of the hospital classrooms; b) a virtual world in which the students have the opportunity to play and go on quests doing activities specially designed that will help them to learn, play, enjoy, and interact. The game's activity type that we propose in this work is not only a way to amuse the kids, but also a way of being in touch with others, and to make them feel that they have goals to achieve in group, and in this way, maintain social relationships.

In this chapter, we are going to present the design of a prototype of multiplayer educative videogames based in the principles of different research areas: a) GBL (Game-Based Learning), which study the learning based on videogames, b) CSCL (Computer-Supported Collaborative Learning), which study the collaborative learning supported by computer, and c) Playability, which study the user experience in videogames. The main research questions discussed in this chapter are the following:

- What are the important characteristics of *"learning" with videogames*? and
- How to integrate the principles of CSCL, DGBL, and playability in the design of serious games for children?

Next, we are going to describe our proposal and the experience developed in the frame of the SAVEH project.

DIGITAL GAME-BASED LEARNING VS. TRADITIONAL LEARNING

According to Heather Coffey (2011), Digital Game-Based Learning (DGBL) is *an instructional method that incorporates educational content or learning principles into videogames with the goal of engaging learners*. Applications of digital game-based learning draw upon the constructivist theory of education. Digital game-based learning

involves activities that can range from completing very simple tasks to the development of intricate problem-solving skills.

James Paul Gee (2003) maintains that good videogames are "machines for learning," since they incorporate some of the most important learning principles postulated by today's cognitive science. Specifically, he states that:

1. Good videogames provide to the users information on demand and as needed, not out of context, as is often the case in the classroom. It is much more difficult for people to remember or understand information that is given out of context or well before it is needed.
2. Good games are capable of presenting users with tasks that are challenging, but at the same time doable. This is essential to maintaining motivation throughout the learning process.
3. Good games convert their users into creators, and not mere receptors. Their actions influence or build the game's universe.
4. Good games feature initial levels that are specifically designed to provide users with the basic knowledge required to allow them to build generalizations that will enable them to face more complex problems.
5. Good games create a "cycle of mastery," in which players acquire routines through which they increase their level so as to accomplish a specific task. When said task is mastered, the cycle is started again with more difficult tasks.

Digital game-based learning creates a learner-centred, learner-guided environment, allowing the freedom to freely explore and experiment within the environment. Therefore, the student must constantly readjust expectations and interactions based on the causes and consequences of each interaction (Gee, 2003).

Research supports the effectiveness of game-based learning in virtual environments compared to the traditional and hands-on training approaches. Some differences between passive training methods, such as classroom lectures and online tutorials, and hands-on training, like learning software and game-based learning, are shown in Table 1 (Trybus, 2011).

LEARNING COLLABORATIVELY WITH VIDEOGAMES

However, the true revolution in gaming are "social videogames," as noted in the book *Digital Culture, Play, and Identity* (Corneliussen & Walker, 2008), where such games already constitute a new way to have fun, make friends, and cooperate (and compete), while promoting self-esteem and interpersonal relations, and which are currently being "played" by over 400 million individuals. Some "social games," like Farmville, Happy Aquarium, Farm Town, Restaurant City, Café World, Country Life, and many others, are linked to social networks (Facebook, Myspace, Tuenti, etc.).

Another line of cutting-edge social online gaming is that of the MMORPG (Massively Multiplayer Online Role-Playing Game). An MMORPG is a type of game in which a large number of players, typically on the order of thousands, interact among themselves via characters in a three-dimensional setting. Second Life (SL) is a particular type of MMORPG in which there is no defined plot; rather, it creates an alternative virtual world called "metaverse" that the players can build as they play. In this "metaverse," the players interact through avatars, socializing, trading, etc. Although SL is the best known of these metaverses, it is not the only one. These virtual worlds, of which the most popular on a global level is the role-playing game World of Warcraft, comprise a new area of research for social sciences, as noted in the introduction and demonstrated by lectures at the symposium on "Analyzing Virtual Worlds: Next Step in the Evolution of Social Science Research," organized by the American Association for the Advancement of Science (AAAS) in Chicago in February of 2010, and by publications such as *The Warcraft Civilization: Social Science in a Virtual World* by Williams Sims Bainbridge (2010) of MIT.

Although not designed for educational purposes but ludic, the use of commercial games like World of Warcraft open up a world of possibilities in education today (Chang, 2008; Corneliussen & Rettberg, 2008; Hui-Yin & Shiang-Kwei, 2010; Golub, 2010; Ducheneau, 2010; Pirius & Creel, 2010; Bainbridge, 2010), such as: students collaborating and discussing ideas, possible solutions, connecting with other students around the world on topics of study, immersing students in a learn-

Table 1. Comparison of traditional training, hands-on, and game-based learning

	Traditional Training (lectures, online tutorials)	Hands-On Training	Game-Based Learning
Cost-effective	X		X
Low physical risk/liability	X		X
Standardized assessments allowing student-to-tudent comparisons	X		X
Highly engaging		X	X
Learning pace tailored to individual student		X	X
Immediate feedback in response to student mistakes		X	X
Student can easily transfer learning to real-world environment		X	X
Learner is actively engaged		X	X

ing experience that allows them to grapple with a problem, gaining higher-order thinking skills from pursuing the solution, among others.

While not targeted at education, nor seeking to cover any type of educational content, Green and Hannon (2007) cite multiple skills associated with being a "guildmaster" (one of the roles in WOW), such as: attracting, evaluating, and recruiting new members; creating apprenticeship programs; teaching children to work together for a common goal; communication skills; understanding multiple perspectives, respecting and even embracing diversity of views, understanding a variety of social norms, and negotiating among conflicting opinions; orchestrating group strategy and organized thinking; managing disputes; etc.

We see the objectives intended through the use of these game types in education, where the improvement of instrumental, interpersonal, informational, and digital competences, which include cognitive skills, methodological skills, technical and language skills, teamwork skills, self-critical capacity, ethical commitment, skills about searching information, selecting it, analyzing it, and extracting it, and social communication and interaction (collaborative work, chats, forums) is paramount. In this sense, through the activities around the videogame, it is possible to contribute to the use of information technology and communication and to develop 21st century skills (González & Blanco, 2012).

In addition, we must not forget the intrinsic social component in every human being that allows us to hold different points of view and attitudes, and which enhance different abilities and promote attitudes of respect and tolerance. This social component can then be incorporated into a videogame as a feature of a "virtual learning community" and cooperative learning (Jonnes & Issrof, 2005) so as to achieve common learning objectives. Working in a group, however, does not in and of itself guarantee cooperative learning. A

context must be defined and the proper methodology employed that adheres to five guidelines (Johnson & Johnson, 1994): positive interdependence, face-to-face interaction, individual and group responsibility, learning of social skills, and review of the group process. Therefore, the elements and characteristics that must be included during the game's design phase in order to achieve effective cooperative learning are:

- **Positive Interdependence:** Achieving this interdependence requires that every member in the group share common recreational and/or learning goals or objectives, group responsibility or "a team life," and evaluation and scoring as a group.
- **Face-To-Face Interaction:** Achieving this type of interaction requires designing situations in the game that promote trust among the group's members and raise the level of commitment with other players such that they all interact similarly and make common decisions.
- **Individual and Group Responsibility:** This aspect is enhanced by establishing roles and by rotating the leader's role among group members, as well as by establishing individual rewards and competitions with other groups.
- **Learning Social Skills:** Promoting social skills requires designing situations involving group planning, strategizing, negotiations, debates, and decision-making, as well as the exchange of roles.
- **Review of the Group Process:** The group's members must be aware of their performance as a group, meaning that activities must be provided where members assess their own mistakes and the group itself can decide to change role assignments and/or objectives in order to improve results.

PLAYABILITY AND LEARNING

We must not forget that the goal of a player is to play and have fun. Thus, to create engaging games we must take into account some key characteristics, like the basics *challenge, fantasy,* and *curiosity* suggested by Malone (1981) or the defined by Jones (1998) or Prensky (2001). According to Jones (1998) the following characteristics are essential to the design of engaging games: a) task that we can complete; b) ability to concentrate on task; c) task has clear goals; d) task provides immediate feedback; e) deep but effortless involvement (losing awareness of worry and frustration of everyday activity); f) exercising a sense of control over our actions; g) concern for self disappears during flow, but sense of self is stronger after flow activity; h) sense of duration of time is altered. Prensky (2001) defined the key characteristics of an engaging game as follows: a) rules; b) goals and objectives; c) outcomes and feedback; d) conflict/competition/challenge/opposition; e) interaction; and f) representation or story.

Following the above reasons and in order to make the learning process as effective as possible when designing an educational videogame, factors such as motivation, attention, concentration, and excitement must be maximized (Norman, 2004). The educational content, therefore, must be "hidden" within the videogame's inner workings, with the videogame mediating the teaching/learning process and proposing cooperative activities that promote learning through group interaction, negotiation, the planning of joint strategies and a shared responsibility for success or failure.

To improve the student's experience with videogames, we must first introduce the concept of playability, which can be defined as a "set of properties that describe the player's experience with a specific gaming system and whose main goal is to amuse and entertain a single player or a group in a way that is pleasing and believable" (González Sánchez, 2010). Therefore, the player experience can be characterized according to seven attributes that affects the playability:

1. **Satisfaction:** Gratification or pleasure derived from playing a game or from some aspects of it (Properties: Fun, Disappointment, Attractiveness).
2. **Learnability:** Player's capacity to understand and master the game's system and mechanics (objectives, how to interact with a game) (Properties: Game Knowledge, Skill, Difficulty, Frustration, Speed, and Discovery).
3. **Effectiveness:** Time and resources necessary to offer players a fun and entertaining experience whilst they achieve the game's various objectives and reach the final goal (Properties: Completion and Structuring).
4. **Immersion:** The capacity of the game contents to be believable, such that the player becomes directly involved in the virtual game world (Properties: Conscious, Awareness, Absorption, Realism, Dexterity, and Socio-Cultural Proximity).
5. **Motivation:** The set of game characteristics that prompt a player to realize specific actions and continue undertaking them until they are completed (Properties: Encouragement, Curiosity, Self-Improvement, and Diversity).
6. **Emotion:** The player's involuntary impulse in response to the stimulus of the game that induces feelings or a chain reaction of automatic behaviours (Properties: Reaction, Conduct, and Sensory Appeal).
7. **Socialization:** The set of game attributes elements and resources that promote the social dimension of the game experience in a group scenario (Properties: Social Perception, Group Awareness, Personal Implication, Sharing, Communication, and Interaction).

The methodology of Player-Oriented Videogame Design (González Sánchez, 2008) proposes incorporating playability throughout the design and development of a videogame as an interactive system. This requires specifying playability requirements for the different facets that allow for an analysis of which playability attributes are affected and how to improve the playability associated with these attributes. These playability facets are the following:

- **Intrinsic Playability:** The playability resulting from the game's very nature, that is, from its rules, goals, and challenges, and how these are projected to the player. It is associated with the design of the game play and to the implementation of the game mechanic, analyzing how the rules, goals, pace, and mechanics of the videogame, are represented.

- **Mechanical Playability:** The playability associated with the quality of the videogame as a software system. It is related to the game engine and underscores features such as the smoothness of cinematic scenes, proper lighting, sound, graphic movements, and behaviour of characters and the environment in the game, and, in multiplayer systems, the communications system.

- **Interactive Playability:** Facet associated with everything involving user interaction, the design of the user interface, dialog mechanisms, and control systems. This is closely associated with the game interface.

- **Artistic Playability:** Involves the artistic and esthetical quality and suitability of the videogame's elements to its nature. These include graphic and visual quality, sound effects, musical score and game songs, the game's history and its narration, as well as how these elements are incorporated into the videogame's environment.

- **Intrapersonal Playability:** Simply personal or perceptive playability. The goal of this facet is to study the perception of the videogame's user and the feelings that the game produces. Its value is highly subjective.

- **Interpersonal Playability:** Group playability. This involves the feelings or perception of the users and the group awareness that are produced when playing with others, either competitively or cooperatively.

We may then conclude that a game's playability results from the value of each of the attributes in the aforementioned facets. Said value must be adapted so as to maximize the player's experience or response when playing. Some new advances on the direction of educational playability are described in Ibrahim et al. (2012). Moreover, we need the equilibrium between educational elements, playful elements, and the emotional aspects that increasing player immersion and motivation in the educational game.

CASE OF STUDY: SAVEH PROTOTYPE

The design of our prototype follows the principles of videogame design (Salen & Zimmerman, 2003), the design methodology focused on the player (González Sánchez, 2010), and the guide of collaborative activity design in videogames (Padilla Zea, 2011; Collazos, et al., 2007). It is aimed to children from 9 to 16 years old, who are going to play in a multiplayer 3D environment.

The players group themselves in groups of 5, and in each level they have to overcome two minigames (challenges), one individual and another in group, to be able to continue to the next phase or level. In each level, different characters present problems more complex and hard to surpass. There is also a Non-Player Character (NPC) who provides help and clues to solve the problems.

In addition, we have considered in the prototype the aspects of playability and its attributes, such as: a) satisfaction, b) learning, c) efficacy in the achievment of goals, d) the sense of immersion through the avatar, the maze, and the obstacles and challenges, e) motivation provided by overcoming challenges, collecting items, competition between groups, and interests, f) emotion produced by the game: happiness, euphoria, hostility or frustration for not achieving the objective, among other feelings, and g) social aspects derived from communication and support between peers, necessary to complete the proposed tasks.

Before taking the 3D videogame prototype to the hospital context, we conducted an initial pilot study with the objective of measuring the playability of our 3D virtual learning videogame prototype, extending this evaluation to the social interactions and emotional aspects (González-Sánchez, et al., 2011).

This pilot study has been conducted with real users and in the scholar context. The prototype developed in Never Winter Nights (NWN) was validated with 25 students (Figure 1), of which 49% were females and 51% males and whose ages ranged from 11 to 12 years old. During the experiment, the users played with the videogame, while we recorded the session on video in order to evaluate the participant's behaviours. We organized the sessions in groups of 5 members that must play with the videogame collaboratively.

We adapted to the children the heuristics and the data gathering techniques. As data gathering techniques we used: interviews, tests, participant observation, and video analysis.

After the session, we made a test with participants, focused on collecting data about the seven

aspects of playability. These results have been normalized (1-0) and resumed in Table 2.

We also evaluated the playability attributes according to their playability facets. The results are shown in Figure 2.

Other aspect observed and analyzed during the sessions was the relative to the interactions. The following types of interactions were observed (see Table 3):

1. **Interacting with Observers (IO):** Participants were observed interacting with observers, usually asking about the game controls, on-screen events, and visual effects.
2. **Observer Triggered Behaviours (OTB):** Observers' comments triggered both verbal and non-verbal behaviours in players.
3. **Shared Experiences (SE):** Players shared experiences with each other by reflecting expressive behaviour (i.e. laughing together)
4. **Cooperation (COO):** Some players shared tips and helped each other through difficulties
5. **Competition (COM):** Players may analyse the score together.
6. **Attempts to Interact (AI):** Players attempt to interact, but the other player ignores them.

Figure 1. Tests realized in the scholar context

Table 2. Quantitative results related to the playability attributes

Attribute	Satisfaction	Learnability	Effectiveness	Immersion	Motivation	Emotion	Socialization
Results (1-0)	1	0.52	1	0.96	0.97	0.95	0.97

Moreover, we observed in the sessions the facial expressions and gestures the participants made, using a list of emotions based on the "circumplex model of affect" by Russell (1980). We measured the degree to which the feeling expressed is positive or negative, and how intense the feeling expressed, distinguishing among:

1. Non-Verbal (Facial Expressions and Gestures)
   a. **Facial Expressions:** Positive (i.e. smiling), negative (i.e. frowning) or neutral (concentrating on the game, relaxed, and not conveying any particular emotion).
   b. **Gestures:** Emotional gestures (i.e. throwing arms up into the air), informational gestures (i.e. pointing, shrugging, head nodding).
2. Verbal (When the Participant Speaks or Makes Any Noise)
   a. **Time:** The time it occurs.

b. **Description:** The description of what was said.

In the next section, we present the main conclusions about the pilot study carried out in the school during the present academic course.

CONCLUSION AND FURTHER WORK

In this chapter, we have presented a proposal of design and use of educational videogames that follows the principles of digital game-based learning, collaborative learning, and playability. We have designed, implemented, and validated a prototype of multiplayer videogame. We validated, mainly, the collaborative activities with the students (children from 11 to 12 years old) into their educational context.

The obtained results of the pilot study were highly satisfactory, encouraging us to use the prototype with students in hospitalization situations

Figure 2. Playability facets in SAVEH prototype

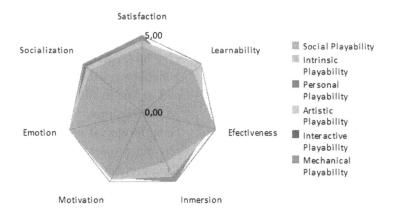

Table 3. Quantitative results related to the observed interactions

Interactions	IO	OBT	SE	COO	COM	AI
Instances (0-1)	0.38	0.32	1	0.86	0.11	0.13

or in home attention. The first step is to connect the student in illness situation with his or her classmates in the school. This way, the hospitalized children could reduce the isolation and could increase their motivation to the learning. Thus, the general state of health could be improved.

As results of experiment, we can note the following:

- At the beginning of the game, children are concentrating on configuring and customizing their own character, showing neutral expressions (~ 98%).
- Upon entering the first stage of the adventure, they look for help, either asking the teacher about how to move and interact with the environment (~ 37%) or seeking help inside the game from Non-Players Characters (NPC) located on stage. In this phase, the expressions and gestures observed are neutral (~ 65%) and negative (~ 35%), maybe due to the initial uncertainty and frustration.
- When a group member gets a clue or solves a puzzle, he or she shows satisfaction with positive expression (~ 97%) and immediately tells his partners (~ 82%). In addition, when they discover possibilities about their custom characters, they share this discovery with partners (~ 47%), showing positive emotions (~ 84%).
- During the group puzzles, which require the interaction of all team members for resolution, players share tips and help each other (~93%).
- Sometimes, players attempt to interact looping for help, but due the concentration in the task he or she is ignored (~13%).

- Due to the activities in the videogame being designed for collaboration, competitiveness has only been observed in the expressions about the number of collected objects by player (~11%).

Currently, we are also working on the automatized extraction of behaviour models of the students in the videogame, such as: a) model of reasoning process for the resolution of problems, based on the social interactions among the users in the collaborative activities; b) the model of the influence of social interaction in the learning process; c) the model of the emotional state of the students in the videogame; d) the model of the social function of each individual inside the group (González & Toledo, 2011). To achieve these goals, we applied a wide spectrum of data mining techniques, including techniques of classification, Markov's Decision Processes (MDP) and Social Networks Analysis (SNA), among others (Eagle & Barnes, 2010).

ACKNOWLEDGMENT

The authors would like to thank all colleagues and students who contributed in this study. We are grateful to Mr. Enrique Robledo and the Nuryana School for your help and support in the experiment and to Mr. Joaquin García for his collaboration coding the prototype of NWN. This work has been developed in the context of the European research project SAVEH, funded by the INTERREG program MAC 2007-2013.

REFERENCES

Bainbridge, W. S. (2010). *The warcraft civilization: Social science in a virtual world.* Cambridge, MA: The MIT Press.

Chang, E. (2008). Gaming as writing, or, world of warcraft as world of wordcraft. *Computers and Composition Online.* Retrieved from http://www.bgsu.edu/departments/english/cconline/gaming_issue_2008/Chang_Gaming_as_writing/index.html

Coffey, H. (2011). *Digital game-based learning.* Retrieved from http://www.learnnc.org/lp/pages/4970?ref=search

Collazos, C., Guerrero, L., Pino, J., Ochoa, S., & Stahl, G. (2007). Designing collaborative learning environments using digital games. *Journal of Universal Computer Science, 13*(7), 1022–1032.

Corneliussen, H. G., & Walker, R. J. (Eds.). (2008). *Digital culture, play, and identity: A world of warcraft reader.* Boston, MA: The MIT Press.

Dondi, C., & Moretti, M. (2008). *Survey on on-line game-based learning.* Retrieved from http://www.unigame.net/html/case_studies/D1.pdf

Ducheneau, N. (2010). Massively multiplayer online games as living laboratories: Opportunities and pitfalls. In Bainbridge, W. S. (Ed.), *Online Worlds: Convergence of the Real and the Virtual* (pp. 135–145). London, UK: Springer. doi:10.1007/978-1-84882-825-4_11

Eagle, M., & Barnes, T. (2010). Intelligent tutoring systems, educational data mining, and the design and evaluation of video games. intelligent tutoring systems. *Lecture Notes in Computer Science, 6095,* 215–217. doi:10.1007/978-3-642-13437-1_23

Gee, J. P., & Hayes, E. (2009). Public pedagogy through video games: Design, resources & affinity spaces. *Game Based Learning.* Retrieved from http://www.gamebasedlearning.org.uk/content/view/59/

Gee, J. P. (2003). *What digital games have to teach us about learning and literacy.* New York, NY: Palgrave Macmillan.

Golub, A. (2010). Being in the world (of warcraft): Raiding, realism, and knowledge production in a massively multiplayer online game. *Anthropological Quarterly, 83*(1), 17–45. doi:10.1353/anq.0.0110

González, C. S., Toledo, P., Alayón, S., Muñoz, V., & Meneses, D. (2011). Using information and communication technologies in hospital class rooms: Saveh project. *Knowledge Management & E-Learning. International Journal (Toronto, Ont.), 3*(1).

González-González, C. S., & Blanco-Izquierdo, F. (2012). Designing social videogames for educational uses. *Revista: Computers & Education, 58,* 250–262.

González Sánchez, J. L. (2010). *Jugabilidad: Caracterización de la experiencia del jugador en videojuegos.* Granada, Spain: Universidad de Granada.

González Sánchez, J. L., Gil Iranzo, R., & Gutiérrez Vela, F. (2011). Enriching evaluation in video games. In [Springer.]. *Proceedings of INTERACT, 2011,* 519–522.

Green, H., & Hannon, C. (2007). *Their space: Education for a digital generation.* London, UK: DEMOS.

Hui-Yin, H., & Shiang-Kwei, W. (2010). Using gaming literacies to cultivate new literacies. *Simulation & Gaming, 41*(3), 400–417. doi:10.1177/1046878109355361

Ibrahim, A., Gutiérrez-Vela, F., González-Sánchez, J. L., & Padilla-Zea, N. (2012). Educational playability: Analyzing player experiences in educational video games. In *Proceedings of ACHI 2012: The Fifth International Conference on Advances in Computer-Human Interactions*, (pp. 326-335). ACHI.

Jones, M. G. (1998). *Creating engagement in computer-based learning environments*. Retrieved from http://itech1.coe.uga.edu/itforum/paper30/paper30.html

Jonhson, D. W., & Jonhson, R. T. (1998). Cooperative learning and social interdependence theory. In Tindale, R., Heath, L., Edwards, J., Posavac, E., Bryant, F., & Suarez-Balcazar, Y. (Eds.), *Theory and Research on Small Groups* (pp. 9–36). London, UK: Springer.

Jonnes, A., & Issrof, K. (2005). Learning technologies: Affective and social issues in computer-supported collaborative learning. *Computers & Education, 44*, 395–408. doi:10.1016/j.compedu.2004.04.004

Malone, T. W. (1981). Toward a theory of intrinsically motivating instruction. *Cognitive Science, 4*, 333–369. doi:10.1207/s15516709cog0504_2

Michael, D., & Chen, S. (2006). *Serious games: Games that educate, train, and inform*. Boston, MA: Thomson Course Technology.

Norman, D. A. (2004). *Emotional design: Why we love (or hate) everyday things*. New York, NY: Basic Books (Perseus).

Padilla Zea, N. (2011). *Metodología para el diseño de videojuegos educativos sobre una arquitectura para el análisis del aprendizaje colaborativo*. Granada, Spain: Universidad de Granada.

Pirius, L. K., & Creel, G. (2010). Reflections on play, pedagogy, and world of warcraft. *EDUCAUSE Quarterly, 33*(3).

Pivec, M., & Pivec, P. (2009). What do we know from research about the use of games in education. In *European Schoolnet: How are digital games used in schools?* (pp. 122-165). Retrieved from http://www.comminit.com/?q=ict-4-development/node/302814

Prensky, M. (2001). *Digital game based learning revolution*. New York, NY: McGraw-Hill.

Prensky, M. (2005). Computer games and learning: Digital game-based learning. In Raessens and Goldstein (Eds.), *Handbook of Computer Game Studies*, (pp. 97-122). Cambridge, MA: The MIT Press.

Rubin, A. M., & Rubin, R. B. (1981). Age, context, and television use. *Journal of Broadcasting, A*(1), 1–13. doi:10.1080/08838158109386424

Russell, J. (1980). A circumplex model of affect. *Journal of Personality and Social Psychology, 39*(6), 1161–1178. doi:10.1037/h0077714

Salen, K., & Zimmerman, E. (2003). *Rules of play: Game design fundamentals*. Cambridge, MA: The MIT Press.

Soller, A., & Lesgold, A. (2000). Modeling the process of collaborative learning. In *Proceedings of International Workshop on New Technologies in Collaborative Learning*. Awaji-Yumetabi, Japan: New Technologies in Collaborative Learning.

Trybus, J. (2011). *Game-based learning: What it is, why it works, and where it's going*. White Paper. New Media Institute. Retrieved from http://www.newmedia.org/game-based-learning--what-it-is-why-it-works-and-where-its-going.html%20

Chapter 15
Benefits of Virtual Worlds in Educational Environments

Vicente Galiano
Miguel Hernandez University, Spain

Victoria Herranz
Miguel Hernandez University, Spain

ABSTRACT

In this chapter, the authors describe the project of a virtual world that they developed in their university and with their students. In this work, they joined concepts like social networks and virtual reality, creating a virtual model of the University Miguel Hernandez (UMH), where students are able to walk around the campus, inside the buildings, chat with other students, and moreover, use videoconferencing rooms where students talk and see other students in the same virtual world. The authors describe this project, called UMHvirtual (available in http://virtual.umh.es), which has been supervised by the authors, implemented by a group of students, and focused on all the university students.

INTRODUCTION

Virtual reality has been widely used in research environments of universities and recreational applications for the general public. However, there have not been many proposals (Dimitropoulos & Manitsaris, 2011) that make use of virtual reality in an integrated platform, available to the public in a university environment and with educational purposes. In this chapter, we will present some platforms that make use of virtual reality, and we will discuss their main characteristics and the similarities and differences with the platform we propose. The following section describes the features and functionality of the platform UMH-virtual showing illustrations and screen captures of the virtual worlds created.

In the project UMHvirtual, we have created a platform and a virtual world that represents the facilities of the Miguel Hernández University, available to the students and to other users or

DOI: 10.4018/978-1-4666-1987-6.ch015

visitors who could be interested in this university or in virtual worlds in educational environments. In this portal, visitors (who can be members of the university community or not) can visit the various campuses of the University, walking between buildings and "chat" with other visitors in a multiuser environment. The talks are conducted in common chats rooms with public or privates instant messages. In addition, if students wish, they can log on to a multiuser videoconferencing room created with OpenMeetings (Caladine, 2008) for each virtual world, so users can chat and see each other in real time. Besides the creation and customization of the characters or avatars, you can create groups, polls, or voting within the community. All these services have been incorporated into UMHvirtual but do not show a significant development with respect to other virtual communities, nor are they focused in particular educational environments.

UMHvirtual proposes new tools available to students and visitors in a virtual world. Firstly, it offers some features to inform and guide visitors through the facilities of the University Miguel Hernández. In this way, the visitor who walks through the virtual worlds gets to know the facilities offered to the university community perfectly. Secondly, UMHvirtual offers educational tools such as videoconferencing between teachers and students, virtual museums, such as the one for mathematics (Galiano, Herranz, Perea, Polo, & Sanchez, 2008), virtual laboratories where students can experience the physical behavior of various laws varying variables for each experiment, or three-dimensional visualizations of molecular structures impossible to visualize otherwise. In addition, each student has a customized avatar and can contact their classmates in a virtual environment to share educational experiences in the same virtual room. In the next section, we will detail more concisely the services that these virtual worlds provide to the students compared to other virtual worlds or other conventional education systems.

BACKGROUND

Virtual reality (Burdea & Coiffet, 2003) has evolved considerably in recent years, mainly in videogames over computers and last generation consoles. Young people and students are used to using virtual reality environments primarily. With this interest in virtual reality, social networks have created several Internet-based virtual reality such as Second Life (Trahan, Adams, & Dupre, 2011), IMVU, Exit Reality, or Habbo.

Second Life is the best-known 3D virtual community. It was created in 2003 and enjoys a wide international attention. One of its main features is that the world is created by its users and they can interact, play, communicate and do business in it as well One of its advantages is that the registration in this community is free and enables users to modify any aspect of the virtual world or even build anything in 3D. Any characteristic related with the physical appearance of the avatars, their movements or sounds are also customizable. Second Life has its own economy and its own currency, called Linden dollars, used by residents to buy and sell items created within the virtual world. This community is different from others because Second life does not use a Web browser. The users need a specific application to run it, with very high system requirements. Despite its virtues, Second Life has not garnered much success as expected, but it was a milestone in the way we navigate and interact with other users on the Internet.

IMVU is another 3D community similar to Second Life, which also has enhanced capabilities to use custom avatars and environments, allowing the user to interact with the person he is chatting with. It also allows members to develop contents to be bought by other members. The approach of this community is to chat and have fun in 3D scenes. Users can shop and dress their own stylish, custom designed avatars, decorate their own 3D space and connect with new people around the world. The main difference with Second Life is that it was originally intended to allow access to content classified as "adult," but after a while, this content was restricted for being considered unfit for IMVU. However, the community has some erotic serving as a lure to the public.

Unlike Second Life, "Exit Reality" runs directly on the Web browser, although it must first install a small plugin that only works with Windows systems. It also has a different approach as it seeks to fulfill the slogan "every website has its own 3D virtual world." After downloading and installing the plugin, the experience is very similar to other 3D virtual communities: Users can move freely around the virtual world, have voice conversations, or decorate their apartment, which becomes the equivalent of their profile user.

In our review, we did not find this virtual world especially designed for educational purposes. Virtual Reality is a technology especially suited for learning because of its ability to capture the attention of students through immersion in virtual worlds, which can help in learning the contents of any matter.

With this technology, students can learn more quickly and assimilate information more easily than by using traditional teaching tools because they use their senses more intensely while immersed in a world of appearances. One of the traditional barriers to the adoption of virtual reality in education is that, due to its high price, this technology is not available to students. We propose the development of a platform accessible to anyone with a computer and an Internet browser, which allows for immersion in a virtual world to supplement his or her college education. One of the many benefits that virtual reality learning environments can provide in any field is a graphical and interactive representation of abstract concepts that students may find difficult to appreciate in real life. For example, at a biology class, students can examine the appearance of the DNA chain, or the arrangement of atoms in a molecule. In the field of mathematics, they can visualize the representation of a function of two variables. There are multiple educational applications that can be performed in a virtual world and we did not find any platform or product that supports them.

A VIRTUAL WORLD FOR EDUCATIONAL CONTEXT

The use of virtual reality in educational institutions has been limited and has not been tested in a massive way to the students.

Virtual Reality is one of the fastest growing fields in recent years, becoming a tool that can reach all users without need for complex equipment or accessories. Taking advantage of these developments that made applications easier and more accessible, the idea of developing a project of Virtual Reality was born at the University Miguel Hernández: The UMHvirtual platform. It offers users the possibility of visiting virtually all of its campuses and locations and get to know their facilities. In addition, the user always has the possibility to move freely or using applications that are deployed virtual guide. Designed to run directly from the Internet browser, it does not require any specific hardware or accessory. With the simple use of a browser, users interact with the environment as if they were immersed in it (Figure 1).

Through a browser, any user can access the home page (http://virtual.umh.es) as shown in Figure 1. We have tried to follow the W3C Guidelines (Caldwell, Cooper, Guarino Reid, & Vanderheiden, 2008) for making Web content more accessible. Moreover, educational environments require specifics To help the visitor to use the platform we explained very clearly the required steps to enter the virtual world. The steps are as follows:

- Installing the VRML viewer plug-in provided in the page.

Figure 1. Home page: http://virtual.umh.es

- Restart the browser.
- Enter the virtual world as a registered user or visitor.

We can see that these simple steps that can be performed by any user without advanced knowledge of computers or virtual reality. The home page also provides links to video tutorials and project information. This principle of simplicity is behind the entire project including the public website shown in the beginning as well as the Web interface that enables the virtual tour. Simplicity and usability (Askar, Donmez, Kizilkaya, Cevik, & Gultekin, 2005; Becker, 2009) has been two fundamentals guidelines in the development process.

A Whole University Virtualized

UMHvirtual seeks to fulfill two main objectives. The first is to spread the university, its facilities, and services through its virtual representation, so any user from Internet can meet and visit a particular building, such as the visit of the University Library. The second objective of this virtualized infrastructure used to offer a virtual environment where students can meet, hold a videoconference with their tutor or classmates, or review their knowledge through virtual experiments. The first objective will be addressed inthis point while the second objective described in the next one.

As Miguel Hernández University has four campuses in different locations (Elche, San Juan, Altea, and Orihuela), we virtualized each one of them independently as different virtual worlds. The project UMHvirtual offers from the home page, a virtual representation of the exterior of the four UMH campuses with a total of more than sixty buildings. UMHvirtual also reproduced the interior of emblematic buildings of the University as Altabix (main Auditorium) and the Rectorate building. In total, UMHvirtual currently has a total of 24 virtual worlds with a level of realism and detail that allow the visitor to get a sense of reality and know the campus even if they have never been there. Because of the many virtual worlds developed and the meticulous detail with which they have been developed, it is not possible to show all of them in this chapter, however we encourage readers to visit the site and enter in the virtual world. Figure 2 shows a collage of some of the virtual worlds we have created. The bottom of the figure shows the entrance hall to the virtual world. Because Miguel Hernández University is a university with four campuses, we designed a virtual entrance hall with pictures on the wall referring to each campus. Thus, clicking on the mural, the visitor or student can access to this virtual world in an attractive and visual way.

In addition, Figure 2 illustrates the virtual worlds that represent building exteriors (gardens, roads, etc.) and interior rooms of the university (theory classrooms and laboratories of practice). As a central element shown in Figure 2, we can see Miguelito. This is the name of the mascot of the university and we use it as a unifying element and a character that helps us during the visit. Thus, in the room shown in the Figure, Miguelito welcomes us, and when user nears the central position, Miguelito greets us and gives us instructions on how to visit virtual worlds.

Usability in Virtual Worlds

We can define Usability as the ease of use and learnability of a human-made object (Buzzi, Buzzi, & Leporini, 2010). As we are talking about software, this software must be more efficient to use (takes less time to accomplish a particular task), easier to learn (operation can be learned by observing the object), and more satisfying to use. The term user-friendly is often used as a synonym for usable, though it may also refer to accessibility. Usability describes the quality of user experience across websites, software, products, and environments. In this sense, we have focused our efforts in implementing a usable Web with intuitive interfaces. Figure 3 shows the interface created for UMHvirtual.

Figure 3 shows four distinct areas. The upper central area indicates the virtual world where meetings happen and provides a link to video conferencing rooms. The central area shows the world in which we operate and on which we can walk and interact with other people and objects. This area displays the user's avatar, which can be

Figure 2. Representation of some virtual worlds

customized in a simple manner. The upper-right of the central area shows the virtual world map with a red dot indicating the user position. In the lower central area, we can find the shortcut buttons to show/hide the chat window, show/hide the map, or making various gestures to other online users (say 'hello,' show anger, etc.). Finally, on the right area there are links for shortcuts to different worlds (user configurable), and information from the virtual world in which we currently are. As the reader may observe, at the moment the website is in Spanish. However, we believe that English translation should be a clear future line work.

One advantage of this interface is that it is purely Web except in the central area, which is represented in VRML (Diez Higuera & Diez Pernas, 2002) and interpreted by the plugin we just installed. As shown in Figure 3, the level of detail of the world and the quality of representation is high. This accuracy in the details results in big vrml files size representing the world. With more

detail or greater number of objects, the number of nodes and elements in the file is greater and the file is larger. We must remember that the user must download only on time the entire vrml file from the server to view the world. Any application that represents a virtual reality must find a balance between the level of detail and speed with which that content is downloaded, or with which the computer can process and generate the virtual world. Is not very useful to create a virtual world with very high level of detail because first, it would take too long to download from server to user's computer, and second, the computer and the graphics card would not be capable to provide a fluent virtual world representation.

Virtual Reality Modeling

As mentioned in previous sections, the goal is to show the UMH in three dimensions, the virtual environment can be recreated by computer using

Figure 3. UMHvirtual web interface

a language modeling three-dimensional objects, such as VRML, X3D, O3D, COLLADA, etc.

A 3D model is a schematic representation visible through a set of objects, elements, and properties that will become a 3D form. The choice of a 3D modeling language will take into account several factors including the language features, the continuing development of new technologies, and especially the price of software. After a lot of considerations about the languages mentioned, we used VRML final as modelling language, due to the standardization and availability of multiple viewers on all platforms and operating systems (Sala, 2009).

The requirements to use the VRML technology are increasingly lower thanks not only to the advancement of its developer base, but also to the evolution of its users and the computer hardware. The set of tools used in creating the 3D campus is large and the process is high demanding but the final result is right when the visitor can access the Web and interact in a VRML environment with other avatars or objects.

The VRML language contains the definitions of the virtual world and the interactions that users can have with objects. Thus, the visitor can notice interaction possibilities with the environment. For example, information points have been established in different worlds through the presence of Miguelito. As shown in Figure 4, when we come to Miguelito, we show a greeting and a few possible destinations which might be of interest. If the user wants to go any of the destinations, user can click on the poster and the tour begins. On this tour, we can see how the avatar moves automatically from the current position to the chosen destination. This is a very visual and practical way to teach visitors how to access to buildings or rooms of a university which they do not know.

Services in a 3D Campus

Often, spreading the word of university services to students and their location within such an institution is often a difficult and involved task. The use of static maps on many websites prevents interaction between student and service. However, we propose implementing interactive services in the UMHvirtual platform. These interactive services are intended to inform and guide visitors.

In the real world, when we approach a building or an administrative department, we do not know the building's name and the services offered to students. It would be easier if when the student arrives at the building he would have access to a panel indicating the services offered and a set of links to the websites of these services. Figure 5 shows an example of this interactive help where the student approaches the Rectorate building. In the bottom-right corner of this figure, we can see an image with the building and two links: one to enter to the building's virtual world and other

Figure 4. User interaction: emerging information points

Figure 5. 3D world in the university campus

which details the administrative services that it hosts. If the student clicks to enter the building, he would enter to a new virtual world inside the building. If he pressed for details, a new window with the services and departments available to the student will be opened. Clicking on the list of services takes to the website of each service.

Another interesting contribution offered from UMHvirtual to students and visitors are intelligent agents that are scheduled for each administrative department. In each administrative service (International Relations, Scholarships, Registration, etc.) we set an avatar that does not really correspond with a real person but it is controlled by an intelligent and automated agent. This agent has been programmed with a high number of questions and it can receive and respond to a lot of questions from chats automatically without human help. Thus in each office we have virtual assistant who

can answer the doubts of the students when asked for specific topics and facilitates the task of informing the student of administrative procedures.

Educational Tools in Virtual Worlds

The second goal we set out for the UMHvirtual project is to provide tools that make teaching more attractive and easier. In virtual worlds, a wide range of possibilities are possible as we are no longer constrained by space or materials issues. Some features have been described in previous sections; here they are described in greater detail (see Figure 6):

- **Group or Individual Virtual Teaching:** As every user has an avatar, they can post virtual school attendance by the presence of the avatar. On the other hand, using the

Figure 6. Meeting students and teacher in the virtual world (a) and videoconference (b)

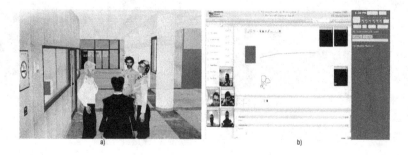

video conferencing room, students and teachers can share their desktop, chat and talk in in general a more dynamic environment than a traditional lecture.

- **Practical (but Virtual) Lessons in 3D:** There are many areas of knowledge that can hardly be viewed in real life: medicine, molecular structures, mathematical functions, and even works of art. However, in a virtual world there are no limitations or budget restrictions. Thus, we create a museum with representations of mathematical functions, another room with art in three dimensions or with the molecular structures of chemical building blocks.

- **Viewing Lectures:** As in real life, during a visit to UMHvirtual, we can see classroom theory lectures taking place. These classes consist of a video projection accompanied by a voice belonging to the teacher who teaches the subject. Figure 7 shows a classroom in which a professor is teaching. When students approach the classroom, the volume gets louder as they approach the sound source, in this case the avatar of the teacher.

Social Networking Presence

Social networking has revolutionized the way people use the Internet and the interactions between users. Social networks like Facebook and Twitter (White, 2010) allow users to communicate his experiences quickly and easily producing a broadcast news feed virally. People spend more than 22% of their time in social networks, generate over 40% of total Internet traffic and currently more than 600 million people use these networks. To benefit from such a high diffusion capacity, we have created a Facebook and a Twitter user called user UMHvirtual, and we have linked it with our site. This is a way to get more directly to students, as they are regular users of these social networks, and allows us to communicate with them more directly and conveniently. As shown in the use and importance of networks, we note that two weeks after the creation of the user and UMHvirtual Facebook page, the page had over 1,800 fans, mostly university students who support the project and therefore that know about it.

Made by Students

We would like to emphasize that 100% of the project has been developed by the university

Figure 7. Recreation of a lecture with video projections and audio

community: two teachers, in this case the authors of this chapter, and a total of 12 students from the Engineering Degree in Telecommunication Engineering. Thus, a project is more appreciated by students when it has been done by themselves. The motivational capacity of a large project driven exclusively by students of the same university that it is targeted to is very high. Students find that their colleagues, students like them, have completed a complex project, and this issue motivates them to work harder and undertake new projects. Moreover, the degree of confidence that comes from seeing how students can do technologically complex projects, improves academic performance, and feeds back with new ideas to be applied in UMHvirtual.

Integration with Wiimote

The use of UMHvirtual is via a standard PC controlled by keyboard and mouse, but we developed a new method for navigating the virtual world. Using the command of the Nintendo Wii console, known as the Wiimote (Nintendo, 2008), the visitor can use the arrow buttons at the top to move around the world through the camera and select the objects or links pointing directly to them.

Nintendo Wii and its remote controller have revolutionized the way people play video games. We think it is possible to use this practical controller in our project. The Wii remote can be connected to the computer using a Bluetooth interface and a PC with Windows XP/7. It can be a desktop PC or a laptop.

We have developed an application for Windows Operative Systems that allows walking on virtual worlds in UMHvirtual using the wiimote and which we have called UMHwalker. Running this application, users log in the site and pressing the arrows keys, the avatar moves along the virtual room. Also, objects can be selected pointing the

wiimote at the screen and pressing the main button. This system has been tested successfully and allows greater immersion and therefore a more intuitive interaction.

FUTURE RESEARCH DIRECTIONS

The platform currently in use has yet to be evaluated by surveying students. The students themselves are responsible for distributing UMHvirtual through social networks like Facebook or Twitter. At the moment, we are evaluating UMHvirtual with students in order to determine the improvement using this virtual environment as an educational tool. In this sense, evaluation results cannot been shown in this work. Our future work focuses on further outreach, incorporation of new services, new access interfaces (such as smartphones). We also are evaluating the integration with new control devices as Kinect (Microsoft, 2012).

CONCLUSION

We described the project UMHvirtual highlighting its main advantages in the university outreach, the communication between students and the creation of a social bond between students and university. We have explained the main tools that UMHvirtual offers to the students using virtual worlds. We have got feedback from mathematics and chemistry students that virtual worlds improve the understanding of their subjects. Moreover, the fact that this project has been developed by students motivates other students in their activity, since they set their expectations of on their own working capacity and quality of their final results from it. In addition, we presented a new interface for navigating virtual worlds improving the sense of immersion with the use of the Wiimote.

REFERENCES

Askar, P., Dönmez, O., Kizilkaya, G., Çevik, V., & Gültekin, K. (2005). Dimensions of student satisfaction on online programs. In Howard, C., Boettcher, J. V., Justice, L., Schenk, K. D., Rogers, P. L., & Berg, G. A. (Eds.), *Encyclopedia of Distance Learning* (pp. 585–590). Hershey, PA: IGI Global. doi:10.4018/978-1-59140-555-9.ch085

Becker, S. A. (2009). Web usability. In Khosrow-Pour, M. (Ed.), *Encyclopedia of Information Science and Technology* (2nd ed., pp. 4077–4081). Hershey, PA: IGI Global.

Burdea, G., & Coiffet, P. (2003). *Virtual reality technology* (2nd ed.). New York, NY: Wiley-IEEE Press.

Buzzi, M. C., Buzzi, M., & Leporini, B. (2010). Accessibility and usability of web content and applications. In Cipolla-Ficarra, F. V. (Ed.), *Quality and Communicability for Interactive Hypermedia Systems: Concepts and Practices for Design* (pp. 64–90). Hershey, PA: IGI Global. doi:10.4018/978-1-61520-763-3.ch004

Caladine, R. (2008). Videoconference, audioconference, and video chat. In Caladine, R. (Ed.), *Enhancing E-Learning with Media-Rich Content and Interactions* (pp. 210–233). Hershey, PA: IGI Global. doi:10.4018/978-1-59904-732-4.ch012

Caldwell, B., Cooper, M., Guarino Reid, L., & Vanderheiden, G. (2008). *WCAG20: Web content accessibility guidelines 2.0*. Retrieved from http://www.w3.org/TR/WCAG20/

Diez Higuera, J. F., & Diez Pernas, F. J. (2002). VRML-based system for a three-dimensional virtual museum. In Shih, T. K. (Ed.), *Distributed Multimedia Databases: Techniques and Applications* (pp. 306–317). Hershey, PA: IGI Global. doi:10.4018/978-1-930708-29-7.ch019

Dimitropoulos, K., & Manitsaris, A. (2011). Designing web-based educational virtual reality environments. In Vincenti, G., & Braman, J. (Eds.), *Teaching through Multi-User Virtual Environments: Applying Dynamic Elements to the Modern Classroom* (pp. 157–178). Hershey, PA: IGI Global.

Galiano, V., Herranz, M. V., Perea, M. C., Polo, I., & Sánchez, J. (2008). *A virtual museum of mathematics: MUMART*. Paper presented at Fifth European Congress of Mathematics. Amsterdam, The Netherlands.

Microsoft. (2012). *Kinect*. Retrieved from http://www.xbox.com/de-DE/kinect

Nintendo. (2008). *Nintendo Wii*. Retrieved from http://www.wii.com

Sala, N. (2009). Virtual reality and virtual environments in education. In Cartelli, A., & Palma, M. (Eds.), *Encyclopedia of Information Communication Technology* (pp. 883–838). Hershey, PA: IGI Global. doi:10.4018/978-1-59904-845-1.ch109

Trahan, M. P., Adams, N. B., & Dupre, S. (2011). Virtual learning environments: Second Life MUVEs to leverage student ownership. In Vincenti, G., & Braman, J. (Eds.), *Multi-User Virtual Environments for the Classroom: Practical Approaches to Teaching in Virtual Worlds* (pp. 62–74). Hershey, PA: IGI Global. doi:10.4018/978-1-60960-545-2.ch005

White, L. (2010). Facebook, friends and photos: A snapshot into social networking for generating travel ideas. In Sharda, N. (Ed.), *Tourism Informatics: Visual Travel Recommender Systems, Social Communities, and User Interface Design* (pp. 115–129). Hershey, PA: IGI Global.

Chapter 16
Scratch:
Learning the Grammar for a New Language

Eurídice Cabañes
ARSGAMES, Spain

Luca Carrubba
ARSGAMES, Spain

ABSTRACT

Videogames, as a new and playful interactive language, have great potential in the education field. On the one hand, we can find educational videogames to cover almost the whole spectrum of topics offered by colleges and academies (although they are used mainly at home and not in the academic environment). On the other hand, playing videogames is in itself a recreational way to generate technical competencies and teach the use of a whole new "digital language." Depending on different countries and cultures, there is a tendency to implement this technology in educational centres in varying degrees. In order to exemplify this implementation, the authors look at "Scratch," a creative videogame program for children with a big community behind it. In the conclusion, they focus on the introduction of videogame language in the educational context, not as educational videogames but as a tool to learn digital literacy and contemporary society.

INTRODUCTION

Technology has obtained increasing importance in our daily life, becoming a principal way to obtain information about the world and to communicate with other people. Technology is so important nowadays that is almost impossible to describe humanity without talking about its technological facet.

Our world is becoming more technological each day. At this moment, we are living in the transition from an analogue technology paradigm to a digital paradigm. We are immersed in what Lévy and Kerckhove (1999) define as the "third

DOI: 10.4018/978-1-4666-1987-6.ch016

age of communication," in which "a new language has taken shape that is even more universal than the alphabet, i.e. the digital language. An age that has followed those of orality and of writing."

This has multiple implications, but in this chapter, we are going to focus on how this technological environment influences education. We will explore how education in this new environment is immersed in a paradigm change in two fundamental ways: through the emergence of a new language and through the idea of 'information saturation.'

New Languages

The so-called "new media," based on the technological advances derived from the digitalization of contents, have brought about a revolution in the domain of audiovisual languages. This implies not only that a new type of content is being developed, but—simultaneously and inextricably—a new way of relating to these contents has appeared.

A good example of this is that the traditional media (print, TV, radio) in their analogical state have often tried to appear as transmitters of information for a passive audience, but after content digitalization, using the possibilities that Internet offers (on-line radios, journals, and TV channels emerge, adapting and creating new languages), they have suffered a fast transformation process. By being enabled to select diverse content to the access to global information, the audience has increasingly been put in the role of 'active users.' This transformation is also apparent within the cultural and entertainment industry, where we can observe, as Antoni Marín (2009) says, that "while some media had evolved from previous realities, others have originally emerged with the digital technology."

In this sense, music, cinema, or even electronic books with their huge hypertextual possibilities are evolving from analoguous to digital media, while others, like video games, would not be possible without digital technology.

The important thing that defines this new media is not the new kind of content that they produce but the new ways to relate to this content. The determinant is the interactivity that emerges from the use of new technologies: "The interactivity modifies not only the way an author deals with her task, but also the contents themselves that she creates and even the role of the spectator. In fact, the latter is now usually more properly called user" (Marín, 2009).

However, we must see to what extent this implies a change in the educational paradigm. As Pérez Tornero affirms (2000): "The privilege that at the educational centers the grammar had over the general semiology, the book over the audiovisual media and the textual writing over the multimedia production, reflects much of the conflict and tends to alienate the education from a society that has strongly enhanced the audiovisual language."

Every education system must carry out a previous analysis of its social context if it is to achieve the aim of providing students with an effective education. As Tornero recognizes, this context is characterized by a massive consumption of the new media that is not accompanied by an appropriate knowledge of their codes and languages, especially when these are languages that are modeling new cognitive styles and configuring modes of appropriation of reality. Therefore, if we live in a time where a new language and new ways to relate with content and information are proliferating, when the new media are gaining increasing supremacy, the education system has to understand this new context, including an education which enables students' competence in the use of these new languages and to enhance the development of technological skills. In this context, education should provide students with a "digital literacy" that allows the use of the new communication and information languages to code and decode messages, as well as to develop a full awareness of its use that involves a critical and creative utilization.

Information Saturation

Technological changes that happen and that we include into our own lives almost with the same speed have lead to a change of the educative paradigm in a second way; until fairly recently, teachers could interact with few information sources. In the current information age, new problems have emerged for educators, who have to manage an overabundance of information and try to find appropriate ways to filter, decipher, and interpret this information. In this way, the new educational context requires a different model of teacher, "whose features overcome the role of a transmitter of knowledge and implement it with a more dynamic dimension: as problem formulator, query provoker, work team coordinator, and designer of experiences" (Pérez Rodríguez, 2009).

If the new technologies create new languages and representation, educational institutions cannot ignore them. They have to integrate and utilize this new language and account for the different communication context. Given the previous points, it is obvious that education must perform important transformations to make it able to provide a critical education in these new languages in order to generate new methods or models of teaching that include them whilst also educating students in basic technological skills.

When we talk about technological or digital skills, we mean the necessary skills to cope properly in the actual digital media environment and interact with the digital content and its different presentations and platforms. This does not just mean teaching the critical skills to discern between useful and irreverent information, for example on the Internet. Other skills are also necessary, skills of negotiation (to know how to enter different groups and spheres and to understand their different rules) appropriate methodology (how to combine different content in a meaningful way), "gaming" (the skill to experiment with the peripheral as a way to solve problems), transmediatic browsing, simulation, collective intelligence, representation, distributed thought, visualization, multitasking, etc.

Furthermore, we are no longer mere receivers of the information created by a small and limited number of producers, not only because ICT have multiplied the number of content generators exponentially, but also because we ourselves are producing these contents.

We must note that these skills are not only useful in an educational environment but also provide means of creative expression. These new technologies are becoming ubiquitous in everything from the workplace, daily life, social engagement, and interpersonal relationships. They constitute skills that allow us to become active administrators of the new media instead of mere "users."

Introducing Video Games in the Educational Context

Inclusion of technologies in the educational context, however, is not an entirely new endeavour. The introduction of Information and Communication Technologies at educational centers has been widely implemented. In the following chapter, we will demonstrate how video games are just one among many other technological media in which we are related to technology. (González & Rodriguez, 2003). Moreover, by specifically concentrating on video games we will explore how they also represent a paradigmatic example of interactive narrative structures, which—within a ludic environment—enable teaching the technical know-how required for the use of computers and facilitate the development of various competencies related to the new media.

There are several different ways of introducing these technologies into the classroom, ranging from using conventional video games for educational purposes to using video games designed specifically as educational tools or, bearing most interest to us, to teaching students how to create their own video games. As Neil Gershenfeld (2009) has pointed out, "It is when people are able to create their own technology that passion gets aroused."

Undoubtedly, playing video games can be fun and educational, but being able to generate your own video games bears an even greater potential at different levels:

Firstly, in our highly technological society in which computers are ubiquitous, it is not sufficient to know how to use the basic tools, but it becomes increasingly necessary to acquire programming knowledge that allows a full-fledged utilization of those tools. Learning to program video games provides knowledge within a very stimulating environment for users.

Secondly, if, as seen above, in the digital eras we are not only consuming content but also producing them, we will need the technical knowledge required to generate contents and express ourselves in the new media. In this respect, learning to program video games is extremely useful in that it involves learning to generate interactive contents.

Scratch

The developers of Scratch, the research group "Lifelong Kindergarten" of the MIT Media Lab, know these advantages and have created a new, user-friendly programming environment that enables the exploration of basic programming principles without the syntax complications typical for other languages.

The idea underlying this 'software' is to leave behind the lines of code and make the programming of animations as intuitive as playing with LEGO toys, that is bringing together 'bricks' that contain all sorts of instructions. This feature makes programming easier and more intuitive than other programming languages, although it requires a learning period. This program has been designed for children from 8 years up, although it can be used by adults as well.

The intention of Scratch creators is to make programming accessible to anyone, since it was designed pursuing educational goals, as Mitchel

Resnick, one of the people in charge of the program, explains: "We want the children to be creators. We want them to do interesting and dynamic things with the computer" (Resnick, 2009).

Epitome

If in the digital era we confront a new language, we should not only understand the values and meanings that are transmitted through this "new media language," but it is also important to know its grammar (basic programming notions), given the fact that unless we master this, we will only be receivers and we will never be able to express ourselves within this language.

That is the reason why learning to program video games is not only a way to develop basic skills for the use of technology, but also provides the necessary knowledge in order to analyze the processes that govern the functionality of video games—and, in general, that of every audiovisual language—and to identify the conceptual framework and the values they support.

BACKGROUND

Before this chapter focuses on video games, we will briefly reflect on the pedagogical capabilities of this medium.

The "Homo Ludens" theory affirms the concept of humans as rational animals by stating that one of the most definitive facets of humanity is its capacity for play. This may seem frivolous but we can also recognize that in 'playing' we learn language, create identity, learn, and improve our social skills as well as we learn about more complex topics such as economy or war.

According to Vygotsky (1993), "the game has some attributes that it shares with other activities of problem solving, but in a more interesting way."

In Vygotsky's experiments with children he proved that the group that had access to materials before the problem statement (i.e.: the children that had the chance to play with it), solved it better than the other groups. This interaction was not just restricted to the instrumental skills; it also influenced language "you control [language] faster when its acquisition is done while performing a ludical activity" (Vygotsky, 1993).

Both the "Homo Ludens" theory and the term itself have been coined by Huizinga. According to him, games and culture are tightly united, in the way that "The big primordial occupations of the human conscience are impregnated in the games (…) so, humanity is created, constantly its expression of existence, a second world invented close to the natural world" (Huzinga, 2007).

The game, according to Huizinga, is one of the first symbolic activities of human kind. The game is the beginning of culture and both are engaged in reflexive interaction. In this sense, the ludical is at the backdrop of all the cultural phenomena, it is crystallized in the research of knowledge, poetry, the juridical life, and the ways of state life. The game is presented as a constituent part of ourselves, as an indispensable tool for learning, and forms part of our culture.

We have seen how the game is an important part of learning and child development. This is broadly accepted, and there are many authors who talk about it in psychology and educational sciences.

Despite this, it is probable that these authors may not have had videogames in mind when they developed their theories; yet, it is apparent that the game analysis parameters could be perfectly applied to videogames without disrupting these theories. If videogames have all the pedagogical advantages of the conventional game, in videogames we can also find other components that make them an even more interesting tool to be introduced in the educative centers.

The advantages of video games over conventional games are:

- As a leisure activity video games have the biggest sales, they are a top entertainment activity, beating even the cinema. Besides,

kids and youths are already familiar with this media.
- Videogame users cover a bigger age demographic than the players of conventional games, for this reason it could implicate a continuous formation (an implication which also puts the focus on possible uses of videogames in corporate life)[1].

Resuming the topic of this chapter, videogames are one of the habitual ways that we use to relate with technology. Videogames are a paradigmatic example of interactive narrative structures that allow, in a ludic environment, to educate students in the technical control of computers and the development of skills related with the new media.

There are many studies in defense of the use of videogames in the classroom (as we will show in the additional reading section), and, despite the fact that their application in the classroom is not widespread, there are a variety of educative videogames that are relevant to most subjects offered in schools and high schools.

The history of educational videogames started with the PLATO project, a project to develop educative contents by the Illinois University, Urbana-Champaign. This was the first project to create educational games. Since then there have been numerous developments, one of the most recent being developed by the MIT (Technological Institute of Massachusetts) who have developed more than 15 conceptual prototypes of educative videogames in a medium, high, and advanced education level. These prototypes cover the educational spectrum from arts and social sciences to science and mathematics. From these studies there have emerged some tools, which could assist students to study different subjects.

Some examples of videogames are: for the smallest children, "Alex builds his farm," "Purple Place," a videogame where the player has to recognize models, shapes, and colours, "Learn music with Pipo," which focuses on teaching basic musical concepts to children from 2 to 12 years old, "Math Blaster," about mathematics which allows children to explore numbers, elemental operations and objects' atstributes, "The Submarine World Adventure," produced by Knowledge Adventure, gives the player information about the seas and oceans of the world as well as the plant and animal life that occurs at those places, "Map Game" about geography, "English Trainings," developed by PLATO, "Tactical Language," "Making History," about history, "Dimexian" about math, "Supercharged," developed by the MIT to teach sciences to university and high school students and numerous others.

This chapter it not trying to itemize all the existing educational games but merely to show a small sample of educational videogames that have been broadly studied, at different times and encompassing diverse subjects, and to enable us to analyze and chart their development.

Our interest is focused not on videogames as a media to teach specific learning content, but on the use of the games itself, and on the increasing function that videogames have in helping to acquire digital skills. This is a fairly recent field of study but we can find some previous investigations about implementations of technology in all scholar's levels and relevant results in CSEDweek (2009), Tucker (2003), Franco et al. (2006), diSessa (2000), Margolings (2008), and Monroy-Hernández (2008). These studies show that learning how to program has also influenced the way children approach other subjects of the school's curricula. There are some examples of projects that are focused on the creation of contents by kids, harnessing low cost and accessible information visualization tools such as Scratch, which have allowed learning, integrating, and using computer graphics principles and interactive techniques for supporting other sciences and various areas of education improvements as, for example, SIGGRAPH Asia Educators Program (2009). Especially regarding Scratch, we can find other workshop proposals like Robertson et al. (2007) or other interesting researches like Resnick et al. (2009), Maloney et al. (2008), Kylie et al. (2007).

VIDEOGAMES CREATION: SCRATCH APPLICATION

According to Neal Gershenfeld (2009), it is when people create their own technology that true interest is awakened. A broad consensus exists about the educational benefits of introducing videogames in the classroom, as well as their potential to improve the acquisition of skills and specific contents.

However, the videogame creation has more advantages:

- In our highly tech society, where computers are omniscient, is not enough to use the basic computer tools but it is also necessary to have programming knowledge to allow us a total and conscientious use of this tool. Learning to program videogames give us this knowledge in a stimulating environment.

- In the digital era, we need the technical knowledge to generate content and express ourselves in the new media's audiovisual language because we are not mere content consumers. Video game programming is useful because it implies video and audio control and the creation of interactive contents.

- In recent years a new computer programming approach emerged which defined a new paradigm computer programming skills should be developed by people with no information background.

There is already a variety of programs available, which we can use to reach this goal, for example RoboMind, Game Maker, E-Slate, Mama, Baltie, Kodu, Alice, Stagecast Creator, Etoys or Scratch. After analyzing all these programs, we finally decided to focus our case study on Scratch; in the following, we give a summary of our analysis of available programs in order of preference (less interesting to more interesting) and the reasons for our decision:

- RoboMind is a simple educational programming environment with its own scripting language that allows beginners to learn the basic principles of computer science by programming a simulated robot. The software is quite limited, and it is not exactly about videogames programming either. It also is proprietary software.
- Game Maker, designed by Mark Overmars at YoYo Games, is commercial software, and is not available for free sothe users that want to learn programming have to pay to get Game Maker.
- E-Slate, Mama, Kodu, Alice are freeware, but they have serious limitations as the language is concerned (the first one is just available in English and Greek, the second one is in English, Hebrew, and Chinese, and the last ones are just in English). All of them are proprietary software and all of them run just on Windows operating systems.
- Stagecast Creator and Baltie are available in more languages and run on windows or MacOS; there is, however, no linux version, and they are also commercial software.
- In the freeware and open source segment, we could only find Etoys, a child-friendly computer environment and object-oriented prototype-based programming language for use in education, or Scratch. Both are good options, both are in a variety of languages, and both have a great community around the program, but we finally selected Scratch as a paradigmatic example of a successful tool for helping kids to develop programming skills, because it has the largest community, which has already developed and uploaded over 1,500,000 projects (MIT, 2011).

Scratch is a computer application for the easy development of video games and hypermedia texts. Using Scratch, it is possible to paint characters (sprites), animate them, build interactive responses to a specific input (from the keyboard, for example) and determine the corresponding output (for instance, the character might "catch" something). While the users do not write code, they still keep a straight "programmer mindset": by placing graphic blocks in a blank area, and by connecting, those users create the functions of the program. This approach represents a high level of abstraction facilitating the accessibility of concepts (informatics programming) leaving users free to focus on the concepts behind the programming language itself rather than worrying about syntax and grammatical errors, which easily occur at the beginning.

Scratch could be considered a social software and educational environment experiment. It enables children no younger than 8 years old to develop video games and interactive stories and share them on the Internet in a way that is easy and safe. It helps to understand how different parts of a video game or story work by programming a prototype and visualizing an idea as well as it allows to understand the logic of video games and interactivity in general. Scratch is educationally oriented and informed by the educators behind the project. It is also community software because the learning methodology is based on the possibility to copy or modify games already done by other users. Scratch is developed by MIT's "Lifelong Kindergarten" Group and utilizes three skill areas identified by "21st Century Learning Skills."

This program defines a new socio-cultural framework for education in the USA, in which different key areas are defined as educational goals, and a priority is defined for each. MIT software follows the guidelines from this framework and identifies three areas as priorities for learning processes in the 21th century:

- Media and Communication
- Thinking and Problem Solving
- Inter-Personal and Self-Directional Skills

Media and Communication

Videogames are hypermedia texts, which require several textual and linguistic competencies in order to be manipulated and/or decoded. As a tool for learning video game programming, Scratch systematically introduces all these elements which are part of the language and lets users familiarize with the process of manipulating different medial elements such as videos, images, and sounds. Accumulating experience in using media objects students learn, probably for first time during institutional education courses, fundamental concepts of media criticque, like media linguistic deconstruction and functional critique. These skills are to be considered very important not just for video game language but for all media-spheres in general in which students move every day, and which represent an important part of the social life in contemporary societies.

In contemporary culture, it is necessary to develop communication skills far surpassing those of writing and reading. Knowing how to deconstruct an image or to create personal paths through different media is some of the needs of everyday life. Video games push students to mix different audiovisual sources in a communication environment controlled by the player. This relation stimulates young creators to consciously choose paths of meaning activated by different materials, helping them to develop basic communication skills. For example, by developing a video game, the creator needs to think about colors, approaching color theory or interaction design elements in early stages of the study course; introducing these concepts during an early age will contribute to develop mature citizens in an information society.

Thinking and Problem Solving

Deconstructing the message, decomposing it in minimal elements, and solving the techno-cultural problems of everyday life are some of the key skills today. All educational systems should pay attention to these aspects. Video games are proving to be a good tool to confront and deal with issues of problem solving and critical thinking in general. Creating a video game, by using Scratch or whatever other tool, means developing an idea, deconstructing it into its most minimal elements and compose the problem and solve every sub-problem systematically. Scratch makes this process easy because it's built upon the abstraction of code, close to the real action the user wants to create; by changing variables or blocks in use the creator can see the results in real-time. This behavior makes the programming language learning curve far easier than classical approaches like textual code and helps to understand information logic by implementing a trial and error methodology at the same time. In order to create a project in Scratch students have to coordinate the inputs with *Spites* (programmable moving objects) by thinking about relations between a player's action and a programmed object's reaction. This process could involve a high level of conceptual abstraction, fomenting decomposition and relational skills over the elements in play. In some way students are invited to make a conceptual map of the elements in play (player, input method, process, output) and draw the connection that occurs between these objects over time (play time). Inputs, sensing, feedbacks are some of the fundamental system concepts students are motivated to play with. These kinds of Seymur Papert conceptual problems are not static but they change dynamically by fostering dynamic learning environments without fixed rules to memorize mechanically.

Interpersonal and Self-Directional Skills

Graphical representation in blocks of the code creates a common language very easy to get for non-IT people, which is also easy to share. The accessibility of a Scratch project is very high, in a short training time the creator/programmer can modify and improve it and by using a common language that does not require previous knowledge of other information languages and by means of a clear categorization, color difference and graphic properties allows everyone to read the program. This condition fosters cooperative work and the possibility to be easily helped by a community of peers when students recognize that necessity. Video game development also requires a clear idea about the final goal of the exercise pushing students to identify the idea in respect to a specific action field. The possibility to share the project through network enhancing, discussion and critique of the work done extends the educational action not only towards the productive phase but also towards the whole creative process.

Scratch, like all the research activities of the "lifelong kindergarten group," is built upon constructionist theory from Seymur Papert (1980). According to this thinking the human learning process is based on learning the know-how rather than the know-what. Construction of the individual, of the conscience, derives from a deductive learning process, where issues correspond exactly in the real world with their uses, and improve educational action. Papert is one of the pioneers in using IT in formal education; since the 1980s he worked on the use of programming languages in primary school. Scratch advanced constructionism by being a tool that simplifies the learning process, mathematical knowledge, programming and more through the direct creation of hypermedia narrative objects. In words of Papert (1980): *"And this is what we're trying to do: find ways in which the technology enables children to use knowledge, mathematical knowledge and other knowledge, not just store it in their heads so that twelve years later it's going to be good for them. Nobody can learn well like that; it's a terrible way of learning. We all like to learn so that we can use what we've learned, and that's what we're trying to do with these children."*

The key point of this approach is what Mitch Resnick, member of the lifelong kindergarten of MIT, terms "technological fluency." Learning key phrases of a natural language cannot be considered to be fluency in this language. Speaking a language means to be able to construct new sentences and meaning based on personal vocabulary. Most people today still do not know how to use a computer; they are able to reproduce some operations, but they are not fluent in using it. Their skills are generally limited to basic features of the operative system, to the use of some office programs and to searching and finding some information on the Internet. Often they are not able to learn new ways to use computers by themselves or to learn a new feature of a program if needed, and neither do they feel comfortable using an unknown application, customizing software for their needs or using a program's features in a different way than usual. They are still unable to create things with a computer, to create images, videos, and sounds; they usually do not debug some operation when it is not working. Mostly they do not modify software or even create a new one.

To be fluent in the use of today's technology means to be able to create digital artifacts based on the individual's own ideas. It is important to have an idea of what to create, to develop the project until it is finished and to choose the right tools to do it. All these operations cannot be considered isolated from their context, but take place within a community of peers. In the process of digital creation, sharing ideas, modifying and extending projects created by someone else, collaborating and helping people from the programming community are basic common and necessary procedures. Every creation should always be relevant to the community.

Therefore, constructivism theory considers learning as an active process in which people build new knowledge through their experiences of the world. Educational systems do not have to transmit knowledge, but must help to construct it.

In the next sections, "Limitations and Problems" and "Solutions and Recommendations," we will offer detailed information about why we consider things like the cost of some of the programs, the commercial or proprietary software or the language of the programs that are just in english or in a limited number of languages to be problematic, giving an detailled explanation of the problems and extended information about the selection of Scratch.

LIMITATIONS AND PROBLEMS

The educational model that we propose supposes an ideal context in which the technological resources are available and the teachers are well versed in using the tools. However, the implementation of this model in different educational contexts faces some problems.

The most evident problem is the availability of the technological resources. The technological availability itself is an important fact in the developing of a country according to the actual economical system's standards. Nowadays in some places of Europe, in South America, broad zones of Asia, and many regions in Africa there is a serious problem about the information-based architecture of new technologies distribution. The technological environment that each context has to work with is different depending on its specific socio-cultural and economic environment.

Other important problems that we find are the program licenses and platform issues that determine the accessibility of software to students. The computer programs that we use in education, the Internet contents managers and other platforms condition our way of relating with the available technology and to acquire information in the digital community. When using commercial software, our participation in the digital community and our endeavours to learn about and understand it are also dependent on commercial factors.

Most of the software used on a daily basis in formal and informal education is commercial and subject to copyright laws. Far from any ideological point of view, we consider this condition problematic in terms of availability of information and tools for students. The hardware and software used at schools and universities should in theory be reproducible at home by the students with little economic effort and should not suppose to be a filter of entrance in education. The software used in education is often platform specific or uses some license that does not allow students to see how it works, or to modify, study, and learn from the program itself. The limitations of the use, the modification, or the redistribution of these programs constitute a control and restriction of the rights of the user over the program. If we want a quality digital education, we cannot allow that this education depends on commercial interests of companies and corporations.

Outside the English and Spanish market, it could be very difficult to find translated software; therefore, we have to consider language accessibility as well. This reveals a cultural background of today's computer technology, which could be, depending on the situation, an important issue for many students who do not speak these languages.

Finally, the technological education of teachers is one of the biggest problems we have to solve when we consider the idea of introducing the new technologies into education. It is not rare that the student controls the computer and its applications better than the teacher. This is due to the few resources that institutions use to update knowledge and to prepare the teaching personell/staff for the challenges of educational paradigm changes.

SOLUTIONS AND RECOMMENDATIONS

To solve these problems we suggest some actions that could improve the basic conditions. We do not have a solution for the unavailability of computers in underdeveloped countries, but we know that nowadays there are some projects to resolve it like the "One laptop per child" campaign that tries to distribute low cost laptops (about 100 dollars) as an energy-saving incentive.

Regarding to the accessibility of software, there is one possible solution, which Scratch has already implemented (and make it a better choice to others similar projects), namely the use of a free software license, like MIT license.

The MIT license is a GPL compatible license issued by the Massachusset Institute of Technology, which also permits to combine the original software with proprietary software. The use of free software licenses for educational context has indeed several advantages. Programs with these licenses usually cost much less than proprietary software, and sometimes this could be a big difference for educational institutions. In general, free software is a community-driven program that acts like a living organism, changing every day and adapting itself to the different conditions. With this kind of program it will be easier for teachers to adopt it on old computers outside the new market without any real need to update their working machine every 2 or 3 years due to the new specifications of upcoming operative system releases. The possibility to freely copy and distribute the program to other people, a student's parents for example, could be very important. Using this kind of software, like Scratch, would actively create a long chain educational system, not school centered but giving the freedom to the student to continue the work/research at home due to the openness of the platform. This has strategic value in an educational system that has to be accessible and inclusive for all.

Scratch offers another advantage, which may be less communicated, but is still important for the educational environment. This software is a cross-platform application and it can be installed and used in all major consumer Operating Systems: Windows, MacOS, and GNU/Linux. An institution, which wants to use the software, does not have to change their previous computer installations to adapt to the product and economically this could be a key value for many educational institutions. Many institutions have already a license contract with some computer company (like Microsoft or

Apple) and in order to use Scratch they do not need to pay an additional fee.

It adapts itself to pre existing IT conditions and does not need any particular technical arrangement. This involves an important aspect for the final user too: students who want to improve their skills can continue to use the software at home without incurring further cost. Students can download Scratch and use it on their home computer as it is. The choice made by lifelong kindergarten group to maintain compatibility between platforms has had an important impact for education. Another important decision was to release the software under MIT license, making the software open source and compatible with other free licenses. Due the openness of Scratch, it is possible to download the code, read it and learn how it has been developed. MIT license defines the user rights, positioning itself as a free software license that manages what users can do with software rather than focusing on what is forbidden. A free software license, like GPL*, lets users 4 basic freedoms: run, study, redistribute, modify. In order to be considered free software, according to the free software foundation declaration, the user must have the right to run the program for any purpose. Users can study the software by accessing the source code. The program can be redistributed to a neighbor and can be modified and distributed as alternative versions, always leaving original authors and credits.

As previously mentioned, outside the English and Spanish markets, it can be very difficult to find translated software; free software applications push software customization on all aspects, starting with the programs language. Language issues could be very important especially in first grade education: using Scratch or a software application in general to learn grammar issue can not be done in ay other than one's native language.. The origin of customization in proprietary software comes from pure commercial interests: small communities are not economically relevant customers for a commercial software publisher. Free software escapes from this condition and lets communities find programs that better adapt to their needs. As an example, Scratch uses different modifications both to single games developed by people and to the core application. The possibility to share student's creations on the Internet is central to the relationship the program tries to construct between its users. It is not just about creating a video game or an interactive story; the key point is to share it with the Scratch online community. In this community, you can find all kinds of Scratch productions, from first demos to semi-professional works. The user is persuaded to share from the beginning: by pressing a button in the main interface, the user is able to publish personal creations to the online community Scratch website host. Other inhabitants of the community will be able to play the game on-line and rate or comment it. If they want, on-line players can download the original code of the game, open it in their Scratch installation, and re-use it, modifying what they want, or just adding features, graphics and gameplay, for later re-publishing. This viral property of the final games makes using scratch the central feature of the educational process, as a tool that is able to improve: remix culture, where sharing knowledge and collective thinking is the main subject. By creating a videogame with open tools like Scratch, users learn not just basic logic and element-analysis in general, but basic mechanisms of collective creation, cultural "mash up" and property distribution. It defines a valuable and prevalent tool in the information community.

Regarding to the technological education of teachers, it is important to develop workshops and courses, as well as the creation of teacher communities (similar to the ones that have emerged around Scratch), where the use of these tools occurs in a collaborative, seamless, and continuous way which allows one to share innovative methodologies, to solve doubt, to state problems, and to provide solutions.

To put this into practice, an economic effort by institution would be needed to educate its staff. It is apparent that despite an educative centre being well equipped in new technologies, this does not mean that its staff is informed about its use, which would make the equipment redundant. As Alonso notes in regard to incorporating new technologies in the educative environment: "the formation is essential, not an added part" (Alonso, 2009).

Furthermore, the tools that are implemented in the creation of videogames within the education system must be free software programs, because, as this would solve a variety of problems that occur when these kinds of activities are introduced in the classroom.

Apart from the evident practical advantages of Scratch, the use of free software is a key characteristic of the new educative paradigm that we defend. This culture, oriented on the idea of sharing knowledge, and opening channels to exchange information is the philosophy that must prevail in the new educative system. The challenge is not to introduce new technologies into the schools, but to create learning practices in an egalitarian way, practices which are not supported by proprietary software.

According to Meiszner, Glott, and Sowe (2008), free software is probably one of the most mature learning ecosystems that exist on the Internet. Free software communities are characterized by providing and distributing the necessary knowledge to create software in a sustainable way. We think the knowledge society needs educational institutions that do not restrict the access to educational content because they understand that the creation of knowledge is is the important part.

After all, a structure open to exchange allows the experts as well as the users to create knowledge in a joint way. If in the use of technologies, collaboration works user to user, in education we advance to the creation of new contents and learning schemes from student to student, opening new important opportunities to enrich the learning of the 21st century (Cobo, 2009).

Free software does not have license costs and can adapt easily to the technological contexts in where we are working. Being modular, it is possible to remove shells when we need to. The translation of software is also easy, which leads to the inclusion of the global community. Perhaps eventually the software developed will be under the control of the user's community, and not a company whose objectives are different from the objectives of an educational institution.

For this reason, we suggest that digital technological education must be based on free software, to respect the freedom of programs, with the possibility of copy, use, change or distribute them. "The battle focuses on the development of applications, not owners. Nobody can make functionality dependent of neither a private support nor the commercial logic" (Alonso, 2009).

We are already beginning to see the efforts of some national governments, like in Brazil or Canada, to escape from the Microsoft monopoly; if we really defend an egalitarian digital education, information and communication technologies must be free from the restrictions of the monopolies associated with the mass media, banks, the advertising industries, instead of generating a new kind of informational conglomerate whose interpretation of "intellectual property" considers the expansion of property more valuable than the access to intellectual products (Martín-Barbero, 2004).

In the following section, we will present the practical case of a workshop for twelve years olds (but which could be adapted to different age groups). It is designed to be very accessible from a technical standpoint, because it only requires a computer for every third child. The ideal duration of the workshop proposed is 60 hours but it could be reduced to 15 hours in order to reach the objectives of the workshop. We will not offer a specification of the time required for each phase of the workshop because this program is intended as an orientation for future educators and should be adapted to the needs of the specific group of kids that participate.

VIDEO GAME CREATION WORKSHOP WITH SCRATCH

Objetives

1. To enhance a critical approach to videogames that allows the students:
    ◦   To identify the conceptual background and the values that are defended in videogames that they are used to playing.
    ◦   To analyze the processes that govern the videogames.
    ◦   To learn to identify the principal parts of a videogame: Avatar, Objectives, game play, etc…
    ◦   To understand the videogame's language and to be able to use this language as a means of expression, valuing its communicative possibilities as a new language.
2. To enhance their own creativity:
    ◦   To learn to value the videogame as an artistic creation and to understand its language.
    ◦   To develop the skills to use it as an expressive and representational media.
3. To develop the basic skills to use Technologies.
4. To develop creativity and self assurance, participation, personal initiative and the capacity to learn to learn, to plan to take decisions and to assume responsibilities, valuing the effort to overcome difficulties.
5. To learn how to do teamwork, to exercise their rights and duties in respect to others and to practice cooperation both interpersonally and collaboratively.
6   To acquire, develop and make a habit of disciplined proceedings at individual and teamwork as a necessary condition for an efficient realization of the learning tasks and as a way for personal development.

Contribution of the Workshop to the Development of the Basic Competences

- It favors a playful response to technology
- Assists to enhance personal autonomy, identity and self-esteem, creativity, and develops skills that allow individuals to participate, make decisions, and choose the correct way to behave in different situations and to take responsibility for the decisions we have taken and the consequences derived from them.
- It contributes directly to the ethical dimension of the social competition; through the emergent "media education," helping students to recognizing the different values that videogames transmit and to evaluate, decode, and deconstruct the technical and conceptual language of the media
- Contributes to the development of the skill of learning to learn and to enhance the awareness of their own capabilities. In addition, it stimulates the virtues and social skills, teamwork and participation helps the subsequent knowledge.
- It favors the basic skill of autonomy and competence because it develops initiatives of planning, decision-making, participation, and responsibility.

METHODOLOGY

In a playful environment, we will try to create a critical conscience by playing familiar videogames as well as independent, educative ones, developed by teachers in a guided way.

Once the students were able to do a basic analysis of the principal parts of a videogame, we will ask the participants to imagine four videogames jointly. Once introduced to the program we are will to use and explain its performance, in three person teams. They will create the videogames under the teacher's assistance.

Progamming

- **First Season:** Each participant brings to the workshop their favorite videogames; we play and analyze them, trying to create in the children a critical conscience. What is beyond the playful component?
- **Second Season:** We show the children videogames of similar mechanics as the ones they have brought at the last season but with a different content (independent, educative, Scratch created videogames) and we will play them while we make a critical exam. What is the difference between them and the ones we played the day before?
- **Third Season:** We will analyze which are the different parts of a videogame, encouraging the children to make the reflections: avatar, prizes, target, etc. Once we identify the principal parts, we encourage them to imagine the game they would like to create. What the avatar would be, what the goals of the game might consist in. The children will be invited to visualize these concepts using software tools to draw that do not require a high skill level.
- **Fourth Season:** We start to work with Scratch, familiarizing the kids with the program, teaching them how to use it. The contents are the following: a) introduction of the interface and functionality of a simple and easy to use example program, b) coordinates (mini games to learn the basic concepts of axis and coordinate), c) giving it movement 1 (how my avatar moves along the axis), e) giving it movement 2 (learn to assign rounds to each movement to make it more effective), f) but when? (keyboard and mouse events)
- **Fifth Season:** Through collective planning four videogames are chosen to be devel-

oped. After that, groups of three children are organized to develop them under the teachers' supervision.

- **Last Season:** The children present the videogame that they have developed and once presentations are finished the children try all the games. We close the workshop encouraging the children to make conclusions collectively from the videogames; the children must justify the values of the games they play, creating a critical attitude to this cultural medium that is so close to them, and making them aware of their own creativity.

We think it is important that this workshop will not be an isolated event but that it will have continuous repercussions in time in three ways:

- **First:** By using Scratch, children can became part of an international community that uses the same program for educative development. This means to get into a shared formative and continuous process, to learn how to relate through this tool with children from other cultures (this will enhance the ideas of exchange, tolerance …)
- **Second:** Generating a documentation that goes beyond videogames created by children by creating a document about the workshop in which the objectives, used resources, methodologies, problems and solutions appear clearly. This document will be useful to improve the workshop and as a tool for teachers, constituting a sociological, philosophical and pedagogical study about the use of this new technology in educative environments.
- **Third:** The games created by the children could be the object of a guided exhibition for children of the same age whose collective reflections would be annexed to the workshop document.

RESULTS

Many kids might have technological skills before the workshops being used to play games and to surf the Internet without problems, in these cases the great advantage is to work with them not just in the technological part but in regard to theoretical aspects too, this means to do an analysis of the games that they use to play and try to create in the children a critical conscience. The acquisition of critical thinking by the kids can be measured by the contexts that they select for their own game and through the dialog with them. In other cases, when we are working with children who come from poverty, or from communities in risk of social exclusion it is possible that their technological skills are not developed as well, but the simplicity of the Scratch program allows them to aquire these skills quite fast. In this case the technical skills or the critical thinking are important objetives to accomplish, but not as important as reinforcing their self esteem and giving them the feeling that they can create something and encouraging them to express themselves by creating the game.. It is really interesting to see how their oun life experiences and their problems appear in the contents of the games that they design. The improvement of their self-esteem is perfectly visible trough direct observation.

In all of the cases, we hope to encounter no great difficulties in measuring the results obtained, on the one hand simply because the direct observation and the conversations with the kids that take place in the constant contact with them during the workshop will provide a lot of information about the skills that the children are aquiring, which allows to adapt the contents and the schedule to their respective needs.

On the other hand, the final product provides interesting information about the skills that the children have obtained during the workshop. These skills are clearly represented by the technological complexity, the contents, characters, enemies, objectives, and story that they select, how they integrate the different digital languages like sound, images, gameplay, etc. in the game, and it clearly shows whether all of them work well together in a coherent manner, etc. In addition, in the Scratch online-community, it is possible to follow the evolution of the children even after the workshop is finished.

FUTURE RESEARCH DIRECTIONS

Scratch represents one of the most successful examples of dataflow programming. This paradigm has proved to be useful to introduce computer programming to many people without specific computer knowledge. Further investigation proposing programming tools that give us the capability to create digital artifacts with increasingly complexity is promoted by this program.

Another important factor in this exploration is to expand the possibilities of these programming environments to make them interact with the real world in an effortless and operative way. This investigation path is being explored from the Scratch developer team itself by the implementation of a micro controller for using data from the real world. A micro controller is a hardware that acts as an interface between sensors (input data coming from physic world) and the application. Since the beginning, Scratch provides this possibility by using the ScratchBoard, now known as Picoboard. It allows users to connect different types of sensors to the program: temperature, light, magnetic, humidity and microphone. Our future investigations will take this direction and we already have done preliminary experiments in the form of personal projects. Based on these preliminary experiences we can glean some of the possible directions for the progress of this kind of software and programming as an IT approach to education. The possibility to use the body as the controller through Microsoft kinect optic sensors and homebrew software by Steven Howell that

connect the 3d cam to Scratch already lets users create motion tracking based games, which is also an interesting option.

CONCLUSION

This article states that education is facing challenges as a result of the change that the digitalization of its contents brought to its paradigms.

Introducing new technologies in educational settings is necessary and represents a clear actual trend, but the educational system cannot limit itself to introduce these technologies without implementing other transformations aimed to change the concept of "teachers" itself. Someone that teaches the students "to learn," to search information discerning the good and the false information, to generate their own content and to share it with others, providing a critical and creative education in the new languages and a new conscious way to relate with the new media.

This chapter has explored that this can be achieved with videogames, but not just by educational games (which may be a good way to introduce students to the new technologies and to make the study of some subjects more dynamic and attractive, but the mere implementation of educational games does not account for an important part of education that we want to emphasize, which is the creation of new contents), but in learning how to make videogames. In this way, students will acquire more holistic technical skills that will allow them to work with the new media because they will learn to work with graphics, videos, music, etc.

As videogame programming can be complex, we propose the use of Scratch, as a freeware (open license?) videogame creation program, which is easy to handle, and is rooted in a big community already formed whose advantages have been described above.

To prove the advantages that the use of this program has we have proposed the creation of a videogame workshop for children that could be implemented in schools and high schools.

With all this, we want to contribute to enhance the trend of educating students in digital skills highly necessary in our contemporary context.

REFERENCES

Alcubierre, D. (2009). *Los videojuegos dentro de la empresa: Integración de una realidad.* Retrieved November 26, 2009, from http://www.cibersociedad.net/congres2009/es/coms/los-videojuegos-dentro-de-la-empresa-integracion-de-una-realidad/979/

Alcubierre, D. (2009). *Los videojuegos dentro de la empresa: Integración de una realidad.* Retrieved from http://www.cibersociedad.net/congres2009/es/coms/los-videojuegos-dentro-de-la-empresa-integracion-de-unarealidad/979/

Alonso, E. (2009). *Segunda ilustración: Cultura digital y progreso.* Paper presented at the IXth Compostela Colloquium in Logic and Analytic Philosophy. Los Angeles, CA.

Cobo, J. C. (2009). *Conocimiento, creatividad y software libre: una oportunidad para la educación en la sociedad actual.* UOC Papers. Retrieved November 9, 2010, from http://www.uoc.edu/uocpapers/8/dt/esp/cobo.pdf

CSEDweek. (2009). *Computer science education week.* Retrieved October 30, 2011, from http://www.csedweek.org/wp-content/uploads/2009/12/CSEdWeek-Two-Pager.pdf

diSessa, A. (2000). *Changing minds: Computers, learning, and literacy.* Cambridge, MA: MIT Press.

Franco, J. F., et al. (2006). Computer graphics, interactive technologies and collaborative learning synergy supporting individuals' skills development. In *Proceedings of the 33rd International Conference and Exhibition on Computer Graphics and Interactive Techniques, SIGGRAPH 2006.* Boston, MA: ACM.

González, M. B., & Rodríguez, P. A. (2003). Un instrumento para evaluar el uso y las actitudes hacia los videojuegos. *Revista de Medios y Educación, 20,* 17–32.

Huizinga, J. (2007). *Homo ludens.* Madrid, Spain: Alianza Editorial.

Jenkins, H. (2007). Confronting the chalenges of the parcipatory culture: Media education for the 21° century. *Nordic Journal of Media Literacy.* Retrieved January 18, 2011, from http://www.newmedialiteracies.org/files/working/NML-WhitePaper.pdf

Kerckhove, D. (1999). *Inteligencias en conexión: Hacia una sociedad de la web.* Barcelona, Spain: Editorial Gedisa.

Kylie, A. P., & Yasmin, B. K. (2007). From super goo to scratch: Exploring creative digital media production in informal learning. *Learning, Media and Technology, 32*(2), 149-166. Retrieved October 31, 2011, from http://www.tandfonline.com/doi/abs/10.1080/17439880701343337

Maloney, J., Peppler, K., Kafai, Y., Resnick, M., & Rusk, N. (2008). Programming by choice: Urban youth learning programming with Scratch. *ACM SIGCSE Bulletin, 40*(1), 367–371. doi:10.1145/1352322.1352260

Margolis, J. (2008). *Stuck in the shallow end: Education, race, and computing.* Cambridge, MA: MIT Press.

Marín, A. (2009). New media ¿viejas o nuevas realidades? *Mosaic, Tecnologías y Comunicación Multimedia*. Retrieved March 26, 2011, from http://mosaic.uoc.edu/2006/10/20/new-media-%C2%BFviejas-o-nuevas-realidades/

Martín-Barbero, J. (2004). *Nuevas tecnicidades y culturas locales: Ejes de una propuesta*. Retrieved February 11, 2011 from http://sociedadinformacion.fundacion.telefonica.com/telos/articulocuaderno.asp@idarticulo=2&rev=61.htm#n1

Meiszner, Glott, & Sowe. (2008). Free / libre open source software (FLOSS) communities as an example of successful open participatory learning ecosystems. *The European Journal for the Informatics Professional, 9*(3), 62–68.

MIT. (2011). *Scratch: Imagine, program, share*. Retrieved November 1, 2011, from http://scratch.mit.edu/

Monroy-Hernández, A., & Resnick, M. (2008). Empowering kids to create and share programmable media. *Interaction, 15*(2), 50–53. doi:10.1145/1340961.1340974

Papert, S. (1980). *Constructionism vs. instructionism*. Retrieved March 22, 2011 from http://www.papert.org/articles/const_inst/const_inst1.html

Pérez Rodríguez, M. A. (2009). *Un nuevo lenguaje para una comunicación global*. Retrieved June 13, 2011, from http://www.uhu.es/agora/version01/digital/numeros/03/03-articulos/monografico/pdf3/perez.PDF

Pérez Tornero, J. M. (2000). El desarrollo de la sociedad de la información del paradigma de la cultura de masas al de la cultura multimedia. In *Proceedings y Educación en la Sociedad de la Información,* (pp. 17-34). Barcelona, Spain: Paidós.

Resnick., et al. (2009). Scratch: Programming for all. *Communications of the ACM, 52*(11). Retrieved October 27, 2011 from http://dl.acm.org/citation.cfm?id=1592779

Robertson, J., & Good, J. (2007). Children's narrative development through computer game authoring. *TechTrends, 49*(5), 43-59. Retrieved October 31, 2011 from http://www.springerlink.com/content/3xh87p7603n60757/

SIGGRAPH Asia Educators Program. (2009). *Education papers*. Retrieved October 25, 2011 from http://www.siggraph.org/asia2009/for_attendees/educators_program/education_papers/details/?type=EducatorsPapers&id=73

Tucker, A. (2010). *A model curriculum for K–12 computer science*. Retrieved October, 30, 2011 from http://csta.acm.org/Curriculum/sub/CurrFiles/K-12ModelCurr2ndEd.pdf

Vygotsky, L. (1993). *Pensamiento y lenguaje*. Buenos Aires, Argentina: Ediciones Librería Fausto.

ADDITIONAL READING

Aguilera Moyano, M. A., & Méndiz Noguero, A. (2011). *Videojuegos y educación*. Retrieved March 04, 2011, from http://ares.cnice.mec.es/informes/02/documentos/indice.htm

Ballestero, F. (2002). *La brecha digital: El riesgo de exclusión en la sociedad de la información*. Madrid, Spain: Fundación Retevisión Auna.

Buckingham, D. (2002). *Crecer en la era de los medios electrónicos*. Madrid, Spain: Morata.

Buckingham, D. (2008). *Repensar el aprendizaje en la era de la cultura digital*. Retrieved March 02, 2010, from http://www.scribd.com/doc/51887967/REPENSAR-EL-APRENDIZAJE-EN-LA-ERA-DE-LA-CULTURA-DIGITAL

Cawkell, T. (2001). Sociotechnology: The digital divide. *Journal of Information Science, 27*(1), 51–53.

Cordes, C., & Miller, E. (2000). *Fool's gold: A critical look at computers in childhood*. College Park, MD: Alliance for Childhood.

Cullen, R. (2003). The digital divide: A global and national call to action. *The Electronic Library, 21*(3), 247–257. doi:10.1108/02640470310480506

Eduteka. (2010). *Scratch en la educación escolar.* Retrieved October 22, 2010, from http://www.eduteka.org/modulos.php?catx=9&idSubX=278

Eisenberg, M. (2003). Mindstuff: Educational technology beyond the computer. *Convergence, 9*(2), 29–53. doi:10.1177/135485650300900205

Gilster, P. (1997). *Digital literacy.* New York, NY: Wiley.

Greenfield, P., & Cocking, R. (1996). *Interacting with video: Advances in applied developmental psychology.* Palo Alto, CA: Ablex Publishing Corp.

Gros, B. (2004). *Pantallas, juegos y educación: La alfabetización digital en la escuela.* Bilbao, Spain: Desclée de Brouwer.

Kafai, Y. B., Peppler, K. A., & Chapman, R. N. (Eds.). (2010). *Origins and guiding principles of the computer clubhouse.* Retrieved February 13, 2010, from http://web.media.mit.edu/~mres/papers/Clubhouse/clubhouse-origins.pdf

Menou, M. (2004). La alfabetización informacional dentro de las políticas nacionales sobre tecnologías de la información y comunicación (TICs): La cultura de la información, una dimensión ausente. *Anales de Documentación, 7,* 241–261.

Papert, S. (1980). *Mindstorms: Children computers and powerful ideas.* Boston, MA: MIT Press.

Papert, S. (1998). *Child power: Keys to the new learning of the digital century.* Boston, MA: Colin Cherry.

Peppler, K., & Kafai, Y. (2007). From SuperGoo to Scratch: Exploring creative media production in informal learning. *Journal on Learning, Media, and Technology, 32*(7), 149–166. doi:10.1080/17439880701343337

Phipps, L. (2000). New communications technologies: A conduit for social inclusion. *Information Communication and Society, 3*(1), 39–68. doi:10.1080/136911800359419

Resnick, M. (2007, December). Sowing the seeds for a more creative society. *Learning and Leading with Technology,* 18–22.

Resnick, M. (2010a). Learning & leading with technology. *International Society for Technology in Education U.S. & Canada,* Retrieved June 24, 2010, from http://web.media.mit.edu/~mres/papers/Learning-Leading-final.pdf

Resnick, M. (2010b). Computer as paintbrush: Technology, play, and the creative society. In D. Singer, R. Golikoff, & K. Hirsh-Pasek (Eds.), *Play = Learning: How Play Motivates and Enhances Children's Cognitive and Social-Emotional Growth.* Retrieved October 10, 2010, from http://web.media.mit.edu/~mres/papers/playlearn-handout.pdf

Resnick, M. (2011). *Rethinking learning in the digital age.* Retrieved May 23, 2011, from http://llk.media.mit.edu/papers/mres-wef.pdf

Resnick, M., Maloney, J., Monroy-Hernández, A., Rusk, N., Eastmond, E., & Brennan, K. … Kafai, Y. (2010). *Scratch: Programming for all.* Retrieved March 09, 2010 from http://web.media.mit.edu/~mres/papers/Scratch-CACM-final.pdf

Sandoval, E. (2009). Conocimiento y comunicación: El lugar del sujeto frente a las tecnologías de información. *Ide@s CONCYTEG Año, 4*(45).

Steven, L. K. (2001). *The ultimate history of video games*. New York, NY: Three rivers Press.

Travieso, J. L., & Planella, J. (2008). La alfabetización digital como factor de inclusión social: Una mirada crítica. In *UOC Papers: Revista Sobre la Sociedad del Conocimiento*, (Vol. 6). UOC.

Turkle, S. (1997). *La vida en la pantalla*. Barcelona, Spain: Paidos.

KEY TERMS AND DEFINITIONS

Accessibility: The possibility to access some information or resource in a inforrmatics ecology system.

Alice: 3D programming environment that makes it easy to create an animation for telling a story, playing an interactive game, or a video to share on the Web.

Baltie: An educational graphic oriented visual programming tool for kids, children, youth and adults.

E-Slate: An exploratory learning environment. It provides a workbench for creating highly dynamic software with rich functionality, by non-programmers.

Etoys: An educational tool for teaching children powerful ideas in compelling ways trougth a media-rich authoring environment and visual programming system.

Free Software: Informatics application with a copyright let user view the sourcecode of the program.

Game Maker: Is a Windows and Mac IDE originally developed by Mark Overmars in the Delphi programming language.

Interactive Stories: Multimedia narrative composed by the mix of images, sounds, videos, and texts.

PLATO: First public supported project of educational software.

Kodu: New visual programming language made specifically for creating games.

Mama: An educational programming language and development environment for developing 3D animations and games.

RoboMind: Simple educational programming environment that will familiarize the kids with the basics of computer science by letting the kids program their own robot.

Scratch: Software application for children and kids to develop videogames and digital narratives.

Stagecast Creator: Easy-to-learn, easy-to-use software tool for making your own games and simulations.

Videogames: Electronic programs that use game logic as man-machine interaction model.

ENDNOTES

[1]   See Alcubierre (2009).

Chapter 17
GAMESTAR(T):
An ARSGAMES Project

María Rubio Méndez
ARSGAMES, Spain

Eurídice Cabañes Martínez
ARSGAMES, Spain

ABSTRACT

There is a distinct tendency to integrate technology into the classroom, but in practice the introduction of the ICT in education is not producing the expected effects. We are confronted with the second digital divide, which consists in the dissociation of the students from the technologies introduced in the educational sphere that do not match their actual technological environment. GAMESTAR(T) has been developed in this context as an ARSGAMES project, which, taking into account the potentialities of video games for education and socialization, proposes a series of weekly meetings that include assembly meetings for decision-making about the club's rules, activities, and materials, thematic courses related to specific domains of knowledge, and the club's sessions, in which children play, assisted by monitors, in an atmosphere of critical and collective reflection. In the following, the authors examine how the club developed, which methodology was used, what problems were encountered, and the solutions applied.

INTRODUCTION

Some of the measures most firmly adopted in view of the need of a digital literacy have been the introduction of digital technologies into the classroom (computers, digital interactive whiteboards, projectors, etc.) and the increasing pressure put on the teaching community to use them, a usage that must be included in the didactic planning of the different subjects, as well as among the objectives of the annual center planning of each educational center. In the main text of the current Spanish educational legislation, the *Ley Orgánica de Educación* (hereafter LOE), the competency in the ICT usage is included as a part of the cur-

DOI: 10.4018/978-1-4666-1987-6.ch017

riculum in different educational stages. These measures seem to demonstrate that the educational advantages of technology have been internalized, especially in a technologically mediated society like ours.

Although it is evident that the introduction of the ICT can have a positive effect on education, the way it is being carried out practically is, in most cases, insufficient and even counterproductive. As pointed out by David Buckingham (2008), we are confronted with a second digital divide which consists in a dissociation of the students from the technologies introduced so far in the educational sphere, for they differ greatly from those they are familiar with and do not match their actual technological environment. Outside of the educational environment, students have generally an extensive access to different resources: they use technology for communicating through social networks, chats, text messages, etc. They play video games, surf through the Internet searching information of their interest, they download and edit multimedia contents, etc. Compared to the amount of resources available outside of the classroom, the technologies used in educational contexts lack all interest for the students, insofar as they are regarded as alien to them, boring and tedious, as well as limited.

In ARSGAMES we both acknowledge the benefits of the technologically mediated education and understand the importance of bridging the second digital divide by making the educational technology, as well as the contents, more attractive to the students.

Although ARSGAMES has always aimed its activity concerning the "serious" research on video games at an adult audience, for a certain while it had been considered to create a link to a younger audience so that it would be able to stimulate a critical and creative spirit among children and teenagers and try to use video games experimentally in different areas of the educational field. This aspiration could materialize thanks to the financial aid "Ayuda a la Creación" of Inter-

mediae Matadero, Madrid, which made possible the GAMESTAR(T) project. ARSGAMES is a Cultural Association composed of professionals, artists, researchers, and students that work on video game research in all of its facets (educational, cultural, economic, artistic, etc.). ARSGAMES organizes events and develops projects related to the world of video games, such as *OpenArsgames, PlayLab,* or *Gamestart.* Even if its range of activities is quite wide, ARSGAMES is specially focused on education with the GAMESTAR(T) project. GAMESTAR(T) is a project that explores the possibilities of video games as a resource for education, socialization and entertainment. Its three main lines of action are:

- **GAMESTAR(T) Club:** A video game club that meets weekly at Intermediae, whose aim is to define how to configure a new, collective space for video gaming that encourages associationism and self-management among its members.
- **GAMESTAR(T) Gameteca**: The "library" containing board games, video games and other resources, located in the Cúpula de Estación Futuro at Intermediae.
- **GAMESTAR(T) School:** Out-of-school workshops focused on learning with video games, which deal with diverse topics such as history, gender questions, health, or how to create video games.

At the outset of the club its objectives were:

- Familiarize the participants with the video games language so as they can think critically about themselves, develop their analytical capacities, and provide them with tools that allow them to modify or even create their own video games.
- Create and stimulate team activities around video games.
- Keep alive the critical spirit towards video games that had been generated by

the OpenArsgames[1] held at Intermediae-Matadero (Madrid) and extend the activities to a younger audience.

These objectives were evolving along the year; they were extended and simultaneously became more complex. From a pedagogical point of view, certain needs were detected that had not been envisaged in the initial project and that refer to aspects connected to the second digital divide and the critical digital literacy, aspects related to the personal development and the educational and affective needs of the students, as well as formal aspects pertaining to the management and coordination of the project. Dividing them into three main groups, the extension of the objectives can be specified as if follows:

- Second digital divide and critical digital literacy.
  - Offer workshops and activities whose tools are designed to be in accordance with those used by the students in their leisure time.
  - Promote "critical gaming" including the reflection on the video games used (content, structure, implicit values, etc.) as a key feature of the activities and workshops of the club.
- Personal development, educational, and affective needs of the students.
  - Involve actively the students in their own learning process, fostering a feeling of belonging to the club in a way that is consistent with the pedagogical principle of "active learning."
  - Design sessions structured so as to incorporate the student's needs, interests and motivations, following the pedagogical principle of "meaningful learning" which consists in showing the relationship of the knowledge to be learned in the club with the stu-

dents' previous knowledge as well as its relevance for real life.
  - Meet the specific needs of the students, their self-esteem, interests, and capacities in order to adapt the activities to them, applying the pedagogical principle of "attention to diversity."
- Coordination and management of the project.
  - Establish sound information channels and means of dialogue between the different instances that facilitate the monitoring and adaptation of the project.

Throughout this chapter the principles that guide the GAMESTAR(T) project will be examined in detail, taking into account the pedagogical foundations it is based on, the methodology applied and the issues it raised along its development. The authors hope this experience is enriching and inspiring for those people interested in pedagogical innovation through the use of technologies in the classroom, especially through video games.

The concept of usability used in this chapter transcends the analysis of the understandability, learnability, operability, and attractiveness of certain software, i.e. the usability of certain video games, and focuses on a specific context of use (an educational context where practice is guided by libertarian pedagogy) in which any video game renders possible to achieve the targeted general and specific educational objectives. In the case of GAMESTAR(T), the usability of certain video game is determined not so much by its intrinsic characteristics (software design, interface intuitiveness, gameplay, or avatar characterization) as by the way it will be integrated in a set of activities. Assembly organization, fostering of critical thinking and cooperative gaming are the fundamental elements to which any video game should be adapted: from a simple shooter designed specifically to deal with health issues (such as *Immune Attack*) to commercial fighting games with a complex gameplay (like *Tekken 5*), video games used can equally meet the requirements imposed by GAMESTAR(T) objectives successfully. Following this guiding principle, in this chapter it will be offered a guide with general criteria that should be taken into account when selecting video games that would be used in an educational context similar to that of GAMESTAR(T) experience. These criteria are more closely connected with pedagogical-methodological aspects of video game implementation than with specific software design features.

The next section, "Background," will examine the current state of the introduction of technologies into the Spanish educational context (paying special attention to video games), the methodological principles that are at the root of the adopted pedagogical model, and the educational advantages that video games can entail for that model. In the section, "GAMESTAR(T) Experience," detailed information about the GAMESTAR(T) experience is offered, specifying the problems encountered, the solutions found, and the results obtained through the implementation of the methodology. The main aim of the chapter is that the GAMESTAR(T) experience can eventually serve as a guide for those who are interested in introducing similar pedagogical models in other educational contexts. Such a guide is available in the section, "Guidelines to Selection and Introduction of Video Games in Educational Environments." Finally, the section, "Conclusion and Future Research Lines," contains a critical assessment of the GAMESTAR(T) experience and a sketch of the principles that, according to the authors, should guide the research on the utilization of video games in education.

BACKGROUND

From the second half of the 20th century, the pedagogical principles and practices have evolved considerably, making education revolve around the personal development of the students rather than the acquisition of knowledge. This new pedagogical model has its roots in an old conception of the human being that had been buried into oblivion in Spain's educational system during Franco's dictatorship: the concept of the human being as an integral being whose multiple dimensions (moral, social, cultural, etc.) must be equally developed without detriment to any of them.

According to Silvio Gallo (1997), the philosophical-pedagogical tradition incorporates two different ways of understanding the human being, the essentialist, and the existentialist conceptions. The former conceives the human being as predefined by an essence that determines its being externally. This conception appears in pedagogical theories which, like that of Plato, understand education as the development of that essence in a process that brings it to its most perfect state, the state that best resembles the idea that forms it. The latter conception, however, considers that there is no human essence: the human being is realized or constructed through action and there is no model to approach to; this model is realized throughout life at the same time as one's own identity. Human beings are open, modifiable, and their only limit is the infinite horizon of their possibilities. The GAMESTAR(T) project completely adheres to this latter conception.

The traditional pedagogy rests upon an essentialist conception of human beings. Nevertheless, the new trends in pedagogy take the existentialism as the starting point, being Rousseau with his *Emile*, the forerunner of this stream of thought. It must be noted that "existentialism" does not mean in this context a strict Sartrean or Heideggerian existentialism, but it should be taken in a broader sense as the conception of human being as a formless being that has to develop itself in its multiple and diverse dimensions, from the cognitive to the moral aspect. The principles of the LOE, such as the *promotion of an integral education knowledge, skills, and values*, support this conception. Thinkers and pedagogues like Francisco Ferrer y Guardia (2009) or Silvio Gallo (1997) identify this view of human beings as a complex, ever changing reality at the basis of the new pedagogy: "The human being is understood as the product of a multiplicity of facets that articulate harmoniously and, for this reason, education must be concerned with all these facets: intellectual, physical, moral, etc." (Gallo, 1997, p. 9). These human facets are closely related and deeply conditioned by the social, cultural, and political context. In a society like ours, the technological or digital dimension should be included and, as shown above, the LOE does so.

The specific characteristics of our technological society make an *existentialist* pedagogical model, which situates students at the core of their own learning process, especially appropriate. This pedagogical model has been defended by different schools of progressive pedagogical thought (Rousseau, 1974; Giner de los Ríos, 1988; Ferrer & Guardia, 2009; Freinet, 1970, 1982). For all these schools, the teacher role should be restricted to that of a mediator of the students' learning process, and it is connected to the principle of pedagogical self-management, according to which the students are the main actors of the learning process choosing what and how they want to learn. Although all these tendencies share a concept of the teaching function, they support different views on how it should be put into practice that depend on their supporting an authoritarian or anti-authoritarian conception of education. In any case, the general, common objective is the individualization of education focused on students rather than on knowledge.

We can confirm that the use of technologies may prove highly beneficial for this pedagogical model, since it allows a direct access to a wide range of knowledge and resources via the Internet. The teacher role would be that of a critical guide that encourages the students' capacities for information analysis, contrasting, and selection, as well as the ability to detect wrong, biased, or deceiving information, etc.

GAMESTAR(T) methodology incorporates the contributions of these pedagogical schools

and models, something that will be better explained in the section devoted to the analysis of the GAMESTAR(T) experience. This pedagogical project derives both from the existentialist pedagogical models and from the new theories on education and technology that demand the introduction of the ICT into the classroom, especially from those that have demonstrated the educational potentialities and advantages of video games opposite to traditional education systems. All this will be examined in detail below.

EDUCATIONAL POTENTIALITIES OF VIDEO GAMES

Since the end of the 20th century, research studies on the educational potentialities of video games have proliferated. There seems to be a general consensus that video games are useful tools in order to develop certain skills and cognitive capacities. Along general lines, and following a study carried out by the Department of Psychology of the University of California (Greenfield & Cocking, 1996), it can be consistently argued that video games help develop the next dimensions of human beings:

- Spatial perception and recognition.
- Development of the visual recognition and the dividing of the visual attention.
- Inductive logic development.
- Cognitive development of scientific-technical aspects.
- Development of complex skills.
- Spatial representation.
- Inductive discovery.
- Development of iconic codes.
- Gender construction.

The Research Group on Video games of the University of Málaga (Spain), led by Aguilera and Méndiz (2004), has conducted a detailed study on the interrelationships between video games and education. Their study reviews the bibliography available about this topic and it draws conclusions in favor of the introduction of video games into the classroom as elements that help develop the next procedural abilities:

- **Reading:** Some video games can be used advantageously to stimulate the reading of books related to them. Reading as a procedural value (Grupo F9, 2000).

- **Logical thinking:** Finding out the way to escape a situation or enter it, working out how to solve a problem, designing a strategy, organizing and planning elements with a view to certain objectives, etc. (Ball, 1978; Estallo, 1994, 1995; Grupo F9, 2000; Le Diberdier, 1998).

- **Observation:** The most exercised skill due to the amount of elements displayed on the screen and to the need to discriminate them visually and spatially (Lowery & Knirk, 1982, 1983; Estallo, 1995).

- **Spatiality, Geography:** Development of cartography and spatial representations: maps, plans, etc. (Ball, 1978; Lowery & Knirk, 1982, 1983; Gagnon, 1985).

- **Vocabulary:** Video games can be used to learn unknown words, which are easily decoded in the context of the game (Ball, 1978).

- **Basic knowledge:** Video games allow the children to acquire basic skills and abilities necessary for their daily experience and development (Griffith, et al., 1983; Estallo, 1995; Bartolomé, 1998; Gros, 2000; Grupo F9, 2000; Le Diberdier, 1998).

- **Orthography:** Spelling and writing correctly the most common words or those that are being learned (Grupo F9, 2000).

- **Problem Solving:** An ever present element in video games that demands from the player a capacity to cope with or escape from difficult situations; this is particularly important in strategy video games (Silvern, 1985, 1986; Estallo, 1995; Bartolomé, 1998; Gros, 2000; Grupo F9, 2000; Mandinacht, 1987).

- **Strategy Planning:** An important mental activity demanded by video games, especially the most difficult ones (Long & Long, 1984; Silvern, 1985, 1986; Estallo, 1995; Bartolomé, 1998; Gros, 2000; Calvo, 2000; Esther-Gabriel, 1994).

The cognitive value of video games is decreasingly questioned or disputed among experts, as it is attested by the numerous studies on this issue quoted in the work of the researchers of the University of Málaga.

Nowadays, the educational plans and strategies are beginning to show a greater interest in this medium owing to its promising potentialities. Video games not only can help us develop abilities and skills or acquire specific knowledge, as we have shown above, but they also bring about significant improvements to the learning process since their specific characteristics stimulate motivation, concentration, creativity, etc. Video games can also facilitate the integration of groups at risk of exclusion. These topics will be dealt with in the next subsections.

IMMERSION

Immersion is an advantageous element of the educational practice that uses video games as a learning tool. This concept can be easily explained: immersion is a psychological phenomenon, which consists in a profound diminishing or a loss of a subject's awareness of the real, surrounding physical environment to the extent that the virtual environment of the video game is "believed" to be real instead. This is equivalent to taking a leap from our everyday life into a virtual world by means of a loss of self-awareness that leads us to a more intense experience that fully engrosses us: it constitutes a leap to another space, where we inhabit fiction. The game acquires significance when we immerse ourselves in it. If such an immersion is possible with conventional games, the level of immersion that could be attained through video games is undoubtedly much higher.

Thanks to the new technological advances, "video games allow the staging of a fantasy digital scenario, being the immersion experience one of its greatest appeals. The surrounding world is put aside and we enter a dimension in which time perception changes. It is a timeless world, so to speak. The surrounding space disappears and another time modality replaces conventional time. The video game on the screen operates some kind of dissolution of the subject in the machine, accompanied by the corresponding timelessness that characterizes these fusion situations" (Balaguer, 2005).

In which sense can the phenomenon of immersion imply an advantage for education? Paying attention to traditional lectures as well as the realization of monotonous, boring tasks is complicated and may lead to diminished students' level of attention, something that can have negative consequences for learning. However, the unattractiveness of a lesson is not the only factor that contributes to lack of attention. Environmental and psychological factors have also an influence on attention processes. One of the acutest problems that can be detected in traditional education is the students' lack of motivation and attention. Therefore, a fundamental objective in education is the search for a way to motivate students and to attract their attention so that they concentrate and remain concentrated. The immersion generated by video games mitigates the negative effects of a pressing environment and facilitates the students' deep concentration on the learning process. If the phenomenon of immersion can be induced through video games, then the students' attention will be focused precisely on that we try to teach them. It may be very difficult to concentrate on a single task for a long period of time, since there are always multiple stimuli that divert

our attention, but we can instead play a video game for many hours without the attention level being diminished, because all our capacities are solicited by the audiovisual environment. Using video games for educational purposes stimulates attention and concentration, which leads to an improved learning.

EXPERIMENTATION WITHOUT CONSEQUENCES

Video games constitute a sphere for experimentation without consequences. As an advantage, this brings along the possibility of a stimulation of the students' creativity that encourages them to risk doing things they would never dare to in *real* situations. Students may get motivated to try to overcome situations or answer to questions just because of the challenge they represent; thus, they familiarize with the cognitive context or framework they are working in, they learn through trial-and-error method, they experiment adopting different perspectives about a single case or phenomenon (provided that the video game allows to repeat or try again) that can offer them a global vision and help develop the so called lateral thinking.

Therefore, it can be argued that video games are a suitable tool for an education that stimulates creativity and involves students and teachers directly in the learning process, promoting active and meaningful learning.

INTEGRATION

Owing to their ludic and interactive elements, video games have become a very powerful tool that influences our conception of reality and the way we form our opinions. According to Juan Alberto Estallo (1995, p. 117), "video games" are tools through which children understand the cultural medium that surrounds them. Video games represent faithfully the social symbolism and the cultural constructions of our context, what should allow us to control their contents as well as their possibilities as value transmitter. Terry Toles affirms that "gaming and entertainment activities configure a subtle expression of the ways a culture perceives reality."

Those potentialities should be seriously taken into consideration: although the current mainstream video games show a clear tendency to sexism and help perpetuate the stereotypes of masculinity as action and femininity as passiveness and submission, a reappropriation of video games may be useful for the elimination of these and other prejudices, and it can transform them into a tool for values education.

"Contra viento y marea" is a good example that deserves closer examination. In this video game, the player has to assume the role of a person (women and men of different ethnic groups can be selected) who must flee from her country in order to preserve her life due to war or political repression. From the flight to the construction of a new life in the host country, players have to face interrogations, painful decisions, the arrival in a foreign country whose language they do not know, the search for accommodation, the prejudices and discrimination of the people, etc. This video game, created by UNHCR (The United Nations Refugee Agency), allows us to go through the experience of being an immigrant, and to understand why people must flee their home country as well as the tough conditions they are subjected to as a consequence. It is, in fact, a great tool to eliminate the dominant pejorative conceptions about immigrants.

This example is sufficient to show how video games that deal with appropriate subject matters can facilitate the integration of marginalized groups. However, the educational potentialities of video games do not end here; video games can be an integration tool in themselves and regardless of their content. Their ludic and interactive elements, together with their social component, promote associationism and group dynamics. As

it will be examined below, GAMESTAR(T) offered an opportunity to confirm that video games can go beyond the social, economic and gender conditions creating social bounds among children of different origins in a shared gaming context. In this sense, the usability of a video game cannot be measured through parameters such as the interface or the gameplay. Given their special characteristics, video games can be integrated into educational practice following other usability criteria that come directly from the educational context and methodology. In order to promote integration, video games should be used taking into account certain usability parameters:

- **Students' Socio-Cultural and Personal Context:** Students' socio-cultural context determines to a great extent their interests and their relationship to video games. From an educational point of view, the usability of certain video game should be assessed on basis of the students' gaming skills in order to select video games that fit them, be it the case of students that have not previously played video games, students with learning difficulties or with functional diversity. The specific characteristics of each student should also be taken into consideration—following the principle of attention to diversity—to select the most appropriate video games; those characteristics can be identified through interviews with the student, family, and social workers. There are video games specifically designed for people with functional diversity, however, it is inadvisable that only the students with functional diversity play this kind of games if an actual integration is to be achieved. Besides, commercial video games that are not specifically designed for people with functional diversity or learning difficulties can be adapted and used so that all students play collaboratively. On the other hand, their socio-cultural level can affect significantly the students' abilities, since the opportunity to play at home depends on the family's economic situation. GAMESTAR(T) incorporates a strategy aimed at promoting domestic usage of video games: loan of video games from the *gameteca*, arrangements with video game shops to offer discounts for the club's members and information about free online video games. Finally, the sociocultural situation has a strong influence on the preferred types of video games. Some video games may be shocking for people from certain social groups. Thus, usability should be also assessed with reference to the video game plot, characters and actions or tasks to be carried out. Teachers should take this into account and, whenever possible, introduce video games designed and developed in different cultures to show the existing diversity of video games beyond the most publicized and popular commercial ones.

- **Students' Ludic, Aesthetic, and Genre Preferences:** It is important that the selection of the video games that are going to be used in a concrete educational context matches the students' interests. Thus, it is possible to contribute to the bridging of the second digital divide, which makes students lose interest in the topics the educational practice deals with. Teachers should try to identify the students' preferences through direct observation, interviews, or questionnaires. In GAMESTAR(T), the assembly organization and free gaming help teachers detect these preferences so that more attractive and successful activities can be designed and arranged.

- **Contents:** Contents should be adapted to the kind of thinking that is going to be encouraged among students. Violent or sexist contents do not need to be necessarily excluded since video games with arguably inappropriate content can be used to draw the students' attention to certain aspects of everyday life and carry out a critical analysis of them. Video games with explicitly sexist content were purposefully selected to be used in GAMESTAR(T) workshop "Girls and Boys: Playing Together," in order to make students think critically about the sexist values that video games implicitly promote, so as they could draw conclusions for everyday life, where those values still persist, from the knowledge and reflection that emerged from gaming.

Since there are not clear parameters that show the difficulty or usability level of video games with respect to the different aforementioned aspects, it is important that, as a sort of preliminary examination, teachers themselves play the video games they wish to incorporate to educational practice to determine whether they would fit its objectives and needs. Likewise, teachers may detect other initially overlooked key issues through gaming together with the students, thus uncovering the advantages and disadvantages certain video games may entail.

THE GAMESTAR(T) EXPERIENCE

The GAMESTAR(T) project began in July 2010, thanks to Flavio Escribano (creator of the original idea of a video game club) and to the financial aid of Intermediae-Matadero. In the beginning, the club held a monthly meeting of the assembly in order to consensually determine the resources that would be purchased to build up the *Gameteca* (consoles, video games, peripherals, etc.)[2], its usage rules, and the general rules of the club. After several monthly meetings, the need for a more frequent activity was evident, so that in March 2011 the club began meeting weekly incorporating ludic activities suggested by the teachers but approved of by all the children. From the outset, the aim of this club was to explore, experiment, and learn using different types of games, turning its members into little researchers that enjoy the different ludic possibilities that exist in our society (emphasizing the potential of gaming as generator of discussion and reflection). The game club tried to stimulate associationism and a collaborative spirit among the club's children, as shown by the fact that they held periodical meetings in which an assembly was formed to discuss and elaborate the rules that regulated the club.

A number of different activities related to video games were organized within the club, including thematic courses. These thematic courses were intended to familiarize students with video games as a gateway to and a tool for formal education (history, arts, mathematics, etc.) and non-formal education (health, socialization, etc.). The courses are the following:

- **Health > Games for Health:** This course presented video games related to health care in a (in the traditional sense) out-of-school context and outside of the hospital, in order to understand the process of becoming ill, being treated, and recovering, acknowledging the importance of every agent involved in it (patient, health staff, family and friends, etc.).
- **Retro-Gaming > Retro Party:** Video games have a history of their own; this course was intended to study the origin of video games paying attention to different aspects, such as aesthetics, hardware power and the evolution and relevance of different gameplay forms. The aim is to discern the future of video games regarding their past and present.
- **Gender > Boys and Girls:** Are there really games specifically designed for boys and girls respectively? How is gender represented in games? This course had a double objective, on the one hand, to show that one can play any type of game independently of the player's gender and, on the other

hand, to try to uncover the discriminatory politics inherent in some video games and to propose solutions accordingly.
- **Little Big Planet > Creation of Levels:** The creation of levels is a very important part of some games. Many games have succeeded rather because of their capacity to provide the players with the possibility to construct their own stages than because of the game itself. This course aimed at stimulating the participants' creativity and generating a desire to modify and experiment with the tools provided by each game, transgressing their purportedly "normal," self-evident use.
- **History > Stories from History**: Video games are among the best educational resources for teaching history in a participative manner. They allow us to actually see Earth's evolution, humanity's most prominent technical and social achievements, and the most important political events that configure our present political geography. Video games have no rival as an interactive medium for teaching of history.
- **Scratch > Creating Your Own Video Games**: Using Scratch, a software tool for multimedia creation developed by the MIT and intended for children from 9 years of age, this course offered the possibility of creating little video games. The aim was to foster creativity, appreciate video games as a medium of creation, understand their language and develop the specific technical skills that are required to use them as a form of expression and representation.
- **Social Relationships within Online Video Games:** In accordance with the philosophy of Game Arenas or online multiplayer video games, we organize tournaments to show the students the need for creating some game rules and a scoring system beyond those incorporated by the games themselves.

The thematic courses mentioned above were held on a monthly basis within the weekly sessions of the club. These thematic courses, together with the meetings of the assembly (also monthly) and the club's activities (using the resources of the *Gameteca*), constituted the three pillars of the GAMESTAR(T) project. GAMESTAR(T) combined self-management of learning and associationism with formal and informal education focused on knowledge, competencies and skills. A ludic atmosphere dominated the sessions, which represented a source of motivation and a means to create cohesion as a group.

It is important to emphasize that the majority of the club's children belonged to a group of people at risk of social exclusion, a circumstance that demanded a special attention to the specific characteristics of each child, always applying the principles of attention to diversity and integration. The methodology that guides the club's activities incorporates all these aspects.

Methodology: Pedagogical Principles

The methodology designed for GAMESTAR(T) is part of a mixed process between ludology and pedagogy which consists of stimulus, action, reflection and feedback, within a scheme that belongs to the world of video games.

- **Stimulus:** An appealing program due to its activities and its content.
- **Action:** Truly participative activities which demand interaction with the audience in order to work properly; an appropriation of the video game language facilitates action.
- **Reflection:** Stimulation of critical and creative thinking through reflection and discussion about all the information and every activity as well as through other activities like the modification of the available video games.

- **Feedback:** Creation of an archive that serves as a physical and virtual document repository that is continually updated and is available for further *a posteriori* analysis and as an information resource for future research.

The project approach is fundamentally based on meaningful learning through video gaming. In our society, video games belong to everyday life, and, as a result, they have been incorporated in the way children and adults confront and conceive the world, to the point that they even codify our understanding of the world. Using video games as a learning tool implies stimulating the process of knowledge acquisition and involving its agents directly in it.

The goal of the project methodology is to foster critical thinking and the analytical skills of the participants so as they can extrapolate them to the world of video games and to the entirety of their experiences. Therewith it is also intended to raise their awareness as responsible and critical video game consumers and as potential professional or amateur video game developers in future as well. For this purpose, workshops are arranged where collaborative and active learning has fundamental importance so that the order and progress of events is guided by the interests, concerns and needs of the participants.

The pedagogical models that GAMESTAR(T) is based on the principles explained in the following section.

"Existentialist" Pedagogical Model

As noted in the section focused on the project's background, GAMESTAR(T) follows a methodology based on the existentialist pedagogical model. In opposition to the traditional educational model where the acquisition and reproduction of knowledge alone were considered the ultimate objective of education, that model does not put knowledge at the heart of education, but the students and the development of their individual character-istics. Such principle requires that teachers take into account each person's cognitive structures, experiential framework, interests, abilities, flair and attitudes, on the one hand, and the diversity inherent in the groups the project has worked with (children at risk of social exclusion that attend a day care center run by the Red Cross), on the other. The origin of this diversity lies in multiple factors such as economic, socio-cultural, geographic, ethnic, and religious factors, just as in the children's different intellectual, psychic, or sensory capacities. Thus, the central role assigned to students in education implies a transformation and an adaptation of the educational environment to them, and not the other way around.

In this type of pedagogy, the teacher function is closely related to the principle of pedagogical self-management, a key feature in the methodolo-gies applied in *Summerhill* by A.S. Neill (2004), in Freinet's (1970) techniques, or in the pedagogi-cal rationalism of Ferrer and Guardia (2009). All these tendencies concur that the teacher should be assigned the function of a mediator or facilitator of learning.

Pedagogical Principle of Anti-Authoritarianism

The principle of anti-authoritarianism constitutes an inseparable part of the education of responsible and free subjects. Those individuals condemned to submission are irresponsible individuals, insofar as they delegate all responsibility on their tutor, that is, the person who dictates and rules they must comply to, and the patterns of behavior they are expected to display. The political trends that have embraced anti-authoritarianism are manifold, from the bourgeois progressivism of *Summerhill*[3] (Neill, 1994, 2004) to the anarchist libertarianism of *Pai-deia*[4] (Luengo, 1990). The key question is how to introduce this system of free self-discipline within the classroom. However, posing this question implies a critical and anti-authoritarian reflection

and the establishment of an educational system open to change. The management of discipline is a highly controversial issue in current pedagogical debates; the authors of this chapter consider that further research on this issue is of fundamental importance for the future of educational practice.

Principle of Pedagogical Self-Management

The principle of pedagogical self-management is developed within the framework of libertarian pedagogy through the self-regulation of learning on the part of the students. This methodology favours an education focused on individual respon-sibility and personal effort and merit. Accounting for these implications, Silvio Gallo (1997) has pointed that another kind of learning is at stake when it comes to pedagogical self-management, namely the socio-political learning of social self-management.

Principle of Context-Based Usability

The principle of usability that the GAMESTAR(T) has followed and applied is based on the idea that any video game is suitable for educational utilization provided that the contents, gameplay, etc. are adapted to the students' socio-cultural context, their ludic preferences and to the kind of thinking that is to be developed. According to this principle, the targeted context, where video games are to be introduced, takes precedence over the technical characteristics of video games themselves. Consequently, assessment of video game usability depends on and varies with the different educational needs. The criteria that guide the selection of video games according to their context-based usability should focus on the pedagogical principles that underlie educational practice, on the students' particular characteris-tics and on the educational context where that practice takes place. Anyway, context-based us-ability should be guided by the aforementioned pedagogical principles for they are a fundamental part of the educational context in which the ludic activity develops.

Although the development of the GAMESTAR(T) project followed the methodology taking always into account these pedagogical principles, the practical application of any theory always gives rise to problems and needs that were not anticipated in the beginning. This was the case of GAMESTAR(T): it was necessary to highlight certain aspects of the methodology, modify some concrete practices that aimed at certain objectives and develop a reflection on unforeseen issues that turned up to be of great relevance in the course of the club's activities. The following section offers an in-depth analysis of these problems, presents the reflections of the GAMESTAR(T) coordinators about them, and reports the measures or strategies adopted in search for satisfactory solutions.

GAMESTAR(T) CHALLENGES

Rethinking the principles that guided the project proved to be necessary due to some difficulties that were encountered throughout its development (both in the workshops and the club's sessions). This led to define more precise the pedagogical and procedural methodology.

One of the most pressing issues, which needed to be dealt with most urgently, was the adaptation of the project to the particular characteristics of the students the project worked with. In the beginning, one of the basic objectives of the GAMESTAR(T) project was to approach video games to the students in an unaccustomed way, presenting them not only as playful tools, but also as cultural products. However, since the group was composed mostly of teenagers at risk of exclusion, the attention to diversity became the core of the pedagogical program. The affective and emotional needs of the group members could not be put aside in favor of the acquisition of certain theoretical knowledge through video games, as it was planned

for the workshops (history, health, history of video games, etc.). The learning methodology should be explicitly oriented to the integration and the improvement of the group's self-esteem. In this sense, video games turned out to be a highly efficient tool with a great number of possibilities that should be carefully analyzed in order to be put into practice optimally.

It is important to emphasize that, in spite of the intrinsic advantages video games entail for this issue, an effort to unite the (theoretical and practical) pedagogical perspectives with the possibilities this medium offers remains absolutely fundamental. Just as what happened after the introduction of technology into the classroom, the second digital divide could deepen if teachers do not take into account the students' situation, previous knowledge, needs and preferences, and two other elements that often neglected, namely what students consider their actual problems are, and what teachers want to encourage in them (in this case of GAMESTAR(T), an improvement in their quality of life as for self-esteem and integration, and an approach to video games from a cultural perspective). One of the most difficult tasks faced by the people involved teaching practice is to develop a general, comprehensive methodological perspective that three challenges: firstly, how to put into practice the theoretical principles of a libertarian pedagogy; secondly, how to integrate video games in that pedagogical theory (which was developed in a context other than ours where the relationship between technology and education was not an issue of concern); and finally, how to put into practice a libertarian pedagogy that integrates video games. Therefore, it is necessary to take advantage of the experiences of other groups and projects, and of the creativity and innovation displayed in the development of one's own practice too.

Hereafter it will be offered a define the problems and controversies we came across and, in the next section, we discuss the solutions we considered most appropriate for our project, solutions that are always guided by the principles of creativity, reflection and incorporation of other existing (theoretical and practical) sources. The different problems can be divided into three main groups: second digital divide and critical digital literacy, personal development and coordination, and management of the project.

Second Digital Divide and Critical Digital Literacy

As shown above, the introduction of video games into the educational environment, even as a key tool, can never be enough to bridge the second digital divide. Students are perfectly able to recognize those video games specifically designed for education (serious games) and the utilization of video games not created as such for educational purposes. Thus, they are reluctant to participate in activities like workshops where video games are used with evident educational objectives, even in those where they are encouraged to play the games they like and usually play themselves. Students always choose and search for the ludic element and prefer free gaming to guided gaming. Undoubtedly, this is a factor education professionals should take into account and learn to take advantage of.

It must be noted that the ludic element inherent in video games offers a great advantage in order to facilitate the teaching and learning process, which consists in reducing the stress and anxiety level the students experiment when they are expected to acquire new knowledge and skills. However, this is not all; in many cases, students, especially if in risk of social exclusion like the project worked with, suffer a high level of stress and anxiety related to the learning process, probably due to an unstable and unsatisfactory school situation, which leads to an immediate rejection of any attempt on our part to provide them with new knowledge. In the case of GAMESTAR(T), students attend a video games club with the preformed expectation of amusing themselves: the club is a place for having fun and

not a place for taking "classes" or acquiring new knowledge, for they associate this to a pressing and stressful context. The educational strategies to be adopted must adapt to this circumstance and benefit from it as much as possible.

During the workshop sessions, it was evident that students initially were reluctant to participate in the activities: they declared explicitly that they had no interest in the workshop and that they preferred playing freely; some of them engaged in other activities like talking to people that did not belong to the club or playing other games that were available at the venue where the workshop took place (table tennis, computer video games, etc.). Nevertheless, the majority of the students eventually participated and enjoyed the workshop sessions. It was in those moments when the second digital divide was most evident, but also their specific personal situation, their fears and hopes with respect to education and the acquisition of knowledge. Bridging the second digital divide was one of the main objectives and challenges of the GAMESTAR(T) project. If the project had not succeeded in closing this gap, then the critical digital literacy would have turned out to be an arduous, almost impossible task to carry out, since it would have been impossible to reach out to the students to make them think about their own gaming, promoting critical gaming, group reflection, and discussion. However, it was possible to take advantage of this situation by means of rethinking and redefining the methodology. In the next section, the strategies applied and the advances made in this area will be examined.

Students' Personal Development: Self-Esteem, Motivation, and Integration

The greatest challenge for the project emerged only when it had already started, that being the reason why the project's design had not included objectives and methodological strategies that referred to it. This challenge was brought about by the students that eventually made up the club. Most of them were going through difficult personal situations: they came from broken families, some among them had especial psychological traits (highly giftedness as well as retardation) or experienced academic failure. In this context, attention to diversity played an essential role in the development of the methodology and the formulation of the club's objectives.

The people in charge of the project found themselves in need of defining clearly and precisely the actual problems and challenges faced when working with students at risk of social exclusion in order to tackle them properly and overcome the difficulties. The trial and error method is not a good choice in education since something extremely valuable is at stake, namely the students themselves. It is advisable to adopt cautious strategies, studying and evaluating the possibilities essayed by other pedagogical projects that have encountered the same situation.

The pedagogical principles that guide Paideia school, the methodology and strategies used in relation to concrete problems (such as those reported by Josefa Martín Luengo, 1990), served as a source of inspiration and helped determine the adopted measures. It was possible to adapt them to GAMESTAR(T) own context with the aim of improving the educational conditions and the personal development of the club's children. Next section offers an analysis of the strategies utilized and the solutions found. The following points describe the found problems and their specific features:

- **Aggressiveness:** Some children of the group attempted to dominate the others assuming the role of the "leader" or the "bully." They behaved aggressively towards their peers and the teachers, sometimes even violently, using expressions and assuming attitudes that were offensive towards the others. While free gaming they took the console controllers off

other students; they chose in the first place the games they wanted, regardless of their partners' interests; they even assaulted physically or verbally (yet without causing tough fights). They adopted a defiant attitude towards the teachers, refusing to participate in the workshops or to adapt to the normal functioning of the club, though they eventually did.

- **Competitiveness:** Together with aggressiveness, competitiveness was one of the most compelling and difficult challenges. Most of the students behaved competitively while gaming and in the workshops: they needed to stand out of the rest by means of winning, and when they did not manage to do so, they got angry and acted violently. This element of competition was fostered in one of the workshops offering video games as prizes for the winners of a little "tournament": the rest of the students refused to acknowledge the victory of the winning group and started to act aggressively, insulting and defying them, shouting and fighting. In consequence of this workshop, it was considered to implement strategies that mitigated the harmful competitiveness: the club, its atmosphere, and dynamics would have been seriously damaged unless urgent measures had been adopted. Offering prizes intensified a counterproductive competitiveness; besides it made the students feel that the club's resources did not belong to them as club members, but they could win and own them privately through tournaments, a circumstance that undermined the feeling of belonging and responsibility.

- **Gender Segregation:** In the beginning, there were only two girls among the club's members; although the number of girls increased as the course advanced, these girls attended the club only sporadically. Boys asserted and enforced a strong masculine territoriality so that gender segregation was evident in the personal relationships as well as in the activities they carried out and the games they chose. This is one of the biggest problems that were faced, which was alleviated braking up gender segregation in many aspects.

- **Motivation:** The students were highly motivated and willing to attend the club's sessions and they remained so along the course. The children manifested openly their wish to participate in the club's sessions; they were happy and enthusiastic and wished that sessions never finish. When the club increased the frequency of its meetings, changing from a monthly session to a weekly session, all the students were receptive and happy about this decision. The only motivation problems were those related to participation in the workshops, which, as shown above, were probably caused by the second digital divide as well as by the students' personal characteristics and attitude towards education.

Coordination and Management of the Project

In reference to the students, we noted some problems that were an obstacle to the development of the club. These problems derive to a great extent from the lack of feeling of belonging to the club that became manifest in a lack of responsibility for its elements. The system of video game loan must be redesigned several times due to a deficient commitment and responsibility on the part of the students. They forgot the games at home or they simply did not return them; they did not report accurately the games that were on loan, to whom, etc. The "king" or the "queen of the game" (the representative of each group in charge of controlling the borrowing) did not fulfill their function efficiently and video games were constantly disappearing. The library lost a

great number of games; this situation jeopardized the workshops, which could not function without games, and was detrimental to free gaming both at the club and at home through the video game loan. However, this lack of responsibility in the management of the club's resources did not imply a lack of conservation of the infrastructure: the video consoles, controllers, and video games were not physically damaged and neither were other peripherals, nor the building where all the meetings were held.

In reference to the teachers and the people in charge of the management and organization of the club, there were few coordination problems and they were easily solved.

Video Game Selection According to Context-Based Usability

Video game selection is one of the most crucial decisions to be taken when implementing a model of pedagogical innovation through video games, such as GAMESTAR(T). This process of selection may be arduous, partly because to scan the range of existing video games is a laborious task, partly due to the fact that it is difficult to find video games with the required characteristics that fit the targeted educational context. However, once they have been found, its implementation in the educational planning is rather easy: one only has to use video games in the habitual or expected way to obtain good results. Video game selection according to context-based usability demands the adaptation of any video game to the educational context, regardless whether they are serious games or commercial video games (fighting video games, racing video games or shooters), being the latter more difficult implement.

In the case of GAMESTAR(T), this posed a challenge from the beginning, since it was not known which people would integrate the club and, therefore, what their socio-cultural situation, needs and preferences would be. In order to cope with the question of personal preferences and tastes, the children were brought to a specialized shop so that they could participate in the purchase of the resources that would compose the gameteca choosing the consoles and video games they liked most. The shop assistant offered the children a guided tour explaining the differences between video game platforms (Play Station 2 and 3, Play Station Portable, Nintendo Wii, Nintendo DS, Xbox 360, etc.) and the content and game-play of many video games. Thus, it seemed that the challenge of video game selection had been overcome. Two unforeseen problems appeared though, namely the adaptation of video games to the duration of the club's sessions and to the students' socio-cultural context:

- **Time Management:** Many video games demanded prolonged gaming to achieve their own objectives (solve puzzles, clear levels, follow a story, etc.). The problem posed by this circumstance is that the students were interested in that kind of video games only if they could play one single video game during a whole session or even during the whole course. For instance, the completion of the objectives of *Zelda: Twilight Princess* (one of the selected video games) requires more than 20 hours of gaming and, besides, if the gaming sessions happen on widely separate occasions, players may lose the thread of the story and their interest in the game. This was also the case of *Animal Crossing: City Folk, The Longest Journey, Prince of Persia: The Sands of Time,* among many others. As a consequence, it had to be examined how such video games could be used in the development of the project.
- **Socio-Cultural Context:** The panorama of the current video game industry, whose titles come mainly from the American or Japanese market, does not represent the cultural environment of the club's members, who belong mostly to the Latin American

or African culture. This issue had to be considered when assessing video game context-based usability. Video games such as *Sing it*, for Play Station 2, were highly popular with the students, who choose to play it in the free gaming sessions, but it did not match their socio-cultural context because all its song's lyrics were in written in a language they did not know (English) and the characters dressing style had nothing to do with theirs. In spite of this, video games with a gameplay similar to that of *Sing it* are specially appropriate to foster the musical, reading and social competencies. On the other hand, they can contribute significantly to integration in that the students play together collaboratively as a group. From the teachers' point of view, the challenge was to take advantage of this type of games adapting them to the students' socio-cultural context.

Owing to the complexity video games' context-based usability can entail, a detailed guide will be offered in the section "Guidelines to selection and introduction of video games in educational environments."

These are the most important challenges that arose in the course of the GAMESTAR(T) project, which needed to be met adapting the methodology and objectives correspondingly, as has been shown in this chapter.

With respect to the relationships, the children established with video games, the way they used them during the free gaming time and the workshops made evident the importance of bridging the new digital divide as a precondition for the advance towards a critical digital literacy. It is essential to understand that the introduction of technologies into the classroom is not a sufficient condition for the critical digital literacy, just as it is not for the motivation and encouragement of the students: it may occasionally be counterproductive unless it is accompanied by a specific pedagogical plan.

The next section is devoted to the presentation and discussion of the different educational strategies adopted in GAMESTAR(T) to cope with its particular challenges.

PEDAGOGICAL STRATEGIES AND SOLUTIONS

The organization through an assembly and the model of pedagogical self-management were two of the mainstays of the project, which were indispensable for its existence and continuity. Consistently with these principles, all strategies, action plans, and concrete measures were put up for discussion and approval both by the coordination team and the students' assembly. Now the principles that governed the assembly will be examined, as well as the way the assembly organized itself and the problems and controversies that emerged in the process of putting in practice these ideas.

The Assembly Model: Pedagogical Foundations

The assembly model has its roots in the libertarian movements that have explored, experimented, and defended its advantages over other models of social organization. In the case of GAMESTAR(T), the focus is on two of the assembly models in the pedagogical practice that have made a greater impact and have become references for the application of this mode of organization in the field of education: *Summerhill* School (UK) and *Paideia* School (Spain). Both schools are guided by the principle of self-management that is realized through decision-making in an assembly. Despite the fact that their respective ideological orientations are quite different, being *Summerhill* a less *politicized* school than *Paideia*, which defines itself explicitly as an anarchist school, the way decisions are taken in both of them is the same: all people that belong to the school gather and sit down to discuss those issues that are of relevance to its functioning (from the curriculum to the organization or the rules), all members are listened equally, their voice has the same effect and each opinion or vote has the same value, independently of the person's age or position in the school. Thus, for example, in *Summerhill* the vote of a seven-year old girl had the same value as that of A. S. Neill himself (founder and director of the school).

The commitment to the assembly consists in accepting everybody's freedom to express their opinions and to comply with the decisions made by the whole group. In *Summerhill* or in *Paideia*, freedom is encouraged, but, above all, the responsibility that freedom entails. This principle governs the assembly and it is the source of the pedagogical self-management. GAMESTAR(T) followed this form of organization and recognized its pedagogical advantages, but also its social and political convenience.

In the first place, the assembly serves as a meeting point and as an event that gives rise to a feeling of belonging to the community, as a space for freedom within it and responsibility for it. Such an organization contributes to the solution of the motivation, integration, and responsibility problems that might emerge within educational communities. Listening to children expressing their wishes, concerns, and suggestions is a fundamental step that must be taken if the educational experience is to be improved. The assembly *must not* be regarded as a "support group" that helps individuals express their feelings, but as a place for decision-making whose strength must be taken seriously, considering the repercussions it may have for the different pedagogical projects that assume it. Children are considered as agents of their own learning process, as free subjects that are capable of taking personal and collective decisions; decisions that must be taken into account and compulsorily and inevitably realized in practice. Important decisions for the development of the pedagogical project, in the case of GAMESTART(T) a video game club, are taken in the assembly and these can modify or even overturn other decisions taken previously by the people that devised the project. Only assuming the force of this principle can a model of pedagogical self-management be achieved that is fully efficient and produces the expected benefits: development of individual freedom and responsibility towards the group, optimal development of the competencies (knowledge as well as skills) and stimulation of the critical spirit.

The assembly cannot be managed in an authoritarian manner; therefore, anti-authoritarianism must remain a key principle. The anti-authoritarian principle is inextricably linked to an education focused on freedom and responsibility. These two concepts make up the fundamental basis of the shared vocabulary of libertarian schools like Paideia. The education of free, engaged citizens presupposes an education focused on individual and social autonomy, and responsibility. Those individuals relegated to a submissive status are irresponsible individuals, since they delegate their responsibilities to their tutors, i.e. those that prescribe the rules they must comply with and, thus, determine the way they are expected to behave. If a critical spirit and personal freedom are to be fostered, that principle should always be present in educational practice and be so experienced by teachers and students.

The advantages of this model of organization can be summarized pointing out that the assembly:

- It is a meeting point and as a common event for all those involved in the teaching and learning process; it is especially appropriate to give rise to a feeling of belonging to the community, of freedom within it and of responsibility for it.
- It constitutes a medium or a channel where information about the group's interests, wishes, and suggestions can be shared, improving communication, mutual respect, and a joint search for solutions.

- It helps develop critical thinking in that it opens the possibility to question and actually transform the foundations and organization of the group, the concrete didactic applications (activities, workshops, classes...), and the time and learning management.

Taking into account the pedagogical advantages offered by the assembly, this model was adopted aiming at solving some of GAMESTAR(T) problems, such as:

- **Lack of Responsibility:** The assembly served the purpose of fostering a feeling of belonging to the club; decisions have been respected and put into practice as far as possible. The system of video game loan and the lack of responsibility for the games was debated several times in the assembly, so that the children drew diverse conclusions and decided to apply different strategies. In this way, the children developed a greater sense of responsibility, which resulted in a greater commitment to, and a greater success of the system of game loan.
- **Motivation:** As shown above in this chapter, the introduction of video games into the teaching practice does not imply an intrinsic source of motivation for involvement in the teaching-learning process. The assembly was instrumental in overcoming some deficiencies, concretely, it was the scenario for the expression of the wish for transformation that the club's members openly manifested, which, in turn, gave the teachers clues about how to direct their practice: fostering the ludic element, team working, self-managing the time and resources...

These are some of the key points that helped understand how to reorient the pedagogical strategies and how to introduce video games into education satisfactorily.

- **Second Digital Divide:** Considering the special situation of the project, this problem appears to be intrinsically connected to that of motivation. Through the meetings of the assembly, it was possible to understand to a great extent what elements of our pedagogical plan were failing and what deficiencies were affecting the introduction of video games into the educational practice. Listening to the children's opinions and suggestions was essential in this respect; observing how they play with video games, what they prefer to do, what they expect from them, etc., is indispensable in order to improve the educational experience adapting the study plan and the concrete activities to the students' interests and preferences. This aspect is crucial to bridge the second digital divide. The assembly model, together with the self-management of learning, opens new and vast possibilities of success.

- **Competitiveness, Aggressiveness, and Self-Esteem:** The feeling of belonging to, and responsibility for the club generated in the course of the meetings (together with other measures) greatly reduced hostility, competitiveness, and aggressiveness. Children felt that all decisions taken were theirs, so they were increasingly keen to participate in the club, not as passive members that only attended to play at a video game club, but as active, committed members that regarded themselves as the makers of the club and those responsible for its correct functioning.

- **Gender Segregation:** This problem can be easily solved in an assembly system where each opinion and vote is equally respected, regardless of sex, social class, or ethnic group. In such a context, students learn to value people for themselves, to listen and respect them equally.

Organization of the Assembly

The organization of the assembly was based on dialogue and discussion conducted by two people in charge of the moderation, being these positions subjected to rotation between meetings of the assembly. The entire club's members, teachers, coordinating staff, and children had the same opportunities to express their opinions, suggestions, or reflections; and decisions were taken in a horizontal, non-hierarchical manner, so that every vote was of equal value, be it of an adult or of a child.

The meetings of the assembly gradually became a key part of the club's development; their frequency was changed from once a month to twice a week, one at the beginning and the other at the end of each weekly session.

Except on very few occasions, the meetings did not last more than half an hour. They followed this order:

- Election of two assembly moderators in charge of taking note of the turns to speak, and of reporting each person's contribution. Sometimes a ballot took place for choosing the moderators, while on other occasions they were simply two volunteers.

- Proposal of an order of the day, respecting certain points that structured the organization and guaranteed its continuity. If someone wanted to make a suggestion outside of the order of the day, it had to be proposed as another point to be dealt with.

- Treatment of the order of the day points strictly respecting the turns to speak, which were requested raising hands, while everybody listen, etc. If necessary, a ballot could be taken.

- In the end-of-session meeting, several points were regularly treated, like the problems that may have emerged along the session, the positive aspects, and the activities for the next session.

Practice of the Assembly Model: Problems and Controversies

Among the biggest problems faced when it came to put into practice an assembly model of organization, was the total immersion of the children and the teachers in a hierarchical and too often authoritarian education and social system. This is by no means a specific problem of GAMESTAR(T), but of every initiative that seeks to implement a self-managed, assembly model. In the first place, our socially structured tendency to organize the teaching-learning relationships hierarchically should be eliminated in favor of the development of a self-managed, horizontal organization that requires the assumption, on the part of the teachers, that they are not more important than the students. Teachers' voice should be put on a level with that of the students. Moreover, teachers should make students understand and assume that they are their equals. In GAMESTAR(T), a continuous process of shared learning took place: teachers and students learned to listen to one another and developed a mutual understanding and respect that contributed to the fact that each person respected herself too. Reinforcing the self-esteem and the awareness of being an equally valuable individual as any other partners was one of the main achievements of the club, even though it is a never ending task that is always be in development.

Examining the core of the practice, it can be seen how this general problem derived in other more concrete and specific problems: the lack of respect towards those that intervened before the assembly, and of motivation to participate in the debates, the lack of order when rising to speak or the scarce active participation. The absence of participation traces back to the fact that the students of the Spanish education system are hardly ever questioned about their interests, nor encouraged to take decisions about their own activities or the way to organize the class and the school. Only patience and, above all, a rigorous application of the decisions made by the assembly could result in a gradual improvement of participation.

GAMESTAR(T) project is still young, but experience, always connected to reflection, may help improve and make the teaching and coordination team, as well as the children, aware of our principles and how to put them into practice.

Organization through assembly and self-management were not the only elements that were introduced as pedagogical strategies to solve the club's problems. Issues such as aggressiveness, self-esteem, and competitiveness required other specific measures:

- **Team Work:** It helped promoting responsibility among the club's members, and reducing the level of aggressiveness. The groups were not permanent and each member assumed different roles in different moments. The elder helped look after the younger, they collaborated to overcome challenges thinking together and some even taught others tricks and cheats for their favourite video games.

- **Elimination of Meritocracy:** A measure proposed in the debates of the coordination team and in the meetings of the assembly that, together with the teamwork, was aimed at solving the problem of competitiveness. While in the beginning prizes and awards were offered to those individuals who deserved them on grounds of their personal merits, these were replaced with awards for the club *as a whole*: the prizes depended on the good functioning of the club and they were to be enjoyed by all members. Any system that fosters meritocracy was thus eliminated, replacing the individualistic egotism with a feeling of belonging to a group, where every person is an important part. This measure was very successful in establishing the club itself as a source of motivation and not exclusively its objects (video games), and it also generated a greater sense of responsibility and better integration.

- **Time Management:** Video games that require prolonged and continued gaming (e.g., *Animal Crossing: Folk City* and *Zelda: Twilight Princess*) were reserved for loan, or for special occasions in which they were taken as elements of analysis of their characters and aesthetic values. In the workshop "Girls and Boys: playing together," *Animal Crossing: Folk City* was used as an example of video game that the industry considers "for girls only" with the aim of making students reflect on video games and gender prejudices.

These were the measures adopted by GAMESTAR(T) for the improvement of the educational experience using video games. As we can see, not all problems derive from the utilization of technology and video games in the educational practice, and, in the same way, the essayed solutions are not only intended for the technological sphere. The authors firmly believe that the introduction of video games, or any other pedagogical resource, whether technological or not, must be accompanied by a critical, theoretical reflection, and by an adaptation of the didactic planning to these new tools. It is no longer possible to think that students will be immediately motivated by mathematics, history or language classes where video games are used: our students demand more freedom, a way to exercise and develop their creativity (for instance, a girl demanded at GAMESTAR(T) video games about "art"). The introduction of video games into the classroom should take into account these factors and react correspondingly.

CONTEXT-BASED USABILITY: TWO EXAMPLES OF CONCRETE METHODOLOGICAL APPLICATION

This text makes use of a specific concept of usability, i.e., context-based usability that refers to the adaptation of video games to a certain educational context, rather than to the selection of video games already designed to adapt to that context. In order to offer a brief introduction to the selection of video games according to this concept of usability, two practical examples of the GAMESTAR(T) experience will be presented. The first refers to the practical development of a workshop; the second refers to the program planning for a series of club's sessions, which was carried out in assembly meetings in collaboration with people of great cultural influence on the club's members: "The Big Bang Case."

Student Usability in a Workshop

All the measures mentioned above began to be consistently applied in the context of the workshop "Girls and Boys: Playing Together." This workshop was paradigmatic with respect to the implementation of the methodology described in previous sections; the maturity of this methodology was reflected in its success.

Along the development of the previous workshop, it could be confirmed that the problems already detected in the functioning of the club were not only reappearing, but also being reinforced due to a bad pedagogical management. Competitiveness, aggressiveness, and gender segregation were present in this workshop, so that it was evident that a new pedagogical approach was urgently needed. As a result of this workshop, GAMESTAR(T) coordinators initiated a shared reflection—supported by the research on the spectrum of possible pedagogical methodologies that are backed up by an undisputed success—that led to an improvement of the GAMESTAR(T) experience.

The workshop "Girls and Boys: Playing Together" will be now presented with the aim of offering a case study that illustrates the methodology and the dynamic of GAMESTAR(T). As explained above, the methodology is based on:

- Assembly meetings at the beginning and at the end of each session.

- Self-managed teamwork.
- Elimination of meritocracy and aggressive competitiveness.
- Selection and introduction of video games according to context-based usability.

Now it will be examined how the workshop was managed and how the methodology was implemented.

This workshop was the first to incorporate an assembly at the beginning of each session. As it was the first assembly, it was decided that two adults would act as moderators so as it could serve as a model for the younger of how the moderation task is supposed to be carried out: take note of the turns to speak, read the order of the day, take minutes, etc.

The order of the day of that session is shown in Figure 1.

During the meeting of the assembly, it was explained what the workshop would consist in and how it would work. Once this was perfectly clear, children began to play. In this workshop girls and boys had to find out the meaning of certain colored labels that had been attached to the video game covers they were playing. For that purpose, they had to play together those video games, discuss, and draw conclusions. Then they had to write down their guesses on a blackboard inside of one the four boxes (blue, red, green, and yellow) that had been drawn on it, and that corresponded to the classification of all the games available, which were: *Tekken 5, Animal Crossing: Folk City, Tomb Rider Legend, Monkey Island 1* and *2, Maniac Mansion, Maniac Mansion: Day of Tentacle, Alice in Wonderland, Worms: Armageddon, The Sims, Mario Kart, Extreme Challenge, Age of Empires 2*, and *Super Mario Bros.* These video games were selected according to the following criteria:

- **Students' Preferences:** Most video games had been selected by the students to integrate the gameteca, so they matched their preferences.

- **Gender Stereotypes:** Video games that represented and perpetuated gender stereotypes were selected to be critically analysed, although strongly sexist video games were avoided (it was decided to exclude these games in order neither to support the companies that produce them nor to let those games be incorporated to the gameteca).

- **Personal Experience of the Teachers:** It is extremely important that teachers themselves play and analyse the games prior to their selection; in the case of this workshop, the teachers in charge of it already had previously played all video games used. Besides, both of them had conducted research on video games and gender, the former through interviews with players (Cabañes, 2009), and the latter through an analysis of the gender features of 25 video games and 50 characters (Rubio, 2011).

The workshop's playful atmosphere was essential for both the formation of groups and its development. The group formation was carried out through a little game: the children picked a card from a hat. The cards contained the name of a well-known video game character (Mario, Sonic, Lara Croft, etc.). Those with the same card joined and formed a group. After that, each group began to play a different video game, though the children eventually mingled and started writing their reflections individually on the blackboard. At the end of the game, a little meeting took place, where several children were selected to present to the assembly the conclusions of their group.

The role of the workshop's coordinator (Eurídice Cabañes) and that of the rest of teachers consisted in accompanying the students while they played, trying to make them think through dialogue, concretely through a series of questions that had been previously prepared: "Why have you chosen that character?," "Do you never choose girls? Why?," "What is happening in the game?," "Do you think all characters wear the

Figure 1. Order of the day

Today we do...

Workshop "Girls and Boys: Playing together" with Euridice

- Explanation of the workshop
- We meet in groups
- We play together
- We draw conclusions

Assembly

Today moderate: **Maria and Flavio**

Order of the day

- **Workshop's evaluation**
- Club's functioning evaluation
- Next activities: **The youngest are coming!**
- Contributions and suggestions

appropriate gear for the activity they have to perform (fighting, racing, exploring, etc.)?" Other strategy consisted just in playing. For instance, while playing *Tekken 5*, boys claimed that it was impossible to win selecting female characters for they were weaker; the teacher only had to grab the controller, select a female character, and achieve overwhelming victories, to show the students that theirs was an unfounded claim whose base was solely a gender stereotype. Such a simple but practical demonstration could produce more immediate and intense reflection that one carried out only through dialogue.

They were able to draw many conclusions, individually, in groups and in the final discussions:

- **Blue:** Video games whose main character is a man. They noted that most video games do not have a female main character. These video games were: *Monkey Island 1* and *2* and *Super Mario Bros.*
- **Red:** Video games whose main character is a woman. They remarked that these games are equally fun as the blue ones and pointed out that boys also play them. These video games were: *Tomb Rider Legend* and *Alice in Wonderland.*
- **Green:** Video games that allowed choosing your character. They noted that you can also choose a girl, but they are far less numerous and always wear provocative

clothes. These video games were: *Mario Kart, Tekken 5,* and *Maniac Mansion.*

- **Yellow:** Video games that the industry labels as intended for boys or girls. Fortunately, nobody discovered the meaning of this label. These video games were: *Animal Crossing: Folk City, Worms: Armageddon, The Sims,* and *Age of Empires 2.*

- That the video game *Maniac Mansion: Day of Tentacle* had no color assigned because there are girls and boys among its main characters, and at least these do not incarnate gender stereotypes.

In the final meeting, these conclusions were discussed, and a joint evaluation was carried out, which confirmed that the workshops objectives had been achieved. These objectives were:

- Be able to perceive video games as biased cultural products and as language that conveys certain discourses; be able to understand and think critically about these discourses.

- Assume the gender perspective about video games and inquire about the values and models they offer, about the reasons for their highlighting some aspects of reality leaving others aside, and about the process that leads people to prefer certain video games over others.

- Realize that one can play and enjoy video games of any genre regardless of the industry or of our sexist society dictates.

- Analyze the representation of male and female identity in video games and detect gender stereotypes; think critically and creatively about possible alternative models of masculinity and feminity in video games.

In order to assess the workshop's functioning and the efficacy of the methodology, the teachers held a meeting where each part of the methodology was discussed: assembly organization, self-managed team work, elimination of meritocracy and aggressive competitiveness, and video game selection according to context-based usability. This evaluation was carried out through direct observation and discussion, without following a fixed questionnaire. The group reached the following conclusion:

The introduction of the assembly meeting at the beginning of the workshop gave the children the possibility to understand the activities to be performed. This was confirmed by direct observation of the fact that children were able to display an orderly pattern of action without asking the adults; there were no more disoriented children that did not know what to do. On the other hand, the students' interventions during the assembly meetings and their obvious high motivation level along the development of the workshop showed that the introduction of the assembly organization was successful: it made them feel more confident.

The formation of groups and the final open discussion helped avoid harmful competition among the children: the objective and the reward of the workshop were to uncover the enigma of the video games colors, an aim that was best attained collaborating with others. Each individual action had an impact on the common objective, thus reinforcing the children's self-esteem and companionship. This was evaluated through direct observation and discussion of the observed facts: aggressiveness and conflict reduction, cooperation between different members of the group, respect of gaming turns, orderly interventions before the assembly, etc.

Video game selection according to context-based usability was assessed through direct observation of the gaming process: it developed without mayor frictions and the students got actively involved in it.

It can be concluded that, owing to the methodological change, the great benefits brought about by the introduction of the assembly model in each session combined with the pedagogical model that uses video games as an educational tool could started to be noticed. The element of social integration of the former combined with the ludic element of the latter, produced a wide scope of action that rapidly evidenced its advantages over other more traditional pedagogical models, such as the authoritarian models based on lectures. In the workshop "Girls and Boys: Playing Together," the participants acquired the knowledge they were expected to learn in a relaxed atmosphere, playing video games among those selected by the workshop's designer; this diminished the level of anxiety and provided them with other emotional and social rewards, like integration, self-esteem, and responsibility.

The Big Bang Case

The Big Bang case can serve as a clarifying illustration of how the club's planning could be adapted to the students' context through video game and resource selection according to context-based usability. As mentioned above, the video games that dominate the market nowadays come from the American and Japanese industries and, as such, they implicitly incorporate a cultural background and express certain values that do not necessarily correspond to the (mostly Latin American and African) ideological and cultural background of the students the project works with. The Big Bang case shows the pedagogical strategy followed to avoid the incompatibility between the values of commercial video games and those of the students concretely with reference to musical culture.

The club's members enjoy playing commercial music video games (e.g. karaoke video games like *Sing it*, dancing video games like *Dance Central*, or video games like *Rock Band*, where gamers play as a full band) owing to their attractive gameplay, yet they identify neither with their musical style, nor with their aesthetic configuration, nor with the song's lyrics, nor with the main characters. In these video games, the characters' appearance follows the American urban fashion trends and the

musical style (pop, rock, etc.) does not correspond to those preferred by GAMESTAR(T) students, namely Latin American music like "reggaeton," Latin hip-hop, etc.

Teachers had no problem in identifying the students' musical preferences through observing their habits (listening to music with their mobile phones and mp3 players) and directly asking them. During the assembly meetings, they suggested introducing Latin music as they already did in their own musical presentations for the end-of-course celebrations. Teachers also observed that a Latin music band called *Big Bang*, which rehearsed at Intermediae-Matadero, was very popular with them and had great influence on them as a sort of cultural icon and model (students asked teachers for Internet addresses to visualize their videos or get their music).

As a result of these observations, GAMESTAR(T) coordinators held a meeting to discuss the possibility of integrating one of the members of Big Bang as a collaborator of the club the following course. Big Bang's role would consist in including new musical styles in the existing music video games (changing the rhythm, song intonation, dancing style, etc.) in order to improve their context-based usability. Besides, it was also suggested that Big Bang, together with the club's member, could make new video games according to their interests and preferences.

It would be carried out within the framework of the assembly where students would decide the way Big Bang would become a part of the club. The context-based usability model makes no sense without direct and active participation on the part of the students, whose identity will determine the usage of the video games.

Summarizing, the proposed model is based on the following scheme:

- Research of the students' socio-cultural context and specific needs.
- Detection of usability problems in the concrete practice.

- Search for solutions based on the results produced by the research on their tastes, preferences, needs, and demands.
- Adaptation of context-based usability in collaboration with the students.

ASSESSMENT OF GAMESTAR(T) EXPERIENCE

In the course of the sessions arranged for the club and the thematic courses, great advances were achieved in making the participants familiar with the world of video games as a cultural experience, and not merely as entertainment merchandise. The club was also successful in fostering critical thinking about the elements that build up the everyday life (being video games a part of it), which involves learning to analyze the ideas they propose and the values they incarnate.

The project showed children, teenagers, and adults the possibilities of video games as meaningful learning tools that involve the students actively in the process of knowledge acquisition. Moreover, it was rendered possible that a group of children be able to create and manage their own game club, feel it as something of their own, and assume responsibility for and active management of the club.

In spite of the problems that emerged in the course of some of the club's sessions, it can be consistently claimed that the general outcome of GAMESTAR(T) was very positive. The experience with the club showed the educational potentialities of video games and their undisputed capacity for social integration.

Self-management of their own club made children feel the space and its resources as something of their own, which implied a greater commitment to the management and preservation of the resources of the gameteca. Most importantly, it also resulted in an improvement of the students' self-esteem and self-conception. These improvements had,

in turn, a positive effect on the reduction of the competitiveness level and interpersonal conflicts. A great level of self-discipline and organization of the activities could be observed during the sessions, especially after the introduction of the assembly meetings at the beginning and at the end of each session. Interpersonal relationships improved to the extent that children of different origins and different social classes developed a group conscience and supported each other.

In the thematic courses, there was an excellent performance and a high level of achievement, though the children's motivation and interest in the workshops varied from person to person. We observed that some children chose to borrow educational video games from the gameteca that had been used in a workshop, showing thus their interest in the subject matter; or that some children explained questions related to a workshop in the free gaming session.

Assessment of Context-Based Usability

In addition to the evaluation of the GAMESTAR(T) experience based on its specific objectives, an evaluation of the selection and usage of video games has been also carried out using context-based usability as a key criterion. In order to evaluate this, a number of indicators have been identified and several criteria have been established to assess them (see Figure 2).

GUIDELINES FOR SELECTION AND INTRODUCTION OF VIDEO GAMES IN THE EDUCATIONAL ENVIRONMENT

Selection and introduction of video games in the educational environment is a crucial challenge that will determine whether this model of pedagogical innovation is a success or a failure. The follow-

Figure 2. Evaluation

Parameter	Criteria	Evaluation
Motivation	Direct observation of students' mood and level of participation in the activities Classroom atmosphere Assessments of the Club's members expressed in the assembly meetings Demand of video game loan Video game selection during free gaming	Positive. Motivation level was always high. Club's members demanded video games for loan during all sessions and participated actively. The video games of the *gameteca* met general acceptance among them and were used during the free gaming time
Adaptation to the socio-cultural context	Direct observation of contrast between the cultural backgrounds of the video games and of the club's members Demands of video games that fit better the students' interests expressed in the assembly meetings Contrast between the expectations of the club's members and the results obtained	Average. Many video games did not match the cultural background of the club's members. They repeatedly demanded the acquisition of new video games closer to their cultural background ("Big Bang case")
Adaptación a las necesidades de aprendizaje	Achievement of the workshop and club's sessions objectives Direct observation of gaming and monitoring of ability development Teachers support to students with special learning needs	Positive. Club's members with (general or specific) special learning needs evolved positively playing video games of increasingly higher difficulty level
Time management	Achievement of learning objectives Interest showed in the video games	Average. Some video games did not meet their objectives owing to their long duration and were used only through loan Some of them have been used successfully in specific workshops
Adjustment to infrastructure	Children's comfort at the venue Smooth gaming	Average. The space reserved at the venue was too small when attendance was high Certain scarcity of resource: there were too few television sets for the many video games and consoles

ing guidelines try to define some basic criteria to select video games successfully for utilization in the educational environment.

Research and Analysis of the Students' Socio-Cultural Context

According to the principles of attention to diversity and of adaptation of the curriculum to the students' specific needs, the main role of the teachers is to identify the socio-cultural context of the students. This context consists not only of the students' living conditions and cultural background, but also their own interests, expectations and needs. In order to detect these factors, it is necessary to carry out an investigative work that includes consulting pedagogical academic sources, direct observation of the environment and the students' activities and interviews with the students and their relatives.

In those cases where such an investigation is unfeasible, an initial questionnaire, which has to be filled by the students, can serve as a preliminary evaluation of the each student's personal situation and of the environment. The questionnaire could contain items like those used in GAMESTAR(T), which, though not explicitly referring to the students' familial and socio-cultural context, can produce relevant information to orient the educational practice, since they reveal the conditions under which the students normally study and their relationship to video games (see Figure 3).

Regarding the personal and socio-cultural context, the essential data that have to be collected are:

- If students have previously had access to technology and to which extent. This will produce useful data to determine the intensity with which each student has to be monitored, as well as the level of complexity of the virtual interfaces to be used. For instance, a student that has never had access to a computer should begin by famil-

iarizing with its different components and playing very simple games like *One Button Bob,* where all actions are performed by pressing a single key.

- If there are cases of students with functional diversity or learning difficulties. Special attention should be paid to the students with functional diversity or learning difficulties that have had none or almost no access the ICT, whose learning curve might be less pronounced. Students with functional diversity may never be able to attain a satisfactory usage of the standard technological interfaces.

- Students' preferences, with the aim of selecting video games similar or identical to those they play in their spare time, which will contribute to bridge the second digital divide.

- Personal and familial attitude towards video games. In many cases, the family's prejudices against video games have a strong influence on children. They enjoy playing games, but, at the same time, they feel guilty about it, for they internalize the negative discourses about video games; such a contradiction gives rise to unhealthy gaming habits—a situation that affects more to girls owing to the gender bias that distances them from technology (Castaño, 2008). Teachers should help children to get rid of the mark of shame implied by their ludic-technological practices. In the same way, teachers should be prepared to detect solitary gaming practices and to reinforce collective gaming and companionship in those cases.

Definition of Learning Objectives

In the first place, the educational objectives must be clearly defined through a critical reflection. These objectives may be general (those that can be included in any educational planning that in-

Figure 3. Questionnaire

Questionnaire for the Gamestart School Workshop
2ⁿᵈ ESO
Extracurricular Activity
I.E.S Juan de la Cierva

Name: _____

Surname: _____

Course: _____

Age: _____

1. How many days a week do you study?
2. How many hours a day do you study?
3. Do you have a specific room for studying? If not, where do you study?
4. Do you enjoy a sufficiently quiet atmosphere when you study? If not, what are the distractions?
5. Do you play board games? Which one/s?
6. Do you practise sport? Which one/s?
7. Do you have a video game console? Which one/s?
8. Do you play video games with friends? How?
9. Do you play video games every day?
10. How many hours a day do you play?
11. What do your parents think about video games?
12. What do your teachers think about video games?
13. Do you think video games are good or bad? Why?
14. Do you think that there are video games for girls and others for boys? Why?
15. Why do you like video games?
16. Do you think one can learn new things through gaming?
17. Mention something you have learned from one or more video games.

corporates technology, in this case, video games) or specific (the subject's objectives that refer to concrete knowledge and abilities).

- **General Objectives:** Among the general objectives there are two that must be included in any educational planning that assumes technology both as a tool and as a end in itself, namely to bridge the second digital divide and to bring about critical digital literacy.
- **Specific Objectives:** Specific objectives depend on the concrete needs of each environment and subject. In the case of GAMESTAR(T), one of the key issues was integration and knowledge transmission that varied with the workshop. For instance, in the workshop Play for health, the specific objectives were to foster critical thinking about drugs, to contribute to

sexual education and to offer basic medical knowledge; whereas in the workshop Stories from history, the specific objective was to transmission of general knowledge about the history of humanity.

It is essential to produce well defined and concrete objectives before selecting the video games that will be used in the students' formation in specific subjects, since according to the criteria for context-based usability, video games should adapt to the previously delimited pedagogical context.

Criteria for Video Game Selection

Once the students' socio-cultural context has been analyzed, and the pedagogical model, objectives, and methodology have been defined, it is possible to move on to video game selection according to the following criteria:

- **Time Management:** Video games should be selected so as they adjust to the time available for educational activities. Video games that require prolonged and continuous gaming to achieve the objectives can be used in long-term and intensive educational programs; on the other hand, video games that imply short games are ideal for short-termed educational plans or long-tem plans with few and infrequent sessions. The possibility of at-home gaming should also be taken into account.

- **Adjustment to Age:** Adjustment to age according to usability can be carried out taking into consideration the video game content, gameplay, aesthetic values, and interface design. PEGI (Pan European Game Information) video game rating system advise only the presence of graphic violence, bad language, sexual content, discrimination, drug use, gambling, and whether the video game can be played online. These rating systems, which may be useful to decide on content, do not indicate whether video games are appropriate with respect to the rest of aspects on which adjustment to age depends. As a consequence, teachers should play the targeted games themselves or at least consult the existing pedagogical literature that deals with such games.

- **Adaptation to Motor Functional Diversity:** If there are students with motor functional diversity in the group, specific video games with adaptive design should be selected or, at least, commercial video games with simple, easy-to-use technological interfaces.

- **Critical Thinking:** Context-based usability assessment allows the adaptation of any video game to the targeted educational environment, providing that it is directed by the teachers towards the learning objectives. The fostering of critical thinking is crucial when trying to introduce violent, sexist, racist, homophobic or classist video games, since their ideological background may influence in a negative way if educational practice is not guided by concrete criteria and strategies that critically challenge, dismantle and eventually discard such interpretations or perspectives. The confection of video game analysis tables containing information about plot or narrative, character design, gameplay, etc. that would be stored in a file repository is very useful. The strategies intended to cultivate critical thinking are the following: discussion and debate, questionnaires, analysis of practical examples or case studies, guided or comparative analysis of video games, monitored gaming with active participation of the teachers, etc. In the case of *serious games*, intended to develop specific skills and to acquire certain knowledge, and that of *persuasive games*, aimed at fostering critical thinking about specific topics, free gaming alone can be an efficient way of achieving their respective objectives; however, critical thinking does not emerge from the mere act of gaming, but it has to be developed through strategies like those just mentioned. The rationale behind this statement is that critical thinking is a second-order thinking process about each video game values, assumptions, implicit and explicit intentions, effects, etc.

- **Attention to Objectives:** Hereafter is a table of video game genres with information about the abilities they contribute to develop, the kind of knowledge that can be transmitted using them and some examples of concrete video games (see Figure 4).

Figure 4. Video games, abilities, and knowledge

Genre	Abilities developement	Examples of Knowledge acquisition	Examples of video games
Shooter	Bodily-kinesthetic intelligence Reflexes Eye-hand coordination Ethics	Health	*Re-Mission* or *Immune Attack* *September 12th*
Platforms	Coordination Means-end planning Team work	History and Geography	*Mario's time machine*
Logic and puzzle	Logical-mathematical intelligence Musical intelligence Spatial intelligence Creativity	Mathematics	*Math Blaster Episode 1: In Search of Spot* or *Professor Layton and the diabolical box*
Strategy	Logical-mathematical intelligence Interpersonal intelligence Intrapersonal intelligence Naturalistic intelligence	History Biology	*Rome total war* or *Hearts of Iron* *Spore*
Sports	Interpersonal intelligence Bodily-kinesthetic intelligence Eye-hand coordination Strategy planning	Physical education	*Wii Sports* or *Pro Evolution Soccer*
Music	Musical intelligence Interpersonal intelligence Bodily-kinesthetic intelligence	Music	*Sing It!* or *Rock Band*
Online and Multiplayer	Interpersonal intelligence Collaborative learning Strategy planning	History	*Age of Empires*
Simulation	Linguistic intelligence Spatial intelligence Musical intelligence Bodily-kinesthetic intelligence Interpersonal intelligence Intrapersonal intelligence	Astronomy Ethics	*Universe Sandbox* *SPENT*

Some Methodological Pedagogical Measures Recommended to Improve Context-Based Usability

It is strongly recommended to use the assembly along the entire development of the educational practice as a method of reflection and decision on video game selection and on the specific implementation in the educational environment.

Other Appropriate Practices

- **Collective Gaming:** Facilitates familiarization of students with video game interfaces unknown to them, and promotes integration, associationism, and coopera-

tion. As a result, it is students themselves that help each other acquire new abilities in a ludic context and in a non-hierarchical way.

- **Cooperative Gaming Practices:** That not only promote associationism and cooperation, but also integration; therefore, it can be very useful to improve deficient context-based usability of specific video games. For instance, in case there were a child with hearing difficulties within the group, cooperative gaming can make up for important auditory signals through a code of tactile signals designed and used by the students themselves in order to improve usability.

- **Active Participation:** Of the teachers in the gaming activity, which leads students to reflection and critical gaming, helps detect their needs, interests, and preferences, creates non-hierarchical social bonds, and suppresses the impression that gaming is being controlled by teachers. This contributes to bridging the second digital divide and eliminates the prejudices against video games that still distress some children.

CONCLUSION AND FUTURE RESEARCH DIRECTIONS

After several months of application, and having ascertained the positive results of the utilization of video games in educational contexts, the authors consider that the GAMESTAR(T) project should keep improving, taking advantage of the experiences and the solutions implemented. This experience opens a broad and complex horizon of research on pedagogical innovation, as well as of development and application both in teacher training and teaching practice.

In the first place, research on pedagogy is essential for the project. Bearing in mind the difficulties encountered, the pedagogical foundations of the criteria, and actions should be sounder. Therefore, the members of GAMESTAR(T) should be encouraged to undertake a deeper commitment to the foundations of the pedagogical plans and their practical application. Integrating video games in education is a novel challenge, which demands a justification that cannot be based solely on its advantages for knowledge acquisition. As shown in this chapter, this advantages are numerous and of great importance, but they would be useless and unsatisfactory if they are not accompanied by a pedagogical basis that takes into account the students' characteristics, interests, preferences and their personal development. Bridging the second digital divide is the true challenge for the introduction of video games into the classroom;

research should concentrate on this issue, analyzing how children establish relationships to video games and why they are so attractive to them, all with the aim of transferring the motivation and interest they generate to an educational context.

On the other side, it is of great importance (and this is the second aspect of GAMESTAR(T)) to train teachers for the usage of video games in classroom. Teacher training should be oriented to an understanding of the meaning of the so called second digital divide and how video games make possible to bridge it. Education plans should include, on the one hand, theoretical knowledge about the pedagogical principles and practices that must be taken into account to improve the teaching experience with video games, the existing video games, its characteristics, the benefits they bring about, the possibilities of creation of own video games, etc.; and, on the other hand, practical knowledge about how to incorporate video games in didactic planning in a efficient and satisfactory manner.

The future lines of research that this project opens:

- Possibilities of bridging the second digital divide through the usage of video games.
- Improvement of the technologically mediated teaching activity through teacher training plans.
- Possibilities of raising the students' level of satisfaction with the educational processes, especially those mediated by technology.

This chapter's conclusions do not limit to a complacent ascertainment of the advantages of the usage of video games in education. It certainly entailed problems that had to be faced and dealt with, which require pedagogical effort to find solutions. The task at hand is by no means easy. That is why it is essential to report the whole process, so as it can serve as a reference for all those interested in introducing video games into the classroom and help develop teacher-training programs.

Following the spirit of the GAMESTAR(T) project, the authors intend to continue with their (theoretical and practical) research on the introduction of video games into education, and to advance to the second stage of the project, i.e. the training and counseling of teachers about the introduction of video games into the classroom. Such work consists in providing teachers with all the indispensable knowledge to accomplish this task through a ludic approach to the video games world, presenting examples of the application of concrete video games to teaching of specific knowledge and skills, informing about how video games are currently being used in different educational projects and which tools are available for creating your own video games.

The GAMESTAR(T) project showed how it is possible to bridge the second digital divide and that, for this purpose, it is fundamental to pay attention to whatever children desire, expect from and look for in video games, how they relate to them and what they demand from teachers.

REFERENCES

Aguilera Moyano, M. A., & Méndiz Noguero, A. (2004). *Videojuegos y educación*. Madrid, Spain: Centro Nacional de Información y Comunicación Educativa. Retrieved April 3, 2011 from http://ares.cnice.mec.es/informes/02/documentos/indice.htm

Balaguer, R. (2005). *¿Por qué atrapan tanto los videojuegos?* Retrieved July 20, 2011 from http://www.psikeba.com.ar/articulos/RBP_videojuegos_subjetividades.htm

Buckingham, D. (2008, September). Repensar el aprendizaje en la era de la cultura digital. *El Monitor,* 17-21.

Cabañes, E. (2009, October 2). *Videojuegos: Las chicas también matan, 5*. OpenArsgames-Mondopixel. Intermediae. Madrid, Spain: Matadero.

Castaño, C. (2008). *La segunda brecha digital*. Madrid, Spain: Ediciones Cátedra.

Estallo, J. A. (1995). *Los videojuegos: Juicios y prejuicios*. Barcelona, Spain: Paidós.

Gallo, S. (1997). *El paradigma anarquista de educación*. Retrieved May 15, 2011 from http://www.flyingmind.com/plataforma/doc7

Giner de los Ríos, F. (1988). *Antología pedagógica*. Madrid, Spain: Santillana.

Greenfield, P., & Cocking, R. (Eds.). (1996). *Interacting with video: Advances in applied developmental psychology*. Los Angeles, CA: Ablex Publishing Corporation & University of California.

Martín Luengo, J. (1990). *Desde nuestra escuela Paideia*. Madrid, Spain: Madre Tierra.

Rousseau, J. (1974). *Emile ou de l'éducation*. Paris, France: Garnier-Flammarion.

Rubio Méndez, M. (2011). *Videojuegos como laboratorio para la construcción de la identidad de género*. Madrid, Spain: Universidad de Salamanca.

ADDITIONAL READING

Ayuste, A. (1994). *Planteamientos de la pedagogía crítica: Comunicar y transformer*. Barcelona, Spain: Graó.

Been, C., & Haring, T. (1991). Effects on contextual competence on social initiations. *Journal of Applied Behavior Analysis, 24*(2), 337–347. doi:10.1901/jaba.1991.24-337

Casey, J., & Ramsammy, R. (1992). *Mac-Mentoring: Using technology and counseling with at-risk youth.* Retrieved from http://eric.ed.gov/ERICWebPortal/search/detailmini.jsp?_nfpb=true&_&ERICExtSearch_SearchValue_0=ED344179&ERICExtSearch_SearchType_0=no&accno=ED344179

Colwell, J. (1995). Computer games, self esteem and gratification of needs in adolescents. *Journal of Community & Applied Social Psychology, 5*(3), 195–206. doi:10.1002/casp.2450050308

Consalvo, M. (2008). Primeras citas e idilios de cuentos de hadas: La sexualidad en los videojuegos. In Álvarez Reyes, J. A. (Ed.), *Catálogo de la Exposición "Try Again".* San Sebastián, Spain: Brizzolis.

Estallo, J. A. (1995). *Los videojuegos: Juicios y prejuicios.* Barcelona, Spain: Planeta.

Ferrer & Guardia. F. (2009). *La escuela moderna.* Barcelona, Spain: Tusquets.

Fileni, F. (1988, January-March). Play as acquisition of mental structures: The case of videogames. *Studi di Sociologia,* 64–74.

Freinet, C. (1970). *Técnicas freinet de la escuela moderna.* Mexico City, México: Siglo XXI.

Freinet, C. (1982). *Las enfermedades escolares.* Barcelona, Spain: Laia.

Freire, P. (1997). *La educación como práctica de la libertad.* Madrid, Spain: Siglo XXI.

Freire, P. (2003). *Pedagogía del oprimido.* Madrid, Spain: Siglo XXI.

Funk, D., & Buchman, J. (1996). Children's perceptions of gender differences in social approval for playing electronic games. *Sex Roles, 35*(3/4).

Gee, J. P. (2003). *What digital games have to teach us about learning and literacy.* New York, NY: Palgrave Macmillan.

Gilster, P. (1997). *Digital literacy.* New York, NY: Wiley.

Giroux, H. A. (1993). *La escuela y la lucha por la ciudadanía: Pedagogía crítica de la época moderna.* Mexico City, México: Siglo XXI.

Giroux, H. A. (1997). *Los profesores como intelectuales: Hacia una pedagogía crítica del aprendizaje.* Barcelona, Spain: Paidós.

Gutiérrez, D., & Javier, E. (Eds.). (2004). *La diferencia sexual en el análisis de los videojuegos.* Madrid, Spain: Ministerio de Educación y Ciencia.

Huizinga, J. (2007). *Homo ludens.* Madrid, Spain: Alianza.

Lacasa, P. (2010). *Los videojuegos: Aprender en mundos reales y virtuales.* Madrid, Spain: Morata.

Marty, J. C. (2011). Hints for improving motivation in game-based learning environments. In *Handbook of Research on Increasing Motivation and Learning Through Educational Video Games: Multidisciplinary Approaches* (pp. 530–549). Hershey, PA: IGI Global. doi:10.4018/978-1-60960-495-0.ch025

McFarlane, A., Sparrowhawk, A., & Heald, Y. (2002). *Report on the educational use of games: An exploration by TEEM of the contribution which games can make to the education process.* Retrieved from http://www.teem.org.uk/publications/teem_gamesined_full.pdf

McLaren, P. (1997). *Pedagogía crítica y cultura depredadora: Políticas de oposición en la era posmoderna.* Barcelona, Spain: Paidós.

Neill, A. S. (1994). *El nuevo summerhill.* Mexico City, México: Fondo de Cultura Económica.

Neill, A. S. (2004). *Summerhill: Un punto de vista radical sobre la educación de los niños.* Mexico City, México: Fondo de Cultura Económica.

Pivec, M., & Pivec, P. (2009). What do we know from research about the use of games in education. *European Schoolnet*. Retrieved from http://www.comminit.com/?q=ict-4-development/node/302814

Prensky, M. (2001). *Digital game based learning revolution*. New York, NY: McGraw-Hill.

Provenzo, E. (1991). *Video kids: Making sense of Nintendo*. Boston, MA: Harward University Press.

Strasburgber, V. (1993). Adolescents and the media. *Adolescents-Medecine: State of the Art Reviews*, (Vol. 4). Philadelphia, PA.

Travieso, J. L., & Planella, J. (2008). La alfabetización digital como factor de inclusión social: Una mirada crítica. In *UOC Papers: Revista Sobre la Sociedad del Conocimiento*, (Vol. 6). UOC.

Turkle, S. (1995). *Life on the screen: Identity in the age of the internet*. New York, NY: Simon & Schuster.

Ulicsak, M., & Wright, M. (2010). *Games in education: Serious games*. Bristol, UK: Futurelab.

ENDNOTES

[1]   In the year 2009, ARSGAMES and Mondo Pixel began to collaborate with Intermediae through its financial aids to creation. Since then, they propose periodical meetings, coordinated by ARSGAMES or by Mondo Pixel, that gather professionals, artists, and amateurs that work around the game art, research on game studies, and game art theory. OpenArsgames is nowadays an indispensable reference for the academic studies on art and video games in Spain. The project consists of a series of presentations given by invited experts that take place the last Friday of every month and deal with different aspects of the video game studies: narratology, cognitive studies, theory of representation, and ludology.

[2]   A game library that hosts a collection of board games, video games, and other resources that are available for usage or loan.

[3]   Summerhill is a progressive, co-educational, residential school, founded by A. S. Neill in 1921. The school is located in Leiston, UK, and it is currently one of the most important democratic schools, where the students together with the teaching staff decide and determine through an assembly its normative and functioning. Nowadays the director of the school is Zöe Neill, daughter of A. S. Neill.

[4]   Paideia is a free, anarchist school located in Mérida, Extremadura (Spain). Paideia was founded in January 1978 by three teachers: Concha Castaño Casaseca, María Jesús Checa Simó, and Josefa Martín Luengo. The school is self-managed in all aspects, from the economic to the educational and the personal.

Compilation of References

Abran, A., Surya, W., Khelifi, A., Rilling, J., Seffah, A., & Robert, F. (2003). Consolidating the ISO usability models. In *Proceedings of the 11th Annual International Software Quality Management Conference*. Software Quality Management.

ACM Interim Review Task Force. (2008). *Computer Science curriculum 2008: An interim revision of CS 2001*. New York, NY: ACM & IEEE Computer Society. Retrieved February 26, 2011, from http://www.acm.org//education/curricula/ComputerScience2008.pdf

Adams, D., & Hamm, M. (1996). *Cooperative learning, critical thinking and collaboration across the curriculum* (2nd ed.). London, UK: Charles C. Thomas.

Aguilera Moyano, M. A., & Méndiz Noguero, A. (2004). *Videojuegos y educación*. Madrid, Spain: Centro Nacional de Información y Comunicación Educativa. Retrieved April 3, 2011 from http://ares.cnice.mec.es/informes/02/documentos/indice.htm

Akerlof, G. A. (1970). The market for lemons: Quality uncertainty and the market mechanism. *The Quarterly Journal of Economics*, *84*(3), 488–500. doi:10.2307/1879431

Akerlof, G. A. (1982). The short-run demand for money: A new look at an old problem. *The American Economic Review*, *72*(2), 35–39.

Alcubierre, D. (2009). *Los videojuegos dentro de la empresa: Integración de una realidad*. Retrieved November 26, 2009, from http://www.cibersociedad.net/congres2009/es/coms/los-videojuegos-dentro-de-la-empresa-integracion-de-una-realidad/979/

Alexander, D. (2002). An accessibility audit of WebCT. In *Proceedings of the Eighth Australian World Wide Web Conference, (AUSWEB)*. Queensland, Australia: AUSWEB. Retrieved from http://ausweb.scu.edu.au/aw02/papers/refereed/alexander/paper.html

Alexander, C., Davis, H., Martinez, J., & Corner, D. (1985). *The production of houses*. Oxford, UK: Oxford University Press.

Alexander, C., Ishikawa, S., & Silverstein, M. (1977). *A pattern language: Towns, buildings, construction*. Oxford, UK: Oxford University Press.

Allison, S., von Wahlde, L., Shockley, T., & Gabbard, G. O. (2006). The development of the self in the era of the internet and role-playing fantasy games. *The American Journal of Psychiatry*, *163*(3), 381–385. doi:10.1176/appi.ajp.163.3.381

Alonso, E. (2009). *Segunda ilustración: Cultura digital y progreso*. Paper presented at the IXth Compostela Colloquium in Logic and Analytic Philosophy. Los Angeles, CA.

Ames, C. (1992). Classrooms: Goals, structures, and student motivation. *Journal of Education & Psychology*, *84*, 261–271. doi:10.1037/0022-0663.84.3.261

Amory, A. (2006). Game object model version II: A theoretical framework for educational game development. *Educational Technology Research and Development*, *55*(1), 51–77. doi:10.1007/s11423-006-9001-x

Amory, A., Naicker, K., Vincent, J., & Adams, C. (1999). The use of computer games as an educational tool: Identification of appropriate game types and game elements. *British Journal of Educational Technology, 30*(4), 311–321. doi:10.1111/1467-8535.00121

Amory, A., & Seagram, R. (2003). Educational game models: Conceptualization and evaluation. *South African Journal of Higher Education, 17*(2), 206–217.

Anderson, L. W., Krathwohl, D. R., Airasian, P. W., Cruikshank, K. A., Pintrich, P. R., Raths, J., & Wittrock, M. C. (2001). *A taxonomy for learning, teaching and assessing: A revision of Bloom's taxonomy of educational objectives*. New York, NY: Longman.

Anderson, R. G., & Biddle, W. B. (1975). On asking people questions about what they are reading. *Psychology of Learning and Motivation, 9*, 90–132. doi:10.1016/S0079-7421(08)60269-8

Anon. (2006). *Gaming with a physical disability*. Retrieved from http://www.game-accessibility.com/index.php?pagefile=motoric

Anon. (2011a). *Serious game*. Retrieved from http://en.wikipedia.org/wiki/Serious_game

Anon. (2011b). *Mobile game*. Retrieved from http://en.wikipedia.org/wiki/Mobile_game

Araujo, R. M., Santoro, F. M., & Borges, M. R. S. (2002). The CSCW lab for groupware evaluation. In *Proceedings of 8th International Workshop on Groupware – CRIWG 2002*. La Serena, Chile: Springer-Verlag.

Armitage, U., Wilson, S., & Sharp, H. (2003). The effects of navigation aids on ownership for learning with electronic texts. In R. Williams (Ed.), *Proceedings of the 2nd European Conference on e-Learning*, (pp. 47-58). Reading, MA: Academic Conferences International.

Askar, P., Dönmez, O., Kizilkaya, G., Çevik, V., & Gültekin, K. (2005). Dimensions of student satisfaction on online programs. In Howard, C., Boettcher, J. V., Justice, L., Schenk, K. D., Rogers, P. L., & Berg, G. A. (Eds.), *Encyclopedia of Distance Learning* (pp. 585–590). Hershey, PA: IGI Global. doi:10.4018/978-1-59140-555-9.ch085

Attewell, J. (2005). *Mobile technologies and learning: A technology update and m-learning project summary*. London, UK: Learning and Skills Development Agency. Retrieved May 6, 2011 from http://www.m-learning.org/docs/The%20m-learning%20project%20-%20technology%20update%20and%20project%20summary.pdf

Baartmans, B. G., & Sorby, S. A. (1996). *Introduction to 3-D spatial visualization*. Englewood Cliffs, NJ: Prentice Hall.

Baenninger, M., & Newcombe, N. (1989). The role of experience in spatial test performance: A meta-analysis. *Sex Roles, 20*, 327–344. doi:10.1007/BF00287729

Baeza-Yates, R., & Pino, J. A. (1997). A first step to formally evaluate collaborative work. In *Proceedings of the ACM International Conference on Supporting Group Work* [Phoenix, AZ: ACM Press.]. *Group, 1997*, 55–60.

Bailey, D. (2004). *Active learning*. In R. Hoffman (Ed.), *Encyclopaedia of Educational Technology*. Retrieved May 6, 2011, from http://edweb.sdsu.edu/eet/

Bainbridge, W. S. (2010). *The warcraft civilization: Social science in a virtual world*. Cambridge, MA: The MIT Press.

Balaguer, R. (2005). *¿Por qué atrapan tanto los videojuegos?* Retrieved July 20, 2011 from http://www.psikeba.com.ar/articulos/RBP_videojuegos_subjetividades.htm

Bandura, A. (2001). Social cognitive theory: An agentic perspective. *Annual Review of Psychology, 52*, 1–26. doi:10.1146/annurev.psych.52.1.1

Baptista, R., & Vaz de Carvalho, C. (2008). Funchal 500 years: Learning through role play games. In *Proceedings of ECGBL 2008*. Barcelona, Spain: ECGBL.

Bär, H., Tews, E., & Rößling, G. (2005). Improving feedback and classroom, interaction using mobile phones. In *Proceedings of the IADIS International Conference on Mobile Learning*, (pp. 55-62). IADIS.

Barnes, C. (1994). *Disabled people in Britain and discrimination: A case for anti-discrimination legislation*. London, UK: Hurst & Co.

Barros, B., & Verdejo, M. F. (1999). An approach to analyze collaboration when shared structured workspaces are use for carrying out group learning processes. In *Proceedings of the International Conference AI-ED 1999*, (pp. 449-456). AI-ED.

Barr, P., Noble, J., & Biddle, R. (2007). Video game values: Human–computer interaction and games. *Interacting with Computers, 19*(2), 180–195. doi:10.1016/j.intcom.2006.08.008

Beasley, N., & Smyth, K. (2003). Students selective use of a virtual learning environment: Reflections and recommendations. In R. Williams (Ed.), *Proceedings of the 2nd European Conference on e-Learning*, (pp. 71-79). Reading, MA: Academic Conferences International.

Becker, S. A. (2009). Web usability. In Khosrow-Pour, M. (Ed.), *Encyclopedia of Information Science and Technology* (2nd ed., pp. 4077–4081). Hershey, PA: IGI Global.

Beck, J. C., & Wade, M. (2004). *Got game: How the gamer generation is reshaping business forever*. Boston, MA: Harvard Business School Press.

Beck, J. C., & Wade, M. (2006). *The kids are alright: How the gamer generation is changing the workplace*. Boston, MA: Harvard Business School Press.

BECTA. (2000). *Managed learning environments (MLEs) in further education: Progress report*. Retrieved 10/08/11 from http://www.jisc.ac.uk/news/stories/2000/07/circular700.aspx

Beekes, W. (2006). The "millionaire" method for encouraging participation. *Active Learning in Higher Education, 7*, 25–36. doi:10.1177/1469787406061143

Bekebrede, G. (2010). *Experiencing complexity: A game-based approach for understanding infrastructure systems*. Delft, The Netherlands: Next GenerationInfrastructures Foundation.

Bekebrede, G., Warmelink, H. J. G., & Mayer, I. S. (2011). Reviewing the need for gaming in education to accommodate the net generation. *Computers & Education, 57*(2), 1521–1529. doi:10.1016/j.compedu.2011.02.010

Belbin, R. M. (2004). *Management teams: Why they succeed or fail* (2nd ed.). London, UK: Butterworth Heinemann.

Belbin, R. M. (2010). *Team roles at work* (2nd ed.). London, UK: Butterworth Heinemann.

Bellinson, J. (2002). *Children's use of board games in psychotherapy*. Northvale, NJ: Jason Aronson Inc.

Bener, A., Al-Mahdi, H. S., Vachhani, P. J., Al-Nufal, M., & Ali, A. I. (2010). Do excessive internet use, television viewing and poor lifestyle habits affect low vision in school children? *Journal of Child Health Care, 14*(4), 375–385. doi:10.1177/1367493510380081

Bentley, R., & Dourish, P. (1995). Medium versus mechanism: Supporting collaboration through customisation. In *Proceedings of the Fourth Conference on European Conference on Computer-Supported Cooperative Work*, (pp. 133-148). ECSCW.

Berger, J. G. (2011). *Key concepts for understanding the work of Robert Kegan*. Report by Kenning Associated. Retrieved on June 20, 2011 from http://wiki.canterbury.ac.nz/download/attachments/6358104/Berger+Kegan+key+concepts+kb.doc

Bernhaupt, R. (Ed.). (2010). *Evaluating user experience in games: Concepts and methods*. London, UK: Springer.

Bettocchi, E. (2006). *Brasil barroco: Um jogo de luz e sombras*. Retrieved from http://www.historias.interativas.nom.br/incorporais

Bickford, P. (1997). *Interface design, the art of developing easy-to-use software*. Chestnut Hill, MA: Academic Press.

Bierre, K. (2005). *Improving game accessibility*. Retrieved from http://www.gamasutra.com/view/feature/2342/improving_game_accessibility.php?print=1

Bierre, K., Hinn, T., & McIntosh, M. (2004). *Accessibility in games: Motivations and approaches*. Retrieved from http://www.igda.org/sites/default/iles/IGDA_WhitePaper.pdf

Biggs, J. (2011). *Student learning research and theory - Where do we currently stand?* Retrieved November 6, 2011 from http://www.londonmet.ac.uk/deliberations/ocsld-publications/isltp-biggs.cfm

Biggs, J. (1999). What the student does: Teaching for enhanced learning. *Higher Education Research & Development, 18*(1), 57–75. doi:10.1080/0729436990180105

Biggs, J. B. (1988). The role of the metacognition in enhancing learning. *Australian Journal of Education, 32*, 127–138.

Biggs, J. B. (1993). From theory to practice: A cognitive systems approach. *Higher Education Research & Development, 12*, 73–86. doi:10.1080/0729436930120107

Bisognin, L., Carron, T., & Marty, J.-C. (2010). Learning games factory: Construction of learning games using a component-based approach. In *Proceedings of the European Conference on Games Based Learning (ECGBL)*. Copenhague, Denmark: ECGBL.

Björk, S., Lundgren, S., & Holopainen, J. (2003). Game design patterns. In *Proceedings of Level Up 1st International Digital Games Research Conference*. Utrecht, The Netherlands: Dordrecht.

Björk, S., & Holopainen, J. (2004). *Patterns in game design*. New York, NY: Charles River Media.

Blackmon, M. H., Polson, P. G., Kitajima, M., & Lewis, C. (2002). Cognitive walkthrough for the web. In *Proceedings of the 2002 ACM Conference on Human Factors in Computing Systems (CHI 2002)*, (pp. 463-470). ACM Press. Britain, S., & Liber, O. (1999). *A framework for pedagogical evaluation of virtual learning environments*. Retrieved 10/08/11 from http://www.leeds.ac.uk/educol/documents/00001237.htm

Blamire, R. (2010). *Digital games for learning, conclusions and recommendations from the IMAGINE project*. Retrieved from http:www.imaginegames.eu

Bloom, B., Furst, E., Hill, W., & Krathwohl, D. R. (1956). *Taxonomy of educational objectives: Handbook I – The cognitive domain*. Reading, MA: Addison-Wesley.

Blum, R. (2000). *Healthy youth development: Resiliency paradigm for adolescent health development*. Paper presented at the 3rd Pacific Rim Conference of the International Association for Adolescent Health. Christchurch, New Zealand.

Blythe, M., Bardzell, J., Bardzell, S., & Blackwell, A. (2008). Critical issues in interaction design. In *Proceedings of HCI 2008, Culture, Creativity and Interaction Design*. HCI.

Blythe, T. (1998). *The teaching for understanding guide*. San Francisco, CA: Jossey-Bass Publishers.

Brassard, G., & Bratley, P. (1996). *Fundamentals of algoritmics*. Hertfordshire, UK: Prentice-Hall.

Brave, S., & Nass, C. (2002). Emotion in human-computer interaction. In Jacko, J., & Sears, A. (Eds.), *The Human-Computer Interaction Handbook: Fundamentals, Evolving Technologies and Emerging Applications*. Englewood Cliffs, NJ: Lawrence Erlbaum Associates.

Brewer, E. W., Hollingsworth, C., & Campbell, A. C. (1995). Incentive motivation psychology: An exploration of corrective learning behavior. *Journal of Southeastern Association of Educational Opportunity Program Personnel, 14*(1), 33–51.

Brewster, C., & Fager, J. (2000). *Increasing student engagement and motivation: From time-on-task to homework*. Northwest Regional Educational Laboratory. Retrieved May 6, 2011 from www.nwrel.org/request/oct00/textonly.html

Brown, D., & Metcalf, J. (2008). Mobile learning update. *Learning Consortium Perspectives*. Retrieved on May 6, 2011 from http://masieweb.com/p7/MobileLearningUpdate.pdf

Bruner, J. S. (1996). *Cultura da educação*. Lisboa, Portugal: Edições 70.

Bruner, J. S. (1975). The ontogenesis of speech acts. *Journal of Child Language, 2*, 1–19. doi:10.1017/S0305000900000866

Bruner, J. S. (1977). Early social interaction and language development. In Schaeffer, H. R. (Ed.), *Studies in Mother-Child Interection*. London, UK: Academic Press.

Bruner, J. S. (1990). *Acts of meaning*. Cambridge, MA: Harvard University Press.

Brusilovsky, P. (2001). Adaptive hypermedia. *User Modeling and User-Adapted Interaction, 11*(1/2), 87–110. doi:10.1023/A:1011143116306

Buchanan, G., Farrant, S., Jones, M., Thimbleby, H., Marsden, G., & Pazzani, M. (2001). Improving mobile internet usability. In *Proceedings of the 10th International Conference on World Wide Web*, (pp. 673-680). New York, NY: ACM Press.

Buckingham, D. (2008, September). Repensar el aprendizaje en la era de la cultura digital. *El Monitor,* 17-21.

Burdea, G., & Coiffet, P. (2003). *Virtual reality technology* (2nd ed.). New York, NY: Wiley-IEEE Press.

Buzzi, M. C., Buzzi, M., & Leporini, B. (2010). Accessibility and usability of web content and applications. In Cipolla-Ficarra, F. V. (Ed.), *Quality and Communicability for Interactive Hypermedia Systems: Concepts and Practices for Design* (pp. 64–90). Hershey, PA: IGI Global. doi:10.4018/978-1-61520-763-3.ch004

Buzzi, M., & Leporini, B. (2009). Editing Wikipedia content by screen reader: Easier interaction with the accessible rich internet applications suite. *Disability and Rehabilitation. Assistive Technology*, *4*(4), 264–275. doi:10.1080/17483100902903457

Buzzi, M., & Leporini, B. (2010). Distance learning: New opportunities for the blind. In Buzzi, M. (Ed.), *eLearning*. Vienna, Austria: IN-TECH. doi:10.5772/7778

Cabañes, E. (2009, October 2). *Videojuegos: Las chicas también matan, 5.* OpenArsgames-Mondopixel. Intermediae. Madrid, Spain: Matadero.

Caladine, R. (2008). Videoconference, audioconference, and video chat. In Caladine, R. (Ed.), *Enhancing E-Learning with Media-Rich Content and Interactions* (pp. 210–233). Hershey, PA: IGI Global. doi:10.4018/978-1-59904-732-4.ch012

Caldwell, B., Cooper, M., Guarino Reid, L., & Vanderheiden, G. (2008). *WCAG20: Web content accessibility guidelines 2.0*. Retrieved from http://www.w3.org/TR/WCAG20/

Callele, D., Neufeld, E., & Schneider, K. (2006). Emotional requirements in video games. In *Proceedings of the 14th International Requirements Engineering Conference*, (pp. 292-295). Washington, DC: IEEE.

Calvino, I. (1991). *O castelo dos destinos cruzados*. São Paulo, Brazil: Companhia das Letras.

Cameron, B. H. (2008). Experience-based learning. In Tomei, L. A. (Ed.), *Encyclopedia of Information Technology Curriculum Integration* (pp. 308–315). Hershey, PA: IGI Global. doi:10.4018/978-1-59904-881-9.ch052

Canossa, A., & Drachen, A. (2009). Play-personas: Behaviours and belief systems in user-centred game design. In T. Gross (Ed.), *Proceedings of the 12th IFIP TC13 Conference on Human-Computer Interaction (INTERACT)*, (pp. 510-523). Berlin, Germany: Springer.

Card, S. K., Mackinlay, J. D., & Shneiderman, B. (Eds.). (1999). *Readings in information visualization*. San Francisco, CA: Morgan Kaufmann.

Caret. (2011). *Student learning*. Report by Centre for Applied Research in Information Technology. Retrieved on June 20, 2011 from http://caret.iste.org/index.cfm?fuseaction=evidence&answerID=7#references

Carmona, M., Heath, T., & Tiesdell, S. (2003). *Public places urban spaces: The dimensions of urban design*. Burlington, MA: Architectural Press.

Carr, N. (2008). Is Google making us stupid? *Atlantic (Boston, Mass.)*, *302*(1), 56–63.

Carr, N. (2010). *The shallows: What the internet is doing to our brains*. New York, NY: Norton and Company Inc.

Carron, T., & Martym, J.-C. (2009). User modelling in learning games. In *Proceedings of the European Conference on Games Based Learning (ECGBL)*. Graz, Austria: ECGBL.

Carron, T., Marty, J.-C., Heraud, J.-M., & France, L. (2006). Helping the teacher to reorganize tasks in a collaborative learning activity: An agent-based approach. In *Proceedings of ICALT*, (pp. 552–554). IEEE Computer Society.

Carron, T., Marty, J.-C., & Heraud, J.-M. (2008). Teaching with game based learning management systems: Exploring and observing a pedagogical dungeon. *Simulation & Gaming*, *39*(3), 353–378. doi:10.1177/1046878108319580

Castaño, C. (2008). *La segunda brecha digital*. Madrid, Spain: Ediciones Cátedra.

Castella, J. C., Trung, T. N., & Boissau, S. (2005). Participatory simulation of land-use changes in the mountains of Vietnam: The combined use of an agent-based model, a role-playing game and a geographic information system. *Ecology and Society*, *10*(1), 27. Retrieved from http://www.ecologyandsociety.org/vol10/iss1/art27/

CEN. (2003). *CEN workshop agreement CWA 14661: Guidelines to standardisers of ICT products and services in the CEN ICT domain.* Retrieved from ftp://cenftp1.cenorm.be/PUBLIC/CWAs/e-Europe/DFA/cwa14661-00-2003-Feb.pdf

CEO. (2001). *The CEO forum school technology and readiness report: Key building blocks for student achievement in the 21st century.* Retrieved May 6, 2011 from http://www.cckln.edu.hk/libweb/Search%20Subject/All%20teachers/21st%20century%20learning/sch%20technology%20report.pdf

Chang, E. (2008). Gaming as writing, or, world of warcraft as world of wordcraft. *Computers and Composition Online.* Retrieved from http://www.bgsu.edu/departments/english/cconline/gaming_issue_2008/Chang_Gaming_as_writing/index.html

Chan, T. W., Roschelle, J., & Hsi, S., Kinshuk, Sharples, M., Brown, T., et al. (2006). One-to-one technology-enhanced learning: An opportunity for global research collaboration. *Research and Practice in Technology-Enhanced Learning*, *1*(1), 3–29. doi:10.1142/S1793206806000032

Chen, M., Cuddihy, E., Thayer, A., & Zhou. (2005). *Creating cross-cultural appeal in digital games: Issues in localization and user testing.* Paper presented at the 52nd Annual Conference for the Society for Technical Communication (STC). Retrieved July 07, 2011, from http://www.markdangerchen.net/pubs/Game_Slides_final3.ppt

Cheok, A., Ishii, I., Osada, J., Fernando, O., & Merritt, T. (2008). Interactive play and learning for children. *Advances in Human-Computer Interaction.* Retrieved from http://www.hindawi.com/journals/ahci/2008/954013/

Chin, J. P., Diehl, V. A., & Norman, K. L. (1988). Development of an instrument measuring user satisfaction of the human-computer interface. In *Proceedings of CHI.* (pp 213-218). CHI.

Chin, J., Diehl, V., & Norman, K. (1988). Development of an instrument measuring user satisfaction of the human-computer interface. In *Proceedings of the SIGCHI Conference on Human Factors in Computing Systems*, (pp. 213–218). SIGCHI.

Choi, K., Son, H., Park, M., Han, J., Kim, K., Lee, B., & Gwak, H. (2009). Internet overuse and excessive daytime sleepiness in adolescents. *Psychiatry and Clinical Neurosciences*, *63*(4), 455–462. doi:10.1111/j.1440-1819.2009.01925.x

Choukroun, J., & Lieury, A. (1985). Rôle du mode de présentation (visuel, auditif, audio-visuel) dans la mémorisation d'instructions. *L'année Psychologique, 4*, 503-516. Retrieved April 24th 2009 from http://www.persee.fr/web/revues/home/prescript/article/psy0003-50331985num85429110

Church, D. (1999). Formal abstract design tools. *Game Developer, 3*(8), 28. Retrieved November 8, 2011, from http://www1.cs.columbia.edu/~cs4995/files/Doug_Church_FADT.pdf

Clanton, C. (1998). An interpreted demonstration of computer games design. In *Proceedings of the Conference on CHI Summary: Human Factors in Computing Systems.* CHI.

Clements, D. H. (1998). *Geometric and spatial thinking in young children.* Retrieved from http://eric.ed.gov/PDFS/ED436232.pdf

Clements, D., & Battista, M. (1992). Geometry and spatial reasoning. In Grouws, D. A. (Ed.), *Handbook of Research on Mathematics Teaching and Learning* (pp. 420–464). New York, NY: Macmillan.

Cobcroft, C., Towers, S., Smith, J., & Burns, A. (2006). *Literature review into mobile learning in the university context.* Retrieved September 25, 2008, from http://eprints.qut.edu.au/archive/00004805/01/4805.pdf

Cobo, J. C. (2009). *Conocimiento, creatividad y software libre: una oportunidad para la educación en la sociedad actual.* UOC Papers. Retrieved November 9, 2010, from http://www.uoc.edu/uocpapers/8/dt/esp/cobo.pdf

Coffey, H. (2011). *Digital game-based learning.* Retrieved from http://www.learnnc.org/lp/pages/4970?ref=search

Cole, I. (2005). *Multidimensional usability model (MUM) questionnaire template.* Retrieved 08/08/11 from http://www-users.york.ac.uk/~ijc4/work.htm

Cole, M. S., Feild, H. S., & Harris, S. G. (2004). Student learning motivation and psychological hardiness: Interactive effects on students' reactions to a management class. *Academy of Management Learning & Education, 3*, 64–85. doi:10.5465/AMLE.2004.12436819

Coley, R., Cradler, J., & Engel, P. (1997). *Computers and classrooms: The status of technology in U.S. schools*. Princeton, NJ: Educational Testing Service.

Collazos, C. A., & Gil, R. M. (2011). Using cross-cultural features in web design patterns. In *Proceedings of Eighth International Conference on Information Technology: New Generations*, (pp. 514-519). Las Vegas, NV: IEEE Press.

Collazos, C., Guerrero, L. A., Pino, J., & Ochoa, S. (2002). Evaluating collaborative learning processes. In *Proceedings of the 8th International Workshop on Groupware (CRIWG 2002)*, (pp. 203-221). La Serena, Chile: Springer Verlag.

Collazos, C., Guerrero, L., Pino, J., Ochoa, S., & Stahl, G. (2007). Designing collaborative learning environments using digital games. *Journal of Universal Computer Science, 13*(7), 1022–1032.

Connell, B. R., et al. (1997). *The principles of universal design version 2.0*. Retrieved from http://www.design.ncsu.edu/cud/about_ud/udprinciplestext.htm

Constantino-González, M., & Suthers, D. (2001). Coaching web-based collaborative learning based on problem solution differences and participation. In *Proceedings of the International Conference AI-ED 2001*, (pp. 176-187). Dordrecht, The Netherlands: IOS Press.

ContestSweepstakes. (2011). *Article history and statistical data about Facebook and Twitter*. Retrieved May 6, 2011 from http://contestsweepstakes.co.tv/article-211-history-and-statistical-data-about-facebook-and-twitter

Corbeil, J. R., & Valdes-Corbeil, M. E. (2007). Are you ready for mobile learning? *EDUCAUSE Quarterly, 30*(2), 51–60.

Cormen, T. H., & Leiserson, C. E. Rivest. R. L., & Stein, C. (2009). *Introduction to algorithms* (3rd ed). Cambridge, MA: The MIT Press.

Corneliussen, H. G., & Walker, R. J. (Eds.). (2008). *Digital culture, play, and identity: A world of warcraft reader*. Boston, MA: The MIT Press.

Corsaro, W. A. (1985). *Friendship and culture in the early years*. Norwood, NJ: Ablex.

Cover, S. (2003). Wireless networks and mobile devices. *Transformations: Liberal Arts in the Digital Age*. Retrieved 10/22/10 from http://www.colleges.org/transformations/issue1/cover/01.html

CPS – TU-Delft Centre for Serious Gaming. (2011a). *Construct-IT*. Retrieved July 18, 2011 from http://cps.tbm.tudelft.nl/site/content/construct-it

CPS – TU-Delft Centre for Serious Gaming. (2011b). *Simport – Maasvlakte 2*. Retrieved July 18, 2011 from http://cps.tbm.tudelft.nl/site/content/simport-maasvlakte-2

CPS – TU-Delft Centre for Serious Gaming. (2011c). *Ventum online*. Retrieved July 18, 2011 from http://cps.tbm.tudelft.nl/site/content/ventum-online

Cradler, J., McNabb, M., Freeman, M., & Burchett, R. (2002). How does technology influence student learning? *Learning and Leading, 29*(8), 46-49. Retrieved May 6, 2011, from http://caret.iste.org/caretadmin/resources_documents/29%5F8%2Epdf

Cradler, J. (1994). School-based technology use planning. *Educational IRM Quarterly, 3*(3-4), 12–16.

Cradler, R., & Cradler, J. (1999). *Just in time: Technology innovation challenge grant year 2 evaluation. Report for Blackfoot School District No. 55*. San Mateo, CA: Educational Support Systems.

Crawford, C. (1984). *The art of computer game design*. Berkeley, CA: McGraw-Hill/Osborne Media.

Crookall, D. (1995). *Debriefing: The key to learning from simulation/games*. Thousand Oaks, CA: Sage.

Crown, S. (2001). Improving visualization skills of engineering graphics students using simple javaScript web based games. *Journal of Engineering Education, 9*(3), 347–354.

CSEDweek. (2009). *Computer science education week*. Retrieved October 30, 2011, from http://www.csedweek.org/wp-content/uploads/2009/12/CSEdWeek-Two-Pager.pdf

Csikszentmihalyi, M. (1990). *Flow: The psychology of optimal experience*. New York, NY: Harper and Row.

Csikszentmihalyi, M. (1991). *Flow: The psychology of optimal experience*. New York, NY: HarperCollins.

Dahlskog, S., Kamstrup, A., & Aarseth, E. (2009). Mapping the game landscape: Locating genres using functional classification. In *Proceedings of DiGRA*. DiGRA.

Daichendt, L. (2011). *Mobile technology use in education*. Retrieved on May 6, 2011 from http://marketingwithnewtechnology.wordpress.com/2011/01/26/mobile-technology-use-in-education/

Daley, A. (2009). Can exergaming contribute to improving physical activity levels and health outcomes in children? *Pediatrics, 124*(2), 763–771. doi:10.1542/peds.2008-2357

Damodaran, L. (1996). User involvement in the systems design process-a practical guide for users. *Behaviour & Information Technology, 15*(6), 363–377. doi:10.1080/014492996120049

Dancik, G., & Kumar, A. (2003). A tutor for counter-controlled loop concepts and its evaluation. In *Proceedings of the 33rd ASEE/IEEE Frontiers in Education Conference – FIE 2003*, (vol. 1), (pp. T3C 7-12). Kansas City, MO: Stipes Publishing.

Danet, B., Ruedenberg-Wright, L., & Rosenbaum-Tamari, Y. (1997). Hmmm... where's that smoke coming from? Writing, play and performance on internet relay chat. *Journal of Computer-Mediated Communication, 2*.

Davis, B. G. (1993). *Tools for teaching*. San Francisco, CA: Jossey-Bass Publishers.

De Cindio, F., Ripamonti, L. A., & Di Loreto, I. (2008). The interplay between the actual and the virtual citizenship in the milan community network experience. In Aurigi, A., & Cindio, F. D. (Eds.), *Augmented Urban Spaces: Articulating the Physical and Electronic City*. London, UK: Ashgate.

De Lera, E., & Garreta-Domingo, M. (2007). Ten emotion heuristics: Guidelines for assessing the user's affective dimension easily and cost-effectively. In *Proceedings of the 21st British HCI Group Annual Conference on People and Computers*, (pp. 163-166). Swinton, UK: British Computer Society.

De Lisi, R., & Cammarano, D. M. (1996). Computer experience and gender differences in undergraduate mental rotation performance. *Computers in Human Behavior, 12*, 351–361. doi:10.1016/0747-5632(96)00013-1

Dearden, L., Emmerson, C., Frayne, C., & Meghir, C. (2005). *Education subsidies and school drop-out rates*. Working Paper vol. 05/11. Washington, DC: Institute for Fiscal Studies.

Deek, F. P., & McHugh, J. A. (1998). A survey and critical analysis of tools for learning programming. *Computer Science Education, 8*(2), 130–178. doi:10.1076/csed.8.2.130.3820

deFreitas, S. (2006). *Learning in immersive worlds: A review of game-based learning*. London, UK: Joint Information Systems Committee. Retrieved on May 6, 2011 from http://www.jisc.ac.uk/media/documents/programmes/elearninginnovation/gamingreport_v3.pdf

DeGani, A., Martin, G., Stead, G., & Wade, F. (2010). *E-learning standards for an m-learning world – Informing the development of e-learning standards for the mobile web*. Tribal Education. Retrieved on May 6, 2011 from http://www.m-learning.org/images/stories/Final_mSCORM_paper.pdf

Deno, J. A. (1995). The relationship of previous experiences to spatial visualization ability. *Engineering Design Graphics Journal, 59*(3), 5–17.

Denzin, N. K., & Lincoln, Y. S. (Eds.). (2006). *O planejamento da pesquisa qualitativa: teorias e abordagens*. Porto Alegre, Brazil: ARTMED.

Department for Education and Employment. (1998) *The learning age: A renaissance for a new Britain*. Retrieved 20/08/11, from http://www.lifelonglearning.co.uk/greenpaper/

Desmet, P. M. A., Overbeeke, C. J., & Tax, S. J. E. T. (2001). Designing products with added emotional value: Development and application of an approach for research through design. *The Design Journal, 4*(1), 32–47. doi:10.2752/146069201789378496

Desurvire, H., & Wiberg, C. (2009). Game usability heuristics (PLAY) for evaluating and designing better games: The next iteration. In Ozok & Zaphiris (Eds.), *Proceedings of the 3rd International Conference on Online Communities and Social Computing*, (pp. 557-566). Berlin, Germany: Springer-Verlag.

Desurvire, H., Caplan, M., & Toth, J. A. (2004). *Using heuristics to evaluate the playability of games*. Paper presented at CHI 2004, Vienna, Austria.

Deutsch, M. (1962). Cooperation and trust: Some theoretical notes. In M. Jones (Ed.), *Nebraska Symposium on Motivation* (pp. 275-320). Lincoln, NE: University of Nebraska Press.

Dev, P. C. (1997). Intrinsic motivation and academic achievement: What does their relationship imply for the classroom teacher? *Remedial and Special Education, 18*(1), 12–19. doi:10.1177/074193259701800104

Dewey, J. (1938). *Experience and education*. New York, NY: Collier.

Di Loreto, I. (2010). *From interactive systems to social interactive systems*. (PhD Thesis). Università degli Studi di Milano. Milan, Italy.

Di Loreto, I., & Gouaich, A. (2010°). *An early evaluation method for social interactive systems*. N°A RR-10016 (2010) 001-010 [lirmm-00486932 - version 1].

Di Loreto, I., & Gouaich, A. (2010b). An early evaluation method for social presence in serious games. In *Proceedings of the 2nd International Conference on Computer Supported Education CSEDU 2010*. CSEDU.

Di Loreto, I., & Gouaich, A. (2010c). A framework for designing social interactive systems. In *Proceedings of ICTEL 2010 Athens - 1st International Conference on Technology-Enhanced Learning*. ICTEL.

Dickinson, D. L. (2001). The carrot vs. the stick in work team motivation. *Experimental Economics, 4*, 107–124. doi:10.1007/BF01669275

Diez Higuera, J. F., & Diez Pernas, F. J. (2002). VRML-based system for a three-dimensional virtual museum. In Shih, T. K. (Ed.), *Distributed Multimedia Databases: Techniques and Applications* (pp. 306–317). Hershey, PA: IGI Global. doi:10.4018/978-1-930708-29-7.ch019

Dillenbourg, P., Baker, M., Blaye, A., & O'Malley, C. (1996). The evolution of research on collaborative learning. In *Learning in Humans and Machine: Towards an Interdisciplinary Learning Science* (pp. 189–211). Dublin, Ireland: Emerald Group. doi:10.1007/978-1-4020-9827-7_1

Dimitropoulos, K., & Manitsaris, A. (2011). Designing web-based educational virtual reality environments. In Vincenti, G., & Braman, J. (Eds.), *Teaching through Multi-User Virtual Environments: Applying Dynamic Elements to the Modern Classroom* (pp. 157–178). Hershey, PA: IGI Global.

Dimitrova, M., Sharp, H., & Wilson, S. (2002). Educational multimedia cognitive walkthrough: Supporting experts to predict valid user problems. In *Proceedings of Human Computer Interaction 2002* (*Vol. 2*, pp. 26–29). London, UK: ACM.

diSessa, A. (2000). *Changing minds: Computers, learning, and literacy*. Cambridge, MA: MIT Press.

Dix, A., Finley, J., Abowd, G., & Beale, R. (1993). *Human-computer interaction*. Upper Saddle River, NJ: Prentice-Hall.

Djaouti, D., Alvarez, J., & Jessel, J.-P. (2011). Classifying serious games: The G/P/S model. In Felicia, P. (Ed.), *Handbook of Research on Improving Learning and Motivation through Educational Games: Multidisciplinary Approaches* (pp. 118–136). Hershey, PA: IGI Global. doi:10.4018/978-1-60960-495-0.ch006

Dondi, C., & Moretti, M. (2008). *Survey on on-line game-based learning*. Retrieved from http://www.unigame.net/html/case_studies/D1.pdf

Dormans, J. (2006). On de role of de die: A brief ludologic study of pen-and-paper roleplaying games and their rules. *The International Journal of Computer Game Research, 6*(1). Retrieved from http://gamestudies.org/0601/articles/dormans

Dormans, J. (2011). Beyond iconic simulation. *Simulation & Gaming, 42*(5), 610–631.

Dornisch, M., & Sperling, R. A. (2006). Facilitating learning from technology enhanced text: Effects of prompted elaborative interrogation. *The Journal of Educational Research, 99*, 156–165. doi:10.3200/JOER.99.3.156-166

Dourish, P. (2006). Re-space-ing place: "Place" and "space" ten years on. In *Proceedings of the 2006 20th Anniversary Conference on Computer Supported Cooperative Work,* (pp. 299-308). New York, NY: ACM.

Dourish, P., Finlay, J., Sengers, P., & Wright, P. (2004). Reective HCI: Towards a critical technical practice. In *Proceedings of CHI 2004 Conference on Computer Human Interaction 2004.* CHI.

Downes, T. (1999). Playing with computing technologies in the home. *Education and Information Technologies, 4*(1), 65–79. doi:10.1023/A:1009607432286

Doyle, C., & Robson, K. (2002). *Accessible curricula - Good practice for all.* Retrieved 06/08/11 from http://www.uwic.ac.uk/ltsu/accessible.pdf

Draganova, C. (2009). *Use of mobile phone technologies in the classroom context, in mobile learning cultures across education, work and leisure.* Paper presented at the 3rd WLE Mobile Learning Symposium. London, UK. Retrieved on June 15, 2011 from http://symposium.londonmobilelearning.net/?page=Programme

Draper, S. W., & Brown, M. I. (2004). Increasing interactivity in lectures using an electronic voting system. *Journal of Computer Assisted Learning, 20,* 81–94. doi:10.1111/j.1365-2729.2004.00074.x

Dromi, G. P., & Krampf, Z. (1986). Programming revisited: The miftan experience. *Social Work with Groups, 9,* 91–105. doi:10.1300/J009v09n01_08

Drury, J., Hirschman, L., Kurtz, J., Fanderclai, T., Damianos, L., & Linton, F. (1999). Methodology for evaluation of collaboration systems. *ACM SIGGROUP Bulletin, 20*(2), 50–51.

Ducheneau, N. (2010). Massively multiplayer online games as living laboratories: Opportunities and pitfalls. In Bainbridge, W. S. (Ed.), *Online Worlds: Convergence of the Real and the Virtual* (pp. 135–145). London, UK: Springer. doi:10.1007/978-1-84882-825-4_11

Dumas, J. S., & Redish, J. C. (1994). *A practical guide to usability testing.* Exeter, UK: Intellect Books.

Duncan-Howell, J., & Lee, K. T. (2007). *M-learning innovations and initiatives: Finding a place for mobile technologies within tertiary educational settings.* Paper presented at the ASCILITE Annual Conference. Singapore. Retrieved on May 6, 2011 from http://www.ascilite.org.au/conferences/singapore07/procs/duncan-howell.pdf

Dunn, S. (2003). *Return to SENDA? Implementing accessibility for disabled students in virtual learning environments in UK further and higher education.* London, UK: City University London. Retrieved from http://www.saradunn-associates.net/uploads/tx_policyreports/CityEU_VLEreport.pdf

Duranti, A. (1986). The audience as co-author: An introduction. *Text, 6,* 239–247. doi:10.1515/text.1.1986.6.3.239

Eagle, M., & Barnes, T. (2010). Intelligent tutoring systems, educational data mining, and the design and evaluation of video games. intelligent tutoring systems. *Lecture Notes in Computer Science, 6095,* 215–217. doi:10.1007/978-3-642-13437-1_23

Ebner, M., & Holzinger, A. (2007). Successful implementation of user-centred game based learning in higher education: An example from civil engineering. *Computers & Education, 49,* 873–890. doi:10.1016/j.compedu.2005.11.026

Egenfeldt-Nielsen, S. (2007). *Beyond edutainment: The educational potential of computer games.* London, UK: Continuum Press.

EIAA. (2010). *New decade heralds the age of digital mobility.* Retrieved on May 6, 2011 from www.eiaa.net/news/eiaa-articlesdetails.asp?lang=1&id=216

Eisenstadt, M. (2007). Does elearning have to be so awful? Time to mashup or shutup. In *Proceedings of the Seventh IEEE International Conference on Advanced Learning Technologies (ICALT 2007),* (pp. 6-10). IEEE Press.

Elkonin, D. B. (1998). *Psicologia do jogo.* São Paulo, Brazil: Martins Fontes.

Elverdam, C., & Aarseth, E. (2007). Game classification as game design: Construction through critical analysis. In *Proceedings of DiGRA 2005.* DiGRA.

Endsley, M. (1995). Toward a theory of situation awareness in dynamic systems. *Human Factors, 37*(1), 32–64. doi:10.1518/001872095779049543

English Encarta Dictionary. (2011). *Motivation.* Retrieved on May 6, 2011 from http://encarta.msn.com/encnet/features/dictionary/dictionaryhome.aspx

Eric_Drav3n, allan_delacruz, & Lethal Intake. (2011, June 13 & 18). *Comments on the stage demo of the newest Tombraider game.* [Online forum comment]. Retrieved July 18, 2011 from http://www.gamespot.com/ps3/action/tomb-raider-2012/video/6318948/tomb-raider-e3-2011-stage-demo

Estallo, J. A. (1995). *Los videojuegos: Juicios y prejuicios.* Barcelona, Spain: Paidós.

Evans, D., & Taylor, J. (2005). The role of user scenarios as the central piece of the development jigsaw puzzle. In Attewell, J., & Savill-Smith, C. (Eds.), *Mobile Learning Anytime Everywhere: Papers from Mlearn 2004.* Mlearn.

Fabricatore, C., Nussbaum, M., & Rosas, R. (2002). Playability in action videogames: A qualitative design model. *Human-Computer Interaction, 17*, 311–368. doi:10.1207/S15327051HCI1704_1

Facer, K., Faux, F., & McFarlane, A. (2005). *Challenges and opportunities: Making mobile learning a reality in schools.* Retrieved on May 6, 2011 from http://www.mlearn.org.za/papers-full.html

Falstein, N. (2002). Better by design: The 400 project. *Game Developer Magazine, 9*(3), 26.

Federici, S. (2005). Checking an integrated model of web accessibility and usability evaluation for disabled people. *Disability and Rehabilitation, 27*(13), 781–790. doi:10.1080/09638280400014766

Federoff, M. (2002). *Heuristics and usability guidelines for the creation and evaluation of fun in video games.* (Master of Science Thesis). Indiana University. Retrieved Februry 08, 2009, from http://citeseerx.ist.psu.edu/viewdoc/download?doi=10.1.1.89.8294&rep=rep1&type=pdf

Felicia, P. (2009). *Digital games in schools: A handbook for teachers.* London, UK: European Schoolnet EUN Partnership AISBL.

Fernández Muñoz, L., & Velázquez Iturbide, J. Á. (2006). Estudio sobre la visualización de las técnicas de diseño de algoritmos. In *Proceedings of Actas del VII Congreso Internacional de Interacción Persona-Ordenador – Interacción 2006,* (pp. 315-324). Salamanca, Spain: AIPO.

Fernández-Muñoz, L., Pérez-Carrasco, A., Velázquez-Iturbide, J. Á., & Urquiza-Fuentes, J. (2007). A framework for the automatic generation of algorithm animations based on design techniques. In Duval, E., Klamma, R., & Wolpers, M. (Eds.), *Creating New Learning Experiences on a Global Scale – EC-TEL 2007* (pp. 475–480). Berlin, Germany: Springer-Verlag. doi:10.1007/978-3-540-75195-3_40

Field, A. (2009). *Discovering statistics using SPSS* (3rd ed.). London, UK: SAGE.

Fincher, S., & Utting, I. (Eds.). (2010). Special issue on initial learning environments. *ACM Transactions on Computing Education, 10*(4).

Fincher, S., & Petre, M. (Eds.). (2004). *Computer science education research.* London, UK: Rouledge Falmer.

Fink, J., & Kobsa, A. (2000). A review and analysis of commercial user modeling servers for personalization on the world wide web. *User Modeling and User-Adapted Interaction, 10*(2-3), 209–249. doi:10.1023/A:1026597308943

Fischer, K. W. (1980). A theory of cognitive development: The control and construction of hierarchies of skills. *Psychological Review, 87*(6), 477–531. doi:10.1037/0033-295X.87.6.477

Flynt, J. P. (2004). *Software engineering for game developers.* New York, NY: Thomson.

France, L., Heraud, J.-M., Marty, J.-C., Carron, T., & Heili, J. (2006. Monitoring virtual classroom: Visualization techniques to observe student activities in an e-learning system. In *Proceedings of the ICALT,* (pp. 716–720). IEEE Computer Society.

Franco, J. F., et al. (2006). Computer graphics, interactive technologies and collaborative learning synergy supporting individuals' skills development. In *Proceedings of the 33rd International Conference and Exhibition on Computer Graphics and Interactive Techniques, SIGGRAPH 2006.* Boston, MA: ACM.

Fredrickson, B. L., & Joiner, T. (2002). Positive emotions trigger upward spirals toward emotional well-being. *Psychological Science, 13*, 172–175. doi:10.1111/1467-9280.00431

French, J. W. (1951). The description of aptitude and achievement tests in terms of rotated factors. *Psychometric Monograph, 5*.

Freudenthal Institute for Science and Mathematics Education of Utrecht University. (2009). *Wisweb*. Retrieved July 15, 2011, from http://www.fi.uu.nl/wisweb/en/welcome.html

Fromberg, D. P. (1992). A review of research on play. In Seefeldt, C. (Ed.), *The Early Childhood Curriculum: A Review of Current Research* (2nd ed., pp. 42–84). New York, NY: Teachers College Press.

Frontend.com. (2001). *Why people can't use elearning*. Retrieved 04/08/11 from http://www.infocentre.frontend.com/uploaded_files/eLearning_white_paper.pdf

Fuller, U., Johnson, C. G., Ahoniemi, T., Cukierman, D., Hernán-Losada, I., & Jackova, J. (2007). Developing a computer science-specific learning taxonomy. *SIGCSE Bulletin, 39*(4), 152–170. doi:10.1145/1345375.1345438

Fussell, S., Kraut, R., Lerch, F., Scherlis, W., McNally, M., & Cadiz, J. (1998). Coordination, overload and team performance: Effects of team communication strategies. In *Proceedings of CSCW 1998*. Seattle, WA: CSCW.

Gabrielli, S., Mirabella, V., Kimani, S., & Catarci, T. (2005). Supporting cognitive walkthrough with video data: A mobile learning evaluation study. In *Proceedings of the 7th International Conference on Human Computer Interaction with Mobile Devices & Services, MobileHCI 2005,* (pp. 77-82). MobileHCI.

Galiano, V., Herranz, M. V., Perea, M. C., Polo, I., & Sánchez, J. (2008). *A virtual museum of mathematics: MUMART*. Paper presented at Fifth European Congress of Mathematics. Amsterdam, The Netherlands.

Gallo, S. (1997). *El paradigma anarquista de educación*. Retrieved May 15, 2011 from http://www.flyingmind.com/plataforma/doc7

Gardner, H. (1999). *Intelligence reformed: Multiple intelligences for the 21ˢᵗ century*. New York, NY: Basic Books.

Gardner, H., & Boix Mansilla, V. (1994). Teaching for understanding within and across the disciplines. *Educational Leadership, 51*(5), 14–18.

Garris, R., Ahlers, R., & Driskell, J. E. (2002). Games, motivation, and learning: A research and practice model. *Simulation & Gaming, 33*(4), 441–467. doi:10.1177/1046878102238607

Gartner Inc. (2010). *Gartner says worldwide media tablet sales on pace to reach 19.5 million units in 2010*. Retrieved August 15, 2011, from http://www.gartner.com/it/page.jsp?id=1452614

Gay, G., Stefanone, M., Grace-Martin, M., & Hembrooke, H. (2001). The effects of wireless computing in collaborative learning environments. *International Journal of Human-Computer Interaction, 13*(2), 257–276. doi:10.1207/S15327590IJHC1302_10

Gee, J. P., & Hayes, E. (2009). Public pedagogy through video games: Design, resources & affinity spaces. *Game Based Learning*. Retrieved from http://www.game-basedlearning.org.uk/content/view/59/

Gentile, D. A., Anderson, C. A., Yukawa, S., Ihori, N., Saleem, M., & Ming, L. M. (2009). The effects of prosocial video games on prosocial behaviors: International evidence from correlational, longitudinal, and experimental studies. *Personality and Social Psychology Bulletin, 35*(6), 752–763. doi:10.1177/0146167209333045

Gesueli, Z. M., & Almeida, R. S. (2003). *As histórias em quadrinhos eletrônicas e o processo de letramento de alunos surdos*. Retrieved from http://www.alb.com/anais14/Sem10/C10019.doc

Gibbons, R., & Katz, L. (1991). Layoffs and lemons. *Journal of Labor Economics, 9*(4), 351–380. doi:10.1086/298273

Gimmestad, B. J. (1990). Gender differences in spatial visualization and predictors of success in an engineering design course. In *Proceedings of the National Conference on Women in Mathematics and the Sciences,* (pp. 133-136). St. Cloud, MN: Women in Mathematics and the Sciences.

Giner de los Ríos, F. (1988). *Antología pedagógica*. Madrid, Spain: Santillana.

Glassner, A. (2004). *Interactive storytelling: Techniques for 21st century fiction*. Boca Raton, FL: CRC Press.

Godinho, E. B. (2008). *Incorporais RPG: Design poético para um jogo de representação*. Rio de Janeiro, Brazil: Pontifícia Universidade Católica do Rio de Janeiro.

Goffman, E. (1959). *The presentation of self in everyday life*. New York, NY: Doubleday.

Goleman, D. (1996). *Emotional intelligence: Why it can matter more than IQ*. London, UK: Bloomsbury.

Golub, A. (2010). Being in the world (of warcraft): Raiding, realism, and knowledge production in a massively multiplayer online game. *Anthropological Quarterly*, *83*(1), 17–45. doi:10.1353/anq.0.0110

González Sánchez, J. L. (2010). *Jugabilidad: Caracterización de la experiencia del jugador en videojuegos*. (PhD Thesis). University of Granada. Granada, Spain. Retrieved March July 15, 2010, from http://hdl.handle.net/10481/5671

González Sánchez, J. L. (2010). *Playability the characterization of player experience in video game*. (Doctoral Dissertation). Granada University. Granada, Spain. Retrieved November 8, 2011, from http://digibug.ugr.es/handle/10481/5671

González Sánchez, J. L. (2011) *Jugabilidad y videojuegos: Análisis y diseño de la experiencia del jugador en sistemas interactivos de ocio electrónico*. Barcelona, Spain: Lambert Academic Publishing GmbH & Co (Ed.)

González Sánchez, J. L., Gil Iranzo, R. M., & Gutiérrez Vela, F. L. (2011). *Enriching evaluation in video games*. In P. Campos et al. (Eds.), *13th IFIP TC13 Conference on Human-Computer Interaction*, (pp. 519–522). Springer.

González Sánchez, J. L., Montero, F., Padilla Zea, N., & Gutiérrez, F. L. (2009). Playability as extension of quality in use in video games. In *Proceedings of the 2nd International Workshop on the Interplay between Usability Evaluation and Software Development (I-USED)*, (Vol. 490), (pp. 37 – 43). Berlin, Germany: Springer.

González Sánchez, J. L., Padilla Zea, N., & Gutiérrez, F. L. (2009). From usability to playability: Introduction to player-centred video game development process. In M. Kurosu (Ed.), *Proceedings of the Human-Computer Interaction International - Human Centered Design 2009*, (pp. 65–74). Berlin, Germany: Springer.

González Sánchez, J. L., Padilla Zea, N., & Gutiérrez, F. L. (2009). Playability: How to identify the player experience in a video game. In T. Gross (Ed.), *Proceedings of the 12th IFIP TC13 Conference on Human-Computer Interaction 2009*, (pp. 356-359). Berlin, Germany: Springer.

González Sánchez, J. L., Padilla Zea, N., Gutiérrez, F. L., Cabrera, M., & Paderewski, P. (2008). Playability: The secret of the educational videogame design. In T. Conolly & M. Stansfield (Eds.), *2nd European Conference on Games Bases Learning (ECGBL 2008)*, (pp. 147-156). Paisley, UK: ECGBL.

González Sánchez, J. L. (2010). *Jugabilidad: Caracterización de la experiencia del jugador en videojuegos*. Granada, Spain: Universidad de Granada.

González Sánchez, J. L., Gil Iranzo, R., & Gutiérrez Vela, F. L. (2011). Enriching evaluation in video games. *Lecture Notes in Computer Science*, *6949*, 519–522. doi:10.1007/978-3-642-23768-3_72

González Sánchez, J. L., Padilla Zea, N., & Gutiérrez, F. L. (2009). Playability: How to identify the player experience in a video game. *Lecture Notes in Computer Science*, *5726*, 356–359. doi:10.1007/978-3-642-03655-2_39

González, C. S., Toledo, P., Alayón, S., Muñoz, V., & Meneses, D. (2011). Using information and communication technologies in hospital classrooms: Saveh project. *Knowledge Management & E-Learning. International Journal (Toronto, Ont.)*, *3*(1).

González-González, C. S., & Blanco-Izquierdo, F. (2012). Designing social videogames for educational uses. *Revista: Computers & Education*, *58*, 250–262.

González, M. B., & Rodríguez, P. A. (2003). Un instrumento para evaluar el uso y las actitudes hacia los videojuegos. *Revista de Medios y Educación*, *20*, 17–32.

Gopinath, B., Baur, L. A., Wang, J. J., Hardy, L. L., Teber, E., & Kifley, A. (2011). Influence of physical activity and screen time on the retinal microvasculature in young children. *Arteriosclerosis, Thrombosis, and Vascular Biology*, *31*, 1233–1239. doi:10.1161/ATVBAHA.110.219451

Gould, J. D., & Lewis, C. (1985). Designing for usability: Key principles and what designers think. *Communications of the AMC*, *2*(3), 300–311. doi:10.1145/3166.3170

Grammenos, D., Savidis, A., & Stephanidis, C. (2009). Designing universally accessible games. *ACM Computers in Entertainment, 7*(1), 8:1-8:28.

Greenfield, S. (2008). *Creating creative brains*. Paper presented at CCI's Creating Value: Between Commerce and Commons conference. Brisbane, Australia. Retrieved July 11, 2011, from http://cci.edu.au/presentations/creating-value-conference-presentations

Greenfield, P., & Cocking, R. (Eds.). (1996). *Interacting with video: Advances in applied developmental psychology*. Los Angeles, CA: Ablex Publishing Corporation & University of California.

Green, H., & Hannon, C. (2007). *Their space: Education for a digital generation*. London, UK: DEMOS.

Greitemeyer, T., & Osswald, S. (2010). Effects of prosocial video games on prosocial behavior. *Journal of Personality and Social Psychology, 98*(2), 211–221. doi:10.1037/a0016997

Gress, C. L. Z., Fior, M., Hadwin, A. F., & Winne, P. H. (2010). Measurement and assessment in computer-supported collaborative learning. *Computers in Human Behavior, 26*(5), 806–814. doi:10.1016/j.chb.2007.05.012

Grudin, J. (1994). CSCW: History and focus. *IEEE Computer, 27*(5), 19–26. doi:10.1109/2.291294

Guerrero, L., Alarcón, R., Collazos, C., Pino, J., & Fuller, D. (2000a). Evaluating cooperation in group work. In *Proceedings of CRIWG 2000*. Madeira, Portugal: IEEE Computer Society Press.

Guerrero, L., Alarcón, R., Collazos, C., Pino, J., & Fuller, D. (2000b). Evaluating cooperation in group work. In *Proceedings of the Sixth International Workshop on Groupware, CRIWG 2000*. Madeira, Portugal: IEEE Press.

Guilford, J. P., & Lacy, J. I. (1947). *Printed classification tests. AAF Aviation Psycological Progess Research Report, No. 5*. Washington, DC: US Government Printing Office.

Guimarães, D. S., & Simão, L. M. (2008). A negociação intersubjetiva de significados em jogo de interpretação de papéis. *Psicologia: Teoria e Pesquisa (Brasília), 24*(4), 433–439. doi:10.1590/S0102-37722008000400006

Gunawardena, C. N., Lowe, C. A., & Anderson, T. (1997). Analysis of a global online debate and the development of an interaction analysis model for examining social construction of knowledge in computer conferencing. *Journal of Educational Computing Research, 17*, 395–429. doi:10.2190/7MQV-X9UJ-C7Q3-NRAG

Gutwin, C., & Greenberg, S. (2002). A descriptive framework of workspace awareness for real-time groupware. *Computer Supported Cooperative Work, 11*, 411–446. doi:10.1023/A:1021271517844

Gutwin, C., & Greenberg, S. (2004). The importance of awareness for team cognition in distributed collaboration. In Salas, E., & Fiore, S. M. (Eds.), *Team Cognition: Understanding the Factors that Drive Process and Performance* (pp. 177–201). Washington, DC: APA Press. doi:10.1037/10690-009

Guzdial, M. (1997). Information ecology of collaborations in educational settings: Influence of tool. In *Proceedings of CSCL 1997*. Toronto, Canada: CSCL.

Hadwin, A. F., Oshige, M., Gress, C. L. Z., & Winne, P. H. (2010). Innovative ways for using gStudy ot orchestrate and research social aspects of self-regulated learning. *Computers in Human Behavior, 26*(5), 794–805. doi:10.1016/j.chb.2007.06.007

Han, D. H., Lee, Y. S., Yang, K. C., Kim, E. Y., Lyoo, I. K., & Renshaw, P. F. (2007). Dopamine genes and reward dependence in adolescents with excessive internet video game play. *Journal of Addiction Medicine, 1*(3), 133–138. doi:10.1097/ADM.0b013e31811f465f

Harré, R., & Langenhove, L. V. (1991). Varieties of positioning. *Journal for the Theory of Social Behaviour, 21*(4), 393–407. doi:10.1111/j.1468-5914.1991.tb00203.x

Harris, D., & Bell, C. (1986). *Evaluating and assessing for learning*. London, UK: Kogan Page.

Harteveld, C., Bekebrede, G., Lo, J. C., Plomber, A.-J., & Jordaan, B. (2011). *Make it fun or real: Design dilemmas and their consequences on the learning experience*. Paper presented at ISAGA 2011: Bonds and Bridges. Warsaw, Poland.

Harteveld, C. (2011). *Triadic game design: Balancing reality, meaning and play*. London, UK: Springer.

Hassenzahl, M. (2003). The thing and I: Understanding the relationship between user and product. In Blythe, M., Overbeeke, C., Monk, A. F., & Wright, P. C. (Eds.), *Funology: From Usability to Enjoyment* (pp. 31–42). Dordrecht, The Netherlands: Kluwer Academic Publishers. doi:10.1007/1-4020-2967-5_4

Hayes, E. (2008). Girls, gaming and trajectories of IT experience. In Kafai, Y., Heeter, C., Denner, J., & Sun, J. (Eds.), *Beyond Barbie and Mortal Kombat: New Perspectives on Gender and Gaming* (pp. 217–230). Cambridge, MA: MIT Press.

Hersh, M. A. (2008). Accessibility and usability of virtual learning environments. In *Proceedings of the 8th IEEE International Conference on Advanced Learning Technologies*. Santander, Spain: IEEE Press.

Hersh, M. A. (2009). *Examples of alternative text descriptions*. Retrieved August 5 2011 from http://www.elec.gla.ac.uk/Events_page/CVHI/cvhi/pages/instructions-for-authors.php

Hersh, M. A. (2010). *Methodological issues in multi-country multi-language participative research with blind and visually impaired people*. Paper presented at SWIIS 2010. Pristina, Kosovo.

Hersh, M. A. (2011). *Participative research with diverse end-user groups: Multi-language, multi-country blind and visually impaired people*. Paper presented at the 17th IFAC Congress. Milan, Italy.

Hersh, M. A., & Leporini, B. (2008). Making conference CDs accessible: A practical example. In *Proceedings of the 11th International Conference on Computers Helping People with Special Needs (ICCHP 2008)*. Linz, Austria: ICCHP.

Hersh, M. A., & Leporini, B. (2009). *Paper template*. Retrieved from http://www.elec.gla.ac.uk/Events_page/CVHI/cvhi/pages/instructions-for-authors.php

Higher Education Academy. (2010). *What is a VLE?* Retrieved 11/08/11 from http://www.ukcle.ac.uk/resources/trns/vles/one.html

Hill, J. L., & Lance, C. G. (2002). Debriefing stress. *Simulation & Gaming, 33*, 490–503. doi:10.1177/1046878102238613

Hofstede, G. (1991). *Cultures and organizations: Software of the mind*. London, UK: McGraw-Hill.

Holden, C. (2001). Behavioral addictions: Do they exist? *Science, 294,* 980-982. Retrieved July 18, 2011 from http://www.sciencemag.org

Holtz, P., & Appel, M. (2011). Internet use and video gaming predict problem behavior in early adolescence. *Journal of Adolescence, 34*(1), 49–58. doi:10.1016/j.adolescence.2010.02.004

Holzinger, A., Nischelwitzer, A., & Meisenberger, M. (2005). Mobile phones as a challenge for m-Learning: Examples for mobile interactive learning objects. In *Proceedings of the 3rd International Conference on Pervasive Computing and Communications Workshops*. Kauai Island, HI: IEEE.

Horrigan, J. (2007). *Older Americans and the internet: A typology of information and communication technology users*. Retrieved from http://www.pewinternet.org/PPF/r/213/reportdisplay:asp

Hromek, R. P. (2005). *Game time: Games to promote social and emotional resilience for children aged 4-14*. London, UK: Paul Chapman.

Hromek, R. P. (2004). *Planting the peace virus: Early intervention to prevent violence in schools*. Bristol, UK: Lucky Duck.

Hromek, R. P. (2007). *Emotional coaching: A practical programme to support young people*. London, UK: Paul Chapman.

Hsi, S., Linn, M. C., & Bell, J. E. (1997). The role of spatial reasoning in engineering and the design of spatial instruction. *Journal of Engineering Education, 86*(2), 151–158.

Hughes, P. (1998). Exploring visual literacy across the curriculum. In Evans, J. (Ed.), *What in the Picture Books*. London, UK: Paul Chapman Publishing.

Hui-Yin, H., & Shiang-Kwei, W. (2010). Using gaming literacies to cultivate new literacies. *Simulation & Gaming, 41*(3), 400–417. doi:10.1177/1046878109355361

Huizinga, J. (2007). *Homo ludens*. Madrid, Spain: Alianza Editorial.

Hupont, I., Cerezo, E., & Baldassarri, S. (2010). *Sensing facial emotions in a continuous 2D affective space*. In *Proceedings of the International Conference on Systems, Man, and Cybernetics,* (pp. 2045-2051). IEEE Press.

Ibrahim, A., Gutiérrez, F. L., González Sánchez, J. L., & Padilla Zea, N. (2011). Playability design pattern in educational video games. In T. Conolly & M. Stansfield (Eds.), *5th European Conference on Games Bases Learning (ECGBL 2011).* ECGBL.

Ibrahim, A., Gutiérrez, F. L., González Sánchez, J. L., & Padilla Zea, N. (2012). Educational playability analyzing player experiences in educational video game. In *Proceedings of The Fifth International Conference on Advances in Computer-Human Interactions ACHI 2012.* Valencia, Spain: ACHI.

Ibrahim, A., Gutiérrez-Vela, F., González-Sánchez, J. L., & Padilla-Zea, N. (2012). Educational playability: Analyzing player experiences in educational video games. In *Proceedings of ACHI 2012: The Fifth International Conference on Advances in Computer-Human Interactions,* (pp. 326-335). ACHI. Gee, J. P. (2003). *What digital games have to teach us about learning and literacy.* New York, NY: Palgrave Macmillan.

IGDA. (2004). *Accesibility in games: Motivations and approaches.* Retrieved March 15, 2010, from http://www.igda.org/accessibility/

Ignelzi, M. (2000). Meaning-making in the learning and teaching process. *New Directions for Teaching and Learning, 82,* 5–14. doi:10.1002/tl.8201

Ihantola, P., Ahoniemi, T., Karavirta, V., & Seppälä, O. (2010). Review of recent systems for automatic assessment of programming assignments. In *Proceedings of the Tenth Koli Calling Conference on Computer Science Education – Koli Calling 2010,* (pp. 86-93). New York, NY: ACM Press.

Ihantola, P., Karavirta, V., Korhonen, A., & Nikander, J. (2005). Taxonomy of effortless creation of algorithm visualization. In *Proceedings of the 2005 International Workshop on Computing Education Research – ICER 2005,* (pp. 123-133). New York, NY: ACM Press.

Inaba, A., & Okamoto, T. (1997). The intelligent discussion coordinating system for effective collaborative learning. In *Proceedings of the IV Collaborative Learning Workshop in the International Conference AI-ED 1997.* Kobe, Japan: AI-ED.

Isbister, K., & Schaffer, N. (Eds.). (2008). *Game usability: Advancing the player experience.* New York, NY: Morgan Kaufmann.

ISO. (1998). *ISO 9241-11: Ergonomic requirements for office work with visual display terminals (CDTs): Part 11: Guidance on usability.* Geneva, Switzerland: International Standards Organization.

ISO/IEC 25010. (2011). *Software product quality requirements and evaluation (SQuaRE): Software product quality and system quality in use models.* ISO.

ISO/IEC 9241-210. (2010). *Ergonomics of human–system interaction: Human centred design for interactive systems.* Clausule 2.15.

ITU. (2010). *Key global telecom indicators for the world telecommunication service sector.* International Communications Union. Retrieved on May 6, 2011 from http://www.itu.int/ITU-D/ict/statistics/at_glance/KeyTelecom.html

Jarboe, S. (1996). Procedures for enhancing group decision making. In Hirokawa, B., & Poole, M. (Eds.), *Communication and Group Decision Making* (pp. 345–383). Thousand Oaks, CA: Sage Publications.

Jarmin. (2012). *Accessibility guide.* Retrieved from from http://jarmin.com/accessibility

Järvien, A., Heliö, S., & Mäyrä, F. (2002). *Communication and community in digital entertainment services.* Retrieved May 10, 2011, from http://www.arts.rpi.edu/public_html/ruiz/public_html/EGDFall09/readings/Creating%20communityUniv.of%20Tampere.pdf

Jenkins, H. (2007). Confronting the chalenges of the parcipatory culture: Media education for the 21° century. *Nordic Journal of Media Literacy.* Retrieved January 18, 2011, from http://www.newmedialiteracies.org/files/working/NMLWhitePaper.pdf

Jensen, J. J. (1986). The impact of computer graphics on instruction in engineering graphics. *Engineering Design Graphics Journal, 50*(2), 24–33.

Johansen, R. (1988). *Groupware: Computer support for business teams.* New York, NY: The Free Press.

Johnson, D., & Johnson, R. (1978). Cooperative, competitive, and individualistic learning. *Journal of Research and Development in Education, 12,* 8–15.

Johnson, D., & Johnson, R. (1995). *My mediation notebook* (3rd ed.). Edina, MN: Interaction Book Company.

Johnson, D., Johnson, R., & Holubec, E. (1990). *Circles of learning: Cooperation in the classroom* (3rd ed.). Edina, MN: Interaction Book Company.

Joinson, A. N. (2003). *Understanding the psychology of internet behaviour: Virtual worlds, real lives.* New York, NY: Palgrave Macmillan.

Joint Information Systems Committee. (2000). *Managed learning environments (MLEs) in further education: Progress report.* Retrieved 11/08/11 from http://www.jisc.ac.uk/news/stories/2000/07/circular700.aspx

Joint Information Systems Committee. (2002). *Briefing paper no 1- MLEs and VLEs explained.* Retrieved 04/08/11 from http://www.jisc.ac.uk/uploaded_documents/bp1.pdf

Jones, M. G. (1998). *Creating engagement in computer-based learning environments.* Retrieved from http://itech1.coe.uga.edu/itforum/paper30/paper30.html

Jones, P., Packham, G., Miller, C., Davies, I., & Jones, A. (2003). e-Retention: An initial evaluation of student withdrawals within a virtual learning environment. In R. Williams (Ed.), *Proceedings of the 2nd European Confrence on eLearning,* (pp. 239-248). Reading, MA: Academic Conferences International.

Jones, K. (1999). With appropriate panache. *Simulation & Gaming, 30,* 327–331. doi:10.1177/104687819903000307

Jones, K. (2004). Fear of emotions. *Simulation & Gaming, 35,* 454–460. doi:10.1177/1046878104269893

Jonhson, D. W., & Jonhson, R. T. (1998). Cooperative learning and social interdependence theory. In Tindale, R., Heath, L., Edwards, J., Posavac, E., Bryant, F., & Suarez-Balcazar, Y. (Eds.), *Theory and Research on Small Groups* (pp. 9–36). London, UK: Springer.

Jonnes, A., & Issrof, K. (2005). Learning technologies: Affective and social issues in computer-supported collaborative learning. *Computers & Education, 44,* 395–408. doi:10.1016/j.compedu.2004.04.004

Jurado, F., Molina, A. I., Redondo, M. A., Ortega, M., Giemza, A., Bollen, L., & Hoppe, H. U. (2009). Learning to program with COALA: A distributed computer assisted environment. *Journal of Universal Computer Science, 15*(7), 1472–1485.

Juul, J. (2005). *Half-real: Video games between real rules and fictional worlds.* Cambridge, MA: MIT Press.

Kagan, J. (1998). *Galen's prophecy.* Boulder, CO: Westview Press.

Kahne, J., Middaugh, E., & Evans, C. (2009). *The civic potential of video games.* Cambridge, MA: MIT Press.

Karoly, L. A., Greenwood, P. W., Everingham, S. S., Hoube, J., Kilburn, S. R., Rydell, C. P., & Chiesa, J. (1998). *Investing in our children: What we know and don't know about the costs and benefits of early interventions.* Santa Monica, CA: RAND.

Katz, S. (1999). The cognitive skill of coaching collaboration. In *Proceedings CSCL 1999.* Mahwah, NJ: Lawrence Erlbaum Associates.

Katz, Y. J., & Yablon, Y. B. (2010). Affect and digital learning at the university level. *Campus-Wide Information Systems, 28*(2), 114–123. doi:10.1108/10650741111117815

Kauchakje, S. (2003). Comunidade surda: As demandas identitárias no campo dos direitos, da inclusão e da participação social. In Silva, I. R., Kauchakje, S., & Gesueli, Z. M. (Eds.), *Cidadania, Surdez E Linguagem: Desafios e Realidades* (pp. 57–76). São Paulo, Brazil: Plexus.

Keegan, C. (2011). *Student learning styles*. Retrieved on May 6, 2011 from http://www.ast.org/pdf/TeachandLearn_Stu.pdf

Kegan, R. (1982). *The evolving self: problem and process in human development*. Cambridge, MA: Harvard University Press.

Kegan, R. (1994). *In over our heads: The mental demands of modern life*. Cambridge, MA: Harvard University Press.

Kegan, R., & Lahey, L. (2009). *Immunity to change: How to overcome it and unlock the potential in yourself and your organisation*. Boston, MA: Harvard Business School Press.

Kegan, R., Noam, G., & Rodgers, L. (1982). The psychologic of emotion: A neo-piagetian view. In Chichetti, D., & Pogge-Hesse, P. (Eds.), *Emotional Development*. San Francisco, CA: Jossey-Bass Publishers. doi:10.1002/cd.23219821606

Keller, J. M. (2008). First principles of motivation to learn and e³ learning. *Distance Education, 29*(2), 175–185. doi:10.1080/01587910802154970

Kelly, B., Sloan, D., Brown, S., Seale, J., Petrie, H., Lauke, P., & Ball, S. (2007). *Accessibility 2.0: People, policies and processes*. Paper presented at the International Cross-Disciplinary Conference on Web Accessibility (W4A). Banff, Canada.

Kelly, B., Sloan, D., Phipps, L., Petrie, H., & Hamilton, F. (2005). *Forcing standardization or accommodating diversity? A framework for applying the WCAG in the real world*. Paper presented at the International Cross-Disciplinary Workshop on Web Accessibility (W4A). Chiba, Japan.

Kent, T. (2003). Supporting staff using WebCT at the University of Birmingham in the UK. *Electronic Journal of e-Learning, 1*(1), 1-10.

Kerckhove, D. (1999). *Inteligencias en conexión: Hacia una sociedad de la web*. Barcelona, Spain: Editorial Gedisa.

Kickmeier-Rust, M. D. (2009). Talking digital educational games. In M. D. Kickmeier-Rust (Ed.), *Proceedings of the 1st International Open Workshop on Intelligent Personalization and Adaptation in Digital Educational Games*, (pp. 55-66). Graz, Austria: IEEE.

Kiili, K. (2010). Call for learning-game design patterns. In Edvardsen, F., & Kulle, H. (Eds.), *Educational Games: Design, Learning, and Applications* (pp. 299–311). New York, NY: Nova Publishers.

King, P. M., & Baxter Magolda, M. B. (1996). A development perspective on learning. *Journal of College Student Development, 37*, 163–173.

Kishimoto, T. M. (2002). Bruner e a brincadeira. In Kishimoto, T. M. (Ed.), *O Brincar e suas Teorias* (pp. 139–154). São Paulo, Brazil: Pioneira Thomson Learning.

Kissane, A., & Finn, E. (2003). Development of a usability model for VLE deployment. In *Proceedings of ILTA, EdTech 2003*. Retrieved 11/05/10 from http://www.ilta.net/EdTech2003/papers/FinnKissane.doc

Klabbers, J. H. B. (2006). *The magic circle: Principles of gaming and simulation*. Rotterdam, The Netherlands: Sense.

Klapproth, D. M. (2004). *Narrative as social practice: Anglo-Western and Australian Aboriginal oral tradition*. Berlin, Germany: Walter de Gruyter Gmbh & Co.

Klein, M. (2005). Os discursos sobre surdez, trabalho e educação e a formação do surdo trabalhador. In Skliar, C. (Ed.), *A Surdez: Um Olhar Sobre as Diferenças* (3rd ed., pp. 75–94). Porto Alegre, Brazil: Mediação.

Klemmer, S. R., & Hartmann, B. (2006). How bodies matter: Five themes for interaction design. In *Proceedings of Design of Interactive Systems* (*Vol. 74*, pp. 140–149). DIS.

Kniberg, H. (2007). *Scrum and XP from the trenches: How we do scrum*. Enterprise Software Development Series.

Knutilla, A. J., Steves, M. P., & Allen, R. H. (2000). Paper In *Proceedings of the Workshop on Evaluating Collaborative Enterprises 2000*. Infrastructure for Collaborative Enterprises.

Kobsa, A. (2001). Generic user modeling systems. *User Modeling and User-Adapted Interaction, 11*(1-2), 49–63. doi:10.1023/A:1011187500863

Ko, C., Yen, J., Chen, C., Chen, C., & Yen, C. (2008). Psychiatric comorbidity of internet addiction in college students: An interview study. *CNS Spectrums, 13*(2), 147–153.

Ko, C., Yen, J., Chen, S., Yang, M., Lin, H., & Yen, C. (2009). Proposed diagnostic criteria and the screening and diagnosing tool of Internet addiction in college students. *Comprehensive Psychiatry*, *50*(4), 378–384. doi:10.1016/j.comppsych.2007.05.019

Kolb, D. A. (1984). *Experiential learning: Experience as the source of learning and development*. Englewood Cliffs, NJ: Prentice-Hall.

Korhonen, H., & Koivisto, E. M. I. (2006). *Playability heuristics for mobile games*. Paper presented at MobileHCI 2006. Helsinki, Finland.

Korhonen, H., Paavilainen, J., & Saarenpää, H. (2009). Expert review method in game evaluations - Comparison of two playability heuristic sets. In *Proceedings of the 13th International MindTrek Conference: Everyday Life in the Ubiquitous,* (pp. 74-81). New York, NY: ACM Press.

Koster, R. (2004). *Theory of fun for game design*. New York, NY: Paraglyph Press.

Koster, R. (2005). *A theory of fun for game design*. Scottsdale, AZ: Paraglyph Press.

Krebs, N. F., & Jacobson, M. S. (2003). Prevention of pediatric overweight and obesity. *Pediatrics*, *112*(2), 424–430. doi:10.1542/peds.112.2.424

Kreimeier, B. (2002). *The case for game design patterns*. Retrieved November 8, 2011, from http://www.gamasutra.com/features/20020313/kreimeier_01.htm

Kriz, W. C., & Hense, J. U. (2006). Theory-oriented for the design of and research in gaming and simulation. *Simulation & Gaming*, *37*(2), 268–283. doi:10.1177/1046878106287950

Kukulska-Hulme, A. (2007). Mobile usability in educational contexts: What have we learnt! *International Review of Research in Open and Distance Learning*, *8*(2).

Kukulska-Hulme, A. (2008). Human factors and innovation with mobile devices. In Hansson, T. (Ed.), *Handbook of Research on Digital Information Technologies: Innovations, Methods and Ethical Issues* (pp. 392–403). Hershey, PA: IGI Global. doi:10.4018/978-1-59904-970-0.ch025

Kukulska-Hulme, A., Sharples, M., Milrad, M., Arnedillo-Sánchez, I., & Vavoula, G. (2009). Innovation in mobile learning: A European perspective. *International Journal of Mobile and Blended Learning*, *1*(1), 13–35. doi:10.4018/jmbl.2009010102

Kukulska-Hulme, A., Traxler, J., & Pettit, J. (2007). Designed and user-generated activity in the mobile age. *Journal of Learning Design*, *2*(1), 52–65.

Kylie, A. P., & Yasmin, B. K. (2007). From super goo to scratch: Exploring creative digital media production in informal learning. *Learning, Media and Technology*, *32*(2), 149-166. Retrieved October 31, 2011, from http://www.tandfonline.com/doi/abs/10.1080/17439880701343337

Laffont, J. J., & Martimort, D. (2002). *The theory of incentives*. Princeton, NJ: Princeton University Press.

Lai, C.-H., Yang, J.-C., Chen, F.-C., Ho, C.-W., & Chan, T.-W. (2007). Affordances of mobile technologies for experiential learning: The interplay of technology and pedagogical practices. *Journal of Computer Assisted Learning*, *23*, 326–337. doi:10.1111/j.1365-2729.2007.00237.x

Lakoff, G., & Turner, M. (1988). Categories and analogies. In Helman, D. H. (Ed.), *Analogical Reasoning: Perspectives of Artificial Intelligence, Cognitive Science, and Philosophy* (*Vol. 3*). Chicago, IL: University of Chicago Press.

Law, E., Roto, V., Hassenzahl, M., Vermeeren, A., & Kort, J. (2009). Understanding, scoping and defining user experience: A survey approach. In *Proceedings of the 27th International Conference on Human Factors in Computing Systems (CHI 2009),* (pp. 719-728). New York, NY: ACM.

Law, R. (2002). *Robin's Laws of good game mastering*. New York, NY: Steve Jackson Games.

Laxton, J., & Coulby, C. (2009). *Mobile learning and assessment: The student perspective in mobile learning cultures across education, work and leisure*. Paper presented at the 3rd WLE Mobile Learning Symposium. London, UK. Retrieved on June 15, 2011 from http://symposium.londonmobilelearning.net/?page=Programme

Lazzaro, M. (2008). The four fun key. In Isbister, K., & Schaffer, N. (Eds.), *Game Usability: Advancing the Player Experience* (pp. 315–345). New York, NY: Morgan Kaufmann.

Lee, S. W., Palmer-Brown, D., & Draganova, C. (2008). Diagnostic feedback by snap-drift question response grouping. In *Proceedings of 9th WSEAS International Conference on Neural Networks*, (pp. 208-214). WSEAS.

Leigh, E., & Kinder, J. (1999). *Learning through fun and games*. Sydney, Australia: McGraw-Hill.

Leontiev, A. N. (2001). Os princípios psicológicos da brincadeira pré-escolar. In Vygotsky, L. S., Luria, A. R., & Leontiev, A. (Eds.), *Linguagem, Desenvolvimento e Aprendizagem* (7th ed.). São Paulo, Brazil: Ícone.

Leporini, B., Andronico, P., Buzzi, M., & Castillo, C. (2008). Evaluating a modified Google user interface via screen reader. *Universal Access in the Information Society, 7*(3), 155–175. doi:10.1007/s10209-007-0111-y

Leporini, B., & Paternò, F. (2003). Criteria for usability of accessible web sites. In Carbonell, N., & Stephanidis, C. (Eds.), *User Interfaces for All*. Berlin, Germany: Springer Verlag. doi:10.1007/3-540-36572-9_3

Leporini, B., & Paternò, F. (2008). Applying web usability criteria for vision-impaired users: Does it really improve task performance? *International Journal of Human-Computer Interaction, 24*(1), 17–47. doi:10.1080/10447310701771472

Lewin, K. (1951). *Field theory in social science: Selected theoretical papers*. New York, NY: Harper & Row.

Lewis, R. J. (1995). IBM computer usability satisfaction questionnaires: Psychometric evaluation and instructions for use. *International Journal of Human-Computer Interaction, 7*(1), 57–78. doi:10.1080/10447319509526110

Linn, M. C., & Clancy, M. J. (1992). The case for case studies of programming problems. *Communications of the ACM, 35*(3), 121–132. doi:10.1145/131295.131301

Linn, M. C., & Petersen, A. C. (1985). Emergence and characterization of sex differences in spatial ability: A meta-analysis. *Child Development, 56*(6), 1479–1498. doi:10.2307/1130467

Loeppky, S. (2006). *Gaming and students with Asperger's syndrome: A literature review*. Retrieved from http://www.usask.ca/education/coursework/802papers/loeppky/loeppky.pdf

Lou, Y., Abrami, P. C., & Spence, J. C. (2000). Effects of within-class grouping on student achievement: An exploratory model. *The Journal of Educational Research, 94*, 101–112. doi:10.1080/00220670009598748

Lyardet, D., Rossi, G., & Schwabe, D. (1998). Using design patterns in educational multimedia applications. In *Proceedings of ED-MEDIA 1998*. Freiburg, Germany: ED-MEDIA.

Madera, C. E. (2009). I will never teach the old way again classroom management and external incentives. *Theory into Practice, 48*(2), 147–155. doi:10.1080/00405840902776483

Malliou, F., & Miliarakis, A. (2005). The MOTFAL project: Mobile technologies for ad hoc learning. In Attewell, J., & Savill-Smith, C. (Eds.), *Mobile Learning Anytime Everywhere: Papers from Mlearn 2004*. Mlearn. doi:10.1109/ICALT.2004.1357716

Malone, T. W. (1980). What makes things fun to learn? Heuristics for designing instructional computer games. In *Proceedings of the 3rd ACM SIGSMALL Symposium and 1st SIGPC Symposium on Small Systems*, (pp. 162-169). ACM Press.

Malone, T. W. (1981). Toward a theory of intrinsically motivating instruction. *Cognitive Science, 4*, 333–369. doi:10.1207/s15516709cog0504_2

Malone, T. W. (1982). Heuristics for designing enjoyable user interfaces: Lessons from computer games. In Thomas, J. C., & Schneider, M. L. (Eds.), *Human Factors in Computing Systems*. Norwood, NJ: Ablex Publishing Corporation.

Malone, T. W., & Lepper, M. R. (1987). Intrinsic motivation and instructional effectiveness in computer-based education. In Snow, R. E., & Farr, M. J. (Eds.), *Aptitude, Learning and Instruction: Conative and affective process analyses* (pp. 243–286). Hillsdale, NJ: Lawrence Erlbaum Associates.

Maloney, J., Peppler, K., Kafai, Y., Resnick, M., & Rusk, N. (2008). Programming by choice: Urban youth learning programming with Scratch. *ACM SIGCSE Bulletin, 40*(1), 367–371. doi:10.1145/1352322.1352260

Malouff, J., & Schutte, N. (1998). *Games to enhance social and emotional skills: Sixty-six games that teach adolescents and adults skills crucial to success in life.* Springfield, IL: Hares C. Thomas.

Mandryck, R. L., Inkpen, K. M., & Calvert, T. W. (2006). Using psychophysiological techniques to measure user experience with entertainment technologies. *Behaviour & Information Technology, 25*(2), 141–158. doi:10.1080/01449290500331156

Manlow, V., Friedman, H., & Friedman, L. (2010). Inventing the future: Using social media to transform a university from a teaching organization to a learning organization. *Journal of Interactive Learning Research, 21*(1), 47–64.

Mann, D., Shakeshaft, C., Becker, J., & Kottkamp, R. (1999). *West Virginia basic skills/computer education program: An analysis of student achievement.* Santa Monica, CA: Milken Family Foundation.

Margolis, J. (2008). *Stuck in the shallow end: Education, race, and computing.* Cambridge, MA: MIT Press.

Marín, A. (2009). New media ¿viejas o nuevas realidades? *Mosaic, Tecnologías y Comunicación Multimedia.* Retrieved March 26, 2011, from http://mosaic.uoc.edu/2006/10/20/new-media-%C2%BFviejas-o-nuevas-realidades/

Markett, C., Arnedillo Sánche, I., Weber, S., & Tangney, B. (2006). Using short message service (SMS) to encourage interactivity in the classroom. *Computers & Education, 46*(3), 280–293. doi:10.1016/j.compedu.2005.11.014

Martín Luengo, J. (1990). *Desde nuestra escuela Paideia.* Madrid, Spain: Madre Tierra.

Martín-Barbero, J. (2004). *Nuevas tecnicidades y culturas locales: Ejes de una propuesta.* Retrieved February 11, 2011 from http://sociedadinformacion.fundacion.telefonica.com/telos/articulocuaderno.asp@idarticulo=2&rev=61.htm#n1

Martin-Dorta, N., Sanchez-Berriel, I., Bravo, M., Hernandez, J., Saorin, J. L., & Contero, M. (2010). *A 3D educational mobile game to enhance student's spatial skills.* Paper presented at 10th IEEE International Conference on Advanced Learning Technologies. Sousse, Tunisia.

Martin-Dorta, N., Saorin, J. L., & Contero, M. (2011). Web-based spatial training using handheld touch screen devices. *Journal of Educational Technology & Society, 14*(3), 163–177.

Martin-Dorta, N., Saorin, J., & Contero, M. (2008). Development of a fast remedial course to improve the spatial abilities of engineering students. *Journal of Engineering Education, 27*(4), 505–514.

Marton, F. (1988). Describing and improving learning. In Schmeck, R. R. (Ed.), *Learning Strategies and Learning Styles.* New York, NY: Plenum.

Marty, J.-C., & Carron, T. (2011). Observation of collaborative activities in a game-based learning platform. *Transactions on Learning Technologies, 4*(1), 98–110. doi:10.1109/TLT.2011.1

Marty, J.-C., Carron, T., & Heraud, J.-M. (2009). Observation as a requisite for games based learning environments. In *Games Based Learning Advancements for Multisensory Human Computer Interfaces: Technics and Effective Practices* (pp. 51–71). Hershey, PA: IGI Global. doi:10.4018/978-1-60566-360-9.ch004

Marty, J.-C., Heraud, J.-M., France, L., & Carron, T. (2007). Matching the performed activity on an educational platform with a recommended pedagogical scenario: A multi source approach. *Journal of Interactive Learning Research, 18*(2).

Masters, G. N., & Hill, P. W. (1988). Reforming the assessment of student achievement in the senior secondary school. *Australian Journal of Education, 32*, 247–286.

Maurício de Souza, P. (2007a). *Tina e os caçadores de enigmas: Mistério cósmico, partes 1 e 2, número 1, agosto.* Rio de Janeiro, Brazil: Maurício de Souza Editora e Panini Comics.

Maurício de Souza, P. (2007b). *Tina e os caçadores de enigmas: Mistério cósmico, partes 3 e 4, número 2, setembro*. Rio de Janeiro, Brazil: Maurício de Souza Editora e Panini Comics.

Maurício de Souza, P. (2007c). *Tina e os caçadores de enigmas: Mistério cósmico, partes 5 e 6, número 3, outubro*. Rio de Janeiro, Brazil: Maurício de Souza Editora e Panini Comics.

Maurício de Souza, P. (2008a). *Tina e os caçadores de enigmas: Criaturas lendárias, número 1, março*. Rio de Janeiro, Brazil: Maurício de Souza Editora e Panini Comics.

Maurício de Souza, P. (2008b). *Tina e os caçadores de enigmas: Criaturas lendárias, número 2, abril*. Rio de Janeiro, Brazil: Maurício de Souza Editora e Panini Comics.

Mayer, I. S., Bekebrede, G., & Warmelink, H. J. G. (2009). Learning in a virtual world: An introduction. In Warmelink, H. J. G., & Mayer, I. S. (Eds.), *Learning in a Virtual World: Reflections on the Cyberdam Research and Development Project* (pp. 1–22). Nijmegen, The Netherlands: Wolf Legal Publishers.

Mayer, R. E., Stull, A., DeLeeuw, K., Almeroth, K., Bimber, B., & Chun, D. (2009). Clickers in college classrooms: Fostering learning with questioning methods in large lecture classes. *Contemporary Educational Psychology, 34*, 51–57. doi:10.1016/j.cedpsych.2008.04.002

Mayes, J. T., & Fowler, C. J. H. (1999). Learning technology and usability: A framework for understanding courseware. *Interacting with Computers, 11*, 485–497. doi:10.1016/S0953-5438(98)00065-4

McFarlane, A., Sparrowhawk, A., & Heald, Y. (2002). *Report on the educational use of games: An exploration by TEEM of the contribution which games can make to the education process*. Retrieved April 13, 2011, from http://www.teem.org.uk/publications/teem_gamesined_full.pdf

McKinney, D., Dyck, J. L., & Luber, E. S. (2009). iTunes university and the classroom: Can podcasts replace professors? *Computers & Education, 52*, 617–623. doi:10.1016/j.compedu.2008.11.004

McLaughlin, J., & Skinner, D. (2000). Developing usability and utility: A comparative study of the users of new IT. *Technology Analysis and Strategic Management, 12*(3), 413–423. doi:10.1080/09537320050130633

McMahon, M., & Pospisil, R. (2005). Laptops for a digital lifestyle: Millennial students and wireless mobile technologies. In *Proceedings of ASCILITE 2005*. Retrieved May, 6, 2011, from http://www.ascilite.org.au/conferences/brisbane05/proceedings.shtml

McMillan, J. (1992). *Games, strategies and managers: how managers can use game theory to make better business decisions*. Oxford, UK: Oxford University Press.

Mead, G. H. (1934). *Mind, self and society*. Chicago, IL: University of Chicago Press.

Mehrabian, A. (1994). *Manual for the revised trait arousability (converse of the stimulus screening)*. Monterey, CA: Alta Mesa Road.

Meijer, S. (2009). *The organization of transactions: Studying supply networks using gaming simulation*. Wageningen, The Netherlands: Wageningen Academic Publishers.

Meiszner, Glott, & Sowe. (2008). Free / libre open source software (FLOSS) communities as an example of successful open participatory learning ecosystems. *The European Journal for the Informatics Professional, 9*(3), 62–68.

Mercer, N. (1994). Neo-Vygotskian theory and classroom education. In Stierer, B., & Maybin, J. (Eds.), *Language, Literacy and Learning in Educational Practice* (pp. 92–110). Clevedon, UK: Multilingual Matters.

Metcalf, C. (2007). *Investigating the sharing practices of family & friends to inform communication technology innovations*. Retrieved from http://blogs.motorola.com/default.asp?item=638638

Michael, D., & Chen, S. (2006). *Serious games: Games that educate, train, and inform*. Boston, MA: Thomson Course Technology.

Microsoft. (2012). *Kinect*. Retrieved from http://www.xbox.com/de-DE/kinect

Middleton, J. A., & Spanias, P. A. (1992). Motivation for achievement in mathematics: Findings, generalizations, and criticisms of the research. *Journal for Research in Mathematics Education, 30*(1), 65–88. doi:10.2307/749630

Milbourne, L. (2005). Children, families and inter-agency work: Experiences of partnership work in primary education settings. *British Educational Research Journal, 31*(6), 675–695. doi:10.1080/01411920500314653

Mirrlees, J. A. (1997). Information and incentives: The economics of carrots and sticks. *The Economic Journal, 107*(444), 1311–1329. doi:10.1111/j.1468-0297.1997.tb00050.x

MIT. (2011). *Scratch: Imagine, program, share.* Retrieved November 1, 2011, from http://scratch.mit.edu/

Mitchell, A., & Savill-Smith, C. (2004). *The use of computer and video games for learning: A review of the literature.* London, UK: Learning and Skills Development Agency. Retrieved on May 6, 2011 from http://www.m-learning.org/archive/docs/The%20use%20of%20computer%20and%20video%20games%20for%20learning.pdf

Mitchell, D. (2008). Generation z striking the balance: Healthy doctors for a healthy community. *Australian Family Physician, 37*(8), 665–667.

Mitchelmore, M. C. (1980). Three-dimensional geometrical drawing in three cultures. *Educational Studies in Mathematics, 11*, 205–216. doi:10.1007/BF00304356

MoLeNET. (2010). *Case studies of innovative e-learning.* Lifelong learning programme. Retrieved on May 6, 2011 from http://www.northamptoncollege.ac.uk/facilities/MoLeNET.aspx

Molnar, A. S. (1997). Computers in education: A brief history. *T.H.E. Journal, 24*(11), 63–69.

Monroy-Hernández, A., & Resnick, M. (2008). Empowering kids to create and share programmable media. *Interaction, 15*(2), 50–53. doi:10.1145/1340961.1340974

Moody, L., & Schmidt, G. (2004). Going wireless: The emergence of wireless networks in education. *Journal of Computing Sciences in Colleges, 19*(4), 151–158.

Mooney, C. (2000). *Theories of childhood: An introduction to Dewey, Montessori, Erikson, Piaget and Vygotsky.* Minneapolis, MN: Readleaf Press.

Morán, S., Rubio, R., Gallego, R., Suárez, J., & Martín, S. (2008). Proposal of interactive applications to enhance student's spatial perception. *Computers & Education, 50*(3), 772–786. doi:10.1016/j.compedu.2006.08.009

Moreno-Ger, P., Burgos, D., Martínez-Ortiz, I., Sierra, J. L., & Fernández-Manjón, B. (2008). Educational game design for online education. *Computers in Human Behavior, 24*, 2530–2540. doi:10.1016/j.chb.2008.03.012

Morrison, T. (2001). *Actionable learning: A handbook for capacity building through case based learning.* Tokyo, Japan: Asian Development Bank Institute.

Muhlenbrock, M., & Hoppe, U. (1999). Computer Supported interaction analysis of group problem solving. In Hosadley & Roschelle (Eds.), *Proceedings of CSCL 1999,* (pp. 398-405). CSCL.

Murray, J. H. (1997). *Hamlet on the holodeck: The future of narrative in cyberspace.* Cambridge, MA: MIT Press.

Nacke, L., Drachen, A., Korhonen, H., Kuikkaniemi, K., Niesenhaus, J., & van den Hoogen, W. … de Kort, Y. (2009). DiGRA panel: Playability and player experience research. In *DiGRA Breaking New Ground: Innovation in Games, Play, Practice and Theory.* London, UK: Brunel University.

Naps, T., Roessling, G., Almstrum, V., Dann, W., Fleischer, R., & Hundhausen, C. (2003). Exploring the role of visualization and engagement in computer science education. *ACM SIGCSE Bulletin, 35*(4), 131–152. doi:10.1145/782941.782998

National Council of Teachers of Mathematics. (2000). *Illuminations.* Retrieved October 8, 2009, from http://illuminations.nctm.org/ActivityDetail.aspx?ID=125

New London Group. (1996). *New literacies end classroom practice.* Retrieved from http://www.newliteracies.com.au/what-are-new-literacies?/138/

Nicotti, J. A., Gonzaga, S., & Gonzaga, P. (Eds.). (2006). *Contos do amor jovem.* Porto Alegre, Brazil: Leitura XXI.

Nielsen, J. (1994). Enhancing the explanatory power of usability heuristics. In *Proceedings of CHI 1994*, (pp. 152-158). Boston, MA: CHI.

Nielsen, J. (1999). Graceful degradation of scalable internet service, WAP: Wrong approach to portability. Retrieved 20/08/11 from http://www.useit.com/alertbox/991031.html

Nielsen, J. (1993). *Usability engineering*. New York, NY: Academic Press Ltd.

Nielsen, J., & Mack, R. (Eds.). (1994). *Usability inspection methods*. New York, NY: John Wiley & Sons, Inc.

Nintendo. (2008). *Nintendo Wii*. Retrieved from http://www.wii.com

Nokelainen, P. (2004). Conceptual definition of the technical and pedagogical usability criteria for digital learning material. In *Proceedings of World Conference on Educational Multimedia, Hypermedia and Telecommunications*, (Vol. 1), (pp. 4249-4254). ACM.

Nokia. (2010). *Game design and user experience*. Retrieved March 15, 2010, from http://library.forum.nokia.com/index.jsp?topic=/Design_and_User_Experience_Library/GUID-21B5CE2C-7141-41CF-A669-2006502C151E.html

Norman, D. A. (2004). *Emotional design: Why we love (or hate) everyday things*. New York, NY: Basic Books (Perseus).

Norman, D. (1990). *The design of everyday things*. New York, NY: Doubleday.

Norman, D. (1999). Affordance, conventions, and design. *Interaction*, *6*(3), 38–43. doi:10.1145/301153.301168

Norman, D. A. (2004). *Emotional design: Why we love (or hate) everyday things*. New York, NY: Basic Books.

Norman, D. A., & Draper, S. W. (1986). *User centered system design*. Hillsdale, NJ: Lawrence Erlbaum Associates.

O'Malley, C., Vavoula, G., & Glew, J. Taylor, J., Sharples, M., & Lefrere, P. (2003). *Guidelines for learning/teaching/tutoring in a mobile environment*. Mobilearn project deliverable. Retrieved on May 6, 2011 from http://www.mobilearn.org/download/results/guidelines.pdf

Oblinger, D. G. (2004). The next generation of educational engagement. *Journal of Interactive Media in Education*, *8*. Retrieved on May 6, 2011, from http://www-jime.open.ac.uk/2004/8/oblinger-2004-8-disc-paper.html

Oblinger, D. G. (2006). Digital games have the potential to bring play back to the learning experience. *EDUCAUSE Quarterly*, *29*(3).

Ochs, E. (2002). Becoming a speaker of culture. In Kramsch, C. (Ed.), *Language Acquisition and Language Socialization*. New York, NY: Continuum.

Ochs, E., Smith, R., & Taylor, C. (1986). Dinner narratives as detective stories. *Cultural Dynamics*, *2*, 238–257. doi:10.1177/092137408900200206

OECD. (1996). *The knowledge-based economy*. Paris, France: Organisation for Economic Cooperation and Development.

Okagaki, L., & Frensch, P. A. (1994). Effects of video game playing on measures of spatial performance: Gender effects in late adolescence. *Journal of Applied Developmental Psychology*, *15*(1), 33–58. doi:10.1016/0193-3973(94)90005-1

Oldenburg, R. (1989). *The great good place: Cafes, coffee shops, bookstores, bars, hair salons, and other hangouts at the heart of a community*. New York, NY: Paragon House.

Oliveira, T. (2003). *RPG (roleplaying game): A aventura do letramento e de (re)construção de identidades sociais no contexto escolar*. Rio de Janeiro, Brazil: Universidade Federal do Rio de Janeiro.

Osgood, C. E., Suci, G., & Tannenbaum, P. (1957). *The measurement of meaning*. Urbana, IL: University of Illinois Press.

Oxford English Dictionary. (2011). *Incentives*. Retrieved on May 6, 2011 from http://oxforddictionaries.com/view/entry/m_en_gb0404550#m_en_gb0404550

Padilla Zea, N. (2011). *Methodology for the design of educational video games on architecture for the analysis of collaborative learning*. (Doctoral Dissertation). Granada University. Granada, Spain.

Padilla Zea, N. (2011). *Metodología para el diseño de videojuegos educativos sobre una arquitectura para el análisis del aprendizaje colaborativo*. Granada, Spain: Universidad de Granada.

Padilla Zea, N., González Sánchez, J. L., Gutiérrez, F. L., Cabrera, M. J., & Paderewski, P. (2009). Design of educational multiplayer videogames: A vision from collaborative learning. *Advances in Engineering Software, 40*(12), 1251–1260. doi:10.1016/j.advengsoft.2009.01.023

Padilla Zea, N., González Sánchez, J. L., Gutiérrez, F. L., Cabrera, M., & Paderewski, P. (2009). Design of educational multiplayer videogames: A vision from collaborative learning. *Journal Advances in Engineering Software, 40*(12), 1251–1260. doi:10.1016/j.advengsoft.2009.01.023

Palfrey, J., & Gasser, U. (2008). *Born digital: Understanding the first generation of digital natives*. New York, NY: Basic Books.

Papert, S. (1980). *Constructionism vs. instructionism*. Retrieved March 22, 2011 from http://www.papert.org/articles/const_inst/const_inst1.html

Parker, A. (2003). Identifying predictors of academic persistence in distance education. *Journal of the United States Distance Learning Association, 17*(1), 55–62.

Patten, T. (2007). *How consciousness develops adequate complexity to deal with a complex world: The subject-object theory of Robert Kegan*. Retrieved on May 20, 2011 from http://terrypatten.typepad.com/iran/files/KeganEnglish.pdf

Pavão, A. (2000). *A aventura da leitura e da escrita entre mestres de role playing games (RPG)*. Rio de Janeiro, Brazil: Entre Lugar.

Pecher, D., & Zwaan, R. A. (2005). *Grounding cognition: The role of perception and action in memory, language, and thinking*. Cambridge, UK: Cambridge University Press. doi:10.1017/CBO9780511499968

Pellegrine, A. D., & Kato, K. (2002). Short-term longitudinal study of children's playground games across the first year of school: Implications for social competence and adjustment to school. *American Educational Research Journal, 39*(4), 991–1015. doi:10.3102/00028312039004991

Pereira, C. E. K. (2007). TNI (técnicas para narrativas interativas). *Rio de Janeiro, 33*(3), 72-85.

Pereira, C. E. K. (2003). *Construção de personagem & aquisição de linguagem: O desafio do RPG no INES*. Rio de Janeiro, Brazil: Pontifícia Universidade Católica do Rio de Janeiro.

Pereira, C. E. K. (2008). *Uma ponte pela escrita: A narratividade do RPG como estímulo à escrita e à leitura*. Rio de Janeiro, Brazil: Pontifícia Universidade Católica do Rio de Janeiro.

Pereira, C. K., Andrade, F., & Ricon, L. E. (1992). *O desafio dos bandeirantes: Aventuras na terra de Santa Cruz*. Rio de Janeiro, Brazil: GSA.

Pérez Rodríguez, M. A. (2009). *Un nuevo lenguaje para una comunicación global*. Retrieved June 13, 2011, from http://www.uhu.es/agora/version01/digital/numeros/03/03-articulos/monografico/pdf3/perez.PDF

Pérez Tornero, J. M. (2000). El desarrollo de la sociedad de la información del paradigma de la cultura de masas al de la cultura multimedia. In *Proceedings y Educación en la Sociedad de la Información*, (pp. 17-34). Barcelona, Spain: Paidós.

Pérez-Carrasco, A., Velázquez-Iturbide, J. Á., & Urquiza-Fuentes, J. (2010). Multiple usability evaluations of a program animation tool. In M. Jemni, D. Kinshuk, Sampson, & J. M. Spector (Eds.), *The 10th IEEE International Conference on Advanced Learning Technologies, ICALT 2010*, (pp. 452-454). Los Alamitos, CA: IEEE Computer Society.

Pérez-Carrasco, A., & Velázquez-Iturbide, J. Á. (2012). Interactive learning of recursion. In *Educational Stages and Interactive Learning: From Kindergarten to Workplace Training*. Hershey, PA: IGI Global. doi:10.4018/978-1-4666-0137-6.ch015

Perkins, D. (1998). What is understanding? In Wiske, M. S. (Ed.), *Teaching for Understanding: Linking Research with Practice*. San Francisco, CA: Jossey-Bass Publishers.

Perkins, D., & Blythe, T. (1994). Putting understanding upfront. *Educational Leadership, 51*(5), 4–7.

Perkins, S., & Saltsman, G. (2010). Mobile learning at Abilene Christian University: Successes, challenges, and results from year one. *Journal of the Research Center for Educational Technology, 6*(1), 47–54.

Perlim, G. (2005). Identidades surdas. In Skliar, C. (Ed.), *A Surdez: Um Olhar Sobre as Diferenças* (3rd ed., pp. 51–74). Porto Alegre, Brazil: Mediação.

Perroni, M. C. (1992). *Desenvolvimento do discurso narrativo*. São Paulo, Brazil: Martins Fontes.

Petrie, H., & Kheir, O. (2007). The relationship between accessibility and usability of websites. In *Proceedings of CHI 2007*. San Jose, CA: CHI.

Petrie, H., Hamilton, F., & King, N. (2004). Tension, what tension? Website accessibility and visual design. In *Proceedings of the International Cross-Disciplinary Workshop on Web Accessibility (W4A)*. New York, NY: ACM Press.

Pew Internet American Life Project. (2007). *Teens and social media*. Retrieved from http://www.pewinternet.org/pdfs/PIPTeensSocialMediaFinal:pdf

Piaget, J. (1951). *Play, dreams and imitation in childhood*. New York, NY: Norton.

Piaget, J. (1952). *The origins of intelligence in children*. London, UK: International University Press. doi:10.1037/11494-000

Piaget, J. (1962). *Play, dreams and imitation in childhood*. New York, NY: W. W. Norton.

Pinelle, D., & Gutwin, C. (2000). A review of groupware evaluations. In *Proceedings of Ninth IEEE WETICE 2000 Workshops on Enabling Technologies: Infrastructure for Collaborative Enterprises*. Gaithersburg, MD: IEEE Press.

Pinelle, D., Wong, N., & Stach, T. (2008). Heuristic evaluation for games: Usability principles for video game design. In *Proceedings of the The 26th Annual CHI Conference on Human Factors in Computing Systems*, (pp 1453-1462). New York, NY: ACM Press.

Pirius, L. K., & Creel, G. (2010). Reflections on play, pedagogy, and world of warcraft. *EDUCAUSE Quarterly, 33*(3).

Pivec, M., & Pivec, P. (2009). What do we know from research about the use of games in education. In *European Schoolnet: How are digital games used in schools?* (pp. 122-165). Retrieved from http://www.comminit.com/?q=ict-4-development/node/302814

Plaza, J. (2003). Arte e interatividade: Autor-obra-recepção. *Concinnitas, 4*, 7–34.

Pokay, P., & Blumenfeld, P. C. (1990). Predicting achievement early and late in the semester: The role of motivation and use of learning strategies. *Journal of Education & Psychology, 82*, 40–43. doi:10.1037/0022-0663.82.1.41

Polson, P. G., & Lewis, C. H. (1990). Theory-based design for easily learned interfaces. *Human-Computer Interaction, 5*, 191–220. doi:10.1207/s15327051hci0502&3_3

Poole, S. (2000). *Trigger happy: The inner life of videogames*. London, UK: Fourth Estate.

Porter, G., Starcevic, V., Berle, D., & Fenech, P. (2010). Recognizing problem video game use. *The Australian and New Zealand Journal of Psychiatry, 44*(2), 120–128. doi:10.3109/00048670903279812

Pratt, J., & Zeckhauser, R. (1985). *Principals and agents: The structure of business*. Boston, MA: Harvard Business School Press.

Preece, J. (1994). *Human-computer interaction*. Reading, MA: Addison-Wesley.

Preece, J. (2000). *Online communities: Designing usability, supporting sociability*. New York, NY: John Wiley & Sons.

Preece, J. (2001). Sociability and usability in online communities: Determining and measuring success. *Behaviour & Information Technology, 20*(5), 347–356. doi:10.1080/01449290110084683

Preece, J., Rogers, Y., & Sharp, H. (2002). *Interaction design: Beyond human-computer interaction*. New York, NY: John Wiley & Sons.

Prensky, M. (2001). Digital natives, digital immigrants part 1. *On The Horizon – The Strategic Planning Resource for Education Professionals, 9*(5), 1-6.

Prensky, M. (2005). Computer games and learning: Digital game-based learning. In Raessens and Goldstein (Eds.), *Handbook of Computer Game Studies*, (pp. 97-122). Cambridge, MA: The MIT Press.

Prensky, M. (2005). What can you learn from a cell phone? Almost anything! *Innovate, 1*(5). Retrieved on June 20, 2011 from www.marcprensky.com/.../prensky-what_can_you_learn_from_a_cell_phone-final.pdf

Prensky, M. (2001). *Digital game based learning revolution.* New York, NY: McGraw-Hill.

Prensky, M. (2001). *Digital game based learning.* New York, NY: McGraw-Hill.

Prensky, M. (2001). Digital natives, digital immigrants. *Horizon, 9*(5), 1–6. doi:10.1108/10748120110424816

Prensky, M. (2006). *Don't bother me mom – I'm learning!* St. Paul, MN: Paragon House.

Prouty, D. (2000). Creativity. *Zip Lines: The Voice for Adventure Education, 40*, 9–11.

Provenzo, E. (1991). *Video kids.* Boston, MA: Harvard University Press.

Purdy, J. A. (2008). *Serious games: Getting serious about digital games in learning.* Retrieved from http://www.corpu.com/newsletter%5Fwi07/sect2.asp

Quaiser-Pohl, C., Geiser, C., & Lehmann, W. (2005). The relationship between computer-game preference, gender, and mental-rotation ability. *Personality and Individual Differences, 40*(3), 609–619. doi:10.1016/j.paid.2005.07.015

Quesenbery, C., Jarrett, J., Ramsey, J., & Redish, G. (2001). *What does usability mean?* Paper presented at the Annual Conference for Social for Technical Communication. Chicago, IL.

Questionnaire for User Interaction Satisfaction. (2011). *Website.* Retrieved 26/08/11 from http://lap.umd.edu/quis/

Rafi, A., & Samsudin, K. (2009). Practising mental rotation using interactive desktop mental rotation trainer (iDeMRT). *British Journal of Educational Technology, 40*(5), 889–900. doi:10.1111/j.1467-8535.2008.00874.x

Rafi, A., Samsudin, K. A., & Ismail, A. (2006). On improving spatial ability through computer-mediated engineering drawing instruction. *Journal of Educational Technology & Society, 9*(3), 149–159.

Rafi, A., Samsudin, K., & Said, C. (2008). Training in spatial visualization: The effects of training method and gender. *Journal of Educational Technology & Society, 11*(3), 127–140.

Rainie, L. (2006). *Digital natives invade the workplace.* Retrieved January 13, 2009 from http://www.informationweek.com/news/internet/ebusiness/showArticle.jhtml?articleID=192700574

Ramage, M. (1999). *The learning way: Evaluating cooperative systems.* (Phd. Thesis). Lancaster University. Lancaster, UK.

Rantzer, M. (1996). *The delta method—A way to introduce usability field methods casebook for software design.* New York, NY: John Wiley & Sons Inc.

Rantzer, M. (1998). Mind the gap: Surviving the dangers of user interface design in user interface design. In Wood, L. E. (Ed.), *Bridging the Gap from User Requirements to Design.* New York, NY: CRC Press.

Rasumsen, E. (2007). *Games and information: An introduction to game theory.* Oxford, UK: Blackwell Publishing.

Rauh, M. T., & Seccia, G. (2005). *Incentives, monitoring, and motivation.* Working Paper, No. 0506008, EconWPA: Game Theory and Information. Retrieved May 6, 2011 from http://129.3.20.41/eps/game/papers/0506/0506008.pdf

Redl, F. (1966). *When we deal with children.* New York, NY: The Free Press.

Reid, W. A. (1987). Institutions and practices: Professional education reports and the language of reform. *Educational Researcher, 16*(8), 10–15.

Reily, L. H. (2003). As imagens: O lúdico e o absurdo no ensino de arte para pré-escolares surdos. In Silva, I. R., Kauchakje, S., & Gesueli, Z. M. (Eds.), *Cidadania, Surdez e Linguagem: Desafios e Realidades* (pp. 161–191). São Paulo, Brazil: Plexus.

Report, H. (2011). *One year or less: Mobiles*. Retrieved on June 20, 2011 from http://wp.nmc.org/horizon2011/sections/mobiles/

Resnick., et al. (2009). Scratch: Programming for all. *Communications of the ACM, 52*(11). Retrieved October 27, 2011 from http://dl.acm.org/citation.cfm?id=1592779

Retaux, X., & Rouchier, J. (2002). Realism vs surprise and coherence: Different aspects of playability in computer games. In *Proceedings of Playing with the Future: Development and Directions in Computer Gaming*. Manchester, UK: Centre for Research on Innovation and Competition.

Rheingold, H. (1993). *The virtual community: Homesteading on the electronic frontier*. New York, NY: Perseus Books.

Richards, R., McGee, R., Williams, S. M., Welch, D., & Hancox, R. J. (2010). Adolescent screen time and attachment to parents and peers. *Archives of Pediatrics & Adolescent Medicine, 164*(3), 258–262. doi:10.1001/archpediatrics.2009.280

Richter, M. G. (1998). Role-play e ensino interativo de língua materna. *Linguagem & Ensino, 1*(2), 89–113.

Ricon, L. E. (2004). Oficina - Transformando conteúdos curriculares em narrativas. In Zanini, M. C. (Ed.), *Anais do Simpósio RPG & Educação*. São Paulo, Brazil: Devir.

Ripamonti, L. A., Di Loreto, I., & Maggiorini, D. (2009). Augmenting actual life through MUVE. In Whitworth, B., & de Moor, A. (Eds.), *Handbook of Research on Socio Technical Design and Social Networking Systems*. Hershey, PA: IGI Global. doi:10.4018/978-1-60566-264-0.ch033

Robertson, J., & Good, J. (2007). Children's narrative development through computer game authoring. *TechTrends, 49*(5), 43-59. Retrieved October 31, 2011 from http://www.springerlink.com/content/3xh87p7603n60757/

Robertson, M. (2010). *Can't play, won't play*. Retrieved July 18, 2011, from http://www.hideandseek.net/2010/10/06/cant-play-wont-play/

Rodrigues, S. (2004). *Roleplaying game e a pedagogia da imaginação no Brasil*. Rio de Janeiro, Brazil: Bertrand Brasil.

Roediger, H. L., & Karpicke, J. (2006). The power of testing memory: Basic research and implications for educational practice. *Perspectives on Psychological Science, 1*, 181–210. doi:10.1111/j.1745-6916.2006.00012.x

Rogers, P. L. (2001). Traditions to transformations: The forced evolution of higher education. *Educational Technology Review, 9*(1).

Rollings, A., & Adams, E. (2003). *Andrew Rollings and Ernest Adams on game design*. Indianapolis, IN: New Riders.

Rollings, A., & Morris, D. (2004). *Game architecture and design: A new edition*. Indianapolis, IN: New Riders Publishing.

Roschelle, J., & Teasley, S. (1991). The construction of shared knowledge in collaborative problem solving. In C. O'Malley (Ed.), *Proceedings of CSCL 1991*, (pp. 67-97). Berlin, Germany: Springer.

Roschelle, J. (2003). Unlocking the learning value of wireless mobile devices. *Journal of Computer Assisted Learning, 19*(3), 260–272. doi:10.1046/j.0266-4909.2003.00028.x

Rosenbloom, A. (2007). Interactive immersion in 3D computer graphics. *Communications of the ACM, 47*(8), 28–31. doi:10.1145/1012037.1012058

Rothschild, M., & Stiglitz, J. E. (1976). Equilibrium in competitive insurance markets: An essay on the economics of imperfect information. *The Quarterly Journal of Economics, 90*, 629–650. doi:10.2307/1885326

Rousseau, J. (1974). *Emile ou de l'éducation*. Paris, France: Garnier-Flammarion.

Rowley, J. (1998). Towards a methodology for the design of multimedia public access interfaces. *Journal of Information Science, 24*(3), 155–166. doi:10.1177/016555159802400302

Roy, M., & Chi, M. T. H. (2005). The self-explanation effect in multimedia learning. In Mayer, R. E. (Ed.), *The Cambridge Handbook of Multimedia Learning* (pp. 271–286). Cambridge, UK: Cambridge University Press. doi:10.1017/CBO9780511816819.018

Ruben, B. D. (1999). Simulation, games, and experience-based learning: The quest for a new paradigm for teaching and learning. *Simulation & Gaming, 30,* 498–505. doi:10.1177/104687819903000409

Rubin, A. M., & Rubin, R. B. (1981). Age, context, and television use. *Journal of Broadcasting, A*(1), 1–13. doi:10.1080/08838158109386424

Rubins, J. (1994). *Handbook of usability testing.* New York, NY: John Wiley & Sons Inc.

Rubio Méndez, M. (2011). *Videojuegos como laboratorio para la construcción de la identidad de género.* Madrid, Spain: Universidad de Salamanca.

Rueda, U., Larranaga, M., Arruarte, A., & Elorriaga, J. A. (2003). Dynamic visualization of student models using concept maps. In *Proceedings of the 11th International Conference on Artificial Intelligence in Education,* (pp. 89-96). AIE.

Ruhl, K., & Suritsky, S. (1995). The pause procedure and/or outline: Effect on immediate free recall and lecture notes taken by college students with learning disabilities. *Learning Disability Quarterly, 18,* 2–11. doi:10.2307/1511361

Russell, J. (1980). A circumplex model of affect. *Journal of Personality and Social Psychology, 39*(6), 1161–1178. doi:10.1037/h0077714

Ryan, G., & Shinnick, E. (2008). The power of incentives in decision making. In Adam, F., & Humphreys, P. (Eds.), *Encyclopaedia of Decision Making and Decision Support Technologies.* Hershey, PA: IGI Global. doi:10.4018/978-1-59904-843-7.ch081

Sahni, S. (2005). *Data structures, algorithms, and applications in Java* (2nd ed.). Summit, NJ: Silicon Press.

Saito, A. (2008). Gamenics and its potential. In Isbister, K., & Schaffer, N. (Eds.), *Game Usability: Advancing the Player Experience* (pp. 357–381). New York, NY: Morgan Kaufmann.

Sala, N. (2009). Virtual reality and virtual environments in education. In Cartelli, A., & Palma, M. (Eds.), *Encyclopedia of Information Communication Technology* (pp. 883–838). Hershey, PA: IGI Global. doi:10.4018/978-1-59904-845-1.ch109

Salen, K. (2007). Gaming literacies: A game design study in action. *Journal of Educational Multimedia and Hypermedia, 16*(3), 301–322.

Salen, K., & Zimmerman, E. (2003). *Rules of play: Game design fundamentals.* Cambridge, MA: The MIT Press.

Salen, K., & Zimmerman, E. (2004). *Rules of play: Game design fundamentals.* Cambridge, MA: MIT Press.

Saliés, T. M. G., & Starosky, P. (2008). How a deaf boy gamed his way to second-language acquisition: Tales of intersubjectivity. *Simulation & Gaming, 39*(2), 209–239. doi:10.1177/1046878107310609

Salomon, G. (1995). *What does the design of effective CSCL require and how do we study its effects?* Retrieved from http://www-cscl95.indiana.edu/cscl95/outlook/62-Salomon.html

Sanchez-Crespo Dalmau, D. (1999). *Learn faster to pay better: How to shorten the learning cycle.* Retrieved from http://www.gamasutra.com/view/feature/3392/learn_faster_to_play_better_how_.php?page=5

Sánchez, J., & Flores, H. (2006). Aprendizaje móvil de ciencias para ciegos. In Sánchez, J. (Ed.), *Nuevas Ideas en Informática Educativa* (pp. 11–21). Santiago, Chile: LOM Ediciones.

Sánchez, J., & Olivares, R. (2011). Problem solving and collaboration using mobile serious games. *Computers & Education, 57*(3), 1943–1952. doi:10.1016/j.compedu.2011.04.012

Santoro, F. M. (2001). *A cooperation model for project-based learning.* (Doctoral Thesis). COPPE Sistemas, UFRJ. Rio de Janeiro, Brazil.

Sawyer, B. (2002). *Serious games: Improving public policy through game-based learning and simulation.* Washington, DC: Woodrow Wilson International Center for Scholars.

Scanlon, E., & O'Shea, T. (2007). New educational technology models for social and personal computing. In *Proceedings of the Seventh IEEE International Conference on Advanced Learning Technologies (ICALT 2007),* (pp. 11-14). ICALT.

Schaefli, A., Rest, J. R., & Thomas, J. (1985). Does moral education improve moral judgement? A meta-analysis of intervention studies using the defining issues test. *Review of Educational Research, 55*, 319–352.

Schell, J. (2008). *The art of game design: A book of lenses.* Burlington, MA: Morgan Kaufmann Publishers.

Schneiderman, B. (2003). Promoting universal usability with multi-layer interface design. In *Proceedings of 2003 Conference on Universal Usability.* New York, NY: ACM Press.

Schneiderman, B. (2000). Universal accessibility. *Communications of the ACM, 43*(5), 85–91.

Schneuwly, B., & Dolz, J. (2004). *Gêneros orais e escritos na escola.* São Paulo, Brazil: Mercado de Letras.

Schuurink, E., Houtkamp, J., & Toet, A. (2008). Engagement and EMG in serious gaming: Experimenting with sound and dynamics in the levee patroller training game. *Lecture Notes in Computer Science, 5294*, 139–149. doi:10.1007/978-3-540-88322-7_14

Scollon, R. (2002). Cross-cultural learning and other catastrophes. In Kramsch, C. (Ed.), *Language Acquisition and Language Socialization.* New York, NY: Continuum.

Scott, G. (2007). *Games get down to business: Simulations growing in popularity as younger workers move up the corporate ranks.* Retrieved on the 16 June 2007 from http://www.theglobeandmail.com/servlet/story/RTGAM.20070502.wgtgames0502/BNStory/GlobeTQ/home

Screen Learning. (2011). *Smart cat profiling.* Retrieved from http://www.screenlearning.com/products/smart-cat.php

Sefton-Green, J. (2004). *Literature review in informal learning with technology outside school.* NESTA Futurelab Research Report 7. Retrieved on April 7, 2009 from http://www.nestafuturelab.org/research/reviews/07_01.htm

Seppälä, P., & Alamäki, H. (2003). Mobile learning in teacher training. *Journal of Computer Assisted Learning, 19*, 330–335. doi:10.1046/j.0266-4909.2003.00034.x

Serious Games, R. A. N. J. (2011). *Sharkworld – A project management game.* Retrieved July 18, 2011 from http://www.sharkworldgame.com/index.php

Sharples, M., Taylor, J., & Vavoula, G. (2005). *Towards a theory of mobile learning.* Paper presented at the mLearn Conference. Cape Town, South Africa. Retrieved on May 6, 2011 from http://www.mlearn.org.za/CD/papers/Sharples-%20Theory%20of%20Mobile.pdf

Sharples, M., Corlett, D., & Westmancott, O. (2002). The design and implementation of a mobile learning resource. *Personal and Ubiquitous Computing, 6*(3), 220–234. doi:10.1007/s007790200021

Shea, D. L., Lubinksi, D., & Benbow, C. P. (2001). Importance of assessing spatial ability in intellectually talented young adolescents: A 20-year longitudinal study. *Journal of Educational Psychology, 93*(3), 604–614. doi:10.1037/0022-0663.93.3.604

Shelley, B. (2001). *Guidelines for developing successful games.* Retrieved from http://www.gamasutra.com/features/20010815/shelley_01.htm

Sheridan, M. K., Foley, G. M., & Radlinski, S. H. (1995). *Using supportive play model: Individualised intervention in early childhood practice.* New York, NY: Teachers College Press.

Shield, L., & Kukulska-Hulme, A. (2006). Are language learning websites special? Towards a research agenda for discipline-specific usability. *Journal of Educational Multimedia and Hypermedia, 15*(3), 349–369.

Shneiderman, B. (1997). Human factors of interactive software. In Shneiderman, B., Plaisant, C., Cohen, M., & Jacobs, S. (Eds.), *Designing the User Interface: Strategies for Effective Human-Computer Interaction.* Upper Saddle River, NJ: Pearson-Addison.

Shneiderman, B. (1998). *Designing the user interface: Strategies for effective human-computer interaction* (3rd ed.). Reading, MA: Addison-Wesley. doi:10.1145/25065.950626

Sicart, M. (2009). *The ethics of computer games.* Cambridge, MA: MIT Press.

SIGGRAPH Asia Educators Program. (2009). *Education papers*. Retrieved October 25, 2011 from http://www.siggraph.org/asia2009/for_attendees/educators_program/education_papers/details/?type=EducatorsPapers&id=73

Silander, P., Sutinen, E., & Tarhio, J. (2004). *Mobile collaborative concept mapping – Combining classroom activity with simultaneous field exploration*. Paper presented at the 2nd IEEE International Workshop on Wireless and Mobile Technologies in Education. Retrieved on May 6, 2011 from http://ieeexplore.ieee.org/stamp/stamp.jsp?arnumber=01281347

Silius, K., Tervakari, A.-M., & Pohjolainen, S. (2003). *A multidisciplinary tool for the evaluation of usability, pedagogical usability, accessibility and information quality of web-based courses*. Paper presented at the Eleventh International PEG Conference. Nashville, TN.

Skliar, C. (1999). A localização política da educação bilíngüe para surdos. In Skliar, C. (Ed.), *Atualidades da Educação Bilíngüe para Surdos* (*Vol. 1*, pp. 7–14). Porto Alegre, Brazil: Mediação.

Skliar, C. (2005). Um olhar sobre nosso olhar acerca da surdez e das diferenças. In Skliar, C. (Ed.), *A Surdez: Um Olhar Sobre as Diferenças* (3rd ed., pp. 5–6). Porto Alegre, Brazil: Mediação.

Skliar, C. B., & Lunardi, M. L. (2000). Estudos surdos e estudos culturais em educação: Um debate entre professores ouvintes e surdos sobre o currículo escolar. In Lacerda, C. B. F., & Góes, M. C. R. (Eds.), *Surdez: Processos Educativos e Subjetividade* (pp. 11–22). São Paulo, Brazil: Editora Lovise.

Smilansky, S., & Shefatya, L. (1990). *Facilitating play: A medium for promoting cognitive, socio-emotional and academic development in young children*. Gaithersburg, MD: Psychosocial and Educational Publications.

Smith, H. (2002). Systemic level design for emergent gameplay. In *Proceedings of the Game Developers Conference 2002*. Retrieved November 8, 2011, from http://www.gamasutra.com/features/slides/smith/index.htm

Smith, H. (2003). Orthogonal unit differentiation. In *Proceedings of the Game Developers Conference 2003*. Retrieved November 8, 2011, from http://www.planetdeusex.com/witchboy/gdc03_OUD.ppt

Smith, S. (2002) *Access all areas: Disability, technology & learning*. Retrieved 11/08/11 from http://www.alt.ac.uk/sites/default/files/assets_editor_uploads/documents/accessallareaslow.pdf

Smith, I. M. (1964). *Spatial ability- Its educational and social significance*. London, UK: The University of London Press.

Snow, C. E. (1989). Understanding social interaction and language acquisition: Sentences are not enough. In Bornstein, M. H., & Bruner, J. S. (Eds.), *Interaction in Human Development* (pp. 83–103). Hillsdale, NJ: Lawrence Erlbaum.

Soller, A., & Lesgold, A. (2000). Modeling the process of collaborative learning. In *Proceedings of the International Workshop on New Technologies in Collaborative Learning*. Tokyo, Japan: ACM.

Sorby, S. (2007). Developing 3D spatial skills for engineering students. *Australasian Association of Engineering Education, 13*(1), 1–11.

Sorby, S., Wysocky, A., & Baartmans, B. (2003). *Introduction to 3D spatial visualization: An active approach*. Clifton Park, NY: Thomson Delmar Learning.

Sparrow, B., Liu, J., & Wegner, D. M. (2011). *Google effects on memory: Cognitive consequences of having information at our fingertips*. Retrieved July 14, 2011 from http://www.sciencexpress.org

Spence, M. (1971). Job market signalling. *The Quarterly Journal of Economics, 87*, 355–374. doi:10.2307/1882010

Starosky, P., Saliés, T. M. G., & Goldfeld, M. (2006). Brincar é coisa séria! O desenvolvimento de L2 de uma criança surda. In M. Goldfeld, & S. Frota (Eds.), *Enfoques em Audiologia e Surdez*, (pp. 418-456). São Paulo, Brazil: Editora AM3 Artes.

Starosky, P. (2005). *Jogos de brincar são jogos de linguagem – O papel da repetição no desenvolvimento de L2 de uma criança surda: Uma abordagem terapêutica interacional mediada por jogos com regras*. Rio de Janeiro, Brazil: Instituto de Letras da Universidade do Estado do Rio de Janeiro – UERJ.

Stasko, J. T., Domingue, J., Brown, M. H., & Price, B. A. (Eds.). (1997). *Software visualization*. Cambridge, MA: The MIT Press.

Stead, G. (2005). *Moving mobile into the mainstream.* Paper presented at the 4th World Conference on mLearning. Retrieved on May 6, 2011 from http://www.mlearn.org.za/CD/papers/Stead.pdf

Steves, M. P., & Allen, R. H. (2001). *Evaluating collaborative enterprises – A workshop report.* Retrieved from http://www.mel.nist.gov/msidlibrary/doc/steves01b.pdf

Stichting RechtenOnline. (2011). *Welkom bij de cyberdam user group.* Retrieved July 18, 2011 from http://www.cyberdam.nl/

Stiles, M. J. (2002). *Disability access to virtual learning environments.* Retrieved from http://www.computing.dundee.ac.uk/projects/dmag/resources/casestudies/stilesfull.asp

Swain, J., French, S., & Cameron, C. (2003). *Controversial issues in a disabling society.* Buckingham, UK: Open University Press.

Swing, E. L., Gentile, D. A., Anderson, C. A., & Walsh, D. A. (2010). Television and video game exposure and the development of attention problems. *Pediatrics, 126*(2), 214–221. doi:10.1542/peds.2009-1508

Swink, S. (2007). *Game feel: The secret ingredient.* Retrieved May 13, 2011, from http://www.gamasutra.com/view/feature/2322/game_feel_the_secret_ingredient.php

Tapscott, D. (1998). *Growing up digital: The rise of the net generation.* New York, NY: McGraw-Hill.

Tapscott, D. (2008). *Grown up digital: How the net generation is changing your world.* New York, NY: McGraw-Hill.

Taylor, J., & Evans, D. (2005). Pulling together: keeping track of pedagogy, design and evaluation through the development of scenarios - A case study. *Learning, Media and Technology, 30*(2), 131–145. doi:10.1080/17439880500093588

Tech, H. (2011). *Twitter user statistics show stunning growth.* Retrieved on May 6, 2011 from http://www.huffingtonpost.com/2011/03/14/twitter-user-statistics_n_835581.html

Terlecki, M. S., & Newcombe, N. S. (2005). How important is the digital divide? The relation of computer and videogame usage to gender differences in mental rotation ability. *Sex Roles, 53*(5/6), 433–441. doi:10.1007/s11199-005-6765-0

Terlecki, M. S., Newcombe, N. S., & Little, M. (2008). Durable and generalized effects of spatial experience on mental rotation: Gender differences in growth patterns. *Applied Cognitive Psychology, 22,* 996–1013. doi:10.1002/acp.1420

Thalemann, R., Wölfling, K., & Grüsser, S. M. (2007). Specific cue reactivity on computer game-related cues in excessive gamers. *Behavioral Neuroscience, 121*(3), 614–618. doi:10.1037/0735-7044.121.3.614

Theofanos, M. F., & Redish, J. (2003, November/December). Bridging the gap: Between accessibility and usability. *ACM Interactions Magazine,* 36-51.

Thiagi Inc. (1999). *Framegame game booklets.* Retrieved July 18, 2011 from http://www.thiagi.com/framegames.html

Thomas, S. (2005). Pervasive, persuasive eLearning: Modelling the pervasive learning space. In *Proceedings of the 3rd International Conference on Pervasive Computing and Communications Workshops (PERCOMW 2005),* (pp. 332–336). Kauai Island, HI: PERCOMW.

Thomas, S., Schott, G., & Kambouri, M. (2007). Designing for learning or designing for fun? Setting usability guidelines for mobile educational games. In Vahey, P., Tatar, D., & Roschelle, J. (Eds.), *Learning with Mobile Devices: A Book of Papers* (pp. 173–181). Mlearning.

Thornton, P., & Houser, C. (2005). Using mobile phones in English education in Japan. *Journal of Computer Assisted Learning, 21*(3), 217–228. doi:10.1111/j.1365-2729.2005.00129.x

Thurstone, L. L. (1950). *Some primary abilities in visual thinking.* Tech. Rep. No. 59. Chicago, IL: University of Chicago.

Thurstone, L. L., & Thurstone, T. G. (1941). *Factorial studies of intelligence: Psychometric monographs 2.* Chicago, IL: University of Chicago Press.

Tingstrom, D. H., Sterling-Turner, H. E., & Wilczynski, S. M. (2006). The good behavior game: 1969-2002. *Behavior Modification*, *30*, 225–253. doi:10.1177/0145445503261165

Toma, A. L. (2007). *A case study - Training aviation English to on-the-job Brazilian pilots.* Paper presented to the second ICAO Aviation language Symposium. Montreal, Canada. Retrieved on May 6, 2011 from http://www.icao.int/icao/en/anb/meetings/ials2/Docs/1.Lage.pdf

Tomita, D. K. (2009). Text messaging and implications for its use in education. In *Proceedings of TCC 2009*. Retrieved on June 20, 2011 from http://etec.hawaii.edu/proceedings/2009/Tomita.pdf

Trahan, M. P., Adams, N. B., & Dupre, S. (2011). Virtual learning environments: Second Life MUVEs to leverage student ownership. In Vincenti, G., & Braman, J. (Eds.), *Multi-User Virtual Environments for the Classroom: Practical Approaches to Teaching in Virtual Worlds* (pp. 62–74). Hershey, PA: IGI Global. doi:10.4018/978-1-60960-545-2.ch005

Traxler, J. (2007). Defining, discussing, and evaluating mobile learning: The moving finger writes and having writ. *International Review of Research in Open and Distance Learning*, *8*(2), 1–12.

Trompenaars, F., & Hampden-Tuerner, C. (2010). *Riding the waves of innovation: Harness the power of global culture to drive creativity and growth.* New York, NY: McGraw-Hill.

Trybus, J. (2011). *Game-based learning: What it is, why it works, and where it's going.* White Paper. New Media Institute. Retrieved from http://www.newmedia.org/game-based-learning--what-it-is-why-it-works-and-where-its-going.html%20

Tsuchiya, S. (2005). Utility deregulation and business ethics: More openness through gaming simulation. *Simulation & Gaming*, *36*(1), 114–133. doi:10.1177/1046878104272667

Tucker, A. (2010). *A model curriculum for K–12 computer science.* Retrieved October, 30, 2011 from http://csta.acm.org/Curriculum/sub/CurrFiles/K-12ModelCurr2ndEd.pdf

Turkle, S. (1997). *Life on the screen: Identity in the age of the internet.* New York, NY: Simon & Schuster.

UPIAS. (1976). *Fundamental principles of disability.* London, UK: UPIAS (Union of the Physically Impaired Against Segregation).

Vahed, A. (2008). The tooth morphology board game: An innovative strategy in tutoring dental technology learners in combating rote learning. In M. Stanfield & T. Connolly (Eds.), *2nd European Conference on Games Based Learning*, (pp. 467-480). Reading, UK: Academic Publishing Limited.

Vallacher, R. R., & Wegner, D. M. (1985). *A theory of action identification.* Mahwah, NJ: Erlbaum.

Vallacher, R. R., & Wegner, D. M. (1987). What do people think they're doing? Action identification and human behavior. *Psychological Review*, *94*, 3–15. doi:10.1037/0033-295X.94.1.3

Van den Hoogen, W. M., Ijsselsteijn, W. A., & de Kort, Y. A. W. (2008). Exploring behavioral expressions of player experience in digital games. In A. Nijholt & R. Poppe (Eds.), *Proceedings of the Workshop on Facial and Bodily Expression for Control and Adaptation of Games*, (pp. 11-19). Enschede, NL: IEEE.

Van Eck, R. (2009). A guide to integrating cots games in your classroom. In Ferdig, R. E. (Ed.), *Handbook of Research on Effective Electronic Gaming in Education* (pp. 179–199). Hershey, PA: IGI Global. doi:10.4018/978-1-59904-808-6.ch011

van Tol, R. A. (2006). *The sound alternative.* Retrieved from http://www.accessibility.nl/games/index.php?pagefile=soundalternative

Vassileva, J., McCalla, G., & Greer, J. (2003). Multi-agent multi-user modeling. *User Modeling and User-Adapted Interaction*, *13*(1), 179–210. doi:10.1023/A:1024072706526

Veen, W., & Vrakking, B. (2006). *Homo zappiens: Growing up in a digital age.* London, UK: Network Continuum Education.

Velázquez-Iturbide, J. Á., & Debdi, O. (2011). Experimentation with optimization problems in algorithm courses. In *Proceedings of the Internacional Conference on Computer as a Tool – EUROCON 2011*. Lisbon, Portugal: University of Lisbon.

Velázquez-Iturbide, J. Á., & Pérez-Carrasco, A. (2009). Active learning of greedy algorithms by means of interactive experimentation. In *Proceedings of the 14th Annual Conference on Innovation and Technology in Computer Science Education – ITiCSE 2009,* (pp. 119-123). New York, NY: ACM Press.

Velázquez-Iturbide, J. Á., Pérez-Carrasco, A., & Urquiza-Fuentes, J. (2008). SRec: An animation system of recursion for algorithm courses. In *Proceedings of the 13th Annual Conference Innovation and Technology in Computer Science Education – ITiCSE 2008,* (pp. 225-229). New York, NY: ACM Press.

Velázquez-Iturbide, J. Á., Lázaro-Carrascosa, C. A., & Hernán-Losada, I. (2009). Asistentes interactivos para el aprendizaje de algoritmos voraces. *IEEE Revista Iberoamericana de Tecnologías del Aprendizaje, 4*(3), 213–220.

Velázquez-Iturbide, J. Á., & Pérez-Carrasco, A. (2010). InfoVis interaction techniques in animation of recursive programs. *Algorithms, 3*(1), 76–91. doi:10.3390/a3010076

Vereniging Deltametropool. (2011). *Project SprintStad.* Retrieved July 18, 2011 from http://www.deltametropool.nl/nl/sprintstad

Vilpola, I., & Ihamäki, H. (2004). *How to remove the major obstacle of learning: Poor usability.* Retrieved 11/07/11 from http://www.elearningeuropa.info/lv/node/2425

Vizcaíno, A., Contreras, J., Favela, J., & Prieto, M. (2000). An adaptive collaborative environment to develop good habits in programming. In G. Gauthier, C. Frasson, & K. VanLehn (Eds.), *5th International Conference on Intelligent Tutoring Systems, ITS 2000,* (pp. 262-271). Berlin, Germany: Springer-Verlag.

Vogel, D., Kennedy, D. M., Kuan, K., Kwok, R., & Lai, J. (2007). *Do mobile device applications affect learning?* Retrieved from http://ln.academia.edu/DavidMKennedy/Papers/1045642/Do_mobile_device_applications_affect_learning

Vorderer, P., & Bryant, J. (Eds.). (2006). *Playing video games: Motives, responses, and consequences.* Mahwah, NJ: Lawrence Erlbaum Associates, Inc.

Vredenburg, K., Isensee, S., & Righi. (2001). *User-centered design: An integrated approach.* Upper Saddle River, NJ: Prentice Hall.

Vygotsky, L. (1993). *Pensamiento y lenguaje.* Buenos Aires, Argentina: Ediciones Librería Fausto.

Vygotsky, L. S. (1976). Play and its role in the mental development of the child. In Bruner, J. S., Jolly, A., & Sylvia, K. (Eds.), *Play – Its Role in Development and Evolution* (pp. 537–554). New York, NY: Basic Books. doi:10.2753/RPO1061-040505036

Vygotsky, L. S. (1986). *Thought and language.* Cambridge, MA: MIT Press.

Vygotsky, L. S. (1998a). *A formação social da mente* (6th ed.). São Paulo, Brazil: Martins Fontes.

Vygotsky, L. S. (1998b). *Pensamento e linguagem* (2nd ed.). São Paulo, Brazil: Martins Fontes.

W3C. (2005). *Introduction to web accessibility.* Retrieved from http://www.w3.org/WAI/intro/accessibility.php

Walker, I. (2008). *The future use of educational assessment games in the foundation stage: An SSAT evaluation project.* Retrieved from http://wiki.ict-register.net/images/4/44/ScreenLearning.pdf

Wang, A. I., Ofsdahl, T., & Mørch-Storstein, O. K. (2008). *An evaluation of a mobile game concept for lectures.* Paper presented at the 21st Conference on Software Engineering Education and Training. Retrieved from November 8, 2011 from http://www.computer.org/portal/web/csdl/doi/10.1109/CSEET.2008.15

Wang, A. I., Øfsdahl, T., & Mørch-Storstein, O. K. (2009). *Collaborative learning through games – Characteristics, model and taxonomy.* Retrieved from http://citeseerx.ist.psu.edu/viewdoc/download?doi=10.1.1.159.4657&rep=rep1&type=pdf

Wang, M., Shen, R., Novak, D., & Pan, X. (2009). The impact of mobile learning on students' learning behaviours and performance: Report from a large blended classroom. *British Journal of Educational Technology, 40*(4), 673–695. doi:10.1111/j.1467-8535.2008.00846.x

Warmelink, H., & Mayer, I. (Eds.). (2009). *Learning in a virtual world: Reflections on the cyberdam research and development project.* Nijmegen, The Netherlands: Wolf Legal Publishers.

Watson, I. (1992). Techniques for helping and controlling children who hate: The craft of Fritz Redl. *Australian Journal of Guidance & Counselling, 2,* 63–70.

Webb, N. (1992). Testing a theoretical model of student interaction and learning in small groups. In Hertz-Lazarowitz, R., & Miller, N. (Eds.), *Interaction in Cooperative Groups: The Theoretical Anatomy of Group Learning* (pp. 102–119). Cambridge, UK: Cambridge University Press.

Wenger, E. (2001). *Communities of practice: Learning, meaning and identity*. Cambridge, UK: Cambridge University Press.

Wenger, E., Mcdermott, R., & Snyder, W. M. (2002). *Cultivating communities of practice*. Boston, MA: Harvard Business School Press.

Wexler, S., Schlenker, B., Bruce, B., Clothier, P., Adams Miller, D., & Nguyen, F. (2008). *Authoring and developing tools*. eLearning Guild Research. Retrieved May 6, 2011 from http://www.cedmaeurope.org/newsletter%20articles/eLearning%20Guild/elg_360_tools_final.pdf

Wharton, C., Bradford, J., Jeffries, J., & Franzke, M. (1992). Applying cognitive walkthroughs to more complex user interfaces: Experiences, issues and recommendations. In *Proceedings of CHI 1992 Conference on Human Factors in Computing Systems*, (pp. 381-388). Monterey, CA: CHI.

White, L. (2010). Facebook, friends and photos: A snapshot into social networking for generating travel ideas. In Sharda, N. (Ed.), *Tourism Informatics: Visual Travel Recommender Systems, Social Communities, and User Interface Design* (pp. 115–129). Hershey, PA: IGI Global.

Whittlestone, K. (2009). *Principles behind the mobile killer application in education in mobile learning cultures across education, work and leisure*. Paper presented at the 3rd WLE Mobile Learning Symposium. London, UK. Retrieved on June 15, 2011 from http://symposium.londonmobilelearning.net/?page=Programme

WHO. (1980). *International classification of impairments, disabilities and handicaps*. Geneva, Switzerland: World Health Organisation.

WHO. (2001). *International classification of functioning, disability and health (ICF)*. Geneva, Switzerland: World Health Organisation.

Widdicombe, S. (1998). Identity as an analysts and a participants resource. In *Identities in Talk* (pp. 191–206). London, UK: Sage. doi:10.4135/9781446216958.n12

Wiser, R. A., & Graesser, A. C. (2007). Question-asking in advanced learning environments. In Fiore, S. M., & Salas, E. (Eds.), *Toward a Science of Distributed Learning* (pp. 209–234). Washington, DC: American Psychological Association. doi:10.1037/11582-010

Wittgenstein, L., Anscombe, G. E. M., & Anscombe, E. (1991). *Philosophical investigations: The German text, with a revised English translation 50th anniversary commemorative edition* (3rd ed.). New York, NY: Wiley-Blackwell.

Wood, M., & Long, N. (1991). *Life space intervention*. Austin, TX: PRO-ED.

Yen, J., Ko, C., Yen, C., Hsiu-Yueh Wu, H., & Yang, M. (2007). The comorbid psychiatric symptoms of internet addiction: Attention deficit and hyperactivity disorder (ADHD), depression, social phobia, and hostility. *The Journal of Adolescent Health, 41*(1), 93–98. doi:10.1016/j.jadohealth.2007.02.002

Yuan, K., Qin, W., Wang, G., Zeng, F., Zhao, L., & Yang, X. (2011). Microstructure abnormalities in adolescents with internet addiction disorder. *PLoS ONE, 6*(6). doi:10.1371/journal.pone.0020708

Zimmerman, B. J. (1990). Self-regulated learning and academic achievement: An overview. *Educational Psychologist, 25*, 3–17. doi:10.1207/s15326985ep2501_2

Zimmerman, W. S. (1954). Hypotheses concerning the nature of the spatial factors. *Educational and Psychological Measurement, 14*, 396–400. doi:10.1177/001316445401400220

Zurita, G., & Nussbaum, M. (2004). A constructivist mobile learning environment supported by a wireless handheld network. *Journal of Computer Assisted Learning, 20*(4), 235–243. doi:10.1111/j.1365-2729.2004.00089.x

Zyda, M. (2005, September). From visual simulation to virtual reality to games. *IEEE Computer*.

Zyda, M. (2005). From visual simulation to virtual reality to games. *Computer, 38*(9), 25–32. doi:10.1109/MC.2005.297

About the Contributors

Carina Soledad González González is the head of the i-TED research group and the Educational Innovation and ICT, the Center of Virtual Teaching, and responsible of the Virtual Campus of the ULL. She has her PhD in Computer Science, specialized in AI and HCI techniques; she did her PhD about the development of an Intelligent Tutoring System (ITS) to support children with SEN. Her main focus area in research is the application of AI techniques, multimedia adaptive interfaces, and social videogames in education. She developed expert systems using Bayesian networks, CBR, and rule-based systems and identification trees. Currently, she is working on a model and evaluation of learning communities in virtual environments of CSCL and 3D games. In addition, she is a manager of the international and national research project in the field of ICT applied to SEN and of online masters courses on 3D and videogames. She has a wide experience in e-learning best practices and LMS systems. Carina has written widely in the field of computer science applied to the educational field.

* * *

Geertje Bekebrede is an Assistant Professor at the Faculty of Technology, Policy, and Management of Delft University of Technology. She finished her PhD research in 2010 on the use of serious gaming for understanding complex infrastructure projects. Currently, her research topic is the use of gaming in education and policy-making, especially in relation to complex decision-making processes. She has been involved in a large number of game design projects for educational and policy purposes. Furthermore, she is involved in several evaluation projects on the effects of gaming. Her research is published in different journals and presented at conferences. She is Chair of the Board of the Dutch Simulation and Gaming Association, Saganet.

Francisco Blanco received his BSc in Physics from the University of Granada and in Anthropology from the UNED (Universidad Nacional de Educación a Distancia). After some years as a software analyst and teacher, he is pursuing a PhD in Computer Science at the University of la Laguna. He is researching how computer games can be used for educational and research purposes and how people interact between themselves and the environment in multiplayer games.

Marcos R. S. Borges is Full Professor in Computer Science at the NCE&IM Postgraduate Program in Informatics of the Universidade Federal do Rio de Janeiro, Brazil. He received his Ph.D. degree in Computer Science from the University of East Anglia, UK, in 1986. From 1994 to 1996, he had served as a visiting research scholar at Santa Clara University, California. His research interests include CSCW, CSCL, and Software Engineering.

Richard Byrne is a graduate of University College Cork. Richard holds an Undergraduate Degree in Computer Science and Economics and a Masters in Financial Economics. Richard is a member of the Social Science Research Network, The CFA Institute, and a candidate of the Chartered Financial Analysts Level 1 program. Richard now works as a Pricing Officer, Associate Level with State Street International (Ireland).

Eurídice Cabañes graduated in Philosophy (University of Valencia, 2007) and wrote her Doctoral Thesis about Computational Creativity in the PhD of Lógic and Philosophy of Science, in 2010. She interned at Imperial College of London in the Computational Creativity Group. Currently, she is the Vice President of ARSGAMES, is part the coordination team of the Observatorio para la Cibersociedad, and belongs to the Editorial Board of TEXTOS. She has organized and participated as a speaker in various conferences and seminars related with philosophy, synaesthesia, art, videogames, etc.

Thibault Carron is an Associate Professor of Computer Science at the University of Savoie. He is an Associate Researcher of the LIP6 Laboratory. He obtained his PhD in Computer Science at the Ecole Nationale Supérieure des Mines de Saint-Etienne in 2001. His current research interests deal with the study of collaborative activity observation. His research results are mainly applied to the educational field and more recently to serious games.

Luca Carrubba is an artist, digital craftsman, and independent researcher and educator. His artistic production focuses on the interaction between audio and video (always sharing the practices and code of both disciplines) in relation to the human perception. His practice expands from the philosophy of DIY (Do It Yourself) to the ideas of DOT (Do it Together), DIWO (Do It With Others), knowledge sharing, accessibility, recycling, social movements, and videogames. He has organised and participated in many workshops about free and open source software/technology/culture in Italy, Spain, Germany, France, UK, Argentina, Brazil, Palestine, Colombia, and China.

Ian J. Cole is a Lecturer in Information and Communication Technology for the Department of Health Sciences at the University of York, where he teaches Informatics. His research interests include virtual learning environments, usability, educational technology, human computer interaction, computer software design, and music technology. He holds a MSc in Multimedia and Educational Software Design and a MA in Music Technology. The majority of work that he is involved in focuses on the student experience, while using virtual learning environments and e-learning software. He has published predominantly on the usability of VLEs and the student experience of using e-learning. In his spare time, he writes experimental music and works on sound design projects.

César A. Collazos is an Assistant Professor of Computer Science at the Universidad del Cauca (Colombia). He received his Ph.D. in Computer Science at the Universidad de Chile. He received his Bachelor degree in Computer Science from Universidad de los Andes in Bogota (Colombia). His research interests include computer-supported collaborative learning and human-computer interaction, especially the modeling, design, and building processes of educative software applications.

Manuel Contero is Full Professor of Engineering Graphics and CAD with the Graphic Engineering Department at the Universidad Politécnica de Valencia, Spain (UPV). He earned a MSc degree in Electrical Engineering in 1990, and a PhD in Industrial Engineering in 1995, both from UPV. In 1993, he joined Universidad Jaume I of Castellón, Spain (UJI) as Assistant Professor, promoting to Associate Professor in 1997. In 2000, he returned to UPV, being appointed Full Professor in 2008. His research interests focus on sketch-based modeling, collaborative engineering, human computer interaction, development of spatial abilities, and technology-enhanced learning.

Ouafae Debdi received the Diploma in Informatics in 2007 with a special studies award. She studied the Master Degree in Information Technologies and Computing Systems in 2008 and the Master Degree in Decision Engineering in 2009, all from the Universidad Rey Juan Carlos, Madrid, Spain. She is PhD student since 2009, as well as a member of the Laboratory of Information Technologies in Education (LITE). Her research interests are innovation in education, educational software to learn programming, software visualization, and human-computer interaction.

Ines Di Loreto received her Ph.D. in Computer Science in 2009 at the University of Milan (Italy) within the area of collaborative systems and virtual communities. For several years, she worked on collaborative serious games, also in the health field (for example for the Mojos project—www.mojos. fr—at the University of Montpellier II, France). Her current research areas include post WIMP interfaces, collaborative systems, and serious games design.

Maria das Graças Dias Pereira, Professor of the Department of Letters at Pontifícia Universidade Católica do Rio de Janeiro (PUC-Rio), member of the Language Studies Post-Graduation Department, research line: Discourse, Daily, and Professional Practices. PhD in Applied Linguistics received from PUC-Rio (1993), Postdoctoral held at ILTEC and Universidade de Lisboa (2008-2009), Master's Degree in Letters from PUC-Rio (1981). Language, Culture, and Work research group leader at CNPq/PUC-Rio. Member of the work group Applied Linguistics Identity Practices (ANPOLL), and of the following associations: Brazilian Association of Linguistics (ABRALIN), Brazilian Association of Applied Linguistics (ALAB), International Pragmatics Association (IPra), Latin American Association of Discourse Studies (ALED), and the International Association of Lusitanists. Dr. Maria Dias Graças develops research in applied linguistics, narrative analysis, interactional sociolinguistics, conversation analysis, and pragmatics. Her areas of interest are discursive practices and identity construction in professional contexts, narrative analysis, social and discursive identity, interaction and new technologies, and national and international migration.

Vicente Galiano is Full Professor of the Physics and Computer Architecture Department at the Miguel Hernandez University in Elche (Spain). He received the Ing. grad. from Polytechnic University of Valencia and the PhD degree in Computer Science in 2007. His main research interests include parallel algorithms for heterogeneous platforms for solving linear and nonlinear systems, high-level interface design in parallel libraries for using them in meteorological and biological applications, and parallel simulations for modeling electronic systems. He is also working on incorporating virtual reality in teaching tools and integrating them with the social networks.

Rosa Maria Gil Iranzo, PhD in Computer Science. She is currently a Professor in the Department d'Informàtica i Enginyeria Industrial at Universitat de Lleida (UdL). She was born in Barcelona, graduated in Physics (Earth, Air, and Cosmos) at the University of Barcelona (UB), earned a Masters in Environmental Management and later a PhD at the University Pompeu Fabra (UPF), has since worked in the fields of Semantic Web and Human Computer Interaction, mainly focusing their latest work in related areas such as design interfaces and emotional cultural elements.

José Luis González Sánchez, PhD in Software Engineering, Lecturer in the Software Engineering Department of University of Lleida, and Research Member of the Research Group in Specification, Development and Evolution of Software at the University of Granada, Spain. He graduated in Computer Engineering at the University of Granada, earned a Masters in Software Development and later a PhD at the University of Granada. He is specialized in interactive systems, user interface design, and user experience, especially in video games. He is a member of the Human-Computer Spanish Association and Academic of Science and Interactive Arts from Spain.

Luis A. Guerrero is an Assistant Professor of Computer Science at the Universidad de Chile. He received his Ph.D. in Computer Science at the Pontificia Universidad Católica de Chile, a M.Sc. degree in Computer Science from Instituto Tecnológico de Costa Rica, and a Bachelor degree in Computer Science from Universidad de Costa Rica. His research interests include the modeling, design, and building processes of collaborative applications, object-oriented technologies, and collaborative learning.

Francisco L. Gutierrez Vela, PhD in Software Engineering, Lecturer in the Software Engineering Department and Research Member of the Research Group in Specification, Development and Evolution of Software at the Department of Languages and Computer Systems, University of Granada, Spain. He is specialized in interactive systems, user interface design, and collaborative design systems. He is interested in the use of videogames and interactive systems applied to education. He is a member of the Human-Computer Spanish Association.

Casper Harteveld is a PhD researcher in the Faculty of Technology, Policy, and Management at Delft University of Technology and is an Affiliate Member of Deltares Institute for Delta Technology. His interdisciplinary research draws on theories from management science, cognitive science, and human-computer interaction. He focuses on the design, use, and evaluation of games in a wide variety of public policy domains but most notably crisis and safety management. He recently wrote a book called *Triadic Game Design* and has established a game-based game design workshop (see http://triadicgamedesign. com). His dissertation deals with the use and evaluation of a game that helps to make sense of risks.

Victoria Herranz is Full Professor of the Mathematics, Statistics, and Informatics Department and Researcher Member of the Center of Operations Research, both at the University Miguel Hernandez in Elche (Spain). She received the PhD degree in Mathematics in 2007 at the University Miguel Hernandez in Elche (Spain). Her main research interests are studying error correction codes and turbo codes and their use in new telecommunications standards, such as as 4G or Wimax. She is also interested promoting new educational techniques with new technologies for students and analyzing the students' behavior using these new tools. She has worked on creating new virtual contents, such as a virtual mathematics museum.

Robyn Hromek is a practicing Educational Psychologist working in Australian schools with a Masters degree in Educational Psychology from the University of Newcastle, NSW. She is an Honorary Associate of the Faculty of Education at The University of Sydney, Australia. While working as an Educational Psychologist she has developed her expertise in the socio-emotional development of children and has drawn on the ideas of Vygotsky, Bandura, Goldman, and Gardner to produce a set of innovative games that readily engage children in the process of becoming the best they may be. Robyn has spoken at numerous international conferences—The International Conference of Moral Education in Nanjing 2011, Fifth European Conference on Positive Psychology in Copenhagen 2010, Second International Conference on Games-Based Learning in Barcelona 2008, and Division of Educational and Child Psychology Annual Conference in Glasgow 2007. She is also the author of three books published through Sage.

Amer Ibrahim is a PhD student at the Department of Software Engineering of the University of Granada. His research subject is Educational Video Games. He is a Member of the Research Group in E-Learning and Video Games at the University of Granada, Spain. He graduated in Information Technology Engineering from the University of Damascus, earned a Masters in Software Development at the University of Granada, and currently is a PhD student at the University of Granada. Interests focus on introducing a new design methodology for educational video games based on playability and player experience.

Norena Martin-Dorta is an Assistant Professor of Engineering Graphics and CAD at La Laguna University (ULL). She earned a degree in Architectural Technology in 1998 from ULL, an MS degree in Library Science and Documentation in 2005, and a Ph.D. in Industrial Engineering in 2009 from UPV. She joined La Laguna University in 2001, and her research interests include development of spatial abilities using multimedia technologies, sketch-based modeling, and technology-enhanced learning.

Jean-Charles Marty is an Associate Professor of Computer Science at the University of Savoie, France. His research interests are mainly in the observation and regulation of collaborative activities. The results of his research are applied to technology enhanced learning, and more recently to game-based learning environments.

Noirin McCarthy is a Lecturer in the Department of Economics and currently teaches on the BA (Economics), MBS (Economics of Business Practice) programme and Masters in Economic Science (M.Econ.Sc) programme. She is an undergraduate of University College Cork (B.Comm) and also holds a Postgraduate Diploma in Health Economics and Evaluation Studies as well as a Masters Degree in Economics (M.Econ.Sc), also from University College Cork. Her research interests include small business economics and labour economics.

Sebastiaan Meijer has been an Assistant Professor at Delft University of Technology since 2008 and is a visiting fellow at CSTEP, India. His research focuses on the use of gaming simulation methods for empirical research and testing of designs. This research is particularly located in the domains of supply chain management, transport systems, and emergency management. He publishes mainly in domain-related periodicals, and collaborates closely with industry to bring gaming simulation into the operating core. He serves as Secretary of the International Simulation and Gaming Association, and regularly lectures on game design in several countries.

Natalia Padilla Zea, PhD in Software Engineering at the University of Granada and Research Member of the Research Group in Specification, Development, and Evolution of Software at the Department of Languages and Computer Systems, University of Granada, Spain. She is specialized in educational video games, collaborative learning, and collaborative educational video games. She is member of the Human-Computer Spanish Association.

Antonio Pérez-Carrasco received the Graduate degree in Informatics in 2008 and the Master degree in Information Technologies and Computing Systems in 2009, both from the Universidad Rey Juan Carlos, Madrid, Spain. He has been a teacher since 2008 at the Escuela Técnica Superior de Ingeniería Informática of the Universidad Rey Juan Carlos. Currently, he is a Member of the Laboratory of Information Technologies in Education (LITE). His research interests are innovation in education, educational software to learn programming, software visualization, and human-computer interaction. He won a second prize given by the Spanish Chapter of the IEEE Education Society to the Best Educational Capstone Project.

José A. Pino is Associate Professor of Computer Science and Director of the Ph.D. program in Computer Science at the Universidad de Chile. His research interests include CSCW, HCI, and Software Industry Studies. He served as President of the Chilean Computer Science Society and President of CLEI (the Latin American Association of Universities Concerning IT). He has co-authored six books and published research papers in journals, including *Journal of the ACM, Communications of the ACM, Decision Support Systems, Interacting with Computers,* and *Information Technology and People.*

María Rubio Méndez is Member of ARSGAMES and Coordinator of the GAMESTAR(T) project, has a degree in Philosophy from the University of Valencia. She completed the Master in Secondary School Teacher Training at the Complutense University of Madrid, in the course of which she wrote a Master thesis on Pedagogical Innovation. She has also received the interuniversity Master´s degree in Logic and Philosophy of Science, where she specialized in the field of Science, Technology, and Society, focusing mainly on Philosophy of Technology, Gender, and Videogames. She is currently writing her PhD thesis on this research field.

Geraldine Ryan holds a PhD in Economics from University of Warwick. Her research interests include small business economics and stock price predictability. She has published a number of pieces on information and incentive problems in economics and knowledge management, financial indicators, and regulation.

Isabel Sánchez Berriel is Assistant Professor of Graphic Programming and Artificial Intelligence with the Statistic, Operational Research, and Computing Department at the Universidad de La Laguna, Spain (ULL). She earned a degree in Mathematics in 1998 from ULL, and she is doing a PhD at the Universidad de Las Palmas de Gran Canaria (ULPGC). In 1998, she joined ULL, Spain, as Assistant Professor. Her research interests focus on mobile programming, videogames, technology-enhanced learning, and natural language processing.

Flavia Maria Santoro is an Associate Professor in the Department of Computer Science of the University of Rio de Janeiro, Brazil. She received her D.Sc. degree in Computer Science from the Federal University of Rio de Janeiro in 2001. Her research interests are in the areas of CSCL, CSCW, computers in education, and distance learning.

Neide Santos earned a D.Sc. degree in Engineering of Production from the Federal University of Rio de Janeiro in 1994. She is an Associate Professor in the Department of Computer Science at the State University of Rio de Janeiro, Brazil. Her main areas of interest include computers in education, educational hypermedia, and Web-based education.

José Luis Saorín is an Assistant Professor of Engineering Graphics and CAD at La Laguna University (ULL). He earned an MS degree in Energy Engineering in 1991, and a Ph.D. in Industrial Engineering in 2006 from UPV. He worked for private companies from 1992, as a project engineer in water supply systems. He joined La Laguna University in 2001, and his research interests include development of spatial abilities and the use of advanced technologies for learning and teaching drawing.

Priscila Starosky, Phonoaudiologist and Linguist. PhD in Language Studies received from Pontifícia Universidade Católica do Rio de Janeiro – PUC-Rio (2011), Master's Degree in Linguistics from Universidade Estadual do Rio de Janeiro – UERJ (2005), Graduation in Phonoaudiology from UERJ (2001). Language, Culture, and Work research group member at CNPq/PUC-Rio. Substitute Professor of Phonoaudiology at Universidade Federal do Rio de Janeiro – UFRJ (2001). Visiting Professor of Phonoaudiology in Post-Graduation courses and Substitute Professor of Applied Linguistics at UERJ – Department of Letters. Dr. Priscila Starosky develops research in applied linguistics, sociocultural studies in the interaction, concerning native language (L1) and second language (L2) in the context of deafness, as well as discursive and identity practices in health and educational contexts.

Pedro Toledo Delgado received the degrees in Computer Science Technical Engineering and Computer Science Engineering from the University of La Laguna (Spain) in 2002 and 2004, respectively. He was a Ph.D student at the same university in 2004, in the Department of Systems Engineering and Control and Computer Architecture. In addition, he collaborated with the DTAI group of the Computer Science Department of the Katholieke Universiteit Leuven during the year 2008, and with the Information Systems Group of the Computer Science Department of the Technische Universiteit Eindhoven, during 2009, 2010, and 2011. His current research interests include reinforcement learning, graph mining, workflow induction, and educational data mining.

J. Ángel Velázquez-Iturbide received the Graduate Degree in Informatics in 1985 and the PhD Degree in Informatics in 1990, both from the Universidad Politécnica de Madrid, Spain. He was a teacher since 1985 at the Facultad de Informática of the Universidad Politécnica de Madrid. In 1997, he joined Universidad Rey Juan Carlos, where he currently is Full Professor and Chairman of the Laboratory of Information Technologies in Education (LITE). His research interests are innovation in education, educational software to learn programming, software visualization, information visualization, and human-computer interaction. Dr. Velázquez-Iturbide is a Member of ACM, ACM SIGCSE, IEEE Computer Society, and IEEE Education Society. He also is the Chairman of the Spanish Association for the Advancement of Computer in Education (ADIE).

Harald Warmelink is an Assistant Professor finishing his PhD research at the Faculty of Technology, Policy, and Management of Delft University of Technology. He researches on the numerous meanings games can have for organizations, most notably the notion and emergence of "playful organizations": a type of organization in which employees value their ability to play so much that the organization becomes highly creative, spontaneous, and pleasurable. Together with several colleagues, he has also evaluated a great many educational games developed and used at Delft University of Technology and several other educational institutes in The Netherlands. He co-edited the book *Learning in a Virtual World: Reflections on the Cyberdam Research and Development Project* with Dr. Igor Mayer.

Ranran Xiong is currently studying for an MSc in Computing Science in University College Cork, having previously studied Systems Management in Henan University of Finance and Economy, Zhengzhou, China. She is interested in data mining, optimization, information systems, and in business management/economics.

Sergio G. Zapata is a Researcher in the Instituto de Informática at Universidad Nacional de San Juan, Argentina, and Professor of Information Systems in the Computer Science program. He is a candidate of a Master degree in Software Engineering. He has more than 15 years of experience in high educations and software engineering.

Index